D1758957

COLLEGE LIBRARY

**Please return this book by the date stamped below
- if recalled, the loan is reduced to 10 days**

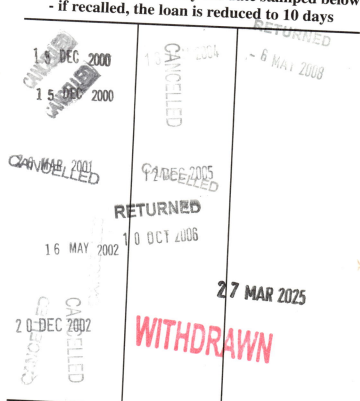

Fines are payable for late return

PAPERS

ON

PSYCHO-ANALYSIS

BY

ERNEST JONES, M.D., F.R.C.P. (Lond.)

PRESIDENT OF THE INTERNATIONAL PSYCHO-ANALYTICAL ASSOCIATION
HONORARY PRESIDENT OF THE BRITISH PSYCHO-ANALYTICAL SOCIETY
FOUNDER OF THE 'INTERNATIONAL JOURNAL OF PSYCHO-ANALYSIS'
CONSULTING PHYSICIAN TO THE LONDON CLINIC OF PSYCHO-ANALYSIS
HONORARY FELLOW OF THE BRITISH PSYCHOLOGICAL SOCIETY

'It is impossible to tell the truth so that it shall be understood and not believed.'
BLAKE

'Ein Nichtverstehen ist oft ein Nichtverstehenwollen.'
FREUD

If ye expect not the unexpected ye shall not find the truth.'
HERACLITUS

FIFTH EDITION

MARESFIELD REPRINTS
LONDON

PRINTED AND PRODUCED IN GREAT BRITAIN
AD/CRP/CBS/77.

DEDICATED

TO

PROFESSOR FREUD

AS A TOKEN OF THE AUTHOR'S GRATITUDE

PREFACE TO THE FIFTH EDITION

THIS should be positively the final edition of this book. In it I have omitted fourteen papers from the previous edition and inserted nine more recent ones. A possessor of the complete set will find that it comprises eighty-nine papers.

In the thirty-five years since the first edition appeared the progress of psycho-analysis, both socially and scientifically, presents many satisfactory features and is slowly fulfilling its early promise, though it will take centuries to bring it to the fruition one can now only glimpse. In this time it has already overcome many obstacles, both internal and external. The one it is faced with at the moment, a serious one, is the temptation of being unduly influenced by current political trends. The essence of these, as I see them, is an over-optimistic belief in the power of the material environment to determine the fate and happiness of mankind. That it can do so in a deleterious fashion is undeniable, as the recent progress in physical science has amply demonstrated. How much, however, it can accomplish in more constructive ways is more doubtful. The teachings of psycho-analysis lay more stress on the internal mental constitution of individuals, on the unconscious processes that depend partly on heredity (so much ignored by environmentalists) and partly on the earliest developmental experiences of the infant. Just as wise parental care accomplishes most in the apparently modest, but difficult enough, way of refraining from doing harm to the growing child and, secondly, in providing conditions as favourable as possible for its spontaneous development rather than attempting actively to further this, so, in my opinion, could governments achieve more by imitating these beneficent procedures in place of ambitious attempts to improve the world by coercive efforts.

Both from outside and inside psycho-analytical circles one hears the cry that more importance should be attached to external circumstances, especially the prevailing cultural traditions, in determining the early development of children : for example, that an Œdipus complex can develop only in a patriarchal society, and so on. That they extensively affect the external form assumed in later life by the individual's peculiarities is evident enough, but I have yet to be shown how their influence is supposed to penetrate to the entirely unconscious phantasies of the infant on which so much of its future nature will depend. No, I think the future will show that psycho-analysis can contribute more to sociology than sociology to psycho-analysis.

ELSTED,
    MIDHURST.
        September, 1948.

CONTENTS

PAPERS ON PSYCHO-ANALYSIS

CHAPTER I

FREUD'S PSYCHOLOGY[1]

THE difficulties inherent in the subject of an essay are frequently mentioned in the introductory sentences by way of excuse for the deficiencies of the exposition. In the present case they are of so peculiar a nature that to mention them here will also serve another purpose—namely, to indicate some of the general aspects of the subject.

The first difficulty—one that necessarily occurs in presenting the views of any progressive thinker—resides in the fact that Freud's views have in the past thirty years undergone a continuous evolution. Most writers who have expounded them have therefore elected to describe them in terms of their historical development, a course which, while lending greater accuracy, has obvious disadvantages, particularly for readers not familiar with the subject. As, however, the later modifications in Freud's views have mainly concerned clinical subjects, such as the ætiology of hysteria and the technique of the psycho-analytic method, with which we are not here concerned, it will be possible to choose the alternative course of attempting to give a more general review of his psychology as a whole.

The second and far weightier difficulty is that Freud's psychology signifies a great deal more than the formulation of a series of new conclusions or the announcement of new discoveries, important as these may be; it involves a radical change in our attitude towards the questions of the structure and functioning of the mind. If, therefore, Freud's views are substantiated by later investigations, they betoken an event of peculiar and far-reaching significance to psychology in general. It is notoriously harder to convey a new attitude or point of view than mere conclusions, or even facts; and yet in regard to our judgement it is a more important matter, for a given conclusion that may appear improbable enough from one

[1] First published in the *Psychological Bulletin*, April, 1910. vol. vii.

point of view is seen in quite a different aspect from another. A corollary of this consideration is that Freud has not only dealt with previously discussed questions—*e.g.*, dream interpretation and the psychology of wit—but has explained what previously had hardly been thought to be problems at all—*e.g.*, the cause of infantile amnesia, the meaning of various absent-minded and other acts in everyday life, etc.

The third difficulty—one really implicit in the last—is that the applications of Freud's psychology are exceedingly diverse, so that the range of subjects included is very extensive. He has, for instance, offered explanations for problems so remote from one another as the origin of myths, the choice of a profession, the sources of artistic creativeness, and the tendency to superstitious beliefs. Of only a few of the subjects, however, has he given any complete or systematic exposition, and the extent to which his principles can be applied refers more to deductions, usually fairly obvious, that follow from these. His expositions are thronged with suggestive hints—of which some are more, some less developed—that are at present being acted on and expanded by both himself and the members of his school. Again, the way in which these different subjects are intimately bound up with one another makes it very difficult to present some without the others. Much of the cogency of Freud's arguments is derived from the astonishing confirmation and mutual support that the application of them receives from widely different fields of study, such as psycho-pathology, dreams, wit, mythology, and everyday life. Just as the true significance of Darwin's suggestions became evident only when their fruitfulness was realised in such different fields as palæontology, comparative morphology, and embryology, so do Freud's hypotheses become irresistibly convincing when one appreciates their capacity to illuminate spheres of human activity that at first sight appear to be remote and unconnected. This third difficulty, the extensiveness of Freud's principles, is one reason why the present exposition can be nothing but the roughest and crudest sketch of the subject indicated in the title of this paper.

Freud is primarily a man of science, rather than a philosopher. In philosophy he might perhaps most nearly be classified as accepting scientific sensationalistic idealism, as represented by Karl Pearson. This is well illustrated by his attitude to such a question as the psychophysical relations of consciousness, or of mental processes in general. He uses the term 'conscious' to denote all the mental processes of which a person is aware, distinctly or indistinctly, at a given moment. Not sharply marked off from these are the pre-conscious (*vorbewusste*) memories, of which a person is not at a given moment necessarily aware, but which can be fairly readily and spontaneously recalled. Unconscious memories are those that cannot be spontaneously recalled by the subject, but which can be evoked by the use of special methods (hypnosis, psycho-analysis, etc.).[1] As we shall presently see, Freud holds that processes of the most complex kind may occur without ever becoming conscious. He is content with this practical finding, and leaves quite open the question as to whether they are ultimately of a mental or physical nature. Leaving on one side the philosophical aspects of the subject, he empirically accepts the obvious fact that it is impossible to describe the processes in question except in mental terms, and so continues to treat of them as if they were mental. Another justification for this he sees in the continuity that experience establishes between conscious and unconscious processes, which may be related to each other in every respect except in the one matter of awareness; the resemblances between them thus far outweigh in importance the differences. He would therefore maintain that both conscious and 'unconscious' mental processes should be treated alike in any epistemological discussion; it is no more obligatory, desirable, or even possible to describe 'unconscious' mental processes in physiological language than conscious processes.

It will be convenient shortly to consider some of Freud's more general and fundamental principles before mentioning their applications. Of these the following seven will be selected, admittedly an arbitrary choice:

1. In the first place, Freud attributes to psychical events a rigorous *determinism*, the word being used in its empirical scientific rather than in its philosophic sense. Psychical processes are never isolated or accidental phenomena, but are as precisely related to preceding and succeeding ones as are successive physical events; there is no more room for 'chance' in the mental world than in the physical

[1] It will be noticed that by definition these resemble Myers' subliminal process, Prince's co-conscious, and Janet's *subconscient*. There exist, however, fundamental differences between Freud's views on the subject and those of other writers; these have been discussed in a striking paper by Hart in the *Journal of Abnormal Psychology*, vol. iv.

one. Freud is therefore never content with such explanations as
would attribute various actions to ' habit,' ' absent-mindedness,'
and the like, but always searches for the motive force itself. As will
presently be indicated, there are certain inhibitions that tend to
prevent one from asking too many questions about the concealed
motives for conduct, and thus lead us to be satisfied with the more
superficial factors or even with mere phrases, such as those just
quoted; the result of this is that many of the answers and explanations given by Freud are apt at first sight to appear superfluous, if
not even far-fetched.

Starting from this point of view he develops his psycho-analytic
method, on which are based practically all his conclusions. He
maintains that, when a subject is asked to make free associations
from a given theme to which he is attending, and wholly to suspend
the active selective criticism that under such circumstances is
instinctively exercised towards the incoming thoughts, the associations must be directly or indirectly related, in a causative manner,
to the initial theme. The connection between this and the associations that occur are often not at all realised by the subject; for this,
however, there are special and definite reasons that will presently
be indicated. Discussion of the psychological principles involved
in the use of psycho-analysis, as well as of other allied topics, must
be reserved for a further paper.

2. Freud's views concerning *affective processes* show certain
important deviations from those currently accepted. He tentatively
states as a working hypothesis that ' there is to be distinguished in
psychical functions something (amount of affect, sum of excitations)
which has all the attributes of a quantity—although we have as
yet no means of measuring it—something capable of being increased,
diminished, displaced, or carried off, and which spreads itself over
the memory traces of ideas, rather like an electric charge over the
surface of the body.' The two words in brackets (*Affektbetrag*,
Erregungssumme) indicate that the property in question can be
described in either psychological or physiological terms. Indeed,
he regards it as something essentially centrifugal in nature, in that
it constantly tends to discharge its psycho-motor energy—characteristically by means of bodily expression—in a manner analogous
to motor and secretory processes. Most significant, however, is
the assumption that it has a certain autonomy, so that it can become
released from the idea to which it was primarily attached, thus

entering into new psychical systems and producing wide-reaching effects. This movement of affect from one idea to another Freud denotes as ' displacement ' (*Verschiebung*), and says that the second idea may in a sense be termed a representative of the first. A simple illustration of the process is when a girl transfers the affective process properly belonging to the idea of a baby to that of a doll, and washes, clothes, fondles, and cares for the doll, and even takes it to bed with her or makes attempts to feed it, thus treating it in all possible respects as she would a baby. An equally familiar observation is the behaviour of a spinster towards a pet animal. In Browning's ' The Last Ride Together,' the same mechanism is beautifully seen: the hero, failing in his ambition to win his mistress, consoles himself with the enjoyment of their last ride, and gradually exalts the significance of this until in a final ecstasy he imagines not only that it is an adequate replacement of his former aim, but that it represents the highest bliss that can be attained on earth or in heaven.

3. Connected with his views on affective processes is the emphasis Freud lays on the *dynamic nature of mental processes* in general. This is best described in terms of the scheme by means of which he depicts the structure of the mind.[1] This scheme he proposes in the most tentative way as merely a working hypothesis, expressly disclaiming any likelihood of mistaking the scaffolding of a theory for the building that will later be erected. Taking the analogy of a microscope or telescope, the theory of which makes use of ideal localities in space, he develops the notion of psychical locality. The mind is a complex reflex apparatus or system, with a seat of entry at one extremity and of discharge at the other; the former is of course the sensorial extremity, the latter the motor. Every mental process tends to set up a movement from one end of the apparatus to the other. To begin with is the perception in its sensorial form; this is not fixed as such, but farther on in the system in the form of a ' memory trace.' The farther forward the process moves, the greater is the extent to which it becomes associated with others; at first the association is of a superficial kind (clang, etc.), later on it is of a higher order (similarity, co-ordination, etc.). A mental process is recalled not in its primary perceptive form, but as a ' memory trace.' Accompanying every mental process is a varying amount of psychical energy, which roughly corresponds with what we term the affect. Excessive accumulation of this energy results

[1] See Chapter XXXV. of the Third Edition for a fuller exposition of this.

in a tension that is experienced as discomfort (*Unlust*), and there is
a constant tendency towards the discharge of this energy (*Abführ*).
The discharge is experienced as pleasure, as relief, or gratification
(*Befriedigungserlebnis*).

The way in which the relief is brought about differs in complexity in the young child and older persons. The infant finds by
experience that satisfaction of a given need—*e.g.*, hunger—is
associated with a certain perception—*e.g.*, the sight of food. The
recurrence of this need therefore brings with it the desire to reproduce the perception associated with satisfaction of it. It is probable
that at first this may occur by ' regression ' of mental processes so
that a hallucinatory perception is produced. Experience, however,
soon teaches that this method is inadequate permanently to still
the need, and that in their capacity in this respect there is an important difference between perceptions externally evoked and those
internally evoked. Internal perceptions are adequate only when they
are durable, as in the hallucinations of the psychoses. The psychical
energy corresponding with the need therefore sets in action further
groups of mental processes, the function of which is to modify
the environment in such a way as to bring about an externally
evoked perception of the kind desired ; for instance, the child
cries until it is fed. The regressive tendency to reproduce the
primary perception by internal means Freud terms the *primary
process* (*Primärvorgang*). The *secondary process*, which inhibits this
tendency and directs the energy into more complex paths, is the
work of a second and quite different psychical system. All the
complicated thought processes that occur, from the memory picture
to the psycho-motor mechanisms that result in changing the
environment so as to bring about the repetition of the desired
perception, constitute merely a *détour*, which experience has shown
is necessary in order to produce the wish-fulfilment. These two
systems, which are already present at an early age, form the nucleus
for what later becomes the unconscious and preconscious respectively.

4. The subject of ' psychical repression ' (*Verdrängung*), which
plays such an important part in all Freud's writings, may be considered as a direct continuation of the previously mentioned one
concerning the relation between the primary and secondary systems,
though it is less hypothetical in nature. The fundamental regulating
mechanisms of mental processes are the tendencies to seek pleasure

by bringing about relief from psychical tension, and to avoid pain by preventing accumulation of psychical energy. These strivings, which have a more or less definite aim, constitute a Wish in the broad sense of the term. When, now, this wish cannot for various reasons be gratified, the tendency of the psychical energy to discharge itself is inhibited, a local damming up takes place, and the mental process in question loses its former power of making free associations. It in this way forms a circumscribed 'complex,' to use Jung's term. Under these circumstances the secondary system cannot make use of the energy of that portion of the primary system, for to do so would only result in the evocation of discomfort (*Unlust*) and it is a chief function of the secondary system to avoid this whenever possible. We have here, then, all the conditions for an intrapsychical conflict, and Freud maintains that, when a mental process is the seat of a competition of opposing affects, blocking (*Sperrung*) of the usual associative activities occurs and the mental process becomes shut off or dissociated. This ostrich-like function of the secondary system therefore results in exclusion of the pain-producing mental process from consciousness. In daily life this mechanism is extraordinarily frequent and shows itself in many ways, the simplest of which is the disinclination for being reminded of disagreeable occurrences we would rather forget. There are many motives for this disinclination, the painfulness of an external situation being the least important ; more important are such mental attitudes as shame, disgust, horror, at the possibility of various internal thoughts and wishes. Emphasis should further be laid on the point, often not sufficiently appreciated, that the action of 'repression' in preventing mental processes from ever entering consciousness is much more important and extensive than that of merely driving out from consciousness those that have once been present there.

'Normal' and 'abnormal' conscious mental events differ only quantitatively, not qualitatively, both proceeding by the same mechanisms of the same psychical apparatus. In both cases the energy of the unconscious mental process (*i.e.*, the Wish) is directed into the complex conscious paths according to the principle of pleasure and pain, the chief difference between the two being that the discharge of energy in the 'abnormal' case takes place by a more circuitous and unusual route than in the 'normal' case. In both cases consciousness exerts a 'censoring' influence

over the dynamic process, allowing it to find expression only in
certain definite ways. The characteristic function of consciousness
is the exercise of this selective censoring influence. Consciousness
may be compared with a sense organ, in that it allows the perception and differentiation of psychical qualities. Its action differs
from that of a sense organ in that it is concerned with the perception not only of externally produced stimuli, but also of internal psychical processes. It is probable that between preconscious
and conscious processes a censorship action is also interposed, of
the same kind. as that between unconscious and preconscious
processes.

5. The manifestation of abnormally repressed mental processes
is to be understood only by consideration of the action of *intrapsychical conflict*. As has already been said, conflict between two
tendencies or wishes results in a blocking and dissociation of the
mental process concerned. The direct route into consciousness
is impeded and the energy passes into a circuitous side-path. The
direction thus taken is, however, rigorously determined by preceding
psychological and physiological factors. The energy may become
linked either with other mental processes or with physical ones.
In the first case, the affect accompanying a given idea, which, being
dissociated, is incapable of becoming conscious (*bewusstseinsunfähig*),
becomes transferred to another one which is assimilable in consciousness (the process known as *Uebertragung*). This is the typical
mechanism underlying the production of obsessions and most
phobias. An insistent impulse to think of a non-permitted subject
shows itself by an obsessive thought about another, associated,
but more acceptable one. The passage from the one idea to the
other occurs through one of the well-known forms of mental
association, usually a lower form, such as extrinsic, and particularly
clang associations. Brill[1] narrates an instance in which a patient,
possessed with licentious impulse relating to a *dog*, suffered from
an apparently innocent obsessive thought concerning *God*.

In the second case the energy finds an outlet in some somatic
manifestation, a process Freud terms 'conversion.' This is the
characteristic mechanism underlying hysterical troubles, where a
given bodily symptom, such as a tremor or an aphonia, is the
expression of a repressed mental complex. Here also, as in the

[1] A. A. Brill, 'Freud's Conception of the Psychoneuroses,' *Medical Record*, December 25, 1909.

purely mental field, the actual direction taken by the discharging energy is determined by the existence of performed associations, such as the usual physical accompaniments of emotion, and the occurrence is favoured by an unusual degree of readiness of the physical response (*somatisches Entgegenkommen*).

In both cases the formation of the unusual associations, which permit the circuitous discharge of psychical energy, takes place outside consciousness, and the subject quite fails to apprehend the significance of the end manifestation, or the connection between it and the primary mental process. Yet the mental events that precede the manifestation may be of the most complex order, fully as much so as conscious ones.

6. Stress should be laid on the importance Freud attaches to *infantile mental processes*. He regards the mental processes, and particularly the wishes, of early childhood life as the permanent basis for all later development. Unconscious mental life is indestructible, and the intensity of its wishes does not fade. Wishes and interests of later acquirement are chiefly significant in so far as they ally themselves with those of childhood life, though the association is, of course, not a conscious one. A great number of the reactions of adult life owe their real force to the adjuvant impulse contributed by the unconscious. Freud, therefore, looks upon the whole of a subject's mental life as a continuity, as a series of associated trends. The appearance of complete discontinuity which it so often presents is an illusion, due to the ignorance of the preceding unconscious influences. For instance, a person may at the age of twenty have his attention for the first time directed in a given line of interest, and may in consequence of this choose a profession and determine his life's career; but the real reason why he reacts in this way to the external influence is that it corresponds with, and becomes associated to, deeper unconscious trends that arose in early childhood life. These views naturally have great importance in their bearing on education,[1] for it is substantially maintained that the main traits of character are permanently determined for good or ill before the end of the fifth year of life. Freud holds in general that owing to our ignorance of the most important mental processes of early childhood, and our own personal amnesia for this period, the significance for later life of these early trends is vastly underestimated.

[1] See Chapters XXXIV.-XXXVI. of the Third Edition.

The amnesia for early mental processes is even greater than is generally supposed, for not only is much actually forgotten, but a selection takes place of such a kind that only the least significant part is remembered. Thus the actual memory for this period is even less valuable than it appears. Further than this, our childhood memories are also less trustworthy than they appear, for later falsifications, distortions, and inventions, arising particularly in the conscious and unconscious phantasies of puberty, impair the reliability of them to a much greater extent than is generally known; it should, however, be added that the technique of psycho-analysis usually enables one to differentiate between an accurate recollection and a falsified one. This infantile amnesia is, according to Freud, not a natural, physiological process, needing no explanation. He considers that, were it not for our extreme familiarity with its happening, we should regard it as by no means so obvious and comprehensible as we at present do. For him it is a curious problem which calls as urgently for solution as that of other less familiar mental events. The cause of the amnesia he sees in the psychical repression that plays so large a part in early education. Children come to the world with potential trends and desires which are innocent enough at an early age, but which are of such a kind that the gratification of them is highly unacceptable to adult standards. Early training largely consists in weaning the child from these desires and directing his mind towards other interests ; the chief of these processes Freud terms ' sublimation.' The primitive trends themselves, such as egotistic enjoyment without regard for others, concern with certain bodily functions, and so on, have to be suppressed, and the mental processes representing them are repressed and become unconsious. This, however, is not effected without a certain cost to the individual, and amongst other penalties paid is the amnesia for infantile mental life. As in other cases, such as, for instance, with hysteric post-traumatic retrograde amnesia, the memories lost are not only those that directly concern the thoughts and wishes now invested with painful and guilty feeling, but also those that are in any way—e.g., in time—associated with these. Further, as was above pointed out, although the desires in question have been repressed into the unconscious, they lose none of their dynamic functions, and, when the sublimation process is not sufficiently potent to provide an outlet for the accompanying psychical energy, other paths of discharge have to be forged, of a kind that for practical reasons are called 'pathogenic.' It is in this way that psychoneurotic symptoms arise, which thus represent in a disguised form the gratification of repressed wishes. One of the chief differences between the indirect expression of an unconscious wish by means of a neurotic symptom and that by means of a sublimated activity is that the latter is useful for social aims, whereas the former is harmful both socially and to the individual.

7. The part of Freud's psychology that has aroused most opposition is his attitude regarding the significance of *psycho-sexual trends*. We are not here concerned with the nature of this opposition, which arises partly from a misconception of Freud's own views, and partly as a result of the peculiarly heavy social ban that is laid on certain aspects of the subject. It should in the first place be stated that he applies the term 'sexual' far more broadly than is customary, and thus includes under it functions that are not generally considered to be of a sexual nature. He does this, however, not in order to distort the usual signification of the term, but because he finds by experience that many psychical manifestations not commonly thought to be derivatives of the sexual instinct are in fact so. He thus extends, not the connotation of the word 'sexual,' but the conceptions denoted by it. His conception of the *idea* 'sexuality' is certainly much wider than the general one, but it is not accurate to say that his use of the word is very different from the current usage. This important matter, the source of much misunderstanding of Freud's views, must be dealt with at some little length, and it may be made plainer by the following illustration. It is taken from a criticism in which the passage occurs, 'Contrary to ordinary usage, Freud speaks of a sexual impulse in childhood,' implying that Freud's departure consists merely in a novel and unjustifiable use of the word. But the departure is, in fact, more than a matter of words, it is a matter of things, of processes, of ideas; the heresy is not one that can be remedied by a dictionary. Freud says in effect: 'Processes which I, in full agreement with the rest of the world, call sexual do actually occur in childhood life, though in the past the existence of them has, for certain definite reasons, been largely overlooked or misinterpreted.' The point can be made clearer still by the following analogy, which in several respects is a fairly close one. Some time after the discovery of nitrogen, in the atmosphere, it was found that it also existed,

in combination with other elements, in solid substances. When this finding was announced, critics might very well have said to the investigator : ' You are distorting scientific language, and are using the word " nitrogen " in a novel and unjustifiably wide sense by applying it to solid substances which are evidently not nitrogen; allow us to inform you that the word denotes, by common accept- ance, a gas, which is to be found in the atmosphere.' To which the investigator would have been right in replying: 'I was acquainted with the meaning of the word when I began my researches, but these have convinced me that the element which both you and I are agreed to call nitrogen may exist not only in its easily observable gaseous form, but also, in certain circumstances, in other forms where its familiar attributes are not manifest, and where its very existence can be determined only by a careful chemical analysis.' When Freud uses the term ' sexuality,' he does so because it just expresses his meaning, and not from any desire to introduce any linguistic changes; whenever he uses a word in a special sense, such as in the case of *Verdrängung* (' repression '), he says so, and gives his reason for so doing. In saying that the analysis of a neurotic symptom reveals as an invariable constituent the presence of a psychosexual process, the customary attributes of which are veiled through the interaction of other mental processes, Freud adopts a position identical with that of a chemist who says that analysis of saltpetre reveals the invariable presence of nitrogen. When he calls certain infantile processes 'sexual,' he does so because he believes that they are intrinsically of the same nature as the processes that everyone calls sexual in the adult.

A little reflection makes it evident that, even if the term is by definition made to refer only to tendencies that have to do with the reproductive instinct, it is impossible to confine it to impulses that directly tend to bring about the reproductive act. For instance, no one with any experience of such a ' perversion ' as fetishism would refuse to call this ' sexual ' in the full meaning of the term, although from its very nature it expresses a negation of the repro- ductive act; the same is true of ordinary masturbation. Even more normal manifestations, which anthropologists have shown to be derivatives of the sexual instinct—such as shame, disgust, etc.— are by no means obviously tendencies that favour the consum- mation of this act, although it may be true that they are indirectly connected with reproduction. On precisely similar grounds Freud holds it justifiable to apply the term ' sexual '[1] to mental processes which, like shame, derive their origin from the sexual instinct, and the only reason why his application of the term is more extensive than that of other writers is that, by his psycho-analytic investigation of the unconscious, he has been able to trace to this origin a number of processes that at first sight do not appear to be connected with it. He has striven to free himself from the prejudice that refuses to recognise the sexual nature of a mental process until this is made so obvious as to be quite indisputable, and he points out how deeply rooted in the human mind is this prejudice.

These preliminary considerations may be thus summarised: Freud lays stress on the dynamic aspects of mental processes, and sees in the tendency of the affects to seek discharge of their tension the motive force determining the flow of mental life; he expresses this in terms of Wishes. He holds that unconscious mental life is rich and complex, and by the interaction between it and consciousness explains the apparent discontinuity of conscious processes, thus adopting a rigorously deterministic attitude towards intuitive and apparently spontaneous mental events. Much of this interaction depends on the result of conflicts between various psychical trends, some of these undergoing repression, so that they can be manifested only along indirect channels. He attributes fundamental importance to the repressed wishes of early childhood life and to the psychosexual systems of activities.

We may now shortly consider some of the fields in which Freud has applied the foregoing principles, and it will be convenient to begin with the subject last mentioned—namely, *Sexuality*. In the first place, Freud holds that the adult mental processes commonly called ' sexual,' which bear a relatively precise relation to reproduction, are the outcome of a development from a broader group of processes in earlier life, of which certain ones have become selected and intensified, while others have become suppressed. In the child are a number of sexual dispositions, the functioning

[1] Freud uses the term *Libido* to indicate sexual desires and longings in all their aspects ; this corresponds in its connotation with that possessed by the word ' hunger ' in relation to the nutritional instinct. Dr. Putnam, in his recent luminous essay on Freud's work (*Journal of Abnormal Psychology*, vol. iv., Nos. 5 and 6), considers that the nearest English equivalent to it is ' craving ' ; perhaps a more exact translation would be ' sexual hunger,' which is the one mostly used by the present writer. For linguistic reasons the adjective ' libidinal,' when used in the present sense, is preferable to ' libidinous.'

of which notably differs from that of adult sexual processes, and
the later development of which is subject to the greatest variability.
A clearer view of these early dispositions is obtained by considering the different kinds of adult sexual perversions. Freud
draws a distinction between the sexual object, the source of attraction, and the sexual aim, the activity in which the impulse manifests
itself ; the difference between these is evident when one dissociates
such an impulse as the masochistic one—*i.e.*, the desire to obtain
enjoyment through experiencing submission or pain—from its
objective, which may be either a male or a female person. Looked
at from this point of view, perversions fall into two groups. On
the one hand are those that show a deviation from the normal
objective, such as homosexuality. Freud thinks that this inversion
of the normal objective can only be explained by assuming that
man has a bisexual predisposition psychically as well as anatomically, and that the normal is reached by the heterosexual component
being developed at the expense of the homosexual one. On the other
hand are those that show a deviation from the normal aim. These
may be divided into two sub-groups. First, there are aims that
pass beyond the normal anatomical regions, such as when kissing
attains a higher sexual value than actual intercourse. The tendency
to overestimate the attractive value of anything belonging to the
loved person—her hair, hand, glove, etc.—may be localised to
a given part, such as the foot, and thus constitute a fetishism.
Secondly, there are the aims that differ from the normal in that they
represent a fixation of the sexual impulse in what should be only
a preliminary stage in the whole process. Perverts of this kind may,
for instance, obtain full sexual gratification from a morbid fascination
of merely looking at a member of the opposite sex under certain
circumstances, and have no desire to do more than this.

Freud finds that the potentialities of all forms of perversion
already exist in the child, which he therefore terms *polymorph
pervers*. Under the pressure of educative influences, however, they
normally become suppressed, and the psychical energy accompanying the impulses is 'sublimated' into other directions of greater
social value. The influences that are specially operative in this respect
are as follows: The tendency to display one's own person or to
seek pleasure in regarding that of others is opposed by the development of personal modesty and shame. The tendency to obtain
enjoyment from various manipulations of and interest in excre-

mental functions[1] is opposed by the development of disgust; and the finding of pleasure in acts that are painful to oneself or to others—masochism and sadism—is suppressed by the cultivation of sympathy with others, with sensitiveness to and horror of suffering. Two other possibilities, however, are open, besides the normal one of sublimation. First, the tendency itself may acquire abnormal strength and may manifest itself in later life as an actual perversion, as indicated above. Secondly, when the conflict between the impulse and the repressing force is especially strong the impulse may find expression in the production of a psychoneurotic symptom, which, therefore, is a disguised form of gratification of the perverse impulse. Hysterical symptoms thus constitute the negative of perversions. These three outcomes are naturally not sharply marked off from one another. One and the same man may show the results of sublimation of a given tendency, which may, for instance, be revealed in the form adopted by an artistic creation, at a time when he is suffering from both a perversion and a psychoneurosis. A correlative of the sublimation process is the development of abnormal traits of character, which have little or no social value; the morbid tendency of some ' Puritans ' to be shocked at the slightest pretext belongs to this group, and is to be regarded as an excessive reaction formation.

The psychosexual life of children differs from that of adults in three main characteristics—in the different nature of the pleasure experienced, in their relative independence of outside persons for this (auto-erotism), and in the fact that they obtain pleasure from much more manifold sources and yet in much less differentiated ways than do adults. At puberty important changes take place in all these respects. The excitations, mechanical and other, that gave satisfaction to the child's desires, now come to contain a disagreeable component (*Unlust*) due to the feeling of tension experienced. They thus constitute merely a ' fore-pleasure ' (*Vorlust*), which impels to further activities destined to produce the ' end-pleasure ' (*Endlust*) that relief of tension brings about. The sexual objective, a member of the opposite sex, now wins greater definition and significance. Lastly, the sources of excitation become

---

[1] One such tendency, to which Freud has given the name ' anal erotism,' has been shown to have an unexpected importance for general psychology, especially in regard to the development of character. Some illustrations of this are given in Chapter XXIV.

more localised, particularly anatomically; this is brought about by repression of the more accessory pleasures in the way indicated above. The greater proneness of women to suffer from psychoneuroses is explained by two characters that their sexual development shows in contrast with that of men. In the first place, the sexual activities of children pertain rather to the masculine type, so that at the time of puberty the augmentation of repression that then takes place has in the woman more to accomplish in suppressing the homosexual component than it has with men. In the second place, a shifting of the primary erotogenic[1] zone takes place with them, from the clitoris to the vagina, whereas this does not occur with men. The changes at puberty being thus more complex in the case of women, the possibilities of erroneous development are much greater.

The sexual thoughts of children are much more extensive and important than is generally believed. Usually in the third and fourth years of life questions begin to occur to them, the parents' answers to which are less satisfying and less often believed by them than is commonly thought. At this time, and shortly after, they begin to withdraw from their parents, and in their own world weave explanations and theories that are more satisfactory to them. These theories frequently contain more of the truth than might be imagined, and are of great significance in later life. Coincidently with the repression mentioned above there occurs repression of, and subsequent amnesia for, these early thoughts. A period of greater or less latency follows, usually from the fifth to the tenth years, when the process of sublimation is at its highest activity. Most adult memories for sexual thoughts seem to have begun in the latter part of this period, the earlier ones having been quite forgotten. In the earlier period sexual phantasies relating to the parents or other members of the family are very frequent, and often determine important reactions and choices in later life.

The next great field that Freud has investigated is that of *Dreams*. I have elsewhere[2] given an account of Freud's work and conclusions on this subject, and so need here mention only the outstanding features of his theory. Dreams are generally thought to be a meaningless conglomeration of psychical processes evoked

---

[1] In earlier writings I had thoughtlessly used the word ' erogenous.' A moment's reflection, however, shows that ' erotogenic ' is a more correct form.

[2] See Chapter X.

by chance somatic stimuli. Freud, on the contrary, finds that they are the disguised expression of highly significant underlying psychical processes. He contracts the ' manifest content,' which is the dream as directly related, with the ' latent content,' which is the group of thoughts reached by psycho-analysis of the dream. In the young child the manifest and latent contents are identical, and the dream plainly represents the imaginary fulfilment of an ungratified wish; the egocentric nature of the wish is equally evident. Freud maintains that every dream represents the fulfilment of an egocentric wish, and that the chief difference between the dreams of adults and those of young children is that in the former case the wish is a repressed one, the presentation of which is disguised so much as to make it unrecognisable until it has been submitted to psycho-analysis.

The mechanisms by means of which is brought about the distortion between the latent and the manifest content are quite precise. The thoughts of the latent content are unconscious, being repressed by the censorship of consciousness. In the waking state they cannot penetrate to consciousness, but during sleep, when the activity of the censorship is relaxed, they can do so, provided, however, they are distorted so that their true meaning is not recognised. The formation of the dream, or dream-making, is purely concerned with translating the latent thoughts into the distorted shape of the manifest content; it performs no intellectual work whatever. Apparently intellectual processes in dreams have been taken bodily from the latent content. The extent to which a given dream is incomprehensible, illogical, confused, and contradictory, exactly depends on the degree of distortion that has taken place, and is proportional to the amount of resistance offered by the subject to disclosing the underlying thoughts.

The four mechanisms of the dream-making are :

1. *Condensation.*—Every element in the manifest content represents the fusion of several in the latent thoughts, and *vice versa*. The latent content is condensed to a tenth or a twentieth of its original extent. The condensation is shown in several ways. For instance, a figure in a dream may be constituted by the fusion of the memories of several different actual persons, either by fusing some traits of one with others of another, or by making prominent the traits common to different persons and neglecting the ones not common to them. The same process frequently affects names,

so that neologisms may be formed exactly analogous to those found in the psychoses.

2. *Displacement.*—The psychical intensity of a given element in the manifest content shows no correspondence with that of the associated elements in the latent content; an element that stands in the foreground of interest in the former may represent the least significant of the latent thoughts, and an apparently unessential feature in the dream may represent the very core of the dream thoughts. Further, the most prominent affect in the dream frequently accompanies elements that represent the least important of the latent thoughts, and *vice versa*.

3. *Dramatisation.*—The manifest content depicts a situation or action, a fact which exercises a selecting influence on the mental processes to be presented. Logical relations between the latent thoughts are as such not represented, but they may be indicated by means of certain special devices. Thus, similarity may be represented by identification, causal relationship by making the one representing group of elements follow on the other, as in the gradual transformation of one scene into another, opposition and contradiction by inverting the two corresponding elements of the already formed dream, and so on. The characteristic that most dreams show of presenting the manifest content predominantly in a visual form Freud terms ' regression,' and explains it by a very interesting theory in which he also discusses the production of psychotic hallucinations.

4. *Secondary Elaboration.*—This is the product of consciousness, and is brought about by the alteration undergone by the dream processes during their apprehension in consciousness. To it is due whatever degree of ordering and consistency there may be found in a dream. It particularly affects parts of the dream that have been insufficiently distorted during the dream-making; its action continues after waking, so that the memory of a dream becomes more altered the greater is the period that has elapsed since it was experienced.

The affect in the manifest content is invariably less intense than that in the latent content; this inhibition is due partly to the tendency to psychical regression during sleep, and partly to the suppressing effect of the censorship. The affect is, as was mentioned above, displaced in the manifest content, but the apparent incongruity in its occurrence and association is solely due to this displacement; in the dream thoughts it is quite congruous and logically justified. The affect itself undergoes no distortion in the dream-making, as does the conceptual content, so that it is of the same nature in the manifest as in the latent content. The forgetting of dreams is, like the distortion of the latent content, a manifestation of the activity of the censorship. The most important part is first forgotten, and often is recalled only during the analysis.

The sources and material from which dreams are composed differ as regards the manifest and latent contents. In every dream appears some incident of the preceding day. Indifferent incidents—*i.e.*, those of little interest to the subject—frequently appear. These may be of the preceding day, or of older date ; in every case they have obtained psychical significance by becoming, on the day of their occurrence, associated with significant experiences or memories. Somatic stimuli—*e.g.*, pain—may sometimes provide material. These, however, are treated like other psychical material, and are woven into the dream under the same conditions; under no circumstances can they alone account for a dream, except in the sense of occasionally being an instigation. Hypermnesia for previously forgotten infantile events is sometimes seen in the manifest content, and much more frequently in the latent content. The groundwork of every dream is of infantile origin. A recent or conscious wish is inadequate to cause a dream unless it is associated with a repressed, unconscious one; this latter is always the real cause, and the superficial one is merely the 'instigator.' The latent thoughts are always of high personal significance to the subject, and are in direct continuity with the rest of his mental life. Dream analysis is the most valuable means at our disposal for penetrating into the unconsious.

The sole function of dreams is to protect sleep by stilling the activity of unconscious mental processes that otherwise would disturb it. When, however, the activity of the endopsychic censorship, which is diminished during sleep, is insufficient to keep from consciousness the latent thoughts, or to compel such distortion of them as to render them unrecognisable, recourse has to be had to the accession of energy that the censor can exert in the waking state, and the sleeper awakes, usually in terror.

In his book on *Wit* Freud has given a valuable contribution to the psychology of this subject and to that of humour; it is extraordinarily rich in new psychological points of view. The pleasure-bringing effect of wit depends partly on the technique and partly on the tendencies of this. Freud has analysed in great detail the various classes of witty jokes, and finds that the technique of their production shows the closest resemblance to that employed in dreams : different forms of condensation, displacement, indirect presentation, reversal into the opposite, failures in thought, production of neologisms, fusion into a unity, etc. According to their aim he divides witty jokes into harmless ones, the aim of which is purely to bring pleasure, and those that have a pronounced tendency; the latter are subdivided into four classes—the obscene, the aggressive or hostile, the cynical, and the sceptical respectively.

The pleasure of wit arises in an economy of psychical expenditure (*Ersparung an psychischem Aufwande*). Four stages in the development of wit may be distinguished. The psycho-genesis of wit leads back to the play with words so characteristic of early childhood life. The suppression of this activity, brought about by the development of logical thought and the knowledge of intrinsic relations between the different conceptions represented by words, is under certain circumstances relaxed in later life, and so arises the simple joke (*Scherz*) in which enjoyment of the old play is again made possible. In the harmless witty jest (*Witz*) the abrogation of the suppressing criticism allows the expression of a given thought of some value ; the difference between joking and wit lies solely in the value of the thought communicated in the latter process. Finally, in wit that has a pronounced tendency, a form that has a more complex mechanism, there is allowed to come to expression a thought that, owing to the force of repression, could not reach expression in a direct way. In the last-named form of wit a certain initial pleasure (*Vorlust*) is obtained through the technique of the jest itself, but instead of this being all, as in the harmless jest, it serves to release further inhibitions, so that a deeper source of pleasure (*Endlust*) is reached.

Wit has a great deal in common with dreams beyond the fact of their both employing the same technical devices. A witty joke suddenly *occurs* to one; it is the product, not of the conscious mental processes, but of the unconscious. The source of the pleasure is also an unconscious one; in wit, strictly speaking, we do not know what we laugh at, and constantly deceive ourselves over the excellence of a joke and the value of the conveyed thought according to the varying part played in the production of our pleasure, on the one hand by the technique of the joke, and on the other hand by its tendency. The most important difference between wit and dreams is that the latter represent an asocial process, the former a social one. Further, dreams serve to guard from pain, wit represents a search for pleasure. Freud makes a number of penetrating remarks on the significance of wit as a social process, its function, and the precise relations between the speaker and hearer, that cannot here be discussed.

Freud further extensively deals with the relation of wit to the comic. The production of the latter and the source of pleasure are, in contradistinction from those of wit, quite conscious. Of the kinds of processes described as comical, ingenuousness stands nearest to wit. It differs from this in being produced free from inhibiting influences and without the application of technical devices ; the pleasure it gives is due to the sight of another setting himself without effort beyond the action of influences that would inhibit the onlooker. Comic processes proper arise from a comparison between our own person and that of the person at whom we laugh, especially when the latter shows an over-expenditure of physical output or a lack of mental. Humour is a defence against the painful or disagreeable ; the energy that would otherwise have produced pain is transformed into a source of pleasure. For humour only one person is necessary, for comicality two, for wit three (the producer of the joke, the imaginary person against whom it is directed, and the person who listens to it).

With wit there is effected an economy of expenditure in inhibition, with comic in thought, with humour in feeling. All three transport us into a state of our childhood, ' in which we did not know the comic, were not capable of wit, and did not need humour in order to make us feel happy in life.'

In another volume Freud has developed a number of interesting and suggestive investigations into the ' Psycho-pathology of Everyday Life.'[1] The principle underlying this work was his discovery that certain inefficiencies in our mental activities and certain apparently purposeless performances, both of which groups seem to have no psychical meaning, show themselves on analysis to have been determined by unconscious motives. These unconscious motives concern unacceptable processes that have been inade-

---

[1] See Chapter II. for a fuller exposition of this.

quately suppressed, and which come to expression by interfering
with the accomplishment of conscious mental activities.

Of the first group may be mentioned the following: Certain
acts of forgetting are due to a half-conscious desire to forget, an
extension of our general tendency not to recall the disagreeable.
The memory that cannot be recalled may itself be of a painful
nature, or may be associated with another of this nature. Difficulty
in recalling well-known proper names is particularly often to be
explained in this way. The actual source of unpleasantness is
usually by no means obvious, and often càn be discovered only
by a little psycho-analysis. It frequently happens during the effort
to recall a given name that another one presents itself, sometimes
in such a compelling way that it is hard to put it aside. Analysis
then shows that the second name is a disguised replacement of the
first, being a compromise between the effort to recall the name
searched for and the unconscious inhibiting impulse. This con-
cealing-memory or ' screen-memory ' (*Deckerinnerung*), in which
one memory appears as a cover for another associated one, may
refer to whole episodes, particularly those of childhood life; it
is one of the ways in which falsification of memory is brought
about. Allied to these defects in recollection are certain mistakes
in action (*Vergreifen*) in which the error principally consists in
omission. Thus many misplacements of objects, with subsequent
inability to find them again, apparently accidental destroying of
objects, and so on, are determined by unconscious motives.

To the second group belong many instances of mistakes in
speech (*lapsus linguæ*), in reading, in writing, and in apprehending
what is said to one (*Versprechen, Verlesen, Verschreiben, Missver-
stehen*). As in the former cases the mistake made is, like an hysterical
symptom, a compromise between the conscious intention and the
unconscious one. Such mistakes, particularly often slips of the
tongue or pen, betray hidden thoughts or wishes against the person's
will. More complicated mistakes of the same nature are various
symptomatic movements, general mistakes in knowledge, when
the person knows well the actual fact that he has incorrectly
described, and elaborately incorrect performances of simple tasks.
With all these errors, as of the ones mentioned above, Freud has
given the analysis of a great number of pretty and instructive
examples, the study of which is invaluable for practical psychology.
He adds in this volume a chapter on the subject of superstition and its

on. For the whole group I have suggested the collective term 'parapraxia,' on the analogy with apraxia.[1]

It will be seen from this that, according to Freud, our mental processes are more rigorously determined than is commonly believed, and that many of them generally thought to be causeless have in fact a very precise and definable cause. The same remark applies to those mental processes where we believe we have a perfectly free choice. A typical instance of this is afforded by the children's game 'think of a number.' Whereas at first sight it would appear that we are free to choose any possible number, careful analysis shows, as was first pointed out by Adler[2] some years ago, that the number actually chosen is always connected with some mental process of considerable personal significance, though this may never have been realised by the subject, and that the choice has been determined by definite preceding mental constellations. I may relate an example of this, obtained from an unbelieving acquaintance. He produced the number 986, and defied me to connect it with anything of especial interest in his mind. Using the free-association method he first recalled a memory, which had not previously been present in his mind, to the following effect: Six years ago, on the hottest day he could remember, he had seen a joke in an evening newspaper, which stated that the thermometer had stood at 986° F., evidently an exaggeration of 98·6° F. We were at the time seated in front of a very hot fire from which he had just drawn back, and he remarked, probably quite correctly, that the heat had aroused this dormant memory. However, I was curious to know why this memory had persisted with such vividness as to be so readily brought out, for with most people it surely would have been forgotten beyond recall, unless it had become associated with some other mental experience of more significance. He told me that in reading the joke he had laughed uproariously, and that on many subsequent occasions he had recalled it with great relish. As the joke was obviously a very tenuous one, this strengthened my expectation that more lay behind. His next thought was the general reflection that the conception of heat had always greatly impressed him; that heat was the most important thing in the universe, the source of all life, and so

---

[1] The German word *Fehlleistung* would thus be rendered by 'parapraxis.'

[2] Adler, 'Drei Psycho-Analysen von Zahleneinfällen und obsedierenden Zahlen,' *Psychiatr.-Neurol. Woch.*, Jahrg. VII., S. 263.

on. This remarkable attitude of a quite prosaic young man certainly needed some explanation, so I asked him to continue his free associations. The next thought was of a factory-stack which he could see from his bedroom window. He often stood of an evening watching the flame and smoke issuing out of it, and reflecting on this deplorable waste of energy. Heat, flame, the source of life, the waste of vital energy issuing from an upright, hollow tube— it was not hard to divine from such associations that the ideas of heat and fire were unconsciously linked in his mind with the idea of love, as is so frequent in symbolic thinking, and that there was a strong masturbation complex present, a conclusion which he presently confirmed. We had just before been talking of sexual topics, a fact which no doubt had unconsciously influenced his choice. His choice of the number was therefore far from being a free one, being, in fact, dictated by a very significant personal constellation.

II. Forgetting

One of Freud's most notable contributions to psychology, and a conception fundamental in his study of the present group of mental processes, was his discovery that, in addition to the other causes of forgetting, ' repression '[1] (*Verdrängung*) plays a most important part. Others before Freud had realised the existence of this mechanism, but it was reserved for him to demonstrate the extent to which it is operative in both normal and abnormal mental life.

Freud regards repression as a biological defence-mechanism, the function of which is to guard the mind from painful experiences. He holds that there is in the mind of everyone a tendency to forget the things that the person does not like to be reminded of—in other words, painful or disagreeable memories. It is true that we often remember against our will matters that we would rather forget, but there are two explanations for this. In the first place, such disagreeable haunting memories are frequently themselves only the replacements of buried and still more disagreeable ones with which they are associated, an occurrence allied to that concerned in the genesis of true obsessions. In the second place, the capacity to forget painful experiences is only of a certain strength,

---

[1] It will be noticed that the word ' repression ' is here used in a rather special sense, to be carefully distinguished from that of ' suppression.' It means in psycho-analysis ' the keeping of certain mental processes from consciousness.'

which differs greatly in different people, and it is not always successful in achieving its aim. It is but rarely that one can forget the death of a dear relative, however desirable that might be, for the associative links to other conscious memories are too well formed. In such cases, what happens is that trivial memories, which by association might serve *unnecessarily* to remind us of the painful event, are apt to get forgotten—the name of the medical attendant, details as to the fatal malady, and so on; the tide of amnesia covers the base of the hill, but cannot reach the summit. By this means an economy is effected in the number of times that the painful memory is recalled to consciousness. Further, it must be remarked that, for reasons which cannot here be gone into, repression acts much more extensively in causing forgetfulness of internal, extremely intimate, and personal mental processes, than of what may be called ' external memories ' known to the world, such as failure, grief, and so on. As is well known, Freud has applied his conception of repression to a number of other fields, notably to the explanation of infantile and hysterical amnesias, which do not here concern us.

A good instance of the recognition of the part played in everyday life by repression has been furnished by Darwin in a passage that does equal credit to his scientific honesty and his psychological acumen.[1] He writes in his autobiography: ' I had, during many years, followed a golden rule, namely, that whenever a published fact, a new observation or thought came across me, which was opposed to my general results, to make a memorandum of it, without fail and at once; for I had found by experience that such facts and thoughts were far more apt to escape from the memory than favourable ones.' Pick[2] quotes a number of authors who more or less clearly recognise that a defensive striving against painful memories can lead to their becoming forgotten; but, as Freud remarks, no one has so exhaustively and at the same time so incisively described both the process itself and the psychological basis of it as has Nietzsche in his ' Jenseits von Gut und Böse ': ' Das habe ich getan, sagt mein Gedächtnis. Das kann ich nicht getan haben, sagt mein Stolz und bleibt unerbittlich. Endlich—gibt das Gedächtnis nach.' [' I have done that, says

---

[1] ' Life of Charles Darwin,' edited by Francis Darwin, 1902, p. 42.
[2] Pick, ' Zur Psychologie des Vergessen bei Geistes- und Nervenkranken,' *Arch. f. Kriminal-Anthropologie u. Kriminalistik*, 1905, Bd. xviii., S. 251.

my memory. I cannot have done that, says my pride, and remains
inexorable. Finally—memory yields.']

The class of forgotten thoughts in everyday life to which this
mechanism mainly applies is, of course, that where the other causes
of forgetting do not provide adequate explanations; in other
words, it principally concerns matters that we should normally
expect to remember. For instance, one would expect some hidden
reason in the case of the name of a near relative or friend being
forgotten much more readily than in the case of that of a casual
acquaintance. The examples of the mechanism may conveniently
be divided into two groups: (1) Forgetting to carry out some
intended purpose (*Vergessen von Vorsätzen*), and (2) forgetting a
given memory.

(1) *Forgetting to carry out an intention.*

A field in which some counter-will frequently leads to forgetting
is that regarding the making or keeping of appointments. A
man unwillingly feels that he should invite a given acquaintance
to a social function he is giving in the near future. He says to him,
' You will be sure to come, won't you ? I am not absolutely certain
of the date at this moment, but I will send you a written invitation
and let you know.' He forgets, until it is too late, and his excessive
self-reproach betrays his unconscious culpability and shows that
the forgetting was not altogether an accident. Maeder[1] relates the
case of a lady who forgot to keep her appointment with the dress-
maker to try on her bridal gown the day before the wedding, recollecting it only at eight in the evening. One must suppose that her
whole heart was not in the marriage, and, in fact, she has since
been divorced.

In my own life I have noted numerous instances of a purposeful
forgetting of appointments. Indeed, I can recall several annoying
quandaries that this habit has led me into. One is perhaps worth
repeating, as showing how complete can be the divorce between
two memories when a ' unpleasantness ' motive is in action. Some
years ago, when in a junior position at a certain hospital, I was
asked by my chief to visit his patients on Friday, as he wished to
attend an important luncheon at the time. It was an exceptional
request, for the rule was that approbation of the committee had
to be obtained before a substitute was allowed to act, and I gladly

---

[1] Maeder, ' Contributions à la psychopathologie de la vie quotidienne,' *Arch. de
Psychol.*, t. vi., p. 150.

consented, quite forgetting that I already had at the same time an appointment, which I was very desirous of keeping, and which would have been particularly inconvenient to postpone. On several occasions during the week, while going over my future engagements, I thought of both these, but never together; the thought would come, ' Let me see, at one on Friday I have to be at such-and-such a place,' and a few hours later a similar thought would come concerning the other place. The two intentions, both of which I was anxious not to forget, were kept distinct from each other, as if in water-tight compartments. When the time came I forgot the hospital appointment, and to my intense chagrin heard that my chief was very annoyed at being called away from his luncheon on account of my apparent unpardonable remissness. The self-reproach one feels on recollecting the forgotten duty on these and similar occasions is indicative of the true significance of the occurrence.

This significance is intuitively realised in the case of lovers. A man who has failed to appear at a rendezvous will seek in vain to be forgiven on the plea that he had forgotten about it—will, indeed, with this plea only increase the lady's resentment. Even if he falls back on the customary psychological explanations, and describes how urgent business had filled his mind, he will only hear in reply: ' How curious that such things didn't happen last year ! It only means that you think less of me.' Similarly, when a man begins to be forgetful about paying accustomed attentions to his wife, overlooks her birthday, and so on, she correctly interprets it as a sign of a change in their relations.

Another field where forgetting occurs to an untoward extent is in giving—a fact that indicates a more widespread objection to giving than is agreeable to our altruistic conceptions. Most of those who have filled secretarial positions have been astonished to find the difficulty there is in collecting subscriptions as they fall due, and the ease with which people with otherwise good memories ' overlook ' such matters. It is far from rare for them even to falsify their memory, and to assert firmly that they have already paid. A few, dimly conscious of their weakness, compensate for it by forming the habit of promptly paying every bill the moment it arrives. In general, however, there is a striking difference between the ease with which one remembers to send to the bank incoming cheques, and that with which one forgets to pay incoming bills.

The same tendency is the explanation of the constant ' forgetting ' to return borrowed books that seems to afflict so many people, a habit which must have distressed most of us who have a good library. This observation will be confirmed by anyone who has tried to establish a permanent library in an institution where many coming and going students have ready access to it.

Almost as common is the habit of forgetting to post letters. Here, also, unconscious motives can sometimes be detected in individual instances. Sometimes one leaves a letter on one's desk for several days, forgetting each time to take it with one ; in such cases it may be counted on that there is some secret opposition to sending the given letter. In one instance of the kind I ultimately posted the letter, but forgot to address the envelope. It was returned to me through the Dead Letter Office. I addressed it and again handed it to my maid to post, but this time without a stamp. I was then forced to recognise that there was in me an unconscious opposition to the sending of the letter, one of which I had previously been unaware, but which manifested itself in external inhibitions. One does not forget to post a letter that one's mind is in full harmony about sending—for instance, a love-letter. One is more apt to forget to send a letter containing a cheque than one containing an account. Often the resistance is of a general order. Thus a busy man forgets to post letters entrusted to him—to his slight annoy-ance—by his wife, just as he may ' forget ' to carry out her shopping orders. Inhibitions of this kind sometimes betray a veiled an-tagonism towards the person whose behests we forget to fulfil. They constitute a way of depreciating the importance of the other person for ourselves, and when pronounced in general they indicate a lack of consideration for others, based on an excessive self-absorption or abnormally high self-esteem.

George Meredith, in his ' Celt and Saxon,' gives a pretty instance of the forgetting of an intention being determined by a counter-will, one which also well illustrates the mechanism of rationalisa-tion described in the second chapter. There are two brothers, one of whom, Phillip, is suffering under the mortification of having been jilted by his fiancée, Adiante. His brother Patrick, who is very fond of him, determines to visit the lady and try to influence her in his brother's favour. He stays as a guest in her father's house, where he finds that she has eloped with another man. In her home is a miniature of the lady; Patrick is greatly struck by its beauty, becomes fascinated by it, and persuades the father to give it him to take to his brother. On reaching home he shows it to his brother, and then says good-night. I now quote from Meredith: ' Phillip checked the departing Patrick. " You can leave that." He made a sign for the miniature to be left on the table. Patrick laid it there. His brother had not touched it, and he could have defended himself for having forgotten to leave it, on the plea that it might prevent his brother from having his proper share of sleep; and also, that Phillip had no great pleasure in the possession of it. The two pleas, however, did not make one harmonious apology, and he went straight to the door in an odd silence, with the step of a decorous office-clerk, keeping his shoulders turned on Phillip to conceal his look of destitution.'

In examples similar to those preceding, the counter-impulse that inhibits the memory is as a rule directed immediately against the conscious intention. In a more complicated series of cases it is directed against some other mental process, which, however, stands in associative relation to the conscious intention ; this mental process is, so to speak, symbolised in the latter. The following are two examples of the kind:[1] Maeder[2] relates the case of a hospital interne who had an important business appointment in the town, but who was not allowed to leave the hospital until his chief, who was out for the evening, returned. He decided to leave his post, nevertheless, and on getting back late in the evening, was astonished to find he had left the light burning in his room, a thing he had never done before during his two years of service. He at once perceived the reason for his omission; his chief always passed by the window on his way to his own house, would see the light burning, and conclude that the assistant was at home. The cause for the inhibition having passed, the subject readily appre-hended it. A patient of mine on a number of occasions made the remarkable omission of forgetting to shave the right side of his face. It was always the same side, and it was the one that was turned towards me during the treatment. Analysis of the occur-rence showed that it was determined by a number of unconscious processes, of which the following was one: The idea of hair was

---

[1] For other examples see Otto Rank, ' Fehlleistungen aus dem Alltagsleben Zentralblatt für Psychoanalyse, Jahrg. II., S. 265.

[2] Maeder, ' Une voie nouvelle en psychologie ; Freud et son école, Cænobium, Gennaio, 1909, Anno. III., p. 100.

connected with various sexual ideas, and the non-shaving of the side turned to me symbolised a disinclination to lay bare his sexual life, the occurrence always synchronising in fact with an outburst of resistance against the treatment.

(2) *Forgetting a given memory.*

We are concerned mainly with striking lapses in memory—namely, regarding matters that as a rule we can easily recall. An instance, which is hard to credit, though I can vouch for the accuracy of it, was related to me by a medical friend. His wife was seriously ill with some obscure abdominal malady, which might well have been tubercular, and, while anxiously pondering over the possible nature of it, he remarked to her, ' It is comforting to think that there has been no tuberculosis in your family.' She turned to him very astonished, and said, ' Have you forgotten that my mother died of tuberculosis, and that my sister recovered from it only after having been given up by the doctors ?' His anxiety lest the obscure symptoms should prove to be tubercular had made him forget a piece of knowledge that was thoroughly familiar to him. Those accustomed to psycho-analysis will surmise that there is more to be said about the matter, but the example will serve to illustrate the influence affective processes have in connection with forgetting.

A lapse of memory that caused a good deal of stir at the time refers to the occasion on which Cardinal Newman (then Dr. Newman) called the Infallibilists ' an insolent and aggressive faction.' When the words were made public, Dr. Newman vehemently denied ever having used them, but some time after he remembered that he had, and admitted it.

It is with proper names that one observes the most striking instances of this process. In the majority of cases the counter-will that prevents a familiar name from being recalled is directed against some mental process that is associated with the one to be recalled, rather than against this itself. On account of some disagreeable experience, we would rather not recall a given name; we may actually succeed in forgetting it, but more often the tendency is shown indirectly in our being unable to recall other names resembling it, and which might bring the undesired one to our mind. In other words, we have to think of the undesired name at times, but we guard ourselves against doing so more often than is necessary.

A hospital interne got to know a nurse, whom he of course

addressed by her surname, and in his work saw her daily for about a year. They later got more intimate, and he now experienced great difficulty in recalling her surname so as to address envelopes to her. On one occasion he was unable to write to her for three weeks ; recourse to her letters was of no use, for she always signed only her Christian name in them. Investigation of the matter brought to light the fact that her Christian name was the same as that of a girl he had previously jilted, and also of another girl he had been passionately in love with throughout his boyhood. This name he could not forget. What had happened was that he had successively transferred his affections from one girl to the other, the three being unconsciously identified in his mind. He was thus always true to his love, and did not wish to recall any fact such as the different surname that would tend to remind him of his faithlessness. The surnames in no way resembled one another.

Brill[1] relates the following example from his own experience: When working at Zurich, he wished to recall the name of an old patient of his, on whose case he had specially worked for some months, but was totally unable to do so. He had painstakingly prepared an account of the case for publication, but at the last moment his chief intervened, and decided to report it before a local society. He was unexpectedly prevented from doing so, and Brill was sent to read the paper at the meeting, this being credited to the chief. In trying to recall his patient's name, the name of another patient, Appenzeller, who was suffering from the same disease, persistently presented itself. In the lengthy psycho-analysis undertaken, one apparently irrelevant memory kept recurring over and over again. This was an actual scene, in which the chief in question had aimed with a shot-gun at a rabbit, and had missed, to the amusement of Brill and the bystanders. The sought-for name ultimately flashed up—*Lapin* (rabbit), the patient being a French-Canadian. The example is instructive in illustrating the associative replacement-formations that come to the mind instead of the proper memory.[2] The sound of the first part of Appenzeller's name resembles the French pronunciation of *Lapin*, and the scene that kept recurring, the failure of the chief to bag the rabbit, sym-bolised the whole incident that was the cause of the inhibition.

[1] A. A. Brill, 'A Contribution to the Psychopathology of Everyday Life,' *Psycho-herapy*, 1909, p. 9.
[2] See p. 42.

The following instance is rather more complex, but shows how fine are the threads connecting unconscious mental processes: A lady was unable to recall the Christian name of a near friend. The full name was Isabell Brown, but she could only recall the surname ; instead of the other, the name Isidore presented itself, to be at once rejected as incorrect. Thus the failure in memory consisted only in the replacement of the syllable ' bell ' by ' dore.' I asked her to associate to the word Brown, and the two names ' Owlie ' and ' Leen ' at once came to her mind. It will be noticed that the first two letters of the first word and the last one of the second word are contained in Brown; the only foreign ones in each case form the syllable ' ly ' in pronunciation—a fact to be borne in mind. The two words were pet names of two common friends, who used to live together with the subject, and it was only in their company that she used to see Miss Brown. Concerning the first one, she said that she was at present pregnant for the first time, and that she was anxious as to the outcome, because certain characteristics in her figure had led her to suspect that pelvic narrowing might give rise to difficulties in the confinement. She also mentioned another friend, Dora D., who had similar characteristics, and Isidora D., a famous classical dancer, whom she knew personally, and whose perfect figure she much admired. The name Isidore, which it will be remembered was the replace-ment-memory, reminded her of the poem by Edgar Allan Poe, ' Beautiful Isidore *Lee* ' (ly). I told her that the correct name of the poem was ' Beautiful Annabel Lee,' so that she had committed another falsification of memory; some inhibition was therefore acting against the syllables ' Anna ' and ' Bell.' Thought of the name Annabel brought to her mind the name of Owlie's sister, Annie Sybil, which is a sound-contraction of Anna Isabell, and at once Miss Brown's proper name Isabell, which I personally did not know, came to her mind. The subject had recently had a painful quarrel with Annie Sybil, in which also the latter's sister had unfortunately become involved; she had always thought it a pity that the sister she disliked had a better figure, and was more suited for matrimony, than the one she was so fond of. There were thus two painful thoughts at the bottom of the amnesia—one the anxiety about Owlie's confinement, and the other that in this respect the disliked sister was more favourably situated.

So far the analysis. I will now venture on the following re-construction of the mistake. The names first recalled by the subject—namely, Isidore Brown—one incorrect, the other correct, were both directly associated to the syllable ' ly,' the former *via* the poem, the latter *via* the pet names of the two friends. The sup-pressed syllable was ' bell.' In view of the fact that the word ' belly ' summarised the whole situation, succinctly symbolising the dis-comforting idea about the friend's confinement, it is difficult to avoid the inference that the amnesia for the syllable ' bell ' had thus proceeded: One must suppose that the thought of Miss Isabell Brown had unconsciously reminded the patient of their common friend and her sister; the diphthong in the surname, further, is identical with that in the former's name, Owlie, and the Christian name resembles the second part of the latter's name, Annie Sybil. The first part of the latter name, Annie, reminded her of ' Beautiful Annabel Lee ' making the word ' belly,' which symbolised the painful thoughts in question. These thoughts, nevertheless, came to expression in the false replacement-memory. First the accent was shifted from the first syllable, ' bell,' of the objectionable word to the second, ' ly,' which was also the second syllable of Owlie's name. This, however, was unsuitable for forming a name by being added to the remembered part ' Isi,' so that a further shifting took place, in which it was replaced by ' dore.' Dora was the name of a friend with similar characteristics to Owlie's, but, in combination with ' Isi,' it was the name of another person, Isidora D., who was strikingly free from them. The subject, therefore, invests her friend with the beautiful and healthy attributes of the famous dancer. One might even go farther, and surmise that the reason why Dore had appeared rather than Dora was because the word ' door,' which is constantly used symbolically for any exit (for instance, of the body, as in the Song of Songs), was better adapted to symbolise the suppressed complex than the word Dora is. An adjuvant reason for the choice of the masculine form Isidore rather than the feminine one Isidora was probably the fact that her attitude towards her friend was a distinctly masculine and protective one. It is fairly evident that the subject was transferring on to her friend emotions—*e.g.*, solicitude about the confinement—that really referred to herself. She had a dread of the same event, and to an expert there are clues in the falsified memory to the particular infantile origin of this. Her identifying herself with the friend was facilitated by two circumstances—first, that she greatly admired the latter's husband (and was thus unconsciously putting herself in her place); and, secondly, that she was devotedly fond of the friend herself.[1] Of especial interest is the fact that the repressed complex, which was responsible for the forgetting, betrayed itself in the replacement-memory, which was, as is always the case, a compromise-formation. To many readers this reconstruction will probably appear as too fine-spun. In my opinion, however, they underestimate the combination of delicacy and rigour with which unconscious and preconscious processes are determined, a conclusion which can readily be confirmed by a painstaking study of similar material.

A simple illustration of the way in which a strong affect will cleave to a name, and be transferred to any other person bearing the same or similar name, is afforded by Shakespeare in ' Julius Cæsar ' (Act III., Scene iii.):

Third Citizen. Your name, sir, truly.
Cinna. Truly, my name is Cinna.
Second Citizen. Tear him to pieces; he's a conspirator.
Cinna. I am Cinna the poet; I am not Cinna the conspirator.
Second Citizen. It is no matter; his name's Cinna; pluck but his name out of his heart, and turn him going.

The same thing happened during the French Revolution. Some confusion had arisen owing to two people bearing the name of Biron. One was known to be guilty, but there was little time for proper investigation. ' Bring them both,' said Fouquier; ' they will pass through it.' They both passed through it—to the scaffold—on the following day.[2]

---

[1] An interesting confirmation of the correctness of the analysis occurred some months later when the baby in question was born. The lady, on mentioning the news to various friends, repeatedly made the slip of referring to her friend as Mrs. M., her own name. She thus expresses her wish that the happy event had happened to her instead of to her friend. M. had also been the friend's maiden name, so that by the mistake the lady further expresses the wish that the friend was still single—*i.e.*, her jealousy at the marriage.

[2] This reminds me of an incident in our own times, which, though not turning on the question of names, is worth recording in illustration of another psycho-analytical thesis—namely, that, as in the last two examples, a strong affect will get transferred on quite illogical grounds and by means of superficial associations; in general it may be said that a strong affect always tends to enforce identification at the expense of discrimination. During the stirring days of the militant suffragettes Lord Weardale was attacked and assaulted at Euston Station by ladies who were under the impression that he was the Prime Minister, Mr. Asquith. A few days later one of the most dis-

A field in which significance is apt to be intuitively attributed to the forgetting of names is that where our own are forgotten. Few people can avoid feeling a twinge of resentment when they find that their name has been forgotten, particularly if it is by some one with whom they had hoped or expected it would be remembered. They instinctively realise that if they had made a greater impression on the person's mind he would certainly have remembered them again, for the name is an integral part of the personality. Similarly, few things are more flattering to most people than to find themselves addressed by name by a great personage where they could hardly have anticipated it. Napoleon, like most leaders of men, was a master of this art. In the midst of the disastrous campaign of France in 1814, he gave an amazing proof of his memory in this direction. When in a town near Craonne, he recollected that he had met the mayor, De Bussy, over twenty years ago in the La Fère Regiment. The delighted De Bussy at once threw himself into his service with extraordinary zeal. Conversely there is no surer way of affronting someone than by pretending to forget his name; the insinuation is thus conveyed that the person is so unimportant in our eyes that we cannot be bothered to remember his name. This device is often exploited in literature. In Turgenev's ' Smoke ' (p. 255) the following passage occurs: ' " So you still find Baden entertaining, M'sieu—Litvinov." Ratmirov always uttered Litvinov's surname with hesitation, every time, as though he had forgotten it, and could not at once recall it. In this way, as well as by the lofty flourish of his hat in saluting him, he meant to insult his pride.' The same author, in his ' Fathers and Children ' (p. 107), writes: ' The Governor invited Kirsanov and Bazarov to his ball, and within a few minutes invited them a second time, regarding them as brothers, and calling them Kisarov.' Here the forgetting that he had spoken to them, the mistake in the names, and the inability to distinguish between the two young men, constitute a culmination

---

tinguished suffragettes, speaking at a meeting at South Kensington, said that ' it was very awkward for Lord Weardale that he should be so like Mr. Asquith. Anybody resembling a Cabinet Minister was not safe in these days. She advised those who resembled members of the Government to make some alteration in their appearance by growing a beard or moustache. Women could not waste their time worrying over whether it was the right man or not (!).' Coming to later times still, we see the same affect radiating over whole nations, so that *all* Germans are supposed to be brutal on the one hand and *all* Englishmen hypocritical on the other.

of disparagement.[1] Falsification of a name has the same signification as forgetting it; it is only a step towards complete amnesia.
The word-contamination in this instance shows a striking psychological intuition of the process termed by Freud ' identification ';
it indicated that in the Governor's eyes the distinguishing characteristics of the young men were so little marked, and the men so unimportant, that he did not think it worth while to make the effort
of differentiating one from the other. Turgenev seems to have been
very familiar with the mechanism in question. In his ' Virgin Soil '
there is an example where it is still more frankly expressed. A
rather forlorn and unprepossessing man called Paklin has just
brought some bad news to Sipyagin, a nobleman. The latter tells
his wife, who asks him how he knows; to which he replies (in
Paklin's presence) ' Mr. . . . Mr. . . . what's his name ? Mr. Konopatin
brought this news.' A little later he is giving various orders, and
runs on thus : ' Eh ? I fancy you spoke, Mr. Konopatin. I'll
take you with me to-morrow, Mr. Konopatin. What do you say ?
I don't hear. You will take some vodka, I dare say ? Some vodka
for Mr. Konopatin ! No ! You don't drink it ? In that case,
Fyodor, show the gentleman to the green-room.' ' Good-night,
Mr. Kono——' Paklin lost all patience at last. ' Paklin !' he
roared; ' my name is Paklin !' ' Yes, yes; well, that's much the
same. It's not unlike, you know.' When they meet the next morning
Sipyagin greets him as follows: ' " Mr. Paklin ! you will come with
me, Mr. Paklin ! Put Mr. Paklin's bag on the box ! I am taking
Mr. Paklin !" he said, with an emphasis on the word Paklin, and an
accent on the letter a, as though he would say, " You've a name like
that, and presume to feel insulted when people change it for you !
There you are, then ! Take plenty of it ! I'll give you as much as
you want ! Mr. Paklin ! Paklin !" The unlucky name kept
resounding on the keen morning air.' One more example from
literature, this time from Meredith's ' The Ordeal of Richard Feverel.'
Mrs. Mount, in talking to Richard, refers to his friend Ripton thus:
' " How's that Mr. Ripson, Pipson, Nipson ?—it's not compli-
mentary, but I can't remember names of that sort. Why do you
have friends of that sort ? He's not a gentleman." '

---

[1] In literature disparagement is often indicated by the forgetting of other matters
besides names. Thus, in Bernard Shaw's ' Cæsar and Cleopatra,' Cæsar's indifference
to Cleopatra is depicted by his being vexed on leaving Egypt at having forgotten
something he has to do. Finally he recollects what it is—to say good-bye to Cleopatra.

Sensitiveness about the correct spelling of one's name is extremely frequent ; we all know the profound difference that members of Scottish clans see between ' Mc ' and ' Mac,' and a practical psychologist realises the importance of being sound on the matter every time he writes such a name. I had thought personally that I was free from sensitiveness of this kind, until a little occurrence some time ago taught me the contrary. An article of mine had been published in a German journal; only my surname was printed, with the letters ' M.D.' (which are not used professionally in Germany) attached, as if they were the initials. The same morning I had occasion to fill up a lunacy certificate, and was surprised at the secretary laughing when I handed it in; I had signed it with my first name only, thus compensating for the omission in the article. This sensitiveness has sometimes deeper roots than mere personal self-esteem; Stekel[1] has traced it to infantile complexes relating to the giver of the name—the father.

The following two instances within my own experience are similar to those quoted from Turgenev. The first relates to Mr. Mayo Robson, the eminent gastro-intestinal surgeon, after whom was named a bobbin he had invented for the operation of entero-anastomosis. Another surgeon, almost equally eminent in the same field of work, and living in the same town, remarked one day in a lofty and contemptuous manner: ' This patient had previously been unsuccessfully operated on by a man called Rayo Bobson, or Bayo Robbins, or some such name.' His motive was evident, and of course quite conscious. In the second instance the mistake in the name was quite unconsciously made as the result of a falsification of memory, but the significance was very similar. It was at a university graduation ceremony, where a number of visitors were present arrayed in multi-coloured and imposing robes. Those so attired formed a procession in double file. A friend of mine, a foreigner, remarked, as Professor Titchener passed, ' Let me see, who is that ? Isn't it Kitchener ?' Many would be inclined to see no significance in the mistake, although my friend knew the names of Lord Kitchener and Professor Titchener fairly well. I have, however, to add these two additional facts: A few minutes before, while talking about experimental psychologists in general,

---

[1] Stekel, 'Warum sie den eigenen Namen hassen,' *Zentralbl. für Psycho-analyse,* Jahrg. I., Heft 3, S. 109. See also his interesting article, 'Die Verpflichtung des Namens,' *Zeitschr. für Psychother. u. med. Psychol.,* February, 1911, Bd. iii., S. 110.

he had allowed himself to make the scurrilous remark that in his opinion they should be called the pantry-cooks of psychology, on account of their menial field of work; the passage from ' cook ' to ' kitchen ' is obvious. Secondly, he had also commented on the martial appearance of this dazzling procession, and I can readily imagine his being especially struck by Professor Titchener's soldierly bearing. It is difficult to avoid the inference that these two trends of thought, present in his mind so recently, played their part in the falsification of the name, which thus betrayed his private opinion of the field of work in which Professor Titchener[1] is so eminent.

Many people have a strikingly bad memory for names, even when their memory is otherwise good. This is generally explained by saying that proper names are among the latest acquired knowledge, so that our memory of them is especially fragile; in accordance with the law of dissolution, these memories are among the first to be lost, a process that constitutes one of the most characteristic signs of approaching senility. This explanation is difficult to harmonise with two facts—first, that in many cases the memory is weak in this connection when it is notably good in regard to other more complex, and later acquired matters, such as scientific formulæ and so on; and, secondly, that the characteristic in question is much more pronounced with some people than with others, and even when they are young. When the opportunity of making a psycho-analysis with some one of this type presents itself, two other matters are brought to light with considerable constancy— namely, that for various reasons the person's own name has acquired an unusual psychical significance, so that it becomes invested with the feeling-tone of the whole personality, and that there is a strong ego-complex present. It would seem, therefore, that the general inability to bear other people's names in mind is an expression of an excessively high estimation of the importance of one's own name and of oneself in general, with a corresponding indifference to, or depreciation of, other people. In my experience I have most often found this characteristic with people having either an extremely common or an extremely rare name, both contingencies

[1] I trust that Mr. Robson and Professor Titchener will pardon my sacrificing the personal privacy of their names in the cause of science. I have purposely selected from a large number of similar instances, two in which the contrast between a rare individual disparagement and an otherwise universal respect is specially striking.

leading to undue sensitiveness in the matter, but I cannot put this forward as being a general rule. It further seems to me probable that the increasing difficulty of retaining names that is such a frequent accompaniment of advancing years may, in part at least, be attributed to the growing self-esteem brought by success, by cessation from the turmoils and conflicts of youth, and by regression to infantile narcissism.

Falsification of memory, as was indicated above, is closely related to forgetting, and is influenced by the same motive. A common instance is the mistakes made with regard to the day of the week. Someone who is eagerly anticipating an event at the end of the week is very apt to think it is Wednesday when it is only Tuesday, and so on ; their impatience at the slowness with which the week is passing manifests itself as an error—in the desired direction—as to the present date.

Not only unconscious falsification of memory, but also deliberate or half-deliberate falsification—*i.e.*, lying—may be dictated by similar influences. Many cases of purposeless and apparently unintelligible lying in particular are often of this nature; Riklin has published a full analysis of one of this kind.[1]

Other mental operations, besides recollecting, may be falsified in the same way, a process designated by Freud as an *Irrtum* (error). Several examples related elsewhere in this paper might be classified in this group, so that one here will suffice. I was buying some flowers, and put two dollars, the exact price of them, on the counter. While they were being got ready, I changed my mind about one bunch, and told the woman serving me to leave it out; it should be said that she was the owner of the shop. On taking the money a few moments later, she said: ' That bunch costs forty cents, so that will make two dollars forty.' Her wish that I were making the order larger instead of smaller was probably concerned in the mistake.

It is of both theoretical and practical importance that the replacement memories which emerge when the mind is striving to recall a given memory that has been repressed always have some associative connections, however distant, with the memory that is being sought for. The following is a striking instance of this : A patient was temporarily unable to recollect the word ' sepia,' and while he was trying to do so four substitutive words, obviously

---

[1] Riklin, ' Eine Luge,' *Zentralbl. für Psychoanalyse*, Jahrg. I., S. 193.

incorrect, came to his mind instead. Two of these were the words 'bastard' and 'Lebanon,' and I propose to describe only the analysis of the latter.

His first association after ultimately recalling the word 'sepia' was the curious feeling that the last two letters ought to be separated from each other—*i.e.*, that *i* (which he interpreted as meaning himself) should not be in contact with *a*. This was followed by a series of associations all of a feminine connotation, indicating that the word 'sepia' was connected with the idea of femininity. His first knowledge of the word dated from childhood from a tube of what he called 'brown sticky stuff' in his sister's paint-box, and I surmised that it was probably related at that time, as is almost invariably the case in childhood, to some forbidden smearing impulse.

The word 'Lebanon' brought the following associations: Cedars of Lebanon; cedar-wood oil; the use of this for the high-power oil-immersion lens; the memory that on the previous day he had spent several hours examining his own semen microscopically to find out how long spermatozoa could remain alive; his current interest in this topic because of his wish not to impregnate a girl with whom he was just entering into an intimate relationship (compare the other substitutive word 'bastard,' and his first association that he was not to be brought into too close contact with something feminine); a passage he had once read to the effect that recurrent masturbation (from which he suffered) led to the emission of a brown fluid instead of semen, a state of affairs to be avoided.

It is known that the idea of impregnation is often unconsciously equated to that of contamination with other bodily material, an association doubtless dating from early childhood theories, and one which persists in its crude form in the perversions of throwing ink, defiling statues, etc.; and it is probable that the inhibition responsible for the forgetting of the word 'sepia' emanated from the group of fears and prohibitions indicated above. But the main interest of the example is the truly extraordinary displacement from these ideas to the word 'Lebanon,' one evidently facilitated by the identity of the first syllable in the three words 'sepia,' 'semen,' 'cedar.'

A few concluding remarks may be added on this mechanism of forgetting. The main points may be summarised in the statements that forgetting is often determined by a painful mental process (*Unlust*) of which the subject is unaware, either at the time only or permanently; that this inhibiting mental process may be a counter-will to recollecting the matter in question, or may be associated with this in a more complex way; and that a false memory presenting itself in the place of the true is a symbolic substitute of this, standing in associative connection with it. Two general considerations indicate that acts of forgetting of the type illustrated above are not, as is commonly supposed, accidental or due to chance. First is the fact that the same one tends to be repeated. If we forget to carry out a given intention, or are unable to recall a given name, the failure is apt to recur, thus suggesting that it has a specific cause. Secondly, is the fact that in at least two spheres of life it is universally recognised that remembering is under control of the will, so that a failure to remember is regarded as synonymous with a not wanting to remember. Freud[1] writes: ' Frauendienst wie Militärdienst erheben den Anspruch, dass alles zu ihnen Gehörige dem Vergessen entrückt sein müsse, und erwecken so die Meinung, Vergessen sei zulässig bei unwichtigen Dingen, während es bei wichtigen Dingen ein Anzeichen davon sei, dass man sie wie unwichtige behandeln wolle, ihnen also die Wichtigkeit abspreche.' [' Both the service of ladies and military service exact that nothing relating to them must be subject to forgetting, suggesting thus that forgetting is permissible with unimportant matters, while its occurrence in regard to important ones is an indication that they are being treated like unimportant ones—*i.e.*, that their importance is being discounted.'] A soldier who forgets to perform a given duty is punished regardless of the excuse. He is not allowed to forget, and whether his not wanting to perform the duty is openly expressed, or indirectly, as by his forgetting, is considered by his officer as comparatively irrelevant. The standard set by women is equally severe; a lover who forgets his lady's wishes is treated as though he openly declared them unimportant to him.

III. ' Lapsus Linguæ '

The everyday occurrence of the defect in psychophysical functioning popularly known as a slip of the tongue has not received much attention from psychologists. The attempts made, by Meringer

---

[1] Freud, *op. cit.*, S. 182.

and Mayer and others, to explain on phonetic grounds the particular mistake made have signally failed, for on the one hand many
cases are to be observed where no phonetic factors are in operation,
and on the other hand careful study shows that such factors are at
the most accessory or adjuvant in nature, and are never the essential
cause.

According to Freud, the word said in mistake is a manifestation
of a second suppressed thought, and thus arises outside the train
of thought that the speaker is intending to express. It may be a
word or phrase entirely foreign to this train of thought, being
taken in its entirety from the outlying thought, or it may be a compromise formation, in which both come to expression. In the
latter case the false word may be a neologism; a common example
of this is where a speaker, intending to use the word ' aggravating,'
says, ' How very aggravoking !' the word ' provoking ' having
intruded itself; many malapropisms are formed in this way, being
the result of uncertainty as to which is the more appropriate word.

The secondary thought that thus obtrudes itself on the intended
speech may, like the motives of repressive forgetting, be of two
kinds: (1) a general counter-impulse (*Gegenwillen*) directed immediately against the speech, or (2) another thought accidentally
aroused by it. In the latter case it can represent either a continuation
of a theme previously in the speaker's mind, or a thought aroused,
through a superficial association, by the theme that is intended
to be spoken; even when it represents a continuation of a previous
theme it will generally, if not always, be found that there is some
association between this and the theme of the speech. It will
readily be understood that in many cases the disturbing thought
is not evident, but can be revealed only by investigation, sometimes
a searching psycho-analysis being necessary.

Cases where the disturbing thought is a direct counter-impulse
are usually easy to interpret. One instance will suffice. A President
of the Austrian Reichstag once finished his introductory remarks
by declaring the session closed, instead of opened ; as the particular
session promised nothing but fruitless wrangles, one can sympathise
with his wish that it were already at an end.

Some cases where the disturbing thought is nearly related to
the intended theme are equally simple. A French governess engaged
on afternoon work in Dr. Stekel's family[1] asked his wife that

---

[1] Related by Freud, *op. cit.*, S. 81.

she might retain her testimonials, saying: ' Je cherche encore pour les après-midis, pardon, pour les avant-midis.' The slip betrayed her feeling of dissatisfaction with the afternoon engagement and her intention to look for another situation for the afternoons as well as the mornings, an intention she proceeded to carry out.

A friend of mine was driving his motor-car slowly and cautiously one day, when a cyclist, who was riding with his head down, furiously, and on the wrong side of the street, ran into him and damaged the bicycle. He sent in a bill for $50.00, and, as my friend refused to pay, he sued him in court. When I inquired about the result of the action, my friend said, ' The judge reprimanded the prisoner for careless riding.' I corrected him, ' You mean the plaintiff, not the prisoner.' ' Well,' he replied, ' I think the fellow should have been arrested for furious riding.'

A lady, when speaking of Bernard Shaw's works, said to me, ' I think very highly of all my writings,' instead of ' all his writings.' She was an amateur writer of short stories.

An unmarried man, a patient, remarked, ' My father was devoted to my wife.' He meant to say either ' his wife ' or ' my mother.' This is a typical instance of a *lapsus* that would pass as being entirely accidental and devoid of significance. I must add, however, that one of the main causes of the patient's neurosis was an unconscious incestuous attachment to his mother, so that his unsuppressed thoughts on the subject of the remark would run in full, ' My attitude towards my mother is the same as that of my father.' No alteration is too slight to have a meaning. The instance narrated above, in which the first letter only of Titchener's name was replaced by a ' K,'[1] belongs to the subject of *lapsus linguæ* equally as much as to that of forgetting.

Such self-betrayals as those just related sometimes afford valuable insight into character and motive. I was present at the International Congress of Neurology in Amsterdam, when the following curious episode occurred: There was a heated discussion regarding Freud's theory of hysteria. One of the most violent opponents, who is noted as having worked long and fruitlessly on the subject of

---

[1] This replacing of the initial letter of a word by that of another word, typically from the same sentence, is known in Oxford as a Spoonerism, on account of a distinguished professor who had the habit of committing the particular slip. As he is still alive, I will refrain from commenting on the psychological significance of the habit.

hysteria, was grudgingly admitting the value of the earlier work of Breuer and Freud—the truth of whose conclusions he had himself confirmed—as a prelude to a vehement denunciation of the ' dangerous ' tendencies of Freud's later work. During his speech he twice said, ' Breuer und *ich* haben bekanntlich nachgewiesen,' ['As is well known, Breuer and *I* have demonstrated'], thus replacing Freud's name by his own, and revealing his envy of Freud's originality.

The following example is more complicated : In talking of the financial standards so prevalent in modern civilisation, I said : ' In yesterday's newspaper there were the headings, " Ten million dollar fire in Halifax; six lives lost." ' It was at once pointed out to me that I had said Halifax instead of Bangor, Maine. Analysis of the mistake brought the following free associations : Until a few years ago I was disgracefully ignorant of the existence of Bangor, Maine, and I remember in college days being puzzled by the reference to Maine in the well-known student song, ' Riding down from Bangor,' as in my ignorance I supposed that this related to Bangor, the university town of Carnarvonshire, Wales. The name Bangor essentially stands in my mind for the original Bangor. It brought up a memory of the recent controversy whether the new National Welsh Library should be established at Bangor, at Swansea (my home town), or at Cardiff (the university town where I studied). This reminded me of interests I have in the contents of this library, in Celtic mythology, which naturally carried me to the valuable library of mythological books that I possess myself. Then I remembered that what had especially struck me in reading about the recent fire was the fact that a valuable collection of books had been destroyed in it, and that this had made me enter a note not to forget to renew my fire insurance, which had recently lapsed, before leaving in the coming week for a fortnight's visit to the United States.

The meaning of my *lapsus* is beginning to emerge. A library fire at Bangor was too near home for my peace of mind, and my unconscious had consolingly relegated it to some other spot. The next problem is to discover the motive for the replacement of Bangor by Halifax, a process that was greatly ' over-determined.' Maine is, from its geographical position, closely associated in my mind with the Maritime Provinces of Canada, and only on the preceding day a Canadian had been demonstrating to me on a map, for the *n*th time, how Maine should rightfully have formed part of these Provinces. Still, that does not explain why I selected Halifax rather than St. John, the other town I know the name of in the Maritime Provinces. One reason, doubtless, was the fact that at the time I was treating a patient from Halifax, Nova Scotia, who had recently been telling me that the houses there were mostly built of wood, and therefore were exposed to the danger of fire. The name Halifax, however, is more familiar to me as an English euphemism for Hell, as in the expression, ' Go to Hal-ifax.' This called up the memory of half-forgotten childhood fears, for, like most Welsh children, I was carefully nurtured with a proper dread of what was called ' the burning fire '; as I grew up I was cheered to learn the groundlessness of this particular dread. My slip of the tongue, therefore, registered my desire that any library fire should be in some other place than in my home, and if possible in a non-existent locality.

An example for which I am indebted to Dr. A. A. Brill is peculiar in that the slip of the tongue represented a resolution in opposition to the conscious intention. A man, who on account of homosexual practices was in constant fear of coming into conflict with the law, invited two lady friends to spend an evening at the theatre. They expressed a wish to see a play called 'Alias Jimmy Valentine,' which dealt largely with convicts and prisons. He was far from comfortable at the idea of spending an evening with such thoughts, but could not well avoid it. On getting into the cab to drive to the theatre, however, he accidentally gave the driver the name of another theatre, and did not notice the mistake until they arrived there, when it was too late to rectify it. At this theatre the play was about the cleverness with which a daughter outwitted her selfish old father. It was not without significance that the subject's attitude towards his own father was one of pronounced hostility, so that his slip of the tongue had the effect of exchanging an evening with a painful topic for one with a topic that he greatly enjoyed.

Several non-scientific writers before Freud had noted the psychological significance of accidental slips of the tongue. Freud[1] quotes examples of this from, for instance, Brantôme and Wallenstein. Shakespeare himself furnishes a beautiful one in the ' Merchant of Venice ' (Act III., Scene ii.). It occurs in the scene where Portia is expressing her anxiety lest the favoured suitor should fare as

[1] Freud, *op. cit.*, S. 94, 113.

badly as the distasteful ones in the hazard set for them by her
father. She wants to tell Bassanio that in the event of his failure
she would nevertheless belong to him, but is prevented from
doing so by her promise to her father. In this mental discord she
speaks:

> ' There is something tells me (but it is not love),
> I would not lose you; and you know yourself
> Hate counsels not in such a quality.
> But lest you should not understand me well,
> (And yet a maiden hath no tongue but thought)
> I would detain you here some month or two,
> Before you venture for me. I could teach you
> How to choose right, but then I am forsworn;
> So will I never be; so may you miss me;
> But if you do, you'll make me wish a sin,
> That I had been forsworn. Beshrew your eyes,
> They have o'erlooked me, and divided me:
> One half of me is yours, the other half yours—
> Mine own, I would say; but if mine, then yours,—
> And so all yours.'

Rank[1] comments on this passage: ' Gerade das, was sie ihm
also bloss leise andeuten möchte, weil sie es eigentlich ihm überhaupt verschweigen sollte, dass sie nämlich schon vor der Wahl
ganz die seine sei und ihn liebe, das lässt der Dichter mit bewunderns-
wertem psychologischen Feingefühl in dem Versprechen sich
offen durchdrängen und weiss durch diesen Kunstgriff die uner-
trägliche Ungewissheit des Liebenden sowie die gleichgestimmte
Spannung des Zuhörers über den Ausgang der Wahl zu beruhigen.'
[' Just what she would like to hint to him gently, because really
she should not speak of it—namely, that even before the choice
she loves him and is wholly his—the poet with wonderful psychological delicacy allows to leak through in the *lapsus linguæ* and
manages by this device to allay the intolerable uncertainty of the
lover as well as the like tension of the hearer.']
     One of our greatest novelists, George Meredith, in his master-
piece, ' The Egoist,' shows an even finer understanding of the
mechanism. The plot of the novel is, shortly, as follows : Sir
Willoughby Patterne, an aristocrat greatly admired by his circle,
becomes engaged to a Miss Constantia Durham. She discovers
in him an intense egoism, which he skilfully conceals from the
world, and to escape the marriage she elopes with a Captain Oxford.
Some years later Patterne becomes engaged to a Miss Clara

[1] Otto Rank, *Zentralbl. für Psychoanalyse*, Jahrg. I., Heft 3, S. 110.

Middleton, and most of the book is taken up with a detailed description of the conflict that arises in her mind on also discovering his egoism. External circumstances, and her conception of honour, hold her to her pledge, while he becomes more and more distasteful in her eyes. She partly confides in his cousin and secretary, Vernon Whitford, the man whom she ultimately marries, but, from a mixture of motives, he stands aloof.

In a soliloquy Clara speaks as follows: ' " If some noble gentleman could see me as I am and not disdain to aid me ! Oh ! to be caught out of this prison of thorns and brambles. I cannot tear my own way out. I am a coward. A beckoning of a finger would change me, I believe. I could fly bleeding and through hootings to a comrade. . . . Constantia met a soldier. Perhaps she prayed and her prayer was answered. She did ill. But, oh, how I love her for it ! His name was Harry Oxford. . . . She did not waver, she cut the links, she signed herself over. Oh, brave girl, what do you think of me ? But I have no Harry Whitford ; I am alone " . . . the sudden consciousness that she had put another name for Oxford, struck her a buffet, drowning her in crimson.'

The fact that both men's names end in ' ford ' evidently renders the confounding of them more easy, and would by many be regarded as an adequate cause for this, but the real underlying motive for it is plainly indicated by the author. In another passage the same *lapsus* occurs, and is followed by the hesitation and change of subject that one is familiar with in psycho-analysis when a half-conscious complex is touched. Sir Willoughby patronisingly says of Whitford: ' " False alarm. The resolution to do anything unaccustomed is quite beyond poor old Vernon," ' Clara replies: ' " But if Mr. Oxford—Whitford . . . your swans, coming sailing up the lake, how beautiful they look when they are indignant !¹ I was going to ask you, surely men witnessing a marked admiration for someone else will naturally be discouraged ?" Sir Willoughby stiffened with sudden enlightenment.'

In still another passage, Clara by another *lapsus* betrays her secret wish that she was on a more intimate footing with Vernon Whitford. Speaking to a boy friend, she says: ' " Tell Mr. Vernon—tell Mr. Whitford." '

¹ The nature of the change of the subject here accurately betrays the content of the underlying affect, *indignation* at Patterne's disparagement of Whitford, just as a mediate association reaction indicates the nature of the complex stimulated.

In relation to these two literary passages I made a personal slip of the tongue that illustrates the probity of the unconscious mind as contrasted with the duplicity of the conscious one. Expounding the subject of *lapsus linguæ* to someone, I said that I had come across two interesting literary examples—in Meredith's 'Egoist,' and Shakespeare's 'Love's Labour's Lost'; when detailing the second I noticed that I had named the wrong play. Analysis of the mistake brought the following memories. On the preceding day, while talking of the sources of Shakespeare's plots, I had made the remark that the only one he had not taken from previous authors was that contained in 'Love's Labour's Lost.' Some six months before, Professor Freud had told me that he had heard from Dr. Otto Rank that there was in the 'Merchant of Venice' an example of *lapsus linguæ* he attributed to the disturbing influence of a suppressed thought, but he could not tell me where it occurred. On looking back I realise that I felt just a touch of pique, though I did not pay any attention to it at the time, at not having observed it myself, and I took the first opportunity to re-read the play, when, of course, I came across the example. The one in the 'Egoist' I had really observed myself. My statement that I had discovered the two examples in question was therefore only three-fourths true. The fact, which I had suppressed,[1] that Dr. Rank deserved some credit, leaked through to external expression in my error of naming the wrong play, substituting Shakespeare's only *original* one. An interesting feature of the example is the fact that a few minutes before I had been relating how a man not over-scrupulous in the matter of priority had betrayed his dishonesty in a treacherous slip of the tongue. No doubt deeper factors than interest in mere scientific priority were also operative in my own case, such as rivalry and an 'English' complex, both of which are matters that play a quite subordinate part in my conscious mental life.

IV. 'LAPSUS CALAMI'

The introductory remarks made on the subject of slips of the tongue apply almost literally to slips of the pen. One principal difference is that the delay interposed by the mechanical acts of writing enables disturbances of co-ordination to occur with especial

---

[1] Naturally I excused this to myself on the ground that pedantic accuracy is uncalled for in conversation, but the facts remain.

readiness, as can be illustrated by a glance over any author's manuscript. The necessity for numerous corrections indicates that, whether owing to the intricacy of the subject-matter or to a lack of clearness in the author's mind, a harmonious flow is far from being attained. General perplexities mirror themselves in half-conscious hesitations about the choice of individual words. Thus, a correspondent, who couldn't decide as to the advisability of a given proposal, wrote to me that it might turn out to be ' umpracticle,' evidently a contamination of ' impracticable ' and ' unpractical.'

A field of frequent errors is that of dates. Many people continue to write the date of the previous year throughout a great part of January. Some recent figures were given in the Press in which it was stated that in the first week of the New Year one in every forty cheques was dated the previous year; in a fortnight's time the average sank to one in sixty. Not all such mistakes are due to the fixation of habit, as is readily assumed; sometimes they signify a disinclination to accept the fact that yet another bygone year has brought them nearer to old age, a reflection that is apt to be prevalent at the turn of the year. Regrets that such and such a date is already past, or impatience that it has not yet arrived, are common motives of such unconscious mistakes. A student dated a letter to me April 11, 1911, instead of April 22. An examination was due in the first week of May for which he was very unprepared, and I attributed his slip to the wish that there was twice as much time ahead of him in which to get ready. That the date he actually wrote was the 11th was no doubt influenced by the presence of these integers at the end of 1911, but it is to be noted even in this connection that his mistake consisted in writing them earlier than he should—*i.e.*, in putting the date earlier. As with the phonetic factors entering into slips of the tongue, the fact that the part wrongly written occurs elsewhere in the same line only predisposes to the mistake. Such factors do not cause the mistake; they only make it easier to assume that particular form.

A lady once told me that an old friend in writing to her had closed the letter with the curious sentence, ' I hope you are well and *un*happy.' He had formerly entertained hopes of marrying her himself, and the slip of the pen was evidently determined by his dislike at the thought of her being happy with someone else. She had recently married.

In a paper on the subject of suggestion I formulated as one of the conclusions the sentence: ' Suggestion plays the principal part in all psychotherapeutic methods except the psycho-analytic one.' In abstracting the article for a neurological journal, a reviewer, who strongly disagrees with the theses I maintained, allowed himself to quote this as follows, ' La suggestion joue le rôle principal dans toutes les méthodes psycho-analytiques,' thus completely reversing my meaning.

In the 1887 edition of Baedeker's ' London ' I happened to notice the following curious slip. The full passage may be quoted : ' Die Sonntagsfeier ist in England bekanntlich streng; alle Geschäfte, Läden, Sehenswürdigkeiten und die City Restaurants sind den ganzen Tag, andere Speisehäuser nur von 1 bis 3 und von 6 bis 11 Uhr geöffnet. Viele Geschäfte schliessen schon Samstag Mittag. Man geht daher Sonntags am besten aufs Land.' ['As is well known, the Sabbath in England is kept very strictly; all the offices, shops, sights, and city restaurants are *open* the whole day, and other eating-houses only from 1 to 3 and 6 to 11. Many places of business close already at noon on Saturday. It is thus better to spend Sunday in the country.'] The last sentence shows that the writer, like most foreign visitors, had suffered much discomfort from the London Sabbath, and in the mistake of writing ' open,' instead of ' closed,' it is plain that the wish was father to the thought.

For the following example I am indebted to Dr. A. A. Brill. A patient wrote to him on the subject of his sufferings, which he tried to attribute to worry about his financial affairs induced by a cotton crisis: ' My trouble is all due to that d——d frigid wave;[1] there isn't even any seed.' What he really wrote, however, was not ' wave,' but ' wife.' In the bottom of his heart he cherished half-avowed reproaches against his wife on account of her sexual anæsthesia and childlessness, and he dimly realised, with right, that his life of enforced abstinence played a considerable part in the genesis of his symptoms.

As with slips of the tongue, no mistake is too slight to be significant. The following four are instances, selected from a considerable number of similar ones, in which it consisted only in the replacement of one letter by another:

A correspondent of mine had published a scientific paper on a

[1] Meaning in the money-market.

sexual subject, and was writing to me about a virulent criticism of it that had appeared ; the critic had used such passionately denunciatory language as to make it evident that the topic of the paper had aroused some strong personal complex. My correspondent's first sentence was, ' Have you seen X's satyrical criticism of my paper ? ' plainly indicating by his unconscious substitution of ' y ' for ' i ' his estimate of the nature of the criticism.

Some few years ago I was writing to an old friend, whom I had always called by his surname. On account of family ties it became more appropriate to address him by his Christian name, and, after a momentary embarrassment natural under the circumstances, I took up my pen and began, ' Dear Fred.' To my amazement, however, I saw that I had slipped in a ' u ' before the final letter of the name. This may seem a very trivial mistake, due simply to the similarity of the two words, but a psycho-analytic conscience tends to be more unsparing in the criticism of its owner, as it is more sparing in that of others. Two memories at once rushed to my mind. One was of a dream I had had two years before, at a time when I was debating with myself whether it would be politic openly to defend the Freudian principles, the truth of which my experience had made me accept. In the dream I was in a swiftly moving motor-omnibus, the driver of which was a ' composite figure,'[1] bearing mostly the lineaments of my friend in question. An angry crowd surrounded us, and threatened the driver for ' going so fast.' It became necessary for me to decide whether to stand aloof or to side with the driver, and I did the latter. I need not give the other details of the dream, but the analysis showed it to be a presentation of my waking dilemma, the driver being a replacement-figure for Professor Freud. I had recently been taken for a long motor ride by my friend, who, by the way, has a German surname, and, though at first I had qualms as to the recklessness of his driving, I soon perceived, to my relief, that this was only apparent, and that he was really an exceedingly skilful and reliable driver. Before the incident of the *lapsus calami*, therefore, he had long been unconsciously associated in my mind with Professor Freud. The second memory was of a letter I had recently written to a Canadian professor of a subject allied to my own. On coming to Canada, I had felt very awkward and constrained at the American custom of formally prefacing a man's title to his name when

---

[1] See Chapter X., p. 221.

addressing him, and it was a long time before I got accustomed to being spoken to by both younger and older colleagues as Dr. Jones or as Doctor. It embarrassed me to have to speak to even fairly intimate friends in this way, and, in the case of the gentleman in question, I frankly told him, in the letter referred to above, that my English prejudices would not let me do it with any degree of comfort. As he was some fifteen years older than myself, I wondered afterwards whether he might resent a younger man taking the initiative of addressing him simply by his surname. The slip of the pen now began to take on a different aspect, and I was obliged to recognise in it the manifestation of a conceited wish that I was on terms of sufficient equality with Professor Freud to allow such a familiar mode of address. I feel certain that no thought of the kind had ever entered my consciousness, to which it is quite strange, though my reaction of shame convinced me of the reality of its existence. The circumstances of the slip of the pen were extraordinarily favourable to its occurrence—the similarity in the names, the previous identification of the men, the occasion of the letter following so soon after the other one, and so on. If it were not for this, I hardly think that such a deeply repressed wish could have come to expression—at least, not so flagrantly.

I am indebted to Dr. A. A. Brill for the following personal example: Although by custom a strict teetotaller, he yielded to a friend's importunity one evening, in order to avoid offending him, and took a little wine. During the next morning an exacerbation of an eye-strain headache gave him cause to regret this slight indulgence, and his reflections on the subject found expression in the following slip of the pen: Having occasion to write the name of a girl mentioned by a patient, he wrote not Ethel, but Ethyl.[1] It happened that the girl in question was rather too fond of drink, and in Dr. Brill's[2] mood at the time this characteristic of hers stood out with conspicuous significance.

A bachelor who had been a lady's guest at a function given

---

[1] Ethyl alcohol is, of course, the chemical name for ordinary alcohol.

[2] In writing my manuscript, I made the slip of replacing the word ' Brill ' by that of ' Bree,' the name of another medical friend. The mistake is evidently a contamination derived from the word-picture of ' Brill on the *spree*,' and is determined by the memory of feeble jests relating to Berlin on the (river) Spree; both the vowel and the consonants of Brill are contained in the word ' Berlin.' It is only right to add, however, that the thoughts of both Dr. Brill and Dr. Bree are intimately connected in my mind with Berlin in ways that discretion prevents me from describing.

by her responded afterwards by inviting her to tea at his house. Meaning to excuse himself for the unconventionality implied, he added, ' I should like to show you my house,' but actually wrote ' *our* house.' Noticing the slip made him realise that his intentions were more serious than he had thought; the relationship soon ripened into marriage.

Mistakes in addressing envelopes are generally manifestations of some disturbing thought that the writer does not mean to express. A young lady was secretly engaged to a medical man, whom we will call Arthur X. She addressed a letter one day, not to Dr. Arthur X, but to Dear Arthur X, thus expressing her desire to let all the world know of their relationship.

Some time ago I was treating a case of exceptional interest in a patient who lived some sixty miles from Toronto, where I then was. On account of the distance the patient, who could not leave his work, was able to visit me only twice a week. I found it impossible to treat him on these conditions, and wrote to tell him so. Instead of writing the name of his town on the envelope, however, I wrote Toronto, displaying my wish that he were more conveniently situated.

V. MISPRINTS

Misprints may, of course, arise from errors made by the writer, the editor, the proof-reader, or the printer. From time to time the Press records amusing instances of a disagreeable truth unintentionally leaking out in the form of a misprint; in Freud's book several examples of this are related.[1] Unlike the other kinds of failure under discussion, one here is rarely in a position to obtain an objective verification of a given interpretation, but sometimes this in itself reaches a high grade of probability. At all events, general principles indicate that the mistake made must be determined by personal constellations of whoever made it, and cannot be altogether accidental.

In a number of the *Zentralblatt für Psychoanalyse*,[2] the title of a book of Gross's was wrongly given as ' Das Freud'sche Ideogenitätsmonument,' instead of ' Ideogenitätsmoment.' As both the writer of the article and the editorial staff (Drs. Adler and Stekel) regarded the conception as a monumental one, it is possible that the overlooking of the mistake is to be correlated with this fact.

[1] S. 66, etc.   [2] Jahrg. I., S. 197.

In a paper of my own on nightmare, I wrote the sentence, ' The association in general between the sex instinct and the emotions of fear and dread is a very intimate one.' This was correctly rendered in the proof, but on the second occasion of reading it the proof-reader was shocked to think that I could make such an obviously outrageous mistake, and altered the word ' intimate ' to ' distant,' in which form it appeared in print.[1]

In a brochure of mine that appeared as a German translation, a mistake was made of a less unfortunate kind. One of my main theses was that the conception of Hamlet represented a projection of the most intimate part of Shakespeare's personality, and so thoroughly did the translator absorb my view of the identity of the two that, when he came to a passage on the death of Shakespeare's father, he unconsciously substituted the name Hamlet for Shakespeare, and rendered the passage as referring to ' the death of Hamlet's father in 1601.' The substitution was overlooked in the proof by two other readers thoroughly familiar with the subject.

The following misprint occurred recently in the *Scotsman* in reporting a speech: ' He had not the wealth of the Plantagenets, nor did he derive any income from American trusts. (Loud *d*aughter).' *Punch* unkindly commented on this replacement of one letter for another (*d* for *l*), ' We knew what was meant without the explanatory parenthesis.'

In the notorious ' Wicked Bible,' issued in 1631, the word ' not ' was omitted from the Seventh Commandment, so that this read, ' Thou shalt commit adultery.' The possibility is not to be excluded that the editor had a personal interest in the subject of the commandment. At all events, he was heavily fined, it being empirically recognised that whether his purpose was conscious or unconscious he was equally responsible for it, and that he had no right, even ' accidentally,' to impute such commandments to Jahveh.

Perhaps a similar theme was running through the mind of whoever composed this passage, which referred to the proposal to tax bachelors : ' Unmarried people usually have just as good reason to be unmarried as those who are married.' The words

[1] The same explanation may hold for a slip concerning the footnote on p. 295 of the Fourth Edition, which had successfully eluded the printers in all the previous editions. This time, however, a *t* was adroitly omitted, making me state as a conclusion of psycho-analysis that ' in his unconscious everyone believes in the *immorality* of his soul.'

' have to be married ' have evidently been omitted from the end of a rather clumsy sentence. A highly interesting misprint of historic importance is detailed by Dattner.[1] At the time when Austria and Hungary were separated, in 1867, special arrangements were made for regulating their common National Debt and their future financial relations. In the Hungarian law on the subject a single word ' effectiv ' was accidentally omitted, the consequence of which would have been to cost Austria between eleven and fifty-two million crowns. The desire of the Hungarian law-makers to come as well as possible out of the transaction unconsciously overcame their probity.

Typewriting, being a form of writing, is subject to the same influences as this. Mistakes made may be due to either a *lapsus calami* or a misreading, in any case being determined by the previous mental constellations of the typist. Thus a typist I once had, having worked long in a lawyer's office, was fond of replacing ' illogical ' by ' illegal,' and, being of a very proper turn of mind, made such mistakes as changing ' a vulgar word ' to ' a regular word.' I have found that distinctness of handwriting is powerless to prevent such mistakes. Prudishness was presumably also the reason why the typist of a Medical Officer of Health substituted ' anti-naval ' for ' ante-natal ' in a letter he had dictated to her (evidently a case of mishearing, for the former word could have no meaning in England in 1917).

One practical aspect of this matter is generally appreciated— namely, that accuracy in correcting proofs can be attained only by getting someone else to do it for one. A mistake once made in the manuscript, and then copied, is very apt to get overlooked by the person who made it. The effective blindness that enabled him to make the mistake, or, more strictly, that enabled an unconscious impulse to come to expression, will very likely continue its action by preventing him from recognising it.

VI. FALSE VISUAL RECOGNITION

In visual perception the same mistakes of affective origin that were discussed in connection with memory are frequently to be observed, and here also they are of two kinds—a failure to see something that for various reasons we do not want to see, and a

[1] Dattner, ' Eine historische Fehlleistung,' *Zentralbl. für Psychoanalyse*, Jahrg. I., S. 550.

falsification of perception in the sense of personal wish-complexes. Examples of the former kind are very common in connection with reading the newspaper. Thus, just when a relative was crossing the Atlantic last year, I saw in the news-headings that a serious accident had happened to a liner, but I had the greatest difficulty in finding the account of it in the paper, overlooking it again and again.

Perhaps the commonest example of false perception is the catching sight of one's name where it really doesn't occur. As a rule, the word that has attracted one's attention is very similar to one's name, containing perhaps the same letters differently arranged. Professor Bleuler[1] relates an example where this was not so, and where, therefore, the essential cause of the mistake must have been of a greater affective intensity; the word was really ' Blutkörperchen,' only the first two letters being common to the two words. He explained it thus: ' In diesem Falle liess sich aber der Beziehungswahn und die Illusion sehr leicht begründen: Was ich gerade las, war das Ende einer Bemerkung über eine Art schlechten Stiles von wissenschaftlichen Arbeiten, von der ich mich nicht frei fühlte.' [' In this case, however, the delusion of relation and the illusion were easily to be traced to their origin: What I was just reading was the end of a remark on a certain kind of bad style in the writing of scientific works from which I felt myself to be by no means free.']

Freud[2] quotes an example from Lichtenberg: ' He always mistook " angenommen " for "Agamemnon," so thoroughly had he read his Homer.' In searching an American newspaper for English political news at the time of the Navy scare in 1910, my attention was caught by the heading ' German Danger'; on looking nearer I saw that it was ' General Danger.' On another occasion I read the heading, ' Future of the Insurance Scheme,' as ' Failure of the Insurance Scheme '; it is easy to discern my sympathy with my medical colleagues in the attack they were at the time conducting on the scheme. Another personal example, with an even grosser mistake, was the following: I was searching the literature to find the earliest instance of a certain superstitious act, and, although I had only been able to trace it to the ninth century, I suspected that it might have occurred still earlier. One

---

[1] Bleuler, 'Affektivität, Suggestibilität, Paranoia,' 1906, S. 121.
[2] Freud, *op. cit.*, S. 133.

day I found in an old French book an account of it quoted from an earlier writer, the reference to whose work contained the words, ' 6ᵉ livre.' I read this as ' 6ᵉ siècle,' and entered it in my notes as such; it was only some time after, on checking the reference, that I discovered the error.

Similar observations can be made in regard to the perception of other objects than written matter, and especially with the recognising of other people. False recognition is quite commonly due to a pervading desire to meet the person in question; a lover who has a rendezvous with his mistress fancies he sees her coming many times over, when really the women he mistakes for her may bear only the faintest resemblance to her.

The failure to greet friends or acquaintances in the street is not always due to not seeing them, and one knows how gradual are the shades between a direct ' cut,' where one person consciously pretends he does not see the other, and a not seeing that is due to a not wanting to see.[1] Women intuitively feel that the difference between the two is unimportant, and are as much offended by the one as by the other; someone who thinks highly of them has no right nòt to see them when they pass.

A striking instance of this affective blindness occurred to me not long ago: It was part of my routine duty to check the invoices for laboratory apparatus as they came in, and hand them over to the assistant superintendent to see that they got paid. On one occasion I had neglected to do this until a small number collected. I then went through them, and took them with me into the assistant superintendent's office. I was very pressed for time, and hoped he would not be there, so that I could simply deposit them on his desk; especially so, as there was a small error in one of them that I had to point out to him, and I realised that his over-conscientiousness would mean a tedious investigation of the error. I felt, however, that I ought to try to find him, and explain the point to him. On going into his office, I saw several men there, went up to one of them who had his back to me, and said, ' Do you know where Dr. X is ?' To my astonishment he replied, ' Why, I am Dr. X.' My not recognising him was facilitated by the fact of his having an unfamiliar hat on, but the actual cause of it I knew well enough.

The phenomenon of *fausse reconnaissance*, or *déjà vu*, which has

---

[1] One might invert the familiar proverb and say, ' What the heart doesn't grieve over, the eye doesn't see.'

perplexed so many psychologists, is closely allied to the same
category. Freud has finally solved this riddle,[1] but, as the explanation
of it is of a more complex order than with the other occurrences
under consideration, I shall not go into it here.

It will be noticed that in this group, as in the other allied ones,
the operative feeling-complex manifests itself in two ways—in
causing the suppression of one mental process and the prominence
of another; it determines what one does see (falsely) as well as
what one doesn't see. In some cases the negative of these two
effects is more striking, in others the positive. A further group of
occurrences may now be mentioned, in which, although strictly
speaking there is no false perception, the positive phenomenon in
question is seen at its acme; it is where one's attention is attracted
in an unusual way to a given object that would have passed unnoticed were it not for the presence of a certain feeling-complex
with which the idea is associated. A simple instance will best
explain what is meant: An English lady who had recently come to
Canada, and who had not yet got acclimatised to the strange life,
was paying a society call. She had to wait a few moments for her
hostess, and on the latter's entry was discovered deeply engrossed
in Pierre Loti's ' L'Exilée,' which she had unearthed from an
unobtrusive corner of a pile of other books. She had never read
anything of Loti's before, and it was purely the title that had
attracted her interest. Brill[2] mentions the case of a New York
embezzler who was discovered by detectives in a Philadelphia
library looking at a book entitled ' Will I ever go back ?' Pur-
suance of this theme, which is obviously impossible here, would
lead us into the psychology of attention and interest, and the
importance played in these processes by feeling; it will be seen,
however, that psycho-analysis has a very considerable bearing on
these problems.

VII. Mislaying of Objects

It is probable that objects are never accidentally mislaid. The
underlying motive manifests itself in two ways—in the act of
mislaying the object, and in the subsequent amnesia; in other
words, a *Verlegen* is a composite of a *Vergreifen* and a *Vergessen*,
the latter being the main feature. As before, the motive may be
a counter-impulse directed against the use of the object, or against

[1] Freud, *op. cit.*, S. 319.   [2] Brill, *Psychoanalysis*, 1912, p. 230.

an idea associated with the use of it. Instances of both will be given, first of the former.

We are all more apt to mislay bills rather than cheques, and in general objects that we don't want to see rather than those we do. Apparent exceptions to this rule, such as the mislaying of valuable objects, come under the second category, where our objection is not to the thing itself, but to what it can remind us of.

A common experience, which has often occurred to me personally, is the following: Whenever I suffer from the effects of over-smoking, I notice that it is much harder to find my pipe; it has got put behind ornaments or books, and in all sorts of unusual places that it normally does not occupy.

A patient of mine was recently very put out at having lost an important bunch of keys. He told me that he urgently wanted them that afternoon to open the lock of a minute-book at a meeting with his auditor and solicitor. I inquired as to the purpose of the meeting. It appeared that an important resolution had been passed at an annual directors' meeting, and that he had omitted to enter it in the minute-book. He was the managing director, and it became a question legally whether a certain action could be taken without the formal consent of the other directors, or whether possibly the minute could be subsequently added by private arrangement with them. At all events, it was an annoying situation, and I felt sure that his dislike of having to face it was connected with the loss of the keys. Further inquiry showed that he had used the keys only once that morning to open his office desk; after doing this it was his custom immediately to replace them in his pocket, the desk being provided with an automatic closing lock. He had missed the keys as soon as he got into the street-car to come to see me, and had telephoned a message for a clerk to search the short distance between his private office and the car-line. The surmise was near that he must have flung the bunch into his desk behind some papers, later closing it in the usual way; on telephoning to have the desk forcibly opened, this was found to be correct.

The following example is a little more complicated: A lady had lost the key of a box containing phonograph records, and had thoroughly ransacked her rooms for it many times during six weeks, but all in vain. The records belonged to a correspondence college, and were a means of learning French pronunciation. They had been put away early in the summer, and now, in the autumn, she wanted them for the purpose of renewing her French studies. Her whole heart was not in these, however, for it happened that she was fond of singing, and hoped to get accepted in an orchestral choir, the rehearsals of which would leave her no time for other studies. As time went on she despaired more and more of being accepted, and fell back on the French as the next best way of occupying her winter evenings. Soon after her definite rejection by the choir she discovered the lost key, which had been carefully stowed away in the corner of an attic. She recollected locking the box in the early summer and thinking that she would not need it again for a long time, but had no memory of putting the key away. She was extremely proud of her voice, and had built on her application being successful. Taking up the French studies denoted failure of her hopes. Her inability to find the key thus symbolised her loathness to believe that her vocal reputation would be slighted.

To lose or misplace a present, especially if it happens more than once, is not generally considered a compliment to the giver, and with right, for it often is an unconscious expression of disdain, disregard, or indifference.[1] When a wife repeatedly mislays her wedding-ring during the honeymoon, it does not augur well for the future happiness of the marriage. Freud[2] relates an example of misplacing where the motive was of this kind, and which, like the last-mentioned example, is interesting in regard to the circumstances under which the object was again found. It concerned a married couple who lived rather aloof lives from each other, any marks of tenderness being of a distinctly lukewarm nature; the fault, according to the husband, lay in the emotional apathy of his wife. One day she made him a present of a book that would interest him. He thanked her for the attention, promised to read it, put it aside, and couldn't find it again. In the next six months he made several vain attempts to find it. At the end of this time his mother, to whom he was devoted, got seriously ill, and was very tenderly nursed by his wife. His affection for his wife rapidly increased, and one evening, coming home from the sick bed with his heart filled with gratitude towards her, he went to his desk, and, without

---

[1] For an example of how complex may be the mental processes behind such a simple occurrence, the reader is referred to a striking analysis by Otto Rank, ' Das Verlieren als Symptomhandlung,' *Zentralbl. für Psychoanalyse*, Jahrg. I., S. 450.

[2] Freud, *op. cit.*, S. 165.

any conscious purpose, unhesitatingly opened a drawer and took out the lost book.

Leaving things behind one is a common type of mislaying. To do so in the street or in a public conveyance has a very different significance from doing so in the house of a friend. In the latter case it often expresses the person's attachment, the difficulty he has in tearing himself away, and the desire or willingness he has to come back. One can almost measure the success with which a physician is practising psychotherapy, for instance, by the size of the collection of umbrellas, handkerchiefs, purses, and so on, that he could make in a month.

VIII. ERRONEOUSLY-CARRIED-OUT ACTIONS

A secondary suppressed tendency may manifest itself in the disturbance not only of writing, but also of any other conscious motor act, an occurrence Freud terms a *Vergreifen*. The intended action is not carried out, or only incorrectly, being entirely or partly replaced by an action corresponding with the suppressed impulse that breaks through. As in the former cases, this secondary tendency is associated either directly or indirectly with the conscious intention, and the faulty action is customarily explained as being due to ' chance,' ' accident,' or ' carelessness.'

A trite example will perhaps best illustrate the type of occurrence. On starting to open a fresh tin of tobacco, I economically reflected that I should first finish the rather dry remains of the previous one. A few minutes later, however, while engrossed in reading, I wanted to refill my pipe, and to my surprise detected myself in the act of opening the new tin, although I had pushed it farther away from me than the other. My checked wish to enjoy the fresh tobacco had taken advantage of my distraction, and so interfered with my conscious intention of filling the pipe from the old tin.

An equally simple example is the following: It is my custom to put scientific journals, as they arrive, on a stool in the corner of my study. On reading them I write on the back the page number of any articles I wish to enter in my reference books; the journals not so marked are put on top of the files to be bound at the end of the year, while the others are placed on a pile at one side of my desk. Once a week or so I go through this pile and enter the references, but, whenever I have neglected this for so long that the pile begins to assume formidable dimensions, I find I have a pronounced tendency to put no more there, and to put on the files any fresh journal I read, whether it has articles that should be entered or not. The motive is obvious—to save myself the trouble of having to enter more than I already have to.

A lady went to post some letters which had come for her brother, and which had to be re-addressed and forwarded on account of his absence. When she got home she found the letters still in her hand-bag, and realised that she must have posted two letters, addressed to herself, which she had opened that morning; they duly arrived on the next day. At the time another younger brother was at home seriously ill with typhoid fever, and she had just written to the elder brother begging him to come home as soon as possible. She knew, however, that on account of urgent business he would not be able to leave immediately, but her posting letters addressed to the home, under the impression that she was sending them to her brother, indicated her keen anxiety that he was already there.

A patient came up from the country to get advice about various obsessing ideas that greatly distressed him. He had been recommended to consult two physicians, another one and myself. The other physician told him ' not to think about the ideas,' and advised him to take a course of physical exercise at a special gymnasium that he kept for the purpose. I, of course, advised psycho-analytic treatment, which has since cured him. He promised us both that he would think the matter over, and let us know what he decided. That night, on getting home, he wrote to each of us—to the other physician that he couldn't yet make up his mind, and to me that he would like to make an appointment to begin the treatment as soon as possible. He put the letters into the wrong envelopes. During the subsequent psycho-analysis it became evident that this ' accidental ' mistake was unconsciously determined by the spiteful desire to let the other physician know what he thought of his advice.

The use of keys is a fertile source of occurrences of this kind, of which two examples may be given. If I am disturbed in the midst of some engrossing work at home by having to go to the hospital to carry out some routine work, I am very apt to find myself trying to open the door of my laboratory there with the key of my desk at home, although the two keys are quite unlike each other. The mistake unconsciously demonstrates where I would rather be at the moment.

Some years ago I was acting in a subordinate position at a certain institution, the front-door of which was kept locked, so that it was necessary to ring for admission. On several occasions I found myself making serious attempts to open the door with my house-key. Each one of the permanent visiting staff, of which I aspired to be a member, was provided with a key to avoid the trouble of having to wait at the door. My mistakes thus expressed my desire to be on a similar footing, and to be quite ' at home ' there.

Two other everyday sets of occurrences may briefly be mentioned where unconscious disturbances of otherwise intended actions are very frequent. The one is the matter of paying out money, and particularly of giving change. It would be an interesting experiment to establish statistically the percentage of such mistakes that are in favour of the person making them, in comparison with that of the opposite sort.

The second is the sphere of domestic breakages. It can be observed that after a servant has been reprimanded, especially when the reprimand is more than usually unjust in her eyes, is a favourite time for crockery to ' come to pieces in her hand.' Careless breakage of valuable china, an event that often perplexes the owner as much as it incenses her, may be the product of a number of factors in the mind of the transgressor, class-envy of valuable property, ignorant lack of appreciation for objects of art, resentment at having to devote so much labour to the care of what appear to be senseless objects of enthusiasm, personal hostility towards the owner, and so on.

IX. Symptomatic Acts

Under the name of *Symptomhandlungen* Freud discusses a series of unconsciously performed actions that differ from the last-mentioned ones in being independent activities, and not grafted on to another conscious one. They are done ' without thinking ' or ' by chance,' and no significance is seen in them. Analysis of them, however, shows that they are the symbolic expression of some suppressed tendency, usually a wish. In many instances the action is a complicated one and performed on only one occasion; in others it is a constant habit that often is characteristic of the person. The mannerisms of dress, of fingering the moustache or clothes-buttons, the playing with coins in the pocket, and so on, are examples of this kind; they all have their logical meaning, though this needs to be read before becoming evident.

Different ways of occupying the hands often betray thoughts that the person does not wish to express or even does not know of. It is related of Eleanora Duse that in a divorce play, while in a soliloquy following a wrangle with the husband, she kept playing with her wedding-ring, taking it off, replacing it, and finally taking it off again; she is now ready for the seducer. The action illustrates the profundity of the great actress's character studies.

Maeder[1] tells the following story of a Zurich colleague who had a free day, and was hesitating between making an agreeable holiday of it and paying a distasteful duty-call on some people in Lucerne. He ultimately decided on the latter, and dolefully set out. Half-way to Lucerne he had to change trains; he did this mechanically, and settled down in the other train to continue his reading of the morning papers. When the ticket-collector came round, he discovered that he had taken a train back to Zurich. His wish to spend the day there and not in Lucerne had proved too strong for his good intentions.

In most of the examples previously mentioned in this paper, and of those encountered in real life, it is possible to discover a motive for the given occurrence that logically accounts for this, but which does not lie particularly deep in the person's mind. In other words, it is, in Freud's language, preconscious,[2] and the subject has no particular difficulty in recognising it as an integral part of his personality. The problem, however, is far from exhausted at this point. It is next necessary to discover the origin of the motive or tendency in question, or to explain why it needs to be expressed at all. In this investigation one reaches the realm of the unconscious proper, and here it often turns out that the error which is being analysed has a deeper meaning—that it symbolises more than the preconscious motive, and expresses tendencies of much greater personal significance; this may be the case, however trivial the error in itself. In some of the preceding examples the preconscious motive disclosed appears trite, and it seems unlikely that such a

[1] Maeder, ' Nouvelles Contributions à la psychopathologie de la vie quotidienne,' *Arch. de Psychol.*, 1908, vol. vii., p. 296.

[2] For the explanation of this and allied terms, see Chapter I., p. 30.

trifling matter should need a complicated psychological mechanism to manifest itself. In the cases of this kind that I have had the opportunity of submitting to a detailed psycho-analysis, I have found that the unconscious associations often shed an unexpectedly instructive light on the full meaning of the occurrence. Unfortunately, however, the motives thus reached are usually of so intimate a nature that discretion forbids the publishing of them.

In still other cases no preconscious motive can be discerned, and the error appears to be quite meaningless until the truly unconscious sources are reached. In the following example[1] the preconscious motive was not discovered until the resistance to the unconscious sources of it was broken down. It is further peculiarly instructive in illustrating what important and fundamental traits of character may be revealed by the analysis of an absolutely trivial occurrence.

A doctor on rearranging his furniture in a new house came across an old-fashioned, straight, wooden stethoscope, and, after pausing to decide where he should put it, was impelled to place it on the side of his writing-desk in such a position that it stood exactly between his chair and the one reserved for his patients. The act in itself was certainly odd, for in the first place the straight stethoscope served no purpose, as he invariably used a binaural one; and in the second place all his medical apparatus and instruments were always kept in drawers, with the sole exception of this one. However, he gave no thought at all to the matter until one day it was brought to his notice by a patient, who had never seen a wooden stethoscope, asking him what it was. On being told, she asked why he kept it just there; he answered in an off-hand way that that place was as good as any other. This started him thinking, however, and he wondered whether there had been any unconscious motive in his action. Being interested in the psychoanalytic method he asked me to investigate the matter.

The first memory that occurred to him was the fact that when a medical student he had been struck by the habit his hospital interne had of always carrying in his hand a wooden stethoscope on his ward visits, although he never used it. He greatly admired this interne, and was much attached to him. Later on, when he himself became an interne, he contracted the same habit, and would feel

[1] In the *Zentralbl. für Psychoanalyse*, Jahrg. I., S. 96, I have published a fuller account of this example.

very uncomfortable if by mistake he left his room without having the instrument to swing in his hand. The aimlessness of the habit was shown, not only by the fact that the only stethoscope he ever used was a binaural one, which he carried in his pocket, but also in that it was continued when he was a surgical interne and never needed any stethoscope at all.

From this it was evident that the idea of the instrument in question had in some way or other become invested with a greater psychical significance than normally belongs to it—in other words, that to the subject it stood for more than it does with other people. The idea must have got unconsciously associated with some other one, which it symbolised, and from which it derived its additional fulness of meaning. I will forestall the rest of the analysis by saying what this secondary idea was—namely, a phallic one; the way in which this curious association had been formed will presently be related. The discomfort he experienced in hospital on missing the instrument, and the relief and reassurance the presence of it gave him, was related to what is known as a ' castration-complex '— namely, a childhood fear, often continued in a disguised form into adult life, lest a private part of his body should be taken away from him just as playthings so often were; the fear was due to paternal threats that it would be cut off if he were not a good boy, particularly in a certain direction. This is a very common complex, and accounts for a great deal of general nervousness and lack of confidence in later years.

Then came a number of childhood memories relating to his family doctor. He had been strongly attached to this doctor as a child, and during the analysis long-buried memories were recovered of a double phantasy he had in his fourth year concerning the birth of a younger sister—namely, that she was the child (1) of himself and his mother, the father being relegated to the background, and (2) of the doctor and himself; in this he thus played both a masculine and feminine part.[1] At the time, when his curiosity was being aroused by the event, he could not help noticing the prominent share taken by the doctor in the proceedings, and the subordinate position occupied by the father; the significance of this for his later life will presently be pointed out.

[1] Psycho-analytic research, with the penetration of infantile amnesia, has shown that this apparent precocity is a less abnormal occurrence than was previously supposed.

The stethoscope association was formed through many connections. In the first place, the physical appearance of the instrument—a straight, rigid, hollow tube, having a small bulbous summit at one extremity, and a broad base at the other—and the fact of its being the essential part of the medical paraphernalia, the instrument with which the doctor performed his magical and interesting feats, were matters that attracted his boyish attention. He had had his chest repeatedly examined by the doctor at the age of six, and distinctly recollected the voluptuous sensation of feeling the latter's head near him pressing the wooden stethoscope into his chest, and of the rhythmic to-and-fro respiratory movement. He had been struck by the doctor's habit of carrying his stethoscope inside his hat; he found it interesting that the doctor should carry his chief instrument concealed about his person, always handy when he went to see patients, and that he only had to take off his hat (*i.e.*, a part of his clothing) and ' pull it out.' At the age of eight he was impressed by being told by an older boy that it was the doctor's custom to get into bed with his women patients. It is certain that the doctor, who was young and handsome, was extremely popular among the women of the neighbourhood, including the subject's own mother. The doctor and his ' instrument ' were therefore the objects of great interest throughout his boyhood.

It is probable that, as in many other cases, unconscious identification with the family doctor had been a main motive in determining the subject's choice of profession. It was here doubly conditioned, (1) by the superiority of the doctor on certain interesting occasions to the father, of whom the subject was very jealous, and (2) by the doctor's knowledge of forbidden topics[1] and his opportunities for illicit indulgence. The subject admitted that he had on several occasions experienced erotic temptations in regard to his women patients; he had twice fallen in love with one, and finally had married one.

The next memory was of a dream, plainly of a homosexual-masochistic nature; in it a man, who proved to be a replacement-figure of the family doctor, attacked the subject with a ' sword.' The idea of a sword, as is so frequently the case in dreams, represented the same idea that was mentioned above to be associated with that of a wooden stethoscope. The thought of a sword reminded the subject of the passage in the ' Nibelung Saga,' where

[1] The term ' medical questions ' is a common periphrasis for ' sexual questions.'

Sigurd sleeps with his naked sword (*Gram*) between him and Brunhilda, an incident that had always greatly struck his imagination.

The meaning of the symptomatic act now at last became clear. The subject had placed his wooden stethoscope between him and his patients, just as Sigurd had placed his sword (an equivalent symbol) between him and the maiden he was not to touch. The act was a compromise-formation; it served both to gratify in his imagination the repressed wish to enter into nearer relations with an attractive patient (interposition of phallus), and at the same time to remind him that this wish was not to become a reality (interposition of sword). It was, so to speak, a charm against yielding to temptation.

X. General Observations

1. *Warrant for Interpretations*

The first criticism of the theses here maintained that naturally presents itself is the question as to the reliability of the individual interpretations. It is not likely that anyone will reject them all as improbable, but, particularly with the more complex analyses, doubt must arise concerning the trustworthiness of the results. This is especially so in regard to the personal, subjective factor in the interpretations, although as a matter of fact the very constancy of the way in which similar conclusions are reached by different observers indicates that this factor is less potent than might be imagined. Experience shows that, when attention is carefully directed to the objective aspects of the analysis, the importance of the personal factor, which from the unavoidable nature of the circumstances can never be entirely eliminated, can be reduced to a degree where it is practically negligible. In most scientific work the personal factor has to be reckoned with, but appreciation of the way in which it acts, especially when this is based on psychological knowledge, as a rule enables it to be excluded to such an extent as not to interfere with conclusions being formulated that are valid enough to stand the objective test of verifiability. It is contended that this statement applies unrestrictedly to psycho-analytic interpretations. It is, of course, to be conceded that the probable accuracy of these interpretations varies considerably in different instances, as conclusions do elsewhere in science. Thus, in a chemical analysis, the conclusion as to whether a given substance is present or not varies in probability according to the quality and amount of evidence obtainable; in some cases the confirmatory tests are so unequivocal that the final decision is a practically certain one, in others it is very probable, in still others it is only a plausible possibility, and so on.

The view that the psycho-analytic interpretations of the class of occurrences under discussion are reliable is based on, among others, the following considerations:

1. The psychological correctness of the principles of the free association method. This is too complex a matter to be gone into here, and I will only refer the reader to Jung's well-known works[1] on the subject.

2. The constancy of the findings by different observers, and the harmony of the conclusions with those reached in the study of other fields—*e.g.*, dreams, psychoneuroses, mythology, etc. It is extremely unlikely that this is due to coincidence, and still more so that it is due to identical prejudices on the part of the different workers, for in the first place this would be postulating a very remarkable uniformity in their individual mental constellations, and in the second place psycho-analytic research brings with it an eradication of personal prejudice, and an appreciation of personal complexes, that is rarely attained elsewhere in the same degree.

3. The increased intelligibility of the processes in question. An occurrence that previously was obscure and meaningless now becomes throughout comprehensible, and an integral part of the rest of the person's mental operations. It is seen to be merely an irregular manifestation of a logical tendency that is an essential constituent of the personality, the unusual features having certain definite reasons for their occurrence. Moreover, the discovery of the underlying motive, and its connection with the manifestation being analysed, is a matter that commonly lends itself to external verification. When, in an analysis, one traces a given error in mental functioning, such as a *lapsus linguæ*, to a thought that the person was desirous of keeping back, it is usually easy to confirm the truth of the conclusion. Very significant in this connection is the unmistakable evidence of the resulting affect in the person, which accurately corresponds with that characteristic of the revealed mental process. Often this is so pronounced that it is quite impossible to doubt the truth of the interpretation made; this especially is a matter where

---

[1] Jung, ' Diagnostische Assoziationsstudien,' Bd. i., 1906; Bd. ii., 1910.

personal experience is more convincing than any possible amount of discussion.

4. The fact that in many fields the principles in question are generally recognised to be valid. Freud's study is only a detailed working-out of laws that were already known to hold true over a limited area. When a man is hurt at finding his name unfortunately forgotten, or at unexpectedly being passed by unrecognised in the street; when a lady is offended by some one who professes regard for her forgetting to carry out her behests or to keep a rendezvous —they are displaying an affect that accords perfectly with the inferences of the psycho-analyst, and with no others. In this correct intuition of mankind lies already the essential nucleus of the conclusions maintained by Freud.

Indeed, it is quite impossible to go through life without constantly making interpretations of just this kind, though usually they are simpler and more evident than those needing a special psychoanalysis. Observation of a very few jokes is sufficient to illustrate this, and we ' read between the lines ' of the people we have to do with, doubting the scientific justification of our right to do so as little as we do in the interpretations of jokes.[1] This holds in the most manifold fields of mental activity. A few examples may be quoted of a kind that could be multiplied indefinitely: With Mr. C. R. Kennedy's play, ' The Servant in the House,' no one can witness it intelligently and doubt that the Hindu servant, who is the principal character, is a presentation of Jesus Christ, or that his name ' Manson ' is a disguised form of the title ' Son of Man.' Yet we should find it difficult to ' prove ' this to a carping critic who is bent on avoiding the obvious inference, and still more to ' prove ' our assumption that the disguise was the product of definite motives in the author's mind. In Mr. Bernard Shaw's play ' Press Cuttings,' one of the characters, the Prime Minister of England, is called ' Balsquith.' When one infers that he compounded the word from the names of two Prime Ministers, Balfour and Asquith, the critic may accuse us of reading into Mr. Shaw's mind views of our own that never existed there.[2] In Shelley's ' Œdipus Tyrannus '

---

[1] In ' Der Witz und seine Beziehungen zum Unbewussten ' Freud has made a detailed study of this subject. As with the occurrences studied in the present paper, he has shown that the insight consciously obtained is often only a partial one, and that the true significance is often related to unconscious sources.

[2] The Royal Censor refused to let the play be acted until the name was replaced by one less open to this personal interpretation—namely, Johnson; the name of the Commander-in-Chief, Mitchener (from Milner and Kitchener) had to be altered to Bones.

what right have we to assume that, in his ridicule of the Ionian Minotaur,[1] the author was satirising the Englishman of his time? When Edward Lear[2] speaks of Excelscue, how is it everyone recognises that he is referring to Fortescue (Excel=XL=Forty= Forte)? Our answer in all these cases is the same—namely, that we feel justified in making the inferences in question because they make something intelligible that otherwise would have no meaning. This answer is perfectly correct, for in the last analysis the justification of every scientific generalisation is that it enables us to comprehend something that is otherwise obscure—namely, the relations between apparently dissimilar phenomena.

To this it may be said that, in such cases as those just mentioned, a logical meaning is given to something that from previous experience we have every reason to expect has one, but that the point in dispute about the 'psychopathological' occurrences of everyday life is whether they have such a meaning or not. Here *a priori* argument can take us no further, and the question can only be referred for solution to actual investigation—a matter usually considered unnecessary, on the pure assumption that the occurrences have no logical meaning. Freud's scepticism made him challenge the necessity of this assumption, and prefer to leave the question open until it was investigated. On doing so, he found as a matter of experience two things—namely, that the realm of psychical determinism is more extensive than is generally supposed, and that awareness of a motive at a given moment is not a necessary accompaniment of the external manifestation of this.

Freud further came to the conclusion that there was a definite cause for the popular belief that so many blunders in our mental functioning are meaningless. He holds that this belief is due to the same cause as the blunders themselves—namely, to repression. Various repressed thoughts are in every one of us constantly coming to expression in the shape of 'meaningless' blunders, the significance of which necessarily escapes us. Being thus accustomed to the occurrences of such matters in ourselves we naturally attach no significance to them in others; we 'explain' these as we do our own, or accept the 'explanations' proffered just as we expect others to accept the 'explanations' of our own blunders.[3]

---

[1] = John Bull.   [2] See Lady Strachey's 'Later Letters of Edward Lear.'
[3] If one wished to be epigrammatic, one might say: 'In the future, reason will be used to explain things; at present, it has to be used to explain them away.' This would be true of a good many matters besides the slips of everyday life.

As to these explanations, little more need be added. Where the factors they have recourse to are operative at all, they act only as predisposing conditions, not as the true cause. Freud[1] gives the following apposite illustration of the actual state of affairs: ' Suppose I have been so incautious as to go for a stroll in a lonely part of the town, where I am attacked and robbed of my watch and money. At the next police-station I give information, with the words: I have been in this and that street, where *loneliness* and *darkness* stole my watch and money. Although in these words I should have said nothing that was not correct, still, from the wording of my information, I run the danger of being thought not quite right in the head. The state of affairs can correctly be described only thus: That *favoured* by the loneliness of the spot, and *unrecognisable* through the protection of the darkness, a thief has robbed me of my valuables. Now, the state of affairs in the forgetting of a name need not be otherwise; favoured by fatigue, circulatory disturbances, and poisoning, some unknown psychical agent robs me of the proper names that belong to my memory—the same agent that on other occasions can bring about the same failure of memory during perfect health and capacity.' Similarly, such a mistake as a slip of the tongue is often attributed by psychologists (*e.g.*, Wundt) to a momentary inattentiveness. It is certainly a question of conscious attention, but Freud[2] has pointed out that the defect is more accurately described as a disturbance of attention than as a diminution, the true cause being the disturbing influence of a second train of thought. The same remarks apply to all the other explanations urged. Several examples were given above in which names and other words differing by only one letter were confounded or interchanged, and evidence was brought forward to show that this external resemblance was merely a predisposing circumstance, and not the actual cause of the mistake. Many such circumstances certainly favour the occurrence of a blunder—that is, they permit a repressed thought to slip partly through. Alcoholic intoxication is notoriously one. Emotional excitement is another. Many blunders, forgettings, and other oversights, are attributed to the confusion of hurry. Thus, for instance, I have noticed that the using of the wrong key, in the examples quoted above, most often occurred when I was in a great hurry (the same was true of the not recognising the assistant superintendent in his office); but if haste

[1] Freud, ' Zur Psychopathologie,' S. 25.   [2] Freud, *op. cit.*, S. 156.

were the true cause, it would be curious that it should bring about a blunder of a kind that defeats its own object; strictly speaking, it is the emotional confusion or excitement engendered by hurry that permits a second repressed impulse to manifest itself in what externally appears as a blunder.

As has been remarked above, there are certain occasions in every-day life when the normal person divines the motivation of un-intentional errors, though these are rare in comparison with the occasions[1] on which it escapes him. Freud[1] has pointed out that there are two other groups of processes in which an *unconscious*, and therefore distorted, knowledge of this motivation is manifested —namely in paranoia and in superstitions. In both these the subject reads a meaning into external happenings that have no such psychical meaning, and, in a very interesting discussion of the subject, Freud produces reasons to believe that this erroneous functioning is due to a projection on to the outside of motives that exist in the subject's mind and are full of meaning there, but which he does not directly perceive.

A little may be said on a feature of some of the analyses quoted that may strike the reader as odd—namely, the remarkable play on words that is so often found. Whoever is surprised at this needs to be reminded of the almost boundless extent to which the same feature occurs in other fields of mental activity—in wit, dreams, insanity, and so on. Even in the serious affairs of everyday life it is far from unusual. Thus, to cite a few business announcements, we see the National Drug Company using as its trade motto 'Nadru,' the National Liquorice Company (N. L. Co.) that of 'Enelco'; we find the Levy Jewellery Company reversing its first name into the more pretentious one of 'Yvel,' and advertisements of 'Uneeda' cigars and 'Phiteezi' boots are familiar to everyone. This tendency to play on words, and to produce a more useful or pleasant result (mirror-writing, ciphers, and rhyming slang,[2] also belong here), is evidently dictated in part by the same 'un-pleasantness' motives—to avoid banal or otherwise unattractive words—that so much stress has been laid on above. It is one that has far-reaching roots in early childhood life. In preconscious and

---

[1] Freud, *op. cit.*, S. 307 *et seq.*

[2] The following are instances from the Cockney type of this: 'Aristotle'=bottle; 'Cain and Abel'=table; 'Harry Nichols'=pickles. Mediate forms are: 'Christmas' (card)=guard; 'Bull' (and cow)=row; 'Malcolm' (Scott)=hot; 'Stockton' (on-Tees)=cheese; 'Rosie' (Loader)=soda, and so on.

unconscious mental activities this play on words—clang associations—is much more extensive than in consciousness, and serves for the transference of a given affect from one mode of expression to a more suitable and convenient one.

2. *Bearing on Psycho-Analytic Method of Treatment*

Three brief remarks may be made on this matter. In the first place, investigation of the errors and slips of everyday life is perhaps the best mode of approach to the study of psycho-analysis, and affords a convenient preliminary to the more difficult, though more important, subject of dreams. The greatest value is to be attached to self-analysis, a fact to which attention cannot too often be called. In the second place, analysis of the occurrences in question is of considerable service in the treatment of neurotic patients. Their behaviour in this respect needs to be closely observed, and frequently a quite trivial occurrence will, when investigated, provide clues to the elucidation of the main problem. Thirdly, consideration of the mechanism of these erroneous functionings makes it easy to understand the way in which psycho-analysis brings about its therapeutic effects. Both the ' errors ' and the neurotic symptoms are the manifestations of dissociated conative trends which are less compatible with consciousness than the rest of the personality opposed to them, are consequently repressed, and can come to expression only in indirect ways and only under certain circumstances. An essential condition for this is non-awareness of the process. Psycho-analysis, by directing the dissociated trend into consciousness, abolishes this condition, and therefore brings the trend under the control of the conscious inhibiting forces. Conscious control is substituted for automatic expression, the significance of which was not realised. These considerations may be illustrated by the tritest of the examples given above—namely, my opening of a fresh tobacco-tin although I wished first to finish the old one. Here it is quite obvious that the rule just stated holds that an essential condition of the erroneous functioning is non-awareness of the significance of the process; I knew that I was reaching for tobacco, but didn't notice which tin it was. The moment I realised the situation, I of course checked the error, and controlled the wish that was taking advantage of my absent-mindedness to come to expression. On a larger scale the same is true of neurotic symptoms; realisation of their significance checks the morbid expression of the underlying impulse. *The cardinal proposition is that consciousness of an aberrant impulse means increased control of it.*

3. *Relation to Health and Disease*

This matter should be fairly evident from the preceding considerations, so that the two corollaries that follow in this respect need only to be stated. The first is that from a psychological point of view perfect mental normality does not exist. In other words, everyone shows numerous defects in mental functioning that are manifestations of dissociated, repressed, psychical material, and which are brought about by the same psychological mechanisms as those operative in the case of the psychoneuroses. A further matter not brought out in the preceding study is that this material is ultimately of the same nature as that from which neuroses are produced. The second corollary is that the border-line between mental health and disease is much less sharp even than is generally supposed. The distinction between the two is really a social one rather than a psychopathological one, just as the distinction between sanity and insanity is primarily a legal one. When the erroneous mental functioning happens to carry with it a social incapacity or disability, the condition is called a neurosis, and when it does not it is called absent-mindedness, eccentricity, personal mannerism, and so on. Further reflections on the significance of these conclusions will here be omitted, as they are not relevant to the main purpose of the paper.

4. *Determinism and Free-Will*

One of the psychological arguments against the belief in a complete mental determinism is the intense feeling of conviction that we have a perfectly free choice in the performance of many acts. This feeling of conviction must be justified by something, but at the same time it is entirely compatible with a complete determinism. It is curious that it is not often prominent with important and weighty decisions. On these occasions one has much more the feeling of being irresistibly impelled in a given direction (compare Luther's ' Hier stehe ich, ich kann nicht anders '). On the contrary, it is with trivial and indifferent resolutions that one is most sure that one could just as well have acted otherwise, that one has acted from non-motived free-will. From the psycho-analytical point of view, the right of this feeling of conviction is not contested. It only means that the person is not aware of any conscious motive. When, however, conscious motivation is distinguished from unconscious motivation, this feeling of conviction teaches us that the former does not extend over all our motor resolutions. What is left free from the one side receives its motive from the other—from the unconscious—and so the psychical determinism is flawlessly carried through. A knowledge of unconscious motivation is indispensable, even for philosophical discussion of determinism.

That the relation between unconscious and conscious mental processes furnishes the key to the problem of psychological determinism has also been clearly pointed out by Kohnstamm,[1] approaching the subject in quite a different way from Freud. He writes: ' Die biologische Betrachtungsweise sieht in den Bewusstseinsdingen nur Bergspitzen, die über einem Nebelmeer sichtbar werden, während das Bergganze—die Gesamtheit der Lebensphänomene—dem unmittelbaren Bewusstsein verborgen bleibt· Wenn man sich auf die Betrachtung von oben her beschränkt, ergibt sich kein natürlicher Zusammenhang, keine Gesetzmässigkeit. Sieht man aber von dem Nebel ab, der die Gründe verhüllt, so erkennt man, wie die Berge aus der Ebene aufsteigen, sich von einem gemeinsamen Grunde abhebend. Man gelangt zu der naturwissenschaftlichen Einsicht von der Einheit dessen, was unter zufälligen Bedingungen teils sichtbar, teils unsichtbar war. Ähnlich sucht die biologische Betrachtungsweise die Bewusstseinsphänomene umzusetzen in raumzeitliche Geschehnisse und Gesetzmässigkeiten, wie sie auch sonst den Gegenstand naturwissenschaftlicher Biologie bilden. So zeigte die gegenwärtige Untersuchung die Zielstrebigkeit unter dem Bilde eines Berges, welcher uns den allgemeinen Reizverwertungstypus des Lebens darstellt und in eine Spitze ausläuft, welche die Willenshandlung bedeutet.' [' The biological way of thinking sees in the facts of consciousness only mountain-peaks, which soar into sight over a sea of mist, while the mountain as a whole—the totality of vital phenomena—remains hidden from the immediate consciousness. If one confines oneself to the view from above, there appears to be no natural connection, no regularity. If, however, one disregards the mist that conceals the base, one recognises how the mountains rise from the plain, and have a common basis. One attains scientific insight of the unity of what, under chance conditions, was partly visible, partly invisible. Similarly, the biological way of thinking seeks to transpose the phenomena of consciousness into regular occurrences of time and space, just as these elsewhere constitute the subject of scientific biology. The present investigation of purposefulness discloses it thus under the metaphor of a mountain, which represents the general reaction of life to different stimuli, and which terminates as a peak that signifies the action of the will.']

5. *Social Significance*

It would be interesting to speculate as to the result of a general knowledge of the unconscious motives that underlie the failures of mental functioning in everyday life; but it is perhaps more profitable to review some of the present results of ignorance of them.

One of these is that both intellectual and moral dishonesty is facilitated to an extraordinary extent. There is no doubt that dishonesty of which the subject is not conscious is much commoner than deliberate dishonesty, a fact of considerable importance in, for instance, juristic matters. The hysteric who cannot move her leg because unconsciously she wishes it to be paralysed, the tourist who oversees a prohibiting notice because he finds such things annoying, and the impecunious man who forgets to pay a bill because he doesn't really want to, are all instances of this. At the same time, the line between the two types of dishonesty is nowhere a sharp one, and in many cases one can only conclude that the subject could with a very little effort recognise the suppressed motive, which is more than half-conscious. In psycho-analytic treatment this is constantly to be observed. The following slight example of it may be quoted: A young American told me of a certain experience she had had in her childhood in company with a boy. I had every reason to believe that this was far from being an isolated one, and asked her whether it had occurred with any-one else. She said, ' Not any time that I can remember.' Noticing the wording of her answer and a certain expression on her face, I asked, ' What about the times that you can't remember ?' She exclaimed, ' Oh, shucks !' and in such a disconcerted tone that I was sure my surmise had been well founded. She then made the remark, ' Well, I really had forgotten the other times till this minute,' the truth of which was probably only partial. The incident made me think of Nietzsche's epigram: ' Man lügt wohl mit dem Munde, aber mit dem Maule, das man dabei macht, sagt man die Wahrheit.' [' One may indeed lie with the mouth, but with the accompanying grimace one nevertheless tells the truth.'] Half-amnesias of this kind are extremely common in daily life.

In spite of the constant endeavour to keep back disagreeable or unacceptable thoughts, these very thoughts betray themselves in blunders of the type under discussion. By the world this self-betrayal is often passed by unnoticed, but it does not escape anyone who has made a study of unconscious functioning. Freud[1] in no way exaggerates when he says: ' Wer Augen hat, zu sehen, und Ohren, zu hören, überzeugt sich, dass die Sterblichen kein Geheimnis verbergen können. Wessen Lippen schweigen, der schwätzt mit den Fingerspitzen; aus allen Poren dringt ihm der Verrat.' [' He who has eyes to see, and ears to hear, becomes convinced that mortals can hide no secret. When lips are silent, the fingertips tattle; betrayal oozes out of every pore.'] Moreover, even with a direct lie, careful observation of the undue emphasis here and the distortion there will usually disclose what the person is trying to conceal, for the lie is a creation of the same mind that at the moment is cognisant of the truth. It is very rare, especially on emotional occasions, for self-control to be so complete as to inhibit all unconscious manifestations, which to an attentive observer will indicate the truth. Strictly speaking, one cannot lie to another, only to oneself, and skilled introspection makes even this increasingly difficult.

An important consequence of this is that everyone is apt to know more about the inner motives of those near to him than they themselves know, inasmuch as everyone is continually performing, at all events, some simple kind of psychical analysis on those around him. This is a fertile source of misunderstandings and friction,[2] especially in family and married life, where contact is much nearer. One person intuitively recognises an intention or tendency in the other that the latter refuses to admit even to himself. When the unavoidable inferences are presented to him, he is indignant, rebuts them as being groundless, and complains that he is misunderstood. Strictly speaking, such misunderstanding is really a too fine understanding. The more nervous two people are, the more often does

---

[1] Freud, ' Sammlung kleiner Schriften,' Zweite Folge, S. 69.
[2] Freud, ' Zur Psychopathologie,' S. 258.

it give rise to schisms, the reasons for which are as categorically denied by the one as they are obvious to the other. This is the punishment for the inner improbity: that, under the pretext of forgetting, absent-mindedness, and so on, people allow tendencies to come to expression which they would do better to admit to themselves and others, unless they can control them.

Most important, however, is the extension of these principles to the sphere of human judgement, for it is probable that repressed complexes play as prominent a part in distortion here as they do in the minor errors of memory mentioned above. On a large scale this is shown in two ways—in the minimum of evidence often necessary to secure the acceptance of an idea that is in harmony with existing mental constellations, or to reject one that is incompatible with these. In both cases it is often affective influences rather than intellectual operations that decide the question. The same evidence is construed quite differently when viewed in the light of one affective constellation from the way it is when viewed in the light of another. Further, when the general attitude towards a question changes in the course of time, this is often due at least as much to modification of the prevailing affective influences as to the accumulation of external evidence; for instance, the average man of to-day does not hesitate to reject the same evidence of witchcraft that was so convincing to the man of three centuries ago, though he usually knows no more about the true explanation of it than the latter did.

Ignorance of the importance of affective factors in this respect, combined with the ineradicable popular belief in the rationality of the individual mind, has the interesting result that strong differences of opinion are attributed by each side to a defect in reasoning capacity on the part of the other. In an exposition of this matter, Trotter[1] writes: ' The religious man accuses the atheist of being shallow and irrational, and is met with a similar reply; to the Conservative, the amazing thing about the Liberal is his incapacity to see reason and accept the only possible solution of public problems. Examination reveals the fact that the differences are not due to the commission of the mere mechanical fallacies of logic, since these are easily avoided, even by the politician, and since there is no reason to suppose that one party in such controversies

[1] Wilfred Trotter, ' Instincts of the Herd in Peace and War,' second edition, 1919, p. 37.

is less logical than the other. The difference is due rather to the fundamental assumptions of the antagonists being hostile, and these assumptions are derived from herd suggestion.'

There is a certain amount of truth in this imputation of stupidity to a person on the opposite side, for in his blind refusal to appreciate or even to perceive the evidence adduced by his opponent he may give an unavoidable appearance of marked stupidity. A further reason for this is that someone under the sway of strongly affective influences thinks not only that anyone differing from him must be deficient in reasoning power, but also that the views of the latter are themselves stupid. In attempting to controvert these, therefore, he unconsciously distorts them until they really are foolish, and he then finds it easy to demolish them. Any man of the period who read only the account of Darwin's views that was promulgated by his theological and scientific opponents must have wondered why it was worth while to attack such obvious nonsense, while our wonder, on the other hand, is that reputable and otherwise intelligent men could have managed so to pervert and misunderstand statements that to us are lucidity itself. Similarly at the present time, if some of the remarkable accounts of Freud's views that are given by his opponents represented anything like what he really holds, the fact would need much explanation that so many scientific men can accept them and yet remain sane.

Yet this astonishing stupidity in apprehending the arguments of opponents, and in defending preconceived views, is only apparent. The men who so grossly misinterpreted Darwin were often men of high intellectual power, and the same is true of many of Freud's opponents; similarly no one can read closely the ' Malleus Maleficarum ' without admiration for the amazing intellectual ingenuity with which the most fantastic propositions are there defended. The process is akin to one that psychiatrists call ' emotional stupidity,' a symptom seen in patients who have no real defect of reasoning power, but who through various affective influences are in a condition that at first sight gives rise to a strong suspicion of some organic defect of the brain.

A further psychological problem of interest in this connection is how to account for the intensity of annoyance, anger, and even hate, that may be engendered by controversial opposition of the particular type discussed above. How irritating it can be to try vainly to get someone to see a point that is perfectly simple and obvious to oneself most people know from ample experience. There would even seem to be a correlation between the amount of heat in this way engendered and the slightness of the difference dividing two people, just as the most bitter wars are between races of similar stock (truer still of civil wars) or between religious sections whose doctrinal differences are apparently of only academic importance. The history of the Balkans shows, for instance, that the races professing the Orthodox creed preferred to be ruled by the infidel Turk rather than by Roman Catholics (*e.g.*, Venetians), and heretics have always been persecuted with a venom that finds no counterpart in the attitude towards heathen countries. It is as though we are willing to understand that people widely different from ourselves cannot grasp arguments that seem convincing enough to us, but what we find hard to tolerate is that those akin to us, and who 'ought to know better,' should behave in this way. The *feeling* it gives us, in the case of either individuals or nations, is that since the matter in dispute is so very obvious there must be an element of sheer obstinacy on the other side that makes them refuse to see the point. The reaction this calls forth is, on the one hand, the belief that they are intellectually inferior and stupid, as explained above, and, on the other hand, the emotions of irritation and anger. I should interpret the latter reaction as an unconscious intuition that the opposition on the other side is really of emotional origin, denoting hostility to our own emotional attitude, as, indeed, it so usually is. In other words, our unconscious correctly interprets the meaning of the situation and appropriately responds with anger, while our conscious mind erroneously rationalises it as one due to the other person's stupidity. The next thing that happens is that we feel increasingly impotent, for, as is well known, the weapon of argument is powerless in the face of 'emotional stupidity'; as Goethe said, 'Against stupidity the gods themselves fight in vain.' The impotence is due to the fact that the weapon is not being directed against the true source of opposition—namely, the unconscious emotional complexes of the other person. (The failure is exactly the same as the physician experiences who tries to dispel neurotic symptoms by means of rational argument; he is not really attacking the cause, which lies in the unconscious.) The feeling of impotence in the face of irrational opposition, of being thwarted for no good reason, still further increases our anger, sometimes to an extreme degree;

this reaction is probably of infantile origin, the resentment and
'tantrums' at first discovering that the world dares to thwart
some of our wishes, a world which originally had gratified them
all to the full.

On observing the general attitude towards people whose
'emotional stupidity' has in the course of time become apparent,
two things are noticeable: In the first place, as was remarked
above, the fault is attributed much more to intellectual inferiority
than to the more important affective causes. Hence the present-day
supercilious pity for the scholastics of the 'dark ages,' an attitude
considerably modified by an objective comparison of the reasoning
powers characteristic of the two civilisations. In the second place,
far greater leniency is shown towards a stupidity that expresses
itself in the form of blind adherence to accepted errors than that
which expresses itself in the form of blind rejection of a novel truth;
in other words, incredulousness is always more harshly judged than
credulousness, though they are both merely different aspects of
the same fundamental failing—namely, lack of true scepticism.
Yet the one is hardly more characteristic of human weakness
than the other—as Nietzsche put it: 'Mankind has a bad ear
for new music'—and it would be hard to convince a student of
human progress that the first manifestation has a greater retarding
influence on this than the second. In any case, these considerations
go to show the fallacy of the popular belief that the will is the
servant of reason, the truth being that reason has always been,
and probably always must be, to a very large extent the handmaid
of the will.

XI. SUMMARY

Only part of the subject-matter dealt with by Freud has been
covered in the present paper. Those interested in it are referred
to his book for richer and more numerous examples, and for the
lucid discussion there given of the theoretical aspects of the subject.
It is perhaps desirable, however, to summarise here the main
conclusions on the topics discussed above.

The occurrences that form the subject-matter of this study,
the general characteristics of which were defined in the introductory section,[1] may be divided into motor and sen-

---

[1] In German the erroneousness of the process is conveniently indicated by the
preface 'ver'—thus, Verdrucken, vergessen, vergreifen, verhören, verlegen, verlesen,
verschreiben, versehen, versprechen, etc. [In English we designate the whole group
by the word 'parapraxes.']

sory.[1] The defects of the former class that enter into consideration are two: (1) The erroneous carrying out of an intended purpose (slips of the tongue and pen, erroneously-carried-out actions); and (2) the carrying out of an unintended purpose (symptomatic acts). The defects of the latter class are also two: (1) Simple failure of perception (forgetting, not seeing); and (2) erroneous perception (false recollection, false visual perception). In each class the distinction between the two kinds of defects is not sharp; thus, in the latter one, for instance, a failure to remember is always accompanied by an over-prominent remembrance of some associated memory, a false recollection. Further, the distinction between the two classes themselves is not a sharp one, both motor and sensory processes playing a part in many instances; thus, in the mislaying of objects, the object is first misplaced, and then the memory of the act is forgotten.

Common to all forms is the fact that the subject, and most observers, either gives an obviously inadequate explanation of the particular occurrence—such as that it was due to ' inattention,' ' absent-mindedness,' ' chance,' and so on—or frankly maintains that it has no explanation at all. On the contrary, psychoanalysis shows that there is not only a definite psychical cause for the occurrence, but that this has always a logical meaning, and may strictly be called a motive. This motive is some secondary tendency or train of thought, of which the subject is not aware at the time. Usually it is preconscious, or, in popular language, unconscious ; in many cases it is unconscious in the strict sense, and is then correspondingly more difficult to reveal. In most cases there are both a preconscious and an unconscious motive, which are associated with each other. The motive is repressed by the subject, the repression being a defence-mechanism that subserves the function of keeping from consciousness undesirable or painful thoughts. The motive may be one of two kinds—either it is a counter-impulse (*Gegenwille*) directed immediately against the mental operation that is intended, or it is an impulse directed against some mental tendency that stands in associative connection with this operation ; that is to say, the association between the two mental processes may be either intrinsic or extrinsic. As a result of the repression, any direct manifestation of the tendency is inhibited,

---

[1] This term is here used in its neuro-biological sense, and hence includes both perceptive and apperceptive processes.

and it can come to expression only as a parasitic process engrafted on another conscious one. The disturbance thus caused constitutes a temporary failure or error of normal mental functioning.

This error can psychologically be compared with a psychoneurotic symptom; the mechanisms by which the two are brought about are almost the same, and the psychical material that is the source of them is closely similar in the two cases. It is maintained that appreciation of the significance of these everyday errors is important for both the practice and theory of psychology; this is especially so in the contribution it furnishes to the problem of psychical determinism, and in the understanding it gives to the deeper, non-conscious motives of conduct. It further throws a valuable light on certain social problems, notably the question of mutual misunderstandings in everyday life, and on the importance of affective influences in forming decisions and judgements.

CHAPTER III

THE THEORY OF SYMBOLISM [1]

I. INTRODUCTION

MY attention was primarily directed to this subject, to the desirability of attaining a fuller understanding of the theoretical nature of symbolism, through observing that it is the interpreting of symbols which calls forth the greatest 'resistance' in psychoanalytic work, and, further, that this is also the centre of the strongest opposition to psycho-analysis in general. This fact—it may be called such, for the observation itself can very easily be checked—is really more curious than might appear, since the meaning of the symbols in question is the part of psycho-analysis that is most independent of individual psycho-analysts; it is a matter that, so to speak, stands outside psycho-analysis, being a body of knowledge that is familiar ground in many other branches of science—e.g., anthropology, folk-lore, philology, and so on. An explanation of the fact itself will be attempted below.

As soon as one begins to go into the subject deeply, however, its interest and importance rapidly widen, more and more problems open out, and at last, especially if the word 'symbolism' is taken in its widest sense, the subject is seen to comprise almost the whole development of civilisation. For what is this other than a never-ending series of evolutionary substitutions, a ceaseless replacement of one idea, interest, capacity, or tendency by another? The progress of the human mind, when considered genetically, is seen to consist, not—as is commonly thought—merely of a number of accretions added from without, but of the following two processes: on the one hand the extension or transference of interest and understanding from earlier, simpler, and more primitive ideas, etc., to more difficult and complex ones, which in a certain sense are continuations of and symbolise the former; and on the other hand the constant unmasking of previous symbolisms, the recog-

---

[1] Amplified from a paper read before the British Psychological Society, January 29, 1916. Published in the *British Journal of Psychology*, vol. ix.

nition that these, though previously thought to be literally true, were really only aspects or representations of the truth, the only ones of which our minds were—for either affective or intellectual reasons—at the time capable. One has only to reflect on the development of religion or science, for example, to perceive the truth of this description.

It is evidently necessary, therefore, that we try to understand more of the nature of symbolism, and of the way in which it operates. Our effort is met at the outset by this difficulty. The term ' symbolism ' has been used to denote very many different things, some of them quite unconnected with one another, and all of them in need of differentiation. Those interested in the various uses of the word may be referred to the historical work of Schlesinger,[1] who has collected some hundreds of different meanings and definitions. Etymology is no guide here, for the earliest meaning of the Greek σύμβολον does not seem to be the present-day one of a sign, but a bringing or weaving together, an implication which can perhaps be traced in the fact that many symbols have several significations; the root of the word, Sanscrit *gal*, Indogermanic *bal*, referred especially to the flowing together of water.

The word ' symbolism ' is currently used both in a wide sense, roughly equivalent to sign, and in a strict sense, as in psychoanalysis, which will be defined later. To give an idea of what different phenomena are included in the former category, we may enumerate the following examples. It is applied in the first place to the idea of various objects, such as emblems, amulets, devices, tokens, marks, badges, talismans, trophies, charms, phylacteries. Then it is used to indicate various figures of speech and modes of thought, such as the simile, metaphor, apologue, metonymy, synecdoche, allegory, parable, all of which are, of course, differentiated by philologists. Mythological, artistic, magical, religious, and mystical fields of thought, as well as that of primitive metaphysics and science, are often called symbolic. There is a symbolism of cubism, of the Catholic Church, of freemasonry, a colour symbolism, and even a symbolic logic. The word is further used to denote various signs, passwords, and customs. Bowing, for instance, is said to symbolise the ancient custom of prostration and hence respect with an absence of hostile intent. Fifty years ago to wear a red shirt or blouse would have been said to symbolise the fact

[1] Schlesinger, ' Geschichte des Symbols,' 1912.

that the wearer sympathised with Garibaldi, just as to-day a black one does in regard to Mussolini. The Venetian ceremony in which the Doge wedded the Adriatic with a ring symbolised the naval power of Venice. In Frankish law the seller of a plot of ground handed the buyer a single stone from it as a symbol of the transaction, and in ancient Bavarian law a twig was similarly used in the sale of a forest. When Louis XI. dispossessed his brother of Normandy, he solemnly broke the ducal ring at an assembly held expressly for the purpose in Rouen in 1469; the act symbolised the complete destruction of his brother's authority. Similar examples of the use of the word could be multiplied endlessly.

Now, amid this maze of meanings, what attributes in common can be found between the various ideas and acts denoted by the word ' symbol ' or ' symbolic ' ? I think I shall find general agreement that the following ones are, if not essential, at least very characteristic, and from them we may advance to a more precise definition of the problem.

1. A symbol is a representative or substitute of some other idea from which in the context it derives a secondary significance not inherent in itself. It is important to note that the flow of significance is from the primary idea to the secondary, *to* the symbol, so that typically a more essential idea is symbolised by a less essential. Thus all sorts of important things may be represented by a shred of material called a flag.

2. It represents the primary element through having something in common with it. Thus it would be a stretch of language to call a mnemonic knot in a handkerchief a symbol of the idea that has to be remembered, although some writers do so.[1] The association may be an internal or an external one. An association, however, which is superficial to the reason may often be of significance in feeling, especially in the unconscious.

3. A symbol is characteristically sensorial and concrete, whereas the idea represented may be a *relatively*[2] abstract and complex one. The symbol thus tends to be shorter and more condensed than the idea represented. The explanation of bowing, given above, well illustrates this.

4. Symbolic modes of thought are the more primitive, both ontogenetically and phylogenetically, and represent a reversion

[1] *E.g.*, Ferrero, ' Les lois Psychologiques de Symbolisme,' 1895, p. 25 *et seq.*
[2] In true symbolism the idea is general rather than abstract.

to some simpler and earlier stage of mental development. They are therefore more often met with in conditions that favour such a reversion ; for example, fatigue, drowsiness, bodily illness, neurosis and insanity, and, above all, in dreams, where conscious mental life is reduced almost to a minimum. A simple observation in this connection is that a tired man usually prefers looking at an illustrated paper, where ideas are presented on a sensorial plane, to reading.

5. In most uses of the word a symbol is a manifest expression for an idea that is more or less hidden, secret, or kept in reserve. Most typically of all the person employing the symbol is not even conscious of what it actually represents.

6. Symbols resemble wit in being made spontaneously, automatically, and, in the broad sense of the word, unconsciously.[1] The stricter the sense in which the term ' symbolism ' is used, the truer is this statement.

In accord with the two attributes last mentioned is the attitude of the conscious mind towards the interpretation of the symbol, in regard to both comprehension and feeling. The wider and more diluted the sense in which the word ' symbol ' is used, the more easily is its meaning perceived and the more readily is the interpretation accepted. With a symbol in the strict sense, on the contrary, the individual has no notion of its meaning, and rejects, often with repugnance, the interpretation.

By the enumeration of these six attributes we have narrowed and defined the field somewhat, but they still apply to a considerable number of different mental processes—in fact, to most forms of indirect figurative representation. *The thesis will here be maintained that true symbolism, in the strict sense, is to be distinguished from other forms of indirect representation,* and that not merely as a matter of convenience, because it is different from the rest, but because the clear conception thus gained of the nature of the differences must prove of value in understanding the most primitive levels in mental development and their relation to conscious thought. Before doing so, and before seeking to define the distinguishing characteristics of true symbolism, it will be profitable briefly to examine a purely linguistic question—namely, the metaphorical use of words;[2] for it is certain that the metaphor is one of the processes—

---

[1] See Ferrero, *op. cit.*, p. 24.

[2] *Cf.* E. B. Maye, art. on ' Enlargement of Vocabulary ' in O'Neill's ' Guide to the English Language,' 1915.

and the most familiar one—that have to be distinguished from symbolism.

The simile is the simplest figure of speech; it logically antedates even the metaphor, and certainly the adjective. In some primitive languages—*e.g.*, Tasmanian—there are no adjectives, similes being used in their stead, the reason, no doubt, being that it is easier to observe a concrete object which can be used in comparison than to abstract the notion of an attribute. The metaphor differs from a simile in the suppression of one of the terms of comparison; we say, for example, ' he buffeted the blows of Fortune,' instead of ' he strove against his ill fortune as he would have buffeted away blows.' A metaphor, therefore, presupposes a simile, which is the more primitive figure; in it the words ' as ' or ' like ' are suppressed, though always implied. In a simile a resemblance is pointed out between things that in other respects are different—*e.g.*, ' lies, like crows, come home to roost '; a mere parallel does not constitute a simile. Our motive in employing a simile is to add ornament, force, or vividness to the phrase, but it is to be supposed that the original motive, as in Tasmania, was to indicate the presence of an attribute by the simple process of comparison. The dream makes frequent use of this latter device, which is, in fact, its usual way of indicating an attribute; often quite a complicated description of a person can be conveyed by identifying—*i.e.*, comparing—him with someone else. This dream mechanism of identification has points of contact with the metaphor also. Thus, if a person's conduct or appearance resembles in some way that of a lion or bull, he may masquerade in a dream in the form of the animal, just as in speech we use such expressions as ' he was a lion in the fight.'

In the evolution, or what philologists call the decay, of the metaphor there are three stages, which are, of course, not sharply marked off from one another. In the first of these a word that is most often used in its literal sense is occasionally used in a figurative one, where its metaphorical nature is at once obvious; an example would be ' the wrath of the gale.' In the second stage both the literal and figurative senses are familiar, so that when the word is used in the latter sense we are conscious of its metaphorical nature only slightly or on reflection—preconsciously, as psychoanalysts would way; thus we speak of ' the depth of the sea ' literally, and ' the depth of despair ' figuratively. In the third stage the figurative sense has become the usual, literal one, and through either ignorance or forgetfulness we are no longer aware of its original literal meaning; thus the word ' melancholy ' does not make us think of black bile, nor does the expression 'acuity of mind ' make us think of a cutting edge. Here the decay of the metaphor is complete, and the figurative ' symbol ' has acquired an objective reality of its own in place of the subjective one of the earlier stages.

The nature of metaphor will be discussed below in connection with the distinction between it and true symbolism. But consideration of the evolution of the metaphor, as just indicated, already teaches us, amongst other things, that the simile is the primary process, there being sufficient likeness between two ideas for them to be treated as at least in some respect equivalent. We note, further, the gradual transference of significance from one use of a word to another, ending in the independence of the original metaphor, which has acquired a reality of its own. This process is no doubt parallel to the gradual extension and evolution of the ideas themselves that are denoted by the words. To show how extraordinarily the uses of a word can ramify from its original simple one, just as other mental processes (interests, ideas, etc.) ramify and extend from a primary one, the example may be taken of the current uses only of the word ' head.' The following are only a few of its numerous applications: the head of the army; the head of a class; the head of a pin; the head of a coin; the head of the table (*i.e.*, the person sitting at its chief end); the heads or headings of an article; the many idiomatic phrases such as ' to give a horse its head,' etc. It would take a volume to expound the ramifications of any of the primary roots of a language.

About the motives for metaphor-making more will be said presently, but a few remarks may be made at this point. A prominent motive seems to be to heighten appreciation on the hearer's part by calling to his mind another image more easily apprehended or comprehended, usually one more familiar in respect of the attribute implied (though by no means necessarily in other respects); or, to present the obverse of the same idea, a metaphor serves to eke out the relative paucity of attributive description. In this sentence the stress falls on the word ' easily '; a metaphor makes the idea, and especially the accompanying affect, more credible, plastic, and *easy*. It overcomes a (relative) difficulty in apprehension or, as the case may be, in presentation; this difficulty may be of either intellectual or affective origin.

II. TRUE SYMBOLISM

The subject of metaphors will be left for the moment in this stage, and that of true symbolism entered on. What I shall here propose to call true symbolism is one variety of the group of indirect representation to which six attributes were attached above. It therefore possesses these attributes together with a number of others that distinguish it from the rest of the group. Before defining these and discussing them in detail, I wish to prepare the reader's mind by remarking that an important characteristic of true symbolism is that the interpretation of the symbol usually evokes a reaction of surprise, incredulity, and repugnance on the part of those unfamiliar with it. An example that well illustrates these features is the interpretation of the familiar Punchinello of the marionette stage as a phallic symbol, on which something may be added by way of exposition.

The conception of the male organ as a ' little man ' is extremely widespread, and, by the process known to mythologists as ' decomposition,[1] it often becomes personified and incorporated in an independent figure. A large number of the dwarfs, gnomes, and goblins so common in folk-lore and legend are of this nature,[2] their characteristic attributes being that they are deformed, ugly caricatures of men, wicked and even malign—yet sometimes willing to be friendly and to yield services on certain conditions, able to perform wonderful and magical feats, and winning their own way in spite of their obvious disadvantages. Sand's description of Punchinello is in these respects typical:[3] ' Il a le cœur aussi sec que son bâton, c'est un égoiste dans toute l'acception du mot. Sous une apparente belle humeur, c'est un être féroce; il fait le mal pour le plaisir de le faire. Se souciant de la vie d'un homme comme de celle d'une puce, il aime et cherche des querelles. . . . Il ne craint ni Dieu ni diable, lui qui a vu passer, sous son nez crochu et verruqueux, tant de sociétés et de religions . . . (speaking of his passion for women) malgré ses bosses et sa figure peu faite

---

[1] See Ernest Jones, *American Journal of Psychology*, vol. xxi., pp. 105, 106.

[2] See, *e.g.*, Freud's analysis of Rumpelstilzchen, *Internat. Zeitschr. f. ärztl. Psychoanalyse*, Jahrg. i., S. 148.

[3] Maurice Sand, ' Masques et Bouffons,' 1860, vol. i., p. 124.

pour séduire, il est si caustique, si persuasif, si entreprenant et si insolent, qu'il a des succès.' Nodier[1] fittingly apostrophises him, ' O Polichinelle, simulacre animé de l'homme naturel abandonné à ses instincts.' His physical characteristics well accord with this interpretation: the long hooked nose, long chin, projecting hump on his back, prominent stomach, and pointed cap.

Punchinello seems first to have made his appearance in England with the Restoration,[2] but his history and that of similar figures is a world-wide one.[3] In England he quickly became assimilated with, and took some of his features from, the English clown and Jack Pudding, just as in Germany he fused with the Hanswurst. In Eastern countries he is met with as Karagheus. The prototype of all modern polichinellos is the Neapolitan *polecenella*, who cannot be traced farther back than the Renaissance. It is highly probable, however, that he is a lineal descendant of the Maccus of the Roman atellanes (introduced in the sixth century), for the statue of Maccus in the Capponi Museum at Rome (found in 1727, but dating from Roman times) shews the closest resemblance to the modern figure.

The attribute of comicality attaching to such figures is of considerable interest in more than one direction. The idea of the male organ as a comic mannikin, a ' funny little man,' is a very common one, and is much more natural to women than to men. The source and meaning of this alone constitutes a problem which cannot be dealt with here, since it would lead us too far away into the nature of the comic in general.[4] The idea itself is a subsection of phallic symbolism, concerning which the reader may be reminded of the following points: There are two broad classes of such symbols, the patriarchal symbols of the eagle, bull, etc., representing the father's power and rights, and the matriarchal symbols representing the revolutionary son. The latter are again divided into two sub-groups: those, such as the devil, the cock, the serpent, etc., which are tabooed and interdicted, and those, such as the goat,

---

[1] Nodier, quoted by Sand, *op. cit.*, p. 147.

[2] It is interesting that in the first recorded mention of him in England (Accounts of the Overseers of St. Martin's, 1666) the showman's name is given as Punchinello, an example of the identification of man with puppet.

[3] Many points have been elucidated since Payne Collier's (anonymous) ' History of Punch and Judy,' 1828, the fullest work on the subject.

[4] See Freud, ' Der Witz und seine Beziehung zum Unbewussten,' 1905, Kap. vii.

the ape, and the ass[1] (the animal sacred to the worship of Priapus, with which the figure of Punchinello is constantly brought into association), which are contemned as ridiculous and comic. I might add that there is a slight trace of the original revolutionary meaning of the matriarchal phallic symbol left in the pose of such comic figures—the most striking example of which was the mediæval court jester—as critics who lash the conventions of society. There is a hint of this point in one of Bernard Shaw's prefaces;[2] it runs: ' Every despot must have one disloyal subject to keep him sane. . . . Democracy has now handed the sceptre of the despot to the sovereign people; but they, too, must have their confessor, whom they call Critic. Criticism is not only medicinally salutary: it has positive popular attractions in its cruelty, its gladiatorship, and the gratification given to envy by its attacks on the great, and to enthusiasm by its praises. It may say things which many would like to say, but dare not. . . . Its iconoclasms, seditions, and blasphemies, if well turned, tickle those whom they shock; so that the Critic adds the privileges of the court jester to those of the confessor. Garrick, had he called Dr. Johnson Punch, would have spoken profoundly and wittily; whereas Dr. Johnson, in hurling that epithet at him, was but picking up the cheapest sneer an actor is subject to.'

We have next to consider the respects in which this example differs from those given earlier in the paper, and it will be well first to examine the definitions offered by other writers. The most exact of these is that given by Rank and Sachs,[3] which I will quote in full: ' Ein letztes, wegen seiner besonderen Eignung zur Verhüllung des Unbewussten und zu seiner Anpassung (Kompromissbildung) an neue Bewusstseinsinhalte überall mit Vorliebe verwendetes Ausdrucksmittel des Verdrängten ist das *Symbol*. Wir verstehen darunter eine besondere Art der indirekten Darstellung, die durch gewisse Eigentümlichkeiten von den ihm nahestehenden des Gleichnisses, der Metapher, der Allegorie, der Anspielung und anderen Formen der bildlichen Darstellung von Gedankenmaterial (nach Art des Rebus) ausgezeichnet ist. Das Symbol stellt gewissermassen eine ideale Vereinigung all dieser Ausdrucks-

---

[1] See Storfer, ' Marias Jungfräuliche Mutterschaft,' 1914.
[2] G. B. Shaw, ' Plays Unpleasant,' 1898, p. viii.
[3] Rank and Sachs, ' Die Bedeutung der Psychoanalyse für die Geisteswissenschaften, 1913, S. 11.

mittel dar: es ist ein stellvertretender anschaulicher Ersatzausdruck für etwas Verborgenes, mit dem es sinnfällige Merkmale gemeinsam hat oder durch innere Zusammenhänge assoziativ verbunden ist. Sein Wesen liegt in der Zwei- oder Mehrdeutigkeit, wie es ja selbst auch durch eine Art Verdichtung, ein Zusammenwerfen ($\sigma\upsilon\mu\beta\acute{\alpha}\lambda\lambda\epsilon\iota\nu$) einzelner charakteristischer Elemente entstanden ist. Seine Tendenz vom Begrifflichen nach dem Anschaulichen stellt es in die Nähe des primitiven Denkens, und als solches gehört die Symbolisierung wesentlich dem Unbewussten an, entbehrt aber als Kompromissleistung keineswegs der bewussten Determinanten, die in verschieden starkem Anteil die Symbolbildung und das Symbolverständnis bedingen.' [' A final means of expression of repressed material, one which lends itself to very general use on account of its especial suitability for disguising the unconscious and adapting it (by compromise formations) to new contents of consciousness, is the Symbol. By this term we understand a special kind of indirect representation which is distinguished by certain peculiarities from the simile, metaphor, allegory, allusion, and other forms of pictorial presentation of thought material (after the manner of a rebus), to all of which it is related. The symbol represents an almost ideal union of all these means of expression: it is a substitutive, perceptual replacement-expression for something hidden, with which it has evident characteristics in common or is coupled by internal associative connections. Its essence lies in its having two or more meanings, as, indeed, it itself originated in a kind of condensation, an amalgamation of individual characteristic elements. Its tendency from the conceptual to the perceptual indicates its nearness to primitive thought; by this relationship symbolisation essentially belongs to the unconscious, though, in its function as a compromise, it in no way lacks conscious determining factors, which in varying degrees condition both the formation of symbols and the understanding for them.']

They then specify the characteristics of true symbols as follows:[1] ' Die Stellvertretung für Unbewusstes, die konstante Bedeutung, die Unabhängigkeit von individuellen Bedingungen, die entwicklungsgeschichtliche Grundlage, die sprachlichen Beziehungen, die phylogenetischen Parallelen (in Mythus, Kult, Religion, etc).' ['Representation of unconscious material, constant meaning, independence of individual conditioning factors, evolutionary basis,

[1] *Op. cit.*, S. 18,

linguistic connections, phylogenetic parallels in myths, cults, religion, etc.'] These attributes will next be examined and commented on in order.

1. *Representation of Unconscious Material.*—This is perhaps the characteristic that most sharply distinguishes true symbolism from the other processes to which the name is often applied. By it is meant, not so much that the concepts symbolised are not known to the individual, for most often they are, as that the affect investing the concept is in a state of repression, and so is unconscious. Further, the process of symbolisation is carried out unconsciously, and the individual is quite unaware of the meaning of the symbol he has employed; indeed, is often unaware of the fact that he has employed one at all, since he takes the symbol for reality. The actual comparison between the idea symbolised and the symbol has never been present to consciousness at all, or else has only been present for a time and then forgotten. In many cases this point of comparison is evident as soon as one's attention is directed to the fact of comparison. In other cases considerable reflection is needed to discover it, and in some cases it is not yet patent—that is to say, any possible points of comparison between the two ideas seem too tenuous to justify the symbolism, even when the fact of the latter is undoubted.

2. *Constant Meaning.*—The statement here implied needs some modification. A given symbol may have two or occasionally even more meanings; for instance, in dreams a room may symbolise either a woman or a womb. In that case the interpretation will depend on the context, the associations, and other material available. A preference for one of these meanings can sometimes be correlated with the social class, the mental circle, or the race to which the individual using the symbol belongs, or it may depend on purely individual constellations. But the possible variation in meaning is exceedingly restricted, and the striking feature is its constancy in different fields of symbolism, dreams, myths, etc., and in different kinds of people. It has further to be remembered that in interpretation it is often a question, not of either this meaning or that, but of both. In unconscious condensation, as shown, for instance, in dreams, there are several layers, in each of which one of the meanings is the true one. When these points are appreciated it will be seen that there is little scope for arbitrariness in the interpretation of symbols.

3. *Independence of Individual Conditioning Factors.*—I find that this attribute is not unambiguously expressed in the words chosen, or else it is a question of the shades of meaning not being identical in the corresponding English and German words. 'Independence of' should be rather 'Non-dependence on,' the point being that the symbolism is not conditioned by individual factors only. The individual has not an unlimited range of choice in the creation of a given symbol, but on the contrary a very restricted one, more important determining factors being those that are common to large classes of men or, more often, to mankind as a whole. The part played by individual factors is a much more modest one. While the individual cannot choose what idea shall be represented by a given symbol (for the reason just mentioned), he can choose what symbol out of the many possible ones shall be used to represent a given idea ; more than this, he can sometimes, for individual reasons, represent a given idea by a symbol that no one else has used as a symbol.[1] What he cannot do is to give a regular symbol a different meaning from anyone else ; he can merely choose his symbols or make new ones, and even in the latter case they have the same meaning as they would with other people who might use them.

This curious independence of symbolic meanings raises in another form the old question of the inheritance of ideas. Some writers—*e.g.*, Jung—hold that anthropological symbolism is inherited as such, and explain in this way its stereotyped nature. For reasons I have developed elsewhere,[2] I adhere to the contrary view that symbolism has to be re-created afresh out of individual material, and that the stereotypy is due to the uniformity of the human mind in regard to the particular tendencies that furnish the source of symbolism—*i.e.*, to the uniformity of the fundamental and perennial interests of mankind. If this view is true, then further study of the subject must yield important conclusions as to the nature of the latter.

4. *Evolutionary Basis.*—This genetic aspect of symbolism will be dealt with at length later on in the paper.

5. *Linguistic Connections.*—We have seen that in symbolism the unconscious notices and makes use of comparisons between two ideas which it would not occur to our conscious mind to bring

---

[1] See Freud, 'Die Traumdeutung,' 5ᵉ Aufl., 1919, S. 240.
[2] *Imago*, Jahrg. i., 1912, S. 486, 487.

together. Now, the study of etymology, and especially of semantics, reveals the interesting fact that, although the word denoting the symbol may have no connotation of the idea symbolised, yet its history always shows some connection with the latter. This connection may be one of different kinds. Thus it may appear in one sphere of thought—*e.g.*, wit—when it is not present in the ordinary use of the word; for example, the well-known ' officers' remounts ' joke current during the South African War illustrates the unconscious association between the ideas of riding and of coitus, although this association is very far from being present in most spheres of thought. It may appear in an older and now obsolete use of the same word, in the root from which the word was derived, or from other words cognate with it.

This may be illustrated from the example of symbolism depicted above. The name Punchinello is an English contamination (see below) derived from the Neapolitan *pol(l)ecenella* (modern Italian *pulcinella*), which is the diminutive of *pollecena*, the young of the turkey-cock (the modern Italian *pulcino* means pullet, *pulcinello* being its diminutive); the turkey-cock itself is a recognised phallic symbol, as, indeed, is the domestic cock, both ideationally and linguistically. The Latin root is *pullus*, which means the young of any animal; the phallus is often, for obvious reasons, identified with the idea of a male child, a little boy or little man. The reason why the name came to be used in this connection is thought to be the resemblance between the nose of the actor and the hooked bill of the bird, and again it may be pointed out that both nose and beak are common phallic symbols.

The name *polecenella*, or its English variant ' polichinello ' (derived *via* the French *polichinelle*), was contaminated with the English word ' punch,' the main meaning of which is a tool for perforating material, with or without the impressing of a design —*e.g.*, to pierce metal or to stamp a die; it used to mean a dagger (another common symbol). The word is short for ' puncheon,' which used to mean a bodkin or dagger, and is now used in carpentry to denote ' a short upright piece of timber which serves to stiffen one or more long timbers or to support a load '; it comes from the late Latin *punctiare*, to prick or punch. Pepys, in his ' Diary,' April 30, 1669, calls punch ' a word of common use for all that is thick and short,' and refers to a gun (by the way, yet another phallic symbol), ' which, from its shortness and bigness, they do call Punchinello.' Suffolk punches are thick-set draught horses with short legs.

To sum up, the four ideas that keep recurring in connection with the name ' punchinello ' are (1) a caressing name for male offspring, equivalent to ' little man,' (2) a projecting part of the body, (3) the motion of piercing or penetrating, and (4) that of shortness and stoutness—four ideas that admirably serve to describe the male organ and nothing else ; indeed, there is no other object to which the curious combination applies of stoutness and pricking. Finally, I may add that two common expressions become more intelligible in the light of the interpretation just given. ' To be as proud (or pleased) as Punch ': overweening pride is intimately associated in the unconscious with exhibitionistic self-adoration. ' He has plenty of punch in him ': in this modern Americanism the word ' punch ' is used as a synonym for the colloquial ' backbone,' ' spunk,' ' sand,' etc.—*i.e.*, symbols of the male organ and its product.

In connection with the phallic signification of the staff wielded by Punchinello, one may remark that the word itself is cognate with the M.H.G. *staben*, to become stiff, both probably coming from a pre-Teutonic root *sta*, which means to stand up. A more familiar piece of knowledge is that the word ' yard,' used as a measure of length, had three centuries ago two other current meanings—(1) a staff, and (2) the phallus. It is still used in the latter sense by sailors ; the Persian word ' khutka ' also means both ' club ' and ' penis.' It is an equivalent of the jester's bauble. In addition to the long nose and staff already mentioned, Punchinello displays several other phallic attributes, the dog Toby being one of them. The fact that such a symbol can in its turn have similar symbols attached to it, a fact strikingly illustrated in the phallic ornaments worn as amulets by Roman ladies,[1] confirms the view taken above of the identification of man with phallus, of the whole with the part.

Even with symbol words where it is hard to trace any association between them and the words denoting the ideas symbolised, such an association is often apparent in the case of synonyms or foreign equivalents. A good example is our word ' room '—a room is a regular unconscious symbol for woman—where one has to go to very remote Aryan sources—*e.g.*, Old Irish—to find any trace of

[1] See Vorberg, ' Museum eroticum Neapolitanum,' Sect. ' Bronzen.'

a feminine connotation; one has only to turn, however, to the German equivalent, *Zimmer*, to find that the compound *Frauenzimmer* is a common colloquialism for woman.

6. *Phylogenetic Parallels.*—One of the most amazing features of true symbolism is the remarkable ubiquity of the same symbols, which are to be found, not only in different fields of thought, dreams, wit, insanity, poetry, etc., among a given class and at a given level of civilisation, but among different races and at different epochs of the world's history. A symbol which to-day we find, for instance, in an obscene joke is also to be found in a mythical cult of Ancient Greece, and another that we come across only in dream analysis was used thousands of years ago in the sacred books of the East. The following examples may be quoted in illustration of this correspondence. The idea of teeth, in dreams, is often symbolically related to that of child-birth, a connection that is hardly ever found in consciousness; in the Song of Songs we read: ' Thy teeth are as a flock of sheep, which go up from the washing, whereof everyone beareth twins, and there is not one barren among them.' The idea of a snake, which is never consciously associated with that of the phallus, is regularly so in dreams, being one of the most constant and invariable symbols: in primitive religions the two ideas are quite obviously interchangeable, so that it is often hard to distinguish phallic from ophitic worship; many traces of this are to be found even in the Old Testament. The idea of father or mother is constantly symbolised in dreams by that of king or queen respectively. The word ' king ' is ultimately derived from the Sanscrit root *gan*, meaning to beget; *ganaka* was the Sanscrit for father, and occurs also in the Vedas as the name of a well-known king. The word ' queen ' comes from the Sanscrit *gani*, which means simply mother. The Czar of Russia is, or rather was until recently, called the ' Little Father,' the same title as the Hunnish Attila (diminutive of Atta=father). The title ' Landesvater '' is commonly used in Germany, just as the Americans still call Washington the ' Father of his Country.' The ruler of the Catholic Church is called the ' Holy Father,' or by his Latin name of ' Papa.'

By adding the six attributes just discussed to the more general six mentioned earlier, we have formulated a conception of symbolism as distinct from the other kinds of indirect representation. The precise differences and relations between them will be discussed

more fully below, and we may conclude this section by a brief
consideration of the actual content of symbolism.

The number of symbols met with in practice is extraordinarily
high, and can certainly be counted by thousands.[1] In astonishing
contrast with this stands the curious fact that the number of ideas
thus symbolised is very limited indeed, so that in the interpretation
of them the complaint of monotony is naturally often heard. The
fact of this remarkable disproportion between the number of symbols and that of symbolised ideas in itself raises many interesting
problems, on which, perhaps, some light may be thrown by the
considerations that will be discussed below in connection with the
genesis of symbolism.

*All symbols represent ideas of the self and the immediate blood relatives,
or of the phenomena of birth, love, and death.* In other words, they
represent the most primitive ideas and interests imaginable. The

[1] There is no satisfactory comprehensive work on the content of symbolism. The
most reliable collection, unfortunately much too unfinished for what is needed, is that
given in Freud's ' Traumdeutung ' (4ᵉ Aufl., S. 262-274), amplified in his ' Vorlesungen
zur Einführung in die Psychoanalyse ' (Zweiter Teil, 1916, S. 164-180). The numerous
examples scattered through Otto Rank's works can also be depended on. In Stekel's
' Sprache des Traumes ' and his 'Angstzustände ' there is an extensive material, useful
to those capable of criticising it. On the anthropological side one may mention the
well-known works by Bachofen, ' Versuch über die Gräbersymbolik der Alten,' 1859;
Burton, ' Terminal Essay of the Arabian Nights,' 1890; Cox, ' Mythology of the
Aryan Nations,' 1870; Dieterich, ' Mutter Erde,' 2ᵉ Aufl., 1913; Dulaure, ' Des
divinités génératrices,' 1805 (much enlarged in a German edition by Krauss and
Reiskel, ' Die Zeugung in Glauben, Sitten und Bräuchen der Völker,' 1909); Faber,
'Origin of Pagan Idolatry,' 1816; Fanin, ' Secret Museum of Naples,' English Trans-
lation, 1872; Fergusson, ' Tree and Serpent Worship,' 1873; Forlong, ' The Rivers
of Life,' 1883; Higgins, 'Anacalypsis,' 1833-1836; Inman, 'Ancient Faiths embodied
in Ancient Names,' 1868, and 'Ancient Pagan and Modern Christian Symbolism'
(the most useful book on the subject), 1869, Second Edition 1874; Hargrave Jennings,
' The Rosicrucians,' 1887; King, ' The Gnostics and their Remains,' 1864; Payne
Knight, 'A Discourse on the Worship of Priapus,' 1786, New Edition 1871, and
' The Symbolical Language of Ancient Art and Mythology,' 1818, New Edition 1876;
Moor, ' Hindu Pantheon,' 1810; Staniland Wake, ' The Influence of the Phallic
Idea in the Religions of Antiquity,' *Journ. of Anthropology,* 1870, Nos. 1 and 2, and
' Serpent Worship,' 1888; Wake and Westropp, 'Ancient Symbol Worship,' Second
Edition 1875; Westropp, ' Primitive Symbolism,' 1885; together with the less
known works by Campbell, ' Phallic Worship,' 1887; Freimark, 'Okkultismus und
Sexualität '; Hermann, ' Xenologie des Saeming,' 1905; Kittel, ' Uber den Ursprung
des Lingakultus in Indien,' 1876; Laurent and Nagour, ' L'occultisme et l'amour ';
Maehly, ' Die Schlange im Mythus und Cultus der classischen Völker,' 1867; de
Mortillet, ' Le Signe de la Croix avant le Christianisme,' 1866; Sellon, ' Phallic
Worship in India,' Memoirs of the Anthropological Society, vol. i., and 'Annotations
on the Sacred Writings of the Hindus,' New Edition 1902; Storfer, *op. cit.*   A number
of recent books—*e.g.*, those by Bayley, Blount, Churchward, Hannay—are of much
less value than their pretensions would suggest.

actual number of ideas is rather greater, however, than might be supposed from the briefness of this summary—they amount, perhaps, to about a hundred—and a few supplementary remarks are necessary. The self comprises the whole body or any separate part of it, not the mind; perhaps twenty different ideas can here be symbolised. The relatives include only father, mother, brothers and sisters, and children; various parts of their bodies also can be symbolised. Birth can refer to the ideas of giving birth, of begetting, or of being born oneself. The idea of death is in the unconscious a relatively simple one, that of lasting absence; it always refers to the death of others, for the idea of one's own death is probably inconceivable as such in the unconscious, being always converted into some other one.[1] Love, or more strictly sexuality, comprises a very considerable number of distinct processes, including some, such as excretory acts, that are not commonly recognised to have a sexual bearing ; it would lead us too far to enumerate and describe them all here, but it may be said that the total conception thus reached closely corresponds with Freud's theory of sex.[2] The field of sexual symbolism is an astoundingly rich and varied one, and the vast majority of all symbols belong to this category.[3] There are probably more symbols of the male organ itself than all other symbols put together. This is a totally unexpected finding, even more so than the paucity of symbolised ideas in general, and is so difficult to reconcile with our sense of proportion that it needs an effort to refuse the easy escape of simply denying the facts, a feat which is greatly facilitated by the circumstance that, thanks to our education, the facts are not very accessible. Rank and Sachs' comments in this connection are of interest:[4] ' Das Prävalieren der sexuellen Symbolbedeutungen erklärt sich nicht nur aus der individuellen Tatsache, dass kein Trieb in dem Masse der kulturellen Unterdrückung unterworfen und der direkten Befriedigung entzogen ist, wie der aus den verschiedensten " perversen " Komponenten zusammengesetzte Sexualtrieb, dessen psychischer Vorstellungskreis, das Erotische, daher in weitem Umfang der indirekten Darstellung fähig und bedürftig ist. Eine weit grössere Bedeutung für die Genese der Symbolik hat die

---

[1] See Chapter XXXII. of the Third Edition, p. 593.

[2] See Freud, ' Drei Abhandlungen zur Sexualtheorie,' 1905, or Chapter III. of the present volume.

[3] See Schlesinger, *op. cit.*, S. 437 *et seq.*

[4] Rank and Sachs, *op. cit.*, S. 12.

phylogenetische Tatsache, dass den Geschlechtsorganen und -Funktionen in primitiven Kulturen eine für unsere Begriffe ganz ungeheure Wichtigkeit beigelegt war, von der wir uns durch die Tatsachen der ethnographischen Forschung und die in Kult und Mythus erhaltenen Reste eine annähernde Vorstellung machen können.' ['The prevalence of sexual meanings in symbolism is not to be explained merely by the individual experience that no other instinct is to the same extent subjected to social suppression and withdrawn from direct gratification as the sexual one, that instinct built up from multiform "perverse" components, and the mental domain of which, the erotic, is therefore extensively susceptible of, and in need of, indirect representation. Much more significant for the genesis of symbolism is the phylogenetic fact that in primitive civilisations an importance was attached to sexual organs and functions that to us appears absolutely monstrous, and of which we can form some approximate idea from the results of anthropological investigations and the traces remaining in cults and myths.']

III. GENESIS OF SYMBOLISM

Having formulated a conception of the nature, characteristics, and content of symbolism, we may proceed to the more difficult questions of its genesis. Our point of departure is that in symbolism a comparison between two ideas, of a kind that is alien to the conscious mind, is established unconsciously, and that then one of these—which for the sake of convenience may be called the secondary idea—may unknowingly be substituted for, and so represent, the first or primary idea. Two questions immediately arise from this statement : Why are two ideas identified which the conscious mind does not find to be similar ? And why does the one idea symbolise the other and never the reverse ?

Taking the former question first, we begin by noting that it is the primitive mind which institutes the comparison between the two ideas, not the adult, conscious mind. This conclusion is confirmed by everything we know about symbolism, the type of mental process, the high antiquity—in both the individual and the race—of the actual symbols themselves, and so forth; even the few new symbols that are made by the adult—e.g., the Zeppelin one—are created by the primitive, infantile mind that persists throughout life in the unconscious.

Just as the simile is the base of every metaphor, so is an original identification the base of every symbolism, though it is important not to confound these two processes. As Freud puts it:[1] ' Was heute symbolisch verbunden ist, war wahrscheinlich in Urzeiten durch begriffliche und sprachliche Identität vereint. Die Symbolbeziehung scheint ein Rest und Merkzeichen einstiger Identität.' [' What to-day is symbolically connected was probably in primæval times united in conceptual and linguistic identity. The symbolic relationship seems to be the remains and sign of an identity that once existed.']

The tendency of the primitive mind—as observed in children, in savages, in wit, dreams, insanity, and other products of unconscious functioning—to identify different objects and to fuse together different ideas, to note the resemblances and not the differences, is a universal and most characteristic feature, though only those familiar with the material in question will appreciate the colossal scale on which it is manifested. It impresses one as being one of the most fundamental and primordial attributes of the mind. In explanation of it there are two hypotheses, which, as they are implicit throughout this section, and, indeed, in the whole essay, may be briefly indicated at this point. The one most usually accepted would refer the phenomenon under discussion, as well as most others of symbolism, to the structure of the undeveloped mind, for which reason it might be termed the static hypothesis; the main feature to which they call attention is the intellectual incapacity for discrimination. The second, psycho-analytical hypothesis, while admitting the importance of this factor, holds that it is in itself insufficient to explain all the phenomena, and postulates other, dynamic factors as well.

In my opinion, not one, but three factors, are operative in this general primitive tendency to identification. The first, which is the only one usually recognised, but which I think is much the least important, is that of mental incapacity. The second, which I shall point out presently, has to do with the ' pleasure-pain principle,' and the third, to which Rank and Sachs call attention, with the ' reality principle.'

The first factor, which I think I shall be able to prove cannot be exclusive, is well indicated in the following passages. Pelletier says:[2]

[1] Freud, ' Die Traumdeutung,' *loc. cit.*
[2] Pelletier, ' L'association des idées dans la manie aiguë,' 1903, p. 129.

'Il est à remarquer que le symbole joue un très grand rôle dans les divagations des aliénés; cela est dû à ce que le symbole est une forme très inférieure de la pensée. On pourrait définir le symbole comme la perception fausse d'un rapport d'identité ou d'analogie très grande entre deux objets qui ne presentent en realité qu'une analogie vague.' We shall see that the disproportion in the importance of the analogy depends on the different points of view of the patient and the doctor rather than on any intellectual inferiority of the former. Jung, from a similar standpoint, writes:[1] 'Die apperzeptive Schwäche drückt sich in einer verminderten Deutlichkeit der Vorstellungen aus. Sind die Vorstellungen undeutlich, so sind auch ihre Unterschiede undeutlich.' ['The apperceptive defect is manifested in a lessened clearness of ideas. If the ideas are not clear, neither are the differences between them.'] He says further: 'Ich will nur hervorheben, dass die *Vieldeutigkeit der einzelnen Traumbilder* ("Überdeterminierung" Freuds)[2] mit ein Zeichen ist für die Undeutlichkeit und Unbestimmheit des Traumdenkens. . . . Wegen der im Traum herrschenden *mangelhaften Unterschiedsempfindlichkeit* können die beiden Komplexinhalte wenigsten in symbolischer Form ineinanderfliessen.' ['I will only point out that the many significations of the individual dream images (Freud's "over-determination")[3] is a sign of the lack of clarity and definition in dream thought. Because of the defective sensibility for differences that prevails in dreams, the contents of both complexes can become confounded at least in symbolic form.'] Both these authors were probably influenced by the common, but fallacious, view of dreams and insanity as *defective* mental products. Silberer, however, approaching the matter from quite another point of view, also writes:[4] 'Ich entferne mich durchaus nicht von der Mehrzahl der Autoren, wenn ich die hauptsächlichste und allgemeinste Bedingung der Symbolbildung, die sowohl den normalen als den krankhaften Phänomenen in der Individual— wie in der Völkerpsychologie gerecht wird, in einer *Unzulänglichkeit* des Auffassungsvermögens seinem Gegenstande gegenüber oder, wie man auch sagen könnte, in einer *apperzeptiven Insuffizienz* erblicke.' ['In agreement with the majority of writers, I see the chief and most general condition of symbol-formation—valid with

---

[1] Jung, 'Über die Psychologie der Dementia præcox,' 1907, S. 72.
[2] This is the same as the condensation, or over-identification, under discussion.
[3] *Ibid.*   [4] Silberer, *Jahrbuch der Psychoanalyse*, Bd. iii., S. 680.

the phenomena of health and disease, in the individual and in the race—in an *inadequacy* of the apprehensive faculty in regard to its object, or, as one might also say, in an *apperceptive insufficiency.*'] We may admit the presence of this factor so far as it goes, but I think it can be shown that what passes for an apperceptive incapacity is very often a non-functioning that is due to other causes than incapacity. It is true that the primitive mind very often does not discriminate, but that is not because it cannot, for when it is necessary it does so to a remarkable extent.

The second factor leading to lack of discrimination is that when the primitive mind is presented with a new experience it seizes on the resemblances, however slight, between it and previous experiences; and this for two reasons, both of which have to do with the pleasure-pain principle. The first of these is that the mind—above all the primitive mind, which is ruled by this principle—notices most what most *interests* it personally, what, therefore, is most pleasurable or most painful. It ignores distinctions between two ideas when they are indifferent to it, and notices only those that are interesting. Where one is so apt to go wrong in this matter is in the assumption, difficult to avoid in practice, that the interests of the primitive mind are necessarily the same as our own conscious ones, the truth being that the relative proportion of interest is often astoundingly different in the two cases. The unexpected associations made by a child when confronted by a novelty are often very amusing to us—for example, the remark that soda-water tastes like a foot that has gone to sleep. Darwin's oft-quoted example of the child who, on first seeing a duck, onomatopoetically named it ' quack,' and then later applied this word also to flies, wine, and even a sou (which had eagle's wings), is rightly explained by Meumann,[1] who points out that the child noticed only what interested him—namely, the flying and the relation to fluid, and so used this word to denote these two phenomena in whatever form they occurred; it was not the duck as a whole that was named ' quack,' but only certain abstracted attributes, which then continued to be called by the same word. The second of the two reasons referred to above is of a more general and far-reaching order. When a new experience is presented to the mind it is certainly *easier* to perceive the points of resemblance between it and previous familiar experiences. One often hears, for instance, such a remark as ' The ideas

---

[1] Meumann, ' Die Sprache des Kindes,' 1903.

in that book were too strange for me to take in on first reading it; I must go through it again before passing an opinion on it.' In such a case if one notices only the points of resemblance there is effected an obvious economy of effort, which is a fundamental human trait: Ferrero[1] aptly refers to it under the terms ' la loi de l'inertie mental ' and ' la loi du moindre effort.' This is, of course, governed by the hedonic pleasure-pain principle, though the fact is often obscured by writers on ethics. The association between ease and pleasure, and between difficulty or labour and pain, is a primordial one, and is well illustrated by the words used to denote them. The word ' painful ' was used in Middle English in the sense of industrious; hence the expressions ' painstaking,' ' painfully correct,' etc. The French *travail*, work, is cognate with the Italian *travaglio*, which means suffering; the Italian word for work, *lavoro*, comes from the Latin *labor*, pain. The Greek πένομαι means both to work and to suffer, as does the Hebrew *assab*. We appropriately refer to child-birth as labour or travail.

The third factor in preventing discrimination is not sharply to be distinguished from the last one, though it refers rather to the ' reality principle.' It is clear that the appreciation of resemblances facilitates the assimilation of new experiences. Our instinctive tendency in such a situation is to link on the new to the old, to search for common ground. If we can relate the new experience in some way to what is already familiar, then we can ' place ' it and understand it; it becomes intelligible. The whole meaning of comprehension and explanation is the referring of the unknown to the known. In this way the process of fusion or identification aids our grasp of reality and makes it possible for us to deal with it more adequately. It is true that it is a process with grave possibilities of defects, it being an everyday occurrence that we assimilate the new too closely in terms of the old, but to assimilate it at least in some degree is the only way in which we can deal with it at all. Rank and Sachs[2] have an illuminating passage on the relation of symbolism to this primary identification in the service of adaptation: ' Psychologisch betrachtet bleibt die Symbolbildung ein Regressivphänomen, ein Herabsinken auf eine bestimmte Stufe bildlichen Denkens, die sich beim vollwertigen Kulturmenschen in deutlichster Ausprägung in jenen Ausnahmszuständen findet, in denen die bewusste Realanpassung entweder teilweise einge-

---

[1] Ferrero, *op. cit.*, pp. 6, 18, 23. [2] Rank and Sachs, *op. cit.*, S. 17.

schränkt ist, wie in der religiösen und künstlerischen Exstase, oder gänzlich aufgehoben erscheint, wie im Traum und den Geistesstörungen. Dieser psychologischen Auffassung entspricht die kulturhistorisch nachweisbare ursprüngliche Funktion der *der Symbolisierung zugrunde liegenden Identifizierung*[1] als eines Mittels zur Realanpassung, das überflüssig wird und zur blossen Bedeutung eines Symbols herabsinkt, sobald diese Anpassungsleistung geglückt ist. So erscheint die Symbolik als der unbewusste Niederschlag überflüssig und unbrauchbar gewordener primitiver Anpassungsmittel an die Realität, gleichsam als eine Rumpelkammer der Kultur, in die der erwachsene Mensch in Zuständen herabgesetzer oder mangelnder Anpassungsfähigkeit gerne flüchtet, um seine alten, längst vergessenen Kinderspielzeuge wieder hervorzuholen. Was spätere Generationen nur noch als Symbol kennen und auffassen, das hatte auf früheren Stufen geistigen Lebens vollen realen Sinn und Wert. Im Laufe der Entwicklung verblasst die ursprüngliche Bedeutung immer mehr oder wandelt sich sogar, wobei allerdings Sprache, Folklore, Witz, u.a., oft Reste des ursprünglischen Zusammenhangs in mehr oder weniger deutlicher Bewusstheit bewahrt haben.' [' Psychologically considered, symbol-formation remains a regressive phenomenon, a reversion to a certain stage of pictorial thinking, which in fully civilised man is most plainly seen in those exceptional conditions in which conscious adaptation to reality is either restricted, as in religious and artistic ecstasy, or seems to be completely abrogated, as in dreams and mental disorders. In correspondence with this psychological conception is the original function, demonstrable in the history of civilisation, of the identification underlying symbolism[2] as a means to adaptation to reality, which becomes superfluous and sinks to the mere significance of a symbol as soon as this task of adaptation has been accomplished. Symbolism thus appears as the unconscious precipitate of primitive means of adaptation to reality that have become superfluous and useless, a sort of lumber-room of civilisation to which the adult readily flees in states of reduced or deficient capacity for adaptation to reality, in order to regain his old, long-forgotten playthings of childhood. What later generations know and regard only as a symbol had in earlier stages of mental life full and real meaning and

---

[1] Note how carefully the authors distinguish in this connection between identification and symbolism.
[2] *Ibid.*

value. In the course of development the original significance fades more and more or even changes, though speech, folk-lore, wit, etc., have often preserved more or less plain traces of the original association.']

The two last factors mentioned, the importance of the pleasure-pain principle and of adaptation to reality in respect to primitive lack of discrimination, throw some light on one of the most puzzling phenomena of symbolism—namely, the extraordinary predominance of sexual symbols. A Swedish philologist, Sperber,[1] has in a remarkable essay elaborated the theory, which has been several times suggested on other grounds by biologists, that sexual impulses have played the most important part in both the origin and later development of speech. According to this theory, which is supported by very weighty considerations, the earliest speech sounds were those that served the purpose of calling the mate (hence the sexual importance of the voice to this day), while the further development of speech roots accompanied the performance of work. Such work was done in common, and, as is still customary enough, to the accompaniment of rhythmically repeated speech utterances. During this, sexual interest was attached to the work, as though, so to speak, primitive man reconciled himself to the disagreeable but necessary task by treating it as an equivalent of, and substitute for, sexual functioning. Words used during these common tasks thus had two meanings, denoting the sexual act and the equivalent work done respectively. In time the former meaning became detached and the word, now applying only to the work, thus ' desexualised.' The same would happen with other tasks, and so a store of speech roots gradually accumulated, the original sexual significance of which had been lost. Sperber then illustrates, with an extensive material, the fact that words having a sexual connotation possess a perfectly astounding capacity for development and extension into non-sexual fields. Partly owing to the careful expurgation of our etymological dictionaries, it is not generally known that an enormous number of common words in present-day use have been derived in historical times from this source, attaining their present meaning through a primary sexual association that has now been forgotten. In the light of work like Sperber's we begin to understand why there is such an amazing number of symbols

---

[1] Sperber, ' Über den Einfluss sexueller Momente auf Entstehung und Entwicklung der Sprache,' *Imago*, 1912, Jahrg. i., S. 405.

for sexual objects and functions, and, for instance, why weapons and tools are always male symbols, while the material that is worked on is always female. The symbolic association is the relic of the old verbal identity; things that once had the same name as a genital organ can now appear in dreams, etc., as a symbol for it. Freud[1] aptly likens symbolism to an ancient speech that has almost vanished, but of which relics still remain here and there.

According, then, to the view here developed, the identification that underlies symbolism is mainly determined by the two factors discussed above, which may be summarised as the tendencies to seek pleasure and avoid pain, and to learn to deal with reality in the easiest and most sparing way. It was just the way in which primitive man must have met the world, the desire for ease and pleasure struggling with the demands of necessity. He succeeded by making a compromise in which he sexualised his tasks. A few examples may be given from the vast subject of the associations between ploughing in particular, or agriculture in general, and sexual activities. Most of the tools used are phallic symbols (the word itself is the commonest vulgar designation), a statement that can easily be proved from folk-lore and mythology, while the conception of the earth as woman, and especially as mother, is universal and fundamental.[2] Sophocles' Œdipus repeatedly speaks of 'the mother-field from which I sprouted.' Shakespeare makes Boult, on the point of deflorating the recalcitrant Marina, say: 'An if she were a thornier piece of ground than she is, she shall be ploughed.'[3] The words for 'plough' in Latin, Greek, and Oriental languages were customarily used also to denote the sexual act,[4] and we still use such words as 'seed,' 'fertility,' 'barrenness' for vegetation as well as for human beings. The association becomes quite manifest in the well-known fertilising magic, a custom that lasted late into civilised times; it consisted in a naked pair performing the sexual act in the field so as to encourage the latter to imitate their example. The Greek words for garden, meadow, field, common female symbols in dreams, were used also to denote the female genital organ.

If, as is here maintained, the individual child re-creates such symbolism anew—*i.e.*, if he (largely unconsciously) perceives

[1] Freud, 'Introductory Lectures on Psycho-Analysis,' English translation, 1922, p. 140.
[2] See Dieterich, 'Mutter Erde,' 2e Aufl., 1913.
[3] 'Pericles,' Act IV., Sc. vi.
[4] Kleinpaul, 'Das Leben der Sprache,' Bd. iii., 1893, S. 136.

these comparisons which are alien to the adult conscious mind—
then it is plain that we shall have radically to revise our conception
of the infantile mind, and especially in regard to sexuality. This
has already been done by Freud on other grounds, after he had
empirically discovered from psycho-analyses that the unconscious
mind of the child, and even the conscious one, is much more sexual
in character than had ever been supposed.[1] In fact, the whole
process to which he has given the name ' sublimation '[2] is probably
an ontogenetic repetition of the one just described, whereby sexual
energy is gradually drained into non-sexual channels. The activity—
tasks in the life of primitive man, games in that of the child—
becomes by degrees independent of this source of interest that is
not inherent in itself, but the ancient association remains in the
unconscious, where in suitable circumstances it may again manifest
itself in the form of symbolism.

It will not have escaped the attentive reader that in this discussion
all the stress has been laid on the defective discrimination shown
by the primitive mind, while nothing has been said about the respects
in which it shows an unwonted power of discrimination.[3] Yet
this also is a striking characteristic of both children and savages,
though not of the unconscious mind. In the latter case, that of
savages, it has curiously been used as an argument in support of
the current theory of the defective intellectual powers on the part
of the primitive, but, in my judgement, closer consideration proves
just the contrary. Herbert Spencer, in his ' Principles of Sociology,'
has collected a series of examples where there are many separate
words for individual acts, but no generic one for the act itself—
thus, thirty words for washing different parts of the body and none
for the act of washing. The Arabians are said to have over 500
words to designate lions in various aspects, but no word for lion;
5,744 for camels, but none for a camel. This is certainly a powerful
argument against any inherent incapacity for discrimination, as the
holders of that hypothesis maintain exists. Whereupon they simply
change their ground, and, being bent on convicting the primitive
of intellectual inferiority, they now quote such facts to show that
he is incapable of abstracting; this is, at all events, a different

---

[1] Freud, ' Drei Abhandlungen,' op. cit.
[2] See Chapter XXXIV. of the Third Edition.
[3] A consideration which in itself finally proves that the prevalent hypothesis of the
primitive lack of discrimination—that this is due to intellectual incapacity—is inadequate to cover the whole ground.

thing from being incapable of discriminating. Thus, Stout[1] writes: 'It certainly appears odd that a lower grade of intellectual development should be marked by superior nicety and precision of discriminative thought. The truth is that these distinctions, so plentiful in savage languages, are due rather to an incapacity for clearly apprehending identity in difference than to a superior power of apprehending difference in identity.' This argument, however, has been very neatly disposed of by Hocart,[2] who has pointed out that the key to the whole question is the matter of interest. Comparing the Fijian language with English, as an example, he shows that the Fijian handles in gross where we do in retail, but that the converse is equally true. Where our interest is very great we have no generic terms, because the differences are so important as to overshadow the resemblances; in such cases the Fijian, with less interest, will use a general and often vague term to cover the whole. The distinction, for instance, is so important among a bull, a cow, an ox, a steer, a calf, a bullock, a heifer, and so on, that we have no single word to denote the species as a whole except cattle, which is collective. Indeed, the same law may be observed to hold good even between different classes in the same country. The laity uses the generic term 'horse,' but a horse-dealer—i.e., someone with a great interest in the matter—has no such generic term; to him a horse is a certain variety of the animal and is different from a stallion or a mare. Similarly, we speak of ships as a class of objects of which there are many varieties, but to a sailor a ship is definitely a vessel with a bowsprit and at least two square-rigged masts; the distinctions between different vessels are to him more important than the resemblances.

It is well known that abstract terms arise originally from concrete ones; we see here that they characteristically arise as a generalisation from a single example: thus, the order of development seems to be concrete, general, abstract. This conclusion can also be supported from consideration of the order of development of the parts of speech. Thus, as Wundt shows,[3] adjectives, which are of relatively late development, had originally the same form as substantives, and were, to begin with, merely special nouns. For example, a brown leaf and a green leaf were two distinct words,

---

[1] Stout, 'Analytic Psychology,' 1902, vol. ii., p. 231.
[2] Hocart, *British Journal of Psychology*, vol. v., p. 267.
[3] Wundt, 'Völkerpsychologie,' Bd. i., Teil ii., 1904, S. 289.

having nothing in common with words for other objects that are red or green. Then one of these 'green' words, one where the element of greenness was very prominent (perhaps with leaves), was extended to other objects when it was wished to call special attention to the green aspect of this object—*e.g.*, a green-leaf cloth—losing in time its substantival connotation of leaf. It is known, for instance, that the Greenlanders have separate names for each finger and that when they want to use a name for fingers in general they employ the name of the principal one (the thumb) for this purpose. They are here reaching from the particular to the general, the first stage of conceiving the abstract.

It will be seen that our custom of using the word 'ship' to denote all sea-going vessels constitutes in type a reversion to the primitive, infantile custom of not discriminating from relative lack of interest, and so, in a sense, is all generalisation. The essential difference between what is called a valuable generalisation—*e.g.*, a scientific one—and the simple grouping together characteristic of the primitive mind resides in the practical worth of the generalisation. To the child, no doubt, its identifications are as useful personally as a great generalisation is to a man of science, but, while they may be equal subjectively, they are not objectively. The second kind takes into better account the facts of external reality, is altogether on a more real and less subjective plane; in short, there is all the difference that exists between the simple pleasure-pain principle and the reality principle. From this point of view there opens the possibility, which cannot be followed up here, of a theory of scientific discovery, invention, etc., for psychologically this consists in an overcoming of the resistances that normally prevent regression towards the infantile, unconscious tendency to note 'identity in differences,' the whole being, of course, worked out on the plane of reality, though the impetus comes from the association between the unconscious ideas that the 'real' external ones can symbolise.

We have next to turn to the second of the two questions raised at the beginning of this section—namely, why it is that of two ideas unconsciously associated one always symbolises the other and never the reverse. To illustrate by an example what is meant: a church tower in a dream, as in anthropology, often—though, of course, by no means always—symbolises the phallus, but a phallus in a dream is never a symbol of a church tower. This fact alone demolishes the hypothesis that symbolism is due solely to any apperceptive insufficiency, from an inability to perceive differences, because in that case there would be no reason why the symbolism should not be reciprocal. The point is clearly put by Ferenczi, who writes:[1] 'One was formerly inclined to believe that things are confounded because they are similar; nowadays we know that a thing is confounded with another only because certain motives for this are present; similarity merely provides the opportunity for these motives to function.' Assuming, then, that two ideas have become closely associated, in the way described above, what are the motives that lead to one of the ideas replacing the other, whereas the reverse never occurs? The answer will, of course, be found only by consideration of the material content of the ideas themselves. The two most prominent features that strike one in regard to these are: First, that the ideas symbolised are the most primordial that it is possible to conceive, and that they are the ideas invested with the strongest primary interest. Secondly, that attaching to them all are powerful affective and conative processes which are in a state of psychical repression, being thus inhibited from entry into the conscious and from free external expression. They are, in fact, the most completely repressed mental processes known.

It is impossible not to connect these two considerations. It is a well-established observation of clinical psychology that when a strong affective tendency is repressed it often leads to a compromise-formation—neurotic symptoms being perhaps the best-known example—in which both the repressed and the repressing tendencies are fused, the result being a substitution-product. From this it is a very slight step to infer that symbols are also of this nature, for it is known that they, like other compromise-formations, are composed of both conscious and unconscious elements. Symbolism certainly plays an important part in many neurotic symptoms; a castration complex, for instance, often results in a phobia of blindness, the eye being one of the commonest somatic phallic symbols.[2] That symbolism arises as the result of intrapsychical conflict between the repressing tendencies and the repressed is the view accepted by all psycho-analysts. It is implicit,

---

[1] Ferenczi, 'Contributions to Psycho-Analysis,' English Translation by Ernest Jones, 1916, p. 237.
[2] See Ferenczi, 'On Eye Symbolism,' op. cit., pp. 228-232.

for instance, in Ferenczi's[1] actual definition of symbols as 'such ideas as are invested in consciousness with a logically inexplicable and unfounded affect, and of which it may be analytically established that they owe this affective over-emphasis to *unconscious* identification with another idea, to which the surplus of affect really belongs. Not all similes, therefore, are symbols, but only those in which the one member of the equation is repressed into the unconscious.' According to him, the most primary kind of symbolism is probably the equating of one part of the body with another, one subsequently replacing the other;[2] there thus comes about an over-emphasis of the upper part of the body in general, interest in the lower half being repressed (Freud's 'displacement from below upwards').

All psycho-analytical experience goes to shew that the primary ideas of life, the only ones that can be symbolised—those, namely, concerning the bodily self, the relation to the family, birth, love, and death—retain in the unconscious throughout life their original importance, and that from them is derived a very large part of the more secondary interests of the conscious mind. As energy flows from them, and never to them, and as they constitute the most repressed part of the mind, it is comprehensible that symbolism should take place in one direction only. Only what is repressed is symbolised; only what is repressed needs to be symbolised. This conclusion is the touchstone of the psycho-analytical theory of symbolism.

IV. FUNCTIONAL SYMBOLISM

The theory of symbolism presented above is manifestly not complete; it does not, for instance, explain why only certain possible comparisons are used as symbols, nor why some symbols are found predominantly in certain fields—*e.g.*, dreams—and others mainly in different fields—*e.g.*, wit. While, however, the theory needs amplifying and supplementing, I would maintain that it does at least begin to introduce order into a confused subject, notably in the distinction it establishes between symbolism and other forms of figurative representation.

Further progress in clarification may be gained by examining the work of what may be called the post-psycho-analytical school of writers, Adler, Jung, Maeder, Silberer, Stekel, with their English followers, Eder, Long, and Nicoll. The feature common to the

---

[1] See Ferenczi, 'On Eye Symbolism,' *op. cit.*, p. 234.   [2] *Idem., op. cit.*, p. 232.

members of this school is that, after gaining some knowledge of psycho-analysis, they have proceeded, by rejecting the hardly-won knowledge of the unconscious, to re-interpret the psycho-analytical findings back again into the surface meanings characteristic of pre-Freudian experience, retaining, however, the psycho-analytical technical terms, though using them with quite different implications. The conception of symbolism has especially suffered from the confusion thus reintroduced, for it has been diluted to such an extent as to lose all exact descriptive value. Thus, Jung makes constant use of the term ' Libido-symbol,' but, as *Libido* means to him psychical energy in whatever form and symbol means simply any form of indirect representation, the term comes to mean merely ' any mental process that is substituted for any other.' He does not hesitate to use the term ' symbol ' in precisely the reverse sense from that in which it is used in psycho-analysis. Take the case of a patient where an associative connection has been established between a given symptom (*e.g.*, inhibition in performing a particular act) and an unconscious incest complex.[1] By the .psycho-analyst the symptom would be regarded as the result of the complex and, in certain circumstances, as a symbol for it; Jung, on the other hand, calls the complex the symbol of the symptom— *i.e.*, according to him, an unconscious idea may be a symbol of a conscious one.

Silberer's work is in some respects in a different category from that of the other writers mentioned, for he is the only member of this school who has made a positive contribution to the theory of symbolism ; unfortunately, incautious presentation of even this has made it possible for other writers, particularly Stekel, to exploit it in a reactionary sense. His work, which is incorporated in half a dozen essays,[2] deserves, however, to be carefully read by anyone seriously interested in the problems of symbolism, and a short abstract of it will be attempted here.

In his first contribution already Silberer set forth the two most original points in his work, both of which he later expanded in

[1] The example is taken from Jung's ' Collected Papers on Analytical Psychology,' Second Edition, 1917, pp. 219, 220.

[2] Silberer, ' Bericht über eine Methode, gewisse symbolische Halluzinations Erscheinungen hervorzurufen und zu beobachten,' *Jahrbuch der Psychoanalyse*, 1909, Bd. i., S. 513; ' Von den Kategorien der Symbolik,' *Zentralblatt für Psychoanalyse*, Jahrg. ii., S. 177; ' Phantasie und Mythos,' *Jahrbuch*, Bd. ii., S. 541; ' Symbolik des Erwachens und Schwellensymbolik überhaupt,' *Jahrbuch*, Bd. iii., S. 621; ' Über die Symbolbildung,' *loc. cit.*, S. 661; ' Zur Symbolbildung,' *Jahrbuch*, Bd. iv., S. 607.

great detail; one relates to the conditions favourable to the production of symbolism, the other to the distinction between different
types of symbolism. As will be seen, he uses the term in a much
wider sense than that given it in the two preceding sections of this
paper. His starting-point was the personal observation that, when
he was endeavouring to think out a difficult problem in a state of
fatigue or drowsiness, a visual picture appeared which, on analysis,
was soon seen to be a pictorial representation of the ideas in question.
To this he gave the perhaps not very appropriate term of ' auto-
symbolic phenomenon.' This itself he divides into three classes,
according to the content of what is symbolised: (1) ' Functional
phenomena,' in which is represented *the way in which* the mind is
functioning (quickly, slowly, lightly, heavily, cheerfully, carelessly,
successfully, fruitlessly, strainedly, etc.). (2) ' Material phenomena,'
in which *what* the mind is thinking is symbolised—*i.e.*, ideas.
(3) ' Somatic phenomena,' in which bodily sensations are symbolised.
Silberer[1] emphatically denies that in this division there is implied
any manner of genetic difference between the three classes; in my
opinion, this is an important error which becomes later the source
of many misunderstandings. He holds, further,[2] that the functional
symbolism never occurs alone, but only as an accompaniment of
the others.

We will next follow Silberer's development of the first question,
concerning the conditions under which symbolism arises. The
first situation he studied was where there was an equal-sided conflict
between the desire to go to sleep and some factor disturbing this,
either mental (effort to work, etc.) or physical. It will be noticed
that this differs from the psychical situation which, according to
Freud, is responsible for dreams merely in that in the latter case
the desire is to continue sleeping ; in both cases it is desire for sleep
versus some disturbance. He soon described the conditions in wider
terms,[3] the conflict being between the effort towards apperception
of any idea on the one side and any factor that made this difficult
on the other; the latter factor may be either temporary, such as
sleepiness, fatigue, illness, and so on, or more permanent, such as
relative intellectual incapacity in comparison with the complexity of
the idea. In his most elaborate analysis of the psychical situation

[1] Silberer, *op. cit.*, *Jahrb.* i., S. 515.
[2] *Idem.*, *op. cit.*, *Jahrb.* ii., S. 558; *Jahrb.* iii., S. 688; *Jahrb.* iv., S. 610.
[3] *Idem.*, *op. cit.*, *Jahrb.* ii., S. 612; *Jahrb.* iii., S. 676.

he formulated the following factors.[1] Symbolism tends to arise either when one's mental capacity is *no longer* equal to grasping a set of ideas that one formerly could, the result of fatigue, illness, etc., or else when the mental capacity of the individual or of the race is *not yet* able to grasp an idea which some day in the future it will. In both cases it will be possible on some other occasion to recognise that the symbolism is either a regression to or a non-emergence from an inferior and more primitive mode of thought, more primitive both in being sensorial instead of conceptual and in being associative instead of apperceptive (in Wundt's terminology). Now, the factors concerned in symbolism can be divided into two groups: (1) What Silberer calls the *positive factors*, those tending to bring a given idea into consciousness or to keep it there; and (2) the *negative factors* that prevent it from entering consciousness in an apperceptive form, and only allow it to enter in a sensorial form—*i.e.*, as symbolism.

Silberer derives the energy of the positive factors from two sources: in the first place from the affect investing the idea in question—*i.e.*, from the dynamic forward-moving tendency of the mental process itself; and, in the second place, from the conscious wish to think in this particular direction. He writes (of the positive factor):[2] ' Er hat den erforderlichen Anspruch auf meine Aufmerksamkeit schon von selbst, durch den Affekt, den er mit sich führt, oder ich erteile ihm diesen Anspruch, indem ich den für mein Gefühlsleben an sich uninteressanten Gedanken kraft meines Willens aufgreife und festhalte, ihn also absichtlich meiner Aufmerksamkeit als interessant empfehle.' [' It either makes the necessary claim on my attention on its own account, through the affect it brings with it, or I grant it this claim by using my will-power to select and hold to a thought which in itself is of no interest to my feelings, and so deliberately recommend it to my attention as an interesting matter.'] This division is simply the psychologist's distinction between passive and active attention. To the psycho-analyst the difference is that in the former case the interest (to the ego) is inherent and direct, whereas in the latter case it is due to an indirect association.

The negative factors he also divides into two classes, both of which result in a state of relative apperceptive insufficiency (see

[1] Silberer, *op. cit.*, *Jahrb.* iii., S. 683, 684, 717; *Jahrb.* iv., S. 608, 611.
[2] *Idem.*, *op. cit.*, *Jahrb.* iv., S. 611.

quotation in Section III.). They are (1) intellectual in kind, either imperfect development (individual or racial) of mental capacity or a transitory weakening of the apperceptive function through a general diminution of mental energy (sleep, fatigue); (2) affective, which either hinder the entrance of the idea by means of the pleasure-pain mechanism (repression) or allow autonomous complexes to rob the function of attention of a part of its energy and so lead to a general diminution of the apperceptive capacity. The affects thus have both a specific and a general effect as negative factors. In addition, they often also act positively, for they themselves may force their way into consciousness, in symbolic guise, instead of the other ideas they have just inhibited. It is clear that in this last point Silberer is referring to repressing forces, to the inhibiting affects that go to make up Freud's ' censorship,' and we shall see that it is to this aspect of the conflict that he devotes most attention. His attitude to Freud's conception of repression and censorship is indicated by his remark that the resistance shewn in dream analysis is the reverse side (*Kehrseite*) of the apperceptive insufficiency.[1]

Silberer recognises that the apperceptive weakness can never be the determining cause of any specific symbol,[2] and was thus led to formulate the statements above quoted regarding the ' positive factor '—*i.e.*, the determining cause. Nevertheless, his predominant interest is with the other side of the subject—namely, with the general conditions that predispose to symbolism. He is chiefly concerned with the factors that *allow* symbolism to occur more readily, rather than with the operative factors that actually bring it about; just as most psychologists deal with the factors that favour the process of forgetting, not with those that actually make us forget. So when he comes to define the different kinds of processes grouped under the name symbolism—the task attempted in this paper—it is from this side alone (of general predisposition) that he attacks the problem. Speaking of the manifold causes of apperceptive insufficiency, he says:[3] ' Und damit ist eigentlich der Schlüssel gegeben zur einheitlichen Auffassung aller der Arten von Symbolbildung,[4] die uns begegnen mögen. Denn nicht in

---

[1] Silberer, *op. cit., Jahrb.* iii., S. 682.   [2] *Idem., loc. cit.*, S. 678.
[3] *Idem., loc. cit.*, S. 683.
[4] The significance of this passage is heightened by the fact that the author is here using the word ' symbolism ' in almost the same comprehensive sense in which the term ' indirect representation ' is used in this paper.

dem Vorgange selbst scheinen mir die wesentlichen Unterschiede bei den verschiedenen Symbolphänomenen zu liegen; d.h. wenn sich auch die Symbolphänomene in Arten unterscheiden, so sind die Unterschiede in ihnen sekundäre Erscheinungen, die nicht die Symbolbildung als solche betreffen. Sondern die Unterschiede liegen primär in denjenigen Verhältnissen, welche die apperzeptive Insuffizienz hervorrufen.' ['It is here we really have the key to a unitary conception of all the kinds of symbol-formation[1] that are to be found. For the essential differences in the different phenomena of symbolism do not seem to me to reside in the process itself— *i.e.*, although these phenomena fall into groups, the differences are secondary manifestations in them which do not concern the symbol-building as such. On the contrary, the differences reside primarily in the factors that bring about the apperceptive insufficiency.'] The classification effected on this basis will be considered presently.

We have next to pursue the development of Silberer's ideas on the nature of the different forms of symbolism, as distinguished according to its content (see above). To the conception of 'somatic phenomena' he adds nothing further, and I will only remark that it is much more closely allied to that of 'functional' than to that of 'material phenomena.' These latter two groups of phenomena correspond so closely with the groupings of symbols based on another mode of classification that they may be considered together with them. In this second classification Silberer[2] divides symbols, not according to their content, as formerly, but according to the factors that have led to the apperceptive insufficiency which he regards as the fundamental basis of all symbolism. The two classes thus distinguished he calls merely the first and second type respectively, but he makes it fairly plain elsewhere[3] that the material phenomenon is characteristic of the former and the functional of the latter. The first type is that which arises on the basis of an apperceptive insufficiency of purely intellectual origin, where the symbolised idea is not hindered by the influence of any affective complex; the second type arises, on the other hand, on the basis of an apperceptive insufficiency of affective origin. So the classification founded on the content (though not the nature) of the positive factors[4] comes to very much the same result as that founded

---

[1] See Note 4, p. 120.
[2] Silberer, *op. cit., Jahrb.* iii., S. 688; iv., S. 609.
[3] *Idem., op. cit., Jahrb.* iii., S. 717.
[4] For the meaning of these terms see above, p. 119.

on the variety of the negative or predisposing factors,[1] and we may use the terms ' material ' and ' functional ' to denote the two types respectively.

We saw above that Silberer's first conception of *functional symbolism* was that it represented the way in which the mind was working (slowly, quickly, etc.). In my experience, and, I may say, also in that of Professor Freud (oral communication), this is a very exceptional occurrence, and one that probably indicates a specially philosophic and introspective type of mind, such as Silberer's own (from which most of his examples are taken). Further, I am more than doubtful whether the functioning of the mind is ever pictorially represented apart from the occasions on which the mind actually feels, or thinks of, this functioning. In fact, I think this can be shewn to be so in the case of an interesting sub-variety of functional symbolism to which Silberer has given the name of ' threshold-symbolism ' (*Schwellensymbolik*),[2] where the passage from one state of consciousness to another—*e.g.*, into or out of sleep—is indicated by appropriate imagery.

However this may be, Silberer soon enlarged the conception of functional symbolism in a quite surprising manner. He began by regarding the process of ' repression ' as a mode of mental functioning, and coined for the pictorial representation of it the term ' cryptogenic symbolism.'[3] He then extended the conception to include practically all functions of the mind except the ideational, and to refer especially to all affective processes.[4] Here it is no longer a question of the *way in which* the mind is working, but of *what* is working in the mind. According to him, therefore, the greater the extent to which affective moments are in play in the production of a given symbol, the more definitely does this belong to the second type of symbolism, characterised by the ' functional phenomenon.' This view is also in harmony with the very interesting remarks he makes on the relation of functional symbolism to gesture, language, mimicry,[5] etc., for, of course, the latter are simply expressions of the emotions.

If, now, we recall the strict sense of the word ' symbol,' as used in the previous section of this paper, it is evident that a symbol of

[1] For the meaning of these terms see above, p. 119.
[2] Silberer, *op. cit.*, *Jahrb.* iii., S. 621-660.
[3] *Idem.*, *op. cit.*, *Jahrb.* ii., S. 580, 581.
[4] *Idem.*, *op. cit.*, *Jahrb.* iii., S. 698, 717, 719.
[5] *Idem.*, *op. cit.*, *Jahrb.* ii., S. 547, 549 ; iii., S. 690.

that kind represents not only the idea symbolised, but also the affects relating to it, or, at all events, some of these. It does this in the same way as the simile indicates an adjectival attribute—namely, by likening the object in question to another one that obviously possesses this attribute, except that in the case of symbolism the one idea is altogether replaced by the other. The affective attitude in this way indicated may be either a positive or a negative one—*i.e.*, it may be either unconscious or conscious, the primary attitude or that resulting from repression. An example of the latter would be the well-known serpent symbol. This symbolises at the same time the phallus itself by means of the objective attributes common to both (shape, erectibility, habits—of emitting poison and of creeping into holes, etc.), and also a subjective attitude towards it, compounded of fear, horror, and disgust, that may in certain circumstances be present—*e.g.*, when the subject is a prudish virgin and the object belongs to a distasteful person.[1] Now, Silberer would call the two things here symbolised material and functional phenomena respectively, and he considers that psycho-analysts pay too much attention to the former to the relative exclusion of the latter; the explanation of this, however, is that in the interpretation of such symbols psycho-analysts are at the moment chiefly concerned with the positive meaning, the negative aspects being dealt with in another connection (resistance, repression, etc.). The noteworthy point here is that Silberer takes into consideration almost exclusively the negative or secondary affects, so that as a matter of practice the term ' functional symbolism ' comes to be almost synonymous with the psycho-analytical ' censorship '—*i.e.*, the inhibiting affects, or, at most, the positive affects that have been *modified* by the censorship.[2] For Silberer, therefore, a psycho-analytical symbol is composed of a material phenomenon (idea symbolised) and a functional one (reactionary affects), both of which are usually conscious processes or nearly so, and he tends to leave out of account the real reason for the whole symbolism—namely, the unconscious, positive affects that are not allowed to appear in consciousness. His overlooking of this essential aspect of the problem accounts also for his curious statement[3] that the

---

[1] The positive affects of the complex are obviously also represented, else there would be no such thing as serpent-worship.

[2] In short, the affects of the preconscious, not of the unconscious.

[3] Silberer, *op. cit., Jahrb.* iii., S. 689, 690 ; iv., S. 614.

universality, or general validity and intelligibility, of a symbol varies inversely with the part played in its causation by affective factors, for it is just these symbols that are most characteristically universal. Relative unfamiliarity with the unconscious itself has here led him grossly to under-estimate the extent to which primitive affective trends are generic, though, it is true, he does verbally admit this in a limited degree.[1]

It is probably also this unfamiliarity, or lack of conviction, which leads Silberer to say that 'material' symbols can change into 'functional' ones, a matter which is worthy of special attention, since examination of it will, I think, reveal the essential differences between true symbolism and metaphor. He writes:[2] 'Es hat sich in neuerer Zeit bei psychoanalytischen Untersuchungen gezeigt, dass Symbole, die ursprünglich material waren, in funktionale Verwendung übergehen. Analysiert man längere Zeit hindurch die Träume einer Person, so wird man finden, dass gewisse Symbole, die zuerst vielleicht nur gelegentlich auftraten zur Bezeichnung irgend eines Vorstellungsinhaltes, Wunschinhaltes, usw., wiederkehren und so zur stehenden Figur oder " *typischen Figur* " werden. Und jemehr sich eine solche typische Figur befestigt und ausprägt, um so mehr entfernt sie sich von der zuerst gehabten ephemeren Bedeutung; umso mehr wird sie zum symbolischen Stellvertreter einer ganzen Gruppe gleichartigen Erlebens, eines seelischen Kapitels sozusagen; bis man sie schliesslich als den Repräsentanten einer seelischen Strömung (Liebe, Hass, Tendenz zum Leichtsinn, zur Grausamkeit, zur Ängstlichkeit, usw.) schlechthin ansehen kann. Was wich da vollzogen hat, ist ein Übergang vom Materialen zum Funktionalen auf dem Weg einer *Verinnerlichung*, wie ich es nenne.' [' Recent psycho-analytic investigations have shewn that symbols which originally were material come to be used in a functional sense. If one analyses someone's dreams for a long time one finds that certain symbols, which perhaps at first made only an occasional appearance to denote the content of some idea or wish, keep recurring, and so become a standing or typical figure. And the more established and pronounced a typical figure of this sort becomes, the more do they recede from the original ephemeral signification, the more do they become the symbolic representative of a whole group of similar experiences, of, so to speak, a mental

[1] Silberer, *op. cit.*, *Jahrb*. iii., S. 690.
[2] *Idem*., ' Probleme der Mystik und ihrer Symbolik,' 1914, S. 153.

chapter, until finally one may regard them as simply the representatives of a mental tendency [love, hate, tendency to frivolity, to cruelty, to apprehensiveness, etc.]. What has happened there is a transition from the material to the functional by means of what I call an internal intensification.') This conclusion is, in my opinion, a fallacious interpretation of a correct observation. The observation is that after a patient has discovered the meaning of a (true) symbol he often strives to weaken and explain away the significance of this by trying to give it some other 'functional,' more general (and therefore more harmless) interpretation. These abstract and metaphorical interpretations do, it is true, bear a certain relationship to the fundamental meaning of the symbol, one which we shall have to examine presently, but the patient's strong preference for them is merely a manifestation of his resistance against accepting the deeper meaning, against assimilating the unconscious. (This very resistance to the unconscious is shewn in Silberer's use of the word ' ephemeral ' in the passage just quoted, for if there is any truth at all in psycho-analysis, or, indeed, in any genetic psychology, then the primordial complexes displayed in symbolism must be the permanent sources of mental life and the very reverse of mere figures of speech.) Some patients become exceedingly adept at this method of protecting themselves from realisation of their unconscious ; when they interpret their dreams, every boat-race becomes the ambition to succeed on the river of life, the money they spill on the floor is a ' symbol ' of wealth, the revolvers that are fired in front of women and behind men are ' symbols ' of power, and, finally, even openly erotic dreams are desexualised into poetic allegories.[1] If, now, the psycho-analyst allows himself to be deceived by these defensive interpretations, and refrains from overcoming the patient's resistances, he will assuredly never reach a knowledge of his unconscious, still less will he be in a position to appraise the relative importance of unconscious trends and those of the surface. By this I do not in any sense mean that the latter are to be neglected, or in their turn under-estimated, but simply that one should not put the cart before the horse and talk of something secondary and less important being *symbolised* by something primary and more important.

Throughout his later work Silberer implies that the process just discussed, of material symbolism changing into functional,

---

[1] See in this connection Jung, *op. cit.*, p. 221.

occurs not merely during the course of a psycho-analysis, but spontaneously as part of the development both of the individual and of the race. What I should call a *levelling* of this sort does, it is true, go on, but the all-important point is that it does so only in the more conscious layers of the mind, so that to describe the process of symbolism in terms of it represents only a very partial truth. The order of events is rather as follows: The ideas or mental attitudes unconsciously represented in true symbols yield, of course as the result of repression, a great many other manifestations besides symbolism. These may be either positive in kind, as the result of sublimation and other modifications, or negative, such as reaction-formations. They, like symbols, are conscious substitutes for, and products of, unconscious mental processes. From this consideration it is intelligible that many of these other conscious products stand in an associative connection with various symbols, both being derived from the same sources. But the connection is collateral, not lineal; to speak of one conscious idea symbolising another one, as the post-psycho-analytical school does, is very much like talking of a person inheriting ancestral traits from his cousin. It is true that a given symbol can be used to represent or indicate (for reasons of convenience, vividness, etc.) a collateral mental attitude derived from the same source; this is, in fact, the chief way in which secondary, metaphorical meanings get attached to symbols. But just in so far as this takes place, the further removed is the process from symbolism. It is very common indeed to find a combination in this respect, so that the figure in question is partly symbolical— *i.e.*, it represents unconscious mental attitudes and ideas—and partly metaphorical—*i.e.*, it indicates other collateral ideas. In some uses the symbolical meaning may be entirely absent, which is what I imply by the word 'levelling'; what Silberer, however, calls the passing of material symbolism over into functional I should prefer to describe as the replacement of symbolism by metaphor— *i.e.*, by an associative connection between collaterals—and the difference is a great deal more than one of words. Further, far more often than might be imagined the symbolical meaning is present at the same time as the metaphorical, though from the nature of things it is much more likely to be overlooked or discounted than the latter. This is very striking in the case of everyday super-stitions, where, in addition to the current secondary interpreta-tions, or even when no conscious interpretation is offered, the unconscious symbolism that constitutes the basis of so many superstitions can be shown to be actively operative in an astonishing number of those addicted to the superstition in question.

These last considerations may now be summarised in more general terms. To begin with, a concrete idea is symbolised by being represented by another concrete idea that usually has a double relationship to it—(1) an objective one, in that the object or process possesses material attributes similar to those possessed by the idea symbolised; and (2) a subjective one, in that the mental attitude towards it is, in some respects, similar to that towards the primary idea. The symbol later becomes secondarily connected, in an associative manner, with other mental attitudes derived from the same source, and is often used to indicate them. With increasing mental development these tend to become more and more general and abstract, for, as the very word implies, all abstract ideas are abstractions of concrete ones, and therefore always ultimately derived from these; so that finally we see a concrete idea, originally used to symbolise a repressed concrete idea, now used to express an abstract thought (either solely for this or, more often, for this in addition to its other function). Hence the common but mistaken view[1] that it is characteristic of symbolism in general to represent the abstract in terms of the concrete. Silberer, by first extending the term ' functional symbolism ' from its original sense to cover the concrete representation of affective processes in general, and by then confining it to the cases where these are secondary in nature, recedes from the conception of true symbolism and reaches once more the popular conception of symbolism as the presentation of the abstract in terms of the concrete.

It is now time to illustrate these points by actual examples, and we may begin by the one last mentioned, that of the serpent. This is one of the most constant symbols of the phallus,[2] and from experiences and thoughts in connection with this object the general conception of ' sexuality ' is largely derived. According to the Jung-Silberer school, the image of a serpent in a dream[3] will symbolise the abstract idea of sexuality more often than the concrete idea of the phallus, whereas to the psycho-analytical school it only

[1] E.g., Silberer, op. cit., Jahrb. iii., S. 662.
[2] Very occasionally it can also symbolise the intestines or their contents, but, so far as I know, nothing else.
[3] I am speaking of cases where the dream image is a symbolic one, which, of course, it need not be.

symbolises the latter, though of course it is commonly *associated with* the former; the practical difference this makes is that, according to the latter school, any meaning of the dream context which is expressed in terms of the general idea is secondary to, derived from, and dependent on a deeper meaning in the unconscious which can only be expressed in terms of the concrete. Again, the unconscious assimilates the general idea of knowledge in terms of the more specific idea of sexual knowledge, which in its turn is assimilated as sexual power; the association is indicated in the Biblical phrase ' to know a woman.' For this reason the idea of the serpent has become associated, especially in the East, with that of knowledge, so that it commonly serves as an emblem of wisdom (as do so many other sexual symbols—*e.g.*, salt). But to say that a serpent may ' symbolise ' *either* a phallus *or* wisdom is to confound two entirely different psychological processes. The relation between them might be further illustrated by comparing these two situations—(1) the case of a man who casually makes use of the colloquial expression ' he is a wily old snake '; here it may well be that the metaphor is purely external, being based on his having heard or read that there is some supposed association between snake and cunning; (2) that of a man who personally and instinctively *feels* that the snake is a fit, natural, and intelligible emblem for the ideas of wisdom and cunning; here one would certainly expect to find that the idea is acting as a true, unconscious, phallic symbol.

A wedding-ring is an emblem of marriage, but it is not a symbol of it. When a man woos a woman he instinctively makes her a present of objects, such as bracelets, brooches, and later an engage-ment-ring, that have the attribute of holding what is passed through them, and unconsciously are symbols of the female organ. At marriage he gives her one of the most perfect symbols of this kind, a plain gold ring, in return for the complete surrender to him of the object it symbolises. The ceremony connotes a group of abstract ideas, fidelity, continuity, etc., with which the ring is now brought into association, and for which it can then serve as an emblem, though never as a symbol.

Most charms, talismans, and amulets are genital symbols, predominantly male. Just as they now bring good luck, or ward off bad luck, so in earlier ages they guarded against the evil powers of magical influences. That these apotropæic qualities were almost exclusively ascribed to genital symbols is due to two circumstances: first, the exaggerated association in the primitive mind between the genital organs and the idea of power or potency; and secondly, the fact that originally nearly all evil magical influences were imagined to be directed against the sexual organs and their functions. As I have shewn elsewhere,[1] for example, practically all the dreaded evil actions of witches in the Middle Ages were symbolic representations of the ' ligature '—*i.e.*, of the attempt to injure sexual potency; they were, in short, castration symbols. The surest safeguard against this calamity was the demonstration, by display, that the threatened part was safe; the mechanism is similar to that of the talion.[2] This train of thought naturally led to charms being associated with the idea of safety in general, particularly as a protection against death or mutilation, as is pathetically shown on a large scale in the present war. Anxious relatives who press a horseshoe or a ' fums up ' on their man when he leaves for the front have not the faintest idea of the meaning of their superstitious act, but that this meaning is not simply an historical one can often be shewn by analysis of their dreams, where the true symbolism becomes apparent; the unconscious often knows what the person is doing so much better than the conscious mind.

To take another current, and more important, analogy. Modern economists know that the idea of wealth means simply ' a lien on future labour,' and that any counters on earth could be used as a convenient emblem for it just as well as a ' gold standard.' Metal coins, however, and particularly gold, are unconscious symbols for excrement, the material from which most of our sense of possession, in infantile times, was derived.[3] The ideas of possession and wealth, therefore, obstinately adhere to the idea of ' money ' and gold for definite psychological reasons, and people simply will not give up the ' economist's fallacy ' of confounding money with wealth. This superstitious attitude will cost England in particular many sacrifices after the War, when efforts will probably be made at all costs to reintroduce a gold standard.[4]

---

[1] ' Der Alptraum in seiner Beziehung zu gewissen Formen des mittelalterlichen Aberglaubens,' 1912, S. 106-110. [' On the Nightmare,' 1931, p. 193.]

[2] It is, in part, identical with that of the perversion called exhibitionism.

[3] See Chapter XXIV.

[4] How this prediction, made in 1915, is being fulfilled is felt by those who carry the burden of taxation on the one hand, and those who experience the misery of unemployment on the other (1923), but few realise the connection between this suffering and the superstition founded in the symbolism here indicated.

We incidentally referred above to the association between the phallus and the idea of power. This is especially close in the case of that of the father, for whom, as was explained above, the idea of the king is an unconscious symbol. His special symbol, the sceptre, thus comes to be the emblem of regal authority—*i.e.*, for the pious respect due to the father. This mental attitude originates, at least in its extreme forms, largely as a reaction against the more primitive and instinctive jealousy and hatred of the father, part of the famous Œdipus-complex.[1] This primitive attitude is expressed in the unconscious of practically all men as the desire to kill, or at least to castrate, the father, a desire that doubtless was literally gratified in primæval times.[2] The mind now recoils from such a horrific conception, and in connection with it we have two beautiful examples of how it deals with this type of truth by diluting its meaning, by changing material symbolism into the harmless functional kind. According to the Jung-Silberer school, the unconscious wish to kill the father merely ' symbolises ' such tendencies as the desire to overcome the old Adam in us, to conquer the part of us that we have inherited from the father, or, even more generally, to overcome a previous point of view. As might have been expected, the same ideas of father-murder or father-castration frequently occur in mythology and the older religions—if not in all religions— and mythologists have similarly deprived them of any literal meaning by interpreting them as harmless and interesting representations of such natural phenomena as the phases of the sun and moon, vegetative or seasonal changes, and so on.

Freud[3] has shown what an essential part this murder impulse has played in the development of religion, not only in primitive systems such as the totemistic, but also in the higher forms, and it is probable that the phallic worship which takes such a central place in earlier religions—and is far from absent in those of our own time—is derived, not only from the extraordinary over-estimation (from our point of view) of the importance of sexual functions characteristic of the primitive mind, but also as a reaction against the hostility toward the patriarchal phallus, and therefore also the divine one; in consciousness adoration for the patriarchal phallus

---

[1] For an exposition of this see Freud, ' Traumdeutung,' 1919, S. 176-185; Rank, ' Das Inzest-Motiv in Dichtung und Saga,' 1912; Ernest Jones, ' The Œdipus-Complex as an Explanation of Hamlet's Mystery,' *Amer. Journ. of Psychology*, vol. xxi.

[2] See Darwin, ' The Descent of Man,' 1871, ch. xx.

[3] Freud, ' Totem und Tabu,' 1913.

becomes over-emphasised just because in the repressed unconscious there is the contrary attitude of hostility. Phallic worship, therefore, was determined by more than one cause, but it was fundamentally concerned with a real phallus. When the facts of Eastern phallic religions began to reach Europe in the nineteenth century, they seemed so incredible that they had at all costs to be re-interpreted into harmless terms, and the view, still prevalent, was adopted that the worship had nothing to do with the phallus as such, but was really directed toward the abstract idea of the divine creative power, which we personify as the Creator, and for which the phallus was a 'symbol' appropriate to simple minds. Reflection shows that the abstract idea in question must itself have been derived from the concrete idea symbolised by the phallic image, so that we have here one more instance of confusion between descendence and collateralism; according to the view just mentioned, the order of development was first concrete phallus, then abstract idea of generation (in so far as it would be admitted that this idea came from the former), then symbol of the abstract idea, whereas to the psycho-analyst the abstract idea and the symbol are related to each other, not as cause and effect, but only as proceeding from a common cause. Indeed, from the standpoint of strict scientific thought, the abstract idea that is here supposed to be symbolised is altogether illusory; we have no experience, in either the physical or spiritual world, of creation, for what masquerades as such always proves on closer inspection to be only transformation.[1] Yet, so hard is it for the human mind to rid itself of such fundamental illusions that the necessity of postulating a creative force is one of the chief arguments adduced in favour of a belief in theism, and even relatively sceptical thinkers like Herbert Spencer feel obliged to fall back on the concept of a 'First Cause.'

We have so far considered the symbol in its relation to the idea unconsciously symbolised, and have reached the conclusion that in the psycho-analytical sense the symbol is a substitute for the primary idea compulsorily formed as a compromise between the tendency of the unconscious complex and the inhibiting factors, whereas the functional interpretation is mainly concerned with the more conscious reactions to and sublimations of the unconscious complex. We have next to deal with another aspect of the problem

---

[1] The whole question is pithily condensed in the expression, 'The wish is *Father* to the thought.'

—namely, the relation of the symbol to the idea it immediately expresses; *e.g.*, no longer with the relation of the serpent symbol to the phallus, but with that of the serpent symbol to the serpent itself. We have, in other words, to consider symbolism in terms of reality-principle, instead of, as before, in terms of the pleasure-principle.

In dreams, myths, and similar material, we find the image of the sun used to symbolise the eye, the father, or the phallus. What bearing has this symbolism on man's conscious thoughts concerning the sun in other respects ? The problem divides itself into two—namely, the question of more or less scientific knowledge concerning the sun, dictated to some extent by man's primary instinct for knowledge, and, secondly, the more practical aspects of how to deal in daily life with the external phenomena in question (heat, shade, darkness, etc.). It is only in civilised man that this distinction holds, and even there only in part, for it is everywhere hard to separate the mere curiosity for knowledge from the practical aspects of the necessity for, or desirability of, knowing. I feel sure that a great deal of what is attributed to man's pure desire for knowledge—the discoveries he makes, and so on—is really dictated much more by the impulses set up by necessity, which may be either external or internal; how well the old adage ' necessity is the mother of invention ' is being illustrated at the present day !

Our problem is especially manifest in regard to what Wundt terms the ' mythological stage of knowledge.' This does not here involve the problem of mythology as a whole, which has more to do in general with the material *versus* functional controversy dealt with above, as Silberer[1] has well illustrated in a number of familiar examples. As he has also well expounded,[2] a most important point to bear in mind in regard to the mythological stage of knowledge is that it is a relative concept. No knowledge is recognised to be mythological by the person who believes in it—at least, not at the moment he does so believe. This, however, is also true of symbolism. It is only when we disbelieve in their objective and literal reality that we recognise them to be symbols, though even then we usually have no idea of what they had been symbolising. So a mythological piece of knowledge is at the time it is accepted,

---

[1] Silberer, *op. cit.*, *Jahrb.* ii., S. 573-586.
[2] *Idem.*, *op. cit.*, *Jahrb.* ii., S. 606, 607; iii., S. 662-666.

and for those who accept it, the only form of truth then possible; it is an adequate form of reality for a certain level of development. A ' higher ' or more objective form of truth would be rejected, for either intellectual or affective reasons, and ' not understood.' Silberer[1] thinks that, on the whole, the first type of symbolism, the material phenomenon, predominates in this process. Taking the idea of symbolism in its strict sense, there is no doubt that, as both Silberer[2] and Rank and Sachs[3] point out, its occurrence in this connection serves the function of rendering it easier to assimilate the perceived material that is being dealt with; the mind assimilates it in terms of the previously familiar. What really happens is that the unconscious assimilates the new material in terms of its own thoughts, the process discussed in Section III. of this paper, the result of which will be the appearance in the conscious of a symbol of the unconscious thought.

So far all is clear, but the point that is disputed in this connection is whether the symbol can bear any relation, and if so what, to the idea (the ' higher form of truth ') that will later, in either the same individual or another, replace the symbol and this mythological stage of knowledge. Can the later, more objective form of knowledge be already implicit in the earlier symbolical presentation of the attempt to deal with the problem ? Silberer does not definitely answer this question, but Jung[4] would unhesitatingly answer it in the affirmative, and, I gather, in all cases.

To my way of thinking, the matter is more complex than would appear from this statement of it. There is certainly some connection in most cases between the symbol and the ' future idea,' but in my opinion it is very much the same as, though not quite identical with, the connection discussed above between the symbol and the functional interpretation. I do not think that the future idea is implicit in the symbol ; on the contrary, the existence of the symbol —to be more accurate, the symbolic use of the symbol—is often the very thing that is preventing the idea from being formulated. As has been explained above, the mind always tends to assimilate a new percept in terms of some unconscious complex, and every step in progress in the line of the reality-principle connotes, not only a use of this primordial association, but also a partial renunciation of it; a surrendering of the personal, subjective factor and an

---

[1] Silberer, *op. cit.*, *Jahrb.* iii., S. 689.   [2] *Idem.*, *op. cit.*, *Jahrb.* iii., S. 692.
[3] Rank and Sachs, *op. cit.*, S. 17.   [4] See specially Jung., *op. cit.*, ch. xv.

attending, which might almost be called sensorial, to the objective attributes of the new percept. Let us follow the example chosen above of the sun. One of the earliest conceptions of this was that it was a mighty eye, the resemblances—in connection with light, etc.—being fairly evident. Later it was regarded as a movable lamp, and later still as a hot gaseous body around which the earth revolves. If in one of these later stages of knowledge the image of the sun appeared in a dream as a substitute for that of an eye, we should, of course, call it a symbol, but in the first stage the ophthalmic idea of the sun would most accurately be described as a symbolic equivalent. Now, how did the progress in knowledge take place, and what is the relation of the symbol to the future idea of the sun? The first stage is simple enough. It is nothing but an identification of the new percept with an old one, a temporarily successful assimilation of it in terms of the older and more familiar one. I imagine that every fresh attribute observed about the sun and its behaviour, every fresh thought about it, was in turn dictated by a similar association, usually unconscious, with some previously familiar idea; or, put in another way, that attention was seriously directed to each fresh attribute through the interest already residing in the previously familiar idea with which the new attribute got associated on the ground of however faint a resemblance, for it is truly astounding how the human mind can escape paying attention to evident, and even important, observations in which it is *not* interested. But, and this is the all-important point, in this second stage the assimilation does not lead to pure symbolism; it is enough to direct attention, and give interest, to the fresh observation, but this is interpreted by a process of ratiocination in conjunction with the facts of external reality, no longer solely in terms of the pre-existing idea, as in the first, more symbolical stage of knowledge. In so far as it is no longer thus interpreted in the older fashion, there is involved a corresponding renunciation, in favour of the reality-principle and its advantages, of the pleasure yielded by the easier and more primitive process of complete assimilation. According to the findings of psycho-analysis, *all* mental progress is accompanied with partial renunciation of some primitive form of pleasure —which is probably the reason why it is so slow—and the process just indicated is no exception to the rule.

The following example also illustrates the same point. Lightning, like mistletoe, was at first, and for thousands of years, imagined to be divine soma[1]—*i.e.*, semen—a notion the last form of which was the conception of a special magnetic or electric fluid; it is interesting, by the way, that the same conception—here termed magnetic fluid, vital fluid, mesmeric fluid, etc.—was long held as the theory of what used to be called ' animal magnetism '— *i.e.*, hypnotism. Increased knowledge as to the nature of lightning essentially connoted, among other things, the partial surrendering of this unconscious assimilation, the giving up of the symbol magnetic fluid, though in the unconscious symbolism that is the basis of neurotic symptoms—*e.g.*, brontephobia—the ancient association between lightning and semen recurs, and it is to be noted that we still popularly conceive of electricity as the flow of a current. Our general question, therefore, of whether the future conception is already implicit in a latent state in the symbol can be answered affirmatively only in a very restricted sense—namely, that part, and often only a small part, of the mental material that will later be converted into the more developed conception is already present, but that the idea as such is certainly not present, even in the unconscious, so that obviously it cannot be ' symbolised.'

Similar remarks hold good in the case of more complex stages in the advance of knowledge, such as scientific generalisations, as also with other conscious tendencies and interests. From one point of view these may be regarded as sublimations from unconscious complexes, developments which are, of course, greatly modified by contact with external reality and by conscious elaboration. They, like symbols, come about as the result of the conflict beween unconscious impulses and the inhibiting forces of repression, but they differ from symbols in that, whereas with the latter the full significance of the original complex is retained unaltered and merely transferred on to a secondary idea (that of the symbol), with the former the psychical energy alone, not the significance, is derived from the unconscious complexes and is transferred on to another set of ideas that have their own independent significance. It is true that here also regression may lead to true symbolism, where the ideas resulting from sublimation may temporarily lose their own intrinsic meaning and sink back to become mere symbols of the complexes from which their energy was largely derived. But in this case they are symbols in the strict sense and do not symbolise

[1] See Kuhn, ' Die Herabkunft des Feuers,' 1859; and the comments on it in Abraham's ' Traum und Mythus,' 1909.

the sublimations, in spite of their indirect association with these. A typical example of the whole process would be the one discussed above in connection with Sperber's views, the case of agricultural work. At first these performances were identified with sexual acts and later achieved an independence of their own, but in neither of these stages could they be called sexual symbols, for they were not being used as pure substitutes; they become symbols only when, as in dreams, myths, etc., they for a time lose their actual meaning (wholly or in part), and are then used as substitutes for the ideas with which they were originally identified.

We have now considered three aspects of symbolism: its relation to the unconscious complex (Sections II. and III.), to the other derivatives of this (functional symbolism), and to external reality. We have last of all to consider briefly a fourth aspect, that to which Silberer has given the name ' anagogic,'[1] and which is very similar indeed to Adler's ' programmatic ' and Jung's ' prospective ' meaning of symbolism.[2] The last two terms are wider ones, and include the ' development of the future idea ' conception just discussed, as well as the anagogic one; we are here concerned, therefore, only with the latter one.

By the anagogic signification of symbolism is meant the mystical, hermetic, or religious doctrine that is supposed to be contained in the symbol. The symbol is taken to be the expression of a striving for a high ethical ideal, one which fails to reach this ideal and halts at the symbol instead; the ultimate ideal, however, is supposed to be implicit in the symbol and to be symbolised by it. Along this path the post-psycho-analytical school[3] loses itself in a perfect maze of mysticism, occultism, and theosophy, into which I do not propose to penetrate; Silberer implicitly and Jung explicitly abandon the methods and canons of science, particularly the conceptions of causality and determinism, so that I may consider myself absolved from the task of attempting to unravel the assumptions that have culminated in their latest views. As the philosophers would say, it is impossible for us to adhere to one universe of discourse.

It is clear that the anagogic aspect of symbolism is only a special case of the general ' future idea ' conception discussed above,

---

[1] Silberer, *op. cit.*, ' Probleme,' etc., S. 138.   [2] *Idem.*, *loc. cit.*, S. 193, 207.
[3] See especially Jung., *op. cit.*, and ' The Principles of the Unconscious,' 1916; Silberer, *op. cit.*, ' Probleme,' etc.

and that the relation between the symbol and the ethical ideals in question is much the same as that already explained as subsisting between it and the various functional aspects, particularly those referring to sublimated interests and activities. In fact, the only difference that Silberer[1] discerns between the anagogic and functional aspects is that the former refer to future mental attitudes and the latter to present ones; when the anagogic ideal has been attained it passes into functional symbolism,[2] a conclusion that confirms my previously expressed suspicion as to the reactionary tendency of his general conception of functional symbolism.

V. REVIEW OF CONCLUSIONS

The main thesis of this paper is that it is possible usefully to distinguish, under the name of symbolism, one fundamental type of indirect representation from other more or less closely allied ones, and that consideration of the points of distinction throws a light upon the nature of indirect figurative representation in general and of symbolism in particular.

Using first the term 'symbolism' in its older broad sense (to include metaphors, etc.), we can make the following generalisations: All symbolism betokens a relative incapacity for either apprehension or presentation,[3] primarily the former; this may be either affective or intellectual in origin, the first of these two factors being by far the more important. As a result of this relative incapacity, the mind reverts to a simpler type of mental process, and the greater the incapacity the more primitive is the type of mental process reverted to. Hence, in the most typical forms the symbol is of the kind of mental process that costs least effort—*i.e.*, is sensorial, usually visual ; visual because in retrospect most perceptual memories become converted into visual forms (most memories of childhood, etc.), this in turn being partly due to the special ease of visual representation. For the same reason symbolism is always concrete, because, as will be explained in a moment, concrete mental processes are both easier and more primitive than any other. Most forms of symbolism, therefore, may be described as the automatic substituting

---

[1] Silberer, *op. cit.*, 'Probleme,' etc., S. 155.   [2] *Idem.*, *loc. cit.*, S. 194.

[3] This generalisation is about equivalent to that implied in Silberer's term 'apperceptive insufficiency,' but he tends to regard this incapacity as the essential cause of symbolism, while I regard it merely as an indispensable condition; I also lay much more stress on the affective causes of it than he does.

of a concrete idea, characteristically in the form of its sensorial image, for another idea which is more or less difficult of access, which may be hidden or even quite unconscious, and which has one or more attributes in common with the symbolising idea.

The essential difficulty that goes with all forms of symbolism is in the adequate apprehending (and therefore also in the conveying) of feeling. This is doubtless to be ascribed to the innumerable inhibitions of feeling which psycho-analysis has shewn to be operative throughout the mind, and which naturally exhibit a more concentrated force in some regions than in others; it is therefore to be expected that the most typical and highly developed forms of symbolism will be found in connection with those regions. Even the weakest form of symbolism, however—for instance, the metaphor —comes into this category. For example, Keats wishes to convey his exaltation at the sense of discovery experienced on first looking into Chapman's ' Homer.' He finds it impossible to do this directly, for any mere direct statement of the fact would leave us cold. He succeeds in transmitting to us some of his own thrill only by likening his sensations to those of someone who has just discovered a new planet or a new ocean.[1] The simile used by Keats strictly stands for an adjective—wonderful, inspiring, or what not—preceding the word ' exaltation '; and the like is true of all similes and metaphors. The problem thus arises: In what way is the replacement of an adjective by a concrete likeness related to the question of inhibited feeling ?

The basal feature in all forms of symbolism is identification. This is one of the most fundamental tendencies of the mind, and is much more pronounced in its more primitive regions. The lack of discrimination connoted by it is only in a very slight degree conditioned by imperfect intellectual development, for the tendency to identify is mainly due to the following two factors, which relate to the pleasure-principle and the reality-principle respectively. In the first place, it is easier, and therefore pleasanter, to note the features of a new idea that resemble those of an older and more familiar one. Further, the mind tends to notice especially those features that interest it because of their resemblance to previous experiences of interest. In the second place, the appreciation of resemblances facilitates the assimilation of new experiences by

---

[1] Here, as is often the case, the inhibition of imaginative feeling that has to be overcome is in the hearer.

referring the unknown to the already known. Even this factor, and obviously the first one, is much more an affective than an intellectual one. These identifications profoundly influence the course of further mental development along both affective lines (sublimations) and intellectual ones (increased knowledge, science).

In so far as a secondary idea B receives its meaning from a primary idea A, with which it has been identified, it functions as what may be called a symbolic equivalent of A. At this stage, however, it does not yet constitute a symbol of A, not until it replaces A as a substitute in a context where A would logically appear. There is an overflow of feeling and interest from A to B, one which gives B much of its meaning, so that under appropriate conditions it is possible for B to represent A. According to the view here maintained, the essential element of these conditions is an affective inhibition relating to A. This holds good for all varieties of symbolism, in its broadest sense.

Affective inhibition can, of course, be of the most varying degree, and on this variation greatly depends the multiplicity of the processes that are grouped under the name of 'symbolism.' When the inhibition is at its maximum there arises symbolism in its most typical form. The distinctions between this and other forms of indirect pictorial representation are qualitative as well as quantitative, and they are so important that it is here proposed that the term 'symbolism' be reserved for it solely.[1] It is already explicitly used in this sense by psycho-analysts, and implicitly by many anthropologists and mythologists, and it seems worth an effort to try to get it generally accepted thus. The two cardinal characteristics of symbolism in this strict sense are (1) that the process is completely unconscious, the word being used in Freud's sense of 'incapable of consciousness,' not as a synonym for subconscious; and (2) that the affect investing the symbolised idea has not, in so far as the symbolism is concerned, proved capable of that modification in quality denoted by the term 'sublimation.' In both these

---

[1] Mr. J. C. Flugel has suggested to me that, as an alternative to my proposal, the term 'cryptophor' be used as a counterpart of 'metaphor,' so that one might speak of cryptophoric as contrasted with metaphoric symbolism, instead of, as I propose, speaking of symbolism as contrasted with metaphoric representation. The drawback I see to his suggestion is that, if the same word symbolism be still used generically for the two classes (for the qualifying adjective would often be omitted in practice), the current confusion between them would only be perpetuated.

respects symbolism differs from all other forms of indirect representation.

The typical attributes of *true symbolism* as modified from the description given by Rank and Sachs, are—(1) Representation of unconscious material; (2) constant meaning, or very limited scope for variation in meaning; (3) non-dependence on individual factors only; (4) evolutionary basis, as regards both the individual and the race; (5) linguistic connections between the symbol and the idea symbolised; (6) phylogenetic parallels with the symbolism as found in the individual existing in myths, cults, religions, etc. The number of ideas that can be symbolised is remarkably small in comparison with the endless number of symbols. They are fewer than a hundred, and they all relate to the physical self, members of the immediate family, or the phenomena of birth, love, and death. They typically, and perhaps always, arise as the result of regression from a higher level of meaning to a more primitive one; the actual and ' real ' meaning of an idea is temporarily lost, and the idea or image is used to represent and carry the meaning of a more primitive one with which it was once symbolically equivalent. When the meaning of the symbol is disclosed the conscious attitude is characteristically one of surprise, incredulity, and often repugnance.

Progress beyond the early stage of symbolic equivalency takes place (*a*) intellectually, by the transference of the symbolic meaning to the idea B becoming subordinated to the acquirement of a ' real,' objective meaning intrinsic in B; (*b*) affectively, by a refinement and modification of the affects investing A (sublimation), which permits of their becoming attached to non-inhibited, conscious, and socially useful or acceptable ideas and interests. Both of these processes connote a partial renunciation as regards the original complex A, with, however, a compensatory replacement of it by other ideas and interests. Whenever there is a failure in this process of sublimation there is a tendency to regress towards the primary complex A, or, rather, this complex, being no longer indirectly relieved, once more tends to reassert itself. Inhibiting forces prevent its doing so in its original form, and as a result of this intrapsychical conflict it may express itself by means of one of its original symbolical equivalents—*e.g.*, B—which then carries, in a substitutive manner, the significance of A and is its symbol. Once this has occurred, further progress can only take place by the same process as that just described, a loosening of the ideational links between A and B, and a renunciation of the need of the complex A for direct gratification. Progress, therefore, in contra-distinction to the views held by the post-psycho-analytical school, does not take place *via* symbolism, but *via* the symbolic equivalents that are the basis of this; symbolism itself, in fact, constitutes a barrier to progress. This is best seen in the blind alley of neurotic symptomatology.

The most important member of this school, from the point of view. of symbolism, is Silberer, whose views have therefore been dealt with at some length in this paper. The differences between his conclusions and my own may shortly be expressed as follows: We are concerned with three groups of psychical material: (1) the unconscious complexes, (2) the inhibiting influences (Freud's ethical censorship) that keep these in a state of repression, and (3) the sublimated tendencies derived from the unconscious com-plexes. In my judgement, the relation of symbolism to these three groups is this: Like the third group, symbols are the product of intrapsychical conflict between the first two groups. The material of the symbol is taken from the third group. The second group, which prevents the first one from coming to direct expression, is to some extent represented in the formation of the symbol; but the dynamic force that creates the symbol, the meaning carried by the symbol, and the reason for the very existence of the symbol, are all derived from the first group, from the unconscious complexes.

The fundamental fallacy of Silberer's work, as it seems to me, is that he tends to confound the process of symbolic equivalency with that of symbolism itself,[1] as was indicated above in regard to the relation between symbolism and mental progress. As a result of this he brings symbolism into a forced relationship with the other product of the unconscious, the third group just mentioned, and tends to regard the symbol as the representative of this further product instead of its being the representative of the first, primary group. Further, on the basis of the (subordinate) part played by the second group in the formation of symbols, and the fact that it is to some extent represented in the symbol, he attaches an altogether exaggerated importance to this second group as constituting the meaning of the symbol, and especially to those aspects of the

---

[1] The same fallacy as that involved in Maeder's confusion of the latent and manifest contents of dreams, and with the same practical result—the attributing of ethical tendencies to a process that has only an indirect relationship with them.

second group (the ethical ones) that are akin to the third group. To put the matter still more concisely: according to the conclusions here reached, the material of a symbol is derived from the third group while its meaning is derived essentially from the first group, to only a very limited extent from the second, and not at all from the third; according to Silberer, the meaning of a symbol is derived mainly from the second and third groups, and only to a very limited extent from the first.

I agree, however, that a symbolic image may be used to represent the second or third group of psychical material in question as well as the first, but in this function it is acting as a metaphor, not as a symbol, and it might then be usefully termed an emblem, token, or sign. When this is so—*i.e.*, when a true symbol is being used metaphorically—all that the second or third group of psychical processes can do is to select for its purposes an already created symbol ; it never contributes, in any important degree, to the actual creation of the symbol. Silberer, in my opinion, confounds the use of the metaphor with that of the symbol, and so mistakes the nature of the true symbol, ascribing to it attributes that properly belong to the metaphor. There are many features in common between the two processes—it would be impossible to confound them otherwise, and the object of this paper would be superfluous— and I do not for a moment wish to maintain that they are totally different in nature. But the differences between them, notably in their relation to the unconscious (together with the other features of symbolism discussed above), are also important.

There are, broadly speaking, two kinds of metaphor, with all gradations between them. With the first kind an analogy is perceived and made use of between two ideas that is true, objective, and of some value; thus, in the phrase ' to find the key to this problem ' the analogy between such a situation and that of discovering how to enter a room difficult of access is of this nature. With the second kind the analogy is only supposed to subsist; it is subjective and often untrue in fact; thus, the phrase ' as wise as a serpent ' is of this nature. Serpents are, in fact, not wiser than most other animals, and the false attribution of wisdom to them is secondary and due to a process of true symbolism, as has been expounded earlier in this paper. With the first kind the association is intrinsic, with the second it is extrinsic, depending, however, on an underlying identity in the source of both ideas (in so far, of course, as they are symbolic).

In a metaphor an abstract adjectival description is replaced by a more concrete simile. Experience shews this to be a more vivid and successful way of conveying the desired meaning and of evoking the appropriate feeling tone. The explanation is that the more primitive method—*i.e.*, recourse to the concrete and sensorial —stands nearer to the sources of feeling. In the evolution, in both the individual and the race, from the original concrete to the general, and from this to the abstract, there is an increasing inhibition of feeling accompanying the greater objectivity. Concrete images are, as a rule, more personal, familiar, subjectively toned, and invested with more feeling than abstract terms. The difference is most plainly seen in the fields where there is most inhibition. There is a considerable difference between damning a man's eyes and merely consigning him to perdition. By the use of suitable abstract circumlocutions, aided by foreign and less familiar technical terms, it is possible to discuss various sexual topics in any society without any difficulty, but—to take the other extreme—the use of some gross obscene word, familiar in childhood, but since discarded, will often bring about a marked uprush of unpleasant emotion.

Therefore, when it is wished to apprehend or convey a vivid impression, a strong feeling, recourse is had to the primitive method of likening the idea to an associated concrete image, because in this way some inhibition is overcome and feeling released; what is popularly called stimulating the imagination is always really releasing the imagination from its bonds. The over-profuse use of metaphors, as that of slang—which fulfils the same psychological function—is well known to be the mark of expressional incapacity; the person belongs to what, in association work, is called the predicate type.

Theoretically and logically the simile is the first stage of the metaphor. But, for the motives expounded above in connection with the process of identification, the two sides of the equation become fused into one at the very onset, with a resulting economy in psychical effort. The savage does not say ' John is like a lion '; still less does he say ' John is as brave as a lion '; he boldly asserts that ' John is a lion.' And when we cannot find language sufficiently vivid to convey our admiration of John's courage, we revert to the primitive method of the savage and say likewise that ' John is a lion.'

One further point. The process known as the decay of a metaphor, whereby the original literal meaning of the word is lost and its figurative meaning receives an accepted and independent significance, is akin to what was described above as the renunciation of a symbolic meaning, whereby the symbolising idea becomes emancipated from its adventitious meaning and achieves a separate existence.

I will now attempt a final *summary* of these conclusions. The essential function of all forms of symbolism, using the word in the broadest and most popular sense, is to overcome the inhibition that is hindering the free expression of a given feeling-idea, the force derived from this, in its forward urge, being the effective cause of symbolism. It always constitutes a regression to a simpler mode of apprehension. If the regression proceeds only a certain distance, remaining conscious or at most preconscious, the result is metaphorical, or what Silberer calls ' functional,' symbolism. If, owing to the strength of the unconscious complex, it proceeds further—to the level of the unconscious—the result is symbolism in the strict sense. The circumstance that the same image can be employed for both of these functions should not blind us to the important differences between them. Of these the principal one is that with the metaphor the feeling to be expressed is over-sublimated, whereas with symbolism it is under-sublimated; the one relates to an effort that has attempted something beyond its strength, the other to an effort that is prevented from accomplishing what it would.

CHAPTER IV

THE GENESIS OF THE SUPER-EGO [1]

IN a paper published some twenty years[2] ago I laid stress on the tentative nature of the contribution I was offering to what was then an entirely new concept, one of the most important that Freud ever made. There is no reason for surprise, therefore, that the experience since gained makes me welcome the opportunity for revising some of those tentative conclusions or extending them in the light of further knowledge. Most of what I wrote concerning the functions and structure of the super-ego still stands, though very much could be added to it, so I propose to confine myself here to the more obscure problem of its genesis.

There can be no more fascinating problem than this in the whole of psychology or anthropology, and that for two reasons. We have good grounds for supposing that to the activity of the super-ego we are mainly beholden for the imposing structure of morality, conscience, ethics, æsthetics, religion—in short, to the whole spiritual aspiration of man that sunders him most strikingly from the beast. The well-nigh universal belief that man is qualitatively different from other animals in possessing a divine and immortal soul itself emanates from this source. Anything, therefore, that can throw light on such a remarkable, and indeed unique, aspect of humanity must needs prove of the highest interest to the student of man and his institutions.

In the second place, the super-ego possesses a further and equally important claim on our interest. There is a darker side to it. The super-ego is man's foe as well as his friend. It is not only concerned with promoting man's spiritual welfare, but is also responsible for much of his spiritual distress and even for the infernal activities that so deface the nature of man and cause this distress. In the obscure depths of the unconscious the super-ego plays a vital part in the conflicts and turmoils characteristic of that region. It is no exaggeration to say that man's mental life is essentially composed of struggling efforts either to escape from or to support the claims of the super-ego.

---

[1] Published in *Samiksa*, the *Indian Psycho-Analytical Bulletin*, vol. i., January, 1947.
[2] 'The Origin and Structure of the Super-Ego,' *International Journal of Psycho-Analysis*, 1926. Reprinted as Chapter VII. of the Fourth Edition of the present book.

Superficially regarded, our life appears to consist of a small section concerned with more or less abstract speculations and reflections and a far larger one concerned with more directly material interests and activities. The subjective element in the former is not very hard to perceive, although it is often denied. But it is seldom understood that even with the latter, subjective, and more usually irrational, elements play a very large part also. Were our reason free to function it would probably be not very difficult to arrange our lives and our institutions so as to provide a vast increase of happiness, achievement and security. But the inexorable claims of the super-ego, irrational as they mostly are, are more urgent than our real interests, which are commonly subordinated to them. And so we have to suffer.

Before coming to our problem it is necessary to be clear on one or two prelusive matters. The super-ego has several conscious derivations—for instance, conscience, ego-ideal, etc.—but it itself has to be carefully distinguished from them. Thus the essential super-ego is an institution of the unconscious, so much so that to make a patient aware of its activities is often an extremely difficult task.

Then we have to be specially careful when we use the word ' morality,' for it is just with the early genesis of this conception that we are concerned. The conscience is plainly the guardian of morality in the fully developed sense of that term: what is socially right (according to the *mores*) and ethically laudable. Now the super-ego is certainly not moral in that sense—in extreme cases, for example, it may even dictate an act of murder as both desirable and commendable—and yet it possesses an important attribute that closely mimics it. That is the sense of urgent ' oughtness,' a categorical imperative. Actually this ' oughtness ' in the super-ego may get attached to attitudes that are either moral or immoral as judged by our reason and conscience, although in both cases it is at least as strong and compelling as any corresponding dictate of the conscience. If, therefore, it is to be called moral it can be only in an extended—irrational—sense of the word. Furthermore, I have been able to trace this pseudo-moral feeling of ' oughtness ' to an earlier stage of development that antedates any sense of right and wrong, one to which I have given the name of ' pre-nefarious inhibition.'[1] It would seem to be in this dark region that we have to search for the beginnings of what later becomes a moral attitude.

[1] Chapter XIV., p. 309.

A paradox that must be faced is that we are able to describe the super-ego only by using two apparently incompatible terminologies, one static, the other dynamic. There is an analogy to this in the dilemma of modern physics which has to describe its ultimates both as particles and as waves, neither alone being able to comprehend all the data. Presumably with psychology as with physics, it indicates the imperfection of our knowledge. On the one hand it seems necessary to describe the super-ego as an object, an introjected object, an entity which can be offered to the id to love or hate or fear in place of an eternal object, originally a parent. And on the other hand we know that this internalised object has no corporeal existence, but emanates from a process of phantasy which is itself the expression of some instinctual drive: here, therefore, we can describe the super-ego only in the dynamic terms of a *process*, a trend with sexual, aggressive, or ' moral ' aims. If it is a thing it is a very living thing, full of activity: watching, warning, guarding, threatening, punishing, prohibiting, ordaining, encouraging, and so on.

The attention paid in the last twenty years by a number of London analysts, notably Melanie Klein, to the processes of introjection and projection in infancy has led to a deeper insight into the origins of the super-ego. In the light of this experience Freud's formulations concerning it now seem to us to call for an important modification in one respect and important extensions in two others.

The first of these points relates to Freud's picture of the super-ego as the resolution of the Œdipus complex. The child, faced with the hopelessness of his Œdipus wishes, both because of the inexorable privation and because of the fear of punishment, effects a renunciation of them on condition that he permanently incorporates something of the parents within himself. This image of love and dread, derived from both parents, though more especially from the one of the same sex, then constitutes the super-ego, which continues to exercise its function of watching, threatening and if necessary punishing the ego when there is any likelihood of its listening to the now forbidden and repressed Œdipus wishes of the id. Freud thus termed the super-ego the heir of the Œdipus complex: its derivative and substitute. Now if all this refers to the fully developed and finished product, the super-ego as it will on the whole remain through life, and also if one reserves the term super-ego exclusively for this finished product, then Freud's formula still stands. But if it means that nothing of the super-ego is to be discerned until the Œdipus wishes are renounced—according to Freud, at about the age of four or five—then the conclusions based on later experience widely depart from it. It is partly a matter of nomenclature, though only partly. Freud would restrict the term super-ego to what I have called the finished product, and he would attach the greatest importance in its genesis to the Œdipus conflicts between the ages of three and five. Nevertheless he would have also agreed that there is some further pre-history both to the Œdipus complex itself (pre-genital difficulties, etc.) and perhaps even to the anxieties and fear of punishment antedating the classical Œdipus situation and preparing the ground for the guilt attributes of the super-ego.

Before taking up the modern modification one is compelled to make to this formula of Freud's I will briefly mention the other two points alluded to above. One concerns the dating of the whole matter. We have now much reason to think that both the Œdipus complex itself, with all its characteristic features (carnal desire for the mother, jealousy and hatred of the father, fear of castration, etc.), and the super-ego in a sufficiently developed form to be clearly recognisable, long antedate the period in which Freud envisaged them and reach back certainly to the second and perhaps even the first year of life. Secondly, the fear of punishment and also other sources of anxiety which play such an essential part in the genesis of the super-ego do not by any means all emanate from the Œdipus situation itself, but have still deeper origins. To put it plainly, the boy has other reasons for anxiety besides the dread of punishment at the hands of his paternal rival; they spring more directly from the relation to his mother alone.

As was mentioned above, the reasons for these extensions and modifications of Freud's formula come from closer study of the processes of introjection and projection. Thanks mainly to the work of Melanie Klein, we have become familiar, not merely with the early age at which they operate, but with the extraordinary and quite continuous interplay between them at every moment of the infant's experiences of life. The introjections are what constitute the super-ego, but—and this is a most essential point—they are far from simple incorporations of external reality, but are to a greater extent incorporations of the infant's projections as well. Once this point is grasped one understands that the infant's own contribution to its future super-ego is more important than those made by the outer world (essentially the parents), a conclusion to which Freud would perhaps have demurred.

We may now return to Freud's view concerning the relationship of the Œdipus complex to the super-ego. He would undoubtedly have agreed that the child's picture of the prohibiting and threatening parent is an exaggerated or distorted one. Though fathers may kill or castrate their boy children they very seldom do; nevertheless every boy feels these eventualities to be likely ones and is in consequence terrified of them. When, therefore, Freud says that the super-ego gains its power of affecting the ego from its representing reality demands,[1] one certainly has to add ' and unreality demands as well ': more accurately, the demands of psychical reality as well as those of physical reality. In my opinion these additions made by the child's imagination to the picture of the parent are much more important and have a longer and more complicated history than Freud believed likely. And, as I pointed out many years ago[2] the earliest phantasies and conflicts exercise a decisive importance on the form taken by the Œdipus complex, its course and outcome.

It is, however, agreed on all sides that these additions exist, so at once we are presented with the problem of their origin. Rather to our surprise, we find to start with that the child has a motive in magnifying external dangers—i.e., in picturing the parent as stricter and more dangerous than he or she actually is. The child can find in this way relief from its fears of internal dangers, which are more intolerable and less assuaged by the reassurance given by the knowledge that the external object (parent) after all has some love and that there are limits to his anger. It achieves this, of course, by the familiar mechanism of projection. The matter, however, is not so simple as this, since the child oscillates in his estimate of internal versus external dangers, especially when the latter includes the projected ones. The external bogy may become so fearsome that the child, evidently with the aim of securing better control over it, introjects it (into its super-ego). Once inside, however, it again becomes intolerably dangerous and the child is compelled to look around for a suitable object in the outer world on to whom it can once more project it. This double process is continually and perhaps endlessly repeated in the endeavour to procure some relief from the anxiety. These desperate expedients show that the child has within

[1] Freud, *Collected Papers*, vol. ii., pp. 251-253.
[2] *Papers on Psycho-Analysis*, Chapter XIV., p. 317.

itself extremely formidable sources of anxiety, for which the formation of the super-ego is one attempted mode of salvation. This
defensive function of the super-ego is the main theme of the present
paper.

Whence come all these fearsome bogies and with them the need
for such desperate defences ? The super-ego is certainly, among
other things, a cruelly persecuting agency which the ego has good
reason to dread. But, after all, the super-ego is only in small part
thrust on to the growing child by outer prohibitions and con-
demnations. It is in a larger part its own creation. Why does it have
to create such a very unpleasant institution inside itself. There must
be a good reason for its doing so strange a thing. Or, put more
objectively, the super-ego must fulfil some highly important function
of value to compensate for its obvious disadvantages.

There can be little doubt that the sense of ' oughtness ' characteristic of the super-ego, the source of what later will be a moral
attitude, is derived from an earlier sense of ' mustness.' Put in other
words, the super-ego's threat to the ego, ' You ought not to do that
and I will punish you if you do,' is a replacement of an earlier:
' You must not do that, for it is harmful (or dangerous).' How is this
transformation effected from fear into the earliest traces of morality,
and what is the nature of the fear in question ? The earliest fears of
the child are on the material rather than the spiritual plane: they
are fears of damage to its interests (privation, deprivation, bodily
injury, and so on). But in the first year of life, love—and the need
for love—begins to play an increasingly important part. This brings
with it a new possibility, the fear of losing love by offending or
injuring the loved and loving object—primarily the mother. And it
is this extension of its needs from the bodily to the spiritual plane
that effects the transformation from ' mustness ' to ' oughtness.'
To provoke the risk of castration is still a non-moral situation:
to run the risk of offending the mother and losing her love becomes
a ' wrong ' thing to do. And in time, as the relationship with the
parents becomes more complex, it becomes quite as important to
abstain from doing wrong things as to avoid doing dangerous ones.
Perhaps the most important region in which this takes place is that
of sphincter control, the earliest ' moral ' training of the infant and
one which takes place long before, according to Freud, the Œdipus
complex is in action, or at all events when it is only in the stage of
inception. Ferenczi, with the intuition of genius, spoke of ' sphincter

morality,' sensing that here was to be found the dawn of moral attitudes. But he had little comprehension of the rich meanings the infant can attach to its excretory activities. They are not simply physical needs, though they derive much of their compulsive nature from this fact, nor simply important components of the sexual instinct (urethral and anal erotism). They are also vehicles of aggressive and destructive impulses, and are still further connected with the cannibalistic incorporations of the parents that precede or accompany them. When to soil the bed signifies to defile, poison or destroy the mother, and at the same time to reveal that one has swallowed and killed the father, then one begins to understand in what weighty tones the nurse's 'moral' training can be conceived.

The super-ego may profitably be regarded both as a barrier against those forbidden and harmful impulses and also as an indirect vent for them. Traces of all the sexual components can be found in its activities even if they are—imperfectly—desexualised. The scopophilic impulse reveals itself in the alert watching and guarding attitude of the super-ego; and the anal-erotic component reactively in the need for orderliness and—most important—in the sense of duty; while the sadistic one is all too obvious in the cruel torturing the super-ego can inflict on the ego. The reaction to the more developed genital impulse is shown later in the moral condemnation of incest, but beside this is the more positive love towards the parental substitute (ego-ideal), etc.

We have now traced the super-ego back to a pre-moral stage, one which I have previously[1] termed a stage of pre-nefarious inhibition, where its main function would seem to be that of a simple barrier against the id impulses, or rather against the intolerable anxiety that these produce in the ego. At this point it becomes merely one defence among others, though one with a peculiar history. Its special features are due to its formation through introjection of parental objects. We may inquire further into the nature of the anxiety in question and of the danger arising from the id impulses. These are problems I have discussed at some length elsewhere, but I will summarise the main conclusions I have reached concerning them.

Whether there is a separate aggressive instinct in man or not, it is certain that the sexual one is, especially in its primordial stage, essentially aggressive in its nature, far more so than psycho-analysts

[1] *Op. cit.*

originally thought. So far as I can judge, there appears to be no satisfactory evidence of aggression occurring apart from some libidinal impulse which would seem to be always the starting-point. There is good reason to suppose that these aggressive components are felt by the infant to be in themselves harmful or dangerous, quite directly so and apart from any effects on either the infant or the loved object. The response to them is anxiety, and at first what may be called pre-ideational anxiety—*i.e.*, without any sense of the nature of the danger. It is we who have to construct from various clues what this danger is. We know that physiologically and psychologically the result of sustained tension from the absence of relief or gratification leads to exhaustion. Some parents take advantage of this knowledge to leave an angry baby alone ' to cry itself out,' in my opinion a very harmful procedure at that age. The dread of this total exhaustion of the libido I have termed the fear of aphanasis, and it is in my opinion the important starting-point of the anxiety against which the super-ego, as well as other defences, is instituted.

CHAPTER V

PSYCHO-ANALYSIS AND THE INSTINCTS [1]

I HAVE chosen the subject of instincts for this lecture because it is in many ways the most interesting as well as the most fundamental, and the most difficult, one in all psychology. Increased knowledge in this field would perhaps more than any other bring psychology into closer relation to cognate mental disciplines, those of physiology, biology, sociology and philosophy. It has for some time now been apparent that mental and physical processes are more likely to become correlated by investigating the instincts, and their emotional expressions, than by the method that appeared so hopeful in the nineteenth century, of studying what may be called the higher phenomena of the mind and cerebral cortex. The close connection between fear and anger, for instance, which has been established on psychological grounds, has been interestingly confirmed by Cannon and his pupils working on purely *physiological* lines. It is further evident that the study of the instincts, a field common to man and the lower animals, offers the most promising chance for getting psychology rightfully placed in the hierarchy of science, namely as one of the *biological* sciences. Then the same study brings us to the tremendous problem of evaluating the relative importance of inherited and acquired tendencies, a problem vital for all *sociological* aspects of psychology. Finally, any results obtained from this study should provide useful data for the most engrossing of *philosophical* speculations, that concerning the relation of body to mind. And this is perhaps the central human speculation of all, since the relationship between one's personality and the immediate body of ' matter ' through which it expresses itself signifies the ultimate problem of how that personality is related to the ' matter ' in question and how the human soul is related to the universe.

Unfortunately psychology has not yet furnished conclusions in any way commensurate in importance to the high aims I have just indicated. There is no sort of agreement among psychologists on whether instincts in the ordinary meaning of the word exist at all— some psychologists regarding their manifestations as being alto-

[1] An address delivered before the British Psychological Society, March 22, 1935. Published in the *British Journal of Psychology*, vol. xxvi.

gether due to acquired habits—or whether if instincts do exist one can say anything definite about their nature or even their number. The most scientific method of studying the matter might appear to be to begin with simple observation of the behaviour they lead to: to concentrate on the motor aspects of instinct. This method has proved very fruitful in the investigation of instinct life in animals, where indeed it is almost the only method available. With human beings, on the other hand, it has not been able to throw any light on the darkness. Its failure here is probably due to the extraordinary plasticity of human instincts. As is well known, the lower we go in the animal scale the more fixed and inevitable are instinctual reactions. Evolution into higher forms seems to be characteristically accompanied by a greater variability and choice of instinctual reaction, a change which has probably itself been an important factor in evolution. In man this variability has reached its highest point and is the biological basis for the general belief in freedom of the will. All this, however, enormously increases the difficulty of ascertaining what tendencies in man are truly primary and innate. Other psychologists have therefore endeavoured to study and classify instincts by introspective methods, particularly of the emotions that usually accompany them. McDougall's promising attempt in this direction led to a correlation of specific emotions with specific instincts, but it was based on too little actual investigation to be of much practical use. Still another line of approach is a combination of these two methods in which attention is concentrated on the apparent *aim* or goal of instincts as judged by the evidences of its direction. Roughly speaking, this is the attitude of most psychoanalysts. One has, of course, to be clear here to distinguish between the goal of an instinct as empirically observed and its purpose in any teleological sense. If one falls into the latter fallacy one will soon find oneself classifying instincts according to their biological value—for instance, their survival value in the Darwinian sense—their social, ethical or even theological value.

My object here is to describe some of the contributions psychoanalysis has made to this obscure problem, so I will come now to my proper theme. It is Freud himself, the pioneer of psychoanalysis, who has made by far the greater part of these contributions. My exposition, therefore, will essentially be of the development of his ideas. Let me begin with two great general considerations which will, by providing a background, help to explain that development.

In the first place, Freud did not, to begin with, regard the investigation of the instincts as his main task in life, which was the elucidation of particular mental phenomena that puzzled him and aroused his interest, notably those of neurotic suffering and of dream life. His study of the instincts was at first incidental to this task, though it gradually forced itself more and more on his notice. It is only of late years, since the War,[1] that it has occupied the forefront of his interest. Although in his earlier work he made innumerable detailed contributions to our knowledge of the ways in which various instincts, particularly the sexual one, manifest themselves, it was only after thirty years of intensive work that he ventured to theorise on the subject. His views, therefore, are not of a hasty or *a priori* nature, and it would surely be wise to attend carefully to the conclusions based on such an unrivalled psychological experience as he possesses. Another proof of his empiric approach is that he has always avoided the usual subjective habit of classifying a number of instincts and has preferred instead a very detailed investigation on the one hand and a very broad and general grouping on the other, wherever this was necessary for his immediate purpose. He displays here a happy combination of the inductive and deductive methods of approach.

In the second place, perhaps from the nature of his work on the neuroses, Freud has always been deeply impressed by the element of *conflict* in human life. We have only to gaze on the present-day world for five minutes, even without reflecting on the lessons of history, to perceive ample justification for this attitude, but Freud has followed this visible external conflict into profounder realms, into the very nature and structure of the mind itself. To him perhaps the most striking feature of the human mind is the incessant conflict within it, more especially in its deeper layers which he terms the 'unconscious.' He thus views life as essentially the expression of conflict not only between man and man, between nation and nation, but still more between one side of man's nature and another side at war with the first. The terms in which he has at various periods formulated the nature of this conflict represent his contribution to the theory of instinct. We can understand that, although his formulations have changed considerably as his ideas developed, his conception of the mind has remained throughout a dualistic one.

[1] Obviously meaning the first World War. *Passim.*

For the first fifteen or twenty years of his researches Freud contented himself with a very simple and broad grouping of instinctual manifestations. Adopting the poet Schiller's well-known antithesis between hunger and love, he divided mental impulses into two groups according as they appeared to promote the preservation of the individual or of the species respectively, a division which has an obvious biological basis. The words he used for the two groups were the ego instincts and the sexual instincts respectively. He expressly admitted that ' the hypothesis of separate ego instincts and sexual instincts rests scarcely at all upon a psychological basis, but is essentially supported upon the facts of biology.' He regarded it purely as a working hypothesis, something with which to start in the task of sorting his observations. He discovered that neurotic suffering proceeded from an unsolved conflict between these two sets, between unrepressed ego instincts and repressed sexual ones, and further researches have amply confirmed the truth of this conclusion. For some years his interest was occupied in the investigation of the various sexual impulses, especially the repressed, unconscious ones, which were at that time little understood. His conclusions on the forms of infantile sexuality, indeed the very existence of this, were for long bitterly opposed, but now have been widely accepted and extended by later workers, by Abraham, Ferenczi, myself and others.

The first time Freud wrote anything about the nature of instincts was in an essay entitled ' Instincts and Their Vicissitudes.' There he established a useful distinction between the *aim* of an instinct, its goal of satisfaction, and the *object* of an instinct, that by means of which it achieves this goal—whether animate or inanimate, the person's own body or someone else's. The source of an instinct is invariably a bodily stimulus, and Freud surmises that each psychological manifestation is accompanied by a physiological one, presumably of a chemical nature. His conception of instinct is therefore in no sense exclusively psychological—rather psychophysiological. He further supposes that the difference in the mental effects produced by different instincts may be traced to the difference in their bodily sources. With the sexual instinct he was able to show this in detail, not merely by defining the sites of the various bodily sources—which he termed erotogenic zones—from which the individual components of that instinct proceed, but also by tracing in a minute particular the contribution each of these components makes to mental activity and especially to character formation. One of the most surprising discoveries in psycho-analysis was that the way in which an infant sucks, or the amount of interest it devotes to one bodily function in preference to another, can profoundly influence that individual's later mental development, even including his temperamental outlook on life (whether optimistic or pessimistic).

The sexual instinct is not at first a unit. It consists of various components, emanating from manifold organic sources. These components at first function quite independently of one another, each as it were blindly seeking for organic pleasure and satisfaction, and it is only later that they combine in the function of reproduction. They at first begin in conjunction with the activity of ego instincts, for instance hunger, with which they have a common source, aim and object, and only gradually do they emancipate themselves from this association to achieve an existence of their own. An infant sucks in food before it sucks its thumb and long before it uses its lips for kissing.

In comparing instincts and their activities with external physical stimuli (and the complex reflex arcs related to them) Freud contrasts the two very neatly. The stimuli instinctual activity provides to the mind come of course from within the organism itself, and furthermore they are fairly constant in their action, not like the single impact or series of impacts that may enter the mind from without. For both these reasons the mind cannot deal with them in the same way as it can with external stimuli, for example by simple withdrawal. No effort of flight avails. It is impelled to influence the outer world in such a way as to force it to give some satisfaction to the instinct and thus allay its stimuli. When this is impossible in a direct fashion the mind has to devise various other means of dealing with the instinctual stimuli.

Of these devices the simplest is repression, setting a distance between the stimuli and the rest of the mind. It is akin to the primitive reaction of withdrawal or flight and is probably a derivative of this. A very important mechanism is that of reversing the direction of an instinct so that it turns towards the self instead of towards the outer world. Freud first described this in connection with certain sexual components, but we now know it plays an even greater rôle with the instinct of hostility. An impulse that derives from both these sources is that of sadism. This can be redirected towards the self, when pleasure is derived from subjugating and even hurting oneself. A later stage of this process is when an object is sought in the outer world who can be induced to inflict the pain and mastery, the person having then adopted what is called a masochistic attitude. The same example can be used to illustrate also a third mechanism, that of reversing the aim of an instinct, from active into passive or *vice versa*. Another example of it is that of the pleasure in gazing, which may change from the desire to look at into the desire to be looked at.

All these sexual component impulses are in a high degree plastic. They can not only interchange among themselves, but—unless a state of affairs known as 'fixation' is present—they can readily replace one object by another. More remarkable is the fact that they can in a sense change their own nature, inasmuch as they can achieve a considerable measure of satisfaction by non-sexual aims, a power familiar under the name of 'sublimation.' This capacity of the sexual instinct for displacement and interchange impressed Freud profoundly and inclined him to postulate a similar capacity on the part of other instincts and emotions. For instance, he speaks of love turning into hate, or *vice versa*, and by this he means a real transformation of one into the other, not a simple replacement of one by the other. This is a part of his theory that some of us find hard to follow, since it would appear to depart from a biological outlook. For long he also held the view that libido, the energy of the sexual instinct, when in a state of repression was converted into anxiety or dread. A quarter of a century ago I suggested as a more likely explanation of the findings on which this view was based that excitation of repressed libido simply stimulated the fear component of the ego instinct, and a few years ago Freud himself came round to this way of regarding the matter. It makes of course no difference to the important clinical observation that morbid anxiety, the essence of ordinary 'nervousness,' is always closely associated with repressed libido.

The second phase in the development of Freud's ideas on instinct dates from 1914, when he published a disturbing essay 'On Narcissism': I will explain in a moment why I use the word 'disturbing.' Self-love appears in its purest form in a sexual perversion Havelock Ellis was the first to describe by the name 'narcissistic,' referring to the well-known myth of the Greek youth who fell in love with himself. But it is easy to detect numerous other manifestations of the same tendency elsewhere. They are to be found in the megalomania of insanity, in the attention the hypochondriac devotes to his body, in various observations easily made on children, on the aged, on patients desperately ill, and even in the phenomena of normal love. Common to all these fields is a remarkable reciprocity between the love of self and the love of others, between what analysts term narcissism and object-libido respectively: when one increases the other diminishes, and *vice versa*. Freud supposed with good reason that the libido to begin with is all collected in the ego, that self-love is the beginning of all love. When it flows outwards we call it object-love, love for other objects than the self. That unfortunately it can flow back again, be once more withdrawn into the ego, is a familiar enough fact. In most marriages there are times later on when one partner reproaches the other that he (or she) does not love as much as formerly, that he (or she) has become ' selfish.' And, as hinted above, there are many typical situations in life, such as in disease, after an accident, in old age and so on, when the tendency to this withdrawal into self-preoccupation and self-love is apt to become pronounced.

Now the reason why I called Freud's essay on narcissism a disturbing one was that it gave a disagreeable jolt to the theory of instincts on which psycho-analysis had hitherto worked. The observations on which the new conception of narcissism was founded were so unmistakable and easily confirmed that we had to accept it unreservedly, but it was at once plain that something would have to be done about the theory to which we were accustomed. For if the ego itself was libidinally invested, then it looked as if we should have to reckon its most prominent feature, the self-preservative instinct, as a narcissistic part of the sexual instinct. Adverse critics of psycho-analysis had always overlooked one half of the unconscious conflicts to which Freud had called so much attention and had charged him, *tout court*, with ' reducing everything to sex,' with ' seeing nothing in the mind but sex.' They were, it is true, supported by the fact that at that time most of Freud's discoveries had been in the field of repressed sexual impulses and very little in the other half of the mind. But he could easily rejoin that his main point was the fact of a conflict between sexual and non-sexual impulses, a ' fifty-fifty ' view of the mind. Now, however, that the ego itself was to be regarded as libidinal, were not the critics right from the start when they denounced Freud's tendency to ' reduce everything to sex ' ? And what had become of his famous conflict ? It is true that the psychoneuroses, his proper field of study, could still be described in terms of conflict, namely that between narcissistic and object-libido. But did this mean that the only conflict was that between one form of sexual instinct and another form, that there was no other source of conflict in the mind ? These and similar questions were thronging our minds just as the Great War broke out, and Freud was not able to give any answer to them until after its termination.

Actually the case was not so serious as I have just portrayed, and the fallacy in my presentation of it is doubtless plain. To say there is reason to suppose that the ego is strongly invested with libido is clearly not the same thing as saying it is composed of nothing else. Various other possibilities remained open. And the critics were quite wrong in asserting that Freud was aiming at a monistic libidinal conception of the mind. On the contrary, he was as obstinately dualistic as ever. But he was hard put to it to demonstrate one side of the conflict, to define any non-narcissistic components of the ego. His scientific career had received an apparent check, by no means for the first time.

The difficulty I have just described only stimulated Freud to further research, and the next point of attack was indicated by the nature of the case. The ground for exploring the conflict between instincts, and thus ascertaining the nature of the latter, had been extensively cleared by the detailed work on one side of the conflict, the sexual one. What about the other side, where so little had been learned ? Clinical psycho-analysis had been so busy in passing by this side in order to reach the repressed sexual impulses that it had largely regarded it simply as an obstacle to its work and had usually designated it as a ' resistance.' Now was the time to examine these resistances more closely. Freud had rather casually described them as moral and æsthetic attitudes which were opposed to the coarseness of sexuality, but it was now necessary to define them more nearly and to learn something about their sources.

Curiously enough, again one of the first things to be discovered about these moral and æsthetic attitudes was their libidinal component, naturally a narcissistic one. Freud in tracing the evolution of narcissistic libido found that the primitive self-love could turn either into object-love or into a form of love still attached to the ego, but nevertheless very different from simple self-love. That is, it became directed to what he called the ego-ideal, not the self as it is, but the self as the person would like it to be. There we meet the moral and æsthetic attitudes in question. For when we ask why the person should love a picture of himself as he would like to be, and not what he is, we soon observe that his picture is an improvement on the actuality just in its moral and æsthetic respects. Really the ego-ideal is much the same as the familiar conscience, or at least it represents an important aspect of this. Further, if the genesis of this picture of the ideal self is studied psycho-analytically it is not hard to perceive its source in the child's attitude towards its parents. Just as the child both fears and loves his parents, so does he develop a mingled attitude of fear and love towards their exhortations and prohibitions, to the ideal behaviour they set before him. And just as the standards they inculcate commonly transcend those they display in their own lives, so does the child's ideal ego transcend in loftiness the picture of his actual parents. So much is this so that when certain conditions are present he will later find it necessary to associate his idealistic attitude with more perfect figures than his parents, with historical heroes, with saints, or with the most perfect figures of all—the Divine ones.

A more important step was made when Freud discovered that many resistances, and indeed the strongest ones, were unconscious. This compelled him to revise the simple antithesis between consciousness and the unconscious as representing the contrast between the ego and the repressed, for now he had to recognise that an important part of the ego itself was unconscious. What concerns us here, however, is that the ego-ideal is also prolonged as it were into the unconscious, if I may use such a topographical analogy. More interesting is the fact that the unconscious part of the ego-ideal, what Freud calls the super-ego, differs markedly from the conscious part. The love component, so evident with the more conscious ego-ideal, is with the unconscious super-ego quite subordinate to fear and severity. The detailed structure of the super-ego, when considered genetically, is in many respects obscure and hard to unravel. There is little doubt, however, that it is brought into being essentially to aid the ego in its dread of the primitive (repressed) impulses directed towards the parents. The parents' prohibitions are internalised, forming thus the first signs of the future conscience, and these are applied to the ego just as those were. It is like an inner voice saying, ' Check those forbidden impulses, else I shall punish you severely.' The punishments in question are precisely those feared from the parents, whether the latter have ever actually threatened

them or not. The super-ego is therefore in large part the incorpora-
tion of the idea of stern parents.

In the present connection the most important feature of the
super-ego is its extraordinary severity and even savagery. So great
is this that the ego's early fear of the primitive impulses is often
replaced by fear of the stern super-ego, of just that institution
originally built up to guard the ego from fear. It was soon perceived,
particularly by London analysts, that the severity of the super-ego
could only in part be derived from the parental attitude towards the
child. It far transcends that in savagery and very obviously so when
the parents are in fact lenient and mild. The savage attitudes could
therefore only be derived from something in the child himself,
being subsequently projected on to an imaginary picture of the
parents and then once more incorporated within.

Detailed analytic studies, strikingly confirmed by those carried out
on young children by Melanie Klein and others, have thrown a great
deal of light on the sources of this severity and have led to the
conception of a primitive *aggressive instinct*, non-sexual in character.
So here at last is something that could be contrasted with the
sexual side of the mental conflicts. Before considering it further,
however, we shall have to retrace our steps.

Freud published his illuminating concept of the super-ego in a
book that appeared in 1923.[1] But, strangely enough, it was not by
this conception and the studies I have just outlined that he arrived
at his present view of the duality of mental structure. Three years
earlier, in a book entitled 'Beyond the Pleasure Principle,' he
offered a very unexpected solution of the dilemma he had produced
in 1914. This solution he reached by a train of very abstract theo-
rising of which I will try to present the gist. He had been trying to
see whether all mental processes were subject to the great pleasure-
pain principle, and further what was the essential purpose and
function of this principle. The first question he answered in the
negative. Certain observations, particularly of dream life, of
children's play and of patients' behaviour during analysis, led him
to postulate another regulating principle besides the familiar
pleasure-pain one, and one more archaic than it. He called the older
principle the *repetition-compulsion*, the blind impulse to repeat earlier
experiences and situations quite irrespective of any advantage that
doing so might bring from a pleasure-pain point of view. As to the

[1] 'The Ego and the Id.'

function of the pleasure-pain principle he discerned this in its tendency to reduce psychic tension or at least to maintain it at as constant a level as possible.

The point common to both these principles is their conservative nature. Both resist interference with a pre-existing state of affairs, and try to minimise or undo the effect of disturbing stimuli. The pleasure-pain principle tries to lower the tension set up by such stimuli, whereas the repetition-compulsion simply tries to restore the previous condition. But, as we shall see in a moment, the two principles are concerned with different sets of stimuli. At this point it occurred to Freud that he had hit on an essential characteristic of our instinctual life. It will be remembered how he described the action of instincts as internal stimulation and contrasted it with that of external stimulation. His new idea now was that it is the instincts themselves that are responsible for the compulsion to repeat, that the essential character of instincts is their conservative, or rather their regressive, nature, the function they fulfil in reinstating earlier conditions. He illustrated this character by the migration of salmon and other fish—the same is true of birds—which we can account for only by assuming that they repeat archaic situations, even those that may be no longer favourable. He suggested that what called instincts first into being was violent stimulation from without, the effect of which was later internalised. Instincts are there to counter these stimuli, to undo the effect of them, and to take the organism back to as near its original state as is possible. If future biological research confirm this hypothesis of regression it will surely prove to be a fundamental addition to our knowledge of the nature and significance of the instincts. The pleasure-pain principle acts at a higher level, at a later stage, being concerned largely with the stimuli afforded by the action of instincts, which it tries to regulate in a way that will most easily provide satisfaction. Thus the older principle is concerned with damping external stimuli, and the later principle with damping the internal stimuli of the former.

Freud has the rare quality of being both a careful and a daring thinker. In the present instance the latter quality was expressed in a most striking fashion. For he did not hesitate to push his hypothesis to the last possible conclusion. He argued that if the aim of instincts is to revert to an earlier state, then there must be a tendency to revert to the earliest state of all, namely to inanimate existence. Thus death is not an unfortunate accident. Life itself inherently leads to death, is actually aiming at bringing about death, even if by a circuitous and complicated path. The aim of life is peace, in the final resort the peace that disintegration of the organic into the inorganic provides. Katabolism has the last word over anabolism.

At first Freud discussed whether this sweeping conclusion could be true of all instincts, but he decided it could not be so of the reproductive instincts, whose aim is, by reverting to the beginnings of life, to start life over afresh. At all events if it were true of these instincts it could hardly be in the same sense, for if their aim is death it is by such an ever-distant route that the term cannot fairly be applied to them in any individual context.

Let us consider a little more closely the reproductive instinct in this connection. That it constantly brings about an earlier form of existence, by creating a fertilised cell from which life starts afresh, is perhaps a more evident feature of this instinct than of any other. But it accomplishes it in a peculiar fashion, by bringing about the fusion of two simple cells in the act of conjugation. And this impulse to unite flesh is surely the most salient attribute of all sexual activities; union is its goal above all else. From this point of view Freud felt himself justified in bringing together the re-creative function of the sexual instinct, its tendency to start ever afresh, with its function of uniting and binding together. He therefore identified the libido, a purely clinical term, with the Eros of the poets and philosophers, the principle that creates, binds together, and sustains all life. He even extended this view of the libido to the rest of the body, making the suggestion—in support of which there is actually much clinical evidence—that every cell in the body has a libidinal charge which plays an important part in its life history.

The outcome of this train of thought was that Freud's final duality was the division of the mind into two sets of instincts which he termed life instincts and death instincts respectively—or, if one prefers Greek names, Eros and Thanatos. For the sake of clearness I will repeat in a sentence the three stages in the development of Freud's ideas concerning the duality of instincts. The first was the contrast between sexual and ego instincts; the second the contrast between object-love, or allo-erotic libido, and self-love, narcissistic libido; and the third is the contrast between life and death instincts, between Eros and Thanatos.

So far, so good, but Freud's next difficulty was this. How precisely was one to allocate the innumerable manifestations of mental life to one or the other of these instincts? Eros was visible and audible enough; as Freud put it, from him proceeds the clamour of life. But what familiar mental manifestation can be recognised as proceeding directly from Thanatos? Freud was at first very much at a loss to answer this simple question. He was inclined, to begin with, to regard the voice of Thanatos as mute, to hold that the death instinct was an immanent principle or force working its will inexorably but nevertheless invisibly. If this were the answer it would, even if true, not be very illuminating, nor could one imagine its having much practical bearing in psychology.

It was at this rather critical juncture that it occurred to Freud to bring together the two lines of work I have just outlined: the purely theoretical one leading to the conception of an immanent death instinct, and the detailed analytic studies of the super-ego with its revelation of a terrifyingly formidable instinct of aggression. How if these two should prove to be the same, that this very visible aggressive instinct be the directing against the outer world of the death instinct that had originally been concerned with destruction of the individual? The turning of the instinct from an inward to an outward direction presents no difficulty, since we are quite familiar with a similar change of direction in a closely allied instinct; I refer to the change from auto-sadism to masochism which I mentioned earlier. And we can quote a similar change in connection with death wishes themselves. It is well established that suicide is the result of murder wishes that have been directed from the objects of them in the outer world and have been turned inward against the self.

I have now stated the theory of instincts that Freud at present holds and would remind you that it is composed of three elements: two premises and an inference. The premises are the existence of a positive tendency towards self-destruction and of an outwardly directed aggressive impulse; the inference is that these two are identical. If biological research should confirm Freud's conclusion it would brilliantly vindicate his imaginative reasoning, and his theory would represent a fundamental progress in our knowledge of instincts. In a somewhat similar case he has already been proved right: when he maintained that the visible resistances patients display against the uncovering of the unconscious are identical with the invisible internal repressions of the unconscious. There is, it is true, this difference: that here he inferred the invisible from the visible, whereas with the death instinct he started with the invisible and then applied it to the visible. The reasoning is more daring in the latter case and will therefore represent a greater achievement if it is borne out.

Much remains, however, before this can be done. The theory, possibly because of its abstruseness, has not received much attention outside the circle of psycho-analysts, and within this circle it has had a mixed reception. A certain amount of adverse criticism has already been devoted to it, and with those analysts who have completely accepted it one is not sure how much of their attitude has not been dictated by the prestige of the author. A respectful hearing is one thing: an uncritical acceptance is another. The theory is certainly not as yet to be regarded as an integral part of psycho-analysis, since it represents a personal train of thought rather than a direct inference from verifiable data. Freud himself first presented the theory in a highly tentative fashion, remarking that he found it hard to say how definitely he believed it himself, but that it was a train of thought that took his fancy. Since then he has incorporated it more resolutely into his general conception of the human mind, although in speaking recently of the death instinct he admits that ' the assumption of its existence is based essentially on theoretical grounds.'

Of the three stages in the theory it is the first one, concerning the innate tendency towards death, that is least securely established, simply because it is so hard to test it directly. Startling as it is, there is a good deal in current thought in harmony with it, and a very similar hypothesis has been put forward by a distinguished biologist, Ehrenberg. Through the recent popularising of cosmic physics the second law of thermodynamics, with its sinister implications, has become a piece of fairly familiar general knowledge, and attempts have been made to derive from it the stability principle of Spencer, Fechner and Petzhold. In its modern form this principle is known as the law of entropy, and the first question that arises is whether the regulating of psychological tension which Freud perceives as the function of the pleasure-pain principle can be brought into relation with the entropy law of physics.

Several psycho-analysts have published critical examinations of Freud's theory, the most closely reasoned being one by Bernfeld and Feitelberg.[1] These authors see no reason for answering in the

---

[1] Bernfeld and Feitelberg, ' Der Entropiesatz und der Todestrieb,' *Imago*, 1930, Bd. xvi., S. 187.

negative the question I just put—they designate it as ' thinkable '—but they distinguish between this conclusion of Freud's about the pleasure-pain principle and his further speculation of an innate and active tendency to death which he derived from it. This latter may or may not be what the pleasure-pain principle subserves—there appears to be no evidence either way—but no form of conflict between any two tendencies, such as Eros and Thanatos, can be assumed in terms of the law of entropy; as our authors put it: ' In the biological-physical conception of a tendency to death ' (for which they would reserve the name ' Nirvana principle ') ' there is no room for Eros.' The conclusions they reach from their searching examination do not support Freud's. For, whereas they find no contradiction between his view of the pleasure-pain principle and the principles of physics, they find nothing to support the Nirvana principle he associates with these, and definitely consider that the conflict he postulates has no connection with the fundamental principles of physics. This, therefore, must stand on its own feet, and must be considered purely in terms of vital phenomena, psychologically or biologically. Whether there is a positive tendency to self-destruction, kept at bay by the life instincts, or whether, as is more generally assumed, the life instincts have only a certain power of keeping going the complicated process of retaining matter in a ' living ' organic form and sooner or later become exhausted, is a problem on which we may reasonably hope to get light from biological and physiological research. In the meantime it would seem premature to express in psychological language a biological principle or tendency that has not been demonstrated in the physiological sphere.

Such premature biologising of psychology is all the more to be deprecated in the present case because of the confusion it so readily engenders. Freud himself is well aware of the speculative nature of his train of thought and distinguishes pretty carefully between this philosophical basis and any possible clinical application of it. Many of his followers, however, misled by the confusion of words, think they are talking of the Nirvana principle of entropy when they are merely referring to the familiar clinical observation of death wishes, directed either against others or against the self. This is a totally different matter, and the gulf between the two has yet to be bridged. To pass from any possible Nirvana or Thanatos principle of biology, correlated with the law of entropy, a silent principle tending towards

absolute peace, from this to the stormy aggressiveness that so
disturbs mental life, is to pass from one world to quite another;
and to identify the two opposites as one is a feat that few could
genuinely encompass.

This leads me finally to the problem of the so-called aggressive
instincts we postulate from a variety of phenomena to which
according to circumstances such words as pugnacity, cruelty, hate,
hostility, destructiveness, animosity, death wishes, etc., can be
applied. How to designate the essence of what is meant here is not
obvious to begin with. The term ' aggressive ' (literally: to advance
towards) commonly means to attack, but it need not imply hatred or
even animosity. In America, for instance, an energetic shop assistant
is called an aggressive salesman, and such a peace-loving body as
the Home Counties Union of Women's Liberal Associations uses
as its telegraphic address the stimulating word ' aggressive.' And
I well remember the criticism psycho-analysts made long ago when
Adler first put forward the idea of a distinct aggressive instinct.
They pointed out that aggressiveness was a generic attribute of all
instincts in activity and so could hardly be a sign of any special
one.

It is hard to say whether the goal of what we call an aggressive
instinct is purely the annihilation of the object towards which it is
directed. For, on the other hand, we perceive this goal at times in
erotic activities, such as, for example, in certain stages of oral
erotism; while on the other hand a person, so far from wishing
annihilation, may feel a lasting bond between himself and a hated
enemy, a curious fact often described in literature. However this
may be, the facts to which the term relates are gruesome enough.
We know from the psycho-analysis of adults, and still more fully
from Melanie Klein's analyses of young children, that antagonistic
phantasies of biting, tearing and destroying other people, primarily
the parents, play a part in the unconscious that is hard to overestimate. Current fashions in anthropology have often been felt
to be in opposition—in my opinion unnecessarily so—with the
doctrines of psycho-analysis, but here the difference of opinion is
unmistakable. For many modern anthropologists teach that man
was originally a peaceful animal on whom a liking for war and
destruction descended within historical times. Psycho-analytic
experience decisively contradicts this complacent view. It teaches
that the aggressiveness which makes the world such an unruly and

alarming abode belongs to the deepest elements in man's nature, and they point to the simple fact, familiar to every nursemaid, that for the first month of its existence the infant responds to life with hate far more readily than with love.

Nevertheless the nosological status of this instinct is by no means clear. Freud holds that ' the tendency to aggression is an innate, independent, instinctual disposition in man,' and if the accent is here laid on the word ' tendency ' no analyst could doubt the statement, since nothing could appear in fact unless there were a tendency to it. More difficult is the question whether such a tendency ever expresses itself spontaneously and in a pure form. That is to say, would anyone, child or adult, ever make an attack with the intent to injure and destroy unless the impulse was either associated with an erotic one, as it constantly is in sadism, or was a reaction to some thwarting or privation that he finds unendurable? These other associations are extraordinarily frequent. Thwarting, whether external or internal, is a state of affairs present from the cradle to the grave, and it always provokes a tendency—whether resisted or not—to violent opposition. The capacity to bear privation with any sort of internal equanimity is seldom developed in any high degree, and aggressive insistence on getting what one wants becomes a magic compulsion, though of course the corresponding impulse may in turn be inhibited or replaced by a reaction formation. Again, the erotising of aggressive impulses is a remarkable general process which accounts for much of the complexity of life. For these reasons it is extraordinarily difficult to detect spontaneous activity of the aggressive instinct in isolation, and I do not myself know of any unequivocal example.

To sum up what I have said about Freud's latest theory. It is characteristic of him to move well ahead of his generation. Sometimes we are able, so to speak, to catch up with him and check his conclusions ourselves: at other times not. The present instance may not be one where his daring imagination has led him to leave firm ground and tread where other investigators cannot follow him. Only more knowledge can decide that. One thing is certain: if a more trustworthy route could be indicated in these obscurities he would be the first to deflect his steps thither; fixity and dogmatism are alien to his nature. In the meantime the purely psychological part of his latest theory may be regarded as assured, that our life consists of nothing but a struggle between love and hate.

CHAPTER VI

PSYCHO-ANALYSIS AND COMPARATIVE PHYSIOLOGY[1]

PSYCHO-ANALYSIS is the department of psychology which offers the best prospect of effecting a liaison with biology, including physiology, since the main direction of its work lies in the unravelling of complex mental processes and in the tracing of their genesis to a small number of primitive impulses which man shares with other animals. The deep prejudice man has against recognising his kinship with the animal world was only partly overcome by the acceptance of the theory of evolution. Actually a compromise was reached, it being grudgingly agreed that man's body may have been derived from non-human origins provided that the same need not hold good for his mind. Here a claim was still asserted for a true uniqueness, and for an independent creation. The findings of psycho-analysis, if taken seriously, are making it increasingly difficult to sustain this belief, and are carrying the theory of evolution through to its logical conclusion by treating both mind and body from a genetic point of view.

We apply the Latin neutral and impersonal term ' id ' to that earliest and deepest layer of the mind that precedes any sense of individual self. The ego or self then slowly develops by the fusion of ' ego nuclei ' which are in connection with various parts of the body, first the mouth and anus, later the hands, eyes, genital organs, and so on.

In spite of this we are unfortunately still far from the desirable state of being able to define the primitive mental elements that would enable us to make a start on the obscure problems of mental heredity in the way open in the fields where physical genes can be isolated. The old term ' instinct,' however much it may be criticised, stands for something real which is still in need of definition. Freud postulated two broad groups of immanent tendencies, one regressing towards simple states and ultimately towards the inorganic—i.e., death—and the other those striving to postpone this goal and even

---

[1] Contribution to the Symposium on the Limitations and Uses of the Comparative Method in Medicine, *Proceedings of the Royal Society of Medicine*, September, 1944, vol. xxxvi., p. 651 (Section of Comparative Medicine, p. 19).

to renew life at its starting-point. Although a similar idea had been put forth previously by biologists as well as by philosophers, we have not yet received an adequate criticism of it from those sides. An allied conception of his is that instincts are essentially conservative in nature in that their aim is to reinstate as far as possible some earlier state of affairs which has had to be abandoned through external pressure or other change in the environment. The periodic breeding migrations of salmon or eels furnish perhaps the most obvious example of this, but Freud thinks that the same principle underlies all instinctual action. It was indeed this conclusion that led him to postulate the tendency to reversion to the earliest state of all, namely lifelessness.

Freud was probably stimulated in this train of thought by his familiarity with a similar, though not identical, tendency that pervades all mental life and plays a very prominent part in psycho-pathological conditions—namely, the tendency to ' regress,' to revert to earlier stages in ontogenetic, and possibly also phylogenetic, development. It is likely that future study of the exact nature of this mental tendency will enable it to be linked up with similar ones in the physiological field and perhaps throw more light on the phenomena of atavism.

Apart from theoretical considerations, however, psycho-analysis can present many concrete studies in the field of instinct that should be of significance to the comparative physiologist. In the epochal struggle between the two principles of, on the one hand, massive fertility combined with an enormous mortality in offspring (as, for instance, with fishes) and the opposite one of a lower mortality combined with greater parental care and often an associated delay in individual development, the latter principle would have seemed to be winning the day were it not for the impressive recrudescence of unicellular organisms and their pathological attacks on larger creatures. It has long been recognised that the human species was the supreme example of this second principle, which indeed may now be in the course of being carried to a dangerous extreme through the inordinate postponement of reproduction leading to a critical infertility.

In the mental field what is called the pleasure-pain principle—the search for pleasure and the avoidance of pain—is, if not all-embracing, of much more comprehensive scope than psychologists used to think. Freud has linked it with the Fechner stability principle of maintaining tension within certain definite limits, and Wilbur has recently correlated it with the more modern biological conception of 'steady states.' Some years ago Ferenczi published a stimulating, though unequal, work in which he proposed to extend these conclusions from the mental field to the physical, and to found a new department of knowledge which he termed 'Bioanalysis.' The point that concerns us here is whether the functioning of individual organs and cells is determined solely by criteria of biological advantage, as is generally assumed, or whether this has to contend with physical tendencies comparable to the pleasure-pain ones of the mental field. Brun and other biologists have produced evidence, chiefly among insects, which strongly supports the latter suggestion by citing extreme cases where organic search for pleasurable sensations has even overwhelmed other tendencies with most deleterious, or even fatal, results to the species concerned. It is a thought that, even on the practical plane, is well worthy of consideration by those whose work is concerned with animal life.

CHAPTER VII

PSYCHOLOGY AND WAR CONDITIONS [1]

I AM exceedingly sensible of the high honour you have done me by inviting me to address you on this auspicious occasion, the centenary of the oldest medical association in the United States. At the outset allow me to make a confession. Although I held a chair in psychiatry on this continent before the last World War, I was never a member of the American Psychiatric Association. This entirely unimportant personal reference is chosen to illustrate a theme of considerable significance—namely, the passage of medical psychology from neurology over to psychiatry. Medical psychology, which happens to have been my special field of work—and by medical psychology I chiefly mean psycho-analysis, because there does not seem to be much medical psychology nowadays outside of psycho-analysis and its imitations—was to begin with more nearly related to neurology than to psychiatry; the pioneering names in it, from Charcot to Freud, and in this country from Weir Mitchell to Morton Prince and J. J. Putnam, are most often those of neurologists. The illusion that medical psychology is essentially an adjunct of neurology was no doubt further fostered by the unfortunate play on-words in the phrase ' nervous disorders ' which encouraged patients to consult physicians whose business it was to know about ' nerves ' in preference to those who might well suspect them of being of unsound mind, thus confirming their own dread. In days when I had to arrange the annual meetings of the American Psycho-analytic and the American Psychopathological Associations, bodies in the founding of which I had the honour of playing a prominent part, I used to see to it that they took place in immediate conjunction with those of the American Neurological Association, of which, by the way, I was proud to be a member. Such an arrangement would, I imagine, seem strange or even unnatural nowadays, and in my opinion rightly so.

Soon after the last war medical psychology in this country, led

[1] An address delivered before the Joint Session of the American Psycho-Analytic Association and the American Psychiatric Association at Philadelphia, May 15, 1944, on the occasion of the Centenary Celebration of the latter Association. Published in the *Psycho-Analytic Quarterly*, vol. xiv.

particularly by Dr. Brill, began to move more and more definitely towards the general body of psychiatry, helping thus to restore to the latter term its original signification of 'mental healing.' For certain reasons this movement approaching coalescence between the two disciplines has proceeded far more rapidly and extensively here than in Europe, where it is only now beginning. In America, for instance, it is obligatory for all psycho-analysts to have had a serious psychiatric training, while in England certainly fewer than ten per cent. have had such training. In Europe, and notably in England, medical psychology in so far as it has extended beyond its own circle has done so in the direction of normal psychology, education, literature, and among the general intelligentsia. Both these movements, the American and the European, are surely laudable and indeed inevitable, since medical psychology in its study of psychoneurotics occupies a position of great strategic importance between the so-called normal and the insane. We know now that these three classes of people have had to cope with the same primordial conflicts, though they have reacted to them in different ways. But it does not seem to be so generally recognised that the psychoneurotic reaction is the simplest and most perspicuous of the three, so that the investigation of the more complex and involved reactions of both the 'normal' and the insane is much more difficult. All the same it is more desirable for the medical psychology to extend in both directions equally rather than preponderantly in one of them, as has on the whole happened in both America and Europe. It should be added that in the past five or ten years there are pronounced signs that we in England are at last following our American colleagues in effecting a wider collaboration between medical psychologists and other psychiatrists, and I am persuaded that this is likely to develop more extensively in the near future.

In an address delivered a few years ago at the opening of the Columbia Institute of Psychiatry[1]—on one of my periodical weekend visits to this continent—I commented at some length on the remarkable status that psychiatry in the United States has attained among the general community, one which is surely unique in the world. Although, no doubt, you yourselves would be very far from satisfied with its status and can see all sorts of ways in which it might and will be improved, nevertheless it has already got much further

---

[1] Jones, Ernest, 'Psychoanalysis and Psychiatry,' *Mental Hygiene*, xiv, 1930. See Chapter XIX.

than in any other country. I am referring here not simply to its own high scientific standards, which are generally recognised abroad, but to the terms it is on with society, the freedom and ease with which psychiatrists are consulted, and the natural way in which they are accepted as a necessary and regular department of general medicine instead of being an isolated caste to be shunned except in the direst contingencies.

Now all this brings with it that American psychiatry, from its inner level, its outer standing, and—last but not least—the extent to which it has been permeated by the doctrines of medical psychology, should be in a specially favourable position for coping with the innumerable problems with which war conditions present it, both the strictly professional ones entrusted to its charge and also the wider, more serious ones where its advice and influence could be of incalculable benefit. To compass this task with honour, it is true, technical and intellectual knowledge will have to be accompanied by a corresponding degree of psychological insight. It is only too easy to be complacent about the fulfilment of this essential condition and not anxious enough lest success in superficial extensity be purchased at the expense of depth.

I wish to consider first the important matter of military psychiatry, and have here to acknowledge my indebtedness to the British Directorate of Army Psychiatry who have generously assisted me with all the information available to them. You will remember that the status of American military psychiatry at the end of the last war was higher than that of any other country, though I understand its activity flagged somewhat in the interval between the two wars. Already in the twenties it seems to have been overtaken by that of Germany, which established in 1929 a special department in the Army entitled Military Psychology. A comprehensive study of this was published in America in 1941, with a bibliography of some 561 German writings on the subject.[1] Very little was done in Britain until the present war was some two years under way. We have a scurrilous saying among us that our War Office begins every war on the basis of the war before last, a saying which, like the rumour of Mark Twain's death, is much exaggerated; but one did, it is true, hear stories of how various authorities were determined to purge the Army of the psychological nonsense that had crept in during the last World War and to put all psychiatric illnesses on a proper basis

[1] 'German Psychological Warfare.' Published by the Committee for National Morale.

of organic neurology as they had been in the good old days of the Boer War. However this may be, there is little doubt—and it was to be expected—that progress in psychiatry had considerable opposition and prejudice to overcome, a trouble which I understand American military psychiatry has also not been entirely spared. One may lay down as an axiom that the better quality a given psychiatric activity displays, and the nearer to the truth are the premises on which it works, the surer it is of encountering irrational opposition. We know that this proceeds from the general dread of mental depths, from aversion to psychological insight, and that it is strongest among those whose mental integrity, often of a very successful order, has been built on defences against those depths. It is therefore to be expected especially in the apparently stable personalities of those who have achieved prominence, political or otherwise, in life.

Military psychiatry in the British Army, when it got going, proved to be particularly enlightened and modern in its outlook. That is to say, it has been extensively influenced by psycho-analytic researches, though for obvious reasons of prudence this taboo word is replaced by the more innocuous term of ' depth psychology.' Every effort is made to express its conclusions in simple everyday language, as being ' obvious commonsense.' Those who accept its conclusions possess psychological insight, often without being conscious of this as such, and perhaps they do not always realise that an accepted truth is generally obvious, however painful the approach to it may still be to others. How irrational the prejudice against modern psychiatry may be is illustrated by the common happening of two opposite arguments being used against it at the same time. On the one hand, when it presented any novel set of considerations to the medical profession, thus broadening the field open to the latter, it would be accused of deserting the sphere of medicine and losing contact with its exponents. When, on the other hand, it came particularly close to any branch of medicine and demonstrated the significance of psychological factors in that branch, it was accused of trying to capture it and displace its lawful owners. Actually the liaison work between the psychiatrists in the Army and both the staff and regimental medical officers is on the whole very satisfactory. Forty years of dynamic psychology have undoubtedly left their mark on the medical profession, and the out and out scoffers are in a diminishing minority. In the Army the medical officers cannot escape seeing the visible results of psychiatric ' commonsense ' on the all-important matters of man power and morale, and are therefore co-operating with psychiatrists to a very gratifying extent. The personal impression I have, from very many sources, of British military psychiatry, both as to its high standards of technical efficiency and the active spirit of helpful good-will pervading it, is a very pleasing one.

The weakest point in our psychiatric organisation would seem to be its numbers. There is in Britain nothing like the number of trained psychiatrists there is in the United States. It is true your Army is much larger than ours, but even so you are probably in a better position to equip it with competent psychiatrists than we are. Apart from India, where we have sent a considerable number to help with the great new armies that are being raised there, I doubt if the British Army, at home and abroad, possesses much more than a couple of hundred psychiatrists, and we could well do with ten times that number. Two simple considerations support this conclusion. When battle psychiatric patients can be treated in the first few days of the breakdown some fifty per cent. can be swiftly returned to duty, while the prognosis among cases that have lasted for a couple of weeks is, especially from a military point of view, a serious one. Yet if one psychiatrist is allotted to forty or fifty thousand men in the field it is evident that very few cases can obtain the necessary treatment in the vital early period on which the prognosis greatly depends. Naturally everything is done to instruct regimental medical officers in elementary therapeutic measures, but during fighting they generally have more than enough of other medical and surgical duties to occupy them fully. Then the fact that fifteen per cent. of all battle casualties and one-third of all discharges from the Army are due to psychiatric illnesses shows the immense size of the problem, which can only increase with time.

I will now review the various activities of our psychiatrists, though this can only be a condensed account, and some of the most interesting data must be suppressed for reasons of military discretion; a fuller account of some aspects has been published in the medical press by Brigadier Rees.[1]

1. *Officers' Selection Board:* The most highly developed, though perhaps not necessarily the most important in the long run, of these activities is in connection with the Selection Boards that examine

[1] Rees, J. R., 'Three Years of Military Psychiatry in the United Kingdom,' *Brit. Med. Journal*, January 2, 1943.

candidates for a commission. Every candidate comes before a Board consisting of a military President, three combatant Testing Officers, two Psychiatrists, two Sergeant Testers, and, where possible, a Psychologist. The Psychologist is here subordinate to the Psychiatrist and refers his findings to him. As you must have found here also in America, there are two kinds of professional psychologists: those we call academic ones, trained in laboratory technique, and those we call clinical, who have taken an interest in the dynamic aspects of the total personality. It is, of course, the latter who are more suitable for psychiatric work, even for those laboratory aspects concerned with set tests. Unfortunately the number of first-class ones is only too few, and that is why not all our Boards are provided with one.

At the beginning of the war there was no dearth of excellent material for officers, but after a couple of years it became plain that considerable care would have to be exercised in selecting new ones if unfortunate results were to be avoided. Some brilliant preliminary investigations by Rodger, Wittkower, and Bowlby showed beyond doubt that psychiatric examinations could be of great value in assisting the military authorities in their choice, and it was as a result of this that psychiatrists were added to the Selection Boards. It was not that the psychiatric examinations were, as was popularly feared by their critics, more severe in the sense of failing more candidates. What was found was that they were more exact in both directions: they not only detected serious defects of personality which might have been overlooked by the military, but they showed that the latter at times overestimated the importance of various deficiencies and so failed a number of candidates who could have become quite satisfactory officers. An example of this difference is that the military attached much higher value than the psychiatrists to what is called ' poor presence,' whereas the latter ascribed more importance to ' poor social qualities.' Another reason for adding the psychiatrists was that at that time we had not had as much battle experience to aid in the selection as the Germans had, and so had to have recourse to other methods.

The Germans had published the psychological tests they used in peace-time, some of which were being employed as early as 1926, and we began by applying their methods. These were discarded after a time, partly because the limited number of our psychiatrists impelled them to search for less cumbersome methods wherewith to examine the enormous number of candidates, but partly for a more interesting reason. The dynamic psychological outlook with which our psychiatrists are imbued rendered them unsympathetic to the old ' faculty psychology ' which still informs the German methods. A little effort enabled them to discard these and to devise their own, based on their different outlook, but they met with more trouble when they had to deal with the faculty psychology so beloved by the military authorities.

I wish to lay stress on this matter, since it is one of the two respects in which our Army psychiatrists have made revolutionary progress in the last couple of years. Like the German psychologists, most military men tend, when selecting officers, to look for specific qualities—the favourites being ' dash,' ' courage,' ' endurance,' ' capacity for leadership,' and the like—and to assess these on some marking system. It sounds very plausible, since beyond doubt these and other qualities are highly desirable in potential officers, but closer inspection raises certain fundamental doubts whether the abstractions are not taking one too far away from reality. Not one of the qualities listed seems essential, and if one tries to ascertain what it is successful officers have in common, one sees it is not so much the possession of certain specific *qualities* as the capacity for *effective behaviour* by whatever way this is achieved. This capacity is a product of the total personality, and therefore it is this that has to be assessed. Every individual is unique in the particular way in which he meets the demands made on him, and it is the characteristic of this personal idiom to which attention needs to be directed. One has to scrutinise the way in which the individual spontaneously fills certain rôles in definite test situations, and this commonsense, and apparently less sophisticated, method proves to be the most scientific because it is nearer to reality than any study of abstract qualities. One may find a certain analogy between this point of view and the reform in the investigation of heart disease introduced by Mackenzie some thirty or forty years ago. Discarding the previous static estimates of cardiac lesions, he concentrated quite empirically on the actual functioning capacity of the heart. Similarly with the budding officer: it is not what qualities he possesses, but how he actually behaves in practice in various typical situations that most matters. One might almost say that it does not matter what neurosis he has so much as how he manages it in actual life. The total personality is the central criterion.

Let us now consider the technique at present used in this selection work. The candidates come in batches of fifty or sixty and mess with the members of the Board for two or three days. On the first evening they undergo a preliminary psychological examination by specially trained sergeant testers, who have usually been professional men in civilian life. These preliminary tests are grouped together under the name of ' Personality Pointers,' and they save a good deal of time. The results are passed on to the psychologist, if present, and then to the psychiatrist. When they are specially good the latter does not need to interview the candidate. The examination in question consists of four parts: (A) The candidate fills in two comprehensive questionnaires. One is an official one for the President of the Board; the other a confidential one for the psychiatrist. In the latter there is the bright idea of asking the candidate to describe his personality as honestly as he can in terms of (a) his best friend, and (b) an adverse critic. (B) Intelligence Tests. Three are used: the Penrose-Raven progressive matrices test, a verbal intelligence test, and a reasoning test. The standard of measurement is the average intelligence of the rank and file; an officer should not fall much below this. It has been found that twelve per cent. of the candidates fail in this test, and that about a fifth of all rejections are due to failures in it. (C) Word Association Test. Jung's method of using this has been improved on by getting candidates to indicate some expressed attitude towards each word, by responding with a sentence instead of a single word. Fifty words are displayed on cards for fifteen seconds each, during which time the candidate has to write down what occurs to him in response to the stimulus. (D) The Thermatic Apperception Test. Hesse introduced this test in the German Army some fifteen years ago, but the method we use is that elaborated by Murray of Harvard. Slides of somewhat ambiguous scenes are presented and the candidate has to exercise his imagination in inventing a story appropriate to each picture.

On the next day the military officers, especially selected for the purpose, carry out various out-of-doors tests. There are group discussions of tactical schemes, a rather gruelling series of tests designed to estimate the candidate's athletic prowess, and there is another, called the ' leaderless group test,' which claims our special attention because it concerns the second of the two important advances to which I referred earlier. Devised by one of our Army psychiatrists, Major Bion, it reveals striking psychological insight, and incidentally illustrates the contrast between the British outlook and the German or, more broadly, between the democratic outlook and the totalitarian one. The test that corresponds to it in the German Army is of a double nature, designed to assay the candidate's responses when under command or when in command respectively. Apparently no other situation is envisaged as thinkable than a definitely superior or definitely subordinate one, and indeed this is perhaps a characteristic military point of view which is as adverse to the very idea of a group without a leader as it is to guerilla warfare or to mob rule. It has in fact taken some time to inculcate a different idea into the military officers who conduct these leaderless tests. In them a group of ten men are given a military task to perform together, crossing a river or what not, and they are left quite free to make their own plans about it. This task is the quasi real or set problem, but it masks the real problem on which the observing officer concentrates. That is the purely social problem of how each individual reconciles his natural desire to distinguish himself favourably in the eyes of the examiner with the desirability of co-operating in a team spirit with the other members of the group so as to accomplish the set task. Instead of following the customary rule of allaying anxiety for the purpose of examination this leaderless test may be said to capitalise the candidate's anxiety so as to ascertain his capacity to deal with it in a critical situation. Various counter-transferences and anxieties are also apt to develop in the military examiners, and the study of them has proved both interesting and of practical value. The candidates of course show all manner of reactions according to their temperament: facetiousness as a guise for self-confidence, embarrassment, the impulse to make themselves prominent and show off, and so on. The examiner soon learns to distinguish between the man who does this for reasons of personal ambition and the one who comes to the fore from motives of helpfulness, as also between the man who voluntarily retires to give others a chance and one who falls into the background because of a deficiency in social contact. The reactions of the rest of the group to a given candidate are as important as his own to it: whether they accept his suggestions, ignore him, and so on. Whether a man leads the others by persuasion, by being recognised as a helpful sociable person, or on the other hand by aggression, appealing to complexes of fear or guilt in the other members, is a matter of evident importance, as is also the question whether a docile man is willing or merely inferior.

From all this emerges the decision whether a given candidate asserts a positive or negative influence in his relation to the rest of the group, whether this is of a group-cohesive nature or a group-disruptive one. Candidates are therefore tested in relation to particular environments and in their attitudes towards superiors, subordinates or colleagues. Our Army psychiatrists attach very special significance to the last of these. If one does wish to use the old nomenclature of qualities one would say that the two things they particularly look for are social adaptability and general resourcefulness. It will be noticed that what is common to both is the mental freedom that permits easy adjustment, whether to persons, to material objects, or to situations.

After these and other military tests, the candidate appears before the whole Board, which considers the various reports. These reports discuss actual findings, not general conclusions or impressions. The number of candidates passed has varied in different years; at present it is perhaps less than half of the total presented. The Board also assesses the suitability of a candidate for particular branches of the Service: plainly a man who would make a good combatant officer would not necessarily be successful in more technical or administrative work, and *vice versa*.

A word about other branches of the Services. Selection methods practically identical with those just mentioned are used with the Royal Marines and with the Women's Auxiliary Services, whom we now call the A.T.S. and you, I believe, W.A.C.S. The Navy does not seem to feel the same need, since those applying for commissions are on the whole of better quality and also they are tested by actual experience in sea warfare beforehand. The Air Force have their own special psychological tests, of which I have no first-hand experience.

2. *Other Selection Work.* There are several branches of this work. (*a*) Fourteen per cent. of the general intake to the Army are referred by the medical officers to the psychiatrists for a report on their suitability for either general or special service. Some form of mental deficiency is probably the commonest condition needing expert investigation.

(*b*) Army Selection Centres examine and report on the cases of men who have already spent about two years in the Army and who have not proved satisfactory.

(*c*) Psychiatrists also play their part in what is called the Selection Testing of Units, work which is rather similar to the Vocational Selection that has been brought to such a high standard in the United States in peace-time. Unsuitable allocation is an obvious loss to man-power in the Army, which in modern times has to be estimated in terms of quality rather than quantity.

(*d*) There is a special examination for men who are to be trained as parachutists, but you will not expect me to give any details of this.

3. *Special Testings.* The consulting psychiatrists in the Army have to report on cases referred to them from the military psychiatric hospitals, as well as, of course, to inspect these hospitals.

4. *Psychiatric Treatment.* Except for cases of exhaustion in the heat of battle, cases in which, by the way, barbitone has proved of great value, the number of neurotic and psychotic patients needing treatment who will be of use for service in what the military authorities call a reasonable period is naturally not great, so that the Army has not at the moment very much interest in this field. Later on it will no doubt assume greater importance. There is little new to report in this work except that some promising results are being obtained by various forms of group rehabilitation treatment, which is proving a useful auxiliary to more intensive individual therapy. Cases of psychoneurosis are some fifteen times as frequent as those of psychosis, and, as was our experience in the last war, it is the ' willing horse ' who holds on to the last before giving way whose case is apt to prove the most intractable. I should also mention some remarkable results from insulin treatment in both military and civilian cases of nervous exhaustion with loss of weight—a reversion to the days of Weir Mitchell.

5. *Morale.* To our knowledge of this all-important subject psychiatrists have contributed in two ways: by studying the subjects who have shown poor morale—*e.g.*, by being absent without leave on repeated occasions—and by special psychological study of the more positive aspects. It is essentially a study of group integration and the factors that heighten or impair this. One of our Army psychiatrists, who knows Germany well at first hand, has made a remarkably penetrating investigation of the morale of the German Army. As one would expect, the conditions favourable to morale and the methods employed to influence it are strikingly different on the two sides in the present war, but since there are few topics that touch more nearly on the question of military discretion it is not one

on which I may expatiate here. I can only say that the work done on it would alone justify the employment of psychiatrists in the Army.

6. *Special Researches*. Last, but far from being least, are the particular investigations carried out under the Directorate of Army Psychiatry. Among these the following may be mentioned as illustrations. The problem of readjustment among repatriated prisoners of war, one with which the United States has not yet had much experience, presents some peculiar difficulties. It may be said that twenty per cent. of them if not adjusted within six months become serious psychiatric cases. The outstanding feature is the sense of being out of touch with both home and the Army—what is called an ' out of the picture ' feeling—with a corresponding absence of group contact. As prisoners their morale was so sustained by a negative attitude to authority, the Nazi guards, that it often persists as a habit. It is hard for anyone to help these men unless he can understand their point of view through having himself passed through the same experience, and such men are chosen for the purpose. We have also learned much about dealing with these problems prophylactically by catering to the men in special ways while they are still in prison camps.

Soldiers serving abroad for considerable periods also present special problems, and this is a matter that concerns America more than the former one. Here suspicions concerning the home front play a prominent part, anger at strikes, resentment at war profiteers, doubts about politicians, fears about the fidelity of their women at home, and the like. Suppressed feelings of guilt at having deserted their families often play a curiously important rôle. The degeneration of the suspicions into paranoid reactions, which depends on the process of generalisation, can be hindered by methods that lay stress on the personal as opposed to the impersonal. Therefore lectures, films, songs, and so on should be based on individual features and should avoid mass representation or general ideas. Some of these reactions will become very important when it comes to demobilisation. Sufferings and privations in common, even with the enemy, are apt to breed a group attitude that will be an impediment to future integration with the home community. It may be, for instance, that returning soldiers will display cynicism about disarming the Germans and Japanese, and will reserve their distrust and resentment for the Army and other national authorities.

A special study has been made of the psychology of mutilated men. Half of these show neurotic reactions bad enough to be troublesome later on. Interesting differences here have been noted between those deprived of an arm and those losing a leg. The former more often show reactions of resentment, depression, and anxiety; the latter those of morbid euphoria or defiance. Only eight per cent. of the whole develop a normal response of resignation and acceptance. Contrary to popular opinion the victims of blindness often show reactions of jealousy and suspicion, as well as of helplessness; the last of these stimulates aggressivity, which is either externalised as bitterness or internalised as depression.

Feelings of not being wanted are common to all these groups: prisoners of war, soldiers far from home, and those crippled. In this connection it is noteworthy that in our experience the soldier's need for female society is not so purely erotic in its nature as has been generally thought: what he often craves for is the sympathetic companionship of a ' nice ' girl, and one has the impression that feelings derived from the mother are at least as important as those related to a sexual partner.

There has been a psychological inquiry into the relations between American and British soldiers, with, I am glad to report, very heartening results.

In addition to these systematic investigations Army psychiatrists often have the opportunity of being useful in connection with special questions that keep cropping up. Early in 1942 some military authority—I am told a converted pacifist—had the misguided idea of initiating what was popularly known as a ' hate campaign '—that is to say, of drilling his men into forms of ' toughness ' and savagery that would have won promotion in a Nazi concentration camp. The English sense of humour, however, was too much for it, and after a month the grotesque episode was brought to an end by a psychiatric report on its futility. Then recently there has been a difficulty in feeding prophylactic drugs to the troops because of a widely spread suspicion that they were designed to deaden sexual impulses. If ever there was a purely psychological problem surely that is one.

I pass now from consideration of the military forces to that of civilians in time of war, and here again my personal experience is derived only from Britain. It is not known, and probably never will be known, whether psychoses have become more or less frequent during the war. The incidence of intake into mental hospitals can of course be arbitrarily regulated according to the pressure. Some large hospitals were entirely taken over for Government purposes and the call-up of doctors has made itself felt in all institutions. These and other factors have disarranged the normal statistics in this field.

The incidence of psychoneurosis also cannot be statistically controlled, even in peace-time. One can only go by general impressions obtained by interchange from other workers in the same field, particularly those in hospital out-patient departments where the largest number are seen. There is no evidence I know of to indicate any increase in psychoneurosis in these five years, and there was a very general impression during the most dangerous period of the war that there was then an actual diminution. Analytical theory would explain this by the reciprocal relationship that exists between so-called 'real' suffering or danger coming from without and neurotic suffering: when fate inflicts suffering there is less need for the self-punishing functions of the neurosis.

The British people have in this war passed through three distinct kinds of trial. The first was the anxiety induced by the demonstration in Poland, Norway, and above all France, that the Germans had devised a successful, and apparently irresistible form of *Blitzkrieg*. This anxiety was most acute before the fall of France, when we saw the Germans marching at will into places like Abbeville, Amiens and the Channel ports in a fashion that in the last war would have seemed quite disastrous. The anxiety was plainly associated with the idea of their invincibility combined with the increasing doubts of the French will to resistance on which we felt we largely depended. Curiously enough it was rapidly and permanently allayed by the actual surrender of France, which produced a palpable feeling of relief. At a time when we had to realise that we stood alone against the invincible and ruthless tyrant a lady made the rather surprising remark to me: 'Thank goodness there are no longer any allies we have to praise.' She was referring, of course, to the exaggerated praise with which we had covered up our distrust. At such a moment of mortal peril the country was seized with a united determination so admirably voiced by the genius of our Prime Minister, and it was this sense of unity that gave us the conviction that there was something we could believe in and trust, namely each other. This conviction was so strong as to be quite impervious to the pessimistic anxieties in the rest of the world concerning our fate, and articles in

American newspapers somewhat gleefully describing the twenty-six different ways in which Hitler could invade Britain had the same effect as water on a duck's back. On paper our chances of winning the war certainly looked thin enough in July 1940, but what emerges from the experience is that for mental peace, confidence and effectiveness the harmony proceeding from internal single-heartedness and group integration of mutual trust is more important than probabilities of actual success or failure.

Soon after this came the second trial, the 'blitz,' as we now call it, on our large cities. Naturally there had been for some time, especially in the period that you termed our 'phoney' war, much speculation about the psychological effect of intensive bombing. In June 1939 a Spanish physician, Dr. Mira, read a paper before the Psycho-Analytical Society in which he gave a very gruesome account of his experiences in Madrid. He presented an interesting classified description of the variety of acute shock conditions he had observed, and we were particularly impressed with the severest of these where mutism and emotional paralysis were followed by practical cessation of all mental activity and even death. Such conditions were certainly uncommon in the London blitz. I cannot say whether differences in national psychology are to be invoked to explain this striking contrast. There were, it is true, some external factors that might well have a bearing on it. They must have felt more helpless in Madrid than in London where the roar of our anti-aircraft defences had a very heartening effect. Then in Madrid the bombing was a prelude to occupation by the enemy, with all that meant, whereas with us we felt in the winter of 1940-1941 that the German invasion was pretty definitely off. There were no disorderly and tragic scenes on the roads as in Spain and France with the advance of the enemy. The mental states we most often observed were simply those of diffuse anxiety, but the people nearly all kept on with their work. They were notably worse among those who had been bombed out two or three times, just as refugees suffer especially if they have been hounded out of two or three countries in succession. In general the population, who after all never saw the enemy face to face, behaved as if the destruction was the result of natural causes, such as fire or other accidents. There was of course a certain amount of exhaustion from lack of adequate sleep over a number of months, but this could hardly be called neurotic. Very notable was the adaptation displayed by children, provided their parents showed no neurotic terror. It was indeed pathetic to see how they assimilated the experiences as if they were part of their normal environment: I remember one child whose first word ever spoken was ' bomb,' uttered as he cheerfully pointed up to the sky.

One came across a small number of definite air-raid phobias, and the instructive thing about them was the ease with which they could be distinguished from the general anxiety states. It is plain that with them the fear is of some internal phantasy which happened to be symbolised by falling bombs. One learns again from this how very much easier it is for the human mind to tolerate external danger than internal dangers, how we always err on the side of generosity in allowing so much anxiety to pass for normal when it is in fact neurotic and avoidable.

The third trial, still proceeding, is that of strain and weariness from the prolongation of war conditions. Although civilians have been much more directly and extensively affected than in the last world war, one nevertheless has the impression that the signs of war weariness for a comparable period are fewer now than then. This might be attributed to two factors: we have not yet had the colossal casualty lists that were so depressing in the years of the last war, and secondly the enemy this time is so much more implacable that the question of a patched-up peace does not arise now as it did to some extent then. In other words, the higher degree of single-heartedness in this war results in a mental harmony that fortifies endurance against discomfort and distress.

The factors that have most adversely affected morale are these. Perhaps the most universal is the depressing effect of the rigid black-out, maintained through summer and winter over years. The bad ventilation within and the longing for the cheerfulness of lights without constitute a steady factor to which adaptation does not improve with the passage of time. In the matter of food there are two elements, the nutritional and the erotic. The nutritional level cannot be very far below the normal, as is evidenced by the health statistics and the absence of epidemics, but it is sufficiently so to diminish the amount of energy generated and also the resistance to minor ailments, particularly respiratory infections. But the poor quality of the food and its monotonous character have turned the act of eating into a habit or duty rather than an enjoyment, especially among the classes of the population accustomed to more variety and higher culinary standards. We know that privation in the sphere of oral eroticism leads characteristically to depression, and some measure of it would appear to be widespread. Even more pronounced is the anxiety engendered among the women who have to rack their brains to provide an edible meal for their menfolk and children. The inability to entertain guests should also be mentioned in this connection, as well as the great restriction of any social intercourse because of travelling difficulties, overwork, and so on. The more social and entertaining classes are further hard put to it by the absence of the services on which they formerly depended. American life is differently organised in this respect, and probably the same class in America is brought up to be more competent in such matters as household repairs and other domestic emergencies. It will be noticed that the factors just mentioned concern discomforts rather than mental conflict, and so show their effects in fatigue rather than in neurosis.

After experiencing a respite of nearly three years London is again passing through a period of bombing, and a comparison between the people's reaction now and at the time of the first blitz is of some interest. The greater number find the present bombing easier to stand and cheer themselves with the favourable comparison with the previous one. The present attacks seldom last for more than an hour instead of all night, night after night, so that adequate sleep can be obtained; the severity is much less, and the toll taken of the invader much higher; the state of the war is quite different, and so on. A small number, however, find the present attacks harder to bear, and this seems to be correlated with an uneasy conscience about our bombing activities, really about the repressed aggression of the people concerned. Treating the attacks as moral punishments they either complain that the second dose is not fair because we have already been ' punished ' in the great blitz, or they take the present one as freshly deserved punishment for what we are now inflicting on German cities.

The partial, though large-scale, evacuation of our cities brought with it a severe test of the qualities, reputed to be well developed among the British, of tolerance, compromise and adaptability. We have not the American tradition of open hospitality and we guard the privacy of our home more jealously. It is one thing to shelter destitute strangers in the flush of an emergency and quite another to share your home for years with non-destitute ones. It was one thing for a woman to care for temporarily adopted children and quite another to share the cooking range with their mother. I have come across several cases of severe and paralysing neurosis arising from these situations. Nor were they made easier when, as occasionally happened, the ' evacuees ' developed the reaction of spoilt children: they then behaved as if nothing could be too good for them or could begin to recompense them for their initial misfortune. Susan Isaacs and others have made specially valuable studies of ' evacuee ' children and of their ambivalence towards their absent or lost parents, and Anna Freud has with Dorothy Burlingham founded a large nursery which also serves for the psychological study of children in these unfortunate predicaments.

I wish finally to review certain wider aspects of psychiatry in relation to war problems which in some future age should well prove to be the most significant of all—namely, those of general sociological import. When a man chooses a career he will do well to reflect on not only the technical interest it offers but also on the bearing it may have on his general interest in life. In this respect psychiatrists may count themselves peculiarly fortunate. Not only do their professional interests compare favourably with any other, but they are in the unique position of possessing keys to the understanding of human behaviour that open wider possibilities of interest, and ultimately of influence, than any other group in the community. It is true that we have hardly begun to appreciate the opportunities open to us in these wider spheres, and also that every attempt to develop them is bound to meet with vehement opposition on the part of society since it involves challenging the underground fears that dominate so much of personal and social life. This opposition, however, will not deter us. And we must be uplifted by the thought that we are the first pioneers in this field. It is centuries since the world at large has presented such a rich material for psychiatric observation as it has in our time, and in those days of long ago there was no psychiatry. In a paper read before your annual meeting two years ago in Boston, Dr. Zilboorg, dealing with the permeation of sociology by psychiatry, remarked on what he called a unique phenomenon in the history of sciences: it is, he said, the first time in history that a purely medical discipline, curative in intent and methodology, has been the means of transforming a whole series of scientific disciplines (sociology, anthropology, criminology, etc.). Other analysts, such as Alexander and Glover, as well as nonanalysts such as William Brown, Baynes, Nathan, etc., have published books of value on current aspects of the same topic. Psychiatry was in the descriptive stage of development until the genius of Freud opened the way to an understanding of the forces at work and gave them meaning. Sociology is still in that descriptive stage, but it is on the brink of the next one when psychiatry will be able to inform it of the inner meaning of the interplay of forces that mould its subject-matter. The present occasion is, of course, not the place for any detailed sociological studies, but I am nevertheless impelled to seize the opportunity to indicate to you some of the vast perspectives now opening up before us and to express the hope that the coming generation of psychiatrists will take full advantage of them.

Cynical philosophers have from time to time expressed the opinion that mankind is more than a little mad, and to-day we are perhaps more willing to heed their remarks than we were in a more complacent past. It is now a good many years since August Stärcke, in Holland, startled his fellow psycho-analysts by proclaiming that psychotic traits and mechanisms were present in all so-called normal people, but since then his conclusion has ceased to be a paradox and has become the subject of serious study. These mechanisms of projection, introjection, self-punishment, etc., which when they dominate the field of consciousness constitute insanity, have been isolated by Freud and his co-workers and their effects and interrelationships closely examined. Melanie Klein, in particular, has laid a firm basis for such studies by making an intensive investigation of their earliest stages in infancy. She has found there such definite imitations of attitudes reminiscent of various psychotic types that she has not hesitated to borrow for her descriptive purpose such nomenclature as ' paranoid position,' ' depressive position,' ' maniac defence,' and so on. Her work is still in many respects the subject of controversy, but I am myself convinced that it will prove of permanent value in our comprehension of the deepest mental layers.

However highly we may treasure as perhaps our most precious possession the procedure known as reasoning, and I would yield to no one in prizing its value, we have now reached a state of psychological knowledge that compels us to recognise that man is essentially not a rational animal: that is to say, the greater part of his behaviour and thought processes are profoundly influenced by affective agencies of a definitely non-rational or even irrational order. To a psychiatrist that means admitting that the unconscious is a constant and formidable factor in human activity. The future may well show that this admission, including the full realisation of it, will prove to mark a decisive step not only in the advance of human knowledge but in the actual control of human conduct. If so, it will be for psychiatrists in due time to teach the world wisdom in the management of human affairs, for who should be better able to do so than those whose daily work consists in handling of the irrational? At present attempted rationalism alternates with prejudice and impulse, and we have such pathetic spectacles as Mr. Chamberlain facing Hitler with an impassable gulf between them. Such methods will have to be replaced by a true emotional understanding which does not flinch from the consequences of its vision. In such situations the significance of counter-transferences and their effects must of course also receive their due recognition. There can be no problem of government, domestic or foreign, that would not be transformed by the acceptance of this knowledge, nor indeed any form whatsoever of human relationships, whether between individuals or between groups.

Of recent years we have been presented with the startling spectacle of irrational and psychotic-like mechanisms dominating the effective part of whole nations. Some of the beliefs that have swept through such nations, beliefs that have not only commanded profound acceptance but have generated the most violent emotions, leading to corresponding conduct, have been of a kind that people uninfluenced by them could only stigmatise as delusional. The identification of Semitic with Satanic, and the fantastic myth of ' Aryan blood ' as the private property of Germans and Japanese, are perhaps the most classical examples. We are taken back to the days of Le Bon's crowd psychology, work which had a *succès d'estime* for the moment but which has been unduly neglected since. We see now that he did not exaggerate in depicting the dangerous baseness of the emotions characteristic of mass infection, though he underestimated—and we should beware of falling into the same error—the exalted and even idealised emotions that can be aroused by the same proceeding.

The group or mass affections that have been most startling in the past quarter of a century, connected with what are called ideologies, have much in common. Indeed it has not been easy for an outsider clearly to distinguish between different ones that are sometimes presented to us as contrasting with each other. What we generally observe is a minority group seizing absolute power and maintaining it by relentless methods: mass propaganda on the unscrupulous lines taught by Le Bon, terrorising of the population by means of a ruthless secret police, and 'liquidation' or torture of all opponents, open or suspected. Sometimes we are told that the aim of the rulers is deification of the People and at other times deification of the State, but some distinctions in aim do not always lead to much visible difference in practice.

It is certain that these mass movements would be impossible in a stable civilisation, and are intelligible only as a reaction to the experience of acute distress, whether of political or economic origin. The factors here were numerous, and it will be a hard task for the historian to determine the hierarchy of their importance: insecurity about the present or future, with the attendant dread of chaos, terrifying inflation with its transvaluation of all economic values, mass unemployment, severe famine conditions, all accompanied by the depressing sense of defeat[1] which the unconscious mind always translates into the significance of punishment for guiltiness. Such a prevailing state of despair provides the classical background for violent action—i.e., a revolutionary movement—and there is a ready response to, or at least acquiescence in, anybody that promises salvation vehemently enough. For the clamour is for salvation from despair. The situation feels too urgent for any sort of scientific inquiry into the most appropriate remedies, just as an uneducated person who is dangerously ill clutches at the quack promises he prefers to a medical diagnosis.

In bygone ages when self-confidence and belief in the goodness of life were not at a low ebb, the profferings of religion were often eagerly accepted. During the decline of the Roman Empire, for instance, there were two competing ideologies, and both were religious: Christianity and Mithraism. Psycho-analysis has had no difficulty in showing that the basic biological complex to which both of these appealed was the father-murder guilt of the Œdipus situation, although they offered contrasting solutions of it. We learn from the Roman example alone that one effect of social distress on the individual is to re-animate this complex, and it offers an important key to many of the great reactions of our time. Much of

---

[1] For reasons obvious only to Italians, Italy, although technically victorious, developed a sense of defeat after the last war.

the passionate violence in the response to external depressing factors emanates from the fount of energy pent up from infantile life but always ready to be re-animated by the appropriate situation. It would seem that religion in our day has lost, perhaps for ever, its power of canalising distress: its solutions are no longer believed in with the necessary fervour. Many writers have nevertheless, it is true, pointed out that some of the emotions nowadays attached to ideologies have a similar origin to the religious ones: the Communists appeal with fanatical conviction to Marx their Allah, or to Lenin his prophet, while the Axis harks back to their ancient divinities Thor and Bellona.

These great social reactions display a close enough resemblance to those of our patients for us to be able to say something about the psychology of them. Above all it is important to grasp that they are not idiopathic, that they do not arise from any inborn propensity to sin on the part of any particular people, although a national tradition and history are of course of importance in determining the reaction. But reactions are what they are, reactions to social situations strengthened by the defence processes that try to protest against the intolerable anxieties and guilts these situations have stirred. It is of great political importance that this should be recognised, since, in any endeavour to hinder future reactions of the same devastating consequences, there will be a much better prospect of success if the situations to which they are reactions are dealt with, than if they are regarded as spontaneous outbursts of devilry. One psychological feature of such reactions was mentioned above: the regression to father hatred, of which the so-called class warfare is a perennial expression. Just as the infant makes its father responsible for all its inevitable privations, anxieties and sufferings, so do most unhappy, unfortunate or unsuccessful people look hurriedly for some scapegoat to take from them any responsibility they may feel for their fate, and they naturally find it in those who have suffered less at the hands of fate. The Nazis had a particularly ingenious, and from their point of view a very successful, paranoid mechanism to further this psychological projection: they asserted that the powers that be had been poisoned by a malignant group of people called Jews. The consequences of their assertion have horrified the world. A second psychological feature of the reactions in question resembles what Melanie Klein has termed the manic defence against depression. The despair and poverty of the ego is dealt with by developing a state of exaltation in it, often after identification with a source of strength such as an appropriate leader, and this is accompanied by a great intolerance of contradiction with a characteristic tendency to violence. Here again we are on familiar social ground.

The practical trouble about these mass reactions is of course the oppression and ill-treatment of other people to which they inevitably lead. Here brutality becomes the centre of the problem. One of the most remarkable features about the Nazi mentality is the extent to which their tradition and training have succeeded in making high degrees of brutality and cruelty ego-syntonic: the processes at work here are in themselves worthy of a special study. In combating such an undesirable state of affairs, by firmness and if need be by force, we encounter great subjective difficulties. The forms of cruelty fostered would often seem to surpass what were thought to be human limits, as they obviously surpass any bestial behaviour of which we have knowledge. Now it may be doubted whether any but the actual victims have the power of imagining such things with any degree of vividness except those who derive a directly sadistic pleasure from the thoughts or accounts of them, and such indulgence has of course little social value. As a rule the mind recoils from the horrors either violently or angrily or, more often, withdraws by all the varieties of denial and discounting to actual complacent ignoring. The remark that ' stories of atrocities are exaggerated ' is occasionally true, and that condones the far greater multitude where the stories are mild under-statements of the truth. How to retain a strong impression that will serve as an adequate spur to action and yet not affect one's mental balance is an as yet unsolved sociological problem. It is in the solving of such a problem and the many other cognate ones that I see a new field opening before psychiatry.

CHAPTER VIII

LOVE AND MORALITY[1]
A STUDY IN CHARACTER TYPES

THE following remarks concern the process whereby a moral attitude towards others is substituted for an attitude of love. This doubtless happens to some extent in the course of every individual development, but there are cases where it dominates the development and gives a characteristic colouring to the whole personality. The process then goes far beyond the mere matter of obedience, of doing things against one's will because some authority orders or compels one to do them. It may become almost the only way in which such a person can express any positive attitude towards another, the giving of pleasure or the displaying of care for the other's interest and welfare. Whatever may be the way in which he manifests these positive attitudes, his inner feeling is one of moral obligation; he manifests them because he feels it is the right and proper thing to do, fundamentally because he feels he ought to. This feeling of ' oughtness,' though in itself often concealed or even repressed, definitely differentiates the attitudes and behaviour from those more spontaneously arising from friendliness, affection or love. It would interest us to know what this remarkable substitution signifies in the character development, how it comes about and what are its consequences in later life.

A simple way to describe the state of affairs would be to say that the id impulses with such people cannot express themselves directly towards others, but have first to undergo extensive modification in the super-ego. There can be no doubt that this is the field where the change from love to morality takes place. It is also evident that it is intimately related to the problem of sadism, since we know that morality itself is inseparably connected with this. In such patients I have always found a strong vein of repressed sadism. This co-exists, however, with a latent capacity for great tenderness of the possessive type, one that is to be distinguished from a true love attitude.

[1] Read before the Fourteenth International Psycho-Analytical Congress, Marienbad, August 6, 1936, and before the British Psycho-Analytical Society, October 21, 1936. Published in the *International Journal of Psycho-Analysis*, vol. xviii., part i.

Because of the sadism there is, consciously or unconsciously, a great fear of the tender attitude or the object to whom it applies being destroyed, and many of the subsequent reaction-formations are designed to prevent this calamity. It is only under the condition of morality that any object-relationship can be preserved. I regard this point of view as important because it provides a clue to the motive for the moral attitude and suggests that it subserves a defensive or preservative function. Thanks to the substitution of this attitude for that of love the latter is never exposed to various imaginary dangers—*i.e.*, those emanating from the destructive impulses. A further protection comes from the extensive component of restitutive tendencies in the moral attitude. They play indeed a central part in it, since the most characteristic elements of the moral attitude is its sense of debt or obligation, the sense of owing something to the other person, of which presumably the latter has previously been deprived by an act of spoliation. These restitutive processes thus imply a sort of contract, whereby one buys off the injured person and thus induces him not to inflict punishment for the act of injury by attacking what is most precious to the evil-doer.

The introjection-projection mechanisms, on which Melanie Klein has laid special emphasis, play a very important part in the substitution process in question. As I indicated earlier, what is more precious to the person may be equally described as tenderness towards an object or the object itself, since the idea of the latter is always introjected in such cases and commonly even identified with the self. Similarly the idea of the external object who has been injured is also introjected and there arises both fear of the destructive powers of this evil internalised object and an impulse to submit to it. The internal loved object is deeply hidden so as to protect it from the evil object.

In my experience the moral substitution of which I am speaking is apt to be specially pronounced if the original oral-sadistic impulses have been extensively displaced on to the anal-sadistic level. I would go so far as to say that anal-erotism and its accompanying reaction-formations are pathognomonic of the whole mechanism, and more particularly of the subsequent revolt against it of which I am next going to speak. The typical complex is the impulse to extract fæces by suction and the corresponding fear of this being done to one.

With many people this substitution of morality for love proves a fairly successful working basis for life. They become reliable and decent citizens who play their part in life well enough. They always suffer, it is true, from the drawback of never greatly enjoying life, and for their neighbours they present the drawback of being more or less hard-hearted and intolerant people.

There is, on the other hand, a considerable class of people of this type who are not successful in the path on which they have embarked. The failure of the mechanism registers itself in a neurosis, more often to the obsessional form. Analysis shows that the failure is due to a protest or revolt against the moral substitution. The revolt comes about in the following way. The characteristic defect of the moral substitution is the tendency of the sadistic elements in the morality to gain the upper hand. When that happens, the restitutive and protective functions of the mechanism begin to fail. The sadism, which had been bound and transformed in the super-ego, reverts to its destructive elements and then threatens injury to either the self or the outer world. As we all know, people with an over-sensitive conscience—i.e., with a strong sense of guilt—are specially cruel and intolerant either to themselves or to other people, sometimes to both. When the sexual impulses have remained on an infantile level and also have not found any extensive sublimation, the directing inwards of the sadism of the super-ego leads to the fear of aphanisis. In these special conditions when this point is reached there is invariably a revolt, especially from the side of the id.

The most visible signs of the revolt against the substitutive morality are conflicts in the sphere of duty. Such people become extremely sensitive to anything being expected of them. The very idea of it is immediately converted into that of being compelled to do something against their will, at times even against what they feel to be their better self—the revolt being by no means always dictated by selfishness. The most striking examples of all are those in which even a personal wish comes to have the significance of an external compulsion. Such a person will start on a plan of gratifying a wish of his, and if it necessitates any continued effort will rebel at the idea of having to carry it out, just as if it were a task he was being expected to perform against his will.

At this point one may observe a variety of types, and I wish to distinguish two particular ones. I do not find it easy to find suitable designations for them. Since in my opinion the revolt in the one type comes from the super-ego, the other from the id, perhaps the

best terms would be the super-ego type of revolt and id type
respectively. This would, however, assume more certain knowledge
than we probably possess. Then again one type might be called the
' moral type of revolt,' the other the ' ethical type,' on the ground
that with the latter the conscious dislike of duty is associated with
a strong preference for the ethical idea of love, whereas with the
former the revolt takes rather the form of a moral condemnation
by the conscience of the sadistic regression in the over-' moral '
super-ego. It will be better perhaps to fall back for the time being
on familiar clinical terms, though at the risk of stressing unduly
the psychopathological aspects of what is strictly a characterological
study. I will therefore designate them here as the *obsessional* and
hysterical types of revolt against morality, ultimately types of defence
against aphanisis.

I have the impression that an essential difference between them is
that with the latter the revolt is more manifest before puberty than
after, whereas with the former it is more manifest after puberty.
This presumably means that the revolt is more intense with what I
am calling the hysterical type, where it sets in earlier. I shall now
proceed to contrast the two types in a number of other respects.
Let me make it clear, however, that I am no longer speaking of the
more ' normal ' hypermoral type of person I described earlier, but
types where there is a *revolt* against such hyper-morality.

The most striking difference between them is the conscience
attitude towards duty. With what I called the obsessional type, the
person consciously wishes to perform his duty and is dismayed at
finding himself prevented by some unknown agency from doing so.
The hysterical type, on the other hand, so dislikes the very idea of
doing anything he is supposed to that he instantly ceases any attempt
as soon as he realises it can possibly be called a duty, and he is
annoyed at anyone who may have introduced this idea, because he
is thereby prevented from doing various other things he might
otherwise have wished to do.

Another way of expressing this difference is that with the obsessional type the revolt is unconscious, whereas with the hysterical
type it is more conscious. In extreme cases this contrast is very
notable indeed.

Parallel with this difference is the fact that ordinary standards of
behaviour, in such matters as financial rectitude, punctuality, social
obligations, etc., are apt to be much higher with the obsessional

than with the hysterical type. The latter may indeed be so non-social or anti-social as to approach the criminal type of character—*i.e.*, they display little repugnance at the idea of criminality.

The manifestations of conscience assume a different form in the two types. With the obsessional there is self-reproach at not being more 'good' in the conventional sense of the word. With the hysterical type there is self-reproach at not being more loving or at not being able to love at all.

There is a greater renunciation of loving and enjoying with the obsessional type, which remains at a more sadistic level. The hysterical type shows more capacity for restitutive activity and approaches more to a genital level. Perhaps that is why the revolt against the cruel morality sets in earlier here and is more intense.

The dread of aphanisis is differently manifested in the two types. With the obsessional one it is purer, taking, for instance, the form of fearing slavery, loss of personality, etc., although one also sometimes sees this re-sexualised as a fear of anal assault. With the other type the dread is more characteristically hysterical, such as the fear of being overcome by sadistic excitement.

The cause of all these differences would seem to be partly constitutional, the one type evidently having a more obsessional disposition and the other a more hysterical one, and partly an economic one concerning the quantity of sadism present and the age at which this gave rise to unsolved conflict.

CHAPTER IX

THE CONCEPT OF A NORMAL MIND [1]

WHAT constitutes a ' normal ' mind, and whether such a thing can actually exist, are questions of considerable theoretical, and sometimes of practical, interest. Even if we conclude that in an absolute sense no mind can be entirely and completely normal, it is nevertheless worth asking what would be the attributes of such a mind. For, with such a standard before us, it would be easier to determine how far a given mind under treatment had progressed in the direction of normality.

Therapeutists are principally concerned with such gross deviations from normality as cause no difficulty in deciding whether or not they are deviations; and that is probably the reason why the present question has not found much consideration in psycho-analytical literature. If a person can never leave the shelter of his home lest a thunderstorm come on and he be struck by lightning, or lest he be run over by a motor-car, his attitude may exhibit a certain inexorable logic, but a logic so unyielding to other considerations would if ' logically ' extended make life impossible, and few criteria of normality could be chosen that would not label such behaviour as ' abnormal.'

In work of this order one feels little need to ponder on careful definitions of normality, and, if asked to produce one, it is easy to be content with such general phrases as ' a mind functioning efficiently,' ' a healthy mind,' ' an organism well adapted to reality,' ' a personality achieving its maximum of happiness,' ' a personality in good contact with the social standards prevailing in the environment.' All these phrases are useful at times and serve to recall to our mind certain standards of value; they prove quite adequate in practice for gross work in psychopathology. Reflection soon shows, however, that they one and all beg the question by assuming that something—*e.g.*, efficiency or health—has been previously defined when in fact it has not.

The case is different when we have to do with variations of conduct that depend on types of character, and in these days, when

---

[1] First published in Schmalhausen's ' The Neurotic Age,' 1931.

character-analysis plays a much larger part in our work than it used to, the judgement of what constitutes normal conduct or normal psychological reactions often presents considerable difficulty. Investigations carried out in this direction, particularly by Edward Glover, Melanie Klein and other workers in England, have led us to adopt a much more sceptical attitude to what passes currently as mental normality and to scrutinise more carefully the generally adopted criteria of normality. They give special point to a criticism of psychoanalysis which was made many years ago by Wilfred Trotter (1916)— one which stands out from the monotonous series of prejudices and misunderstandings that usually do duty for criticism in this field. Trotter suggested that the conclusions of psycho-analysis would be more cogent if they did not so often imply an unthinkable acceptance of the normality of the social environment. He evidently meant to advocate that to achieve a comprehensible judgement in psychology one needed only to analyse the so-called 'normal' as well as the obviously neurotic, and that to judge the latter by the standard of the former might well introduce serious fallacies in the generalisations formulated. His actual words are as follows: 'To those who have approached Freud's work solely by the path of medicine the idea that it can give anyone the feeling of a certain conventionality of standard and outlook and of a certain over-estimation of the objectivity of man's moral values will seem perhaps merely absurd. That this is an impression which I have not been able altogether to escape I record with a good deal of hesitation and diffidence and without any wish to lay stress upon it. Psycho-analytic psychology has grown up under conditions which may very well have encouraged the persistence of the human point of view. Originally its whole activity was concentrated upon the investigation and treatment of disease. Many of its early disciples were those who had received proof of its value in their own persons, those, that is to say, who had been sufferers from their very susceptibility to the influence of human standards. The objective standard of validity by which the system was judged was necessarily that of the physician—namely, the capacity to restore the abnormal mind to the "normal." Normal in this sense is of course no more than a statistical expression implying the condition of the average man. It could scarcely fail, however, to acquire the significance of "healthy." If once the statistically normal mind is accepted as being synonymous with the psychologically healthy mind (that is, the mind in which the full capacities are available for use), a standard is set up which has a most fallacious appearance of objectivity. The statistically normal mind can be regarded only as a mind which has responded in the usual way to the moulding and deforming influence of its environment—that is, to human standards of discipline, taste, and morality. If it is to be looked upon as typically healthy also, the current human standards of whose influence it is a product must necessarily be accepted as qualified to call forth the best in the developing mind they mould. Writers of the psycho-analytic school seem in general to make some such assumption as this.'

Trotter's remarks were useful as a warning to slipshod thinking in analytical circles, a commodity by no means unknown, but they do not constitute a valid criticism of psycho-analysis itself. Three rejoinders may be made to them. To begin with, they hardly did justice to the practical consideration that in gross pathological work, with which psycho-analysts were for years mainly concerned, it was quite safe to contrast extreme neurotic deviations with the socially ' normal,' an attitude which in no way precluded a subsequent estimation of the latter on analytical lines. In the next place, there were never wanting indications in the psycho-analytical literature that these more general questions were merely being held in suspension without prejudice to further investigation. No one familiar with Freud's own writings, for instance, could be in doubt concerning his very open-minded attitude—one sometimes dubbed pessimistic—on the supposed normality of the normal or the ultimate validity of accepted social standards of civilisation. Already in one of the first of his books, the ' Traumdeutung ' (1900), he quotes with evident approval a passage from Zeller on the normal mind: ' An intellect is rarely so happily organised as to be in full command of itself at all times and seasons, and never to be disturbed in the lucid and constant processes of thought by ideas not merely unessential, but absolutely grotesque and nonsensical; indeed, the greatest thinkers have had cause to complain of this dream-like, tormenting and distressing rabble of ideas, which disturbs their profoundest contemplations and their most pious and earnest meditations.' And a paper of great sociological interest written not long afterwards (1908) evinced a penetrating scepticism on the subject of prevailing social standards. He betrayed this underlying attitude time and again in his works, culminating in a recent book (1929) for which he has been much reproved by the cheerful believers in easy progress.

Amongst other psycho-analytical writers who have dealt with the same theme, an essay by Stärcke (1921) should be mentioned as providing reflections on the normal mind searching and sceptical enough to satisfy the most exigent. Stärcke came to the conclusion that Western civilisation is built on an attitude towards life characteristic of a particular form of obsessional neurosis which he defines under the name of ' metaphrenia,' extending thus and rendering more precise the comparison of civilisation with disease that Ruskin, Edward Carpenter and other English sociologists had made. In a highly interesting study of the various definitions that psychiatrists, jurists and others have attempted of insanity he has no difficulty in demonstrating their arbitrariness and maintains that the only tenable definition of an insane person is a person who threatens to unmask the unconscious (*i.e.*, insane) mentality which the community finds intolerable. Finally, even if we were not in a position to adduce these examples—and it would be easy to cite others—and even granted slipshod thinking on the part of psycho-analysts, it would still remain true that there is nothing in the method of psycho-analysis itself that binds the theory to any preconceived conception of normality in the average human mind. And, as I remarked above, recent work has amply demonstrated in detail the independence of psycho-analysis from any such preconceptions.

If now we cast back to the series of casual definitions of normality mentioned above it is easy to perceive that they fall into two main groups: (1) those depending on the criterion of happiness, and (2) those depending on that of adaptation to reality. By reality we can in this connection only mean psychological reality, and this in its turn may be reduced to mental contact with the individuals comprising the particular environment of the subject. Such contact does not necessarily imply acceptance of the environmental standards, but it does imply a sensitive perception of them, and a recognition of their social significance, when deciding on a course of conduct or when estimating the impression a given response to other people will make on them. The mental attributes here concerned evidently depend on a feeling-relationship with other human beings which needs further definition, but which must be of central importance in deciding on any criterion of normality; it is a matter to which we shall have to return later. The first criterion, that of happiness, is doubtless also one that relates to certain fundamental qualities, but there are difficulties in the way of using it quite empirically. In the first place a subjective judgement must come into play—apart, of course, from gross deviations—in estimating whether a given person is happier or less happy than is to be expected from his particular fate in life, in estimating how much influence is ' normally ' exerted by this or that misfortune, grief or difficulty. We reach in this way the general philosophical consideration of the value of life, of whether it is more ' normal ' to be an optimist or a pessimist, to enjoy life or to endure it. With the milder forms of cyclothymia we may often make the interesting observation that the patient in his depressed mood has a vivid sense of now being more normal, of perceiving life as it really is, and of recognising that in his gayer mood he was merely being influenced by various illusions that distorted his perception of reality. Nevertheless, deep analysis constantly shows that even the philosophic pessimism about life is bound up with internal inhibitions of enjoyment and self-content which, from their origin and their fate after analysis, can only be regarded as artefacts in the evolution of the individual. And we find, further, that lasting impairment of the natural zest of life—I use the word ' natural ' deliberately, having in mind what we know of the importance of the pleasure principle in biology—is more often the result of such internal inhibitions than of externally inflicted misfortune, however severe and however lasting.

The concept of ' efficiency ' would appear to stand midway between the two just mentioned, of happiness and of psychological adaptation. Efficiency in life is not easily thinkable with anyone who is either excessively influenced by other people or is quite insensitive to their feelings, for both of these attitudes proceed from unsolved conflicts in the psychological relationship to others and merely represent different reactions to these unconscious conflicts. Nor is it compatible with a state of mind destitute of all gusto, where no achievement seems much worth while. It should further be remembered that in using any concept of efficiency as a criterion of normality it is important to distinguish between merely external success in life, where opportunity plays such a large part, and internal success—i.e., the fullest use of the given individual's powers and talents. All these considerations lead one to infer that behind the expression ' happiness ' and ' feeling-relationship ' there probably lie attributes of central importance to our present theme.

We observed earlier that the usual therapeutic standards of normality, relating as they mostly do to obviously pathological material, are necessarily of a low order, and it is desirable to illustrate this consideration further. Our test of therapeutic success, as is well known, is not simply the removal of manifest symptoms, but the providing of channels from the unconscious to consciousness free enough to ensure a permanent flow of energy from the one level to the other that will make the subsequent re-forming of any psycho-neurotic symptom impossible. Such symptoms are of course not an inevitable product of development; they represent the last desperate device for dealing with unsolved conflicts between anxiety and guilt on the one hand and various libidinal forces on the other. When the anxiety and guilt which have caused the undue repressions have been sufficiently dissolved by analysis, and the conflict between them and the libido thus lessened, the latter becomes redistributed more diffusely instead of being expressed in psycho-neurotic symptoms. Now it constantly happens in the course of analysis that the patient receives what might be called bonuses in addition to the actual benefit he expected on coming for treatment. The reasons for this gratifying state of affairs are twofold. The patient is sure to discover a number of symptoms he had not previously recognised to be such; he has perhaps thought of them before under names like ' idiosyncrasy,' ' peculiarity,' ' lack of interest,' ' dislike,' and so on. In the analysis these are of course resolved just like other symptoms. The second reason is that it is impossible to confine the analytic freeing to the specific energy locked up in the manifest symptoms themselves. As is well known, the curiously indirect technique of psycho-analysis does not permit of this, and the fortunate result is that there comes about a general freeing of the personality in addition to the relief from the actual symptoms. We thus obtain a visible proof of what William James long ago surmised—namely, that there is in everyone a very considerable quantity of psychical energy locked up, not at the disposal of the personality. We can even specify the way in which this has come about. The diminution in the amount of free energy is due to waste through internal friction: with pronounced unconscious conflicts much energy is either held in latent suspense by repression or else is expended in the endeavour to create neurotic substitutes for more direct modes of expression; while on the other hand a corresponding amount of energy is used up in maintaining the repressions (anti-cathexis).

How unsuspectedly precarious may be the state of balance in a relatively stable personality can best be appreciated by carrying out

a series of character-analyses. Nowadays we have far more opportunity for this through patients consulting us on account of social
disharmony, with or without manifest psycho-neurotic symptoms,
or with apparently normal candidates who present themselves for
the study of psycho-analysis. In work of this kind one is often
astonished to observe how a comparatively good functioning of the
personality can exist with an extensive neurosis, or even psychosis,
that is not manifest. Various reaction- and character-formations
cover over the underlying neurotic or psychotic condition, which
often makes a dramatic appearance at even an early stage of the
analysis.

All the considerations brought forward up to this point are, or
should be, truisms to the psycho-analyst, and I wish now to mention
one which has not received adequate notice in psycho-analytical
literature. A thorough analysis, we know, has the effect not only of
removing any manifest psycho-neurotic symptoms, but of so dealing
with the fundamental conflicts and complexes as to bring about a
considerable freeing and expansion of the personality. In so doing
it leads to changes of a general order in the character and even
intellect, notably in the direction of increased tolerance and open-
mindedness. But it could be used for a still further purpose which,
in my opinion, would be of great interest and value if attempted.
Mainly because of the time consumed, an analysis is customarily
brought to an end when the unconscious conflicts have been resolved
and when the empirical results desired are achieved. There is no
motive as a rule to make use of the work done by applying it in
detail to the conscious (and pre-conscious) layers of the mind. An
impartial observer cannot fail to be struck by the disconcerting fact
that analysed people, including psycho-analysts, differ surprisingly
little from unanalysed people in the use made of their intelligence.
Their greater tolerance in sexual and religious spheres is usually the
only mark of a change in the use of the intellect. In other spheres
they seem to form their judgements, or rather to maintain their
previous convictions and attitudes, on very much the same lines of
rationalised prejudices as unanalysed people do. Fads and cranky
attitudes, of course, one can count on being altered by an analysis,
and opinions on subjects directly connected with analytical problems,
such as mental responsibility in crime, are sure to be modified. But
I am thinking rather of the main mass of opinions on current topics
and events of the kind that make up social life and conversation,

opinions which are demonstrably far from objective and which there is every reason to think are extensively influenced by the distorting effects of unconscious complexes. Here it is striking to observe how little advantage is commonly obtained from psycho-analysis in comparison with what one knows must be potentially available. Analysts and other analysed persons often continue to hold heatedly the same convictions and to employ in support of them the same rationalised arguments as unanalysed people in such matters as political controversy: the sacro-sanctity of private property and the capitalistic system, or, on the other hand, the panacea of communism; the relative advantages of free trade and tariffs; the fallacies of a managed currency, of the gold standard, or of bimetallism; in the varying attitudes towards the manifold fields of art; in feelings about fashions or differences in social class; in the conventional estimates of historical and political personages and events; in the important sphere of national prejudices and convictions; in views about foreign problems (the relation of one's own country to others). As the last war showed, analysts are as pacifist in peace-time and patriotically militarist in war-time as their fellows, and for just the same reasons. Even in the sphere of pathology itself analytic scepticism has not been pushed far: one can, for instance, find medical analysts who fully share their colleagues' superstitions about the climatic origin of influenza or rheumatism, not to mention innumerable other ones.

I have no doubt that it would be an extraordinarily interesting experiment, and one of great profit socially, to conclude an analysis by applying its findings to the various conscious and pre-conscious convictions of the kind just mentioned, to elucidate and estimate the part played by the unconscious in forming them. But who would bell the cat? Who is himself sufficiently objective and well-informed[1] to undertake such a task? Still, the same question might once have been asked in regard to exploring the unconscious itself. A pioneer was found then, and he will doubtless be found again. Then we shall learn much of value about the relationship of unconscious complexes and social interaction, and thus gain knowledge that would aid us in the study of normality.

Even without this knowledge, however, I think it is possible to make a beginning in constructing the desired concept of normality. We have abstracted from the customary definitions the attributes of

[1] It may be remarked that both the acquiring (and especially the non-acquiring) and the selecting of knowledge are extensively influenced by unconscious complexes.

happiness, of efficiency in mental functioning, and of a positive social feeling-relationship, and have postponed analytic consideration of them. If we now attempt this, we may hope to attain more stringent criteria of normality than is otherwise possible.

We will begin with the last mentioned of the three attributes, the *relation to one's fellows*. In his important contribution to our knowledge of evolution in the normal, Abraham (1925) cautiously stated that the most complete development presupposes ' a sufficient quantity of affectionate and friendly feeling,' and he correlated this with the degree to which narcissism and ambivalence have been transcended in the course of development—a process of which he gave a signal example in his own life.

We are unfortunately far from possessing any method of quantitatively measuring degrees of friendliness and affection, or any way of estimating the amount one would expect to find in a ' normal ' personality or the proportion between it and other components. Nevertheless we are in a position to make a number of qualitative statements that have a definite value in giving an approach to this difficult problem. Let us begin by considering Abraham's formula. We can at once say that the greater part of what used to be called narcissism, or self-love pure and simple, is of a secondary nature. It is a matter rather of regression brought about as a flight from difficulties in the Œdipus situation which the child has not been able to surmount. Similarly the retaining of an ambivalent attitude, an alternation or entanglement between love and hate, is also a regressive flight into the primitive instinct of hate, which is used as a defence against the difficulties in question. The precise nature of these difficulties, and what the surmounting of them signifies, we shall presently discuss.

We can further say that certain forms of what may be called excessive friendliness and conciliatoriness, including a good deal of philanthropic benevolence, however agreeable such qualities may be socially, are not really simple manifestations of the love instinct. They are exploitations of this instinct, the main function and meaning of which is the repression, by ' reaction-forming,' of unresolved sadism. The sadism often enough comes to expression in other spheres, such as with the professional philanthropist who makes his home life a misery by his morose disagreeableness, or with the notorious truculence of so many political pacifists. This simple consideration, easily confirmed in actual analyses, at once precludes us from estimating the amount of friendliness in a given personality merely by observing what is apparent; as with dreams, the latent content is far from being identical with the manifest. An apparently soft and yielding nature is by no means necessarily the mark of a loving nature. It may simply mean that the unconscious sadism has been retained in its primitive state, needing the energy of reaction-formations to keep it there, instead of being transformed into the valuable character traits of firmness and strength with which to meet the difficulties of life or, if necessary, to resist the will of one's adversaries.

On the other hand it is equally certain that much of what passes as ' strength of character ' is an illusion. Such traits as obstinacy, pugnacity, extreme ' individualism,' cynicism, hardness of heart, insensitiveness to the feelings of other human beings, however useful they may on occasion be to their owner, are often little more than defences against love of which the person is too afraid—or, more strictly, of possible consequences of this love.[1] A matter-of-fact attitude of being ' superior to sentiment ' is often a buttressing of the personality, a self-justification in the presence of deep-seated fear.

We thus see that the degree of friendliness and affection is to be estimated by the *internal freedom* of such feelings rather than by the quantity of them that may be manifest. It will then be found that this freedom is accompanied by a slowness of response to hostility or even to opposition. The assimilation and control of the unconscious sadism, the same thing that allows love and friendliness to flow easily, begets an inner confidence and security that enable the person to endure opposition calmly and to be so un-intimidated by hostility as to render aggressive opposition on his part unnecessary except in extreme and urgent situations. It will be seen how different this confident sereneness is from the neurotic conciliatoriness of the type described above, though a superficial observer may at times confound the two. Psychologically they are poles apart, one being born of confidence, the other of fear.

A word should be said here on the matter of homosexual and heterosexual affection respectively. Experience would appear to show that there exists a certain correlation between the two, so that, for instance, it is rarely possible for a man both to love women and

---

[1] In his study of Baudelaire, René Laforgue (1931) has delineated with striking insight the deep fear of surrendering oneself to happiness.

to hate men. Clinically the question is often more confused than this. Thus a man may unconsciously work out both sides of his nature on the opposite sex only; ignoring men, he may then attain a certain expertness in sexual technique—uncontrollable passion often alternating with impotence in a way that attracts many homosexual women—but fundamentally he is ambivalent or even hostile to women and never truly loves them.

These few remarks are only an abstract from the volume that could be written on the complicated problems of love and hate, of friendliness and animosity. I cannot conclude them, however, without making some slight reference to what is perhaps their most important social aspect, and one of the most difficult psychological aspects of the problem—namely, the assessing in the ' normal ' of the relations between the interests of the individual and those of society. For a full discussion of the problem, especially in its sociological and biological aspects, the reader is referred to a paper by Flugel (1921). From the point of view of psycho-analysis it is established that neurotic tendencies can lead to extreme attitudes in either direction. It can be shown, for instance, that selfishness at the expense of the community may be due to unconscious fear and repression, while on the other side quixotic self-sacrifice may proceed from unconscious guilt. That is not to say that every extreme attitude is necessarily neurotic. If we take the most extreme of all, the sacrifice of life for country in war, are we to say that the man who refuses to join in what he regards as a meaningless massacre is more normal than the man who feels that life is not worth living unless he has done all in his power, at every cost, to help his particular country win a particular fight ? Doubtless more people would say so in time of peace than in time of war, but I may quote my own experience of analyses since the last war, which indicate that the contrary view does not apply to war-time only. I have analysed several conscientious objectors who had to recognise in the course of the analysis the neurotic basis of their attitude and who declared at the end of it that if called on to make the same decision again they would make a different one, whereas I have never analysed an ex-combatant who at the end of the analysis adopted the attitude of a conscientious objector. When we come to consider the problem of conscience, with which the present one is in essence identical, I will suggest a criterion for testing the normality of the relation between individual and social interests, and would only add here the reflection that the line of demarcation may prove to be somewhat different in the two sexes—it being possible that with a normal man loyalty attaches to a larger group than with a normal woman.

We now pass to the second of the three attributes mentioned earlier—namely, that of *mental efficiency*. As we have seen, it is related to the other two, and at this point I intend to bring forward only one consideration, which seems to concern it more directly than others that could be mentioned. We assume, for good reasons, that all the energy employed in the pursuit of any activity is ultimately derived from primitive unconscious sources, and it is therefore plain that the optimum condition for the ' efficient ' expenditure of this energy must be an unimpeded flow of it. Any state of affairs in which the flow is constantly hampered to some extent, or is exposed to temporary interruption, will be one where efficiency is temporarily or permanently below its potential maximum. Now the difference between these two conditions is the difference between sublimation and displacement. A great deal of what commonly passes for sublimation is really displacement, or at best imperfect sublimation. There are two essential distinctions between these processes. In displacement the psychological significance of the external conscious activity remains more or less that of the original unconscious impulse: the one is little more than a substitute for the other and is thus subject to whatever conflicts, compulsions or inhibitions may influence the latter. This explains why fiery energy may at times be devoted to an external activity, in what is inherently a compulsive fashion, and yet may be fickle or temporary in its course; the person is really reacting to an unconscious complex, with its urges and inhibitions, rather than to the external stimulus. The second distinction is related to the first, but is less easy to define. It is that in true sublimation not only has the external activity or interest come to have a greater significance than the original unconscious source from which the energy is derived, but also that the nature of the energy has undergone some qualitative change. Freud speaks of desexualised energy in connection with sublimation. This is very likely the essence of the matter, but it is plain that we are still some distance from understanding the precise nature of the change. Whatever it may be, it is certainly compatible, oddly enough, with the zest of the original wishes being retained to the full.

Finally we have to consider the first mentioned of the three attributes, *happiness*, the one I would select in spite of Bernard Shaw's dictum to the contrary as probably the most important of the three. It need hardly be said that by happiness we do not here mean simple pleasure, but a combination of enjoyment—or rather the capacity for enjoyment—with self-content. The reason why these two things go together is that where self-content is deficient it means that unconscious guilt is operative, which will surely impair the capacity for enjoyment, either at times or always.

Two conclusions are forced on us here by psycho-analytical experience: first, that impairment of happiness, in the broad sense just given to it, is always due to the triad of fear, hate and guilt (in psycho-analysis ' guilt ' is a shorthand expression for ' unconscious feelings of guiltiness that give rise to the need for self-punishment '); and, secondly, that the difficulties in development responsible for the inhibiting effect of this triad are in essence those of the Œdipus situation. The interrelationships between the members of the triad in question, with which I have attempted to deal in a previous paper (1929), are quite extraordinarily complicated and are characterised by a curiously recurrent stratification. This is not the place to recapitulate them and I must content myself here with a few summary statements. Although in clinical practice an upper layer of fear—e.g., with phobia—is certainly secondary to deeper guilt and hate, an ultimate analysis nevertheless shows that fear is the most fundamental member of the triad. Personally I have long shared the opinion, expressed more than half a century ago by a German writer, Dick (1877), that anxiety is the Alpha and Omega of psychiatry, and that the various complex fixations of attitude we have to resolve in analysis are in the last resort defences against intolerable anxiety; I would unhesitatingly extend this view to the field of normal psychology and maintain that on the way in which any individual deals with the primordial anxiety of infancy more depends than on anything else in development.

As was pointed out earlier, many unsocial attitudes—e.g., selfishness, antagonism—are really defences against something within, which the individual has found intolerable and so has been unable to master. In measuring, therefore, freedom from anxiety, one cannot be content with observing the merely manifest freedom, but must also take into account the cost at which this apparent freedom is maintained—i.e., the presence or absence of secondary defences. The hate group, with all its varieties and ramifications, well illustrates this. The infant's chief help in dealing with its difficulty of enduring libidinal privation or frustration, with the anxiety to which it leads, is to have recourse to the reaction of hate (anger, etc.), a fact probably related to the large component of sadism in its libido. This, however, leads to further fear (of retaliation and self-injury) and becomes sexualised in its turn, thus affording a sadistic outlet. Much of it is then turned inwards, constituting unconscious guilt—with both its sadistic and its masochistic sides.

Unconscious guilt plays such a large part in analytic work, and is so evidently the foe to freedom, that patients often raise the question whether conscience in any form is not to be regarded as a morbid entity. And indeed the word ' conscience ' may well be taken as the crucial point of the present discussion, for round it centre all the problems of the relationship of the individual to society, of gratification and restraint, and the fundamental reactions to anxiety. It is commonly defined as the conscious part of the super-ego, being thus distinguished from unconscious guilt. The definition is certainly imperfect and is also not quite accurate in either direction. At least two further considerations must be taken into account. One can distinguish between a super-ego actuated (especially in its relationship to other human beings) by guilt based on fear and one actuated by affection, by what may be called negative and positive tendencies respectively. Parallel with this is the distinction between a still sexual super-ego and a desexualised super-ego.

In previous writings I have sustained the view that the deepest difficulty of the child in its earliest development is to endure libidinal tension in the presence of privation without having recourse to one of two reactions: on the one hand to bring about an artificial inhibition with the consequent fear of loss, or on the other to develop the defences of guilt and hate which in their turn lead to further intolerable situations. And I have suggested that this primordial difficulty may be described as a vague dread of what I have called the issue of aphanisis—*i.e.*, paralysis brought about by continued and unrelieved over-excitation.

When these two defensive reactions in their turn create difficulties, the outcome is a neurosis, so that from this vantage-point we surmise that the psychological problem of normality must ultimately reside in the capacity to endure—in the ability to hold wishes in suspension without either renouncing them or ' reacting ' to them in defensive ways. Freedom and self-control are thus seen to be really the same thing, though both are badly misused concepts.

We reach the conclusion that the nearest attainable criterion of normality is fearlessness. The most normal person is, like Siegfried, ' *angstfrei*,' but we must be clear that we mean by this not merely manifest courage, but the absence of all the deep reactions that mask unconscious apprehensiveness. Where these are absent we have the willing or even joyful acceptance of life, with all its visitations and chances, that distinguishes the free personality of one who is master of himself.

It may now well be asked whether a criterion born of psychopathology can possess more than a very limited validity, and what is its relation to other criteria that may be arrived at by other disciplines. Personally I should not be inclined to rank psychopathology low in this matter. In an address recently delivered in America (1930) I instituted a plea for the precedence of psychopathology, with its technique for exploring the depths, over any form of psychology of the normal, which has to be content with the surface of far more distorted and obscure material. A biological criterion, such as, for example, the maximum survival-value to the species, suffers from the shifting standards and aimlessness of evolution, or else it approximates to the one here put forward--namely, the fullest possible development of the organism. As to philosophical or æsthetic criteria, it would not be hard to show that the subjective idealism on which they are based represents only individual forms—of therefore limited validity—of the criterion here advanced.

Dr. Schmalhausen had asked me to give my opinion on the question of whether a normal mind exists. I have dealt with the problem on somewhat different lines, but perhaps I may be allowed in conclusion to attempt a personal answer to his question. It will conduce to clearness if we subdivide the question into three: what is a normal mind ? does such a thing actually exist ? and can such a thing ever exist ?

My answer to the first of these questions is that by adopting the criterion of unimpeded development we have advanced some distance towards establishing an objective standard of normality. Very much has still to be learned about the different ways in which that standard can be attained and the different forms it can assume according to the interplay of inherited characteristics and the influences of the particular environment. But the problem does not appear to be an insoluble one. In centuries to come, when the social and educational sciences take note of the findings of depth psychology, the knowledge gained by studying this problem will be perceived to be of inestimable practical value, and will rank as not the least of the gifts which psycho-analysis has bestowed on the world.

The second question is the easiest of the three to answer, and definitely in the negative. We have no experience of a completely normal mind. If we think at random of well-known names having some title to the claim, from possessing unusual freedom and balance of personality, or sanity of judgement, or from exhibiting other marks of normality in a pre-eminent degree—names like Bright, Darwin, Faraday, Freud, Goethe, Huxley, Leonardo da Vinci, Napoleon, Shakespeare, Washington—a psycho-analyst would have no difficulty in demonstrating some measure of deflection in development with each of them, and often enough manifest neurotic reactions. Nor does psycho-analysis, even in young children, offer at present any prospect of removing every trace of the deepest layers of anxiety.

The third question should perhaps be subdivided into two. (1) Is there any reason to suppose that a mind could be ideally normal in the absolute sense ? As we do not meet absolute perfection elsewhere in the universe, even in Newton's Laws of Motion, it would be astonishing ever to find it in such a wry locality as the mind of man. (2) Is there any reason to expect normality, in the more limited and almost clinical sense here adopted, in the future when early mental development is better understood and seriously cared for ? I do not know.

REFERENCES

Abraham, K. (1925). (Trans. 1927.) 'Character-Formation on the Genital Level of Libido-Development,' *Selected Papers,* p. 416.

Dick (1877). *Allg. Z. Psychiat.,* vol. xxiii., p. 231.

Flugel, J. C. (1921). 'On the Biological Basis of Sexual Repression and its Sociological Significance,' *British Journal of Medical Psychology,* vol. i., p. 225.

Freud, S. (1900). (Trans. Third Edition, 1932). 'The Interpretation of Dreams,' pp.81-2.

Freud, S. (1908). (Trans. 1924.) '"Civilised" Sexual Morality and Modern Nervousness,' 'Collected Papers,' vol. ii., p. 76.

Freud, S. (1929). (Trans. 1930.) 'Civilisation and its Discontents.'

Jones, Ernest (1929). 'Fear, Guilt and Hate,' *Int. J. Psycho-Anal.,* vol. x., p. 383.

Jones, Ernest (1930). 'Psycho-Analysis and Psychiatry,' *Ment. Hyg.,* N.Y., vol. xiv., p. 384.

Lafourgue, R. (1931). (Trans. 1932.) 'The Defeat of Baudelaire.'

Stärcke, A. (1921). (Trans. 1921.) 'Psycho-Analysis and Psychiatry,' *Int. J. Psycho-Anal.,* vol. ii., p. 361.

Trotter, W. (1916). 'Instincts of the Herd in Peace and War,' pp. 78-9.

CHAPTER X

FREUD'S THEORY OF DREAMS [1]

FREUD's theory of dreams occupies a nodal position in his psychology, constituting as it does a point of conjunction for his various conclusions on normal and abnormal mental life respectively. From it as a starting-point he has developed outlooks that call for the earnest consideration of psychologists, for it is extensively conceded that if his conclusions are true they carry with them a revolutionary change in our knowledge of the structure and functions of the mind. These broader aspects of his theory will not here be considered, the present paper being intended merely to delineate the main outlines of the dream theory proper. Owing to the richness of the subject-matter even this purpose can here of necessity be but very imperfectly attained, so that the following description can at best only serve as an introduction to the study of his ' Traumdeutung.'[2] No just criticism of the theory can be made without a careful perusal of this volume, in which Freud has in detail entered into all the manifold problems relating to dreams, has presented the evidence on which his conclusions are based, and has fully discussed rival views and anticipated the possible objections that may be raised to his own. A few illustrative examples, drawn from the writer's experience, will accompany the present paper, but in order to economise space no actual dream-analyses will be detailed, it being proposed to do this in a subsequent paper.

The method Freud uses in the investigation of dreams is that termed by him Psycho-Analysis, and on the question of the reliability of this method rests that of the validity of his conclusions. No account of psycho-analysis itself can be given here, for that alone would exact a long exposition, but it should explicitly be stated that the technique of this method is a complex and intricate matter the acquirement of which is not, as many writers seem over-readily to

[1] Amplified from a paper read before the American Psychological Association, December 29, 1909. Published in the *American Journal of Psychology*, vol. xxi.
[2] First edition, 1900 ; fifth edition, 1919. It is advantageous to read before this more difficult volume Freud's ' Vorlesungen zur Einführung in die Psychoanalyse,' Zweiter Teil, ' Der Traum,' 1916. (English translation, ' Introductory Lectures on Psycho-Analysis,' 1922.)

assume, an easy task, but one requiring much practice, patience, and experience. In no branch of science can the testing of the results obtained by the use of an entirely new and difficult technique be satisfactorily submitted to an off-hand trial on the part of someone quite untrained in this, and it is strange that it does not occur to those who do not directly confirm Freud's conclusions as soon as they ' try psycho-analysis ' that the fact may be due, not, as they hastily infer, to the erroneousness of those conclusions, but to a more humble explanation—namely, that they have not mastered the technique. Articles purporting to disprove Freud's conclusions have been published on the basis of a casual scrutiny of three or four dreams; Freud, on the other hand, published nothing on the subject until he had made a careful study of over a thousand dreams. In my opinion the ' Traumdeutung ' is one of the most finished pieces of elaborate work ever given to the world; it is in any event noteworthy that in the twenty years that have elapsed since it was written only one other investigator, Silberer, has been able to make any addition —and that only a very minor one—to the theory, while not one constituent element of the theory has been disproved.

It is commonly believed in scientific circles that the mental processes of which dreams are composed arise, without any direct psychical antecedent, as the result of irregular excitation of various elements in the cerebral cortex by physiological processes occurring during sleep. This, it is maintained, accounts for the confused and bizarre nature of the mental product, and any apparently logical connection and order that frequently appear to some extent in dreams are explained by the supposition that the mental processes in question are represented in cortical elements that stand in close, anatomical or physiological, relation to one another, and so are simultaneously stimulated by the peripheral stimuli. Hence any problem as to the psychical origin of the mental processes, still more as to the *meaning* of the dream as a whole, is by the nature of things excluded as being non-existent, and any investigation along such lines is condemned as savouring of antiquated superstitions about the ' reading of dreams ' unworthy of educated people. To this attitude Freud, as must every consistent psychologist, stands in sharp opposition. He contends that dream processes, like all other mental processes, have their psychical history, that in spite of their peculiar attributes they have a legitimate and comprehensible place in the sequence of mental life, and that their origins are to be traced psychologically with as much certainty and precision as those of any other mental processes. The very possibility of this is sometimes doubted on the ground that the material to be investigated is so very uncertain and indefinite in its nature. Not only has one no guarantee that the dream has been accurately observed, remembered, and reported, but in most cases one can be pretty sure that what has actually happened is just the opposite of this—that, namely, parts of the dream are forgotten altogether, other parts are falsified in the memory, and so on, the result being that the material offered for investigation is only a partial and distorted copy of the original. However, apart from the fact that at least some dreams are clear throughout and precisely remembered, one has to accept empirically this feature of indefiniteness and study it like any other; the explanation Freud offers of it will be mentioned presently.

From one point of view dreams may be grouped into the following three categories. First may be distinguished those that are throughout both sensible and intelligible; such especially are the dreams of children. The very occurrence of such dreams, in which the mental processes fully resemble those of waking life, although they are never confounded with them, is in itself a strong argument against the view that dreams result from the isolated activity of single groups of brain cells. Secondly, there are dreams which are connected and have an evident meaning, but one the content of which is curious and surprising, so that we cannot fit them into the rest of our waking life. A person dreams, for instance, that his brother has been gored to death by a bull; he cannot account for his having come by such a curious notion, nor can he at first sight relate it to any waking thought. Thirdly, there is the most frequent type of dream, where the mental processes seem disconnected, confused, and senseless. These two latter types of dreams have a peculiar quality of strangeness and unreality; they are foreign to the other mental experiences of the subject, and cannot be inserted into any place in his waking thoughts. It is as though the subject has lived through a different range of experience, in another place or in another world, which apparently has no connection with the one to which he is accustomed. Now, Freud holds that this sense of foreignness is an illusion due to very definite causes, and that the mental processes which go to form dreams are really in direct continuity with those of waking life.

In tracing the antecedents of dream processes Freud makes use, as has been said, of the psycho-analytic method, which essentially consists in the collecting and ordering of the *free* associations that occur to the subject when he attends to any given theme and abrogates the selecting control over the incoming thoughts that is instinctively exercised by the conscious mind. If this method is applied to any component part of a dream, however senseless it may appear on the surface, mental processes are reached which are of high personal significance to the subject. The mental processes thus reached Freud terms the ' dream thoughts '; they constitute the ' latent content ' of the dream in contradistinction to the ' manifest content,' which is the dream as related by the subject. It is essential to keep distinct these two groups of mental processes, for on the appreciation of the difference between them rests the whole explanation of the puzzling riddles of dreams. The latent content, or dream thought, is a logical and integral part of the subject's mental life, and contains none of the incongruous absurdities and other peculiar features that characterise the manifest content of most dreams. This manifest content is to be regarded as an allegorical expression of the underlying dream thoughts, or latent content. The distortion of the dream thoughts into the dream proper takes place according to certain well-determined psychological laws, and for very precise reasons. The core of Freud's theory, and the most original part of his contribution to the subject, resides in his tracing the cause of this distortion mainly to a ' censorship ' which interposes an obstruction to the becoming conscious of unconscious psychical processes. This conception he arrived at from the analysis of various abnormal psychical manifestations, psychoneurotic symptoms, which he found to be constructed on a plan fully analogous to that of dreams. It may be remarked at this point that, quite apart from any views about the cause of the distortion, the nature and functions of the dream thoughts and other problems, the fact itself of the distortion is certain, and cannot be doubted by anyone who carefully observes a few dreams. That, for instance, the vision of a strange room in a dream is a distorted presentation of several rooms that have been actually seen, from each of which various individual features have been abstracted and fused together so as to present a new and therefore strange room, is the kind of observation that can easily be verified. Before considering, therefore, the nature of the latent content it will be well shortly to describe the distorting mechanisms by means of which it becomes transformed into the manifest content.

A dream is not, as it appears to be, a confused and haphazard congeries of mental phenomena, but a distorted and disguised expression of highly significant psychical processes that have a very definite meaning, although in order to appreciate this meaning it is first necessary to translate the manifest content of the dream into its latent content, just as a hieroglyphic script yields its meaning only after it has been interpreted. The mechanisms by means of which the manifest content has been formed from the underlying dream thoughts may be grouped under four headings.

The first of these is called *Condensation* (*Verdichtung*). Every element of the manifest content represents several dream thoughts; it is, as Freud puts it, ' over-determined ' (*überdeterminiert*). Thus the material obtained by analysis of a dream is far richer and more extensive than the manifest content, and may exceed this amount by ten or twenty times. Of all the mechanisms it is the easiest to observe, and to it is mainly due the sense of foreignness that dreams give us, for it is a process with which our waking thought is not familiar.[1] The representation in the manifest content of the extensive material comprising the latent content is brought about by a true condensation, rarely by the mere omission of part of the latent content. The condensation is effected in several ways. A figure in a dream may be constituted by the fusion of traits belonging to more than one actual person, and is then called a ' composite person ' (*Sammelperson*). This may occur either by the fusion of some traits belonging to one person with some belonging to another, or by making prominent the traits common to the two and neglecting those not common to them; the latter process produces a result analogous to a Galton's composite photograph. The same process frequently occurs with names: thus Freud mentions a dream in which the person seemed to be called Norekdal, which had been formed from the names of two of Ibsen's characters, Nora and Ekdal; I have seen the name Magna formed by fusing Maggie and Edna, and similar instances are common enough. The neologism thus produced closely resembles those met with in the psychoses, particularly in dementia præcox, and like these may refer to things as well as to persons. Lastly in this connection it should be remarked that certain of the elements in the manifest content are especially

---

[1] For a discussion of condensation see pp. 106-109.

rich in associations, as if they formed particular points of junction (*Knotenpunkte*); they are in other words the 'best-determined' elements. These are intimately related to the most significant elements in the underlying dream thoughts, and also frequently show the greatest sensorial vividness in the manifest content.

Condensation subserves more than one function. *In the first place* it is the mechanism by means of which similarity, agreement, or identity between two elements in the latent content is expressed in the manifest content; the two elements simply become fused into one, thus forming a new unity. If this fusion has already taken place in the latent content the process is termed *Identification*; if it takes place during the construction of the dream itself the process is termed *Composition* (*Mischbildung*): the former process rarely concerns things, chiefly persons and places. In the process of identification a person in the dream enters into situations that really are proper to some other person, or behaves in a way characteristic of this second person. In the process of composition the fusion is revealed in the manifest content in other ways; thus a given person may appear in the dream, but bearing the name of some second one, or the figure in the dream may be composed of traits taken some from the first, others from the second person. The existence of a resemblance between two persons or places may thus be expressed in the dream by the appearance of a composite person or place built up in the way just mentioned; the important feature that the two have in common, which in this case is the essential constituent in the latent content, need not be present in the manifest content, and indeed usually is not. It is clear that by this means a considerable economy in presentation is effected, for a highly complex and abstract resemblance may be expressed by simply fusing the figures of the persons concerned. Thus, if two persons both show the sentiments of envy, fear, and malice towards the subject of the dream, these sentiments may be expressed by the appearance in the manifest content of a composite figure of the two persons. In this composite figure there may be traits common to both persons, such as colour of hair or other personal characteristics, but the essential resemblance in the underlying dream thoughts is as a rule not evident in the dream. The superficial resemblance presented in the dream is frequently thus the cover for a deeper and more significant one, and gives the clue to important constituents of the dream thoughts. The process in question may also represent merely the wish that there were such a resemblance between the two persons, and therefore, the wish that they might be exchanged in their relation to the subject. When, for instance, a married lady dreams that she is breakfasting alone with some man friend, the interpretation is often a simple matter. *In the second place* condensation, like the other distorting mechanisms, subserves the function of evading the endopsychic censorship. This is a matter that will presently be further discussed, but it is plain that a repressed and unacceptable wish that two persons or places may resemble each other in an important respect, or may be interchanged, can be expressed in the manifest content of a dream by presenting an insignificant resemblance between the two.

It might be assumed from the description given above that the process of condensation takes place in one direction only, that each element in the manifest content represents a number of elements in the latent content in the same way that a delegate represents the members of his constituency. This, however, is not so, for not only is every element in the manifest content connected with several in the latent content, but every element in the latter is connected with several in the former. In addition to this, frequently associations exist between the different elements of the entire structure of the dream, so that this often has the appearance of a tangled network until the full analysis brings law and order out of the whole.

The second distorting mechanism is that termed *Displacement* (*Verschiebung*). In most dreams it is found after analysis that there is no correspondence between the psychical intensity of a given element in the manifest content and the associated elements in the latent content. An element that stands in the foreground of interest in the former, and seems to be the central feature of the dream, may represent the least significant of the underlying dream thoughts; conversely an apparently unessential and transitory feature in the dream may represent the very core of the dream thoughts. Further, the most prominent affect in the dream, hate, anxiety, and so on, as the case may be, often accompanies elements that represent the least important part of the dream thoughts, whereas the dream thoughts that are powerfully invested with this affect may be represented in the manifest content of the dream by elements of feeble affective tone. This disturbing displacement Freud describes, using Nietzsche's phrase, as a 'transvaluation of all values.' It is a phenomenon peculiarly frequent in the psychoneuroses, in which a lively interest or an intense affect may be found associated with an unimportant idea. In both cases a transposition of affect has taken place whereby a highly significant idea is replaced by a previously indifferent and unimportant one. Often the association between the primary and secondary ideas is a very superficial one, and especially common forms of this are witty plays on the speech expression for the two ideas, and other kinds of clang association. As is well known, Jung has demonstrated[1] that this superficial association is usually the cover for a deeper hidden bond of high affective value. This mechanism of displacement is the cause of the puzzling fact that most dreams contain so many different and hardly noticed impressions of the previous day; these, having on account of their unimportance formed but few associations with previous mental processes, are made use of in the dream-making to represent more significant ideas, the affect of which is transferred to them. Displacement also explains much of the bizarreness of dreams, notably the remarkable incongruity between the intensity of the affect and the intellectual content; a person may in a dream be terrified at an apparently indifferent object, and quite at ease in the presence of what should be alarming danger.

Two special forms of displacement should be separately mentioned because of their frequency. One is the representation of an object or person thought of in the latent content by the device of allowing a part only to appear in the manifest content, the process known as *pars pro toto*, which is one of the forms of synecdoche. The other is representation by means of allusion, a process known linguistically as metonymy; it has just been referred to in connection with superficial association. There are still two other ways in which a latent dream element can be converted into, or replaced by, a manifest element—namely, visual dramatisation through regression, which will presently be considered, and symbolism. Symbolism, which Freud calls the most curious chapter of the dream theory, forms such a special and important topic that I have considered it at length elsewhere;[2] at this point I will only remark that, for some as yet unknown reason, dream symbolism differs from other symbolism in being almost exclusively sexual.

Condensation and Displacement are the two main mechanisms by means of which is produced the distortion during the passage from the latent to the manifest content. The extent to which a given dream appears confused, bizarre, and meaningless as a rule varies

---

[1] ' Diagnostische Associationsstudien,' 1906, Bd. i.   [2] Chapter III.

with the extent to which these two mechanisms have been operative in its formation. The following fragmentary extracts from some dream analyses will illustrate the processes in question:

(1) *I was in the country in Massachusetts, and yet seemed to be in the east not of America but of England. Above a group of people was vaguely outlined the word Ölve or Ölde* (which may be expressed as Öl̦e). This dream affords a particularly striking illustration of displacement, for every element in it directly led in the analysis to thoughts about the Netherlands, although no indication whatever of this country appeared in the manifest content. Massachusetts brought to my mind its capital Boston, and the original Boston in Lincolnshire.[1] That reminded me of Essex,[2] these two counties being the most low-lying (Netherlandish) ones in England. In Essex lives a friend through whom I had got to know well a number of Flemish people. On the day preceding the dream I had written a letter to someone in Maldon, a town in Essex, a name the sound of which brought to my mind Moll Flanders. The costume of the people in the dream was taken from a certain picture of Rembrandt's, which brought up a number of recent and old memories. Öl̦e was a condensation of Alva, the tyrant of the Netherlands, and Van der Velde, the name of a Flemish painter of whose works I am fond, and also of a particular Flemish friend: two days previously I had seen in the hospital a Dutchman with a very similar name. In short, turn which way I would, all parts of the dream stubbornly refused to associate themselves with anything but Netherland topics, the further analysis of which resolutely led in only one direction.

Associated, therefore, with only one word in the manifest content of the dream, which at first sight appeared to be meaningless enough, are a number of mental processes that occupy a significant place in my waking life. These, and many others which for personal reasons I cannot mention, are connected with the element in the manifest content of the dream by means of exceedingly superficial associations, chiefly ridiculous plays on words of a kind I hope I

---

[1] That in the dream-making I was presumptuous enough to confound an American State with an English county is an illustration of the irresponsible liberties taken by the mental processes concerned in this production, and shows how completely they differ from our waking thoughts.

[2] I might add that the latter part of the word ' Massachusetts ' has a sound not very dissimilar to that of ' Essex '; further, that the meaning of the first part of it, ' chu ' (which in Boston is pronounced as if it were spelt ' chew '), resembles that of the other word (' ess ' is the stem of the German verb ' to eat ').

should never be guilty of when awake. Anyone, however, who is interested in the psychology of wit, or familiar with the unconscious phantasies of hysterics or the flight of ideas met with in mania and other psychoses, will not find it strange that the superficial associations and preposterous plays on words so characteristic of those fields of mental activity are common enough in yet another field—namely, that of dream formation. The question whether the associations that occur during dream analysis are made only then, and take no share in the actual formation of the dream, will not here be discussed; it is one of the objections with which Freud fully deals in the ' Traum-deutung.'

(2) The play on words in these dreams, which may surprise those not familiar with dream analysis, is further illustrated in the following example: *A patient dreamed that he was in a village in the neighbourhood of Paris that seemed to be called Marinier. He entered a café, but could only remember of its name that it contained an* n *and an* l. As a matter of fact, he had just been planning to visit Paris, where he would meet a particular friend who lived there. The patient was fond of making anagrams, and was very given to playing with words, both consciously and still more unconsciously, so that it was not hard to divine that the invented word Marinier together with the letters *n* and *l* were derived from a transposition of the letters in Armenonville. This was confirmed by his next remark, to the effect that on his last visit to Paris he had dined enjoyably with this very friend at the Pavillon d'Armenonville.

(3) A patient, a woman of thirty-seven, dreamed that *she was sitting in a grand stand as though to watch some spectacle. A military band approached, playing a gay martial air. It was at the head of a funeral, which seemed to be of a Mr. X; the casket rested on a draped gun-carriage. She had a lively feeling of astonishment at the absurdity of making such an ado about the death of so insignificant a person. Behind followed the dead man's brother and one of his sisters, and behind them his two other sisters; they were all incongruously dressed in a bright grey check. The brother advanced ' like a savage,' dancing and waving his arms; on his back was a yucca-tree with a number of young blossoms.* This dream is a good example of the second of the three types mentioned above, being perfectly clear and yet apparently impossible to fit into the patient's waking mental life. The true meaning of it, however, became only too clear on analysis. The figure of Mr. X veiled that of her husband. Both men had promised much when they were young, but the hopes their friends

had built on them had not been fulfilled; the one had ruined his health and career by his addiction to morphia, the other by his addiction to alcohol. Under the greatest stress of emotion the patient related that her husband's alcoholic habits had completely alienated her wifely feeling for him, and that in his drunken moments he even inspired her with an intense physical loathing. In the dream her repressed wish that he would die was realised by picturing the funeral of a third person whose career resembled that of her husband's, and who, like her husband, had one brother and three sisters. Further than this, her almost savage contempt for her husband, which arose from his lack of ambition and other more intimate circumstances, came to expression in the dream by her reflection of how absurd it was that anyone should make an ado over the death of such a nonentity, and by the gaiety shewn at his funeral not only by all the world (the gay air of the band; her husband is, by the way, an officer in the volunteers, while Mr. X has no connection with the army), but even by his nearest relatives (the brother's dancing, the bright clothes). It is noteworthy that no wife appeared in the dream, although Mr. X is married.

In real life Mr. X, who is still alive, is an indifferent acquaintance, but his brother had been engaged to be married to the patient, and they were deeply attached to each other. Her parents, however, manœuvred to bring about a misunderstanding between the two, and at their instigation, in a fit of pique, she married her present husband, to her enduring regret. Mr. X's brother was furiously jealous at this, and the pæan of joy he raised in the dream does not appear so incongruous when we relate it to the idea of the death of the patient's husband as it does in reference to his own brother's death. His exuberant movements and ' dancing like a savage ' reminded the patient of native ceremonies she had seen, particularly marriage ceremonies. The yucca-tree (a sturdy shrub common in the Western States) proved on analysis to be a phallic symbol, and the young blossoms represented offspring. The patient bitterly regrets never having had any children, a circumstance she ascribes to her husband's vices. In the dream, therefore, her husband dies unregretted by anyone, she marries her lover and has many children.

(4) The following two dreams illustrate the formation of neo-logisms: The patient, a woman of thirty-nine, dreamed that *she was sitting on a stage with four others, rehearsing a play they were to take part in; it seemed to be called ' The Wreck of the Kipperling.' Her title-rôle was*

called Kipper. She felt foolish and embarrassed. This feeling she had several times recently experienced, circumstances having placed her in an awkward and compromising situation in regard to a man and woman, for both of whom she cared. Years ago, when in school in France, she had greatly suffered from feeling awkward and silly at having to read aloud in class from French plays, a language she imperfectly pronounced. Three days before the dream she had been reading a volume of satirical poems by Owen Seaman, and being a foreigner had had considerable difficulty in understanding and appreciating them. This had distressed her, for her friends thought very highly of them. Her embarrassment culminated at the reading of one of the poems, in which Rudyard Kipling is depreciated and entitled ' Kipperling '; she much admired Kipling's writings and had felt foolish when her two friends assured her he was crude and vulgar. She resented his being nicknamed Kipperling, and said, ' Fancy giving a poet the name of a silly little fish.' From the fusion of Kipling and Kipperling, and perhaps influenced by the fact that the latter name had been employed by *Seaman,* she had coined for herself in the dream the title of Kipper. Kipper (dried herring) is frequently used in London slang to denote foolish people (' silly kipper ').

(5) In another dream the same patient imagined she was called ' *Hokerring,*' a neologism produced by fusing the two words ' smoked herring '; this process may be represented thus:

$$\text{(SM) OKE (D)}$$
$$\text{H\qquad ERRING}$$

(The parentheses indicate letters omitted in the neologism.) The term smoked herring reminded her of a bloater, and of a rather vulgar word in her native language meaning nude, pronounced bloat. This brought up infantile memories of shyness and a sense of foolishness that were connected with nakedness.

The construction of the manifest content out of the latent content Freud terms the *Dream-work (Traumarbeit).* In this, two other principal mechanisms are concerned in addition to those just mentioned of condensation and displacement. The first of these may be called *Dramatisation (Darstellung).* It is a familiar observation that the manifest content of most dreams depicts a situation, or rather an action, so that in this respect a dream may be said to resemble a theatrical representation. This fact exercises a selecting influence on the mental processes that have to be presented (*Rücksicht auf Darstellbarkeit*), for dramatisation, like the arts of painting and sculpture, is necessarily subject to definite limitations, and therefore special expedients have to be employed to indicate mental processes that cannot be directly portrayed. Just as a painter has indirectly to convey abstract mental processes by adopting certain technical devices, so a dramatist has to select and modify his material in order to make it conform to the restrictions of his art, as for instance when an action extending over years has to be presented in a couple of hours. In a dream the mental processes are dramatised so that the past and future are unrolled before our eyes in a present action; an old wish, for instance, that relates to the future is seen realised in a present situation.

It is further well known that the manifest content of most dreams is predominantly, though not exclusively, of a visual nature, and the particular process of expressing in a dream various thoughts in the form of visual pictures Freud terms *Regression*, wishing to indicate by this the retrograde movement of abstract mental processes towards their primary perceptions. The network of dream thoughts is in this way resolved into its raw material. This process of regression is characteristic of dreams as contrasted with other mental constructions formed by means of similar mechanisms, such as daydreams, psychoneurotic symptoms, and so on, though it sometimes occurs in the last named in the form of hallucinatory visions. In his discussion of the nature and function of regression Freud develops a number of important theoretical considerations regarding the structure of the mind, which, however, cannot here be gone into. He traces regression, both in dreams and in visions, partly to the resistance of the censorship, and partly to the attraction for the mental processes thus represented exerted by infantile memories, which, as is known, characteristically preserve their original visual type. In the case of dreams, though not of course in the case of waking visions, it is probable that the regression is further facilitated by the cessation during sleep of the forward movement from the sensorial to the motor side.

Under the heading of dramatisation may also be included the representation of various intellectual processes. We shall presently see that the intellectual operations (judgement, etc.) that are frequently met with in the manifest content of dreams originate not in the dream-making but in the underlying dream thoughts; no intellectual work is performed in the dream-making proper. In the dream thoughts there are of course all kinds of intellectual processes, judgements, arguments, conditions, proofs, objections, and so on. None of these, however, finds any special representation in the manifest content of the dream. As a rule they are entirely omitted, only the material content of the dream thoughts being represented in the dream, and not the logical relations of these. The dream-work, however, sometimes makes use of certain special devices to indicate these logical relations indirectly; the extent to which this is done greatly varies in different dreams and in different individuals. The logical relations between the constituents of the dream thoughts, just as between those of waking thoughts, are displayed by the use of such parts of speech as ' if,' ' although,' ' either,' ' because,' etc., which, as has just been said, find no direct expression in the manifest content. Instances of the devices in question are the following: Logical concatenation between two thoughts is indicated by the synchronous appearance of the elements representing these in the manifest content; thus, in the third dream related above, the husband's death, the second marriage, and the subsequent children, three logically related thoughts, are represented by three groups of elements that synchronously appear in the manifest content. Causal connection between two dream thoughts is usually not indicated at all. When indicated it is done by making the one representing element follow on the other. The commonest way of doing this is by one clause being represented in an introductory dream (*Vortraum*), the other in the main dream (*Haupttraum*); it should, however, be remarked that this splitting of the manifest content does not always indicate causal connection between the corresponding dream thoughts. A less frequent device is the bringing about of a transformation of the one element into the other; the transformation must be a direct one, not a mere replacement, as when one scene passes gradually into another, not as when one scene is simply replaced by another. Evident absurdity in the manifest content signifies the existence of mockery or scorn in the dream thoughts, as was illustrated in the third dream related above. An alternative in the dream thoughts is not expressed in the manifest content; the representing elements are merely brought together in the same connection. When an alternative (either—or) appears in the manifest content it is always the translation of ' and ' in the dream thoughts; thus in the second dream related above I felt that the third letter in the word outlined was either *v* or *d*, and both of these were present in the latent content.

Opposition and contradiction between dream thoughts may be indicated in two ways in the manifest content. When the contrasting thoughts can be linked with the idea of exchange, then the representing elements may be fused into a unity, a process described above under the name of identification. Other cases of opposition, which fall into the category of the converse or reverse, may be indicated in the following curious way: two parts of the already formed dream that are connected with the dream thoughts in question are inverted. Inversion of mental processes in dream-making subserves other functions than the one just mentioned: it is, for instance, a favourite method of increasing the distortion; the simplest way of disguising a mental process is to replace it by its obverse. Some subjects seem to employ this distorting mechanism to an inordinate extent, and many dreams can be interpreted merely by inverting them. The inversion may concern either space or time. An instance of the former occurred in the third dream related above, where the yucca-tree (phallus) was attached dorsally instead of ventrally. Instances of both may be seen in the following dream by the same patient:

(6) *She stood at the seashore watching a small boy, who seemed to be hers, wading into the water. This he did till the water covered him and she could only see his head bobbing up and down near the surface. The scene then changed into the crowded hall of an hotel. Her husband left her, and she ' entered into conversation with ' a stranger.* The second half of the dream revealed itself in the analysis as representing a flight from her husband and the entering into intimate relations with a third person, behind whom was plainly indicated Mr. X's brother mentioned in the former dream. The first part of the dream was a fairly evident birth phantasy. In dreams, as in mythology, the delivery of a child *from* the uterine waters is commonly presented by distortion as the entry of the child *into* water; among many others, the births of Adonis, Osiris, Moses, and Bacchus are well-known illustrations of this. The bobbing up and down of the head into the water at once recalled to the patient the sensation of quickening she had experienced in her only pregnancy. Thinking of the boy going into the water induced a reverie in which she saw herself taking him out of the water, carrying him to a nursery, washing him and dressing him, and installing him in her household.

The second half of the manifest dream therefore represented thoughts, concerning the elopement, that belonged to the first half of the underlying latent content; the first half of the dream corresponded with the second half of the latent content, the birth phantasy. Besides this inversion in order, further inversions took place in each half of the dream. In the first half the child *entered* the water, and then his head bobbed; in the underlying dream thoughts first the quickening occurred, and then the child *left* the water (a double inversion). In the second half her husband left her; in the dream thoughts she left her husband.

Last among the dream-making mechanisms is that termed *Secondary Elaboration (sekundäre Bearbeitung)*. It fundamentally differs from the other three in that it arises from the activity, not of the underlying dream thoughts, but of the more conscious mental processes. This remark will be more comprehensible when we presently consider the forces that go to make a dream. When the dream is apprehended in consciousness it is treated in the same way as any other perceptive content—*i.e.*, it is not accepted in its unaltered state, but is assimilated to pre-existing conceptions. It is thus to a certain extent remodelled so as to bring it, so far as is possible, into harmony with other conscious mental processes. In other words an attempt, however unsuccessful, is made to modify it so as to render it comprehensible (*Rücksicht auf Verständlichkeit*). This secondary elaboration is closely allied to the process I have described as rationalisation.[1] As is well known, there is a pronounced tendency on the part of the mind to distort foreign experiences in such a way as to assimilate them to what is already intelligible; in hearing or seeing a sentence in a strange tongue the subject imagines analogies to familiar words in his own, a falsifying process that frequently is carried to excess, leading to curious misunderstandings. To this secondary elaboration is due whatever degree of ordering, sequence, and consistency there may be found in a dream.

In connection with the secondary elaboration may be mentioned the allied process discovered by Silberer and named by him ' threshold symbolism.' He has shewn that the last portion of the manifest content of a dream, just before waking, can represent the idea of waking; instances are: crossing a threshold, leaving a room, starting on a journey or arriving at a destination, etc. It is further possible, though not yet demonstrated, that the same process may

[1] See Chapter II. of the Third Edition.

occur in the midst of the dream itself, portraying variations in the depth of sleep, tendency to break off the dream, etc.

Reviewing now as a whole the process of dream-making, we have above all to lay stress on the fact that in the formation of a dream no intellectual operation of any sort is carried out; the dream-work is concerned solely with translating into another form various under-lying dream thoughts that were previously in existence. No creative work whatever is carried out by the process of dream-making; it performs no act of decision, calculation, judgement, comparison, conclusion, or any kind of thought. Not even the elaboration of any phantasy occurs in the dream-making, though a previously existing phantasy may be bodily taken over and woven into the dream, a fact that gives the key to the explanation of highly wrought and yet momentary dreams, such as the well-known guillotine one related to Maury. Any part of a dream that appears to indicate an intellectual operation has been taken bodily from the underlying latent content, either directly or in a distorted form; the same applies to speech phrases that may occur in a dream. Even some of the waking judgements passed on a dream belong to the latent content. To repeat, there is in the dream-work nothing but transformation of previously formed mental processes.

The dream-work proper is thus a process more distant from waking mental life than even the most determined detractor of dream activities would maintain. It is not merely more careless, incorrect, incomplete, forgetful, and illogical than waking thought, but it is something that qualitatively is absolutely different from this, so that the two cannot be compared. Dream-making proceeds by methods quite foreign to our waking mental life; it ignores obvious contradictions, makes use of highly strained analogies, and brings together widely different ideas by means of the most superficial associations, for instance by such a feeble play on words as shocks the waking mind with a keen sense of ridiculousness. The mental processes characteristic of dreams would if they occurred in a conscious waking state at once arouse grave suspicion of impaired intelligence; as Jung has clearly pointed out,[1] they are in fact processes that are frequently indistinguishable from those met with in advanced stages of dementia præcox and other psychoses.

Besides the detractors of dreams there are others who adopt the opposite attitude and ascribe to dreams various useful and valuable

[1] ' Psychologie der Dementia præcox,' 1907.

functions. As we shall see later, Freud holds that there is but one function of dreams—namely, to protect sleep. Several members of the post-psycho-analytical school, however, notably Maeder—and in this country Nicoll—maintain that dreams serve such functions as the formation of tentative efforts at the solution of various disturbing problems or dilemmas. In my opinion, the fallacy in this conclusion lies in confusion between the latent content of the dream and the dream-work itself. Certainly in the latent dream thoughts there are to be found the processes described by Maeder, just as numerous other kinds of intellectual operations, but this in no sense proves that the dream itself is constructed for the purpose of developing them. Dream-work is nothing but a translation.

The affect in dreams has many interesting features. The incongruous manner in which it may be present when it is not to be explained by the ideas of the dream, or be absent when from these ideas it might have been expected, has already been noted above, and is quite elucidated by psycho-analysis, which reveals that in the underlying dream thoughts the affect is logically justified and is congruous enough. The apparent incongruity is solely due to the distortion of the conceptual content, whereby a given affect becomes secondarily attached to an inappropriate idea. The third dream mentioned above well illustrates this fact; the incongruity with which Mr. X's death was joyfully celebrated by his brother explains itself as soon as one realises that the figure of Mr. X in the dream represented that of another man in the latent content. The affect investing the latent content is always more intense than that present in the manifest content, so that, although strongly affective dream thoughts may produce an indifferently toned dream, the reverse never occurs —that is to say, an affective manifest content never arises from an indifferently toned latent content. Freud attributes this inhibition of the affect in dream formation partly to the cessation in sleep of the forward movement from the sensory to the motor side—he regards affective processes as essentially centrifugal—and partly to the suppressing effect of the censorship, which will presently be further considered. Another important matter is that the nature of the affect as it appears in the manifest content is the same as that of the latent content, although, as has just been said, the intensity of it is always less there than here. The influence of the dream-work on the original affect is thus different from that on the rest of the dream thoughts, in that no distortion of it takes place. As Stekel puts it in a recent article,[1] ' *Im Traume ist der Affect das einzig Wahre.*' [' In dreams the only true thing is the affect.'] The affect appears in the same form in the latent as in the manifest content, although through the mechanisms of transference and displacement it is in the latter otherwise associated than in the former. It should, however, be remarked that a given affect in the manifest content may represent its exact opposite in the latent content, but on closer analysis it will be found that the two opposites were already present in the latent content, and were both of them appropriate to the context; as is so often the case in waking mental life, exactly contrasting mental processes in dream thoughts are intimately associated with each other. In such cases of inversion of affect, although both occur in the latent content, the one present in the manifest content always belongs to a more superficial layer of the unconscious, so that it is the inverted affect that yields the underlying meaning of the dream. Thus a repressed death wish may be masked by grief in the manifest dream, and fear in the latter is one of the commonest coverings for repressed libidinal desire.

Having mentioned some of the mechanisms that bring about the distortion of the latent content into the manifest we may next shortly consider the material and sources from which a dream is composed. Again we have sharply to distinguish between the sources of the manifest content and those of the underlying dream thoughts; the latter will presently be dealt with apart. Three peculiar features shown by the *memory* in dreams have especially struck most observers: first the preference shown for recent impressions; secondly, that the experiences are otherwise selected than in our waking memory, in that subordinate and hardly noticed incidents seem to be better remembered than essential and important ones; and thirdly, the hypermnesia for previously forgotten incidents, especially for those of early childhood life.

The first two of these features may be considered together, for they are intimately connected. In every dream without exception occur mental processes experienced by the subject in the last waking interval (*Traumtag*); other recent experiences that have not occurred on the day actually preceding the dream are treated in just the same way as more ancient memories. There must therefore be some special quality that is of significance in dream formation attaching

[1] *Jahrbuch der Psychoanalyse*, Bd. i., S. 485.

to the mental experiences of the preceding day. Closer attention shows that the experience in question may be either psychically significant or quite indifferent; in the latter case, however, it is always associated with some underlying significant experience. The dream-instigator (*Traumerreger*) may be (1) a recent significant experience that is directly represented in the manifest content, (2) a recent significant experience that is indirectly represented in the manifest content by the appearance there of an associated indifferent experience, (3) an internal significant process (memory) that regularly is represented in the manifest content by the appearance of an associated, recent, indifferent experience. In each case, therefore, a recent experience (*i.e.*, from the preceding day) appears directly in the dream; it is one either significant in itself or else associated with another (recent or old) significant one. The selection of incidents of subordinate interest applies only to incidents of the day before the dream. Older incidents, that at first sight appear to be unimportant, can always be shown to have *already* become on the day of their occurrence psychically significant through the secondary transference on to them of the affect of significant mental processes with which they have got associated. The material from which a dream is formed may therefore be psychically significant or the opposite, and in the latter case it always arises in some experience of the preceding day.

(7) An example of an incitement from the dream-day that is also of interest in connection with the subject of memory is the following: I dreamed that *I was travelling in Bavaria and came to a place called Peterwardein*. On waking I felt quite sure I had never seen such a name and regarded it as being probably a neologism. Two days later I was reading a book on Turkish history, when I came across the name of the place, which is an ancient fortress in South Hungary. As I knew I had been reading the same book on the evening before my dream, my interest was aroused and I turned back to see if the name had occurred earlier in the book. I then found that on the evening in question I had skimmed over a page containing a number of Hungarian place-names, of which Peterwardein was one, so that without doubt my eye must have caught the name and noted it, although I had absolutely no memory of it. I then thought of the Hungarian town Grosswardein, and eliminating the syllables common to the two names I saw that the dream must have contained an allusion to a certain Peter Gross, whom I had met in Bavaria,

and whose father[1] had been born in Hungary, a fact in which I had special reason to be interested.

The explanation Freud gives of these facts is shortly as follows: The meaning of the appearance in the manifest content of indifferent mental processes is that they are employed by the dream-work to *represent* underlying processes of great psychical significance, just as in battle the colours of a regiment, themselves of no intrinsic value, stand for the honour of the army. A more accurate analogy is the frequent occurrence in the psychoneuroses of the transposition of a given significant affect on to an indifferent idea; for instance, intense dread of a harmless object may arise as a transposition, on to the secondarily associated idea of this object, of a dread that was fully justified in relation to the primary idea. In short, the process is another form of the displacement mechanism described above. Just as in the psychoneuroses, so also in the dream the primary underlying idea is of such a nature as to be incapable of becoming conscious (*bewusstseinsunfähig*), a matter that will presently be further discussed. Freud explains the regular occurrence in the dream of a recent experience by pointing out that this has not yet had time to form many associations, and therefore is more free to become associated with unconscious psychical processes. The circumstance is of interest as indicating that during the first sleep after a mental event, and unnoticed by our consciousness, important changes go on in our memory and conceptual material; the familiar advice to sleep over an important matter before coming to a decision probably has an important basis in fact.

The third feature, namely the hypermnesia particularly for experiences of early childhood, is of cardinal importance. Early memories, which the subject had completely forgotten, but the truth of which can often be objectively confirmed, not infrequently occur with startling fidelity even in the manifest content. This fact in itself should suggest the ontogenetic antiquity of dream processes. In the latent content the appearance of such forgotten memories is far more frequent, and Freud holds it probable that the latent content of every dream is connected with ancient mental processes that extend back to early childhood. The following instance may be given of this:

(8) A patient, a man aged thirty-seven, dreamed that *he was being attacked by a man who was armed with a number of sharp weapons; the*

The brilliant Otto Gross.

assailant was swarthy, and wore a dark moustache. He struggled and
succeeded somehow in inflicting a skin wound on his opponent's left hand.
The name Charles seemed to be related to the man, though not so definitely as
if it were his name. The man changed into a fierce dog, which the subject
of the dream succeeded in vanquishing by forcibly tearing his jaws apart so
as to split his head in two. No one could have been more astonished
at the dream than the patient himself, who was a singularly inoffen-
sive person. The name Charles led to the following free associations:
A number of indifferent acquaintances having this as their Christian
name—a man named Dr. Charles Stuart, whom he had seen at a
Scottish reunion, at which he had been present on the day before
(this man, however, wears a beard)—another man present at the
reunion whose personal appearance had many traits in common
with his assailant in the dream—the Scottish Stuart Kings Charles I.
and Charles II.—again the acquaintance Charles Stuart—Cromwell's
designation of Charles King I., ' that man Charles Stuart '—the
medical practitioner of his family, whose name was Stuart Rankings,
and who had died when the patient was nine years old. Then came
the memory of a painful scene, previously quite forgotten, in which
the doctor had roughly extracted two teeth from the terror-stricken
patient after forcibly gagging his mouth open; before he could
accomplish this the doctor had had his left hand badly bitten. The
date of this occurrence could from extrinsic evidence be referred to
the patient's fifth year. From a number of reasons that cannot be
given here it became clear that the dream thoughts altogether
clustered around this childhood experience. The assailant in the
dream was no other than the doctor whose treatment of the patient
was nearly thirty years after his death thus fearfully avenged in the
latter's dream.[1] The play on his name Stuart Rankings (Rank-kings),
which enabled him to become identified first with the Stuart King
Charles, and then with Charles Stuart, and finally to be called in the
dream plain Charles, is interesting. It should be added that the Dr.
Charles Stuart mentioned above is a dental surgeon, who a week
previously had in the patient's presence performed a painful tooth
extraction on the latter's wife; on the day before the dream he had
inquired of the patient concerning his wife's health. The identification of the man with the dog in the latter part of the dream was

---

[1] The deeper interpretation of the dream will be easy to those familiar with psycho-
analysis, especially when I add that the dream was accompanied by appalling dread,
and that the first association to ' hand ' was ' neck.'

greatly over-determined. The doctor in question was a noted dog fancier, and had given the patient a fine collie to whom he became greatly attached; he led a very irregular life, and the patient often heard his father refer to him as a gay dog; finally he died 'like a dog,' from an accidental overdose of poison, in the presence of a number of people who were from ignorance powerless to render the slight assistance that would have saved his life.

The source of some dream material is to be found in somatic stimuli during sleep, though by no means so frequently as many writers maintain. They are, however, in no case the whole cause of the dream, but are merely woven into its fabric in exactly the same way as any other psychical material, and only when they fulfil certain conditions. The exaggerated claims sometimes made out for the importance of these stimuli are easily disproved by, for instance, the following considerations. A sleeper may react to a given somatic stimulation when this is of a lively nature, such as bad pain, in one of several different ways. In the first place he may altogether ignore it, as often occurs in bodily disease; secondly he may feel it during, or even throughout, sleep without dreaming at all;[1] thirdly he may be awakened by it; and fourthly he may weave it into a dream. Even in the last instance it enters into the dream only in a disguised form, and it can be shewn that this disguise depends on the nature not only of the stimulus but of the rest of the dream. The same stimulus may appear in different dreams, even of the same person, under quite different forms, and analysis of the dream regularly shows that the form adopted is altogether determined by the character and motive of the dream. In short, the dream makes use of the somatic stimulus or

---

[1] In some, though by no means all, of the so-called 'battle dreams' that have recently been the subject of much controversy this may perhaps be the case—that is to say, that an actual memory of a terrible situation is faithfully reproduced during sleep. This occurs only in severe cases of 'shell shock' when the patient is constantly striving in waking life to obliterate the painful memory so far as he can, but is no longer able to do so when tired and in a state of lowered consciousness—e.g., light sleep. In most cases, however, two further features are to be discovered on closer examination. In the first place, it will be found that, although the dream is mainly a replica of actual experiences, there are usually some superadded elements present that do not belong to these experiences. This means that an attempt, however unsuccessful, is being made to transform the painful and sleep-disturbing memory into something more harmless—i.e., a true dream is being constructed. The prognosis of the 'shell shock' is better when this is the case. In the second place, if the anxiety battle dreams persist for a long period one may suspect that the traumatic effect of the experience is being increased by the action of unconscious complexes with which the painful memory has become associated. In both these cases the dream comes under the formula of Freud's theory as here described.

not according to its needs, and only when this fulfils certain require-
ments.

A somatic stimulus can not only furnish psychical material to be
used in the dream-making, but may occasionally serve as the
effective instigator of the dream. These are usually what Freud terms
'comfort dreams' (*Bequemlichkeitsträume*), where the stimulus
(mostly a painful one) is transformed into a symbol of something
pleasurable, and is so prevented from disturbing the dreamer.
Even here, however, the occurrence of a somatic stimulus can rarely
explain the whole dream, for as a rule it at most merely arouses a
complex train of thought that is already present, and out of which
the dream is constructed; when it cannot do this it awakes the
sleeper. The following example will perhaps make the process
clearer:

(9) A man *saw in front of him* in a dream *a Greek altar composed of
a solid mass of writhing snakes. There were nine of them, and they finally
assumed the shape of a pyramid or triangle.* He woke at this point
suffering from severe colicky pains in the abdomen, and, being a
medical man, the resemblance at once flashed across his mind
between the idea of contracting coils of intestine and that of writhing
snakes. One can hardly doubt that there was here a genetic relation
between the somatic stimulus and the dream, especially as the visual
projection of internal sensations into a region in front of the person
is known to occur frequently both in dreams and in insanity.
According to the physiological view we have here an adequate
explanation of the dream. The psychologist, on the other hand,
notes that there are features in the dream (the altar, the number nine,
the triangular form) quite unexplained by this ætiology, and which
he is, or should be, disinclined to attribute to 'chance.' Freud
would say that the wish to sleep, which is the real cause of every
dream (see later), had attempted to transform the disturbing sensations into a more satisfactory imagery, and so to incorporate them
with an agreeable train of thought in the unconscious as to deceive
the sleeper and spare him the necessity of waking; in the present case
the pain proved too insistent for this to be possible, except for a
short time. That at all events some psychological mechanism was
at work is shewn by even a slight examination of the unexplained
features in the dream. The thought of them at once reminded the
subject that on the preceding day a young lady had asked him why
the number nine was so prominent in Greek mythology; he replied

that it was because nine, being composed of three times three, possessed in a high degree the properties of the sacred number three. At this point he felt embarrassed lest she should go on to inquire why three was a sacred number, for, of course, he could not tell her of the phallic significance of this, with its relation to religious worship in general and to snake-worship in particular, and he had no simple explanation ready to his mind. Fortunately, either her curiosity was satisfied by the first answer or her attention was diverted by the general flow of conversation (it was at a dinner-party), so the dilemma did not arise. The train of thought thus aroused and brought to an abrupt stop evidently had very intimate associations, for the dream is plainly a narcissistic and exhibitionistic one; in it the subject identifies himself with the god Priapus who was adored for his masculine attributes (here represented by the typical phallic symbol of the snake). The avoidance of haste in being content with the first superficial explanation that offers itself will always shew that, as here, dreams are concerned with much more significant matters than intestinal colic.

I observed many beautiful examples of the same mechanism as the result of the air raids over London, especially those taking place during deep sleep either late at night or early in the morning. Some of my patients proved extremely ingenious in converting the noisy stimulus of warning signals and barrage gunfire into reassuring dreams, so avoiding the disagreeable necessity of waking, with its unpleasant consequences of having to get up on a cold night and take shelter, of fear, anxiety, and so on. One typical feature of such dreams was that in the earlier stages of the raid, when the firing was more distant, the disturbing stimuli could be quite successfully transformed into other imagery, while as it got louder and louder the resemblance between it and the imagery became more and more evident—*i.e.*, the disguise was less and less perfect, until the noise was so great that the person awoke. They resemble in this respect those sexual dreams in which the early part of the dream consists of quite disguised symbolism, the meaning of which becomes more and more evident as the stimulus becomes more insistent, until the person awakes with a seminal emission.

(10) A patient, a woman aged forty, dreamed that *she was buying Christmas presents in a fair. Before her was a box containing, in two rows one above the other, six bull's-eye lanterns or electric torches, of which only the front glass could be seen. At this point a report of artillery was heard*

and she exclaimed ' Goodness ! That must be a raid.' Someone close by, however, said ' Oh no, don't you know they are beating the drums in honour of the end of the war ?' (or else *' of the victory,'* the patient having the impression of both phrases). *She was again alarmed by a second report, but was once more reassured. She then recollected that she had heard about the arrangements for the celebration,* and was thinking about the details when she was awakened by someone knocking at the door. By this time the dream had so successfully dissuaded her of any possibility of a raid that she never thought of it on waking—she didn't even hear at first the loud firing that was going on—but supposed that the lady whose rooms were below had forgotten her flat-key and wanted to be let in (there being a common door-key to both sets of rooms). She was firmly persuaded of this until she opened the door below and found that there was a raid alarm. The reports in the dream were doubtless those of the near guns, whereas she had been able to transform the more distant earlier sounds into harmless imagery.

The imagery itself was a compromise between military thoughts and pleasanter personal ones. The news had come the day before of the victorious end to the campaign in German East Africa, though, of course, there had been no celebration of it. The box was one she was just sending to the front, and was to contain, among other things, an electric torch. The appearance of the packed objects was greatly over-determined: ammunition shells in their cases, the muzzles of guns (as a child she used constantly to see these in the sides of old wooden battleships near her home), the box of eggs out of reach that Alice tries to buy in Looking-Glass World, bull's-eye lanterns and magic lanterns that fascinated her as a child, six-chambered revolvers, all played a part; in childhood she was excited by stories in which a revolver was suddenly whipped out (she had later learnt to use one herself in connection with private theatricals that took place at a happy period of a love affair which, however, ended unfortunately). The patient was at the time suffering from ungratified sexual desire, and there was reason to think that the object she was reaching towards in the dream was a symbol of a (soldier's) phallus.

(11) A patient, a man of thirty-four, dreamed that *a boatload of women and children were escaping under rifle-fire, the scene taking place in India during the Mutiny. They managed to escape, after which he was concerned with the problem of how to publish the news of their terrible*

sufferings in the English newspapers without too greatly harrowing the feelings of the civilian population. The scene then changed and he was charged *with the task of deciding how best to punish the mutineers. Some were blown from the mouth of cannons* (as happened historically), *and others were to be mown down by guns drawn up in a city square. The latter performance was in progress, and he was debating whether there was any danger to the civilian population through shell splinters* when he awoke to the booming of the barrage. The allusions to the German outrages on civilians and women by sea and through the air are evident, but a temporarily successful effort was made by the dream to convert such thoughts into a less disturbing historical story of events that took place sixty years before and thousands of miles away.

Having partly answered the question of *how* a dream is built we may take up the more difficult one of *why* it is built, or, more accurately put, the problems concerning the forces that go to make a dream. It is impossible to do this without first referring to Freud's views on psychical repression (*Verdrängung*) and unconscious mental processes; these views in themselves call for a detailed exposition which cannot here be given, so that this part of the present paper will be even more incomplete than the rest. Freud uses the term ' conscious ' to denote mental processes of which we are at a given moment conscious, ' preconscious ' (*vorbewusste*) to denote mental processes of which we can spontaneously and voluntarily become conscious (*e.g.*, a memory out of one's mind for the moment, but which can readily be recalled), and ' unconscious ' to denote mental processes which the subject cannot spontaneously recall to consciousness, but which can be reproduced by employing special devices (*e.g.*, hypnosis, psycho-analysis, etc.). He infers that the force which has to be overcome in the act of making the last-named processes conscious is the same as that which had previously opposed an obstacle to their becoming conscious—*i.e.*, had kept them repressed in the unconscious. This force or resistance is a defensive mechanism which has kept from consciousness mental processes that were either primarily or secondarily (through association and transposition) of an unacceptable nature; in other words, these processes are un-assimilable in consciousness. Returning now to the subject of dreams, we have first to remark that Freud empirically found an intimate and legitimate relation between the degree of confusion and incomprehensibility present in a given dream and the difficulty the patient experienced in communicating the free associations leading to the dream thoughts. He therefore concluded that the distortion which had obviously occurred in the dream-making was related to the resistance that prevented the unconscious dream thoughts from becoming conscious; that it was in fact a result of this resistance. He speaks of the resistance that keeps certain mental processes unconscious as the ' endopsychic censorship.'[1] In the waking state the unconscious processes cannot come to external expression, except under certain abnormal conditions. In sleep, however, the activity of the censorship, like that of all other more conscious processes, is diminished, though it is never entirely abrogated. This fact permits the unconscious processes (the latent content) to reach expression in the form of a dream, but as they still have to contend with some degree of activity on the part of the censorship, they can reach expression only in an indirect way. The distortion in the dream-work is thus a means of evading the censorship, in the same way that a veiled phraseology is a means of evading a social censorship which would not permit a disagreeable truth to be openly expressed. The dream is a compromise between the dream thoughts on the one hand and the endopsychic censorship on the other, and could not arise at all were it not for the diminished activity of the latter during sleep.

Distortion of the dream thoughts by means of the mechanisms of condensation and displacement is by no means the only way in which the censorship manifests itself, nor is this distortion the only way in which the censorship can be evaded by the dream processes. In the first place we have already noticed above one of its manifestations under the name of secondary elaboration. This process continues even in the waking state, so that the account of a dream as related directly after waking differs from that related some time after. The fact of this change in the subsequent memory of a dream is sometimes urged as an objection to the interpretation by psycho-analysis, but the change is just as rigorously determined, and the mechanism is as precisely to be defined, as that of any other process in the dream-making. For instance, if the two accounts are compared, it will be found that the altered passage concerns what might be called a weak place in the disguise of the dream thoughts; the

---

[1] Considerable objection has been raised—e.g., by Bleuler, Rivers, and others—to Freud's use of the word ' censorship,' but so far as I can see it is rather to the word than to the conception. It is not to be imagined that Freud understands by this term anything in the nature of a specific entity; to him it is nothing more nor less than a convenient expression to denote the sum total of repressing inhibitions.

disguise is strengthened by the subsequent elaboration by the censorship, but the fact of the change points to the need for distortion at that given spot, a point of some value in the analysis.[1] Instead of subsequently altering this weak place the censorship may act by interposing doubt in the subject's mind as to the reliability of his memory about it; he may say ' The person in the dream seemed to carry such and such an object, but I am not sure that I haven't imagined that in thinking over the dream.' In such cases one is always safe in accepting the dubiously given point as unhesitatingly as the most vivid memory; the doubt is only one of the stages in the disguise of the underlying dream thoughts.

An interesting way in which the censorship may act is by the subject receiving the assurance during the dream that ' it is only a dream.' The explanation of this is that the action of the censorship has set in too late, after the dream has already been formed; the mental processes which have, as it were unwittingly, reached consciousness are partly divested of their significance by the subject treating them lightly as being ' only a dream.' Freud wittily describes this afterthought on the part of the censorship as an *esprit d'escalier.*

The last manifestation of the censorship is more important—namely, the tendency to forget dreams or part of them; it is an extension of the doubting process mentioned above. Freud traces this tendency to forget, as also that shown in many forgetting acts of waking life,[2] to the repressing action of the censorship. As was mentioned above, the fragmentariness of the remembered dream, together with the uncertainty and actual falsification in the memory of it, are frequently urged as casting doubt on the reliability of any psychological analysis of dreams, but if a truly empiric attitude is adopted towards the material obtainable, as elsewhere in science, it will be found that these features are in a sense part of the nature of the dream itself and have to be explained just as other features have. One should always remember that it is the same mind that produces

---

[1] I have elsewhere (' Ein klares Beispiel von sekundärer Bearbeitung,' *Zentralblatt für Psychoanalyse,* Jahrg. i., S. 135) narrated an instance of this in which a patient was unconsciously impelled, in the act of relating a dream that had occurred nearly twenty years before, to alter a certain feature in it. She knew that she was changing this, but had no idea why she did it; the analysis showed that it concerned a weak place which, if left in its original form, would, in the current circumstances, have at once betrayed the meaning of the dream thoughts. Though consciously she was quite unaware of the nature of these, her intuition had felt the danger.

[2] See Chapter II.

both the dream and the subsequent changes in it, whether these are additions or falsifications.

Freud's explanation can often be experimentally confirmed. When a patient informs the physician that he had a dream the night before but that he cannot recall anything of it, it frequently happens that the overcoming of a given resistance during the psycho-analytic treatment removes the barrier to the recollection of the dream, provided, of course, that the resistance concerns the same topic in the two cases; the patient then says, ' Ah, now I can recall the dream I had.' Similarly he may suddenly during the analysis of the dream, or at any time subsequent to the relation of the dream, supply a previously forgotten fragment (*Nachtrag*); this latter fragment invariably corresponds with those dream thoughts that have undergone the most intense repression, and therefore those of greatest significance. This occurrence is extremely frequent, and may be illustrated by the following examples:[1]

(12) A patient, a man aged twenty-six, dreamed that *he saw a man standing in front of a hoarding with a gate-entrance on his left. He approached the man, who received him cordially and entered ' into conversation ' with him.* During the analysis he suddenly recalled that the hoarding seemed to be the wall of an ' exhibition,' into which the man was entering to join a number of others. The significance of this added fragment will be evident when I mention that the patient, who had frequently indulged in pædication, was a pronounced *voyeur.*

(13) A patient, a woman aged thirty-six, dreamed that *she was standing in a crowd of schoolgirls. One of them said, ' Why do you wear such untidy skirts ?' and turned up the patient's skirt to show how worn the under-skirt was.* During the analysis, three days after relating the dream, the patient for the first time recalled that the under-skirt in the dream seemed to be a nightdress, and analysis of this led to the evocation of several painful memories in which lifting a nightdress played an important part; the two most significant of these had for many years been forgotten.

As was mentioned above, the censorship can be evaded by the dream thoughts in other ways than the usual one of distortion. They may appear in the manifest content in their unaltered form, but their significance be misunderstood by the subject when he recalls the dream. For instance, a person may dream that he sees his brother dead, the actual dream thoughts being the wish that the

---

[1] A more striking instance is related in Chapter XIII. of the Fourth Edition.

brother may die. The subject fails to realise that the picture corresponds with a wish, even a repressed one, partly because the nature of this is so horribly unlikely that it does not occur to his consciousness, and partly because the dream is accompanied by an emotion, anxious grief, which is apparently incongruous with a wish. Such dreams are always intensely distressing (*Angstträume*), and in a sense it may be said that the dread here replaces the distorting mechanisms of condensation and displacement.

Although Freud attaches great importance to the action of the endopsychic dream censorship in causing the transformation of the latent into the manifest content of the dream, he does not attach an exclusive importance to it in this respect. He recognises that other factors are also at work in making the dream thoughts unintelligible to the waking consciousness. One of these factors was mentioned above in connection with regression, and it is clear that ideational material that is presented to consciousness in the regressive form of the raw material of its sensorial imagery could not be understood. Another important factor leading to distortion is the process of symbolism, one that seems to be bound up with the very nature of the unconscious mind itself and undoubtedly related to its ontogenetic and phylogenetic history.[1]

We have finally to consider the most important problems of all, those relating to the latent content or dream thoughts. The first thing that strikes one about these is their intense psychical significance. A dream never proceeds from trifles, but only from the mental processes that are of the greatest moment and interest to the subject. Dreams never deal with trivialities, however much they may appear at first sight to do so. The explanation of why incidents of subordinate interest occur in the manifest content has been given above. More than this, the dream thoughts are processes of the greatest *personal* interest, and thus invariably egocentric. We never dream about matters that concern only others, however deeply, but only about matters that concern ourselves. It has already been mentioned that the underlying dream thoughts are perfectly logical and consistent, and that the affect accompanying them is entirely congruous to their nature. Freud, therefore, not only agrees with those writers who disparage the mental quality of dreams, holding as he does that the dream-making proper contains no intellectual operation and proceeds only by means of the lower forms of mental activity, but

[1] For a discussion of this see Chapter III.

he also agrees with those other writers who maintain that dreams are a logical continuance of the most important part of our waking mental life. We dream at night only about those matters that have most concerned us by day, though on account of the distortion that takes place in the dream-making this fact is not evident. Lastly it may be added that all the dreams occurring in a given night arise from the same group of latent dream thoughts, though they usually present different aspects of them.

There are certain differences between the dreams of a young child and those of an adult. In the child, at all events before the age of four, no distortion, or very little, may take place, so that the manifest content is often identical with the latent content. In correspondence with this fact we find that children's dreams are logical and co-ordinate, an observation that is hard to reconcile with the commonly received opinion that dream processes arise from a dissociated activity of the brain cells, for one can see no reason why dreams should be a meaningless conglomeration of disordered and lowered mental functioning in adults when they are obviously not so in the child. Further, with young children it is easy to recognise that the dream represents the imaginary fulfilment of an ungratified wish; the child is visiting a circus that the day before he had been forbidden to go to, and so on. Now, Freud maintains that the latent content of every dream represents nothing else than the imaginary fulfilment of an ungratified wish.[1] In the child the wish is an ungratified one, but it may not have undergone repression, that is to say it is not of

[1] It seems necessary to keep calling attention to the fact that Freud's generalisation about dreams representing wish-fulfilments refers to the latent content of the dream, to the dream thoughts from which the dream proceeds, and not to the manifest content, for one constantly hears the irrelevant objection that dreams do not seem always to deal with wishes, one often expressed in the question ' How can a fear dream indicate a wish, when something is happening in it that the dreamer very much doesn't want to happen ?' It is only after analysis that the latent content of the dream is known, and it is only to the latent content that the wish-fulfilment theory applies.

A more serious objection is afforded by the class of dreams, of which the so-called ' battle-dreams ' are a good instance, where the whole dream appears to consist of nothing but a representation of an actual experience. Here Freud considers (' Beyond the Pleasure-Principle,' English translation, 1922) that the dream function (that of transforming thoughts in such a way as to preserve sleep) is unable to deal with the traumatic thoughts in question, probably because these have not yet been sufficiently incorporated into the mind. Indeed, we might well refuse the name of ' dreams ' at all to such intense obsessive memories that break sleep, just as one would to similarly acting painful sensations in diseases or isolated painful thoughts (*e.g.*, grief), which may pervade sleep without giving rise to a dream proper. In such cases the dream function simply fails to act.

such a nature as to be unacceptable in consciousness; in the adult the wish is not merely one that could not be gratified, but is of such a nature as to be unassimilable in consciousness, and so has become repressed. It frequently happens that even in the adult a wish-fulfilment appears in the manifest content, and still more frequently that a wish-fulfilment not present in the manifest content, but revealed by psycho-analysis, concerns a wish of which the subject is quite conscious; in both these cases, however, full analysis always discloses that these wishes are merely reinforcements of deeper, unconscious ones of an associated nature. No wish, therefore, is able to produce a dream unless it is either unconscious (*bewusstseins-unfähig*) or else associated with an allied unconscious one.

It has sometimes been alleged by Freud's opponents that his generalisation of all dreams representing a wish-fulfilment is the outcome of observing a few dreams of children, and that his analyses merely consist in arbitrarily twisting the dream, to gratify some *a priori* notion, until a wish can be read into it. This suggestion is historically untrue, for Freud came to the analysis of adult dreams from the analysis, not of children's dreams, but of adult psycho-neuroses.[1] He found that his patients' symptoms arose as a compromise between two opposing wishes, one of which was conscious, the other unconscious, and that they allegorically represented the imaginary fulfilment of these two wishes. He further found that an essential factor in their production was a conflict between the two wish-systems, of such a kind that the unconscious one was forcibly prevented from becoming conscious; it was unconscious because it was repressed. It frequently happened that the psycho-analysis of the patients' symptoms directly led to their dreams, and on submitting these to the analysis in exactly the same way as any other mental material he discovered that the construction of them showed close resemblances to that of the neurotic symptoms.[2] In both cases the material examined proved to be an expression of deeper mental processes; in both cases these deeper processes were unconscious, and had in reaching expression undergone distortion by the endo-

---

[1] As may well be imagined, a number of Freud's individual conclusions had been anticipated by previous writers, particularly by artists. In the ' Traumdeutung ' he deals fully with the scientific literature on the subject. Prescott (' Poetry and Dreams,' *Journ. of Abnormal Psychology*, vol. vii., Nos. 1 and 2) has published an interesting paper on the relation of poetry to dream-production, using English poetry as an example.

[2] These resemblances are expounded and illustrated in Chapter XI.

psychic censorship. The mechanism by means of which this distortion is brought about is very similar in the two cases, the chief difference being that representation by visual pictures is much more characteristic of dreams. In both cases the unconscious mental processes arise in early childhood and constitute a repressed wish, as do all unconscious processes, and the symptom or dream represents the imaginary fulfilment of that wish in a form in which is also fused the fulfilment of the opposing wish.

Dreams differ from psychoneurotic symptoms in that the opposing wish is always of the same kind—namely, the wish to sleep. A dream is thus the guardian of sleep, and its function is to satisfy the activity of unconscious mental processes that otherwise would disturb sleep. The fact that sometimes a horrid dream may not only disturb sleep, but may actually wake the sleeper, in no way vitiates this conclusion. In such cases the activity of the endopsychic censorship, which is diminished during sleep, is insufficient to keep from consciousness the dream thoughts, or to compel such distortion of them as to render them unrecognisable, and recourse has to be had to the accession of energy that the censorship is capable of exerting in the waking state; metaphorically expressed, the watchman guarding the sleeping household is overpowered, and has to wake it in calling for help.

Freud couples with his discussion of dream problems a penetrating inquiry into many allied topics, such as the nature of the unconscious and the function of consciousness, that cannot here be even touched upon. I would conclude this imperfect sketch of his theory of dreams by quoting a sentence of his to the effect that ' *Die Traumdeutung ist die Via Regia zur Kenntniss des Unbewussten im Seelenleben.*' [' The interpretation of dreams is the Via Regia to the knowledge of the unconscious in mental life.']

CHAPTER XI

THE RELATIONSHIP BETWEEN DREAMS AND PSYCHONEUROTIC SYMPTOMS [1]

At first sight the resemblances between dreams and psychoneurotic symptoms appear to be of a very superficial kind, and it is the obvious differences between them that most naturally take our attention. Nevertheless, a psychological study of the two manifestations discloses a far-reaching similarity between them in almost all respects; in fact the more closely one investigates the psychogenesis of them the more one is impressed by the extraordinary resemblances, and the more difficult does it become to define the essential differences between them. That the study of normal dreams is highly important, both for the understanding of all kinds of mental disturbances and for the treatment of the psychoneuroses, is growing more and more evident, and I shall presently touch on some of these practical aspects.

Our knowledge of the psychogenesis of both dreams and neurotic symptoms we principally owe to the laborious work of Freud, and I shall here largely confine myself to the exposition of some of his conclusions. He has dealt fully with the manifold problems of dream life in a book devoted to the subject,[2] and some five years later, in the ' Bruchstück einer Hysterieanalyse,'[3] he illustrated in detail his views on the relationship between dreams and hysteria, and showed the value of dream analysis for the elucidation of this neurosis. I will try to deal with the present theme in the form of a series of statements. These may be grouped under four headings, and I need hardly add that they will have to be far from exhaustive either in number or extent.

I. General Characteristics

In the first place one might remark on the fact that both dreams and neurotic symptoms frequently appear to the lay mind to be remarkably meaningless, illogical, or even absurd. For instance, in a

---

[1] An address delivered before the Wayne County Society, at Detroit, May 15, 1911. Published in the *American Journal of Insanity*, July, 1911.

[2] Freud, ' Die Traumdeutung,' 1900, 5ᵉ Aufl., 1919.

[3] Reprinted in the ' Sammlung kleiner Schriften zur Neurosenlehre,' 2ᵉ Folge, 1909.

dream one may see an historic personage, say George Washington, talking familiarly to one's brother, and in a place that neither had ever visited. Similarly a neurotic patient, who in the ordinary way is courageous enough, may be seized with an irrational terror at the sight of some object for which he has a specific phobia—for instance, a cat. On a healthy person the incomprehensibility of such bizarre occurrences produces an unavoidable impression of unreasonableness, and he has an instinctive difficulty in taking either of them seriously, certainly in devoting to them that earnest attention which they really deserve. We describe this illogical or incongruous feature by saying that the occurrences in question cannot be related to the rest of the person's conscious thoughts; it is something apart, strange, and apparently quite disconnected. This statement is perfectly true, and the alternative hypotheses are either that such manifestations are in their very nature throughout bizarre and illogical, or that they are the product of normal logical thoughts which for some reason have become distorted. Freud has produced evidence to shew that the latter hypothesis is probably the true one, and that the obvious gaps between the occurrences and the rest of the person's mind can be filled in by bringing to light various thoughts that previously were unconscious.

A further resemblance between dreams and neurotic symptoms lies in the conception of them that was until recently generally prevalent among scientific men, and which still widely obtains. This is based on the former of the two hypotheses just mentioned, the one that accepts the manifestations in question at their face value. It may be stated as follows: They are both disordered products of an imagination that is functioning improperly because of certain non-mental circumstances. In sleep, when the mind is at rest, various physical excitations disturb in an irregular manner different groups of certain brain cells, the result of which is the anomalous, fitful, and disconnected series of mental processes that we call a dream. In the psychoneuroses the same thing takes place, except that the physical excitations are of a morbid kind (due to malnutrition, toxins, etc.), so that we call the result a disease. In both cases it is denied that the manifestations are susceptible of a psychological interpretation, that they have a precise psychical history, or that there is any logical meaning behind the odd and inconsequent series of mental processes.

This familiar conception received a rude shock at the hands of

Freud when he published his observations shewing that, though dreams and neurotic symptoms have all the appearance of disorder and disconnectedness, this appearance is not primary, but is itself the result of the action of certain definite mental agents. The two manifestations are rather the *altered* products of mental processes that are entirely consequent and highly significant parts of the personality. By means of psycho-analysis they have been traced to their origin, when it becomes plain that they have a perfectly definite psychical history, and an entirely logical meaning. There are thus two main problems: first the nature and significance of the sources of the manifestations in question, and secondly the nature and significance of the alteration or distortion that these original mental processes have undergone before attaining their final appearance.

Both manifestations have a remarkable tendency to be forgotten. With dreams this is such a characteristic feature as to need no dwelling on; everyone who has tried systematically to recall his dreams will have noticed how treacherous is his memory of them, and what a usual occurrence it is for the remembrance of even a vivid dream completely to disappear within a few minutes after waking. In the case of neurotic symptoms this feature is not so generally recognised, but careful observation shews that it is almost as constant, though not so pronounced, as it is with dreams. However detailed the anamnesis taken in the first few interviews with the patient, one regularly finds later that it is incomplete and that all sorts of early symptoms have been ignored or forgotten. The same holds in respect to the duration of symptoms; patients almost always under-estimate this. A typical instance is that of a patient of mine who stated he had had trembling of the hand for the past three months, and never before; it turned out later that he had had it for the past six months, and on two former occasions for two or three months each time. Further, the memory of dreams and of neurotic symptoms not only fades in intensity, but becomes distorted as time goes on. This occurrence is also better known in the case of dreams, where Freud has given it the name of ' secondary elaboration.' The memory of neurotic symptoms is similarly fallacious: different ones are misplaced in time, confounded with one another, and so on. The history of a neurotic illness laid bare after a prolonged investigation has often quite a different appearance from the incomplete and incorrect one given by the patient during the first interviews.

This curious tendency to forget and alter mental processes that at the time of their occurrence were so valid as to absorb the whole attention of the person is certainly noteworthy, and in itself would suggest an inner connection between the two processes. We shall see that the significance of the tendency is the same in the two cases, it being a manifestation of the repression of underlying mental processes which are symbolised by both dreams and neurotic symptoms. The vulgar tendency to belittle dreams and symptoms, which was mentioned above, is also an expression of the same psychical force. Further, the two tendencies, to falsify the memory of the two manifestations, and to forget them altogether, have exactly the same psychological significance, both being results of the repressing force.

Dreams and neurotic symptoms shew intimate psychological connections with superstition, both on the surface and in their essence. That dreams have always been a fruitful source of superstition is well known. Even at the present day belief in the telepathic nature of some dreams, and in their service for foretelling events, is far from extinct. In more subtle ways dreams may influence the waking thoughts in a manner that can only be described as superstitious; I have recently published some striking instances of this.[1] It has been said that all neurotic patients are at heart superstitious, and although this is probably an overstatement, still with some forms of neurosis—e.g., obsessions—the superstitiousness of the patients is quite extraordinary. One of my patients could not stand with his face to the north because it might bring some harm to his father; he could not cross the street without first counting eight, for otherwise ill-luck would happen to him; and so on. Cases of the kind are familiar enough.

The intrinsic relations between superstition and the two manifestations in question, though highly interesting, are too involved to discuss here, and I must refer you to the suggestive chapter on superstition in one of Freud's works.[2]

II. CLINICAL RELATIONS

It is not very rare for a neurotic symptom actually to date from a given dream, an occurrence first fully described by Féré in 1886. As an instance I may mention the case of a patient of mine who

[1] See Chapter X. of the Third Edition.

[2] Freud, ' Zur Psychopathologie des Alltagslebens,' 7ᵉ Aufl., 1920. See also Ernest Jones, ' Der Alptraum in seiner Beziehung zu gewissen Formen des mittelalterlichen Aberglaubens,' 1912, and ' Die Bedeutung des Salzes in Sitte und Brauch der Völker,' *Imago*, Jahrg. i., Heft 4 and 5.

whenever he had a certain dream, to the effect that he was being hanged, always suffered for some time after from an hysterical paralysis of the right arm. In discussing in a recent paper[1] this type of occurrence, I pointed out that it is incorrect to regard the dream as the *cause* of the symptom that subsequently arises. They both have a common cause in some buried thoughts. The process, however, is of considerable interest as showing that the same thoughts can come to expression in both a dream and a neurotic symptom, thus illustrating the near relationship of the two.

Certain neurotic symptoms even in their external appearance strikingly resemble dreams. In hysteria, for example, curious conditions occur which so resemble dreams as to be thus named. Loewenfeld[2] gives the following description of them: ' Die Aussenwelt macht nicht den gewöhnlichen Eindruck, das wohl Bekannte und täglich Geschehene erscheint verändert, wie unbekannt, neu, fremdartig, oder die ganze Umgebung macht den Eindruck, als sei sie ein Phantasieprodukt, ein Schein, eine Vision. In letzterem Falle besonders ist es den Patienten, als ob sie sich in einem Traume oder Halbschlafe befänden, hypnotisiert oder somnambul seien, und sie sprechen dann auch zumeist von ihren Traumzuständen.' [' The outer world fails to make its accustomed impression, things that are well known and seen every day seem altered, as if unknown, new, strange; or the whole environment gives the impression of being a product of the imagination, a sham, a vision. In the latter case especially the patients feel as if they are in a dream or half-sleep, as if they have been hypnotised or are somnambulic, and they mostly also speak then of their dream-states.'] Abraham,[3] who has submitted these conditions to a searching investigation, points out further resemblances they have to reveries or day-dreams, to twilight states, and to noctambulism. He finds that the condition passes through three fairly well-defined stages: first, one of exaltation of the imagination; then one of dream-like withdrawal from the outer world, during which the environment seems unreal, strange, and altered; and finally a third, one of vacuity, in which the thoughts stand still and the mind seems a blank. The first two stages are pleasurable, the third disagreeable. His analysis of the content of consciousness

[1] See Chapter X. of the Third Edition.

[2] Loewenfeld, ' Ueber traumartige und verwandte Zustände,' *Centralbl. f. Nervenheilk. u. Psychiatr.*, 1909.

[3] Abraham, ' Ueber hysterische Traumzustände,' *Jahrbuch der Psycho-analyse*, Bd. ii., S. 1.

during these stages shows that, like neurotic symptoms in general and also dreams, it represents the symbolic gratification of various repressed ambitions and desires.

The reverse occurrence to this is still more frequent, in which, namely, a neurotic symptom appears directly in a dream. This is most often found with various fears; for instance, a person who is afraid of heights dreams that he is on the edge of a precipice and about to fall. In such cases the analysis of the dream furnishes a specially direct clue to the nature and origin of the corresponding symptom.

Not only may the 'superficial content (called by Freud the manifest content) of a dream be identical with that of a given symptom, as in the example just mentioned, but a dream that appears in no way to resemble any symptom may arise from the identical underlying mental processes that are the cause of a symptom from which the patient is at the same time suffering. The significance of this fact for the treatment of neurotic symptoms will be dwelt on later.

III. Structure

Recent impressions, often in themselves quite trivial, are adjuvant factors in the production of both dreams and neurotic symptoms. Most observers have noticed how frequently casual recent thoughts and impressions, which passed unnoticed at the time, are met with in dreams, and Freud has found that in every dream there is represented some mental process, either trivial or significant, of the day before. Similarly neurotic symptoms often owe their occurrence to some recent and often trivial impression, such as the reading or hearing about a given illness, a slight shock, grief, or fright (often called imitation or suggestion). In both cases there is a considerable tendency, on the part of both the observer and the person concerned, to regard this recent impression as the cause of the dream or symptom. Strictly speaking, it is never more than the exciting cause, which acts by evoking a manifestation of deeper and much more significant mental processes.

Both dreams and neurotic symptoms are a compromise-formation, being produced by the interaction of two opposing sets of forces. One of these, the real source of the dream or symptom, is composed of certain buried mental processes, called by Freud the ' latent content,' which have a strongly marked dynamic or conative trend.

The actual characteristics of this latent content will be pointed out in the next section. The other set of forces, called by Freud the endopsychic censorship, consists of various social and ethical inhibitions, the effect of which is to prevent the passage into consciousness of the mental processes comprising the latent content. In other words, the latter consists of thoughts, desires, and wishes of a kind that are highly unacceptable to the conscious personality, and which, therefore, are ' repressed ' in the unconscious; the patient has great difficulty in admitting their existence, sometimes even in conceding the possibility of their existence. The dream or symptom is thus an allegorical presentation of the latent thoughts. These cannot come to direct expression, so they are hinted at by means of circumlocutions, euphemisms, and metaphors quite analogous to those in which we hint at forbidden themes in polite society. That is the meaning of the distortion referred to above. When the distorted product is resolved into its elements, when the underlying mental processes are unravelled, and the latent content laid bare, it is always found that they have a perfectly definite and logical meaning, and furthermore that they are always of an intimate nature and of high significance to the personality. Whatever the superficial appearance of a dream or symptom may be, the underlying causes of it are never trivial. The following simple dreams illustrate this conclusion.[1]

(1) A woman, aged thirty-one, dreamed that *she met a Mrs. R., who invited her to come and take a bath together*. This is not so senseless as it appears. The associations supplied by the patient were as follows: ' Mrs. R. is about to be confined. I helped her sister once at her confinement. That is supposed to bring luck. It is one of the things done to cure sterility. After her confinement I bathed together with her for the same reason (a Jewish superstition). To have a child is my dearest wish, especially as my husband and my woman friends despise me for my childlessness, and taunt me with it. I have been to many doctors and had two operations, but so far nothing has helped.'

(2) A girl of twenty dreamed that *she and her sister were to get $150 for diving from the roof of an aquarium in public. A friend who was present remarked that the sister was being badly paid for her work, which was*

---

[1] As with all the other examples given here, no attempt is made to render the ful analysis. The patients' contributions and my own interpretations, however, are kept distinct from each other.

precarious, and the patient replied: ' Well, you know, we can always dive.'
The patient was very fond of diving at the baths, an act which gave
her a markedly voluptuous sensation. All that the sum of $150
reminded her of was that when she was fifteen a man friend took
her out for the evening, repeatedly kissed her, and on saying good-
bye put $1.50 into her purse to buy some chocolates with, adding:
' I wish I could afford to give you a hundred times as much.' The
sister was at the time the paid mistress of a certain man. The dream
is thus a fairly open expression of the girl's realisation that the same
avenue for earning money was open to her.

(3) The same patient dreamed that *an Angora cat was restlessly
moving to and fro in a room. Presently he struggled to reach a window and
then jumped out into the street.* She described it as an awful nightmare,
from which she awoke with a feeling of paralysis in the legs. She
owned an Angora cat, which was ' very beautiful and graceful, with
blue eyes.' She herself was pretty and graceful, and had blue eyes.
She identifies herself with the cat, and projects on to him thoughts
that really concern herself. The cat was fond of standing at an open
window, enjoying the air. Late one night he alarmed her by jumping
through it and escaping. Her sister laughed and said, ' He has gone
to lead a gay life on Broadway.' She replied, ' Yes, cats can go out
at night whenever they like, but we can't, we should only be called
fallen women.'

This dream illustrates one of the causes of the frequent fear of
falling, which may occur as either a symptom or a dream, physical
and moral falling being unconsciously associated, so that the idea of
the former can be used to represent that of the latter.[1] Another
dream of the same patient shows this even more plainly. (4) *She
stepped out of an upper window, picked up an umbrella that was lying there,
opened it, and dropped to the ground. She fell on to the cellar steps in the
front of the house. A man picked her up, and they went down the street
together.* On the previous day she had annoyed her father by incon-
veniently borrowing his umbrella. The thought of a raised umbrella
first reminded her of parachutes, and that a friend of hers had
recently made a balloon ascent with her husband (a noted aviator)
on their honeymoon; then of a Zeppelin-shaped balloon filled with
candy, that a man friend had just given her. She had wondered
whether a Zeppelin balloon was sharp enough to penetrate one of
the ordinary shape if there was a collision. Finally it became evident

---

[1] This is illustrated in the old saying: ' When a maiden falls, she falls on her back.'

that an opened-up and raised umbrella was associated in her mind with the erect male organ; in fact she had heard jokes in which the two were compared. As to the cellar entrance, she was struck by the curious fact of this being in the front of the house in question, instead of at the side, as it is in real life. The house was identified with herself and her own body, as is so naturally the case with women, to whom the home is an integral part of themselves. That the lower entrance to it symbolised the site of her (moral and physical) fall on the street (in which she was aided by a raised umbrella and a man) is quite intelligible. Going together with a member of the opposite sex (especially on the street) has long been a symbol for the sexual act; indeed, the word coitus itself is derived from *coire*—to go together. The three dreams thus represent the wild *demi-mondaine* instinct that with many ardent women slumbers at the back of the mind.

The individual details of the mechanisms[1] by means of which the latent content becomes transformed into the disguised manifest content are strikingly similar with dreams and neurotic symptoms. One of the more obvious of these is that known as ' condensation.' Every single feature of a dream and of a neurotic symptom representing more than one group of mental processes is, as Freud expresses it, ' over-determined.' One can never talk of *the* cause, for there are always numerous co-acting agents. Each feature is a highly condensed representation of an extensive series of other thoughts, a fact which renders the full exposition of the structure of any dream or symptom a matter of great practical difficulty. Thus in a dream a given strange figure may be formed by the fusion of attributes taken from several different people, the result being a composite person; the same applies to all other elements of the dream. Sometimes the extent to which the condensation is carried is quite extraordinary. The analogy between the neologisms that occur in dreams, and those so frequent in insanity, has often been commented on; the genesis and structure of them is similar in the two cases. In the neuroses neologisms are relatively rare; they are chiefly met with in the obsessional neurosis. The following is a simple instance of condensation, in the dream of a homosexual patient:

(5) He dreamed that a *man, whose name seemed to be Lysanias, was advancing towards him.* Of the name he said that nothing was known of it beyond the fact that it is mentioned in Luke iii. 1 as that of a

---

[1] See Chapter X. for an account of these complex processes.

tetrarch of Abilene; it should be said that the patient was a professional Bible-reader. Remembering, however, that nothing occurring
in a dream is without significance, I asked him to supply free associations to the names. The first one brought the words lyceum and
licentious; his school (not in this country) was called a lyceum.
When a schoolboy, he had been in the habit of resorting to an
abbey ruin in the neighbourhood for the purpose of indulging in
sexual practices with an older boy called Leney. The name Lysanias
(tetrarch of Abilene), therefore, expressed the fact of his having been
licentious when at the *lyceum* by going to the *abbey* with *Leney*. An
isolated instance of this sort may be due purely to coincidence, in
spite of the immediate associations furnished by the patient, but
when we find similar occurrences in every dream without exception
that is submitted to analysis it becomes extremely difficult to regard
this explanation as adequate.

Another equally prominent mechanism in both dreams and
neurotic symptoms is that known as ' displacement.' By this is
meant the replacement of one idea by another, more satisfactory or
acceptable; the affect belonging to the original idea is displaced
on to the second one. The directing of interest away from forbidden
thoughts into the sphere of sport is an instance of this mechanism,
which plays a large part in everyday life. It is one of the ways in
which the symbolism is brought about that is so constant a feature
in dreams and neuroses. Displacement is illustrated in all the dream
examples here related; further instances are the following:

(6) The last-mentioned patient dreamed that *he was at the side of
a dirty-looking, sluggish river. He seemed to know that the Sanitary
Inspector had said it was full of disease germs. The banks were covered
with silvery, iridescent, fishes' eggs. A gigantic dog-fish raised itself out of
the stream and attacked him.* The river reminded him of the River Wey,
which gave the associations: milky-way—curds and whey—semen
(germ). Fishes' eggs always made him think of drops of semen
(masturbation). He had a morbid repugnance for all fish, finding
them loathsome. A boy, with whom he had had sexual relations in
school (the patient playing a passive part), was nicknamed Fishy,
on account of his large mouth and fish-like eyes. As to dogs, he
had had a terror of them ever since one had bitten him badly when,
in boyhood, he was gratifying his sexual curiosity with it. The
whole dream thus symbolised a sexual attack of a kind he had since
come to regard as repulsive.

(7) A woman, aged thirty-five, dreamed that *she was driving in a trap with a tall, dark man. The horse was a bay. They came to a level crossing and saw a warning notice with only the word ' near ' on it. A train came dashing along. The man tried to cross, but the horse refused and turned round just in time, thus saving them.* The man recalled to her a cousin who had once proposed to her when they were out driving. The word ' near ' made her think of ' a near relative.' She thought it wrong to marry a near relative, on account of the risk to the children, and for this reason had refused her cousin's offer, although she was very fond of him. The bay horse reminded her of one she was greatly attached to as a girl, and which was named after her; also her own name before marriage was Bay. In the dream she thus identifies herself with the horse, who saves them from disaster.

It is impossible for me to go here into further detail in regard to these various mechanisms, and I will only add two further remarks on the subject. The mechanism of inversion is an extremely common one in both dreams and neurotic symptoms. The inversion may concern either space or time. For instance, the second part of a dream or of an hysterical attack[1] may represent the first part of the logical underlying thoughts. The other matter is that the affect in both dreams and symptoms is always true. If a patient has a morbid fear of a trivial object, either in a dream or when awake, this fear is always justified in fact; that is to say, there is some associated object or idea in real life that he has every right to be afraid of. The unreasonableness arises only through the fear having got displaced on to a trivial associated idea; the person dares not admit to himself what he is really afraid of. For instance, a woman patient of mine, having every reason to be afraid of a certain treacherous object that has the capacity of penetrating the body, with dangerous results, contracted a phobia of—knives. To laugh at neurotic patients for their ' ungrounded ' fears is to display a complete ignorance of the significance and genesis of the symptom.

IV. LATENT CONTENT

The associated ideas obtained by any careful study of dreams lead one at first to a number of mental processes that have taken a share in building the dream. Up to the present, however, it has not been found possible to reach the true latent content or underlying meaning

[1] See Freud, ' Hysterische Phantasien und ihre Beziehung zur Bisexualität,' *Zeitschr f. Sexualwissenschaft*, 1908, Heft 1.

of dreams by the use of any other method than the psycho-analytic, a method which, like other complex procedures, has its own technique that requires to be carefully learned. The material obtained by more superficial studies is found to be quite heterogeneous, and the conclusion may hastily be reached that the latent content has no characteristic features, that any kind of mental process, a fear, anxiety, wish, and so on, can give rise to a dream. On the contrary, the true latent content that lies behind this material, and which is laid bare by psycho-analysis, is found to be specific and homogeneous, and always has certain definite and characteristic features. The preceding remarks apply equally as well to neurotic symptoms as to dreams. The features common to the latent content of both are as follows:

1. The latent content is always unconscious; that is to say, it consists of mental processes unknown to the person, and of which he cannot become aware by direct introspection but only by means of certain indirect modes of approach.

2. These mental processes are never indifferent to the person, but are highly significant, and are ' repressed ' in the unconscious on account of their being unacceptable to the conscious mind.

3. The latent content is of infantile origin, later additions being merely reinforcements of earlier infantile trends. The following is an instance of how infantile material can lie behind an apparently meaningless dream:

(8) The last-mentioned patient dreamed that *she was pregnant, and that she was suffering from nausea. She thought to herself, ' Surely the baby is not coming out this way.'* Analysis of the dream led to long-forgotten infantile thoughts, in which she had imagined conception and childbirth to be processes analogous to the ingress and egress of food, and taking place at the same alimentary orifices. The hysterical vomiting (æsthetic disgust), from which she suffered in waking life, originated in the same buried complex.

4. The latent content of neurotic symptoms is invariably, and of dreams usually, of a sexual nature, although in both cases, of course, other material is also included. It should be remembered that this statement refers principally to the infantile form of sexuality, which differs widely from the adult type.[1] I am aware that this generalisation, like all other new ones, is bound to give the appearance, to those who are shocked by its strangeness, of being an obvious

[1] See Chapter I., and Freud, ' Drei Abhandlungen zur Sexualtheorie,' 2ᵉ Aufl., 1910.

exaggeration, but it is a matter that can only be settled by facts, not by preconceived opinions; so far as my experience goes the facts conclusively point to the truth of it. To the other examples of it I have already related the following may be added:

(9) A patient, aged thirty-three, dreamed that *she was in a bathroom, and that an enormous spider, with huge legs, kept falling on to her and entwining itself around her. She called to her son for help, and endeavoured to get the spider into the bath, which was made of tin.* The spontaneous and quite unprompted associations to the elements of this 'harmless' dream were as follows: Her mother-in-law had a tin bath the surface of which she was fastidious about keeping immaculate. The patient's son, a boy of eight, had recently soiled and scratched it by standing in it with his boots on. She used to find very repugnant the maternal duty of taking her boy, when a baby, to the bath-room for other purposes. The word 'tin' brought to her mind the word 'nit.' (The frequency with which reversal occurs in unconscious mentation was mentioned above; it is an interesting subject, which deserves a special discussion.) She had suffered badly from nits when at school, and had often to be taken to the bath-room to have her hair treated; the experience had caused her great disgust. The enormous spider called to her mind her husband, from whom she is separated. He is an unusually big man; she loathed his embraces, which gave her the feeling of being grasped by a spider. After them she used to take not only a douche, but a full bath, to wash away any traces of his contact. She had been in the habit of calling her son to her room to protect her by his presence whenever she found her husband's embraces quite unendurable. The dream thus discloses itself as a disguised reminiscence of very intimate experiences.

The following is an example of a bisexual dream, in which, namely, the actor plays both a masculine and feminine part.

(10) The patient, a farmer of twenty-four, dreamed that *he saw an immense lion. His feeling was that it had been a family pet, but that as there was a latent danger about it he ought to shoot it. The rest of the family did not seem to appreciate the danger or to agree with him that it was necessary to destroy the animal. His mother appeared on the scene, weak and ill, as she had been the year previous to her death. She was quite indifferent to the danger, and he could not understand this, especially in view of her weakness. With difficulty he persuaded her to let him lead her out of the danger zone. Then his father appeared, who though dubious about the necessity of taking any action, began to load a rifle. The patient now became more apprehensive,*

doubted his capacity to tackle the animal himself, and decided to leave the job to a more reliable marksman—namely, his father. After a consultation they called to their assistance their dog. He and his mother had to prepare the dog for the fight, and this now turned inexplicably into a small lion, the other animal disappearing from the scene. The preparation consisted in fitting top-boots on to the new lion's feet, and at his mother's suggestion he tried to do this. He succeeded with one boot, though not so as to satisfy the lion. The next one was still more difficult to get on, but he managed to get it on by means of swinging the foot to and fro inside it. This movement irritated the lion, which seized his head and crushed it. The patient's feeling was one of mixed apprehension and submission. A later addition: *in the first part of the dream the animal was half a lion and half a snake; it had definite features of both these, the tail and hind parts, for example, having altogether the appearance of a snake, the head being half leonine and half snake-like, the teeth and claws being leonine, and so on.* It thus resembled the fabulous monsters of mythology, creatures probably also born of dreams. To connect this bizarre dream with the waking thoughts of a prosaic young Canadian farmer, and to regard it as an expression of his psychosexual life, might perhaps seem a gratuitous and not very likely undertaking, but even the few facts I can here relate show that it was far from impossible, as indeed the full analysis proved. The lion, with its half-menacing, half-undecided expression, at once recalled to the patient his father, whose head and cast of features have a strikingly leonine appearance. (This resemblance in the father both I and a common acquaintance had previously noticed quite independently of the patient, to whom I had never mentioned it.) The thought of a snake also brought to his mind his father's cold, beady eyes, and his insinuating ' sneaky ' manner of getting his way when he was not in a position to bully; in outbursts of anger the patient had frequently called him a snake. He was constantly on bad terms with his father, and the troubles that resulted constituted the main symptom for which he was being treated. He had always slept with his father, and when the latter went into the mother's bedroom, which was divided off by a board partition, the overheard sounds caused in him both physical excitement and jealousy.

The dream expresses four phantasies, an auto-erotic, a feminine, a masculine, and a bisexual. The top-boots that he was fitting on to the foot (an ancient phallic symbol) of the small lion represented a condom, which he had worn when masturbating, so as to heighten the illusion of the imagined vagina (sheath); it also reminded him of a snake-skin. In being attacked by the lion-snake he played a feminine part. The contact of his father's penis in bed had always excited him; he had frequently compared the appearance of it to a snake and had woven all sorts of grandiloquent phantasies about it. As a boy of nine he had pictured to himself, half fearfully, half voluptuously, that there was a large snake in his bed, and later on had suffered from the fear that a snake might creep into his mouth or anus when he was asleep out of doors. In the dream his protection of his mother from the large animal (the father, the dangerous family pet) and his co-operation with her in handling the small one (himself) shows him in a masculine part. In real life he had in fact remonstrated with his father for going to the mother's room against her will when she was weak and ill. The conclusion of the dream represents a mixed, bisexual phantasy. The crushing of the head between the lion's jaws brought the following associations: a frog in the jaws of a snake—a boa-constrictor he had seen swallowing a mass of raw beef—gripping his penis in the act of masturbation—a game he used to play with an older boy, which consisted in getting the latter to grip his head between his thighs: ' it felt like having one's penis held tight ' (the head is a well-known phallic symbol). This theme was connected with both masochistic and sadistic phantasies, though principally the former.

It is probable that a great number of dreams, just as most neurotic symptoms, are connected with infantile incestuous wishes. These came to fairly evident expression in the dream just related, as also in the next one.

(11) The patient, a woman of twenty-three, dreamed that *she was walking alone in a dark thicket. She thought how terrible it would be to meet a negro there, as she was unprotected. One appeared, armed with a pickaxe, and grabbed her by the arm. She struggled to escape, but thought to herself that ' it would not be so terrible if she were to collapse.' She reached a high board fence and pushed open a door, which had rusty nails.* The patient was a Southern girl, who from a child had never been allowed to go out without carrying a revolver. The association between negroes and rape was naturally a very close one in her mind. She had ' a horror of anyone being killed on her account ' (the fear covering a repressed wish), and recollected several instances of lynching near her home. There was in general in her mind a very intimate association between the ideas of sexual relations and violence. As a child she had frequently overheard conjugal acts on the part of her parents, and had

interpreted them as a violent sexual assault; the fact that her parents often used to quarrel fiercely, her father striking and wounding her mother, no doubt contributed to this conception. The grabbing of her arm in the dream brought to her mind an occasion on which she had tried to defend her mother, and her father had roughly seized her by the (same) arm, violently twisting it. The negro in the dream at once reminded her of her father, the short white beard, the working-clothes, and pickaxe, as well as his build and movements, being exactly the same. The fence recalled one of the same appearance as in the dream, in front of which she had, when a girl of fifteen, seen a man exposing himself; she had ' absent-mindedly ' stopped and asked him if he wanted to speak to her. The rusty nails brought back the fence at the home, which ' it wouldn't take anything to break down.' Further dreams, in which her father stabbed her or her mother with a knife, etc., shewed that in her repressed imagination she had identified herself with her mother, and wished that her father would commit the same kind of assault on her as on her mother; in fact she was constantly, and in the most wanton way, provoking disagreements and quarrels with her father. In the course of the treatment the patient fully realised, and confirmed by recalling a number of forgotten memories, the incestuous origin of her family troubles; since the analysis she has been on excellent terms with both her father and mother.

5. The latent content of both dreams and neurotic symptoms consists of an imaginary gratification of one or more repressed wishes. As was previously mentioned, all kinds of other material may enter into their composition, and wishes that are not repressed frequently find an imaginary gratification in them, but the latent content itself is always a repressed wish-fulfilment.

Of all the relationships between dreams and neurotic symptoms the most important practically is that in many cases the latent content of both is identical; that is to say, the mental causes (repressed complexes) of a neurosis will sooner or later come to expression in the patient's dreams. Before discussing the corollaries that follow from this fact I will illustrate it by some more instances.

(12) This example is taken from the same case as (7) and (8). One of the patient's chief symptoms was a feeling of powerlessness, at times amounting to a complete paralysis, in both arms. This was at first manifested only while playing the piano, a recreation of which she had been particularly fond. She dreamed that *she was in a large*

hall. At one end, opposite to her, was a maroon-coloured church organ. There were several upright pianos, and one baby grand piano, at which she was playing. Her boy was kicking at it from the side, and she reproved him saying, ' You ought not to abuse such a beautiful instrument.' The free associations to the elements of this dream were: Organ. ' I don't know why it was maroon-coloured, for our organ is painted grey. I have always been passionately fond of organ music. To hear it gives me a delicious soft feeling. I used to get into the church alone, and try to play on the organ. (Pause.) The word is also used for a certain part of the body.' Reproving the boy (who was nine years old). ' I have been greatly exercised of late lest he might acquire any bad habits in school as I did at his age (masturbation), and last week spoke to him on the subject; I used words almost the same as those in the dream.' From these and other associations it was not hard to infer that the acts of masturbation and of piano-playing had become unconsciously associated in her mind. I told her so, and she answered, ' Well, I didn't tell you that when I woke from the dream I found I had been doing it in my sleep.' This proved to be an important step in the discovery of a number of thoughts, phantasies, and incorrect ideas relating to masturbation, all of which were concerned in the genesis of the hysterical paralysis; roughly put, her loss of power in piano-playing, which gradually extended to other functions, was in a way a punishment for playing with her fingers in another, forbidden direction.

(13) The following example is taken from the same case as the last. *She was seated at a table which was covered with food; the table was made of rough boards as at a picnic. She played in this food as though on a piano. Her fingers got unpleasantly sticky, and covered with some stuff that seemed like either fine hay or shredded wheat.* The rough board table reminded her of picnics she used to go to when a young girl; she used to play see-saw with a boy-cousin on a board taken from the temporary table, and this used to cause genital excitement. The latter idea brought to her mind other similar onanistic acts (on chairs, steps, etc.). Stickiness was associated with both this and the idea of semen. Fine hay called to her mind the hen-nests in which she used to search for eggs, and shredded wheat the threads of babies' clothes. There are thus two themes, masturbation and conception. These were connected in her mind by the curious belief she had held as a girl that illegitimate pregnancy might result from masturbation. Fears in this direction had made her life a misery for several years

till at the age of seventeen she learned the truth; in the preceding dream the belief was indicated by her playing on a ' baby ' piano (a baby and the part of the body where it is born are often unconsciously associated). The connection with food dated from a much older complex. When a child of five she had developed the idea that babies grew from food taken into the body. Her vomiting symptom arose from this complex, as was remarked in example (8). The dream is thus a condensed biographical account of her views and experiences on the subject of sexuality and child-birth.

(14) The patient, whose history I have elsewhere related,[1] suffered from an anxiety state with pronounced gastric symptoms. She dreamed that *she was going to the beach to bathe. On her way she stopped to buy some milk. They gave it her in several bottles; all these were white, except one, which was violet-coloured. When she reached the sea a small boy ran out of the water to meet her.* The dream represented a birth phantasy, as many dreams do in which a child emerges from the water.[2] In the preparation for the event it was only natural that she should need a quantity of milk, but the curious circumstance of one of the bottles being violet-coloured needs an explanation. Nothing in a dream is without import, and this instance is a good example of how an apparently insignificant feature may be connected with the most important underlying thoughts. The immediate associations were: ' violets are my favourite flowers; my husband's poison bottles (he was a doctor) were blue; in milk shops I have never seen blue or violet bottles, but they sell buttermilk in brown bottles; buttermilk was prescribed for my stomach trouble and I loathe it, it nauseates me.' It is possible that the violet colour was composed from a mixture of the blue and brown; at all events we shall see that the corresponding ideas are intimately associated with one another. Like the last-mentioned one, this patient also had constructed an infantile hypothesis of pregnancy on the view that the baby grew in the abdomen out of food, but, keener than her, she had surmised that some special substance had been added to the food to fructify it. On the analogy of the mixing of urine and fæces, and of the watering and manuring of vegetation, she inferred that the new substance was a fluid, and as the doctor was evidently concerned in the matter she concluded it must be some kind of medicine. Throughout her childhood she had a remarkable fascination for medicines, and drank all she could get at. As a reaction to

[1] Chapter XIX., p. 427, of the Fourth Edition.   [2] See Chapter X., p. 231.

this in later life she acquired a loathing for any medicinal substance that in any way resembled the appearance of semen, the infantile complex being now buried; instances of this were buttermilk, flax-seed emulsion, and koumiss, all of which were forced on her with the object of bettering her stomach trouble. As to the blue poison bottles of her husband (who, it should be remembered, was a doctor), it turned out that poison (a medicinal fluid which when swallowed produces serious effects) also belonged to the same group of ideas; it is this association that is at the basis of the common delusion of insane patients that they are being poisoned—*i.e.*, that a certain fluid is being forced on them against their will. The same association is the explanation of the old beliefs in ambrosia, nectar, love-potions, and other magical drinks. A flower or bud was in her dreams a common symbol for a baby, as it is in poetry. The violet colour in the dream was thus greatly over-determined. The insight gained into the nature of the psychogastric symptoms from the analysis of this dream alone was of considerable value for the question of treatment.

The importance of the fact that the latent content of many dreams is identical with that of the neurotic symptoms from which the patient is at the same time suffering is a twofold one, it being equally significant for pathology and for therapeutics. A knowledge of the nature, mechanisms, and meaning of normal dreams is indispensable for the understanding of the manifold problems of the neuroses, and also, it may be added, of the psychoses.[1] An adequate study of these problems is only possible when the unity of the laws applying to both normal and morbid processes is appreciated, and nothing demonstrates this unity more clearly than the study of dreams. Through it one realises that the same forces are at work in the normal, in the neuroses, and in insanity, and that there is no sharp line dividing any of these. Not only is the principle of cause and effect just as rigorous with bizarre morbid manifestations as it is in normal, mental life, but the various psychological laws according to which it operates are precisely the same in both cases. Further, the study of the patient's dreams is the readiest and most direct route to the unconscious, where the conflicts are taking place that form the basis

---

[1] Hughlings Jackson once made the significant remark, which unfortunately was never acted on by his colleagues: ' Find out all about dreams, and you will then understand insanity.' Freud, in his ' Traumdeutung,' maintains that it is hopeless to approach the psychology of insanity unless one has a knowledge of the genesis and structure of normal dreams.

of the surface symptoms; it is therefore of prime importance for the investigation of the individual pathogenesis.

For therapeutics the study of dreams is of the greatest value in two ways. First, the deeper knowledge and comprehension of the sources of the disorder must of itself put one in a better position to deal with them. In few maladies are the pathogenic factors so darkly hidden as the neuroses, and many modes of treatment (*e.g.*, persuasion) can only be described as a blind fight with unseen foes. When the morbid factors are appreciated and precisely defined our power of managing them is considerably increased. Secondly, the mere carrying out of the dream analyses is a therapeutic measure of very great value. To understand this curious circumstance one has to remember that the cause of a neurosis does not reside in the material that is repressed so much as in the fact that it *is* repressed. The conflict between the repressed wish and the opposing resistance of the censorship is the essential matter, and the symptoms constitute a compromise between these two forces; from another point of view it may be said that they are symbolic expressions of the repressed wishes. If, now, the resistance of the censorship can be sufficiently overcome (as has to be done in a dream analysis) to permit the fusion of the two groups of conscious and unconscious processes that previously were kept apart, so that the patient realises the thoughts and feelings that he had previously kept from himself, then a symbolic compromise-formation (symptoms) becomes superfluous and indeed impossible. This principle is the essence of the psycho-analytic method of treatment. All those who carry out this treatment are in fact agreed that the most valuable part of it lies in dream analysis. One can often treat a case of neurosis mainly by dream analysis, attaining a complete cure thereby.

After having dwelt on the resemblances between dreams and neurotic symptoms it becomes desirable to point out some of the differences between them. The most obvious of these is of course the fact that dreams belong to normal phenomena, neuroses to abnormal. On this matter, however, there is a great deal to say. In the first place, certain dreams are decidedly pathological in nature. For instance, nightmares[1] and other severe anxiety-dreams occur only in subjects who show other evidences of an anxiety-neurosis (commonly included under the heading of neurasthenia), and there

---

[1] See Ernest Jones, 'On the Nightmare,' *Amer. Journ. of Insanity*, January, 1910. (Published in book form, 1931.)

is reason to believe that increased knowledge of dreams will show that certain types are indicative of definite forms of neurosis or insanity. Then, again, some neurotic symptoms—*e.g.*, the hysterical dream-states previously referred to—are hardly to be distinguished from dreams in either their nature or their appearance, and others, as was mentioned above, actually date from dreams. Most significant, however, is the circumstance that both dreams and neurotic symptoms arise from the identical mental material, and by means of identical psychological processes. The repressed wishes that the neurotic finds necessary to express in external symptoms is expressed by the healthy person in dreams. The two are merely different ways of obtaining an imaginary gratification of the same buried wishes. One may in fact describe dreams as the neuroses of the healthy, just as a neurosis is a dream of the invalid. Further, the healthy person is, strictly speaking, never normal. Freud[1] has shown that the buried desires in question come to expression in health in a variety of manifestations, absent-minded acts, forgettings, slips of the tongue or pen, and so on, the psychological mechanisms and significance of which are exactly similar to those of neurotic symptoms. We thus see that in many respects consideration of dreams furnishes a very uncertain criterion to separate health from disease.

An almost equally obvious distinction is that dreams belong to sleep, and neurotic symptoms to waking. Here also we are on unsure ground. Many neurotic symptoms—*e.g.*, night terrors, noctambulic wanderings, nocturnal paralyses, certain kinds of nocturnal, epileptiform fits—definitely belong to the region of sleep, and others, such as various automatic and twilight conditions, occur in mental states that are hard psychologically to distinguish from sleep. On the other hand, there is a most intimate connection, both in essence and appearance, between night-dreams and day-dreams or reveries. Some of the most typical dreams, particularly night-mare, occur by day (day-mare) as well as by night, and in all stages between deep sleep and full waking; often the subject is quite unable to tell whether he was awake or asleep at the time or in an intermediate state half-way between the two.

An interesting feature of dreams is their pronouncedly visual character. Most dreams, though by no means all, shew this to a high degree; in a dream we see things before us as on a stage. This feature is exceptional in the neuroses, though it finds its counterpart

[1] Freud, ' Zur Psychopathologie des Alltagslebens,' 7° Aufl., 1920.

in hysterical hallucinations; in insanity hallucinations are of course common enough, and indeed, even in health they are not exceedingly rare. In analysing the psychogenesis of hallucinations Freud found that it proceeds by the same symbolising mechanisms, and that the content of them is just the same, as in dreams; indeed the relationship between insane symptoms in general and dreams is so close that one can with quite fair accuracy define an insanity as a dream from which the patient has not awakened. Freud's explanation of the sensorial nature of hallucinations is the same as his explanation of the ' regression ' that is the cause of the visual feature of dreams.

Conscious mental processes play a greater part in the subsequent remodelling of dreams than in that of neurotic symptoms. This is a statement, however, that requires much modification. In some dreams the ' secondary elaboration ' plays no part at all, whereas in some forms of neurosis, particularly the obsessional neurosis, it plays an extraordinarily important part.

Consideration of the apparent differences between dreams and neurotic symptoms, therefore, leads us to the same conclusion as consideration of their resemblances to each other did—namely, that the relationships between the two are far-reaching in extent and in significance. The truth of Freud's conclusions as to the nature and mechanisms of unconscious processes is strongly confirmed by their validity being demonstrated in two regions of mental functioning apparently so disparate as dreams and neuroses. He has produced evidence to shew that the same principles hold good in even more distant fields—namely, in the origin of many forms of criminality, in the formation of myths, fairy-tales, folk-beliefs, and superstitions, and in the creation of literary and artistic productions. In all these the driving force comes from the unconscious, all are essentially methods of an active phantasy for stilling ungratified desires; the psychological mechanisms changing, disguising, and distorting the primitive childhood tendencies are the same, and with each it is probable that the sexual instinct is of fundamental importance. With right could one of our greatest psychologists say:[1]

> ' Lovers and madmen have such seething brains,
> Such shaping fantasies, that apprehend
> More than cool reason ever comprehends.
> The lunatic, the lover, and the poet,
> Are of imagination all compact.'

---

[1] ' A Midsummer Night's Dream,' Act V., Scene 1.

CHAPTER XII

THE NATURE OF AUTO-SUGGESTION [1]

From time to time in the course of the past fifty years or more a fresh wave of interest has been aroused in the subject of auto-suggestion. These waves fall into four or five fairly well-marked periods, but it is not proposed to give any historical description of them here. On reviewing the literature produced by these different periods one does not, I am afraid, get the impression that the last half-century has seen any serious addition to our knowledge of the subject, which remains much as it was in the days of Baragnon, [2] seventy years ago, who discussed it under the name of *auto-magnétisation*.

That being so, it would be tempting to seek elsewhere than in scientific curiosity for the source of the interest that periodically continues to be taken in the subject, and one might in this connection throw out the following suggestions. Assuming that there really is a phenomenon of auto-suggestion, and that its therapeutic value can compare with that of the usual suggestion treatment, then it is clear that the use of it presents two features that are bound to make a wide appeal. In the first place, the idea caters to the universal desire for ' free will ' and flatters the narcissistic sense of omnipotence by according with its favourite conception of the ego as a self-sufficing and self-acting agent, independent of the outer world and able to gratify all its wishes by the incantation of magic verbal formulæ. [3] In the second place, it specifically delivers the patient from the most dreaded form of outer dependence—namely, the sexual transference which psycho-analysis has shown to underlie what must for the sake of convenience be termed hetero-suggestion. [4]

[1] Read before the Medical Section of the British Psychological Society, March 22, 1923. Published in the *International Journal of Psycho-Analysis*, vol. iv.
[2] Baragnon: Étude du magnétisme animal,' 1853, p. 198 *et seq.*
[3] On the narcissistic importance of words see Ferenczi, ' Contributions to Psycho-Analysis,' 1916, p. 194 *et seq.*
[4] I cannot refrain from remarking here on the very imperfect acquaintance with psycho-analytic writings displayed by McDougall in his statement that this theory of transference is ' based *merely on the fact* that some subjects show signs of erotic excitement when in hypnosis, and on the Freudian prejudice,' etc. 'A Note on Suggestion,' *Journal of Neurology and Psycho-pathology*, vol. i, p. 4.

The motives just indicated probably apply to the physician as well as to the patient, for in treating numbers of patients *en masse* by ' auto-suggestion ' he can gratify the hypnotist's sense of power without needing to become aware of the accompanying personal (and sexual) dependence of the patients. The medical dread of this transference relationship is well known, and I surmise that we may also attribute to it the fact that so many hypnotists have, during the past forty years, insisted on their preference of ' suggestion in the waking state ' to hypnotism proper; one need only instance the names of Bernheim, Bramwell, Forel, Van Renterghem, and Vogt.

Leaving aside these questions of popular fashion and motive, we may turn to consideration of some of the still unsolved problems relating to auto-suggestion. In proposing discussion of these problems I am further moved by the consideration that so far they have received no attention from the standpoint of psycho-analysis.

The first problem of all is, of course, whether there is such a thing at all as auto-suggestion—*i.e.*, whether there is an endopsychic process shewing the characteristics that distinguish what we ordinarily call suggestion. When I raised this question in opening the discussion on auto-suggestion at a recent meeting of this Society my remark was evidently taken in jest, but I noted that both the reader of the paper (Dr. William Brown) and all the other speakers confined what they had to say to the subject of hetero-suggestion, so that my question cannot be regarded as unjustified; incidentally, McDougall has expressed a similar scepticism.[1]

It is impossible to proceed, therefore, without first coming to some understanding about what are the essential characteristics of suggestion in general. Here, unfortunately, there is a lack of agreement in some important particulars,[2] and it is easy to see that the view adopted by a given author in these respects determines his attitude towards the problem of auto-suggestion. The difference of opinion mainly exists over which should be regarded as the most important and characteristic of the processes comprising suggestion. It is generally agreed that these can be grouped under three headings. In the first place there is the emotional *rapport* existing between the subject and the operator, the state termed by Durand (de Gros)[3]

[1] McDougall, *op. cit.*, p. 9.
[2] See Bernard Hart, ' The Methods of Psychotherapy,' *Proc. Roy. Soc. Med.* (*Psych. Sect.*), vol. xiii.
[3] Philips (a *nom de guerre*), ' Cours théorique et pratique de Braidisme,' 1860, p. 29.

hypotaxia and by myself[1] affective suggestion. This is indubitably the stage that precedes any other process, and on its existence the later processes depend. Secondly, there is the acceptance of the idea suggested, the process termed by Durand[2] ideoplasty and by myself[3] verbal suggestion. Thirdly, there is the ultimate effect realised by this idea after it has been incorporated into the personality.

I will now quote four of the most notable definitions that have been given of suggestion, and it will be seen that they fall into two groups, according as the main importance is attached to the second or third of these processes respectively. Bernheim[4] gave the broad definition of suggestion as ' l'acte par lequel une idée est introduite dans le cerveau et acceptée par lui.' McDougall,[5] with evidently the same point of view, has rendered this more precise in the statement that ' Suggestion is a process of communication resulting in the acceptance with conviction of the communicated proposition *independently of the subject's appreciation* of any logically adequate grounds for its acceptance.' In contrast with this attitude stands Janet's[6] conception of suggestion as the ' développements complets et automatiques d'une idée qui se font en dehors de la volonté et de la perception personelle du sujet.' Similarly Th. Lipps[7] regards suggestion as ' die Hervorrufung einer psychischen Wirkung, die normaler Weise nicht aus der Weckung einer Vorstellung sich ergibt, durch Weckung dieser Vorstellung ' (' the evocation, by arousing an idea, of a psychical effect which normally would not result from the arousing of such an idea '), and he further[8] insists that ' nicht die Weckung der Vorstellungen, sondern diese weitergehende psychische Wirkung ist das Charakteristische der Suggestion. Diese psychische Wirkung ist das eigentlich Suggerirte ' (' it is not the arousing of the ideas, but this further psychical effect,

---

[1] ' The Action of Suggestion in Psychotherapy,' *Journal of Abnormal Psychology*, 1910, vol. v., p. 219. Reprinted as Chapter XV. of the Fourth Edition.

[2] Philips, *op. cit.*, p. 44.

[3] *Loc. cit.* The only exception to this is with Moll's *Stamme Hypnose*, in which not a word is spoken, and this affords one of the many interesting transitions between hetero- and auto-suggestion.

[4] Bernheim, ' Hypnotisme, Suggestion, Psychothérapie,' 1903 edition, p. 24.

[5] McDougall, *op. cit.*, p. 10.

[6] Janet, ' État mental des Hystériques : Les Accidents mentaux,' 1894, p. 30.

[7] Th. Lipps, ' Suggestion und Hypnose,' *Sitzungsbericht der bayerischen Akademie der Wissenschaft*, 1897 (1898), S. 394. It is a matter for regret that this essay, doubtless because of its relative inaccessibility, is not more widely known, for it contains the most searching discussion of the subject yet provided by any psychologist.

[8] *Idem, op. cit.*, S. 392.

that is the characteristic of suggestion. This psychical effect is what is really " suggested " '). There can be little doubt that the emphasis laid here by Janet and Lipps on the further effects or action (*Wirkung*) of the suggested idea represents a definite advance on the intellectualistic conceptions of Bernheim and McDougall. Even if the latter would maintain that they too have in mind a psychical effect of the idea introduced, it is plain that their definition refers chiefly to one effect only—namely, disturbed judgement—and does not take into sufficient account the other abnormal effects, such as hallucinatory sensations, influence on bodily processes, etc.

Lipps made two further steps in the nearer definition of the psychical action or effect (*Wirkung*) in question. In the first place, he points out[1] that what is remarkable in connection with suggestion is not the actual nature of the effects, which can all be produced by other means, but the *way* in which they are produced. It is the conditions under which the effects follow an idea that are peculiar to suggestion, for these effects would not follow the idea under other conditions. The characteristic of these conditions he sees in a special combination of intact psychical energy with diminished psychical excitability.[2] By the latter phrase he means an inhibition of the counter-ideas which normally would oppose the action of the suggested ones. This inhibition is, of course, related to the contrasting freedom with which ideas are accepted from the operator, and is thus the secondary result of the state of *rapport* mentioned above. He therefore includes these two additional conclusions in his final definition of suggestion, which is:[3] ' Die Hervorrufung einer über das blosse Dasein einer Vorstellung hinausgehenden psychischen Wirkung in einem Individuum, durch Weckung einer Vorstellung seitens einer Person oder eines von dem Individuum verschiedenen Objektes, sofern diese psychische Wirkung durch eine in ausserordentlichem Masse stattfindende Hemmung oder Lähmung der über die nächste reproducirende Wirkung der Suggestion hinausgehenden Vorstellungsbewegung bedingt ist ' [' The evocation in an individual, through an idea being aroused by another person or an object distinct from the individual, of a psychical effect that goes beyond the mere existence of this idea,

[1] Th. Lipps, ' Zur Psychologie der Suggestion,' *Zeitschr. f. Hypnotismus*, 1897 Bd. vii., S. 95.

[2] *Idem*, ' Suggestion und Hypnose,' *op. cit.*, S. 520.

[3] *Idem*, ' Zur Psychologie der Suggestion,' *op. cit.*, S. 117.

provided always that this psychical effect is conditioned by an extraordinary inhibition or paralysis of the ideational movement which passes beyond the proximate reproductive effect of the suggestion ']. He explicitly included auto-suggestion in this definition in a way which will presently be noted.

The actual phenomenology of the effects of suggestion are too well known to need recounting here. Concerning their nature Lipps has shown in detail that all of them, even the eliciting of hallucinatory sensations, represent the normal logical consequences of the suggested ideas, differing only from the usual consequences of the same idea in that, through the inhibition of the criticising ideas customarily operative, they are allowed to proceed to their logical termination without hindrance. We may therefore conclude that the characteristic of suggestion lies in the free development of the effects of communicated ideas, the forces usually hindering this development being neutralised by the presence of the *rapport*, or concentration on the idea of the operator. It is generally agreed that this *rapport* consists of an emotional bond; as is well known, psychoanalysts consider the bond to be sexual in nature and due to the re-animation of an infantile attachment to a parent.

Our formulation of the three processes thus runs in order: *rapport*; inhibition of all mental processes except those suggested; free development of the latter. We are now able to reduce the difference of opinion noted above to differences in the view held of the way in which the *rapport* operates; all are agreed that it is in this that the operative force resides. From this point of view the two schools of thought may be contrasted somewhat as follows: According to one, the main thing is the remarkable influence exerted by the operator or hypnotist; granted this and the rest follows, the ideas developing to their logical conclusion by the sheer force imparted to them. According to the other school, the main thing is the subject's peculiar attitude towards the operator; it is this which neutralises any critical ideas inimical to his. Psycho-analysts may certainly be classed as belonging to the latter school. Some thirteen years ago, for instance, I wrote:[1] 'We can no longer regard the subject as a helpless automaton in the hands of a strong-willed operator; it is nearer the truth to regard the operator as allowing himself to play a part, and by no means an indispensable one, in a drama constructed and acted in the depths of the subject's mind.'

[1] *Op. cit.*, p. 220.

From what has been said it is not astonishing that the two views just described lead to contrasting attitudes towards the subject of auto-suggestion. Those who expound the former of the two views tend to decry the importance of auto-suggestion or else to deny its existence altogether, to depreciate its practical value, and to attribute most of its phenomena, whether therapeutic or pathogenic, to some more or less disguised form of hetero-suggestion. In this group of authors may be mentioned Baragnon,[1] Camus and Pagniez,[2] McDougall,[3] and Grasset;[4] the last named of these goes so far as to hint that auto-suggestion is in most cases the result of previous hypnotism. Janet[5] would appear to take up an intermediate position; he ascribes at least a great many pathological processes to auto-suggestion, apart from the intervention of an idea from without. Forel[6] also holds that ' Jede Suggestion wird durch Autosuggestion des Hypnotisierten ergäntz und modifiziert ' [' every suggestion is added to and modified by auto-suggestion on the part of the hypnotised person ']. At the other extreme there is Baudouin,[7] the leading exponent of auto-suggestion, who holds the diametrically opposite view that ' hetero-suggestion, even during induced sleep (*i.e.*, hypnosis), is still an auto-suggestion.' Similarly Levy-Suhl[8] maintains: ' Jede Suggestionswirkung beruht letzthin in einer Auto-suggestion ' [' every effect of suggestion rests ultimately on an auto-suggestion '].

We thus return to the problem of what phenomena, if any, are to be classed as belonging to auto-suggestion. The matter is certainly not to be settled by simply asking whether the operative ideas have originated from without or from within. In the first place, this is often very hard to determine, and in a certain sense it might even be maintained that all ideas take their ultimate source from the outer world. Secondly, the question does not touch the essential part of the problem, for clinical psychology no longer regards ideas as active agents in themselves; any activity they may exhibit is due only to their being representatives of some impulse or other. We must

---

[1] Baragnon, *loc. cit.*
[2] Camus and Pagniez, ' Isolement et Psychothérapie, 1904, p. 57.
[3] McDougall, *loc. cit.*
[4] Grasset, ' L'hypnotisme et la suggestion,' 1904, p. 131.
[5] Janet, *op. cit.*, p. 71.
[6] Forel, ' Der Hypnotismus,' 11 Auflage, S. 122.
[7] Baudouin, ' Suggestion and Auto-Suggestion,' Eng. Trans., 1920, p. 204.
[8] Levy-Suhl, ' Die hypnotische Heilweise und ihre Technik,' 1922, S. 33.

therefore concentrate our attention on the nature of the dynamic factors at work, and in this way seek to determine whether two classes of them can be detected, corresponding with hetero-suggestion and auto-suggestion respectively. Several writers—e.g., Baudouin[1]—insist that the ideas produce their effect only through acting outside the field of consciousness, but being unfamiliar with what goes on in this unconscious layer of the mind they were unable to throw any light on the nature of the forces operative in the transformation of the ' idea ' into its effect—i.e., the ' realisation ' of the idea. Lipps[2] holds that in auto-suggestion, just as in hetero-suggestion, there is a general inhibition of mental excitability, particularly of the ideas antagonistic to the ones being ' suggested.' In hetero-suggestion this is brought about through a high degree of psychical investment of the idea of the operator; in psycho-analytical terminology, a hyper-cathexis of the idea of the operator is correlated with a hypo-cathexis of all ideas in conflict with his. Now, is there a group of phenomena, to be called auto-suggestion, in which there is a corresponding hyper-cathexis of a given idea to account for the general hypo-cathexis that Lipps maintains to be present, and, if so, what is known of the nature of this idea ? The only suggestion he makes in this connection[3] is that the part of the ego communicating the idea is to be regarded as a foreign object to the part that receives it, but he throws no further light on this remarkable splitting of the personality. Baudouin[4] repeatedly insists also on the essential importance of relaxation in the practice of auto-suggestion, and it is evident that this relaxation is identical with the inhibition of mental excitability described by Lipps. Baudouin's[5] conception of the concentration of attention necessary in addition to the general relaxation—the two features which in his opinion comprise the essentials of the practice of auto-suggestion—corresponds further with what we have called hyper-cathexis of a particular idea, but he never mentions any idea to which this applies except the idea which is being ' suggested.'

It might be supposed that psycho-analysis, adhering as it does to the second of the two schools described above, the school that lays stress on the part played in the depths of the subject's mind, would at once lend countenance to auto-suggestion as a phenomenon which

[1] Baudouin, op. cit., p. 26.
[2] Lipps, op. cit., S. 117.
[3] Idem, op. cit., S. 96.
[4] Baudouin, op. cit., pp. 131, 132, etc.
[5] Idem, op. cit., pp. 27, 141, etc.

obviously supports the view in question. On the other hand, it would appear to contradict the psycho-analytical view concerning the significance of the idea of the operator, at all events unless it can be shown that in auto-suggestion there is a hyper-cathexis of another idea which is equivalent to that of the operator.

It is time to turn from this general discussion of the problem and consider the actual data bearing on it. It must be said, however, that it is by no means easy to ascertain these. To begin with, McDougall's[1] criticism that in so many of the examples cited of auto-suggestion one cannot exclude the operation of hetero-suggestion is evidently justified; it obviously applies to a great part of Coué's performances. Indeed, this factor has also to be taken into account when a person practises ' auto-suggestion ' after reading a book of instructions, for the idea of the authority behind this book must often play a considerable part. McDougall further objects to the wide application of the term ' auto-suggestion ' to such phenomena as the ready acceptance of propositions which are congruent with any strong conative tendencies; that the wish is father to the thought is comprehensible without invoking any such process as ' auto-suggestion.' Lipps[2] makes a similar protest, one which would seem to apply to a large number of the examples quoted by the various writers on the subject, Baudouin,[3] Bonnet,[4] Parkyn,[5] etc.

If now we attempt to exclude these two groups, a task not easy to carry out, what phenomena have we left that may serve our purpose? They would seem to reduce themselves to two. In the first place there are the descriptions of experiments carried out on themselves by various medical investigators. We have many such accounts, from Cardan,[6] in the sixteenth century, who is said to have cured himself of gout by this means, to Liébault's[7] self-cure of migraine. The best accounts are perhaps those given by Baudouin,[8] Birot,[9] Bléch,[10] Lagrave,[11] and Lévy[12] On reading through these

---

[1] McDougall, *op. cit.*, p. 9.

[2] Lipps, ' Suggestion und Hypnose,' *op. cit.*, S. 392.

[3] Baudouin, *op. cit.*   [4] Bonnet, ' Précis d'auto-suggestion volontaire,' 1911.

[5] Parkyn, ' Auto-Suggestion,' 1916.   [6] Cardan, ' De Subtilitate,' 1550, lib. xxi.

[7] Liébault, ' Du sommeil provoqué,' 1866.   [8] Baudouin, *op. cit.*

[9] Birot, *Annales du Magnetisme*, 1815, t. ii., p. 253.

[10] Bléch, ' L'auto-suggestion comme moyen thérapeutique physique et moral,' *Rev. de l'hypnotisme*, Fév., 1897.

[11] Lagrave, ' Quelques expériences d'auto-hypnotisme et d'auto-suggestion,' 1890.

[12] P. E. Lévy, ' L'education rationelle de la volonté,' 1898.

and other accounts one may learn something about the effects that are to be produced by means of ' auto-suggestion,' but very little indeed on the point at present under consideration. Practically no idea is mentioned on which the mind is concentrated, except the particular ones to be ' suggested.' This evidently does not provide us with the motive force for which we are seeking, so one would infer that the hyper-cathexis in question must take place entirely in the unconscious. The inference should not be astonishing, for it will be remembered that the same is to a great extent true of hetero-suggestion and hypnotism.

The second set of phenomena are those known under the name of auto-hypnosis. They should be more promising, for more reasons than one. I agree with Freud's[1] view—in contradistinction to Bernheim's—that the state of suggestibility is simply a *forme fruste* of hypnosis. In any case there would seem to be better prospect of elucidating the psychology of either suggestion or auto-suggestion by studying the state in which the manifestations are magnified. It was for a similar reason that in my previous study of suggestion[2] I largely confined myself to the problem of hypnotism.

Phenomena that come into consideration from the point of view of ' auto-hypnosis ' are met with in four circumstances: (1) Medium-istic trances; (2) hysterical dream states; (3) religious and mystic ecstasies; (4) a miscellaneous group in which states of exaltation are indulged in more or less as a habit, either in connection with nar-cotics or not.

The first of these has to be excluded on the ground that in the accounts given of them attention is devoted almost entirely to the messages purported to be delivered in this way, the mental state itself of the subject being a matter of only subordinate interest. The second state has been studied analytically by Freud[3] and Abra-ham,[4] and the latter author specifically draws a comparison between them and hypnosis. The conclusions arrived at by these studies which interest us most here are that the dream states in question represent substitutive gratifications of day-dreams which formerly ended in masturbation. The earlier phases of the state are pleasur-

[1] Freud, ' Group Psychology and the Analysis of the Ego,' Eng. Trans., 1922, p. 100.
[2] *Op. cit.*
[3] Freud, 'Allgemeines über den hysterischen Anfall,' reprinted in his ' Sammlung kleiner Schriften,' Zweite Folge, 1909.
[4] Abraham, ' Ueber hysterische Traumzustände ,' *Jahrbuch der Pscyho-analyse,* 1910 Bd. ii., S. 1.

able, but the culmination, which replaces the sexual act once indulged
in, is usually accompanied by considerable degrees of anxiety. The
intense concentration of attention (which Abraham terms *Besetzung*
—*i.e.*, cathexis) or self-absorption, which—just as in ' auto-
suggestion '—is the counterpart of the withdrawal from the outer
world, is exclusively concerned with the more or less conscious
sexual phantasy. It is known that phantasies preceding or accompanying masturbation are predominantly incestuous in origin, hence
the feeling of guilt attaching to them, so that we are led to the same
conclusion here as is reached from the study of the ordinary hypnotic
rapport—namely, that the essential feature of such states is the
revival of the infantile repressed idea of the parent. Indeed,
Abraham[1] points out that these hysterical states may either occur
spontaneously or be induced through the presence of some person
by whom the subject feels himself to be ' hypnotised.' Two features,
therefore, stand out here—the importance of auto-erotism and of
incestuous attachment to the father. We also note once again the
great difficulty of distinguishing between hetero- and auto-suggestion, and this must incline us to the conclusion that either there is
only one process concerned in all the phenomena grouped under
these two names, or else, if there are two, they must be extremely
closely related.

In the third set also, the religious ecstasies, it is difficult to exclude
the possibility of an important part being played by the idea of an
external person—namely, God. This is of course more evident in
the trances of Christian saints than in those of other mystics, but it
is worthy of note that even in the Indian form of mysticism the
word ' yoga ' is defined as ' the experimental union of the individual
with the divine.'[2] This fact need not lead us immediately to exclude
the group in question from the category of ' auto-hypnosis,' but it
is one to be borne well in mind when discussing the possible
relation of hetero- to auto-suggestion. I do not propose here to
enter on a discussion of religious ecstasy, especially as the material
exists in a readily accessible form.[3] I need only remind you of two
of its most characteristic features. The first is that a sexual undercurrent is plainly in evidence in all the accounts given by saints and

---

[1] *Idem, op. cit.*, S. 30.

[2] William James, ' The Varieties of Religious Experience,' 1902, p. 400.

[3] Görres, ' Christliche Mystik,' 4 Bde., 1836-1842 ; Ribet, ' Mystique Divine,'
1890.

mystics themselves, and that, as Pfister[1] has shown in his interesting study of Von Zinzendorf, the sublimations often enough undergo regression into the crudest sexuality. The second feature is the extraordinarily intense feeling of union that characterises the most exalted states. I will quote only one illustration of this, from Saint Teresa,[2] the greatest expert in this field of experience: ' In the orison of union, the soul is fully awake as regards God, but wholly asleep as regards things of this world and in respect of herself. . . . She is utterly dead to the things of the world and lives solely in God. . . . I do not even know whether in this state she has enough life to breathe. It seems to me she has not: or at least that if she does breathe she is unaware of it. . . . Thus does God, when He raises *a* soul to union with Himself, suspend the natural action of all her faculties. She neither sees, hears, nor understands, so long as she is united with God. . . . God establishes Himself in the interior of this soul in such a way that when she returns to herself it is wholly impossible for her to doubt that she has been in God and God in her.' It would seem that in such orisons object-love tends to revert to the more primitive stage of identification, a point which we shall see to be of some importance. The same is apparently true for the milder states to which Catholics refer under the name of ' recollection.'

An even closer resemblance to ' auto-hypnosis ' is presented in the well-known yoga system of the East.[3] The two preliminary states of *prâtyâhâra* and *dhâranâ* correspond with the relaxation and concentration respectively which are the essentials in the practice of auto-suggestion. The final state, called by the Vedantists *samâdhi* and by the Buddhists *dhyâna*, has been thus described:[4] ' Then we know ourselves for what we truly are, free, immortal, omnipotent, loosed from the finite, and identical with the Atman or Universal Soul.' We see here a regression to the most primitive and uncritical form of narcissism. Some years ago I had the good fortune to treat a patient who had graduated highly in the yoga hierarchy. In the psycho-analysis of his case, which I published at length,[5] two features were specially prominent in this connection, and these were the same two as we noted above in respect of the hysterical dream

[1] Pfister, ' Die Frömmigkeit des Grafen Ludwig von Zinzendorf,' 1910.
[2] ' Œuvres de St. Teresa,' Bouix édition, t. iii., pp. 421-423.
[3] On the resemblances see Kellner, ' Yoga: Eine Skizze,' 1896.
[4] Vivekananda, ' Raja Yoga,' 1896; cited by James, *op. cit.*, p. 400.
[5] *Jahrbuch der Psychoanalyse*, 1912, Bd. iv., S. 564.

states. The part played by the idea of God-Father in the auto-hypnotic state was unmistakable, and, further, the patient manipulated to an extraordinary extent the various yoga instructions in terms of what Sadger has called secondary auto-erotism.

The task of isolating a pure form of auto-hypnotism, and of distinguishing it from ordinary hypnosis, continues to elude us, but we will try our luck once more with the fourth set of phenomena indicated above. In the cases of this class collected by William James,[1] he attaches considerable importance to mystical states induced by various narcotic drugs, particularly alcohol, nitrous oxide, and chloroform. This is worthy of note, for we now know the close dependence of these states on repressed homosexuality, and, further, the nearness of the latter to narcissism. Of the instances he quotes of sporadic and apparently spontaneous trance states, the most perfect account is that given by John Addington Symonds, and those familiar with the writings of this author will remember what a part is played in them by repressed homosexuality. Symonds' own description of the state contains the following passages: ' In proportion as these conditions of ordinary consciousness (*i.e.*, space, time, sensation, etc.) were subtracted, the sense of an underlying or essential consciousness acquired intensity. At least nothing remained but a pure, absolute, abstract Self. The universe became without form and void of content. But Self persisted, formidable in its vivid keenness, feeling the most poignant doubts about reality.' It was typical of his states of trance that they ended in an anxiety attack, just as the dream states described by Abraham. In them we get hardly any hint of the idea of an outside being; the whole of consciousness is confined to the idea of self. On the other hand, the curious personal experiences described by the Canadian alienist, Bucke,[2] have clearly a reference to the outer world. In them he came to realise that the universe is ' a living Presence,' and became conscious in himself of eternal life. The account he gives of his union with what he terms the cosmic consciousness is probably only an attenuated form of what a more strictly religious person would have felt to be union with God.

What inferences may now be drawn from the consideration of the data at our disposal ? The first conclusion I think we are justified in coming to is that it is extraordinarily difficult to draw any sharp

[1] James, *op. cit.*, p. 387 *et seq.*
[2] Bucke, ' Cosmic Consciousness: A Study in the Evolution of the Human Mind,' 1897.

line between hetero- and auto-suggestion. The relationship is so very intimate as to make it probable that the agents operating in the two cases are merely variants, and not distinct forces. This conclusion has more far-reaching consequences than might appear at first sight, so I will briefly review the evidence for it. It is both clinical and psychological. Clinically every physician who endeavours to teach his patients how to use auto-suggestion, as I did myself some twenty years ago, will probably be able to confirm my experience of finding how very hard it is to estimate the importance of the part played by the idea of the physician in the patient's mind, and to distinguish between this and the other factors at work. The gradation between hetero- and auto-suggestion in such situations seems to be quite imperceptible. The same is true of the hypnoid states of hysteria, which may occur either in the presence of another person by whom the subject feels himself to be influenced, or else quite spontaneously. Even in the cases of religious trances we have noted the interrelation between intense self-absorption on the one hand and concentration on the idea of an external person on the other. Then, again, the actual manifestations of the two conditions are quite identical. They may be said to include all the effects that mental functioning can potentially bring about in both the mental and the physical fields, from the most complete delusional and hallucinatory formations in the former, to the gravest interferences with all kinds of bodily functions in the latter, and in rare cases even with life itself. Psychologically the two conditions are quite identical but for one single point. In both there is a hyper-cathexis of one train of thought with hypo-cathexis of most others. The state of relaxation, or—to use Lipp's more accurate terminology—of physical inhibition, is doubtless the reason why the judgement of external reality can be so profoundly affected, and with this is also lost the criticism of endopsychic ideation, including repression. It will be noted that these two latter functions are two out of the six with which Freud credits that part of the ego which he terms the ego-ideal. In hetero- and auto-suggestion there is equally the consciousness of surrender of the sense of will and feeling of effort. The one point in which the two conditions differ is in respect of the idea on which concentration has taken place. With hetero-suggestion we know that this is the idea of the Father *imago*,[1] which has been aroused through

---

[1] For the sake of simplicity, and also because it is the more important in this connection, the idea of the Father alone is referred to instead of that of both parents.

contact with a suitable substitute. With auto-suggestion, all the evidence points to the idea being that of the actual Self.

I next propose to sketch a theory that shall take into account the preceding considerations. If I am right in concluding that the unconscious hyper-cathexis is of the idea of the Father in hetero-suggestion, and of the Self in auto-suggestion, then we must search for some point of intimate contact between these two ideas. A clue in this direction is afforded by Freud's[1] formula that the hypnotist replaces the ego-ideal. For if we enquire into the matter and origin of the ego-ideal, we discover that it is compounded of two constituents, derived from the Father and the Self respectively; so that here we have a nodal point connecting the two ideas.

It will be remembered that the original (primal) narcissism of the infant becomes in the course of development distributed in four directions, the actual proportion in each of these varying enormously with different individuals. *One* portion remains in an unaltered state attached to the real ego; this is probably the one concerned in the genesis of hypochondria. A *second* portion is deflected from any direct sexual goal and becomes attached to the idea of the parent, leading to adoration, devotion, and general over-estimation. It is important to bear in mind that to begin with this process is much more a matter of narcissistic identification than of any form of object-love. A *third* is transferred on to an ideal ego, and is one of the constituents of the ' ego-ideal.' The *fourth* is gradually transformed into object-love. Now the second and third of these commonly fuse during the latency period of childhood or even earlier. The form assumed by the resulting ego-ideal is largely derived from the ideas and mental attitudes of the father, the bond being affected through the second portion of narcissistic libido mentioned above—that attached to what may be called the father-ideal. On the other hand, the energy that gives the ego-ideal its significance is wholly derived ultimately from narcissistic libido. There are three routes for this: (1) directly from the original narcissism of the primary ego (third portion mentioned above); (2) via the attachment to the father-ideal (second portion); (3) via the regression of narcissistic identification with the father that often takes place after a disappointment at the lack of gratification of object-love (fourth portion).

When the hypnotist, as Freud says, takes the place of the ego-ideal,

[1] Freud, ' Group Psychology,' *op. cit.*, p. 77.

what happens is presumably this: the thought of him becomes identified in the unconscious with that of the father, and in this way the constituents of the ego-ideal which were built up in connection with the idea of the father—its form and two out of the three narcissistic components enumerated above—are re-animated. Perhaps, incidentally, this is the reason why it is so difficult for the hypnotist to give effective suggestions that obviously conflict with the father-ideal, such as criminal and immoral suggestions.

Leaving for a moment this question of the mechanism whereby narcissism becomes re-animated, a matter to which we shall presently return, I wish to say a little about the effects of the process. Many clinicians are inclined to divide the effects of ' auto-suggestion ' into two groups, which might be called pathogenic and therapeutic respectively. To take the pathogenic ones first: the notion is that ' auto-suggestion ' may create various neurotic symptoms by allowing certain ' morbid ' ideas to realise their full effects unchecked by others which normally would counteract them. Perhaps as good an example as any is the case of the oft-quoted medical student who imagined he was acquiring every disease except housemaid's knee. I would recommend that we should not use the term ' auto-suggestion ' for this class of phenomenon, for the following reasons. The essence of such symptom-formation consists in a conflict between repressed libidinal wishes and the repressing force exerted from the side of the ego, particularly of the ego-ideal. From one point of view the symptoms might roughly be called a punishment inflicted on the personality by the ego for the striving towards gratification on the part of the repressed forbidden wishes. The fears of our medical student, for instance, represent the threat of castration (disease) as a punishment for repressed Œdipus wishes (incest with the mother and castration of the father). The morbid ideas that were allowed to develop during the reading of his textbooks merely afforded suitable material that could be used by his ego for this purpose. So that to refer to the whole process as one of ' auto-suggestion ' is to confine attention to one aspect of the process, and not to the most important aspect. The resultant symptom is only *in part* ego-syntonic—*i.e.*, in harmony with the ego—the repressed wishes being not at all so, while the term ' auto-suggestion ' should surely be applied only to mental processes that are wholly ego-syntonic. Further, one misses here the note of omnipotence so characteristic of the typical forms of ' auto-suggestion.'

What we have called the therapeutic effects of ' auto-suggestion,' on the other hand, differ in both these respects. They are marked to begin with by a belief, more or less profound, in the omnipotence of thought. The catch formula ' Every day in every way I grow better and better ' means, if it means anything, ' I have only to *wish* to become stronger, handsomer, cleverer, self-confident, and free from any suffering, and it will be so; my wishes are all-powerful and brook no obstacle.' Then, in contrast with ' pathogenic auto-suggestion,' the therapeutic tendencies in question are throughout ego-syntonic.

Successful auto-suggestion presupposes harmony even between the narcissism of the ego-ideal and that which has remained attached to the real ego. It is the conflict between the ego-ideal on the one hand and the real ego with its associated allo-erotism on the other that is responsible for neurotic states. How fraught the union is with the consequences we know from Freud's[1] studies of mania. The two states in which man's sense of power over both himself and his environment, and often his actual power, is at its maximum are, first, acute mania, and, secondly, the exaltation that follows on sudden conversion to a significant idea, most often a religious one. In both these cases, however, there has previously been a specially deep cleavage between the actual ego and the ego-ideal, so that the reconciliation between the two results in a tremendous accession of energy through the release of the primary narcissism from the tyranny of the ego-ideal. Yogi are reputed to display something of the same sense of power and self-content, which in their case is due to a union brought about by the more gradual process of auto-suggestion.

On the basis of the foregoing considerations I would formulate the following theory: SUGGESTION IS ESSENTIALLY A LIBIDINAL PROCESS: THROUGH THE UNIFICATION OF THE VARIOUS FORMS AND DERIVATIVES OF NARCISSISM THE CRITICISING FACULTY OF THE EGO-IDEAL IS SUSPENDED, SO THAT EGO-SYNTONIC IDEAS ARE ABLE TO FOLLOW UNCHECKED THE PLEASURE-PAIN PRINCIPLE IN ACCORDANCE WITH THE PRIMITIVE BELIEF IN THE OMNIPOTENCE OF THOUGHT. *Such ideas may either develop to their logical goal (beliefs, judgements, etc.) or regress to their sensorial elements (hallucinatory gratification). The essential part of the unification in question is that between the real ego and the ego-ideal. The condition under which it takes place is that the repressed*

Freud, ' Group Psychology,' *op. cit.*, pp. 107, 108.

allo-erotic impulses are to be renounced. This is made possible by a regression of their libido in the direction of auto-erotism, which results in a further reinforcement of the narcissism. If the primary narcissism has been released and re-animated directly, by concentration upon the idea of self, the process may be termed auto-suggestion; if it has been preceded by a stage in which the ego-ideal is resolved into the earlier father-ideal, the process may be termed hetero-suggestion.

If this view proves to be correct, then the old question of whether most hetero-suggestion is really auto-suggestion or whether most auto-suggestion is really hetero-suggestion must be regarded in another perspective. It is, in the first place, a much less important problem than has often been thought, for that the essential agent in both is narcissism is a more fundamental consideration than the question of the particular way in which this has been mobilised in a given case. It is highly probable that the process of re-animating narcissism may proceed to varying depths in different psychological conditions; that suggestibility varies greatly in different persons is of course well known. The fact that primary narcissism is more fundamental than the father-ideal itself, and our clinical experience that the chief part even in hetero-suggestion is played by agents within the subject's mind, are considerations which incline one not to contradict Baudouin's opinion that more weight must be attached to auto-suggestion than to hetero-suggestion, though one should add the modification that perhaps the latter process may prove in most cases in practice a necessary stage in the evocation of the former.

Freud[1] thinks that the uncanny and enigmatic qualities that cling to the idea of hypnosis can be accounted for only by assuming that the regression to the infantile conception of the Father re-animates the inherited attitude towards the primal Father of the horde in savage times. The view here expressed could be brought into accord with this by supposing a similar re-animation of the well-known enormous narcissism of primitive man, with his absolute belief in the magical omnipotence of thought.

The theory here propounded perhaps throws some light on two further problems: the relation of hypnosis to sleep and to 'will-power' respectively. That the hypnotic state is psychologically exceedingly akin to sleep is well known, and is indicated in the very word itself. The fact has given rise to much speculation, but it

---

[1] *Idem, op. cit.*, pp. 95-99.

should become more comprehensible when one recollects that sleep is the most complete expression of narcissism known—*i.e.*, of the state which we here suppose to underlie that of hypnosis.

Without wishing to embark on a discussion of the nature of will, I may briefly state my agreement with Lipp's[1] view that the sense of will, and of striving or effort altogether, really emanates from a consciousness of inhibition, or—put in more modern language—an intuition that in respect of the idea in question the conscious ego is inhibiting other, unconscious, mental processes. At all events it is plain that the will is specially connected with the conscious ego, and particularly the ego-ideal. Most authors lay great stress on the practical importance, in both hetero- and auto-suggestion, of avoiding, so far as possible, any sense of effort, exercise of will-power, or even of forced attention, and this might well be correlated with the view here expressed of the necessity for suspending the activity of the ego-ideal. The exhortations of a patient's relatives that he should ' use his will-power ' or his ' self-control ' succeed only when the strength of the ego-ideal is definitely greater than that of the repressed libidinal wishes, as it is in the normal. It is natural that the relatives should ask for this desideratum, but they overlook the fact that the very existence of neurotic symptoms shews that in all probability the two sides of the conflict are more evenly matched than they hope. It is only rarely that much can be accomplished by simple methods of reinforcing the ego-ideal—*i.e.*, the repressions.

Finally, the theory here advanced leads me to attempt some re-statement of our formulations regarding the mechanism of mental healing in general. The essential problem is the fate of the repressed allo-erotic (usually incestuous) impulses which conflict with the ego-ideal and constitute the important dynamic factor in every neurotic symptom. Only a part of them can be directly sublimated, a solution which the patient has already tried, though, it is true, under unfavourable psychological conditions. Now it would seem that all possible means of dealing with the situation therapeutically reduce themselves ultimately to two, and to two only. Either the libidinal energy of these impulses may be, more or less completely, reconverted into the narcissism from which they proceeded, this being affected by a regression in an auto-erotic direction, or else the assimilative capacity of the ego-ideal may be raised. These two principles are, as will be shown in a moment, mutually contradictory

[1] Lipps, ' Suggestion und Hypnose,' *op. cit.*, S. 428, 472.

and therefore to a large extent incompatible with each other, and this explains why it is fundamentally impossible to combine the two methods of treatment based on them, those of suggestion and psycho-analysis respectively. One may lay down the dictum that if the patient is not treated by psycho-analysis he will treat himself by means of suggestion, or—put more fully—he will see to it that he will get treated by means of suggestion, whatever other views the physician may have on the subject.

When a neurotic patient comes for any kind of treatment, he will soon transfer unconsciously on to the idea of the physician various repressed allo-erotic tendencies—*i.e.*, he will take the physician as a love-object (provided, of course, that the treatment continues long enough). If the treatment is not psycho-analysis, one of two things will happen. The patient may become aware of affection for the physician. Then probably symptoms will improve, libido being withdrawn from them and transferred to the idea of the physician. I suspect, however, that in these cases true educative treatment by suggestion or any allied method is rarely successful. What usually happens is that the improvement is dependent on continued contact with the physician, and even this has to be of a specially satisfactory kind. When the physician's attention is withdrawn, the symptoms tend to reappear. The alternative to this course of events is that the allo-erotism regresses to the stage of narcissistic identification with the physician—that is, the father-ideal. The educative suggestions then made are more likely to have a lasting effect, the reason being that the stage to which the patient's libidinal organisation is reduced approximates closely to that of true narcissism, so that when he leaves the physician he still has himself as a love-object. This is certainly the direction that most neurotics spontaneously take, for it spares them the suffering of symptoms, the distress at having to recognise their repressed allo-erotism, and the pangs of disappointed love. It is the great reason, as I hinted at the outset of my paper, why auto-suggestion is so widely preferred to hetero-suggestion, with all its potentialities of allo-erotism. The practical drawback to auto-suggestion clinically is that it is in so many cases harder to mobilise the narcissism in this way than by means of hetero-suggestion. The drawback to any form of suggestion is that what peace of mind it gives is purchased at the expense of an important part of the personality being impeded in development, with consequent lack of stability; the allo-erotism that should progress to object-love, altruism, and the various sublimations of life regress towards auto-erotism, with all its stultifying potentialities.

In psycho-analysis, on the other hand, the aim of the treatment is to effect some reconciliation—or at least tolerance—between the ego-ideal and the repressed allo-erotism. As in other forms of treatment, the allo-erotic transference tends to regress to the stage in which the analyst is identified with the father component of the ego-ideal—*i.e.*, with the father-ideal, and this tendency has to be carefully watched by the analyst. When the ego ideal begins to raise serious protests against accepting the repressed tendencies that are being brought to light by the analytic procedure, the well-known state of resistance ensues. Now the most securely entrenched form of resistance,[1] one to which there is a tendency in all analyses, is that in which the patient identifies the analyst with his real ego, projects on to him his own repressed mental processes, and then severely criticises him from the standpoint of his ego-ideal. This situation is the most formidable met with in psycho-analytic work, for all object-relationship between analyst and patient may be suspended, and the analyst cannot proceed until this is re-established. As it is characteristically accompanied by such manifestations as arrogant conceit, the analyst often says that a limit has been set to analytic possibilities by the patient's narcissism, overlooking the vital consideration that the narcissism is not a primary one, but has been secondarily resorted to as a defence against repressed allo-erotism. It may be said, therefore, that the success of an analysis depends very largely on the extent to which the analyst can manage to preserve an object-relationship to himself in the patient's mind, for it is just this relationship that has to be brought to consciousness and harmonised with the ego-ideal.

It will thus be seen that the aims of the hypnotist and the analyst are diametrically opposed. The former really seeks to strengthen the patient's narcissism, the latter to divert it into more developed forms of mental activity. The psychological situation (narcissistic identification) most favourable to the one aim is fatal to the other.

I have considered here the contrast between suggestion and analysis in its therapeutic aspects only. It is probable, however, that it is applicable over far wider fields. The contrast between auto-erotism

---

[1] An excellent description of the manifestations of this is given by Abraham, ' Über eine besondere Form des neurotischen Widerstandes gegen die psychoanalytische Methodik,' *Internat. Zeitschr. f. Psychoanalyse*, 1919, Bd. v., S. 173.

and allo-erotism, on which it rests—*i.e.*, between infantilism and adult life—may be correlated with the whole difference in outlook and conduct between the mental attitude of introversion and exclusion of reality, on the one hand, and adjustment to the world of reality on the other: between what may be called the Eastern and the Western methods of dealing with life.

CHAPTER XIII

THE PSYCHOPATHOLOGY OF ANXIETY[1]

THE first task here should be to attempt to clarify the relationships between allied concepts, those of anxiety, fear, dread, fright, panic, apprehensiveness, etc. In psychopathology the term 'morbid anxiety,' or 'anxiety' for short, is widely employed to designate a particular collection of phenomena, one which can be distinguished from those grouped under the name of fear. It was selected for this purpose partly because of its etymological relationship to the more expressive German word 'Angst' and partly because it, better than any other, refers to the state of mind rather than the attitude towards an object, this being the point one wishes to emphasise in the morbid condition in question. It is generally agreed that at least two features serve to make this distinction:

1. *Disproportion between the external stimulus and the response.* In pronounced cases this is very evident, for example in the claustrophobic distress induced by mere presence in a closed room, and indeed acute attacks of anxiety often occur when it is impossible to ascertain any external stimulus of danger whatever. In more doubtful cases opinions may vary on this matter of disproportion. How much distress, for instance, should be allotted as normal for someone exposed to an air raid during the war, or still more for those exposed to the appalling conditions of the actual front, without recourse being had to pathological factors? Generosity is prone in such cases to make considerable allowances for the situation and to pass over responses of anxiety as natural and inevitable which perhaps a more critical mood would scrutinise more strictly. Psycho-analysts, who have to investigate these states in great detail, have come to encouraging conclusions as regards mankind in this respect and take a very favourable view about its capacity to resist the stimulus of external danger without fear reactions being evoked, provided only that the internal functioning of the mind is healthy in a respect that will presently be mentioned. They thus present a

---

[1] Read before a Joint Meeting of the Royal Society of Medicine, Psychiatric Section, and the British Psychological Society, Medical Section, April 9, 1929. Published in the *British Journal of Medical Psychology*, vol. ix.

very high standard of man's bravery and maintain as the result of their therapeutic experiences that very much of what passes for 'normal' timidity and apprehensiveness is really a neurotic and curable state of affairs. They are not content to take for granted many manifestations of fear that are commonly accepted as being within the range of the normal, and they cannot help observing that there would appear to be what might be called a conspiracy of leniency on the part of society in this matter by which these manifestations are not scrutinised at all closely. It is plain that psychologists also have in the past been very willing to acquiesce in the same low standards and to take many manifestations of fear at face value; in consequence, misleading inferences have been drawn concerning the nature and extent of operation of the fear instinct.

2. *Disharmony between bodily and mental manifestations.* Here again the estimate has often perforce to be made on purely subjective grounds. As a result of general experience one allots a certain degree of bodily disturbance to a certain degree of mental apprehension and then notes that this proportion is in many cases deranged. As with the former attribute, this is easy to observe in extreme cases, for example, where a patient displays extensive bodily disturbance of the kind we associate with fear, dryness of the mouth, sweating, polyuria, etc., and yet is very little aware of conscious fear. It would be still easier to observe, and would therefore make a deeper impression on the medical mind, were it not for the readiness with which the anxiety nature of these physical manifestations is over-looked clinically. It took, for instance, some years before those responsible were able to perceive the anxiety basis of the cases of 'disordered action of the heart' so common in the war, and it is an everyday experience to come across cases where such anxiety symptoms as chronic diarrhœa, psychical impotence, sweating, and flatulent dyspepsia are wrongly diagnosed on a physical basis. The greater prominence of bodily manifestations in cases of morbid anxiety as compared with those of normal fear is certainly very striking and cannot fail to arouse the impression of a thwarted instinct, as though some impediment to the usual expression forced the instinct to find an outlet in a bodily direction to a greater extent than would otherwise have happened. I do not think, however, that sufficiently accurate observations have yet been made for us to establish with any sureness a direct correlation between the dis-harmony in question and the extent to which the response is

pathological. It would be very valuable clinically if this could be done, but the difficulties in the way of recording accurate observations of blood pressure, sweat glands, etc., with someone in a state of fear are obvious, and animal experiments are useless here because of the impossibility of estimating the mental state. But it would be useful to know at least whether the disharmony in question is invariable—*i.e.*, whether pathological anxiety can occur with conscious fear out of proportion to bodily manifestations. I do not think this can happen, but I do not know.

3. In addition to these well-recognised features there is another one which is of special interest. It may be described as an internal disharmony among the manifestations themselves. I refer not merely to the disharmony mentioned above as subsisting between the mental and the physical groups as a whole, but to the general impression one has of inco-ordination within each of these groups. These do not appear to be constituted for any biological purpose in the way we can perceive the normal manifestations of fear to be. The inco-ordination is, perhaps, easier to observe in the mental sphere. There is neither activity nor passivity in any co-ordinated sense, but a curious admixture of over-excitation with paralysis. In the physical sphere the dissociation may go so far as to produce a mainly monosymptomatic picture. A patient may, for instance, complain of pollakiuria or cardiac angina, and one may have to make very searching enquiries before it can be established that there are also traces of other anxiety manifestations. The importance of these observations is that they strongly suggest a disorder of the fear instinct rather than a simple exaggeration of it.

Coming now to the pathology of the condition, I need not trouble you with the innumerable pre-Freudian hypotheses on the subject,[1] for I think they have been for years universally discarded, except perhaps by neurologists. For the most part they debated the question whether morbid anxiety, which was regarded as an over-excitation of the nervous centres, is due to the action of normal stimuli on pathologically over-excitable centres or to the action of pathological stimuli—*e.g.*, intestinal toxins—on normal centres. The difficulty in tracing pathological stimuli inclined the majority of writers on the subject to predicate a pathological nervous system, probably inherited as such. This debate became irrelevant when Freud discovered that it was not necessary to predicate either a

---

[1] A discussion of them will be found in Chapter XIX, of the Fourth Edition.

pathological nervous system or pathological stimuli, for the evidence pointed unequivocally to the conclusion that the condition is induced by the action of normal physiological stimuli on a normal nervous system; all that could be called pathological were the social situations responsible for the form of stimulation.

As is well known, Freud's first contribution to the problem was made on a purely physical basis. Studying the anxiety syndrome isolated in ' neurasthenia ' by Hecker, Freud separated it altogether from this disorder and showed that it had a distinct and character- istic pathogenesis. This anxiety neurosis occurred whenever undue sexual excitation was combined with deficient opportunity for discharge, an observation which has been confirmed from so many independent quarters that, in his ' Introductory Lectures ' (p. 335), Freud was able to say: ' So far as I know, the fact that a connection exists between sexual restraint and anxiety conditions is no longer disputed.' He laid stress on the element of frustration which is common to all the situations in which the neurosis arises, so that the anxiety could be described as what was found in place of frus- trated libido. He tried to explain the neurosis in terms of the chemi- cal or physiological components of libido and would, I think, still adhere to this. That is to say, he assumed that in sexual excitation certain chemical substances are generated or liberated and that when these could not be dissipated along their accustomed paths anxiety arose. Anxiety was thus for him a substitute for libido when this was frustrated and was presumably developed out of it; to put it more accurately, the physiological basis of anxiety was generated from the physiological basis of libido by some unknown process of chemical transformation.

In investigating the genesis of more complicated mental states such as the phobias, Freud found close parallels for the mechanism of his anxiety neurosis. Without going into the detailed structure of these conditions one may say that they present the same picture of anxiety making its appearance as a substitute for a thwarted libidinal impulse. Freud insists that there is an intimate connection, the nature of which will be discussed presently, between these two things in every phobia, and in my opinion any careful investigation of these states cannot fail to confirm his conclusions. With his usual caution, however, Freud has refused to generalise from this finding and does not maintain that all anxiety has this source, but only the morbid anxiety of the psychoneuroses. Elsewhere he speaks of the anxiety found, for instance, in dreams, as being a substitute for *any* unconscious impulse, libidinal or otherwise. I confess that, although I have discussed this idea with him personally, I have never been able to grasp it to my satisfaction. In any event it is not an important matter in practice, for most unconscious—*i.e.*, repressed—impulses are either libidinal or else impulses—*e.g.*, those of hate—which arise as a reaction to libidinal ones. Freud has not developed this other idea further, so that in considering his work we have to confine ourselves to the relation between repressed libido and morbid anxiety as seen in the psychoneuroses.

Until quite lately he had always held the view not merely that this morbid anxiety arose in consequence of the repression of libido, but that it was actually derived from it by some process of transformation perhaps akin to the transformations of energy with which we are familiar in the physical world. This is a view with which I have at various times in the past twenty years expressed disagreement[1] on the ground that there was insufficient evidence to justify our postulating a process at such variance with the biological theory of instincts. According to this, instincts are specific modes of reacting to the environment that have been evolved as such through ages of attempts at adaptation and, although their manifestations can, in the higher animal, be extensively modified, deflected and also fused with those of other instincts, this is a different thing from a radical transformation of one into another. I have, on the contrary, suggested that morbid anxiety is a perverted manifestation of the fear instinct, which, in the case of neurotic conflicts, has been stimulated to activity as a protection against the threatening libido. This protective nature of anxiety has, of course, always been recognised by Freud, his view being that the ego when unable to deal otherwise with an overcharge of libido responded by converting it into anxiety and then proceeded, by the well-known mechanisms of phobia formation, to 'bind' this. It seemed to me unnecessary to postulate this change, since the situation could be adequately described by simply saying that the anxiety was an expression of the ego's effort at defence. In his latest volume[2] Freud has fully accepted this view and abandoned his previous more complicated one. We are thus brought back to the simple conflict between ego and libido in the course of which the former responds by, among other ways, developing a reaction of fear.

E.g., Loc. cit.   'Hemmung, Symptom und Angst,' 1926.

We shall have to consider later the nature of this conflict and raise the question what precisely is the ego afraid of when it dreads libido, but at this juncture I wish to point out that the formula just reached gives us an opportunity of again contrasting, in a more fruitful way, morbid anxiety and normal fear. For the latter, Freud uses the expression ' real fear,' referring to the external reality of the danger stimulus. He has presented a delicate analysis of real fear, and I paraphrased this in a former paper,[1] read during the war before this Section of the Royal Society of Medicine, from which I now propose to quote. ' Morbid anxiety, as we see it in the psychoneuroses, is a defensive reaction of the ego against the claims of unrecognised libido, which it projects on to the outside world—*e.g.*, in the form of phobias—and treats as if it were an external object; it is, in a word, the ego's fear of the unconscious. But there appears to be an important difference between it and " real " dread in that the latter concerns only the ego itself, arises only in connection with external danger to the ego, and has nothing to do with the desires of repressed libido. One is tempted to say that the latter (real dread) is a normal protective mechanism that has nothing to do with the abnormal mechanism of morbid anxiety. Here, however, as elsewhere, the line between normality and abnormality is not so absolute as might appear, and consideration of the matter leads one to examine more closely into the nature of real dread itself. We then see that this can be dissected into three components, and that the whole reaction is not so appropriate and useful as is commonly assumed. The reaction to external danger consists normally of a mental state of fear, which will be examined further in a moment, and in various activities suited to the occasion—flight, concealment, defence by fighting or even sometimes by attacking. On the affective side there is to begin with a state of anxious preparedness and watchfulness, with its sensorial attentiveness and its motor tension. This is clearly a useful mental state, but it often goes on further into a condition of developed dread or terror which is certainly the very reverse of useful, for it not only paralyses whatever action may be suitable, but even inhibits the functioning of the mind, so that the person cannot judge or decide what he ought best to do were he able to do it. The whole reaction of " real " fear is thus seen to consist of two

---

[1] ' War Shock and Freud's Theory of the Neuroses.' Read before the Royal Society of Medicine, Section of Psychiatry, April 9, 1918. ' Papers on Psycho-Analysis,' 3rd edition, chap. xxxii.

useful components and one useless one, and it is just this useless one that most resembles in all its phenomena the condition of morbid anxiety. Further, there is seen to be a complete lack of relation between development of dread and the degree of imminence of danger, nor does it bear any relation to the useful defensive activities. Thus, one does not flee because one is frightened, but because one perceives danger; in situations of extreme danger men very often respond with suitable measures of flight, fight, or what not, when they are not in the least degree frightened; on the other hand, the neurotic can be extremely frightened when there is no external danger whatever. The inference from these considerations is that even in situations of real danger a state of developed dread is not part of the useful biological mechanism of defence, but is an abnormal response akin to the neurotic symptom of morbid anxiety ' (pp. 471, 472).

Freud further suggested that the developed dread sometimes found in situations of real danger is derived, not from the repressed libido that is directed towards external objects, as happens in the psychoneuroses, but from the narcissistic part of the libido that is attached to the ego. You will observe that he was still at that time using the conception ' derived from,' but it is not hard to translate this into the terms of defence I have indicated above. I ventured to apply this suggestion to the understanding of the war neuroses, and the theory I then developed was shortly afterwards confirmed by workers in Germany and Hungary,[1] whose investigations, owing to war conditions, were carried out independently of my own and of each other's; incidentally, I think this fact has a certain value as evidence of the objective validity of the psycho-analytic method. The view I put forward was that the only men who suffered from war shock were those whose libido, organised on a homosexual-narcissistic basis, was so attached to the ego as to become stimulated when the latter was threatened—i.e., in situations of real danger. The mechanism of the real anxiety in such situations is more complicated than might at first appear. It would be natural to suppose that the response of anxiety was one directly invoked by the stimulus of external danger, so that it would seem unnecessary to invoke any libidinal factor, narcissistic or otherwise. Several facts, however, speak against this simple view of the matter. First of all, as was remarked above, we have the consideration that the reaction of

Abraham and Ferenczi respectively.

developed anxiety is not the inevitable or in any sense the normal mode of responding to normal danger. Secondly, the incidence of this condition—*i.e.*, war shock—in the army as regards both frequency and type of subject afflicted. Thirdly, actual investigation of such cases, which demonstrates the abnormalities in the narcissistic libido among them, so that I felt justified in describing the condition as a narcissistic neurosis.

This conclusion is fortified by considerations drawn from allied fields. Recurring for a moment to the more fully investigated cases of ordinary psychoneurosis, we know that anxiety arises in relation to over-development of a libidinal cathexis. Now the curious thing is that the latter can happen either from direct erotic excitation or from what might be called the opposite of this—namely, a threat to the libidinal organisation. That direct stimulation should increase the available quantity of libido is, of course, fully intelligible, but how comes it that a threat to it has the same effect? Whatever may be the explanation, the fact seems clear enough: a threat causes a libidinal investment at the point threatened, as though—to speak figuratively—the libido protects itself by increasing its strength. The fear reaction on the part of the ego is secondary to this increase and clinically we find that at least as much morbid anxiety is a response to an excess of libido provoked by threats as to that provoked by erotic excitation, a circumstance which if pondered on will yield many interesting ethical reflections. The anxiety of war shock, and probably also that of hypochondria, appears to belong wholly to this negative context, and for the sake of clarity I will recapitulate the steps in which I conceive it to appear. First, perception of external danger. Secondly, normal fear response of mental alertness and physical preparedness (glycogenic stimulation, etc.). Thirdly, an over-investment of the ego with narcissistic libido as a protective response to the threatened danger. Fourthly, the evoking of ' developed ' or morbid anxiety on the part of the ego as a response to the excess of narcissistic libido.[1] This last response is obviously useless, and indeed detrimental, so far as the external danger is concerned, and consideration of it brings us back

---

[1] These considerations show how simplistic is the view of those writers, such as Rivers, who attempt to describe the neuroses in terms of self-preservation alone and who imagine that there is some inherent conflict between this conception and the psycho-analytic one. Here the conception of self-preservation, valuable enough in itself, is taken at face value without any need being felt to investigate the relation between what is meant by this term and the other components of the organism.

to the question that I postponed earlier in my remarks—namely, the precise relation of it to the internal 'danger' of excessive libido.

This question resolves itself into two. In what sense is the (relative) excess of libido conceived of as a danger? And can we form any biological conception of the function of the resulting morbid anxiety? It is, of course, evident that a person's libido, even in the adult sense, could be dangerous to his interests if uncontrolled: a man may ruin his career or lose his life in this way. One has to reckon in this connection not only with the direct consequences of the uncontrolled libido—complicated situations with the woman, pregnancy, etc.—but still more with the complications with other people, the men nearest to the woman and society at large. Behind this rational façade, however, much more remote and even more powerful mental forces are at work. It does not need much experience of neurotics to discover that their fears, even in the cases that appear to relate to current situations, are essentially of an infantile nature. When elucidated they are invariably shown to relate to various libidinal infantile situations, whether real or imaginary, and it becomes evident that this situation was in infancy, and still is in the unconscious, regarded as being absolutely intolerable. In the face of it the child is helpless, alarmed and at the end of its resources. The erotic wishes exciting the child are impossible in the nature of things to gratify, and it is this unrelieved need of gratification that is found intolerable. To put it more physiologically, the child has only a very limited capacity for enduring afferent excitation with no opportunity for any efferent discharge. There is reason to think that the ultimate nature of the danger to the organism is that it may lose what even the ego itself does not want to lose—namely, the capacity for erotic gratification. And it is further plain that the source of this danger lies in the sadistic, or aggressive, component of the sexual instinct. It would appear that to the infant strong excitation without relief is tantamount to destruction of the very capacity for obtaining relief. I have suggested the term 'aphánisis'[1] to denote this ultimate fate; the most familiar clinical manifestation of it is the castration complex.

We are not here concerned with the complicated methods the child devises to cope, however inadequately, with this state of affairs; to do so would, in my opinion, be to write the whole of

See Chapter XXV., p. 440.

psychology. We are concerned only with the first step in the response, and that is the group of reactions which later on will be called morbid anxiety. Perhaps the most striking feature here is the apparent lack of purpose and co-ordination in the manifestations. They must surely remind us of the very earliest reactions of the infant to distress of any kind, and if we consider them in this light we can perceive certain functions they perform. Some of them, notably the over-activity of the excretory organs, furnish a limited gratification which at the same time relieves tension and affords reassurance. Others, for instance the respiratory manifestations, call the attention of the environment to the urgent need for help. In more extreme states still we find a higher degree of paralysis, the protective nature of which is known from biological instances—*e.g.*, in rabbits. Here it seems plain that the last resource of the child, as of the neurotic, is reached in the form of what may be called an artificial aphánisis; the disturbing impulses are inhibited by a general inhibition of vital activity.

Freud has directed our attention to a still earlier situation in life from which many of the characteristic features of anxiety would appear to be copied or perhaps even derived. That is the event of birth itself. In this bold and apparently far-fetched suggestion Freud was anticipated by no less a man than Erasmus Darwin. What seems to me to be needed is a careful correlation of the phenomena of birth and of morbid anxiety with the various manifestations of the fear instinct as seen in animals. Only in this way shall we get final light on the puzzling problem of the relation between internal danger and external danger, of the conflict between the interests of the individual organism and the threat provided by the activity of racial impulses.

CHAPTER XIV

FEAR, GUILT AND HATE [1]

I

ANYONE who has seriously tried to unravel the complicated relationships subsisting between any two of these emotional attitudes will agree that the problem is one of exceptional difficulty. I hope, nevertheless, that the considerations to be brought forward here will contribute in some measure in elucidating at least the nature of the complexities in question and thus in furthering the approach to the more fundamental problems that lie behind them. As in our daily analytic practice, and indeed in all forms of scientific investigation, to get problems clearly stated is by no means the least difficult part of the task, nor is it the least important part.

Let us first consider the more purely clinical aspects of these relationships. The heart of the difficulty soon reveals itself. It is that—to speak statically—there exists a curious series of layer formations definitely connected one with the next, the connection being often in the nature of a reaction. This holds good for each of the emotional attitudes in question, so that one may be found at a given level in the mind, another at a deeper level, the former again at a still deeper level, and so on. It is this stratification that makes it so hard to tell which is the primary and which is the secondary of any two groups. To put the matter more dynamically, it is the complex series of interactions among these attitudes that makes it hard to determine chronologically their developmental relationships.

Let me now illustrate these generalities. If we have a patient suffering from any form of fear neurosis, of bound or unbound ' morbid anxiety,' we know from our experience that guilt must surely be present also. It is sometimes easy to demonstrate this, sometimes extremely hard, but we know that if the analysis is consistently pursued this proposition will be proved to be true. I am not maintaining in the abstract that fear cannot exist apart from guilt, but I should certainly maintain that clinically observed fear, a neurosis in which fear is one of the symptoms, always has guilt

[1] Read at the Eleventh International Congress of Psycho-Analysis, Oxford, July 27, 1929. Published in the *International Journal of Psycho-Analysis*, vol. x.

behind it. As Shakespeare long ago pointed out, ' Thus conscience does make cowards of us all.' Yet the matter is not so simple. It cannot be that an emotional reaction so phylogenetically ancient as fear is can be solely dependent on, or generated by, one so recently acquired as guilt is, one the very existence of which—at all events in a fully developed form—is doubtful in other animals than man. We have here an example of how a biological outlook may serve as a check on clinical investigation and warn us against a possibility of readily going astray. Our scepticism is confirmed by still deeper analytic research, particularly into the earliest stages of infantile development, where we find extensive evidence indicating that the guilt itself proceeds from a yet earlier state of fear. And it is worth while remembering in this connection that the guilt can be extraordinarily deep. A patient may have succeeded so extensively in expressing unconscious guilt conflicts in terms of conscious fear, may be so completely convinced that his difficulties arise from fear and nothing else, that it may in certain cases take years of analysis to make the underlying guilt conscious. Were it not that this procedure does not necessarily in itself solve the therapeutic problem the analyst might well have rested from his labours and felt satisfied that he had found a complete answer to his problem of the genesis of the phobia—namely, that it originated in guilt.

A similar gratification can be observed with hate. This is one of the commonest covers for guilt, and the way in which it functions here is easy to understand. Hatred for someone implies that the other person, through his cruelty or unkindness, is the cause of one's sufferings, that the latter are not self-imposed or in any way one's own fault. All the responsibility for the misery produced by unconscious guilt is thus displaced on to the other, supposedly cruel person, who is therefore heartily hated. The mechanism is, of course, very familiar in the transference situation. We know that behind it there always lies guilt, but further analysis still shows, in my opinion always, that the guilt itself is dependent on a still deeper and quite unconscious layer of hate, one that differs strikingly from the top layer in not being ego-syntonic.

In the last of the three possible combinations, of fear and hate, the same thing is to be observed. Hate, notably in its milder forms of ill-temper, irritability and anger, is commonly enough a cover for, or a defence against, an underlying state of apprehensiveness. This may occur either chronically, as in a disagreeable and irritable character, or acutely, as when a sudden alarm evokes an outburst of anger in place of panic. Yet we have good reason to think that the underlying fear is rarely, if ever, present unless there is a still deeper layer of hate, of the same ego-dystonic type mentioned just above.

In all these three cases, therefore, it is not hard to demonstrate the presence of three layers of which the first and third are of the same nature. In one of the three cases fear constitutes the deepest layer, in the other two hate. But we are here only at the beginning of our problem, for the state of affairs just presented does no more than illustrate the nature of the complexity in it; it tells us nothing about the final chronological or ætiological relationships. For this a deeper analysis is necessary, and this time I shall find it easier to consider each of the three emotional attitudes separately. We may begin with that of hate, for it would appear to be the least complicated of the three.

II

We have seen how various manifestations of the *Hate* impulse can cover both anxiety and guilt, but that there is reason to suppose that in all such cases there is present below these a still deeper layer of hate. It is highly probable that the more superficial one is derived from the latter, so that it might from one point of view be described as a breaking through of what had been repressed. It is, of course, not simply a break through, for there are several notable differences between the two, the aim towards which it is directed, the conditions under which it appears, and so on. Among these the most important doubtless is the relation to the ego. What we have called the superficial—*i.e.*, conscious—layer achieves in most instances, at least at the moment when it is being experienced, an extraordinary degree of ego-syntonicity. There are few emotions in life that can give the subject such intense conviction of being in the right, that carry with them such a complete sense of self-justification, as anger—the acme being reached in what is called righteous indignation. By definition this is quite otherwise with the deeper, unconscious layer of hate. If now we try to reconstruct the precise relationships between the two layers, we shall come to the following conclusions: The primary hate is probably the instinctive purpose of the infant, usually in the form of rage, to frustration of its wishes, particularly its libidinal wishes. This primary ' reactive ' impulse commonly fuses with the sadistic component of the libido to make what we meet with clinically as sadism. In the overcoming of the thwarting object there are therefore two sources of erotic satisfaction, the original, previously thwarted, one and the pure sadistic one. Later on, however, this gratification is interfered with by guilt. The secondary, conscious reaction of hate is an attempt to deal with the guilt, or, rather, the impotence it has caused. Its method of revolting against the guilt is to project this outwards, to identify the forbidding agency with another person, who is then identified with the original thwarting person in connection with whom the guilt has been generated to start with. It is in this sense that we can speak of the secondary hate layer as a return of the repressed, but it is strictly conditioned by creating a phantasy of the other person being in the wrong or by manœuvring reality so as to bring this about.

It is curious, and seemingly a paradox, that guilt can be relieved by an exhibition of the very thing—namely, hate—which was the generating occasion of the guilt itself. We are familiar with the talion principle in psychology and with the exactness with which the punishment is made to fit the crime. We have here an example of a very similar principle, which might be termed the *isopathic principle*,[1] according to which the cause cures the effect. If hate causes guilt, then only more hate, or rather hate otherwise exhibited, can remove the guilt. The most remarkable example of it is the idea unconsciously cherished by every neurotic, part illusion, part truth, that love is the only cure for guilt, that only by pursuing (and being allowed to pursue) a sexual goal will he ever be relieved of his suffering. The idea is compounded of a pleonastic platitude (' if I feel free and sanctioned in a sexual situation I shall feel no guilt ') and an illusion, that privation or frustration must necessarily signify guiltiness. I may quote another example of this isopathic principle, one also closely connected with the themes here under discussion. In a previous paper, on the Origin and Structure of the Super-Ego, I insisted on the essentially defensive nature of guilt, on its being generated to protect the personality from the privation which this characteristically interprets as frustration (*e.g.*, at the hands of the father). Now clinically in the neuroses, and always in the transference situation, we observe this guilt mainly in the indirect perspective of projection; the prohibiting, condemnatory and

At the Congress I used the phrase ' homœopathic principle,' but Dr. Federn has reminded me that homœopathists reserve the term ' isopathy ' for the particular part of their principles here concerned.

thwarting functions of the guilt-arousing agency, the super-ego, are mirrored in the patient's vision of the analyst. More than this, if the self-punishing tendencies are at all highly developed, we may expect to find that the patient will provoke the outer world—*i.e.*, father-substitutes—to inflict punishments on him, and it is easy to see that this is done in order to diminish the sense of guilt; by provoking external punishment the patient saves himself from some of the severity of internal (self-) punishment. We get three layers very alike to the other sets of three mentioned above: first dread of external punishment (*e.g.*, by the father); then guilt and self-punishment to protect the personality from the outer one, the method of religious penance; and finally the evoking of external punishment, a disguised form of the original one, so as to protect the personality from the severity of the self-punishing tendencies. The father is invoked to save the person from the thing that saved him from the father! As in vaccine therapy, the disease is cured by administering a dose of its cause, and, just as there, the success of the cure depends on the dosage of the morbific agency being brought under voluntary control.

The last part of this excursion, which I hope will help us in our further considerations, leads us to the second of our themes, namely *Guilt*. I should expect to find general agreement among analysts in clinical and analytical observation that the sense of guilt is the most concealed—though not necessarily the deepest—of the three emotional attitudes we are considering. My experience is that human consciousness tolerates either fear or hatred more readily than the sense of guilt. A feeling of inferiority, of general unworthiness is the utmost that the majority of patients can achieve in this direction, and from their extreme sensitiveness to the very idea of criticism one can only infer that the risk of really—not merely verbally—admitting that they are in the wrong constitutes a formidable threat to the personality. This intolerability varies a good deal, of course, among different people, and I have very much the impression that one of the chief factors on which the variation depends is the strength of the sadism present. If this observation proves to be correct[1]—that is, that the intolerability of guilt varies directly with the savagery of the sadism present—then one could not fail to connect it with Melanie Klein's opinion that the genesis of the

---

[1] Freud has pointed out a similar connection in the case of obsessional neuroses (' Hemmung, Symptom und Angst,' S. 50).

super-ego is to be found in the sadistic rather than in the phallic stage of development. In this connection one must raise the question whether guilt can arise purely as a way of dealing with—a defence against—the primary anxiety of unsatisfied libido or, on the other hand, is it always and inevitably associated with the hate impulse? I should be inclined to answer both these questions in the affirmative, but with the important modification that one is thereby distinguishing two phases in the development of guilt. In the former case it would not really be correct to speak of guilt in the full sense: one needs some such expression as a ' prenefarious ' stage of guilt. This must closely resemble the processes of inhibition and renunciation; the formula would appear to be the categorical ' I mustn't because it is intolerable.' It attempts thus to avoid the primary anxiety, but the situation becomes more complicated when an object relationship begins to be set up. Here sadism combined with rage at frustration breaks through, love of the other person[1] conflicts with dread of punishment at his hands (castration and withdrawal of the loved person), and the second stage, that of fully developed guilt, is constituted. Here we may describe the formula as ' I shouldn't because it is wrong and dangerous.' Love, fear and hate[2] are all equally necessary for this consummation, so that it would not be wrong to describe the super-ego as a compound of all three, its peculiarity being the making internal of attitudes previously directed outwards. As was remarked earlier, there is little doubt that the self-punishing function of guilt is destined to protect the individual from the risk of punishment from without, just as it is with religious penance.

It is at this point that we encounter the first of the more ultimate problems. How comes it that the process designed to protect the personality from an impossible situation, which may for present purposes be defined as the fear evoked by hate, becomes itself unendurable? So much so that the individual in self-defence against this salvation reverts to the very attitudes, fear and hate, he was being protected from. How can these be at the same time more intolerable and less intolerable than guilt? It can only be that we are confounding two things under the one term, that of guilt. I suggest that the two things are the two stages indicated above, that

[1] It seems to me highly unlikely that guilt ever appears in relation to an object who is simply hated: ambivalence is an essential condition of guilt.

[2] It is interesting that the word ' innocent ' denotes ' not hurting.'

of renunciation and that of self-punishment respectively. If so we should expect a certain inverse correlation between the two. There is a great deal of evidence to bear this out, and indeed Reik and Alexander go so far as to see in the self-punishing tendency a device to spare the subject the necessity of renunciation; that is to say, he punishes himself so as to procure for himself the necessary condition for indulgence. It has further to be remembered, as was hinted earlier in this paper, that the secondary appearance of fear and hate is by no means identical with the deeper layers of these. It is in a sense much more artificial: the danger of external punishment to which the subject exposes himself, for instance, is rarely serious, certainly not in comparison with the grim reality that the original danger seems to the unconscious. They are, in other words, much more ego-syntonic than the primary layers, much more under the control and regulation of the ego.

We now have to consider the third and last theme, that of *Fear*.[1] Let us begin by putting the question: does fear (of injury) always signify the idea of retaliation—*i.e.*, does it always imply a previous attitude of hate, or even of guilt as well ? Theoretically there appears no good reason why it should, and with many animals—*e.g.*, rabbits —it would seem a very gratuitous assumption. Nevertheless, if we adhere to our clinical findings, at least in all ages beyond the very earliest infancy, we are bound to admit that we never find the one without the other, so that we have to postulate the presence of hate, and probably also guilt, whenever we come across fear. This is perhaps because pure privation so rapidly comes to signify deprivation and frustration and hence evokes anger and hate. If privation proves too hard to bear and leads to fear we may be sure that in practice both hate and guilt are also present. This clinical observation is, however, no proof that *early* anxiety is secondary to either hate or guilt, as it would often appear to be in the upper layers of the mind. On the contrary, all the evidence, notably that of infant analyses, points to its preceding these.

Coming now to the subject of fear itself, the first problem is to distinguish between fear of an external danger, an event proceeding from without, and fear of an internal danger, one arising from the development of a certain internal situation. There is no doubt that

---

[1] It will be plain that I constantly use the word ' fear ' in this paper in the clinical sense of anxiety and apprehension, not necessarily in the biological sense of alertness with its appropriate responses.

failure adequately to appreciate this distinction has greatly retarded our progress in the past. It has been so illuminatingly drawn by Freud in his ' Hemmung, Symptom und Angst ' that I need only refresh your memory by quoting one passage from that work (S. 120): ' Der Angst wurden so im späteren Leben zweierlei Ursprungweisen zugewiesen, die eine ungewollt, automatisch, jedesmal ökonomisch gerechtfertigt, wenn sich eine Gefahrsituation analog jener der Geburt hergestellt hatte, die andere, *vom Ich produzierte*, wenn eine solche Situation nur drohte, um zu ihrer Vermeidung aufzufordern.' [' Thus we attributed two sources of origin to anxiety in later life. One was involuntary, automatic and always economically proportionate, and arose whenever a situation analogous to birth had established itself. The other was produced by the ego as soon as a situation of this kind merely threatened to occur, in order that it might be avoided.'] Our patients sometimes give us a conscious hint of it in their complaint of being ' afraid of fear,' or ' afraid of being afraid.'

Before inquiring into the nature and function of the fear or anxiety response let us be clear about the nature of the danger. Freud (*op. cit.*, S. 126) gives the name of ' traumatic situation,' characterised by helplessness and completely vague indefiniteness about the object of the dread, to that in which the subject is unable to cope with a mass of over-excitation for which no discharge can be provided. It is evidently the primordial situation, though he thinks it can recur in later life, particularly in the somatic anxiety neurosis. The typical fear in the psychoneuroses, on the other hand, he terms ' a danger situation,' where anxiety is purposively produced by the ego so as to warn the personality of the possible approach of the traumatic situation and the desirability of taking precautions to avoid it. These two evidently correspond to what we have provisionally termed the internal and external dangers respectively. Freud insists that the dread in the psychoneuroses is always dread of an outside intervention, that the libidinal impulse is ultimately a source of danger not in itself but only because of the intervention it may give rise to (*op. cit.*, S. 67). There would appear to be two fundamental ways in which the external danger expresses itself, and we shall see that they both lead to the re-establishment of the primary internal one. Either the object who can provide gratification—*e.g.*, the mother in the boy's case—is withdrawn, or else a parent, there the father, threatens to take away the organ necessary for the obtaining of the gratification. In either event the result is the same: in the former a state of privation is set up directly, in the latter indirectly through deprivation. But privation is another name for the original traumatic situation, that of intolerable libidinal tension consequent on the blocking of efferent discharge. We can thus say that the danger to which Freud alludes when speaking of the ' Kastrationa-angst des Ichs ' (*op. cit.*, S. 40) is that the ego may lose the capacity, or opportunity, for obtaining erotic gratification. The fear is lest the excitation of libido that cannot or is not allowed to obtain gratification may lead to the interference with the libido that can: to put it shortly, the libido that is not ego-syntonic constitutes a danger to the libido that is. This may be expressed clinically as a direct fear of impotence, but the more interesting variety is where the fear is lest the personality itself be lost, lest the loftiest ideals or the most laudable enjoyments be interfered with. Analysis shows that in such cases these always represent *imperfect* sublimations of the incest wishes themselves, for they constitute the kernel of the narcis-sistic investment of the ego. That is why the danger in question can be equally well described as one to the ego or to the libido; strictly speaking, it is to the ego's possession of libido, to its capacity for achieving libidinal gratification whether of a sensual or of a sublimated kind.

Now this is exactly what I wished to designate by using the term ' aphanisis.' Some colleagues have expressed surprise that just I, who have always insisted on the concrete nature of the unconscious, notably in connection with symbolism, should now describe part of its content by such an abstract Greek term. My reasons were two. In the first place I find it necessary to insist on the absoluteness of the thing feared, and this thing is something even wider and more complete than castration, if we use this word in its proper sense. The penis can be very extensively renounced by men, even in the unconscious, its place being taken by other erotic zones in exchange, and with women the personal significance of it is almost altogether secondary. The ultimate danger with which we are here concerned is to all possible forms of sexuality, not only to the inaccessible, forbidden ones, but also to the ego-syntonic ones and the sublima-tions of these. It means total annihilation of the capacity for sexual gratification, direct or indirect, a matter on which we shall again have to lay emphasis when we come to consider the primary traumatic situation. In the second place it is intended to represent an intellectual description on our part of a state of affairs that originally has no ideational counterpart whatever in the child's mind, consciously or unconsciously. It is therefore quite a different thing from an analytic interpretation of the unconscious in the usual sense. In the anxiety neurosis, for instance, there is, according to Freud, an automatic creation of an emotional state of anxiety rather than a state of fear with the idea, either consciously or unconsciously, of any specific danger. Whether this is so there or not—and it seems to me likely enough—we have to admit that it must be so in infancy, at a period that precedes any ideational thought whatever; I refer not merely to the birth situation itself, about which so much is still doubtful, but to many months afterwards when we can observe a state that may be called pre-ideational primal anxiety (*Urangst*). It is only later, when the situation is becoming externalised and the anxiety is created by the ego as a ' signal ' (Freud) for warning purposes, that we can speak of ideational fear, one which then usually has a specific reference.

Having cleared some of the ground concerning the ' danger,' we can now pass to closer consideration of the dread itself, and this brings us to the primary ' traumatic situation.' There is little doubt that, as Freud has from the beginning insisted, this early anxiety is quite directly connected with the simple situation of libidinal priva tion. One says ' connected with,' but the precise nature of the relationship between the two constitutes the second of the more fundamental problems we encounter in the course of the present considerations, and one of the most obscure in the whole field of psycho-analysis. I have for many years expressed the view that Freud's formula of the conversion of repressed libido into anxiety was untenable on both psychological and biological grounds, and he has himself recently withdrawn it (*op. cit.*, S. 40), though he still makes a reservation in the case of primal, automatic or objectless anxiety (*op. cit.*, S. 41, 88). The question therefore arises whether the known biological significance of the fear instinct as a defensive response, together with the entirely defensive significance of ' signal ' anxiety in the psychoneuroses, should not lead one to attempt the same solution in the case of primal anxiety. The situation itself can be defined: it is that of helplessness in the face of intolerable libidinal tension for which no discharge is available, no relief or gratification of it. Freud speaks of the ' Unbefriedigung, des Anwachsens der Bedürfnisspannung, gegen die er ohnmächtig ist ' (' non-gratification, of a growing tension due to need, against which it is helpless ') (*op. cit.*, S. 82) and says that the real kernel of the ' danger ' is ' das Anwachsen der Erledigung heischenden Reizgrössen ' (' an accumulation of amounts of stimulation which require to be disposed of ') (*op. cit.*, S. 83). Can we get any further than this ? Why is the tension in question intolerable, and in what sense is it alarming ? Is the evidently inhibiting effect of the anxiety in some way a defence against whatever is intolerable, or is it a simple, so to speak mechanical, consequence of over-excitation that is blocked ? I believe it is both. If we consult the sister science of physiology—and perhaps we are justified in doing so when dealing with such a profound pre-ideational region—we learn that a similar situation there, which can of course be experimentally induced, ends in exhaustion of the stimulation itself; a hungry man ceases to be hungry when food is unobtainable for long, and fasting experts are presumably men who can tolerate the initial stage of excitation and reach that of gastric anæsthesia better than others can. With the libido, however, this would be tantamount to total annihilation of it, and all possibility of erotic functioning would be gone, sub-jectively for ever. It may be that it is this resulting state of aphánisis, corresponding exactly with that brought about by external danger in the ways described above, against which the primal anxiety constitutes a defence.

There are two other points of view which would appear capable of throwing light on the problem. If we inquire into the con-stituent phenomena of anxiety we find, as I have described elsewhere in detail,[1] that both the mental and physical ones can be divided into two groups, that of inhibition and that of over-excitation respec-tively; the contrast between the diminished flow of saliva and the increased flow of urine will serve to illustrate the point. This must have some meaning. A second consideration is afforded by the following suggestion. It continues the train of thought already hinted at, according to which it may be possible to show that even primal anxiety has, if not a purpose in the psychological sense, at least a function to perform. It would not be strange if the ego, in the truly desperate situation in which it finds itself, made every imaginable effort to alleviate it. These efforts, I suggest, may be divided into two groups, which overlap the division of the actual phenomena into the two groups mentioned above. They are (1)

[1] See Chapter XIX of the Fourth Edition.

attempts to isolate the ego from the excitation; these represent the flight aspects of the fear instinct, would if successful bring about a state akin to hysterical anæsthesia, and must be the dawnings of what Freud terms the primal repression (*Urverdrängung*), and (2) attempts to deal more directly with the excitation itself, either by affording limited avenues of discharge or, more aggressively, by damping down the excitation itself. The first of these groups needs no further explanation, but it is necessary to amplify the account of the second one. Many of the over-excitation phenomena—*e.g.*, mental excitement, pollakiuria, etc.—must afford some measure of libidinal discharge, and Freud has suggested (*op. cit.*, S. 129, footnote) that even the paralysis of inhibition may be exploited in a masochistic sense. We are reminded of the circumstance, which has not, I think, been explicitly formulated, that the same is true of all forms of defensive mechanisms. Reik and Alexander have, for instance, forcibly pointed out that guilt has not only the effect of inhibiting the forbidden impulses; it has also invented a special mechanism, that of punishment, whereby they can, at least in some measure, be gratified. In regression, which, as Freud has clearly pointed out, is a form of defence, there occurs a leak on the lowlier but more accessible levels to which the libido has receded. In guilty self-castration itself the subject obtains the benefit of functioning erotically on the feminine plane. As to the damping-down process, the essence of every inhibition, I regard this as the earliest stage of the renunciation which later on is an essential part of the process whereby the unavailing incest wishes become transformed into more useful psychical activities. The central importance of it in the genesis of the neuroses will presently claim our further attention.

If the conception put forward here is valid we reach the conclusion that what the infant finds so intolerable in the primal ' traumatic ' situation, the danger against which it feels so helpless is the loss of control in respect of libidinal excitation, its capacity to relieve it and enjoy the relief of it. If the situation is not yet allayed it can only end in the exhaustion of a temporary aphanisis, one which doubtless signifies a permanent one to the infant. All the complicated measures of defence that compose the material of our study in psychoanalysis are fundamentally endeavours to avoid this consummation. Primary anxiety, no less than the later ' signal ' anxiety, belongs essentially to these defensive measures. Repression, which, as Freud has recently pointed out, takes its place in the series of defences, is one of the consequences of anxiety.

III

It remains to co-ordinate the relations subsisting between fear, guilt and hate, and to formulate the generalisations that would appear to emerge from the reflections I have detailed above.

We have observed that two stages can be distinguished in the development of each of these three mental reactions. With fear there is first the primal aphánistic dread arising from the intolerable tension of unrelieved excitation, and, secondly, when this privation has become identified with external frustration, the ' signal ' dread of this danger. With hate there is first the anger at frustration, and, secondly, the sadism resulting from the sexualising of the hate impulse. With guilt there is first what we have termed the pre-nefarious inhibition, the function of which is to assist the early fear reaction and which in effect is hardly to be distinguished from it, and, secondly, the stage of guilt proper, the function of which is to protect against the external dangers.

It will be noticed that only fear and guilt exhibit the phenomenon of inhibition. When this develops further into the renunciation undertaken with the object of deflecting the wishes into more promising directions the outcome may prove satisfactory. Perhaps it is because this element is lacking in the hate-sadism reaction, and also because from its very nature it tends to provoke the external danger still more, that this reaction has such unfortunate consequences both socially and pathologically (obsessional neurosis, paranoia and melancholia). Clinically it commonly appears as the only available alternative to inhibition and guilt, as a defence or protest against them, but the reverse of this may also occur, where inhibition and guilt alternate with each other as a defence against the dangers of sadism.

The critical point in the whole development is evidently that where the internal situation becomes externalised, where privation gets equated to frustration. Just because it is more accessible, more easily influenced, and a welcome aid in the task of obtaining the relief of gratification, the infant must find the situation altered to its advantage, though, it is true, it then encounters old dangers in a new form. In dealing with these the phantasy of the strict parent plays an important and, indeed, indispensable part. The magnification of the external dangers increases the advantages gained by externalising the situation and also, by the development of the super-ego, points the way to coping with the difficulties in their new form. Just as the reactions of adolescence are determined by those of the infantile sexual phase, so must those of the external—*i.e.*, Œdipus—situation of fancy be influenced by those of the preceding internal situation. For instance, the greater the primal anxiety the more will the imago of a strict parent be used in the Œdipus situation; the more sadistic the earlier reaction the more difficult will it be to deal with the guilt of the latter, and so on. We are thus led to lay stress on the importance of the earliest reactions. It was a revelation when Freud established the fundamental truth that all fear is ultimately fear of the parent, all guilt is guilt in respect of the parent, and all hate is hate of the parent. We are beginning to see, however, that even these very early attitudes must themselves have a pre-history, one which in all probability greatly influences them.

To complete the list of our conclusions the considerations should be recalled that were brought forward at the beginning of this paper. There I called attention to the various layers of secondary defence that covered the three attitudes of fear, hate and guilt, and pointed out that the defences themselves constituted a sort of ' return of the repressed.' We have seen how deep must be the primary layers of these three emotional attitudes, and also that two stages can be distinguished in the development of each of them. The relationship of the secondary layers would appear to be somewhat as follows. Any one of these primary attitudes may prove to be unendurable, and so secondary defensive reactions are in turn developed, these being derived, as was just indicated, from one of the other attributes. Thus a secondary hate may be developed as a means of coping with either fear or guilt, a secondary fear attitude (' signal ' anxiety) as a means of coping with guilty hate, or rather the dangers that this brings, and occasionally even a secondary guilt as a means of coping with the other two. These secondary reactions are therefore of a regressive nature, and they subserve the same defensive function as all other regressions.

It is worth calling attention to the part played by the libido in connection with the three emotional attitudes in question. Each one of them may become sexualised. With fear there is the masochistic aspect of paralytic inhibition and the somatic discharge in the fear reaction itself, with guilt there is moral masochism, and with hate the development of sadism.

Freud has recently commented on the remarkable fact that we are even yet not in a position to give a satisfactory answer to the apparently simple question of why one person develops a neurosis and another not. I am convinced that when we are able to give a final form to this answer it will prove to lie in the infant's response to the primal ' traumatic ' situation, and consequently to the Œdipus danger that later develops out of it. The main conclusion of the present paper is that fear, hate and guilt can all be regarded as reactions to this primal situation, as means of coping with it. The fundamental problem is evidently how to sustain a high degree of libidinal tension without losing control of the situation. If the infant is so helpless as to stand in danger of the spontaneous aphanisis of exhaustion he will resort to desperate measures and will then run the risk of oscillating between two unfavourable reactions. On the one hand he may depend too much on the artificial aphánisis of inhibition, and this will, in its turn, bring with it loss of control over the disturbing wishes through losing possession of them, through disappearance of the wishes themselves. On the other hand, he may pursue the easier path of developing in an excessive degree the defensive reactions of fear, hate and guilt, the path leading surely to neurosis. It would probably be more accurate to say, not that he oscillates between these two ways, but that the former is the primary one and that he is impelled to adopt the latter one only when that fails. This would account for the prominence of the ' all-or-none ' reaction so characteristic of severe neuroses and of the demonstrable fear of moderation that neurotics display. To control or guide a wish, or to hold it in suspense when necessary, signifies to a neurotic to admit into play the reaction of guilt which to him appears the only conceivable motive for controlling an impulse. Of this he has a well-founded dread, because he has never learnt to control the inhibiting tendency that constitutes its essence and in which is inherent the danger of artificial aphánisis. The very thing in which he originally sought salvation has become his greatest danger.

If the train of thought here presented is substantiated it must have important bearings on the practical problems of therapeutics. The most difficult aim of therapeutic analysis is to induce toleration, first for the reaction of guilt, then for the hate and fear that underlie it, and the greatest obstacle we encounter is the patient's lack of confidence in the possibility of controlling the originally defensive inhibiting tendency. The battle is half won when he realises that there are other than moral reasons for restraining the gratification of an impulse; it is wholly won when he fully realises that this capacity for restraint, instead of being the danger he has always imagined, is, on the contrary, the only thing that will give him what he seeks: secure possession of his personality, particularly of his libidinal potency, together with self-control in the fullest sense of the word. Then only is he able to deal adequately with reality, both in his own nature and in the outer world.

CHAPTER XV

COLD, DISEASE AND BIRTH [1]

It is only appropriate that a paper written as a contribution to the *Festschrift* prepared in honour of Dr. Ferenczi should couple on to one or other of his characteristic views, and the present one will do so in several respects. It is to Ferenczi more than to anyone else that we owe our dawning realisation of how subtle are the inter-relations between psychical and physical disorders, an important realm we are only beginning to explore. He has shewn that both mental and bodily diseases may sometimes be due to the same factors, to unsatisfied cravings, a mechanism quite different from the familiar hysterical conversion. I propose to indicate a still more indirect way in which certain mental tendencies may lead to serious bodily disease—namely, through false associations of a symbolic kind concerning the idea of disease, associations leading to conduct which unwittingly exposes the person to the danger of contracting disease through infection.

The class of infective disease here referred to is that acquired by the respiratory route, about the scope of which something will be said later. This kind of disease is acquired by simply breathing infected air, and the chance of its happening is immensely increased by inadequate ventilation in the presence of infection. Nothing, therefore, could better favour the chance of acquiring the infection than the prevailing belief, or superstition, that such diseases have an ætiology of exactly the opposite kind—*i.e.*, that they are due to the malignant influence of cold air, or what are popularly known as draughts. Since this belief still lingers even in medical circles, something may first be said about it from a purely pathological point of view. Without taking up the extreme position that the popular belief is entirely superstitious and untrue (though I personally consider it to be so), I will maintain here only that the patho-logical importance commonly ascribed to cold air is enormously exaggerated.

---

[1] Published in the *Festschrift* prepared by the Hungarian Psycho-Analytical Society (of which the author is an honorary member) on the occasion of Dr. Ferenczi's jubilee (*Internationale Zeitschrift für Psychoanalyse*, vol. ix., Heft 3).

Three sets of considerations seem to me to make this conclusion inevitable: (1) Experimental work in both human beings and other animals, (2) sceptical reflection on the nature of disease, and (3) recollection of the history of the belief in question. I will begin with the last of these. When a popular belief on a given subject fades in exact correspondence with the growth of precise scientific knowledge on that subject, one may suspect that the function of the belief had been simply to fill a gap in lieu of definite knowledge, particularly if the subject was one of great psychical importance to humanity. One need only instance the enormous restriction in applicability that religious explanations of natural phenomena undergo when these phenomena are investigated by other means. The huge mass of folklore on the subject of health shews both how important man has always felt this matter to be, and also how impossible it has been for him ever to tolerate ignorance in this sphere. This hiatus he was always compelled to fill. Knowing practically nothing about the causation and treatment of disease, he invented more or less fantastic explanations to remedy his ignorance. The way in which these false explanations are determined will be illustrated later. In this series one of the ætiological agents most believed in, and one that was supposed to account for a vast range of diseases, was cold air. In the medical literature of only a century ago it is quite astonishing to find what an extraordinary number of diseases was supposed to be brought about in this way. Even in the last generation of medical textbooks one finds this ætiology given for a variety of such bacteriological conditions as peritonitis, tuberculosis, hepatic abscess, pericarditis, pleuritis, gastritis, and a large number more. Many obviously irrational elements in these beliefs indicate their superstitious nature. Thus night air was thought to be peculiarly deadly; malaria, for instance, was thought to proceed from the inhalation of this noxious substance until the impossibility of acquiring it in the absence of the necessary kind of mosquito was demonstrated. It is interesting to note that cold air striking, like an enemy, in one localised direction (*i.e.*, ' draughts ') is especially dangerous, notably if it strikes from behind. This also applies to cold air reaching certain particular areas of the body, such as the feet and the back of the neck. Air entering through an aperture, most of all through a keyhole, is more dangerous than other varieties. If we consider one instance only of the ætiology described fifty years ago, we will see how out of accord it is with our present knowledge of pathology. I will select the teaching that oöphoritis might follow the wearing of unsuitable nether garments during menstruation. If these garments were open instead of closed, the dangerous air might penetrate into the vagina, ascend the patent cervical canal, circulate in the body of the womb, and work its way along the tortuous Fallopian tubes until it reached the sensitive ovary itself.

Naturally the advent of bacteriology was bound to exercise a powerful modifying influence on these beliefs, but so implanted were they in the human mind that recourse to some rationalisation proved necessary. So it was maintained that cold air, though not the specific cause of these diseases, acted by lowering the resistance of the organism to ubiquitous infective agents, and thus determined whether the patient was to suffer from the disease or not. So in practice the new knowledge altered little, and people guard against this supposed source of disease almost as carefully as they did in the days before Pasteur and Koch. Yet experimental research on both human beings and other animals shows that it takes an inordinate degree of cold, a degree which is never approached under civilised conditions, to lower the body temperature of the organism, and that nothing short of this makes any appreciable difference to its resistance against pathogenic infection.

The effects of false beliefs have usually been very mixed. Mankind has often suffered severely from them, but has often received compensatory benefits in the form of comfort and happiness. In the present instance the balance has gone heavily in the former direction, for here incommensurably greater suffering has resulted than from any other single belief, true or false. It has been computed that, when all the immediate and remote complications and sequelæ are taken into account, quite three-quarters of all physical disease and death originate in respiratory infection—one of the most gigantic facts in the history of human suffering.

Can psychology throw any light on the origin and meaning of this fateful error? The first possible explanation that occurs to one may be mentioned to begin with, though it is evidently a superficial one. It has to do with a pure error in logic. A prominent symptom of the acute stage with most of these infections is shivering and sensitiveness to cold (the well-known stage of rigor). This initial phase of the illness is commonly mistaken for the pathogenic chill supposed to be the cause of the disease. Further, it cannot be chance that the belief in the danger of cold air has lingered longest in respect of purely respiratory disease, and is held most strongly of all in connection with the mild infection that actually goes by the name of 'a cold.' Here there is an additional reason for confusion over ætiological agents. Cold air (just as bright sunlight) can stimulate the respiratory and ocular mucous membranes to such an extent as to produce many of the less important, though striking, manifestations of this familiar condition; thus, running at the eyes and nose, nasal tickling, sneezing, and even coughing. Although it is fairly easy to distinguish this short-lived state from the genuinely toxic condition called a cold, it is likely that the superficial resemblance between the two furthers the ætiological confusion in question, and makes it easier to ascribe the second one also to the physical agents that obviously produce the first.

No modern psychologist, however, would for a moment be content with this purely intellectualistic explanation, apart altogether from the fact that it is applicable only to a certain class of diseases. We know now that formal errors in logic are due not to intellectual deficiency, but to the operation of emotional factors. As Ferenczi[1] well says: 'One was formerly inclined to believe that things are confounded because they are similar; nowadays we know that a thing is confounded with another only because certain motives for this are present; similarity provides the opportunity for these motives to function.' We have, therefore, to search further for a more complete explanation of such a strong and deep human characteristic as the one we are considering. The only writer I know of who has attacked the problem psychologically is Trotter.[2] He suggests that man's discomfort and fear in the presence of cold air may be related to the danger of being isolated from the safe warm herd, so that the belief here under discussion would be a direct manifestation of what he terms the herd instinct. If we translate Trotter's 'herd' psychoanalytically into terms of the family, ultimately the mother, his suggestion may prove to be related to the one that will be propounded here.

The assistance to be expected from psycho-analysis will naturally be sought by determining what contributions could have been made to the belief in question by the unconscious. We have to consider what ideas in the unconscious correspond with the elements of the

[1] Ferenczi, ' Contributions of Psycho-Analysis ' (Engl. trans.), 1916, p. 237.
[2] W. Trotter, ' Instincts of the Herd in Peace and War,' 1916, p. 31.

statement ' cold air causes disease.' The unconscious equivalents of the last-mentioned idea are familiar to us from numerous psycho-analyses. Though the wish-fulfilment mechanism of the unconscious may occasionally connect certain forms of disease with agreeable ideas—such as in the well-known association between the ideas of cancer and pregnancy—yet there is little doubt that the commonest and most fundamental unconscious conception of disease is that of a crippling injury. The injury is instinctively imagined to have been inflicted from without, either with a sadistic or with a hostile intent. The records of primitive folk-lore and superstition teach us how constantly the supposed inflicter of the disease (and also of death) are figuratively personified (Róheim). The injury, like all injuries, ultimately signifies castration (Rank).

From the latest researches we have learned that the idea of castration has a much wider connotation in the unconscious, particularly in its genetic aspects, than used to be thought. In addition to ideas directly concerned with the loss of the penis (threats, fears of retaliatory punishment, etc.), there are three other important sources from which this complex is fed. They are: removal of fæces, identified with the penis (Jones), weaning from the nipple (Stärcke), and loss of the mother's body at birth (Alexander). It is to Ferenczi's[1] imagination that we owe our first proper appreciation of the psychical significance that the act of birth must have for the infant, and he has traced the consequences of this in the later development of the individual. From his work, and of course from Freud's, we have come to realise how great must be the suffering and resentment experienced by the infant on being expelled from paradise, and how strong is the perennial desire to return there. After the painful act of birth has been gone through, the most prominent demonstration to the infant of the ' castration ' it has just undergone—in being deprived of the nest it formerly owned as part of its total self—is certainly the sensation of cold air. The uncomfortable stimulation produced by this change in temperature betokens the revolution in its state of being, and on its (unwilling) response to it its very life depends. Small wonder that the dominant impression thus received on the threshold of life remains for ever after connected with the ideas of discomfort, insecurity, danger, or even bodily harm.

[1] Ferenczi, ' Entwicklungsstufen des Wirklichkeitssinnes,' *Internat. Zeitschr. f. Psychoanalyse*, 1913.

CHAPTER XVI

JEALOUSY[1]

IF a foreigner ventures to develop a psychological theme before a French audience, in the land *par excellence* of psychology, he will need to justify himself with more than usual care. What, then, will you think of his audacity when he selects as his theme the one chosen for this lecture ? For if there is any of the human sentiments about which the French are supposed to know everything worth knowing, surely it is jealousy. Your poets, writers and psychologists have explored it both intensively and extensively, and their intuitive genius has flashed illumination on its secrets. After what they have written, can anything be said that is not banal ? Yet I tell myself that even if I said nothing new I could nevertheless count on your interest. That your interest in the theme is perennial and inexhaustible is shown by the part it plays in your public life. I do not know if anyone has ever calculated what proportion of your theatre is occupied with the theme of jealousy, but it must be greater than that of any other theatre. And what would be the circulation of any newspaper if it excluded *crimes passionels* from its contents ? Perhaps some would buy it from curiosity to see what else of interest there could be in the world to fill a whole newspaper. You have even evolved a special jurisprudence in this connection, though I understand it is not actually yet incorporated into your laws.

The theme may therefore be presumed to be interesting to you. But this consideration alone would be a poor excuse for my having chosen it, for it would mean exploiting a ready-made interest. On the contrary I have the high ambition of stimulating in you a new interest in this well-worn theme, and the reason why I dare cherish such an ambition is that, thanks to the new science of psychoanalysis, I have something new to offer you. For the truth is mightier even than national pride. And the truth is that, with all her brilliant contributions to science, especially to that of psychology, France has not a monopoly of knowledge. It happens from time to time that discoveries of great importance are made in other countries, and

[1] Address delivered at the Sorbonne, March 21, 1929, and before the British Psycho-Analytical Society, May 15, 1929. Published in the *Revue Française de Psychanalyse*, 1929, Tome III.; *Psyche*, 1930-31, vol. ii.

then France is faced with a somewhat painful situation. Like all great lovers, France prefers to give rather than to receive, and when she is asked to receive knowledge won in a foreign country she consents to do so only after transforming the gift so as to impart to it something of her own peculiar genius. I do not doubt that this will be the case also with psycho-analysis and, indeed, its leading exponent in France, M. le Dr. Laforgue, has already occupied himself with this task by adapting the new knowledge to the characteristic idiom of French thought.

Why psycho-analysis is a discovery of great importance can be told in a word or two. It is because it has shown that what we have hitherto known as our minds is really but the small part of a totality. In the future we shall have to refer to them by the more modest title of conscious mind, realising that this conscious mind is only a relatively small and selected portion of our whole mind, that it is in great part derived from a deeper layer which we now call the unconscious, and that it owes to this its driving force. The nature of this unconscious, absolutely and totally unknown to the conscious mind, has been laid bare to us by Professor Freud, of Vienna, whose genius forged a method for exploring this previously dark and inaccessible territory. To make our understanding of any psychological process complete, therefore, we now have to add to what we may know about it by conscious introspective methods all that can be found out by the psycho-analytic method about its origins, derivations and unconscious associations. This work has not only answered many questions previously obscure, but has made us realise that there are a number of questions which till now we had not even put, because being content with our knowledge we did not know that these questions existed.

Let me at once illustrate this last remark by proceeding to the theme of the lecture itself. So much is known about jealousy, its relation to love and hate, the exact circumstances under which it arises, and so on, that it would be easy to come to the conclusion that everything essential about it is already known. But I can put a number of questions to which I do not think it would be easy to give a really satisfying answer. To begin with, is it really known why some people are more jealous than others, or why women suffer more frequently from this complaint than men? It certainly is not to be correlated simply with the strength or the fidelity of the love: some of the best lovers are rarely jealous, and some of the weakest appear to be more interested in jealousy than love itself. When men are betrayed is it known why one man proceeds to shoot the woman, another the interloping rival? This certainly does not depend on the external situation, but on something obscure in the psychology of the individual man. Is there any psychological difference between the jealousy of a lover who does not yet know whether his wooing is going to be preferred to his rival's and the jealousy against a rival who later intrudes and threatens to take from him the woman he has already won; or between the jealousy founded on suspicions, often groundless, and the outburst on the occasion of an open betrayal? It is even difficult to say to what extent jealousy is a normal phenomenon, an inevitable accompaniment of love, and if so how this differs in its nature, apart from its external manifestations, from what psychologists call morbid jealousy, a condition which may at times amount to actual insanity.

These few questions alone are enough to remind you that there are many kinds as well as degrees of jealousy, and one is led to ask whether there can be any single underlying principle to account for this variety. I may say at once that in my opinion investigation of the unconscious processes on which all these manifestations depend justifies one in announcing a single key which can unlock all the main secrets. Before disclosing this, however, I propose to lead you first from the manifestations themselves to consideration of the deeper factors concerned, and I will begin with contrasting the more familiar 'normal' jealousy with the extreme forms of insane jealousy; that will give you some idea of the magnitude of our task.

It will be simpler to consider separately the problems in the two sexes and we will start with the classic situation of the eternal triangle, two rivals for a woman's love. My first remark will be one that will astonish those of you who are not acquainted with psycho-analysis. It is that we have the best reasons to conclude that when a man finds himself in this situation it is not for the first time in his life. Every little boy finds himself in the same situation, for he has had two parents of opposite sexes and he cannot escape an attitude of jealousy in his desire for the exclusive possession of his mother's love. This is just as true whether his father is still present or already dead, or even if he is brought up by another woman than his own mother. An emotional attitude towards the father is then developed which contains all the elements present later in the adult situation. They are fear, hostility and guilt. The little child does not, of course, manifest these emotions in the open manner that an adult may, though signs of them often enough leak through to the surface and can be detected by the attentive observer. They soon enter into what we term a state of repression, are buried and forgotten, and usually remain entirely unconscious for the rest of the person's life. They are, however, none the less actively operative for that. We consider that this primal situation is the archetype for all later life, and that on the particular way in which the child deals with it will depend his reactions and behaviour when confronted in later life with all the manifold problems and difficulties that occupy so much of the sphere of love. All the typical attributes of his love-life are thus determined in early infancy. You will agree now that this first conclusion is strange and astonishing, that if it is true it belongs to knowledge that is unrecognised, and probably also that the conclusion is repellent as well as strange. Yet this discovery of Freud's was forestalled nearly two centuries ago, of course by a Frenchman. Diderot, in *Le Neveu de Rameau*, writes of a little boy: ' Si le petit sauvage était abandonné à lui-même, qu'il conserva toute son imbécillité et qu'il réunit au peu de raison de l'enfant au berceau la violence des passions de l'homme de trente ans, il torderait le cou à son père et coucherait avec sa mère.' In these words we have a perfect description of what psycho-analysts call the Œdipus complex.

It is easy to enumerate the elements of which jealousy is made up in the simple situation when a dangerous rival appears. The first sign is fear at the thought of losing the loved object, and this will turn into the pain of grief if she has been lost. Accompanying this is hatred of the rival and perhaps also of the faithless woman. Then, more secret but probably more important than either of the other two elements, there is the wound to self-esteem and self-love, to what in psycho-analysis is called narcissism. I am going to lay a great deal of stress on this element and hope to elucidate it further. In doing so I find support in the words of a great French writer, La Rochefoucauld, who very aptly said: ' Il y a dans la jalousie plus d'amour-propre que d'amour.'[1] Shand, the Scottish psychologist, writes in a similar vein: ' It is due to the desire of self-love to possess certain things exclusively for self . . . that jealousy principally arises.'[2]

This feeling is tantamount to what we call a feeling of inferiority,

---

[1] La Rochefoucauld, ' Maximes,' cccxxiv.
[2] Shand, ' The Foundations of Character,' 1914, p. 258.

a sense of diminished worth, and at times the person is aware of a sense of self-criticism as though he were wondering what fault on his part could have led to this state of affairs. This observation is in accord with the results of psycho-analytic investigation, which show that all such feelings of inferiority ultimately proceed from a latent sense of moral inferiority, from the reservoir of guiltiness rarely absent from the unconscious and which many people spend most of their lives in evading. The unconscious guilt is derived from the early reactions to the Œdipus complex in infancy, and the constant fight between it and human desires constitutes the unconscious conflict on the results of which mainly depend an individual's capacity for happiness.

So far the description is readily intelligible: fear or grief, wounded self-esteem and anger. It is all so evident that no need is felt for any special explanation, although I have perhaps already hinted that the full analysis even of this simple situation will prove it to be more complete than it appears. At all events, it is clarity itself in comparison with the extreme or insane form of jealousy, to which I now invite your attention. Here we see the same elements magnified into a caricature, but with the striking feature added of groundlessness, for it is well known that the most insatiable jealousy may co-exist with absolute fidelity of thought and deed on the part of the loved person. The fear here takes the form of a mad suspiciousness that overthrows all reason, that finds food in the most innocent trifles, and that distorts, misreads, misjudges evidence to such an extent that no sanity remains. The anger and hatred may culminate, as we know, in savage murder. The wounded narcissism is less in evidence, being evidently protected by the hate which, like most hate, presents itself as righteous. Now in the true delusional type of jealousy, psycho-analysis has made a very remarkable discovery, one, I think, never anticipated before Freud's work on the subject. It has been able to show that the jealousy process is dictated far more by interest in the rival than by interest in the woman—that, in short, it is a perverted expression of a repressed homosexuality. The chain of events that underlies it is as follows: The subject has a strong homosexual tendency which he has repudiated so completely as to bury it in the unconscious—*i.e.*, to make himself quite unaware of its existence. As a reaction to it, or compensation for it, or defence against it—all expressions are equally correct—he has in a forced way tried to love a woman. This has perhaps succeeded for a time until the buried tendency reasserts itself, often in response to some new stimulation, some change in the environment, or perhaps some diminution in the woman's attractiveness. This type of man, who, incidentally, is often too fond of drink, makes a special appeal to many women, particularly those with a highly developed maternal instinct. They instinctively feel that he needs help and encouragement, and their vanity assures them that they are the destined saviour. Such marriages are, however, built on an insecure foundation, love of the adult type is hardly possible in them, and the *dénouement* we are now concerned with is far from being the only one that can ensue. When the collapse comes the interest in the other man is, in the nature of the case, not allowed to manifest itself in a positive fashion. The resulting symptom of morbid jealousy can be described in many ways, all accurate according to the point of view adopted. One can say that it constitutes a violent repudiation of the homosexuality: it says, in effect, ' No, I do not love that man: on the contrary I detest him.' Or one can say that the man identifies himself with his wife and through her plays, in his imagination, a feminine part with the other man. In other words, he projects on to his wife the desires he has to repudiate in himself. He says: ' It is not I who am in love with that man, it is my wife who is.' His forbidden love for the man comes to expression under the mask of exaggerated love for his wife, if we accept the conventional judgement that jealousy is a measure of love.

The actual manifestations of this delusional jealousy are aften so mad and the underlying factors I have just outlined are so foreign to ordinary consciousness that one might well despair of being able to establish a common bond between it and the familiar everyday jealousy to which I first referred. Nevertheless psycho-analysis has been able to show that the factors underlying even ordinary jealousy are more subtle and complex than is generally supposed, and that in their nature they are not so very far removed from those responsible for delusional jealousy. It would indeed be strange if it were otherwise, for it is pretty plain that the extreme form is essentially an exaggeration of the simple one. All the main elements of suspicion, fear, grief, anger and shame are present with both, and it would be unlikely if this unique constellation of emotions that we call jealousy could arise in two entirely separate ways and from two entirely different sources. I can at once point to one psychological mechanism common to the two forms, the one we referred to above under the name of projection. We saw how the masked homosexual projected on to his wife his repressed love for the other man. Now what is very frequent, possibly even universal, in simple jealousy is that the man projects general feelings of infidelity on to the woman, feelings he does not always avow to himself. It is undoubtedly the Don Juans of this world who cannot trust women; they cannot believe in their fidelity because they cannot believe in their own: they project on to them their own faithless and fickle desires. Who was it sang ' La donna è mobile, quant 'è il vento '? Rigoletto's duke, whose only pastime was the pursuit of women. A cynic might say that such men mistrust women because their experience has shown them how easy it is to seduce them, but this logical rationalisation only covers the deeper psychological factors. If, therefore, this particular mechanism of projection can occur in both forms, perhaps we shall find that the origins also of the two have more in common than might at first sight appear.

To develop my argument I must next consider some general propositions on the subject of love itself. Here again I am going to be bold and venture to think that it will be possible to say something new about love to, of all audiences in the world, a Parisian one. Now what I have to say is something sad, and that is that there is much less true love in the world than there appears to be, and even much less true passion. Investigation of the deeper layers of the mind teaches one that love and passion can fulfil many other functions than their own, which means that they can be conjured up for other motives than the normal one of love. And it is by no means easy to distinguish what we might thus call secondary love from primary love, especially as they commonly occur together, completely fused with each other. Let us take the case of ordinary politeness, the mildest manifestation there is of affection. We all know the difference here between genuine politeness, what the French so gracefully call *politesse du cœur*, and the artificial mannered politeness. More interesting is the observation that the latter is commonly employed to mask an unfriendly attitude, to cover disdain, suspicion, dislike, apprehension or even hostility. This is notably so with well-bred, well-controlled men, whose first reaction to a threat is an increase of stiff politeness. In one of his poems[1] Rudyard Kipling has wonderfully illustrated this psychological mechanism in reference to the training of self-control that is

[1] ' Et dona ferentes.'

said to be characteristic of the English ideal; the last two lines are:

' Cock the gun that is not loaded, cook the frozen dynamite—
But oh, beware my country, when my country grows polite !'

What is evidently true of politeness is even truer of more intense grades of affection and of love itself. Often and often rivalry, disaccord, jealousy, and hatred of a degree that would make life together difficult or impossible are dealt with unconsciously by using these emotions to stimulate the exactly contrary one of affection, which is the most obvious mask for them and the most complete defence against them. As a result the hateful emotions are kept at bay, suppressed or even buried in the unconscious. This state of affairs is naturally commonest in family life, where the people concerned are forced to live together; one might say that they have to love each other so as to avoid hating each other. I hope that these remarks do not shock you, nor do I want to be misunderstood as having generalised too extensively. I only wish to remark that there is far more hatred in the unconscious mind than is generally known, and that the most characteristic defence against it is the development of an overcharge of affection, of a greater amount than would otherwise be there. One has to remember that any close contact between human beings brings a restriction of the personality that is apt to breed resentment. It is rare for such close contact to be represented without providing numerous reasons for resentment, friction, disagreements, oppositions and so on, all of which are mild expressions for some degree of hatred. What in consciousness is felt as annoyance is in the less restrained unconscious already hatred. The question has even been raised whether it is possible for love to exist at all without there being also an accompanying undercurrent of hate, naturally of varying intensity according to the disposition of the person concerned. One could quote many passages from the great writers which would support this supposition. Racine, for example, in his ' Andromaque '[1] makes Hermione say:

' Ah ! je l'ay trop aimé pour ne le point haïr.'

In the same play[2] he also indicates the alternative between love and hate in these words of Pyrrhus:

' Songez-y bien: il faut desormais que mon cœur,
S'il n'aime avec transport, haïsse avec fureur.'

---

[1] Acte ii., Sc. 1.   [2] Acte i., Sc. 4.

One might say that what is meant in this last passage is merely the familiar fact that a person often reacts with hate to disappointed love, as was so well expressed by Congreve in the oft-quoted lines:

> ' Heaven hath no rage like love to hatred turned,
> Nor hell a fury like a woman scorned.'

But this is just what I mean when I speak of the frictions, oppositions and dissatisfactions so rarely separable from love. They all arise from disappointment at the love not proving the perfect ideal they had imagined and expected, with consequent resentment against the person responsible for the disappointment. It is evident that this will be the greater the greater the disproportion between the ideal and the actual. Ultimately, therefore, the resentment depends on the distance of the previous ideal from reality and on the person's capacity to exchange the one for the other; to accept the positive side of what reality offers and to neglect the unobtainable. Of the two the second factor, that of adaptability, is in practice much more important than the first, the loftiness of the ideals. Ideals do not harm so long as one does not expect them to be realised, so long as one does not build on them. Now excessive dependence on ideals for the achievement of happiness is a thing that varies greatly among different people, and, as it underlies the greater part of jealousy, we shall have to inquire more closely into its nature.

This leads us to a second accessory function of love. We have seen that love can fulfil not only its own proper function, that of bringing happiness by gratifying the instinct of love, but other accessory ones, such as the masking of hate. The second accessory function we are now concerned with is the part it plays in affording reassurance and security about one's self-value, particularly in the erotic sphere. I want to distinguish this sharply from what might be called the normal function of love, and that is not easy because it is often concealed behind this. Let me put the matter another way by differentiating two things that are often confounded, desire and need. One can perhaps see this distinction most readily in such spheres as drinking and smoking or similar indulgences. One man will drink wine because he enjoys the pleasure it adds to his mood—in other words, for a positive reason. Another will drink because without it he is unhappy, unfree in himself, weighed down by what Janet calls ' un sentiment d'incomplétude '—in short, he drinks for a negative reason, because he is dependent on it, cannot do without it, *needs* it. The same is true of love. Normally, a man loves because it expresses his desires, not his needs. He wants, it is true, an external opportunity to express his desire for self-completion in its fullest terms, but he does not feel particularly incomplete without this. It is otherwise with a man who is driven to search for a suitable object in order to relieve his doubts about his own value, to reassure himself about his erotic capacity, to give himself the inner security that he otherwise lacks. To him love is a therapeutic cure for a morbid state of affairs, not simply the fulfilment of desire. The first man has in any case the *internal capacity* for self-expression even when the external opportunity for gratifying it may be absent. But the second man has not this internal capacity of his own accord; he hopes that it will be engendered or bestowed on him by the external opportunity for gratification. He thus becomes dependent on the external opportunity—*i.e.*, on the object of affection—in the same way as a morphinomaniac becomes dependent on his dose. His passion, his craving, his declarations may very well be more vehement than the first man's, but the observant eye can perceive the difference and does not account him a good lover for all his protestations. The most striking feature about his love is that, strictly speaking, it is not love at all, but a craving to be loved. He is not interested in the object of his affection as such, only in her relationship to himself. I am of course describing extreme forms of the type, but I am afraid that attentive observation reveals some degree of this attitude often enough in life. It is this type that is the victim of jealousy, and for that reason we must continue our analysis of the mental state in it.

What, then, is the secret of the doubt, the inferiority, that he seeks to remedy at the woman's hands? The obvious answer is his erotic capacity, but the matter is by no means so simple as this. Closer examination shows that the sense of deficiency is connected with an inner self-dissatisfaction, a self-criticism that betrays some conflict within the self. And actual psycho-analysis of such cases reveals the inner nature of this conflict in the unconscious itself. One can say definitely that all sense of inferiority, mental or physical, is ultimately based on a sentiment of *moral* inferiority, on a sense of guilt of which the person is often entirely unaware. This guiltiness relates fundamentally to the parents; it arises in early childhood in connection with the difficulties in development to which I alluded earlier, and few people get entirely rid of it. Mental health and freedom, with the capacity for happiness that this brings, is essentially dependent on freedom from unconscious guiltiness. With this goes a compensatory self-love. It is the self-love, self-esteem and self-respect that is wounded and damaged by the unconscious guilt, hence the person's sensitiveness to criticism and his constant demand for approval or recognition in various forms. Hence also the unsparing nature of the hatred aroused when one is betrayed; if love is pitiful, self-love is certainly pitiless. La Rochefoucauld[1] justly observed that ' la jalousie est le plus grand de tous les maux, et celui qui fait le moins de pitié aux personnes qui le causent.'

You will say that I am here describing neurotic and therefore abnormal people, but it is often easier to perceive the nature of the more subtle processes of the normal when they are placed under the magnifying glass of neurosis: in their essence the two are identical. Let us take, therefore, someone suffering in the way I have described and try to ascertain what precisely he is impelled towards. He seeks from the loved woman something vital to him that can be described by many terms, for they are all equivalent in this connection: security (from fear), certainty (from doubt), peace of mind (from the troublings of the unconscious guiltiness), potency, freedom. All these precious gifts are identified with the woman, or, rather, with the assurance of her absolute love for him and fidelity to him. I add here the word fidelity because lack of confidence always sets up a throw-back, what we call a regression, to earlier stages in the development of the love instinct. The two features of this that concern us here are, first, the regression to the childish desire to be loved in place of the desire to love, and, secondly, the insistence on the lowly instinct of possessiveness, and so, on exclusive possession of the object. One begins to see now how feverishly important the woman's fidelity is to such a man. To lose it is not simply to lose the most desired thing that the world outside can give, it is also to lose the confidence in one's own personality. This is the fear that underlies jealousy. But there is even worse than this. The loss in question risks in such a person exposing the moral inferiority and guiltiness that is the primary cause of the lack of confidence; and this is something that no human being can endure and towards the concealment of which most of our strivings are directed. Unless he rapidly takes steps to protect himself against it, the next stage in the jealousy situation would be shame. To quote

[1] La Rochefoucauld, ' Maximes,' mdiii.

again La Rochefoucauld:[1] ' On a honte d'avouer que l'on ait de la jalousie.' Socially also a jealous lover or husband mostly cuts a ridiculous figure. France is perhaps the only civilised country where this is less so and where there is even a certain approval of jealousy if it is cast on a sufficiently tragic scale. Jealous people take full advantage of this. Certainly there would be fewer crimes of passion —i.e., of jealousy—in France were it not that the jealous person has a certain confidence that he can in this way obtain social sympathy and approval and so ease the pangs of shame and guilt that threaten to emerge behind his manifest desires. The psychological process can be described quite simply. The more wicked and dastardly he can make out the conduct of the other persons concerned to be the more is he relieved from responsibility; the onus and odium are on them, not on himself. He has lost what was necessary to his peace of mind, but there is an alternative way open to him to obtain this— namely, by displacing his unconscious dislike and disapproval of himself on to the object of affection. This is one reason why the persistence of the jealous person produces at times an acute impression of someone who actually wants to be assured that the betrayal has taken place. He almost implores the woman to assure him that this is so and is obviously dissatisfied when she denies it, however truthfully. At this stage it is not so much the betrayal that he cannot endure, but the state of uncertainty. In the most classic case in literature, Shakespeare's ' Othello,' we find this vividly expressed:

> ' I had been happy, if the general camp,
> Pioneers and all, had tasted her sweet body,
> So I had nothing known.'

One sees from these considerations that such a man has two alternative and competing ways of attempting to solve his unconscious conflict, or, put in simpler language, of achieving a stable self-confidence. The one is by being assured that he is loved, the other is by finding some justification to hate. The one closed to him is the normal one of loving. Of his two methods certainly the fundamental one, to which he constantly recurs, is the solution by means of being loved, ideally by the woman who most reverses the rôle of the forbidding mother. Unfortunately, however, quite apart from external chances of fate, there is an internal tendency that can interfere seriously with this proposed solution. For there is often a fear of being loved too greatly, a fear of having his person-

[1] La Rochefoucauld, ' Maximes,' cccclxxii.

ality ' possessed ' by the love object, which really means ' disapproved of.' In this case the cure would be worse than the disease; the very thing that was meant to restore his self-confidence threatens to take away the little he has. There is thus what is called an ambivalent attitude towards the idea of being loved, a craving for it and a dread of it; it represents at once the highest security and the greatest danger. It is this ambivalent attitude that renders the position of such a person so insecure and predisposes him to the pangs of jealousy. If it is not strong then jealousy will not arise unless there is a reasonable cause, but it will then be exaggerated; if it is strong, jealousy will arise in any event, even if imaginary grounds for it have to be invented.

Traces of this ambivalent attitude are common enough and account for the apprehension of marriage and postponement of it that a majority of young men display. It is, as I have just remarked, stronger in those disposed to jealousy. This did not escape the observation of the master-psychologist, Shakespeare. Othello, at the moment of his elopement, says:

> ' But that I love the gentle Desdemona,
> I would not my unhoused free condition
> Put into circumscription and confine
> For the seas' worth.'

In an interesting sub-variety of the type the apprehension is hidden beneath a compensatory mask of over-confidence. Schnitzler, in his play ' Paracelsus,' has described this type excellently, and has very clearly shown how the concealed lack of confidence with its concomitant jealousy may nevertheless emerge in certain circumstances. In the play these are provided by the hypnotist's revealing the buried thoughts of infidelity in the wife's mind, thoughts which hardly pass a normal range but the knowledge of which is quite enough to disturb the husband's equanimity. The hypnotist, realising the significance of insecurity in this connection, plays on the husband's fears by alternatively arousing and allaying his suspicions until his mental equilibrium quite breaks down. Whereupon he admonishes him on the mistake of being over-confident— *i.e.*, of gratifying his self-love at the expense of love for his wife. We thus see that the insecure attitude under discussion may lurk where it is least expected.

After this excursus into the realm of neurotic jealousy we may now return to the possibility of finding some unitary formula that will unite the extremes of so-called normal jealousy on the one hand and delusional or insane jealousy on the other. I have purposely chosen the neurotic jealousy for our investigation, because it stands midway between these two extremes and shows the characteristics of both: it is both an exaggeration of the normal and an adumbration of the insane. You will remember that the salient feature of the insane type was the projection outwards of repressed homosexual desires. How does this idea agree with the psychology of the other two? Well, when I pointed out that the neurotic man attempts to achieve potency through the method of becoming loved instead of expressing it by the usual way of loving I might just as well have said that he seeks to achieve it by inverting his sex—*i.e.*, his sexual attitude. Naturally this change varies greatly in extent and may be in no wise apparent except to those who know how to appreciate slight indications; it is, for instance, commonly masked by the vehemence of the pleadings and cravings. Nevertheless that is the essence of the change that has taken place in the unconscious. By it is avoided the responsibility of claiming the right to what may be called the primary desires, those pertaining to the person's own sex, for, owing to the incest attachment, these are the most deeply forbidden of all. If this inversion is carried up to a certain point, and responded to— *i.e.*, sanctioned—by the woman, the man acquires all the confidence of which he is capable. If, however, it passes beyond this point, in which case the woman assumes a masculine meaning in the man's eyes (this being often contributed to by his tendency to select women with a somewhat masculine inclination), then fear is aroused, the original fear of deprivation which started the whole difficulty in childhood. His defence against this is flight. The commonest step to be taken first is to develop impulses of infidelity so as to free himself from what he now feels to be a threatening bondage. Much more marital infidelity is of neurotic origin than is generally supposed; it is not a sign of freedom or potency, but quite the reverse. This tendency is in itself one of the factors leading to jealousy, as I explained earlier, for it is often projected on to the wife and she is suspected of impulses which are perhaps being repressed in the man. The further step in the flight is in the homosexual direction. What is the real meaning of this? The ultimate source of the fear and guilt that lie behind all these reactions is the relationship to another potential man and it is derived from the boy's attitude towards his father. So long as there is an unconscious fixation on childish attitudes it is hard for him to picture a woman quite apart from another man to whom she secretly belongs; this is simply another way of saying that he cannot refrain from reproducing the situation of childhood when the woman he loved belonged to another man who was never far away. The homosexual tendency we have noted is really an impulse to placate this ' other man '—*i.e.*, the father—by identifying himself with the woman, by replacing his masculine attitude towards the mother by a feminine one towards the father. In his love life he needs, as I indicated formerly, a certain masculinity in the woman; this is the father she carries about with her. The woman's love protects him from his guilt and the fear of the father. If this love is unsuccessful he has to reproduce a triangular situation, often delusionally, so as to deal along homosexual lines with the father. If the love is less unsuccessful, he is fairly safe until a rival appears on the scene. The situation then becomes intolerable to him. Instead of reacting in a manly way by using his love of the woman to make her happy, and devoting himself to this sole aim, he becomes concerned with the man rather than the woman, and with her attitude towards him and the other man rather than with her personality itself. He reproaches her with not loving him enough. Psychologically this means a reproach that she no longer by her love protects him from the feared and hated father.

If matters go further he protects himself against his fear and guilt by developing anger. You will remember that I described the three psychological stages in jealousy as consisting first of the fear of loss, secondly of shame and wounded self-esteem that is derived from the unconscious guiltiness, and thirdly of anger which protects him against both by justifying his hatred, putting him in the right and thus once more restoring his self-esteem.

Whether this anger will be directed more against the woman or against the man depends on the level to which his psychosexual development has proceeded. If the inhibition is a deep one, so that the homosexual solution has gone far, then he will turn on the woman and in certain cases will even kill her. If he has proceeded further along the normal line of development, his fear of the father is less and his aggressive opposition to him will be allowed to express itself against the rival.

I have for the sake of simplicity considered the psychological problems of jealousy in terms of the man, but there is little to add about the woman's problems because they are essentially of the same order. The source of the conflicts in childhood is the same, as are also the attempted solution by sexual inversion and the consequent dependence on the partner's approval. For both physiological and psychological reasons the woman is normally—*i.e.*, usually—more dependent on this approval than is the man, and this I take to be the essential reason why women are so much more prone to jealousy than men.

I should like now to sum up in a few words the gist of what I have had to say. It is my experience that jealousy is a much less normal phenomenon than is commonly supposed, that for the greater part it rests on an abnormal and neurotic basis. It betokens a failure in the development of the capacity to love, a lack of self-confidence due ultimately to unconscious guiltiness that has not been overcome from childhood days, and an undue dependence on the love object that indicates a tendency in the direction of sex inversion. This last feature becomes plain enough in insane jealousy, but I consider it is present in a milder degree in the other forms also. In short, jealousy is a sign of weakness in love, not of strength; it takes its source in fear, guilt and hate rather than in love.

CHAPTER XVII

PSYCHO-ANALYSIS AND MODERN MEDICINE [1]

THE word ' modern ' is introduced into the title of this address to indicate an important change that has come over medicine in the past twenty or thirty years. Nowadays stress is laid far more on the functional and dynamic aspects of disease than on the more static aspects of any ' lesions ' that may be concerned. One may describe this change as a closer approach to reality. The capacity for functioning—present and future—has become the practical issue of clinical medicine, the criterion by which disease is estimated: a heart or liver is bad if it is working badly or is likely to work badly. The advance made in clinical psychology is along a parallel line to this. Psycho-analysis, which is the essence of modern clinical psychology, lays stress on the active functioning of the personality for its criterion of the severity of any mental disorder. More than this, it conceives of such disorder in terms not of lesions or labelled states, but of dynamic, striving impulses in the mind. Its psychopathology is cast throughout in dynamic terms, even to the problems of ætiology. Just as modern medicine goes beyond the static picture of lesions and seeks to understand the disturbance in organic function, so does psycho-analysis pass by the older mental categories of perception, cognition, etc., and seek to understand the dynamic processes of the mind—the motivation, purposes, and tendencies that produce a particular mental attitude or reaction.

I do not propose to give here any account of psycho-analysis, for many are now accessible.[2] My object is rather to comment on some aspects of the contact between it and general clinical medicine. We may consider three features here: the assistance psycho-analysis gives in dealing with a hitherto obscure field of clinical medicine; the light it throws on the interaction of mind and body in cases of organic disease; and the extent to which it is widening the field of medical practice.

---

[1] An address delivered before the Paddington Medical Society. Published in *The Lancet*, January 6, 1934.

[2] See, for instance, Helene Deutsch, ' Psycho-Analysis of the Neuroses,' 1932; Freud, ' Introductory Lectures on Psycho-Analysis,' 1929, and ' New Introductory Lectures on Psycho-Analysis,' 1933; Ernest Jones, ' Papers on Psycho-Analysis,' 3rd edition, 1923; Karin Stephen, ' Psycho-Analysis and Medicine,' 1933.

Clinical Psychology

That one branch of medicine did not, until recently, share in the enormous advance general medicine had made in the past century is well known. I refer, of course, to psychological medicine, and particularly to the vast field of neurotic disorder. How large this is cannot easily be computed, but I have many times known experienced practitioners estimate the neurotic complaints and suffering for which they are consulted, irrespective of whether organic disease is present or not, as varying between 60 and 90 per cent.—at all events the large majority. Even if we say that the body is one half of the organic personality and the mind the other half, then it follows that general medicine—by studying physiology and pathology—offers the possibility of understanding one half, clinical psychology the other half. Those who reflect on this state of affairs, feeling their helplessness in the face of it, have naturally disliked their ignorance of what it all signifies and have automatically adopted some attitude to give them some ease of mind in the matter. One common attitude is simply to deny the significance of it, to depreciate in all possible ways the importance of mental suffering. How easy it is to overlook the profound loathing that lies behind an hysterical vomiting, the unendurable tension that can express itself only in a compulsive tic, the fear and hate behind ejaculatio præcox, or the murderous impulses masked by an agoraphobia. Such practitioners casually recommend a patient tortured with obsessions to play golf or to go for a sea cruise; more troublesome hysterical patients are immured in nursing-homes, where a hypothetical malnutrition of the brain—more imaginary than the actual trouble from which the patient is suffering—is remedied by the administration of milk and phosphates. When the futility of such methods becomes too evident then the practitioner is only too apt to fall back on moral disapprobation, and abusive words are spoken of the patient's laziness, obstinacy, and general moral turpitude— a mode of treatment not much more effective than the first one.

Over this vast field psycho-analysis offers the medical profession just what it lacks—both understanding of these disorders and the power of dealing with them. The trouble is that the profession is as yet only very imperfectly aware of its lack. Having acquired its own rough technique for avoiding psychotherapeutics it tends to resent being told that neurotic disorders can be both understood and cured, since this necessitates the taking of a deal of trouble. To accept this news puts a much greater responsibility on the practitioner than he used to feel when he could persuade himself that neuroses either did not exist or that the patient was only to be blamed for them.

MENTAL PAIN

In the symptomatology of somatic disorders pain occupies a peculiarly central position. When the danger signal of pain is presented no one can be satisfied until he has ascertained the significance and cause of it. Now bodily pain can be masked in many ways, for the body automatically does what it can—by, for instance, inhibiting certain movements, etc.—to diminish any tendency to pain. And the same is true of the mind. Mental pain when acute is called unhappiness; perhaps a better word would be simply ' dis-ease ' in the original sense of this. When a patient is uneasy of mind we are faced with a problem. But the mind is far more ingenious than is the body in masking pain and thus assisting the practitioner's tendency to discount its central symptom of disorder. The importance of unhappiness runs parallel to the patient's strong motives for depreciating and diminishing it in any way possible. In its most acute forms, for instance, in the agony of agitated melancholia, it is of course not to be overlooked. But there are so many ways in which the practitioner can be misled, apart from his own proclivities in this direction, that most mental pain or disease is overlooked; one may unhesitatingly assert that it would be a gross exaggeration to say that even 5 per cent. of it gets appreciated at its true value.

All neurotic symptoms come about in the endeavour to escape some underlying mental pain. One class is so effective as to be well known for this very feature. That is the remarkable phenomenon where mental disturbances are replaced by physical ones, the ' conversion ' or somatic form of hysteria; what the French call ' la belle indifférence des hystériques ' illustrates the success of the manœuvre. Even more astonishing are the cases where mental dis-ease is marked by its very contrary, by forced and excessive gaiety, by various deceptive forms of pseudo-happiness, and so on. It is a daily occurrence to hear of the last tragedy of all, suicide, happening when just before the victim gave the impression of being ' in the best of spirits.'

Instincts and Conflicts

Psycho-analysis finds the ultimate source of mental trouble—whether neurotic or psychotic—in a disorder of the instinctive life. And of all mental processes it is the instincts—the inborn endowment of the mind—that lie nearest to both the psychological and the biological way of thinking. If we try to picture the physical correlative of the instincts, which as psycho-somatic manifestations they must surely have, we would nowadays do so in terms of biochemistry, the characteristic feature of modern medicine, rather than in those of the static histological studies of the cortex so hopefully pursued thirty years ago. The more simple, and almost reflex, instincts, such as appetite for food, rarely get disordered in any primary fashion, though of course they are often secondarily involved in disorders arising elsewhere. The instincts that matter in the present connection all concern our relations with other human beings. They may usefully be divided into two groups: those displaying a positive attitude towards our fellow-beings, such as sexual, social, and friendly impulses; and those displaying a negative one, such as aversion, fear, hate, disgust, flight, or quarrelsomeness. An interesting combination of the two is presented by the moral group: this displays both positive elements, such as honesty, loyalty, sense of duty, and so on, and also negative ones, notably the tendency to criticise adversely, to condemn, or even to persecute. In psychopathology the instincts of most concern are those of sexuality, hate, fear, and morality; but, since the last can probably be resolved into derivatives of the others, we are left with the three of chief note.

Now it is interesting to observe that each of these instincts, whether positive or negative in kind, may manifest itself in one of two opposite ways, which may be called sthenic or asthenic respectively. The sthenic effects are bracing and stimulating; the asthenic effects enervating and debilitating. A man may, for example, be firm and determined with a cold, hard hatred, or he may be ineffectively trembling with anger. Similarly fear may make every muscle taut and ready, every sense alert, and the mind at its highest pitch of quick response to thought; on the other hand, it can notoriously paralyse every function. Whether the operation of an instinct leads to harmonious effectiveness or to disintegration appears to depend on one central factor—namely, on whether it is acting as an expression of the personality approved of by the self or, on the contrary, in opposition to important constituents of the personality. We call it ego-syntonic in the former case, ego-dystonic in the latter. It is of some theoretical interest, and also of some diagnostic value in practice, that prominent physiological accompaniments of emotion —sweating, trembling, tachycardia, and the like—occur mainly with ego-dystonic manifestations of instinct activity. From these simple considerations we begin to see the enormous importance of *mental conflict*, a conception which occupies a central position not only in psycho-analysis, but in all modern psychopathology. What this word connotes furnishes the key to the understanding of most problems of the psychoneuroses, of the psychoses, and even of normal psychology. Emotions, also depressing ones, may be stirred by other causes than conflict: strain, grief, anxiety, and so on. But distress does not itself constitute neurosis. On the other hand, closer examination will show that it is being intensified by some associated conflict. It is, of course, easier to ascribe mental trouble to simple and obvious factors, but it is seldom correct to do so. Thus none of the endless cases of ' nervous breakdown due to overwork ' is really brought about by this factor—it is invariably associated with some hidden source of conflict.

These intrapsychical conflicts, even those assuming an apparently current form, all originate during the early development of the mind. Certain internal antagonisms and incompatibilities then established have never since been resolved. In fact the method adopted for dealing with them excludes the possibility of solution, since it consists largely in accepting them as insoluble and merely building up a series of defences, insulating one part of the mind from the other, and so on. In this fashion it is hoped to keep at bay those instincts that appear to be antagonistic or dangerous to the ego. Such methods, in which *psychological repression* plays a large part, have a certain amount of success, but always at a cost which varies from one individual to another and in the same individual from one period of life to another. Something may be observed of the effects of these deep conflicts, particularly when they produce distressing neurotic or psychotic troubles, but the conflicts themselves are invisible to both the observer and the patient, since they take place in what nowadays is termed the *unconscious* region of the mind. The period when they are generated is always the first three or four years of life, after which the structure of the personality has been estab-lished for good or ill. Usually medical practitioners take note of a current situation, grief, disappointments, etc., or else fly to an explanation in heredity. The paramount importance of the intervening period of early development is commonly overlooked, and was so altogether until Freud directed attention to it. And yet that important events must take place in those early years should not be surprising when we remember that the individual child has in the first five years of life to accomplish the transition from the animal to civilised man, to achieve in that short time what has taken mankind anything from 50,000 to 500,000 years.

The central content of the repressed impulses may be summed up in two words: incest and murder. When we reflect that these refer to loved parents, that bitter hostility has to fight against the strongest feelings of dependence and affection, it is not astonishing that no easy solution can be found. On the physical side also there are many bewildering ideas with which the young child has to grapple: the problems of cleanliness, clashing with the extraordinary significance that excretory processes have for the infant; the instinctive knowledge of coitus, with the unknown dangers accompanying the idea of penetration; the sex differences, with their implication of castration. Small wonder that no child escapes an 'infantile neurosis,' tantrums, fears, eating difficulties, destructiveness, etc., manifestations which every adult does his best to discount. If one describes the unconscious conflicts in this sphere of repressed impulses as essentially taking place between love and hate, or between the sexual impulse and fear, one will cover a great deal of ground by this brief generalisation.

The course of *symptom-formation* in psychopathology is of peculiar interest, being much more circuitous than one would expect. If the defences built up in infancy against the unconscious conflicts are effective enough then no manifest neurosis need exist, though some measure of inhibition is always to be found. The occasion for the onset of a clinical neurosis is most often some form of privation or thwarting. This is usually an external thwarting, though in one interesting circumstance—namely, when a person gives way at the height of success—it has an internal source (the forbiddenness of success). In any event the occurrence comes to have an internal meaning, to represent punishment, as if it were an internal forbidding due to guilt or fear. Misfortune is always taken in a moral sense; the person (or race) adopts an attitude of moral condemnation either towards himself or others. Then the latent unconscious conflict is reactivated: thwarting and forbidding versus the forbidden impulses. The latter 'regress' to their original infantile form, and the unconscious builds an imaginary (hallucinatory) wish-fulfilment of them. The clinical symptoms represent—in a symbolic or masked way—the compromise between this primitive wish-fulfilment and the forbidding and repressing agencies of the mind.

I will not dwell longer on these rather complicated matters, but I wished to lay stress on the essential importance of infantile unconscious conflicts in relation to the problems of psychopathology, and to indicate that only by exposing them fully and finding some solution of them can one hope to bring about a radical cure of the distressing maladies they so often generate.

PSYCHO-ANALYSIS AND BODILY DISEASE

The second way in which psycho-analysis has an important bearing on medical practice is in relation to bodily disease. It must be rare for bodily disease to last long without its becoming complicated by some form of neurosis, and the question arises of the precise relation between the two conditions. Bodily disease would seem to have three main effects on the mind, and each of them may in turn set up a complex train of reactions.

Deprivation.—In so far as bodily disease produces manifestations that the patient can perceive, whether active symptoms or merely restriction of strength, movement, etc., it imposes limits on his previous freedom and well-being. This deprivation may then serve as a starting-point of a neurotic development in the way I indicated previously when speaking of privation in general. It is accepted by the unconscious mind as a punishment for guilty impulses, an attitude which may become conscious among unsophisticated people, as when they offer sacrifices and make atonements during an epidemic to avert the wrath of God at their sins. Compensatory phantasies are stirred in the unconscious, the purport of which is to deny the guilt or defy the punishment. These reverberate into the deepest layers of primary conflict, and the neurotic symptoms resulting therefrom are attempts to express a compromise between the two sides of the conflict. Perhaps the commonest clinical result is where the physical symptom is directly 'exaggerated'—*i.e.*, intensified by the addition of neurotic suffering. Pain is commonly so intensified, a fact which often gives rise to practical difficulties in estimating its clinical significance. A rheumatic arm may develop an hysterical anæsthesia or paresis, and there is the whole gamut of conversion phenomena to choose from.

Fear.—It is not possible for any affliction of the body to occur without its stirring some degree of fear in the unconscious, and often enough a certain amount of it penetrates through to consciousness. Even the very thought of such affliction, without its being actually present, is often enough to stir fear, as witness the extensive series of pathophobias (among which dread of syphilis and cancer are assuredly the most frequent). The very word ' heal ' means to make ' whole '—*i.e.*, to restore the threatened integrity of a unity and prevent the loss of any part. Psycho-analysis has thrown much light on the nature of this fear. The unconscious apprehends any affliction of the body, notably accidents and surgical operations, but also simple diseases, as assaults the ultimate aim of which is mutilation. And the essence of the mutilation is damage to an erotic organ, most typically castration or destruction of the womb. These irrational fears are again connected with infantile guilt, and so go to reinforce the factor of deprivation I mentioned earlier.

Opportunity for Suffering.—Suffering plays a very remarkable and complex part in the human economy, and it has been the subject of extensive psycho-analytic research. In spite of the natural and powerful revulsion of the mind against any suffering, a revulsion which has led to the elaborating of many forms of defence, nevertheless certain agencies in the mind have not failed to exploit certain forms of suffering—probably as a protection against others. It may, for example, be made to minister to the deep need for self-punishment which is so much more prevalent than is recognised. The tendency to self-punishment, which may express itself physically by avoidable accidents, etc., or—more often—in the various subtle ways of self-thwarting in life, has as its purpose the allaying or neutralising of the unconscious sense of guilt, one of the most intolerable forms of suffering. Then, again, the painful sting of punishment, misfortune, and suffering is often dealt with by ' libidinising ' the act or process in question—*i.e.*, by investing it with erotic feeling. One form of this is familiar as the sexual perversion of masochism, where suffering, pain, or humiliation is sought, not for its own sake, but for the sake of the accompanying erotic gratification. Every surgeon, whether he recognises them or not, must encounter many cases where the patient is secretly bent on having some operation or other under various more or less plausible pretexts, and it may happen that the situation happily coincides with some repressed trend of sadism in his own nature.

THE ENLARGED SCOPE OF MEDICINE

The third respect in which psycho-analysis bears on medical practice is the vast extension it gives to the field of practice. So much is this so that a considerable proportion of patients who apply for analysis would never have regarded their problem as coming within the ordinary medical purview. It is becoming plainer that many difficulties in life that would previously have been called social or moral problems, or thought to be due to unalterable individual peculiarities, are really in great part the product of mental complexities that fairly come into the field of psychopathology. Moreover, they can be beneficially treated by regarding them from this point of view.

The reason for this is that if a neurosis or psychosis is left to run its own course it tends to evolve through a stage of clinical symptoms and personal suffering—where also it would be recognised as in some sense ' medical '—then through a further stage of anti-social attitudes or behaviour (hatred and aversion), and to culminate in some form of pure inhibition. Inhibition is the ultimate goal; but the neurosis traverses various more or less stormy stages before reaching it. Symptoms signify unhappiness: inhibition signifies the renunciation of happiness—and of all the efficiency that goes with it.

The social difficulties I have been referring to concern these later stages of the neurosis. Perhaps the commonest example of them is marital unhappiness. In certain phases this may reveal itself in gross ' medical ' manifestations, notably impotence or anæsthesia, though even here one may remark that there are so many forms and degrees of these that they are often overlooked clinically, and further that medical practitioners commonly under-estimate both the frequency and the significance of such troubles. More often, however, sexual difficulties fall into the background of the picture, and the dissatisfaction works itself out as envy and bickering over petty matters, most often in regard to money. Regressions to infantile patterns are exceedingly common in married life; indeed in some degree they occur in the vast majority. The mate becomes unconsciously identified with the corresponding parent, and the imperfectly solved ambivalence towards that parent—with its buried hostility, anxiety, and dependence—is transferred to the mate. I am touching here on a very large theme, but what I wanted to make plain is that a large amount of so-called marital incompatibility, with its destructive effect on happiness and social efficiency, is really of psycho-pathological origin, and that this knowledge opens an extensive new field of work to the medical profession.

There are many other new fields of which the same may be said. Difficulties, inefficiencies, or even pronounced inhibition are very common in daily work, with the most serious personal and social effects. Difficulties in 'getting on' with one's fellows, perhaps especially with superiors, perhaps especially in public, or perhaps in general social life, are also exceedingly common. Sexual perversions, a subject on which there is no teaching given in our medical schools, and the very names of which are often unknown to medical practitioners, are to be found both in a manifest form and, much more often, in disguised forms that produce other manifestations such as alcoholism, drug addiction, eccentricity, etc.

I have mentioned a few of the new fields which have become more accessible to medical work since psycho-analysis has deepened our understanding of them and pointed the way to therapeutic help. It does not require any special far-sightedness to look forward to the time when, as a result of these extensions, the medical profession, particularly the medical psychologist, will play a far more important part than now in the body politic. Even the field of legislation, and of international relationships, is one where our knowledge and advice will come to be of very considerable assistance. But one must confess that at present the medical profession appears to be signally unaware of the perspective opening out before its eyes, as well as unresponsive to the vast opportunities now presented to it.

CHAPTER XVIII

THE UNCONSCIOUS MIND AND MEDICAL PRACTICE [1]

I shall divide what I have to say here into two groups: considerations bearing on the relation between the patient and the doctor, and those concerning the relation between the patient and himself, especially his disease.

Before coming to these topics themselves, however, I must first say something about the meaning of the unconscious mind in general. So immediate is the feeling of our own personality, and so intimate is our first-hand acquaintance with our thoughts and emotions, that it is exceedingly hard to bring home to oneself the idea that all this self-knowledge is only very partial, that the most important part of our conscious mind is merely a selection of what has been allowed to filter through from the unconscious mind, the primary fount of all our mental processes. Now what is this unconscious mind to which so much significance is nowadays attached since Freud's epoch-making discovery of it? To begin with, it represents our inborn instincts as they first manifest themselves in the dawning mind of the infant. But these never develop smoothly, as they seem to do with other animals. It is plain that in the past 50,000 years there have been brought about many extensive changes and modifications, if not in our inborn instincts themselves, certainly in the adult expression of them. The difficulties we perceive in the early mental development of the individual must be related to the fac. that most of these extensive changes that the race took 50,000 years to accept have to be hurriedly recapitulated in the individual in the short space of five years.

In the contact between these instincts and the outer world, and perhaps for more intrinsic reasons, difficulties and conflicts arise from the start. The apprehending of outer reality is for long preceded by a period in which the mind is ruled by phantasy, and phantasy of such a grotesque and exaggerated nature as to seem quite incredible to our conscious mind. This is one feature of the unconscious that makes it so hard to believe in the reality of its mani-

[1] An address delivered before the Swansea Division of the British Medical Association, March 31, 1938. Published in the *British Medical Journal*, June 25, 1938.

festations and still harder to take them seriously enough to appreciate their grim significance.

DEFENSIVE MECHANISMS

This phase of development is dominated by the problem of what in psychopathology is termed ' anxiety,' doubtless an expression of the remarkable activity on the part of the fear instinct. The majority of the mental changes that go on at this time consist of the building up of a large variety of defences against anxiety, and these defences, or ' mental mechanisms,' play an extremely important part throughout later life. Let me illustrate these at this point by a simple example —the reciprocal process of introjection and projection. When the infant's mind is terrified at feeling something bad, painful, and dangerous inside itself or its body, it often responds by seeking to take in something it conceives to be good and helpful from another person so as to assuage or neutralise the bad thing. I purposely say ' thing,' since the primitive mind never works in abstract terms, such as ' evil impulse,' ' hate,' etc., but always in concrete physical ones. Thus when a kind mother reassures a frightened child he does not feel that she has given him love with which to allay his terrors, but an actual part of her body, milk or flesh, which he feels to be good, helpful, and strong. This attitude of taking in or absorbing something from another person so that it is then felt to be a part of oneself is what we mean by the word ' introjection.' ' Projection ' is the reverse process. Here the mind deals with the bad thing by denying the possession of it and ascribing it to another person. I recently came across a pathetic example of this, and am sure you have all met with somewhat similar ones. A man was dying of a very painful cancer and was being given some relief by means of large doses of morphine. In a state of drug delirium he imagined it was his nurse who had the dread disease, and he uttered the most heartfelt expressions of sympathy and pity for her sufferings. Here in a critical hour the mechanism of projection succeeded perfectly in extruding from his personality all sensation of pain and distress, on the condition, however, that his unavoidable perception of them was deflected towards the outer world.

When these defensive mechanisms function imperfectly or break down, then the underlying anxiety breaks through or else there is mental pain—that is, suffering. I put at the outset these matters of anxiety and suffering, with the defences against them, in the foreground because I think this is the most instructive point of view from which to regard the various problems of psychopathology in general, and, I will add, even those of the psychology of the so-called normal as well.

Some of the defensive mechanisms are, when extensively employed, characteristic of the psychoneuroses, others of the psychoses. Neuroses and psychoses may become manifest, giving rise to specific symptoms, or they may show themselves more indirectly by producing what we call neurotic or psychotic character traits. In my opinion evidence of one or other of these conditions is to be found in every human being, and commonly enough all of them; it is simply a matter of degree. Now we know that in childhood the occurrence of manifest neurosis is universal: there is no child who escapes suffering from one or other of the familiar symptoms of night terrors, food phobias, and so on. What has only recently been appreciated is the extent to which still younger children—in the first two or three years of life—are affected by mental mechanisms especially characteristic of the psychoses. It would be inaccurate— or at all events loose language—to describe this, as some authors have done, as a psychotic stage of development. But one can at least say that in these phases the infant is more or less dominated by phantasies and convictions of a kind that, were we to encounter them in the adult, would have to be called insane delusions. Many years ago a Dutch psycho-analyst, Stärcke, startled us by asserting that the mentality of the normal is built on a psychotic basis. Nowadays, unfortunately, the sight of the world is such as to make this assertion less obviously absurd even to others than psychologists. There seems to be little doubt that there are temporal fluctuations in the extent to which these underlying mental attitudes shimmer through in social and political forms, and that we are at present in a favourable position for observing them.

The grandiose achievements that men of genius have in all ages encompassed in the spheres of art, of thought, and of science cannot but bring inspiring and elevating reflections to any contemplative mind. The sense of wonder is vastly heightened when one admits what formidable difficulties human beings encounter in the course of their development, and what an unstable basis most of them have to build on. It is extremely instructive to examine from this point of view the various institutions of civilisation, such as that of marriage, of religion, of class and caste, and—last but not least—the numerous political theories and devices of government. Such a study reveals both how complex are the methods by which man seeks to fortify himself against his inner weaknesses and also how ingenious are the ways in which he has socialised those defences.

We must now withdraw from these spacious perspectives and concentrate on the more purely clinical topics before us. I alluded to them only to indicate that we are concerned here with fundamental problems of human biology, of which neurotic troubles constitute only one aspect. I should have said ' only a minor aspect ' were it not for the important fact that we owe to the neuroses, through their greater perspicuity and accessibility, the most fruitful approach to the deeper problems of human nature. Much of the interest of psychopathology proceeds from this consideration.

Medical Neglect of Psychology

When psychological factors play such a large part in medical practice it is astonishing how little attention is devoted to them in medical circles and in the medical curriculum. It is of course very hard to estimate in precise figures the proportion of ill-health that may be ascribed to psychological disorder. A distinguished physician recently gave as his opinion that it is as high as 80 per cent., but such an estimate certainly needs closer definition. I do not know what proportion of the populace is considered to be in completely perfect physical health. I should suppose it to be a rather small minority, but I am sure that those in perfect mental health consitute a much smaller minority. Most patients, therefore, who seek medical advice present a varying combination of both mental and physical troubles. Let us look at the matter in a different way for a moment. We know that the actual distress of which a patient complains often bears no close correlation to the illness which the physician thinks necessary to treat, especially since his bias must for many reasons be heavily in favour of treating the physical condition rather than the mental. There is no doubt that a much higher percentage of the patient's complaints are psychological in nature than the diagnoses made by physicians would indicate. Not that this would necessarily signify their greater importance. The relative importance is something that has to be judged in each case. If a patient with a cancer presents also some neurotic manifestations we go straight for the cancer. On the other hand, the fact that a severe and crippling neurosis may be accompanied by some slight bodily disturbance such as indigestion does not mean that the latter should necessarily claim precedence in therapeutic attention. The rarely attained ideal would be that judgement should be passed by someone equipped to estimate the significance of both mental and physical factors. At present the mental causes of ill-health are pitifully neglected, the attention paid to them being infinitesimal in comparison with that devoted to the physical causes.

A great many reasons are given for this state of affairs, most of which contain some truth: the difficulty of acquiring an adequate knowledge of medical psychology and of applying psychotherapeutic methods, the apparent contradictions and obscurities in medico-psychological writings, the time needed for dealing with neurotic patients, and so on. It is little wonder that medicine has always hoped to evade these tasks by discovering a remediable physical ' basis ' for neurotic suffering, and that it clutches at every hint, endocrine or other, in this direction. This seems to me to be an attitude that combines an undue optimism with an undue pessimism. It is partly based on an over-medical view of psychoneurosis being a ' disease ' in the ordinary sense, the social and biological aspects not being taken into account. It is easy to see the point if one considers examples from other fields, examples that are more than analogies. Among the many problems that civilisation has to deal with one may instance social conflicts, criminality, education, and the risks of distress and destruction due to the unsatisfactory uses that many ruling politicians make of their reasoning powers. Now it is no doubt arguable from a medical point of view that the difficulties I allude to are ultimately due to lesions in the brain or malfunctioning of the ductless glands. But to sit down and wait until these somatic causes are discovered, and—what is by no means the same thing— efficacious remedies found for them, would seem to be both a policy of despair and a dream of hopefulness. A teacher who adopted any such attitude about those of his pupils who were slow at learning French or coping with arithmetic would soon be dismissed from his school on the ground that he was lazily seeking excuses to evade his duty of finding psychological solutions for the difficulties in question. It may well be that in the future we shall regard the present-day attitude of the medical profession towards psychoneurotic difficulties as similarly misplaced.

No, the real reason for the medical neglect of psychology is, in my opinion, a very simple one. It is that, just as their patients, physicians too are human beings. And by that I mean that, without in the least being aware of it, they shrink from the unconscious mind and have built up their life on the basis of more or less successful protections against it. The dark phantasies and fierce impulses and dread fears of the unconscious, carefully repressed from consciousness, are completely unknown; at the most some distant issue of them, such as irritability, insomnia, intolerance, etc., may be perceived. Anything that tends to draw one, however slightly, nearer to the unconscious is automatically avoided, and the position of security is fortified by so-called practical matter-of-fact attitudes or by any other means that may present themselves. There is no reason for supposing that members of the medical profession differ from the rest of the community in all this.

THE 'NIGHTMARE' PHENOMENON

The only remark one might add is that one particular mode of defence offers itself to them with greater readiness than to other people: I mean the chance of displacing or projecting mental phenomena on to the somatic sphere. I will quote a classic example of this, which I have studied in great detail (Jones 1931)—namely, the phenomenon called 'nightmare.' Actually this is an expression of a violent conflict between a certain unconscious sexual desire and intense fear; the admixture of these two components is infinitely varied, so that all transitions are found between the simple erotic dream, the anxious dream with seminal emission, and the pure fear dream. Until a couple of centuries ago the world saw in these manifestations the action of lecherous demons, who indeed often appear in the dream in various guises. It represented an important advance in thought when a scientific age sought for a more natural-istic explanation and contested the popular belief in devils, demons, and witches. But if ever there was a case of emptying the baby out with the bath water it was here. Medical thought discarded not only the fancied demons but also the sexual conflict that was the essential cause, and they did this by taking full advantage of their readiest projection mechanism—somatic attribution. From now on nocturnal emissions were attributed to physical tension in the seminal vesicles, prostatic or urinary pressure, and the like, while nightmares were put down to gastric pressure on the heart, intestinal toxæmia, and a large variety of other processes implicating every system of the body. In this we safely get far away from the frightful struggle between incestuous desire and castration fear that provides the actual dynamics of the phenomena. The mediæval writers, with their insistence on the *personal* sexual wishes as the causative agent, were perhaps after all nearer to the truth than modern physicians. Both used projections, on to demons or somatic processes respectively, but at least the earlier writers retained a hold on the psychological and sexual nature of the phenomena which was lost in the later medical projection.

This historical excursus will also serve to illustrate a momentous consideration to which I wish to draw special attention. It is that in medical practice we are concerned not alone with the patient's unconscious mind, with its incalculable influence on the clinical situation, but also with that of the physician. Most of all, perhaps, we are concerned with the subtle and extensive interaction of the two. On the physician's side this produces its effect not merely in the practical handling and treatment of individual patients, but in what is possibly an even more important sphere—that of diagnosis and pathology, particularly ætiology. It will, however, be easier to expound this theme after we have considered the various attitudes the patient's unconscious displays towards disease and therefore to the person treating the disease. I will next take these two topics in order: the influence of the patient's unconscious on his relation to himself (including any disease present) and on his relation to the physician.

INFLUENCE OF THE PATIENT'S UNCONSCIOUS

The first of these two topics naturally divides itself into the problem of neurosis itself and the attitude of the patient's unconscious to physical disease. To understand the latter one must have some knowledge of the former. There are fortunately many descriptions of the psychopathology of neurosis now available (Deutsch, 1932; Freud, 1929; Jones, 1938; Mitchell, 1921; Stephen, 1933), and I shall confine myself here to emphasising certain fundamental features of the condition. First of all, neurotic manifestations do not themselves constitute a disorder except in a purely clinical and descriptive sense; actually they are only the visible symptoms or signs of an underlying disorder, just as jaundice is a sign of hepatic disturbance. They result from an excessive inner *tension* which has been provoked by some intolerable thwarting or *privation*. The tension itself proceeds from an unresolved *conflict* which has often been stirred to fresh activity by some current situation. They express in a variously disguised way both sides of this conflict, and thus are always what may be termed *compromise-formations*. In the conflict the important elements are sexuality, aggression, fear, and love, but these are involved in such an extraordinarily complicated fashion that one cannot describe the two sides of the conflict in any simple terms.

These four or five sentences state in an exceedingly condensed form the most essential basis of our knowledge about the meaning of psychoneuroses; but it is a basis that has been reached only as the result of extremely detailed studies of the characteristic unconscious mechanisms that determine the structure of such formations, and the state of affairs is actually much more complex than I have just indicated. Let us look at it in another way. Thwarted and repressed impulses provide the active dynamic urge that starts everything going. These meet with opposition from other instinctive attitudes, and the conflict generates first fear, then mental pain and misery. This is the disorder itself, but then there comes into play a whole series of defences, one or two of which I mentioned earlier, and the manifest neurosis as we see it clinically is the resultant combination of all these factors, containing elements from each one of them. It expresses, therefore, something of the primary repressed impulses, something of the resulting anxiety and distress, and something of the defensive attitudes. The proportion of these varies considerably in different cases. In one the gratification of the repressed wishes is prominent, so that the neurosis brings unmistakably positive advantages to the patient, who is correspondingly loath to renounce it. In another the anxiety breaks through and dominates the clinical situation, either directly or in the form of protective phobias. In yet another case the defensive mechanisms play the largest part, and then the clinical type is apt to assume the form of what we call a character neurosis.

Factors in Neurosis Formation

It is important to distinguish between the current and the essential factors in neurosis formation, just as it is to distinguish between the exciting and essential causes of tuberculosis or heart disease. In the ætiology of neurosis we commonly, though by no means always, find current factors, such as overwork, over-excitement, privation, grief, misfortune. Yet none of these can by itself produce a neurosis. It evokes one only if certain specific conditions are present in the unconscious—namely, a serious unresolved conflict dating from childhood, one with which the current factors can become associated. The process set up is what we call ' regression.' The emotional responses reanimate the older ones and revert to an older type. This is the reason why a real cure of any neurosis necessitates the exposure of the essential childhood basis and the resolving of conflicts then left in an unsatisfactory state.

The central content of the repressed impulses may be summed up in two words: incest and murder. When we reflect that these refer to loved parents, that bitter hostility has to fight against the strongest feelings of dependence and affection, it is not astonishing that no easy solution can be found. On the physical side also there are many bewildering ideas with which the young child has to grapple: the problems of cleanliness, clashing with the extraordinary significance that excretory processes have for the infant; the instinctive knowledge of coitus, with the unknown dangers accompanying the idea of penetration; the sex differences, with their implication of castration. Small wonder that no child escapes an ' infantile neurosis,' tantrums, fears, eating difficulties, destructiveness, etc., manifestations which every adult does his best to discount.

If a neurosis proceeds successfully to its logical extreme it ends in a state of inhibition, more or less extensive according to the severity of the conflict. It seems plain that the function of a neurosis is, on the one hand, to retain in an unaltered infantile form certain repressed impulses, and on the other to keep at bay the anxiety and distress that these impulses are prone to bring in their train. It is often very remarkable what extensive inhibitions people will bear before they consider them as symptoms and seek for therapeutic help. Permanent sexual frigidity or a sexual perversion that confines gratification to the narrowest possibilities, the crippling effects of a phobia that may forbid all social life or even going out of doors (as with an agoraphobia): these and many similar restrictions are cheerfully borne if only the impulses and dread they cover are thereby successfully kept out of sight and never enter consciousness.

The Patient's Attitude towards Treatment

These considerations about the nature of neuroses enable us to understand a prominent and peculiar feature in the patient's attitude towards therapeutic help. It is of course common enough with physical disorders for there to be a conflict between patient and doctor over the question of what is to be treated. The patient naturally wishes to be relieved of whatever symptoms are giving him distress, whereas the doctor is more concerned with abolishing the cause of the symptoms than with merely alleviating them. No doubt the actual treatment will vary with the strictness of the doctor's professional code of ethics, since it is undoubtedly easier to fall in with the patient's wishes and alleviate the symptoms than to insist on giving him the trouble of having the underlying causes investigated and dealt with. Still, there is no doubt about what the medical attitude ought to be in such a situation, even if in practice doctors sometimes depart from it. Now with the neuroses the conflict between doctor and patient is much sharper. It must be very rare in organic disease for no wish for cure to exist in the patient's mind, but with neuroses this state of affairs is the rule. One may say that they constitute the only condition where the patient comes for help to sustain the disease and resists every effort to cure it.

To give up a neurosis would signify to the neurotic mind, which has not been able to encompass any alternative, to surrender certain cherished wishes and also, since this is inherently unthinkable, to dispense with the only protection it knows against the accompanying anxiety and mental misery. When a person is disturbed by neurotic symptoms his distress is only in part due to the painful effect of the symptoms themselves. What disturbs him far more is the inner feeling that his defensive systems are beginning to break down, which is indeed what the presence of manifest symptoms means. What brings him for help is his need to strengthen and reinforce these defences—that is, the neurosis itself.

This curious situation is further complicated by an even more peculiar feature—one which leads to a unique problem in therapeutics. With organic disease one can reckon not only on the patient for some will towards cure, but still more so on the part of the doctor; unless he panders to the patient's preference for the alleviation of symptoms his whole attitude is in favour of curing the condition. Now with the neuroses it is different. Here also there is agreement between doctor and patient, but unfortunately this time in the opposite direction—namely, of avoiding a cure. In a certain very important sense doctor and patient are psychologically in a similar position. Both have had to fight against their unconscious fears and to build up various complicated defences against them in the course of their early development. Both therefore show the strongest disinclination to open up these defences and expose the repressed material behind them. It is far easier to turn the other way, to discount or deny the significance of any signs of underlying emotions, to get away as far as possible from them, to strengthen and encourage what is called the ' will-power.' This is of course what the patient in particular wants, since it is the only way he knows of to combat the neurotic affliction. And, with one single exception, this also has been the aim, avowed or otherwise, of all the various methods of psychotherapy from the beginning of medical history.

Psycho-Analysis

The exception is, of course, psycho-analysis. And by psycho-analysis I mean *real* psycho-analysis, not the strange things that nowadays often pass by that name. The aim of psycho-analysis is in exactly the opposite direction to that of other forms of psychotherapy. It is to uncover and resolve the conflicts that underlie the whole neurosis. In this way it strengthens the ego, including the ' will-power,' not by the method of direct encouragement which has such palpable limitations, but by diminishing the unconscious anxieties that are the real cause of its weakness.

This procedure, however, cannot be carried out except by some-one who is prepared to face calmly the contents of his own unconscious mind, and who has had the personal experience of resolving the conflicts and anxieties in it. Without this his endeavours to help his patients would constantly be thwarted, unknown to him, by the powerful inner forces making for the opposite solution to the analytic one. At first sight no doubt it seems strange to ask that a doctor should have to undergo the same treatment as that which he proposes to employ with his patients. In no other branch of medicine is such a thing thought of. When it happens, as for instance with pulmonary tuberculosis, then certain advantages are perceived—the doctor is perhaps better able to appreciate the difficulties of the regime—but no one would dream of suggesting that the staff of a sanatorium must necessarily be tuberculous. With psycho-analysis, however, the whole situation is radically different. The very tool the analyst employs in the treatment is his own unconscious mind, and if this is not clear, perspicuous, and able to function quite smoothly he will be in the position of a histologist using a rusty and muddy microscope: everything will be distorted by artefacts.

RELATION BETWEEN THE UNCONSCIOUS MIND AND ORGANIC DISEASE

I should like now to say something about the relation between the unconscious mind and organic disease. Bodily processes are of the greatest interest to the mind, and especially so to its primitive, infantile, and unconscious layers. They are therefore one of the commonest ways by which unconscious mental attitudes find expression. We are very familiar with some forms of this—for instance, in conversion hysteria, where an unbearable loathing may express itself as chronic vomiting, or a wish to expel imaginary poison may lead to chronic colitis. But it is certain that the effects of unconscious attitudes go far beyond this, and it is at present impossible to set limits to our knowledge concerning the extent to which they may influence bodily processes. It is, for instance, probable that the greater part of ordinary dyspepsia takes its origin in this way. Much work in this direction has recently been done on very varied conditions, ranging from asthma and thyroid syndromes to duodenal ulcer.

Where, on the other hand, the organic disorder is essentially of physical origin we still have the question of how the mind reacts towards it, since this may not only influence the patient's attitude to treatment but may also exacerbate the physical condition itself or complicate it by the addition of neurotic symptoms. The unconscious invariably interprets every physical illness as a personal attack, which it colours with a projection of its own aggressivity. In other words, someone has either malevolently or sadistically assaulted the person. This, it is felt, is equivalent to introducing a bad poisonous material that will corrode all that is good within, will exhaust and drain vital material, and prevent the acquiring of beneficial sustenance. The unconscious then conceives of help in coping with the invasion in one of two ways: the doctor is either to offer something good that will neutralise the malevolent foreign body or to display a violence greater than this. We are familiar with these two broad types of treatment, psychologically regarded, and perhaps also with corresponding types of doctor. The one is illustrated by a soothing cough medicine or a gentle manipulative massage, the other by most medicines or by surgical operations. I say ' most medicines,' for it is a familiar experience that a medicine with a pleasant taste is apt to be suspected of impotency.

There are three features in organic disease that are prone to activate a latent neurosis. In the first place every form of injury or illness signifies privation or deprivation in one form or another, whether it be interference with sleep, with freedom of movement, of eating, of working, or of other activities. Now, as I remarked earlier, privation is the characteristic starting-point for all neuroses. It sets in action the typical mechanisms of regression back to infantile phantasies and wish-fulfilments with all the symbolisms and disguises that clothe neurotic processes. With the details of these we are not here concerned.

In the second place the unconscious invariably responds to any kind of physical illness or injury by generating anxiety. Some of this is of course conscious, but much more is unconscious. We know that one of the two main functions of every neurosis is to provide a barrier or support against unconscious anxiety, so that is a second way in which organic disorders stimulate any latent neurosis.

Finally, most physical illness causes either pain or some other kind of suffering, and thus provides material for the various tendencies in the unconscious that seek for suffering. This search for suffering is perhaps the most remarkable trait in human nature, being so paradoxically antibiological, but it is hardly possible to exaggerate its importance psychologically, and even the most experienced of us are constantly being surprised by its power and range. It has several sources. There is the curious component of the sexual instinct called masochism, which is far more subtle and widespread than is commonly thought. Then there is the tendency to self-punishment which plays a large part not only in neuroses but in everyday psychology. It comes from the fact that an important part of the conscience is itself unconscious, and that part is far more primitive and ruthless than the conscious part with which we are familiar, though of course even the latter can at times inflict considerable suffering and penance by remorse. Most subtle and dangerous of all, however, is the tendency of the mind, from fear and other motives, to turn its repressed aggressive impulses against itself instead of against the outer world. Suicide is of course its extreme form, but it has a thousand other manifestations. It is a motive that has always to be watched for, since in both neurosis and organic disorder it may succeed in baffling the most skilled therapeutic efforts.

The Unconscious Mind of the Doctor

I have not time to develop the interesting theme of the ways in which irregular functioning of the unconscious mind of the doctor may interfere with his clinical judgement in making diagnoses and deciding on treatment, but I am persuaded that the potential skill of most doctors is considerably reduced by such aberrant activity. The commonest example is probably the way in which doctors share popular superstitions about the danger of cold air, but the grimmest example of all is, of course, when the patient's death results from such mistakes; but short of this I think one could trace more errors in medical practice to unconscious interference with knowledge than to lack of knowledge itself.

Conclusion

In summing up I would repeat the two main contentions of my paper: that there are few cases in which the unconscious mind of the patient does not play a part in the clinical situation, and, further, that the fact of the doctor possessing an unconscious mind is one the importance of which is commonly overlooked.

References

Deutsch, Helene (1932), 'Psycho-Analysis of the Neuroses,' London.
Freud, Sigm. (1929), 'Introductory Lectures in Psycho-Analysis,' London.
Jones, Ernest (1931), 'On the Nightmare,' Hogarth Press, London.
Jones, Ernest (1938), 'Papers on Psycho-Analysis,' Fourth Edition, London.
Mitchell, T. W. (1932), 'Psychology of Medicine,' London.
Stephen, Karin (1933), 'Psycho-Analysis and Medicine,' Cambridge.

CHAPTER XIX

PSYCHO-ANALYSIS AND PSYCHIATRY[1]

Without wishing to make an invidious list of the many institutions in America devoted to psychiatry, I think it may be said that this is the third great institute of psychiatry to be inaugurated in this country, the third of the institutes which, by the magnificence of their foundation and the searching spirit that informs them, are destined to arrest attention even beyond the world of psychiatry. It was my privilege, nearly seventeen years ago, to participate in the opening exercises of the first of them, the since renowned Phipps Clinic. The honour I now feel at being invited to play a part on the present occasion moves me to unburden myself of some general reflections, but they are such as have a direct bearing on the proper theme of this address. On revisiting this country for the first time since that event at Baltimore, I cannot refrain from reviewing in my mind the changes that have taken place in that time in the world of American psychiatry, a world to which I once myself belonged.

It is not my duty here to comment on the important technical advances in knowledge that have taken place in these years, but it might be of interest if I related my impression of three important events that have occurred in the general position of psychiatry in America. The most outstanding of these, and one on which this country has every right to congratulate itself, is what might be called the social consolidation of the profession of psychiatry. So much impressed is the outside observer by this that it does not seem unmerited to say that America has actually created a new profession. In a very important respect one can almost say that the profession of psychiatry does not exist in any other country in the world. You, and still more my European colleagues, may be astonished at such a statement, but I make it because the respect in which it is true is in my judgement of far-reaching significance. It is this: If we consider for a moment the three great fields of the psychoses, of the psychoneuroses, and of so-called normal psychology, with its vast

---

[1] Address delivered at the opening exercises of the Institute of Psychiatry, Columbia University, New York, December 4, 1929. Published in *The State Hospital Quarterly*, January, 1930, and in *Mental Hygiene*, 1930, vol. xiv.

social implications, then one is bound to admit that the presence of a relationship between them is perceived much more widely in America than in Europe. You observe I say ' more widely,' not ' more deeply,' for the scientific study of this relationship has certainly been carried much further in Europe, even though only by a small group of workers. Still, the fact remains that in America both the medical profession and society at large have accorded a much more general recognition than elsewhere to the community of interests subsisting between these branches of study. In Europe, broadly speaking, the psychoses are the care of the psychiatrists; the psychoneuroses are vigorously claimed by both neurologists and asylum psychiatrists, the battle being complicated by the appearance of a small, but increasing, number of specialists in that department; and academic psychology—with minor exceptions, such as limited contributions to industrial psychology—remains as aloof from the concerns of mankind as it does in America.

The importance I attach to the observation just made is this: I am convinced that progress in any one of the three fields in question can be only very partial and limited until the relationship between them is fully explored. It is easy to pay lip service to the existence of this relationship, but it is quite another matter to take it seriously and investigate its deeper meaning. Yet only in this way can we come to understand that the normal, the neurotic, and the psychotic have reacted differently to the same fundamental difficulties of human development, and to penetrate into the exact nature of these difficulties. Parenthetically, I wish to express here my conviction that the strategic point in the relationship between the three fields is occupied by the psychoneuroses. So-called normality represents a much more devious and obscure way of dealing with the fundamentals of life than the neuroses do, and it is correspondingly a much more difficult route to retrace. The psychoses, on the other hand, present solutions so recondite and remote that it is very hard for the observer to develop a truly empathic attitude towards them, and unless this can be done, any knowledge remains intellectualistic, external, and unfruitful. If a man's main interest is in the psychology of either the normal or the psychotic, it is fairly safe to predict that his understanding of the deeper layers of the mind will remain strictly limited. In America, however, thanks to the broad conception of psychiatry there prevailing, a psychiatrist is less exposed to these dangers. Society will see to it that he is chiefly occupied with the problems of the psychoneuroses, though his interest will extend along the mental-hygiene movement in the one direction and into the field of the psychoses in the other. The problems of social adaptation, or maladaptation, will therefore always stand in the foreground of his attention.

It would be tempting to inquire how this broad conception of psychiatry came to be developed only in America. It is definitely a matter of the last twenty years. I am not familiar enough with the details of growth in this period to venture a firm opinion on the point, but my impression is that the change has been brought about by a developing attitude on the part of society in general quite as much as by the influence of a few outstanding personalities. It appears, in fact, to be an expression of the American social conscience. It is easy for Europeans to wax satirical over this conscience, for assuredly the raw guilt out of which it is evolved has at times produced manifestations grotesque enough to warrant any satire. But to ignore this feature would be a venial error compared with the blunder it would be to ignore or underestimate the vast positive value of that social conscience. After all, perhaps the greater part of social progress emanates from an uneasy conscience, from dissatisfaction with a state of affairs unpleasant to our feelings or repugnant to our cultural sentiments. In the present case, for instance, the widespread social recognition that the psychiatrist's work—whether it is concerned with mental hygiene, with the therapy of the psychoneuroses, or with the care of the psychotic— constitutes an essential unity would seem to have proceeded in large measure from a dawning realisation that there exists in the community a vast amount of mental suffering to which attention needs to be directed.

The mention of the word ' suffering ' induces another reflection. It is noteworthy that, whatever pressure may have come from the side of society, the psychiatric movement in America to which I am now referring is essentially a medical one, is indeed an immense extension of the scope of the medical profession. It is not at first sight evident why this had to be so. *A priori* it might have seemed just as likely, and even more logical, if the increasing light thrown on mental problems had come from the side of the pure psychologist. Just as in physiology, where an accurate knowledge of the normal processes of bodily functions must precede the study of their derangements in disease, it might have been supposed that the proper order would have been for psychologists to obtain insight into the structure and development of the normal mind and then for this knowledge to be applied to the investigation of various departures from the normal. The reverse of this has happened. Almost all insight into the deeper structure and development of the mind has come from psychopathology, and it is only through this knowledge that we are beginning to understand something of the more obscure problems of the normal mind. It may sound paradoxical, but I venture to predict that in a not far distant future psychopathology, particularly of the psychoneuroses, will constitute the standard study of psychology, the basis from which the student will proceed later to the more obscure and difficult study of the so-called normal, and moreover I should not be altogether surprised if America achieved this consummation before any other country.

There are two objective grounds why this prediction is a very safe one to make. Investigation of the deeper layers of the mind has shown irrefragably that the basic elements out of which our minds are developed persist with the psychoneurotic—in the unconscious, it is true—in their original form to a much greater extent than they do with the normal, and further that they present themselves in a magnified and perspicuous aspect as if under a clear lens, so that from every point of view they are far more accessible to examination there than with the normal. Fundamental complexes and mechanisms, the effects of which radiate throughout the whole mind, can be very plainly demonstrated in the psychoneurotic when the same processes can often be only dimly inferred in the normal, and yet anyone who urges the objection that there is a qualitative difference between the two classes is merely displaying his omission to investigate the relationship between them.

The second ground on which the prediction can be based is even more interesting. We know nowadays that the reason why psychology has lagged so extraordinarily behind all other branches of science is because there exist in the mind—both, be it noted, of the subject and the object—the most formidable obstacles which interpose themselves in the path of any exploration designed to penetrate below the surface. Unlike any other man of science, therefore, the psychologist is from the beginning cut off from the object of his study—the human mind. So far as our present experience goes, there is only one motive strong enough to overcome these obstacles —that of wishing to be delivered of suffering; even the keenest scientific curiosity offers only a very partial substitute for this motive. Now in the history of the world the theme of suffering has been the special concern of three classes of men: of poets, of priests, and of physicians. Until recently it has been the first of these three, the poet, who has contributed most to our understanding of mental suffering, and we owe some of our most precious insight to his flashes of genius. But he is, after all, primarily concerned, not with the understanding of suffering, but with the transmuting of it into beauty or whatever else would raise it to another plane. Few have thought more profoundly about the function of poetry than Keats, and he tells us:

> '. . . they shall be accounted poet kings
> Who simply tell the most heart-easing things.'

The priest's interest, too, has been mainly therapeutic. Starting with a vested interest in a particular cure, he has been chiefly engaged in transmitting his cure to those in need. Nevertheless, the more profound theologians, having—so to speak—a scientific interest in their work, have also furnished us with much knowledge concerning the nature and sources of suffering. They have rightly laid especial stress in this connection on the importance of moral problems, notably on the problem of evil—nowadays called the problem of the sense of guilt. The physician likewise did not proceed very far so long as his attitude was a purely therapeutic one, showing once more how the passion for therapeutics—laudable as it is on humanitarian grounds—has often proved the bane of medicine and has blocked progress in real prevention and cure based on knowledge. Those over-anxious to heal cannot pause to find out how to do so. It is only when the desire to relieve suffering was infused by the scientific thirst for knowledge that we began to have serious insight, not only into the meaning of all this suffering, but— what is still more important—into the dynamic factors that move both the depths and the surface of our minds. In this achievement there is, in my opinion, one man's name that will be for ever pre-eminent, and that is the name of Freud, now so contemned, but in the future to be honoured above all his contemporaries.

This expansion of psychiatry into what were previously non-medical fields was either stimulated by or, at all events, responded to the special social sense of the American people. It is appropriate, however, in addressing the new Psychiatric Institute of the New York State Hospitals to remember that, although the names of workers elsewhere—such as Dr. White, of Washington, and Dr. Putnam and Dr. C. Macfie Campbell, of Boston—will not be forgotten in this connection, the main inspiration for the broadening and humanising of the conception of psychiatry in America emanated from the forerunner of this institute—namely, the Psychiatric Institute of the New York State Hospitals, situate on Ward's Island. That inspiration will always be associated with the names of Dr. Adolf Meyer and Dr. August Hoch, together with their brilliant pupils, Drs. A. A. Brill and George H. Kirby, who now, by their presence on the staff of Columbia University, link the two institutions that have co-operated in founding this impressive and promising institute. In saying this I would not have you think that I underestimate the important part played, particularly in the mental-hygiene movement, by lay co-operation. Although I think it desirable that the movement in question should always remain essentially a medical one, I am not one of those who think that laymen should be jealously excluded from psychiatric work, for I have ample experience of their value even on the therapeutic side itself.

The second event of the past few years to which I wished to make a short reference was the use American authorities made of psychopathology and psychology in the war. It is well known that this was more extensive and more enlightened in America than in any European country, and I mention it here only as an illustration to confirm the thesis just put forward of the remarkable extent to which psychiatry in America has become associated with the national life and has ceased to be regarded as a narrow speciality.

The third event is perhaps the most interesting of all and will bring me closer to the theme proper of this address. I mean the extent to which knowledge of psycho-analysis has permeated psychiatry itself in America. When I was last here, before the war, psycho-analysis had certainly established a foothold, particularly in New York, but they have extended this foothold only very slowly in the time that has elapsed since then. On the other hand, the extent to which a varying degree of knowledge of psycho-analysis has been accepted by American psychiatrists at large is truly noteworthy and is something for which there is no parallel in any country in Europe. Oddly enough, however, I think it could well be maintained that this open-mindedness on the part of American psychiatrists redounds less to their credit than might at first sight appear. For it looks sometimes as if they had purchased this open-mindedness by indulging in certain superficiality, in fact at the expense of their imagination. To put the matter cursorily, and therefore very partially, it might be said that European psychiatrists have been loath to accept psycho-analysis just because they realised it was a grim business, an affair of tremendous import from which they preferred to keep aloof; whereas American psychiatrists welcomed it as a novelty, but have failed to realise adequately its significance. This remark, like all such facile generalisations, is distinctly unfair, but what interests me is the modicum of truth it contains. If you find it over-sharply expressed, perhaps you will allow me to put the matter in a more objective way. What concerns us here is the precise relationship of psycho-analysis to psychiatry, the extent to which psychiatry can profit from psycho-analysis, and —last, but not least—the danger it is in of not securing this profit. I propose that we consider these questions in this order.

It has been said that the relationship of psycho-analysis to psychiatry resembles that of histology to anatomy. The point of similarity is evident; the one studies the finer details, the other the gross outlines. Let us see how far the analogy can carry us. It is hard for us nowadays to picture what anatomy was like before the discovery of the microscope, but we know enough to realise something of the revolution this instrument effected. It was not merely that far more became known about the actual anatomical structure of the various organs; more important than this was the contribution histology made to our knowledge of function and genesis. This is a matter too obvious to need stressing, but the point I am making here is that just the same is true of psycho-analysis. The addition to our knowledge through the detailed study of the finer content of various mental processes—*i.e.*, the purely interpretative side of psycho-analysis, the revealing of the latent content of dreams, delusions, and so on—interesting as all this may be, is relatively unimportant in comparison with the illumination psycho-analysis has thrown on the more vital problems of motivation and psychogenesis; in other words, it can explain, not only what has happened, but also why it happened. The exploration of the unconscious layers of the mind, made possible for the first time by psycho-analysis, has yielded knowledge of such inestimable value for psychiatry and psychology that it is hardly exaggerating to term it a revelation. We are in fact introduced to a new world, the world of the unconscious, where all the important events take place the results of which are simply documented in consciousness.

Though it is of course impossible for me here to substantiate these extensive claims by citing any of the endless detail of which psycho-analytical work is composed, may I at least try to specify a little more definitely something of the nature of the contributions psycho-analysis has, in my judgement, made to the subject of psychiatry and to select for this purpose three particular considerations. It will be understood that I am using the word psychiatry here in the broad sense previously indicated and not merely as denoting the field of the psychoses. I am also speaking purely of its psychological aspects; of the relation of these to its organic aspects I shall say a word in conclusion. Well, to me the outstanding achievement of psycho-analysis in psychiatry is that it has given us for the first time a real comprehension of the meaning of mental morbidity. One may even go further and say it has taught us that mental morbidity has a meaning. Before the advent of psycho-analysis the prevailing view was that psychopathological symptoms had no psychological meaning; they were supposed to represent—from a psychological point of view—meaningless manifestations of a breakdown on the part of the mental apparatus. Various toxic and other organic influences were supposed to derange the brain, and the resulting symptoms were believed to be as meaningless as from a musical point of view the jangling sounds are meaningless that result from a clumsy weight crashing on to a piano. The infinitely detailed investigation of such symptoms by means of psycho-analysis has shown that they are full of meaning to their finest ramification, that they are throughout informed with purpose, with intent, and with aim. The achievement of imaginary gratification, the allaying of guiltiness and remorse, the protection against the most terrible dangers—all these are processes that we are as yet very far indeed from being able to express in any other than psychological terms.

One of the most startling discoveries psycho-analysis has made of a general nature is that most of the phenomena comprising a mental disorder are symptoms, not in the Greek sense of morbid casualties, but in the modern sense of indicators. But they are indicators, not so much of disease, except by implication, as of a healing process. This is a point of view that had hardly been suspected before psycho-analysis, and it is one that has important therapeutic as well as pathological bearings. It means not merely that the delusions of the paranoiac, the phobias of the hysteric, and the obsessions of the obsessional neurotic are not the disease, but signs of a disease—so much had been conjectured previously—but that they are the products of an attempt to heal the underlying trouble. Appreciation of this must radically affect our attitude toward such phenomena in our therapeutic endeavours. By merely thwarting them (*e.g.*, by suggestion) an apparent success may be achieved that is purchased by a worsening of the disorder itself underlying them, one that may then manifest itself in more sinister ways.

In the second place, we know at last something—in fact, a great deal—about the nature of this underlying disorder, the disease itself, if we use the word in a broad and not too medical a sense. It may fairly be said that before psycho-analysis not even the site of the lesion was known, to say nothing of the nature of the lesion. This site is nothing more nor less than the unconscious mind, a region of the universe the very existence of which was only vaguely surmised before psycho-analysis explored and defined it, and yet one that is almost certainly of greater practical importance to humanity than consciousness itself. The disorder underlying all mental morbidity can be defined as a failure on the part of the ego to deal in any final manner with certain fundamental intra-psychical conflicts that are the inevitable lot of every human being. These conflicts arise from the difficulty in adjusting the claims of the sexual instinct in its earliest stages with those of other psychical forces. The integrity of the ego needs on the one hand secure possession of certain sexual impulses, or their derivatives, and on the other a secure relation to external reality. It is threatened if the conflict in question is not solved, and the ultimate danger menacing it is paralysis of mental functioning, a hypothetical condition to which I have given the name aphanisis, one to which some approximation is found in the dementia of psychotics and the inhibitions of psycho-neurotics. All mental morbidity is, therefore, a state of schizophrenia, although Professor Bleuler has proposed to reserve this term for the most striking of its forms. What we meet with clinically as mental disorder represents the endless variety of the ways in which the threatened ego struggles for its self-preservation. In the nature of things, therefore, our conception of it can be cast only in terms of active dynamic strivings.

The third psycho-analytical contribution to psychiatry I would cite is its extension of psychopathology into the realm of ætiology. It has long been surmised that certain psychoses were due to errors in development—indeed, with idiocy it is obvious—but the investigations of psycho-analysis have been able to establish this as a general proposition. What is termed ' fixation,' with the closely allied ' regression,' is a fundamental concept in psycho-analysis, and from this point of view it may fairly be said that all mental morbidity signifies an arrest in development. A potential neurotic or psychotic is someone who still carries about with him a conflict that is normally solved in infancy; he is someone who has never successfully passed a given stage of infantile development. Various precipitating factors decide whether this state of affairs will come to expression in the form of symptoms early or late in life. The relation between the arrest in ontogenetic development and particular difficulties in the phylogenetic history of humanity opens up a fascinating chapter, to which psycho-analysis has already made promising contributions. To sum up the three considerations just advanced, psycho-analysis has provided psychiatry with an interpretative, a dynamic, and a genetic point of view.

We may now profitably compare what I have said about American psychiatry and about psycho-analysis respectively. American psychiatry has the distinctive feature of breadth. It has already absorbed the psycho-neuroses in its scope and is making serious encroachments into normal psychology. The three fields have to be united, and American psychiatry and psycho-analysis are the two movements that are most alive to this truth. It was dimly perceived many years ago by Hughlings Jackson when he made his famous remark: ' Find out about dreams and you will find out about insanity.' It was Freud who found out about dreams and applied his findings to insanity, but it is to be noted that he found out about dreams by applying a psychopathological method derived from the study of the neuroses, thus uniting the three fields. If one takes the trouble to appreciate at their full value the three psycho-analytical points of view I have just sketched, it must be evident that psycho-analysis, while coinciding with its aims in the psychiatric ones we considered earlier, is still broader in its scope. Any attempt, therefore, to dismiss psycho-analysis to a corner of a chapter on the therapeutics of psychiatry, as if it were an alternative to hydrotherapy or a subvariety of suggestion, is simply to exhibit ignorance of its meaning and significance. When the doctrine of evolution made its appearance, it had either to be denied *in toto* or else to fertilise the whole of biology, to cause natural history, embryology, and comparative anatomy to be viewed afresh in a flood of light; even its bitterest opponents, to do them justice, realised that to have regarded it merely as a contribution of detail would have been simply foolish. Yet there is to-day a real risk of a corresponding blunder being committed with psycho-analysis. The forces of repression that veil first the existence and then the significance of the unconscious are hard to overestimate in their strength and subtlety; to accept a discovery with lip service and subsequently to discount the importance of it is only one, though a potent one, of its workings. To my mind there has never been any likelihood of psycho-analysis being stifled even by the most relentless opposition. But there is a very real danger, particularly in America, lest the gifts it can confer on psychiatry be put aside for long through complacent acceptance without proper appreciation of their value. This, in one word, is the message I make bold to bring from psycho-analysis to American psychiatry.

I have said something about the relation of psycho-analysis to the psychological aspects of psychiatry. What, now, is its relation to the organic aspects? I need not correct here the common misconception that psycho-analysis ignores the organic factors in mental disorder. Psycho-analysis has, it is true, to point out that attention has been too exclusively focused on them in the past, to the neglect of the psychological factors, and it has tried to restore a due proportion between the two sets. The same holds good for bodily disease in general, for it is probable that mental factors play a considerable, and possibly even an important, part in this field also. Into the vexed question of the connection between mind and body I do not propose to enter, my point of view here being purely clinical and empirical. But how is one to bring together the two indisputable facts that unconscious conflicts and bodily poisons may both operate in the production of mental disorder?

I hinted earlier that the ego, the kernel of the personality, on the integrity of which mental health depends, has two essential tasks to perform and two corresponding difficulties or dangers to cope with. It has to assimilate, and to respond adequately to, stimuli proceeding from two very different sources, from perceptions of the outer world and from stimuli arising in the inner world, respectively. It has not only to do this, but also to bring these two sets of stimuli into some sort of harmony with each other. Psycho-analysis finds that these tasks are much more formidable than is commonly thought, and that they are very rarely carried out with any degree of smoothness. It can point to endless imperfections in the performance of this task—for it is in essence a single task, the uniting of the inner with the outer world of the demands of the instincts with the demands of reality. When the imperfections are gross, mental morbidity will surely result. When they are less so, the issue, wavering in the balance, may be influenced by changes in the forces with which the ego had to deal. Changes may occur in the demands on the part of reality, through the fluctuating circumstances of life and of human relationships, and changes may take place in the insistence of the inner needs, for example, at various times of life—puberty, climacteric, and so on. But not only may there be all these manifold variations in the task set the ego, but the capacity of the ego to perform it may also be affected by factors directly influencing it itself. By these I mean somatic factors, principally—so far as we know—toxic ones. We are all familiar with the profound alterations in mental functioning that can be induced in this way, but the contribution psycho-analysis has been able to make is to indicate the nature of these alterations. They are the very same as those in the other case we considered previously, where the ego, without being weakened by any somatic influences, has proved unequal to its great task. The mental morbidity represents—in the organic just as in the psychogenic cases—the triumph of the imperfectly controlled unconscious impulses.

That this conception of mental morbidity can, thanks to recent researches, be seen to reign over the whole field, in both the psychogenic and the organic realm, is a scientific generalisation of supreme theoretical interest. The knowledge gained from it must enable us to direct our prophylactic and therapeutic efforts more intelligently than before. The immediate practical application of the knowledge is another matter. The work done by Ferenczi and Hollós on the psychology of dementia paralytica and by Tausk and Kielholz in respect of the alcoholic psychoses has shown that the mental manifestations of these disorders are in no way to be explained as a direct result of the toxins concerned; they are expressions of individual conflicts which can no longer be coped with by an ego weakened by the cerebral poisoning. Obviously this discovery has no immediate bearing on the necessity of dealing with the toxins, but nevertheless the suggestion that the more stable is the relation between consciousness and the unconscious the less liable is the mind to be disturbed by toxins may well prove to have important practical applications in the future. At the other end of the scale, there is no doubt that where the ego shows spontaneous failure to cope with this task, the approach can, at least at present, only be psychological. In the intermediate cases, where the ætiology is more mixed, the decision of which is the most suitable mode of attack will of course be a matter of judgement, and there will be some in which both are indicated. There is no contradiction whatever between the psychological and the organic point of view; they are of necessity interrelated.

We have not, however, exhausted this interrelationship by the consideration just advanced, which is concerned with only one way in which bodily factors can affect the mind. Quite apart from the direct influence of such factors in weakening the ego, we have to remember that the very existence of any bodily disturbance is in itself a psychological fact the importance of which to the mind may be very great and indeed momentous. On the other side, that the mind can affect the body is well recognised, though in my opinion the extent to which it can do so is still very much underestimated. It is not merely that psychogenic disorders—e.g., hysteria—often express themselves by disturbance of bodily function where the physical symptoms actually symbolise various mental processes. There are many other ways in which mental disorder—e.g., in the anxiety states—can affect somatic functioning more directly and can produce even structural changes with or without the co-operation of somatic factors. Finally, there remains what may perhaps prove to be the most important consideration of all. I refer to the probability that conceptions generated in the field of psychopathology— such as, for example, the connection between the pleasure principle and relief of tension—may in the future be applied to corresponding mechanisms in the somatic field and thus become established as biological principles of unconjecturable significance.

From all these considerations it will be evident that pathological psychiatry—i.e., that part concerned with somatic changes—forms an essential link between internal medicine on the one hand and psycho-analysis on the other, indeed, one might say between medicine and psychology in general. It will not be the only one— genetics or endocrinology, for example, may rival it in importance in the future—but it will surely remain an indispensable one. More novel, however, is the conclusion that psycho-analysis must become an increasingly important link between medicine and psychiatry on the one hand and the whole of society on the other. There are already a few feeble links of the kind, physical hygiene being perhaps the most prominent. But when one reflects that there is no aspect of human endeavour that can long remain unaffected by psycho-analysis—from ethnology to politics, from education to sociology, from art to economics, from philosophy to religion; in short, the whole fabric of civilisation—then we must see that to-day we are witnessing the birth of an enormous widening of medical endeavour and of the significance of medicine in the body politic. And in this widening, psychiatry, as the chief link between psycho-analysis and medicine, will, I trust, play an honourable part.

CHAPTER XX

THE CRITERIA OF SUCCESS IN TREATMENT [1]

I DO not know whether this symposium came into being because of my division into 'therapeutic' and 'analytical' results in the Clinic questionnaire. Although the distinction between the two cannot be sharply drawn, I nevertheless think that it has some value. Though it is not identical with this, it approximates to the comparison between the patient's estimate of the success achieved and the analyst's, estimates which seldom coincide exactly because of the latter's greater knowledge and higher standards. Nor is the matter the same as the question when to bring the treatment to an end, though it is evidently cognate with it.

On the purely therapeutic side I would attach the main importance to the patient's subjective sense of strength, confidence and well-being. By well-being I mean of course the potential capacity for enjoyment and happiness, since the actual amount of happiness obtainable will not depend on internal factors only. This subjective sense signifies that more energy is at the disposal of the ego than was previously, while there is correspondingly less cathexis of id and super-ego ' positions ' independent of ego control. The state of affairs can be described equally well in terms of greater freedom on the part of the ego or of greater self-control of the total personality. The two conceptions are synonymous: self-mastery means freedom for self-expression and freedom from internal compulsions. A harmonious conscience has to a great extent replaced the unconscious super-ego. The ego has expanded at the expense of the id and super-ego. The energy of the id is discharged towards the outer world *via* the ego and not independently of it. All these statements are merely different ways of saying the same thing.

A consideration to be borne in mind is that one may be misled by mere external activity and capacity. Many severe neurotics can compass a high degree of quite valuable activity and reach high standards of ability. Our test is rather whether all this is sheer achievement alone or, on the other hand, an expression of a freely functioning personality which is pouring positive feeling into the

[1] Introduction to a Symposium of the British Psycho-Analytical Society, March 3, 1936.

activities in question. The capacity for achievement in itself can be dearly bought at the expense of severe affective inhibitions or at the expense of serious incapacity in other spheres of life.

The free flow of positive feeling through the ego is the counter-part of the diminution of anxiety. Accepting for the moment Freud's old conception of anxiety as the conscious currency of all repressed affects, we perceive that previously unconscious affects are now allowed to flow into consciousness instead of provoking anxiety. As we all know, the most accurate test of this is the patient's reaction in the presence of suitable frustrations or abstinences. Mental health and the capacity for continence go together.

Undoubtedly the sphere where these tests can best be applied is the sexual one. This is not only because crippling of sexual capacity is the central core of all neurosis, but because few spheres can rival this one for the value it gives to life. If one cannot love then life loses most of its meaning. Here again we have to distinguish between apparent and real capacity. Many neurotics are sensually potent and lead a very active life in this respect. But our test, as before, is whether this activity is an expression of feeling that radiates through the whole personality in a harmonious fashion, stimulating and satisfying its most diverse aspects. If the patient has developed this potential capacity he is likely to be free and in control of himself in other respects also. It means further that he must have dealt satisfactorily with the evil and aggressive side of his nature.

I have left the matter of symptoms to the last because, as I think we should all agree, the importance of removing symptoms is far from being the best test of therapeutic success. We know that there are endless ways in which they can be removed, that they often disappear or vary spontaneously, and that anyone who chose this as the only way of measuring the value of a therapeutic method would not be displaying much insight into the real significance of neurotic illness and would be adopting a superficial and external view of it. On the other hand it is possible to err in the opposite direction and to dismiss the importance of symptoms in a too cavalier fashion. What really matters is not so much the presence or absence of symptoms as the nature of them when present and the amount of psychical significance attaching to them. The psychological structure of a neurotic symptom is, as we know, that of a compromise. It is compounded of a repressed impulse and a counter force.

Often the amount of energy investing it is derived more from the former source, often more from the latter. In general I would consider it more unsatisfactory to leave uncured a symptom of the latter sort, where the reaction is predominant, than one of the former, since symptoms—at least those of minor import—are often harmless outlets, almost safety-valves. If, however, the total quantity of energy attached to the symptom is great I should not take such a light view of it, since it means that the personality is being deprived of a very measurable quantity of psychical energy. Again, I should regard symptoms which bind a quantity of anxiety as grave and a failure to remove them as serious. Examples of this are symptoms where the feature of dependence is prominent, such as drug manias or alcoholism. In such cases even a vast improvement is not very gratifying so long as anything at all is left of the original propensity, experience showing that the tendency to relapse after the imperfect analytic treatment is to be seriously reckoned with. Finally, one might remark on the curious obstinacy so often shown by the main symptom for which the patient originally consulted the analyst. In my experiences this has mostly been the last symptom to disappear. It seems to have an almost mystical significance for the patient, one which is of course commonly heightened by the symptom being taken as a battle-ground between patient and analyst, a test-case of the fight between the resistance and the analysis.

Let us now consider the matter of analytical success. What are the most trustworthy criteria of this? One Freud laid down was that the amnesia of the third and fourth years should be removed and the events of most traumatic importance in those years be brought into relation with the subsequent neurosis. It is a criterion of undeniable weight and one perhaps not always given due attention. But analytical success goes beyond the pathological field altogether. It betokens an understanding not only of whatever symptoms may be present, nor even of pathological character traits, but of the developmental lines of all the subject's main interests in life. From this point of view it is easier to think of a cognitive criterion here than it is with purely therapeutic problems. Thus one may demand a knowledge of the paths of direct association which may be traced like red lines through the life-history of every individual, so that ultimately one can see his whole life as a gradual unfolding or extension of a relatively few primary sources of interest. Pursuing this idea to its logical conclusion, Ferenczi once asked Freud whether an absolutely complete analysis would reveal a unitary source of dominant importance in every individual's life, and Freud replied socratically that by asking the question he had given the answer. Similarly one would demand to know the precise relation of phantasy to events, or—as we call it nowadays—the relation of internal to external reality. All this insight should of course be shared equally by patient and analyst.

I should like to say something now concerning the relations between therapeutic and analytical success. One quite valid reason for desiring the latter is the desire to satisfy scientific curiosity. But we know that scientific and professional standards do not invariably coincide. It is a truism that the patient's interests should always lie in the forefront. Our laudable zeal for analytical success, however, can at times somewhat blur this fact. Let us therefore for the moment measure our conclusions by this criterion alone. We must then ask whether our attitude should always be to press for the maximum of analysis à l'outrance or whether it should be subject to modification according to the individuality of the patient. In the first place we must be influenced by our knowledge that the more deeply and fully can we analyse a given patient the more satisfactory is the therapeutic result. Analytical success betokens the highest degree of the favourable results I described just now when speaking of the therapeutic criteria. One may then expect a confident serenity, a freedom from anxiety, a control over the full resources of the personality that can be obtained in no other way than by the most complete analysis possible.

All this being so, how then can one hesitate from postulating the quite simple ideal of complete analysis in every case? And yet, this would, in my opinion at least, over-simplify the problem with which the actual facts face us. After all, the analyst's wishes and ideals are by no means the only factor in the situation. Other factors are the strength of motive, especially unconscious motive, for the changing of set psychological attitudes, the varying capacity of the ego to deal with the deepest anxieties, the comparison of the sacrifices that the greater duration of analysis entails with the probable advantages— a comparison that depends in turn on many further factors such as age, position in life, etc.—the quality and adequacy of the defences against the deepest layers, and probably more obscure quantitative factors which we are only now beginning to discern. My own practice is to try to take such factors into account when appraising

what would be best for the given patient. In general one aims at
carrying the analysis as far as one can. And when one sees that too
much energy is locked up in the deepest levels and that the defences
against the resulting anxiety are inadequate, then one must say that
the patient has little to lose by aiming at a maximum analysis. There
are, however, cases where a quite satisfactory working capacity has
been achieved, where the patient is adequately adjusted to what
remains to him of life, and where the attempt to disturb and modify
the deepest defences would be tantamount to a severe cost for the
sake of a somewhat doubtful idealism. In such cases one would,
before insisting on a complete analysis, have to be confident not
only of both one's own and the patient's capacity to carry it through
successfully, but also of one's judgement that the advantage would
definitely outweigh the disadvantage. After all, analytic work should
teach us to value balanced judgement above all fanaticism, even that
of the most laudable kind. This consideration, of course, in no way
deters us from striving to acquire the further knowledge that may
enable us to cope with the obstacles before which we now have to
pause.

CHAPTER XXI

PSYCHOLOGY AND CHILDBIRTH [1]

As your experience must have taught you, variations and difficulties in childbirth are brought about not only by the familiar obstetric agencies of a physical nature, but also by less palpable influences to do with the personality of the patient. It is not merely that neurotic attitudes, for that is what I am referring to, cause difficulties in the personal relationship with the patient and make her hard to guide, control and help. More serious are the indirect effects they may have on the course of labour itself, and indeed of the whole pregnancy as well. They are commonly dismissed as nuisances, but if doctors and nurses were to regard in this light all difficulties met with in their attempts to help patients their work would be both wearisome and ineffective. To try to cope with difficulties by studying and understanding them, on the other hand, is far more interesting as well as being beneficial. I hope to show you that the neurotic difficulties in connection with childbirth are much more complex and interesting than is generally thought.

Childbirth is naturally such a tremendous emotional experience that its effects are apt to deverberate to the very depths of a woman's nature, and these depths originate in the beginnings of life. One may say that a woman's emotional reaction to childbirth is essentially determined by certain elements in her earliest development, although these elements, belonging to that dark region we call the unconscious mind, are completely unknown to her and indeed are of a quality quite alien to her conscious personality.

You will ask at this point what childbirth, an affair of adult life, has to do with infantile development: the answer is, a great deal. It is now known that in the first three or four years of life various sexual sensations, impulses, and attitudes of mind which in adult language we can only describe as ' ideas,' play a very important part. They are all buried and forgotten subsequently, but they profoundly influence the mind for the rest of life. Those who suppose, for instance, that the maternal instinct operates only after marriage must be quite forgetting the significance of dolls in a little girl's emotional

[1] Delivered before the West Sussex Midwives Association, Horsham, January 28, 1942. Published in *The Lancet*, June 6, 1942.

life. Jealousy alone is enough to stimulate interest in the source of babies, possibly in the hope of being able to prevent such undesired occurrences, and there are deeper motives still for interest in these matters: curiosity is perhaps the motive easiest to understand, but it is certainly not the only one. Now young children know instinctively, as well as from direct observation of pregnancy, where babies come from, and they are never really deceived by stories about cabbages or storks. Evidently the child can have no knowledge of the womb or any other internal organ. The ' inside ' is everything—it may be called a ' sack ' conception—and the child's knowledge of this is derived solely from such experiences as eating, colic and defæcation: in other words, its idea of the inside of the abdomen is essentially an intestinal one, and this in its turn colours in important ways the later attitude to pregnancy and labour. When they nevertheless ask where babies come from it is partly to obtain permission for the knowledge they already have and partly as a substitute for the more puzzling questions of how the baby gets out of the body and how it got in.

The favourite infantile theories of childbirth, as they might be called, are that the child is expelled through the only opening known at that age, namely the anus, or that someone cuts the abdomen open, a kind of Cæsarean section, the navel being the centre of operation. We may call these alternatives the anal and sadistic theories respectively, and both play a part in the later attitudes towards childbirth.

Mutual envy between the sexes is common in early childhood, and of course in more disguised ways in later life. The male one, envy of the female's capacity to give birth to children, is less recognised than its counterpart. It seems often to find adequate indirect expression in the creative productivity widely open to men, but traces of it are often to be found in its unaltered form. It may well contribute to the various motives at work in the curious savage custom of couvade, in which the husband up to the last moment acts the part of the wife in labour. Here a plea might be entered for the much neglected theme of the treatment of husbands during labour. Some of their anxiety and distress can be alleviated if one recognises that much of it originates in remorse at the sadistic elements that have co-operated in bringing about their wives' happy but painful state. The anatomical envy of little girls is fairly well known, though it is easy to forget the central part it plays in women's envy of men which they prefer to explain on more rationalistic grounds. There are many reasons for it in childhood, but a prominent one that concerns us here is the little girl's belief that possession of a penis would give her more power to control her sphincters and guard against the ' accidents ' that so commonly get charged with terrific meaning in her mind. So strong is this wishful thinking that in the unconscious mind it may prevail against the four great experiences in feminine life that would logically destroy it and convince her of her feminine rôle. These experiences, while gratifying the desires that accompany normal female functioning, also unfortunately cater to the deepest fear in the female heart—that of being torn open and damaged internally. They are: (1) the child's observation that she is anatomically endowed with an open place (often neurotically misconstrued as a wound) in lieu of visible external structures; (2) menstruation, with its disconcerting flow of blood; (3) the first coitus, involving rupture of the protective hymen; (4) childbirth with all its pain and danger. I will not refrain from remarking that, especially in the last three of these, malicious females are seldom wanting who play on the fears of the individual concerned by retailing beforehand gruesome stories of horrors and perils.

The influence emotional processes exert on the course of pregnancy and labour depend in the last resort on the woman's attitude towards the vital content of her body, the unborn babe. Does she, deep in the unconscious, feel it to be something ' good,' invested with love and pride, or something ' bad,' associated with hatred and danger ? It is evidently akin to the sociological question concerning the increasing repugnance to bearing children, one which in another generation or two may well lead to a critical social and national situation almost rivalling that of the present war. Behind the important economic and social factors in this repugnance lie deeper ones to which the psychologist can point. The relationship to the husband is the most obvious of them. At a deeper level the responsibility of becoming and being a mother has in the unconscious mind often to cope with the forbidden wish to oust the mother herself and take her place, a conflict which adds its inhibiting effect to others. Then there is what I have just called the woman's deepest fear concerning her body, which often lurks behind the more superficial excuses concerning the effects on her figure, mammary and abdominal cicatrices, perineal tears, and so on.

If her attitude towards the unborn child is purely positive, the course of the pregnancy and labour is, apart from physical complications, smooth, and is accomplished with love and pride. More often, however, though in very varying degrees, the child has become unconsciously identified with the fanciful introjected 'internal object' to which Melanie Klein has called so much attention, and the attitude towards it gets coloured by the mixed feelings with which these internal objects (breast, penis, fæces, etc.) are invested. These fanciful ideas of internal objects, of things inside one, which play a very important part in the mental development of children, are of course the concrete expression of emotional attitudes towards the parents—love, hate, envy, guilt, and so on—and they are the chief source of the fears that haunt children. The internal damage to which I have more than once referred is one of the feared effects of what is inside the body and what it may do there; explosive accidents from loss of control of the sphincter muscles often acquire an exaggeratedly terrifying meaning in this sense, one which is re-echoed during the process of labour.

All this may be put in a simpler way by saying that in labour the woman's true character is revealed. If it is harmonious and loving, all goes well. If it contains conflicting elements of hate, resentment, envy and fear, then they reflect themselves in disturbances of the labour process.

Let us now apply these considerations to understanding the actual effects of such factors on the processes of pregnancy and labour. If a woman has unconsciously ideas of hatred, guilt or fear concerning the fruit of her womb (or the other, older internal objects with which it has become identified), how do they affect the physiological processes at play? They may do so in one of two opposite ways: by inhibiting the nervous mechanism of the normal expulsive movements, or by exaggerating these in a violent, inordinate and ill-timed fashion. Which of these two effects will come about will depend on the psychology of the complex in question. If the unconscious hopes —if I may so translate its attitude into conscious intelligible language —that it can achieve wholesomeness by expelling the bad things, then we have the second, violent effect. If, on the other hand, it more pessimistically fears that the bad thing will by act of expulsion damage the body, or if it dreads exposing to the outer world the badness that has been harboured (hence so many women's fear of birthmarks, deformities and other imperfections in the baby), then we have the former, retentive effect.

The phenomenon of inhibition is familiar enough: it is what

obstetricians term primary inertia. A less well recognised effect is that of constipation, and this is intelligible when we remember how extensively the alimentary canal is identified with the inside of the body in the unconscious—*i.e.*, the infantile mind.

Irregular and ill-timed violence in the expulsive movements is among the causes of secondary inertia, and even apart from that extreme effect, it may grossly impair the harmony that should attend the process of childbirth. In pregnancy also the same psycho-physiological tendency may be seen at work. Much of the vomiting of pregnancy—I do not of course refer to pernicious vomiting of hepatic origin and the like—usually ascribed to reflex action has really a psychological origin in the unconscious effort to expel the foreign, and therefore ' bad,' object. Lastly, the frequency of mis-carriage in certain women is also often connected with the same tendency.

CHAPTER XXII

SOME PROBLEMS OF ADOLESCENCE [1]

BEING deeply sensible of the honour bestowed on me by being asked to address this joint meeting, I have reflected that the subject of my remarks should be one worthy of the importance of the occasion, and also one of sufficiently wide bearing to insure the interest of workers in different fields. One possible source of misapprehension in my title should be cleared away to begin with. It concerns the use of the word ' problem ' in this connection. Many of you, particularly perhaps among the members of the Educational Section, may expect that with this word I have in mind something of an executive order, and that I intend to convey my opinions on how best to deal with various ' problems ' facing the teacher, for instance, or on the guiding of adolescents through various ' problems ' and difficulties with which they are likely to be faced. Such a paper would presumably be called a ' helpful ' one, but I am afraid I shall disappoint those of you who look for one of this kind. The sense in which I here intend to use the word ' problem ' is that of a nodal point of ignorance, to which an ' answer ' consists of a correlation, one which for popular purposes is conveniently expressed in terms of what is called causation.

It is worth dwelling a little on the difference between the two points of view just indicated, for it has a definite bearing on most of the questions of interest in connection with adolescence. As is well known, the special danger besetting all forms of applied science is that too much emphasis is apt to be laid on the ' applied ' and too little on the ' science.' With all the affairs of life that deeply engage our interest—for instance, those of health, of education, or of politics—the impulse to do makes us impatient of the desire to know. We usually prefer to act without knowledge rather than to seek knowledge first and act after; we may at times be willing to make use of knowledge if it can be acquired without too much effort, but only too often the insistent necessity of acting somehow at all costs

---

[1] Delivered before a joint meeting of the General, Medical and Education Sections of the British Psychological Society, March 14, 1922. Published in the *British Journal of Psychology*, vol. xiii.

is paramount over the knowing precisely what the results of the action may be.

In contrast with this instinctive tendency, the object of science is knowledge and nothing else whatever. Once knowledge has been attained it can, of course, be subsequently taken into account when deciding on this or that plan of action, but this involves a quite different category of mental activity which it is expedient to keep distinct from the former. To come nearer to our subject of to-night: it occurs to me that there must exist already a number of societies, congresses, clubs and magazines, in sufficient profusion to afford abounding opportunity for the discussion of the *art* of dealing with adolescence, educationally or otherwise, and that there is ample room for one society, such as ours, whose sole aim should be the pursuit of knowledge for its own sake, where the desire to know should be allowed full sway with the temporary abrogation of all other impulses. The bearing of these considerations will, I trust, become evident in the remarks to follow.

A second expectation more general among my audience I do not propose to disappoint. It will be anticipated that no psycho-analyst is likely to treat of adolescence without mentioning the word ' sex,' and to do so would, in my opinion, be like playing ' Hamlet ' without the Prince of Denmark. The educated world has agreed upon a conspiracy of silence about the sexual life of childhood— *i.e.*, before puberty—and the subject is rarely referred to unless explicitly to deny its existence. Even the sexual life of adults is regarded as so unimportant as not to be worth discussing in most textbooks of psychology. Now, if the sexual instinct ever plays a significant part in the life of man it surely is during the age of adolescence, for biologically the essential characterisitc of this age is that it represents the achieving of sexual maturity. Few, indeed, are the problems relating to adolescence that can be solved without taking into account some sexual factor or other.

There are innumerable detailed problems of adolescence to which time could profitably be devoted, but most of them are concerned with one or other aspect of the great developmental process that we call ' growing up.' It seems to me, therefore, most fitting that I should attempt here to consider the general nature of this cardinal process, for any effort to attain a better understanding of it must necessarily be of assistance in the study of the many other problems that stand to this one rather in the position of corollaries to a main proposition.

I wish, therefore, to ask in what precisely does this ' growing up ' consist, what are the forces bringing it about or impeding it, and to what extent and with what results is it usually achieved? What is actually effected during this transitional stage of adolescence, when the child becomes the man? Perhaps we can best approach this question by inquiring into the chief differences between the beginning and the end of the process, between the child and the man. There are, of course, many such. Some of them are less valuable for our purpose, for they are only very gradual in kind, and are largely matters of increasing age and experience. Others are more characteristic, and justify us in determining the extent to which a given person has grown up, the extent to which he has cast off or retained childish traits; it is to these differences that we have to pay special attention. Not that they also are not gradual in kind, for Nature makes no leaps here any more than elsewhere, but the change is sufficiently striking to enable us for practical purposes to distinguish them in another class from the former ones.

One might think that it would be no very formidable task to establish the most notable differences between a child and an adult, but I can say that on attempting it I have found it extremely difficult. Many of the points that at first sight seemed secure enough turned out on closer inspection to be more than uncertain. Often one knows perfectly well whether a given reaction of capacity is more typically childish or grown up, but to define the essence of it is quite another matter. What I have to put forward for your consideration here, therefore, is especially tentative, and I will ask you to receive it as such.

Closer examination of the difficulty of this comparison shows that, as is often so, the matter has not been justly stated. We are not comparing sufficiently pure elements. The whole of life up to the time of puberty is not a single element, nor is the whole of it after this date. Both periods should be further divided into two, the former into infancy and late childhood, the latter into adolescence and fully adult life.[1] If we contrast late childhood with adolescence,

---

[1] I use the word ' infancy ' to cover the years up to five, ' childhood ' those up to twelve, and ' adolescence ' from twelve to eighteen. Twelve is chosen rather than fourteen on the ground that the changes incidental on puberty show themselves earlier in the mental than in the physical sphere.

we do not come to at all the same conclusions as we do if we contrast the other, earlier period of childhood with the other, later period of adult life. Reflection along these lines will, I maintain, show that it is, on the other hand, infancy and adolescence that have to be contrasted with late childhood and adult life. In order to secure the most pronounced contrasts for our present purpose, therefore, I will mainly consider those between the two extremes—infancy and fully adult life.

Let us begin with one of the more obvious differences—namely, the greater development of intellectual powers in the adult. This is the aspect on which I feel personally to be least qualified to speak, and I have a becoming respect for the enormous amount of experimental research that has been carried out on this subject. Scales have been established by means of which the progress of intelligence from year to year can be estimated, and the intellectual age of various individuals compared with their actual age. Efforts have also been made, by Burt, Yule, and others, to devise methods for isolating the common factors in the different forms of intelligence testing and for estimating the correlation between these and other mental traits. But with all deference to this work, I wish to submit two remarks of a sceptical nature in regard to some of it. Rightly or wrongly, I feel convinced that there yet remains much to be done in the way of critically examining the nature of many of these tests from the purely psychological side. They are, I think, too often regarded from an external and matter-of-fact point of view, often from an exceedingly adult point of view, without due consideration being paid to the very subtle ways in which the reaction to the tests may be influenced by delicate affective, and commonly quite unconscious, factors. Speaking more generally still, I would say that my psycho-analytic work has given me a very high opinion of the intelligence of children, and has taught me that there are some important respects in which it commonly becomes positively blunted by increased age, or rather by that ' education ' which is an inescapable accompaniment of this increase. I have been impressed over and over again by the bold initiative of thought, by the sceptical and searching spirit of inquiry that can be displayed by a young child, of which the same person never shows a trace throughout his later life. It is true that one has to set beside this the child's suggestibility and credulity—though the latter is often more apparent than real—and the effects of these soon put an end to his earlier freedom of thought. Nevertheless, this sort of experience does suggest to me that much of the experimental work on intelligence needs a further analysis of the nature of the elements that are being measured and of the possibly different processes that may be included in the category of intelligence. It is remarkable how little we really understand of the ideational aspects of the mind when one reflects how exclusively the attention of psychologists has for centuries been concentrated on these aspects; possibly, indeed, it is just because of this exclusive concentration that we know so little.

The *second* feature that occurs to me as distinguishing the adult from the child is the higher degree of what may be called integration in the former. By this I mean a greater co-ordination among the various component parts of the mind. With adults the mind seems to work more as a whole than with children, so that a given action is more likely to be related to the rest of the personality than it is with children, where it may be mainly the expression of a single more or less disconnected impulse. Something can be said about the nature of this integration. It is essentially dependent on a heightened capacity for inhibition, as may be seen if we contrast the extreme cases of a deliberate action in a well-balanced adult and the impulsive conduct of the infant. (In later childhood there is often a very considerable degree of integration, often much more than in the immediately succeeding years of adolescence; this correlation between infancy and adolescence on the one hand, and between later childhood and adult life on the other, is one to which we shall return later.) Now, in the contrast we are depicting there are two prominent features. The impulsive action of the infant is often concerned only with the impulse itself; in it no account is taken of other tendencies or reflections, and it approximates more or less closely to the dissociated autonomous 'complex activity' so familiar in paraphrenia and other mental disorders. In the second place, it is obviously hard to control, and clamours for *immediate* expression; the young child is notoriously extremely impatient of delay or postponement. I would venture to connect these two features and to suggest that the small extent to which the individual impulses are brought into relation with the rest of the mind in infancy is closely connected with the fact that the child has not yet learned to tolerate excitation without an immediate response—*i.e.*, to be able to interpose a delay between the excitation and the motor or emotional response. What the precise connection is between the increase of

co-ordination and of inhibition is a matter calling for a more
technical discussion than is possible here. I will only add that the
greater power of inhibition—*i.e.*, the capacity to endure a greater
amount of psychical pain—is an essential part of the developmental
process of subordinating the pleasure-pain principle to the reality
principle.

The suggestion may be put forward at this point that a fuller
understanding of this problem of integration will probably throw
much light on the difference in intellectual power at different ages,
for the higher reasoning powers, the capacity to think in general
and abstract terms, seem to bear a close relation to the power of
concentrating, a faculty in which co-ordination and inhibition play
a very important part.

The *third* distinguishing attribute is not such a compact one as the
last. It has to do with certain features common to various emotional
and imaginative traits in each class. If we compare the phantasy life
in children and adults, especially young adults, it may at first sight
appear to be a mental aspect equally developed in both, but there
are certain characteristic differences in the two cases. The phantasies
of childhood are much more obviously egocentric than those of later
years. A young man or woman will often weave an elaborate fiction
in which they do not recognisably appear, but with children the hero
is hardly distinguished, if at all. Then, as a rule with children we
miss the note of yearning or aspiration, that reaching out to something beyond the individual self, an endeavour even to attain to the
infinite, with which we are familiar particularly in late adolescence.
It may assume manifold forms here—religious, artistic, poetical, or
purely social—but in all of them the characteristic marks are the
feeling that the self is incomplete or even unsatisfactory, and the
intense desire to get into contact with something—an idea or a
being—outside the self. With this goes usually a much greater
development of altruism, and the essence of the whole group we are
now considering may well be the development of a higher capacity
for loving and the desire to love, as distinct from the older desire
to be loved which is such a prominent feature of childhood.

In this connection we must also think of the relation of phantasy
to reality at different ages. On the whole it would appear that the
life of phantasy is gradually brought into closer relation with the
facts of real existence at two different periods during the development
of the individual: first, during the transition from infancy to later

childhood, and then, more definitively, during the transition from adolescence to later adult life. This change also betokens a progression similar to the one we have just noted from preoccupation and satisfaction with the self to a greater interest and love for the outer world; in other words, an unfolding of the personality so that the flow of feeling outward away from the self is facilitated. Numerous differences of detail are, of course, to be correlated with this great evolution; I will only instance the greater selfishness and cruelty of children as compared with adults.

A *fourth* group of differences comprises the more specific changes in the individual's relationship to his fellow-beings. The most prominent feature here surely is the diminution in the degree of dependence shown. I purposely say diminution, for there are very few adults, if any, in whom traces of the old childish feeling of dependence are not still to be found, and quite pronounced degrees of it are common enough at all ages. The change represents one of the most important of all the differences between children and adults, and the extent to which it has been brought about is one of the criteria on which we must rely clinically in deciding how successfully a given person has performed the task of growing up. Relics of the older attitude are commonly seen, not merely in such gross manifestations as timidity or embarrassment in the presence of superiors, but in manifold forms of undue sensitiveness to public opinion, the opinion of the neighbours, or even of the servants. Or the person shows the need of outer support in everything he undertakes: he does not venture to rely on or even to use his own powers of initiative, he dares not act for himself, he dares not think alone, and in extreme neurotic cases he dares not even walk alone. The manifestations in the intellectual sphere alone are of infinite variety; all degrees of stupidity occur, which are really expressions not of a defect as they appear to be, but of an affective inhibition of ideation. The number of people who can make a genuinely free use of their mental powers in thinking is extremely small.

Psycho-analysis of both the milder and the more strongly marked forms of dependence has done much to elucidate its nature. One conclusion stands out with especial clearness—that all forms of psychical dependence are fundamentally due to persistence of the infantile attachment to one or other parent, particularly to the fear of being disapproved of by that parent, and thereby losing his or her love. The change from dependence to independence, which is such

a cardinal constituent of the process of growing up, is thus seen to
be closely related to the question of attachment or detachment in
reference to the parents.

The character traits of enterprise, responsibility, initiative, and
self-reliance are, as a rule, distinctly more pronounced in the male
sex. Furthermore, of the external influences that can affect their
development, the most striking are experiences in the sexual sphere,
notably the acceptance of masturbation and the abandoning of the
early sense of guilt in connection with this, the first act of coitus,
marriage, and the birth of the first child; the death of the significant
parent is also to be noted as often playing an important part here.
These considerations alone suggest that possibly the phenomena in
question are connected with the psychosexual life, and we shall
presently see that there are other grounds for coming to this
conclusion.

We thus come to the last, but by no means the least, of the
features we are enumerating—namely, the fact of sexual maturity.
This is the most outstanding and undeniable difference between
children and adults, and we have, therefore, to define it more
closely. Not long ago this would have seemed a very simple task.
It would have been said that the difference consisted in the absence
of sexuality in the child and its presence in the adult. Since the
researches of Freud and his school, however, this position is no
longer tenable. We have now to recognise that there exist in all
societies strong motive forces impelling adults on the one hand to
restrict in every way possible the manifestations of sexuality in
childhood, and on the other to blind themselves to the sexual
nature of these manifestations; between these two methods the
recognition of infantile sexuality has been reduced practically to
a vanishing point. How far this attitude on the part of adults
represents a useful biological function or is merely a sociological
phenomenon, originating in jealousy and perpetuated by repression,
is an important question which has been interestingly considered by
Mr. Flügel in his recent book, ' The Psycho-Analytic Study of the
Family.' What we have here to consider is the nature of the transition in the sexual life that occurs during the development from
child to man.

As is well known, the conclusions arrived at by psycho-analysts
on the subject of sexuality in childhood are as follows: During the
first four or five years of life the sexual life of the child, both

physically and mentally, is an exceedingly rich one, and passes through a series of characteristic stages; the nature of these stages will be presently alluded to. Its manifestations differ very considerably from those familiar in adult life, and resemble rather those of primitive man or of our pre-human ancestors; they are thus decidedly atavistic in type, an additional reason why their sexual nature has been so extensively overlooked. When the second half of childhood has been reached, they have largely disappeared from view. Some of the constituents of the infantile sexuality have been deflected into entirely non-sexual channels—*i.e.*, sublimated; others have been repressed, and survive only in the unconscious mind; a few still find expression in a furtive manner withdrawn from adult view; and the only ones that are allowed to preserve an open existence do so under the condition that an inhibition is interposed between them and their natural goal. The ones last mentioned comprise the affectionate impulses of childhood, the desire to be loved, to receive and bestow suitable caresses, which are permitted and even encouraged by the parents and other authorities. They are characterised by the desire to be loved being far more pronounced than the desire to love, or—what is much the same thing—by the self playing a more important part in the relationship than the object, and, as has been remarked, by the inhibition of the tendency of the impulse to attain an openly sexual goal.

The physical changes at puberty, important as they are, do not concern us here, but equally important changes on the psychological side accompany them. They usher in the process which is to end by replacing the type of sexual life we have just described as characteristic of late childhood by that of adult life. When the process is completed, which normally is between the ages of sixteen and eighteen, three things have happened: impulse is no longer inhibited in respect of its sexual goal; it is directed towards strangers instead of to the parents and persons of the immediate environment as formerly; and the capacity to love has grown stronger at the expense of the desire to be loved, especially in the male sex.

But before these important changes can be brought about the transitional stage of adolescence has to be passed through, and this is affected in a highly interesting manner. At puberty a regression takes place in the direction of infancy, of the first period of all, and the person lives over again, though on another plane, the development he passed through in the first five years of life. As this correlation between adolescence and infancy is the most distinctive generalisation to which I wish to call your attention in this paper, I should like to dwell on it at some little length; it is one to which I would attach considerable importance as affording the key to many of the problems of adolescence. Put in another way, it signifies that the individual *recapitulates and expands* in the second decennium of life the development he passed through during the first five years of life, just as he recapitulates during these first five years the experiences of thousands of years in his ancestry and during the pre-natal period those of millions of years. I believe this to be true of other mental aspects than the purely sexual ones, though it is in the latter sphere that it is most definitely to be observed. It is, of course, obvious that by the word ' recapitulates ' one does not mean simply ' repeats,' any more than in speaking of the embryo recapitulating his infrahuman ancestry we mean that he literally repeats it. It is just because the process of recapitulation in all three cases is far from being an identical repetition of the former ones that the significance of the features common to the earlier and later stages is not evident and has so long been overlooked. The differences are plainly due to the circumstances in which the development takes place in the two stages being themselves very unlike.

Let us now compare in more detail the sexual development during infancy and adolescence respectively. In both of them five stages are passed through, and these are essentially similar in both cases. Any description of them, however, must necessarily be schematic, for one should constantly remember that the richness, complexity and variability in the factors modifying the process of development prevent its being accurately summarised in any simple formula. Nevertheless, when it can be clearly followed it will be found on the whole to contain indications of the five stages in approximately the order given here, though it should again be added that there is never a sharp distinction between the various stages, that they usually overlap extensively, and that they may even all coexist together. After making these qualifying reservations, we may enumerate the stages. The first is that of diffuse auto-erotism, in which the various orifices of the body play the chief part. This is followed by the various sub-stages to which the term ' pregenital ' has been attached; of these the most fully studied is the anal-sadistic phase, which is marked by the prominence of the sadistic impulse combined with the numerous physical and mental derivatives of anal-erotism. In the third stage the genital zone proper has achieved a primacy over the others, and narcissism is fully established. Closely related to this is the homosexual phase, the distinctness of which varies considerably in different individuals. The final stage is the heterosexual one in which an object chosen from the members of the opposite sex becomes of the greatest interest, and the sexual impulse is directed towards her or him respectively.

As was remarked above, these stages are passed through on different planes at the two periods of infancy and adolescence, but in very similar ways in the same individual. The evidence for this statement is derived from actual investigation of the sexual development in particular persons. It is found empirically, for instance, that when a person has special difficulty in passing through the masturbatory phase of adolescence, information obtained about his childhood shows that he had a similarly pronounced difficulty in this respect in the earlier period too. Again, if in adolescence the homosexual trend is especially prominent, it is found that the same was true of his early childhood, and so on. It is on the basis of numerous experiences such as these that I venture to propound the general law mentioned above, that adolescence recapitulates infancy, and that the precise way in which a given person will pass through the necessary stages of development in adolescence is to a very great extent determined by the form of his infantile development. Some further description is necessary to amplify the schematic account given above of the sexual development during adolescence. That the autoerotic phase belongs to the earlier stages of adolescence rather than the later is familiar enough knowledge. With it goes the tendency to introversion and a richer life of secret phantasy, together with the greater preoccupation with the self and the varying degrees of shyness and self-consciousness which are so often prominent features during adolescence. The anal-sadistic phase varies in intensity, but it is characteristic enough for the nice, gentle lad of ten to change into the rough and untidy boy of thirteen, to the great distress of his female relatives; extravagance, procrastination, obstinacy, passion for collecting, and other traits of anal-erotic origin often become especially prominent at this age. The narcissism may be shown in either a positive or negative way: the bumptiousness, conceit, and cocksureness of youth are as well-recognised characteristics of this stage in development as are the opposite ones of self-depreciation, uncertainty, and lack of confidence; the two sets commonly alternate in the same person. The homosexual phase is more often positive than negative, and is far commoner during adolescence than at any later age; that it varies enormously in intensity in different individuals is, of course, well known. The heterosexual impulse commonly shows the following difference in its fate at the two periods of life: at both it most often breaks through the barriers of prohibition and reaches a directly sexual goal, but whereas in childhood this part of the impulse usually becomes increasingly subordinated to the constituents that are inhibited in respect of this goal—*i.e.*, to family affection and the like—in adolescence it is for psychological reasons the directly sexual ones that grow progressively stronger, often entering into severe conflict with the other set before harmony is finally established by a fusion of the two in successful love.

Five features of difference between children and adults have now been mentioned, and I should like to apply to each of them in order the conclusions just reached concerning the relation between adolescence and infancy. The first two features, those of intellectual change and greater integration, may be considered together. I remarked that inhibition played a central part in regard to the latter feature, and probably an important one in regard to the former also. Now it is surely noteworthy that the two periods of life at which the acquirement of inhibition is most active are those of infancy and adolescence. The lessons learnt in both may differ in their individual form, but they are of a similar order. In its development into childhood the infant learns to hold in suspense the action of various stimuli on the mind (and, of course, nervous system), to endure it without immediate motor or emotional response, to postpone such response to the most satisfactory moment, and to co-ordinate it with other forces operative in the mind. The adolescent passing into manhood or womanhood acquires a still higher degree of this capacity to tolerate stimulation and inhibit response. The most typical example from infancy would be the acquirement of control over the acts of excretion, where every feature of the description just given is illustrated. In adolescence a great part of both the natural changes and the training deliberately inculcated may be summed up under the term ' acquirement of self-control,' and it is not necessary for me here to attempt to enumerate, or even to quote from, any of the thousands of examples of this with which you are all familiar. One might, perhaps, suggest that there is this difference in the process at the two ages—namely, that in infancy greater emphasis seems to be laid on the acquirement of control over volitional *motor* outflow, while in adolescence it is laid on the acquirement of control over *emotional* outflow. The child learns to restrain action when it is inexpedient, the adolescent learns to restrain the display of emotion (not only when inexpedient in this case, but always).

This growth in the power of inhibition at the two ages in question must certainly be correlated with the circumstance that they are the two most emotional ages of man; in fact, it would seem as though the inhibition is related to the rush of emotion so characteristic of these periods of life, for there is much reason to think that emotion itself is due to the inhibition of instinctual impulses. A process that is closely connected with inhibition, being indeed in all probability one of its manifestations, is that of ' repression,' and again infancy and adolescence are the two ages at which this takes place on the most extensive scale. How successful it is in regard to infancy is well known. The greater part of the first five years, and always the most important part, is invariably forgotten, and remains inaccessible to consciousness (the definition of ' repression '), while commonly enough not a single trace is left of the whole period. In adolescence a second great wave of repression sets in, reaching a height never attained at any other period of life. Ideas which were tolerable enough to consciousness up to puberty—for instance, the desire for the pleasure of parental caresses[1]—now become repressed for ever, and ideas which later on will once more be freely admitted to consciousness—*e.g.*, sensual ones—are often quite banned.

The two characteristics of the third feature were the greater development of altruism, of interest and love for one's fellow-beings and the outer world in general, and the increasing replacement of phantasy by adaptation to reality, the replacement of the pleasure-principle by the reality-principle. Both of these are more plainly manifested later on in adolescence and during the transition from it to adult life, just as in childhood they are related to the transitional period following infancy. It seems to me that they can well be correlated with the change in the sexual life from the manifestations most connected with the self, including auto-erotism, narcissism,

[1] I do not, of course, mean that the acts themselves become intolerable, though even that occasionally happens.

and to a great extent even homosexuality (for this can almost be classified as a variety of narcissism), to allo-erotism—*i.e.*, the need for a love-object. This correlation evidently throws light on the first phenomenon, which is largely a matter of extending the libidinal attachment from the self to surrounding objects. The relation of phantasy to reality also comes to be closely connected with the sexual life, although, as Freud has pointed out, it is not originally so. In the competition between the experiences and enjoyments of phantasy and those of real life, one of the great factors that ultimately gives the victory to the latter is the evolution from auto-erotism to allo-erotism. The accessibility of the source of satisfaction—*i.e.*, the self—in the earlier of these phases renders the person largely independent of the outer world, whereas with the development of the allo-erotic phase the necessity for adaptation to the outer world becomes an increasingly pressing one, and to this must probably be ascribed much of the transition to the reality-principle. In the evolution from auto-erotism to manifest hetero-sexuality phantasy plays the part of a bridge, just as it does in that from forbidden incestuous to permissible object-love.

About the fourth feature, that of dependence, much misunderstanding has prevailed. The child has in this respect, as in so many others, been judged from the point of view of the adult. Because the adult sees plainly that the infant cannot subsist without adult care and help, he is apt to assume that the infant must realise this and feel extremely dependent on the adult, being only very gradually weaned from this dependence. In other words, he considers the question of dependence in terms of adult reality, and projects the same attitude on to the child's mind. In my opinion, however, this is a very partial view of the state of affairs. The infant's needs are so automatically satisfied, and the distinction he draws between self and outer world is so rudimentary, that he is much more likely to have a sense of power than of helplessness, as we all probably should if our wishes were only gratified with the ease and certainty on which the infant can count. I think that the feeling of dependence, which is only a later feature in the child's development, is not primarily related to the fact that he has to rely on parents for his material welfare, food, clothes, and so on, for this fact he takes very much for granted, and it does not produce very much psychological reverberation. Psycho-analysis, particularly of cases where the attitude of dependence has been specially pronounced, shows that it is to a far greater extent related to the need for love, and that it is a characteristic phenomenon of the allo-erotic or Œdipus phase of infancy. Normally it diminishes progressively between the ages of six and twelve, but with the onset of puberty it reasserts itself in other forms, among which the familiar displacement of the feelings of adoration and dependence from the father on to the idea of God is perhaps the most typical. Although this need for personal love to which we refer must psychologically be classed as a part of the sexual instinct, yet the impulses comprising it differ from what are commonly called sexual impulses in being more or less completely inhibited in respect of any sexual goal; the aim is emotional rather than physical union. The regression which takes place during adolescence to the infantile Œdipus relation to the parents is chiefly manifested on the positive side only in relation to the father (with the boys) as hostility and rivalry; the attitude towards the mother at this period is mainly a negative one, a rejecting of caresses and intimacies that up till then had been permitted. At the same time greater activity begins to be shown towards other love objects, and the desire to love increases at the expense of the desire to be loved. When the fully adult stage is reached, the incestuous attachments are abandoned; a strange love object is found, who is loved not only with feelings of an ' inhibited ' nature, but also with those of a directly sexual kind. When this process is complete, then adult independence is achieved in all respects. Dependence can, therefore, be defined as persistent incestuous attachment of the libido, and independence as the disposal of it in some other direction. This non-incestuous disposal of it may be either in relation to a love object, or it may take the form of sublimation; most often it is both.

These conclusions, if true, have an important bearing on the theory of education. A child can, of course, educate himself, but by education is usually meant the influencing of a child by another person for certain specific purposes. I would maintain that the essential motive force made use of in this relationship, whether at home or in the school, is the attachment of what we have called ' inhibited libido ' of incestuous origin, the same factor that is responsible for the phenomenon of dependence. If the libido is not converted into this form, or evolves out of it, then—other factors being equal—by so much is the child the less educable. Limits are set to education, therefore, in two opposite ways—by auto-erotic

functioning or by allo-erotic and non-incestuous functioning—both
of which provide channels for the libido that are not at the service
of the teacher. The second of these is, of course, much the rarer
during school life, and any sign of it on the part of pupils is vigorously opposed by all teachers. The former, however, is a common
enough phenomenon at the school age, and is, therefore, from one
point of view, the greatest foe that the teacher has to encounter,
which is the reason why teachers denounce it in unmeasured terms
as the unpardonable sin. That their efforts to deal with it meet with
very limited success is well known, and this must in great part be
ascribed to the fact that they refrain from making any study of the
nature and significance of the phenomenon.

From this simple statement it is not to be inferred that manifest
sexuality (either auto- or allo-erotic) and educability are purely
reciprocal functions. This matter is complicated by the circumstance
that excessive repression, carrying with it complete suppression of
all forms of manifest sexuality, is very apt to involve also the
‘ inhibited libido ’ on which educability depends. Indeed, I should
be inclined to ascribe the notorious fact that children are usually
much more ‘ troublesome ’ and ‘ difficult ’ from twelve to fifteen
than from eight to eleven to repression of their ‘ inhibited libido ’
at the former age rather than to the struggle for manifest sexuality,
with the revolt this entails. Incidentally, I might add that the present
law and custom of regarding the period from five or six to fourteen
as an educational unit is not at all in accord with the conclusions of
clinical psychology, which suggest that the period from five or six
to twelve is not comparable with that from twelve to eighteen,
and cannot profitably be dealt with on the same educational
lines.[1]

It will thus be seen that excessive repression and imperfect
repression equally diminish the capacity to be educated. Future
researches of a more exact kind will doubtless be able to establish
an optimum between these two extremes, one at which educability
will be at the highest point attainable by each particular child.

Something should be said here, if only a few words, on the

[1] Sir Percy Nunn, the distinguished educationalist, who was present when this
paper was read, at once appreciated the importance of this consideration, and the
weight of his influence led to its being acted on in the arrangement of the London
County Councils. Since then educationalists in other parts of England have also re-
arranged their courses on the same model and even our Public Schools have now
adopted this point of view.

important subject of the various forces acting on the adolescent in connection with the process of growing up. These are both external and internal, the latter being probably the more important. Each set also comprises two groups of forces, acting in the direction of growing up and against this respectively, so that there are four groups in all—two favouring and two hindering the growing up, two internal and two external. On the one side there is the vital unfolding of the personality, recapitulating the history of the species, which manifests itself even in early childhood in the form of ambitious phantasies and performances. This is the strongest force of all, and normally it prevails; it is aided both by the disinterested affection of the parents, which recognises what is to the child's ultimate advantage, and by their ambitiousness operating through the mechanism of self-identification. On the other side there is the conservative tendency to cling to former phases of development, and the reluctance to exchange these for new and unknown ones—at all events, until there is some assurance that the pleasures surrendered will be replaced by fresh equivalents. This tendency, which includes what Freud indicates under the terms ' regression ' and ' fixation,' as well as other processes as yet insufficiently studied, is certainly far stronger than is commonly supposed. It is powerfully reinforced by pressure brought to bear in the same direction by parental influence, perhaps more from the side of the mother. The parental motives hindering the growing up of the child are in the majority of cases stronger, and often much stronger, than those favouring this development. Their two chief constituents are jealous rivalry and the reluctance to give up the pleasure previously derived from the children, both, of course, being usually denied by the parent. The pleasure that the parent obtains from his children, and more especially from her children, is often in inverse proportion to the age of the children, and furthermore, the renunciation of it commonly betokens a loss rather than an exchange. The upshot of the whole matter is that in most cases growing up is effected by an integral ' urge ' on the part of the child or adolescent against an almost equally strong internal resistance, and also against serious external opposition. Little wonder that successful accomplishment of the process belongs to the rarities of human existence. Throughout the years of adult life the fight continues of freeing the personality from the restrictions that operate to excess during childhood and adolescence, until this evolutionary impulse to grow up is met by the counter-force of the involutionary process which conducts us through ' second childhood '[1] to the grave.

The foregoing considerations raise from a new point of view the problem of the biological significance of puberty. In the majority of animals puberty, in the sense of capacity to reproduce the species —*i.e.*, sexual maturity—takes place subsequent to birth—at a point the distance of which from it varies enormously in different species. The pre-puberty period is, I think, longer in man than with any other animal, constituting some 20 per cent. of the total duration of life. The strongest attempts are made on the part of society to extend it until it covers as well the most active years of sexual life— those from fifteen to thirty-five. Whether this is a biologically harmful tendency, one due to purely sociological and psychological factors, would make an interesting question for discussion. More germane, however, to the present topic is the consideration that man appears, so far at least as my knowledge goes, to be the only animal in which the earliest manifestations of sexual life do not proceed smoothly up to the stage of full maturity. In man, on the contrary, as was pointed out above, sexual development has to be gone through twice over, with a more or less complete break—Freud's so-called ' latency period '—in between. Instead of the development progressing evenly and culminating in puberty, what happens is that a rehearsal of the whole process is performed in the first years of life, and then, on reaching puberty, the individual has to start again at the beginning and go through the drama in a more serious and sometimes tragic fashion.

In conclusion I would say that I am very aware of the sketchiness of the outlines I have drawn in this paper. In the endeavour to deal with such a vast and important field I have been obliged to express many points in such a summary and schematic way as to deprive the statements made of the accuracy which could only be attained by introducing the modifications and qualifications impossible in a short exposition.

[1] If the views here expressed are correct, this should more properly be termed the 'third childhood.'

CHAPTER XXIII

THE PHANTASY OF THE REVERSAL OF GENERATIONS [1]

In a previous paper[2] I called attention to the importance of a peculiar phantasy which is not at all rare among children, to the effect that as they grow older and bigger their relative position to their parents will be gradually reversed, so that finally they will become the parents and their parents the children. Since this was published I have come across a number of illustrative references to the theme, and I should like to mention some of these before discussing the significance of the phantasy. It should be noted that there are several component parts, or degrees, of the phantasy—the gradual reversal in size, the extension of this to the belief that the child is in imagination the actual parent of its parent—*i.e.*, equivalent to its own grandfather—and the consequences of the phantasy in adult life, especially as regards the attitude towards children and the belief in re-incarnation.

A good description of the phantasy itself was given a few years ago by James Sully:[3] ' A number of children, I have found, have the queer notion that towards the end of life there is a process of shrinkage. Old people are supposed to become little again. One of the American children referred to, a little girl of three, said once to her mother: " When I am a big girl and you are a little girl I shall whip you just as you whip me now."[4] I have collected a number of similar observations. For example, a little boy that I know, when about three and a half years old, used often to say to his mother with perfect seriousness of manner: " When I am big, then you will be little; then I will carry you about and dress you and put you to sleep." And one little girl asked about some old person of her acquaintance: " When will she begin to get small ?" Another

---

[1] Read before the Psychiatric Society, at Ward's Island, New York, February 8, 1913; published, in part, in the *Internat. Zeitschr. f. ärztl. Psychoanalyse*, Jahrg. i., Heft 6.

[2] Chapter XXVII., p. 520, of the Fourth Edition.

[3] James Sully, ' Children's Ways,' 1906, pp. 64-66.

[4] This remark supports my opinion that one of the important determining factors of the phantasy consists in hostility and revenge-wishes directed against the parents (see Chapter XXVII., p. 520, of the Fourth Edition).

little girl asked her grown-up cousin, who was reading to her something about an old woman: " Do people turn back into babies when they get quite old ?"

' Another interesting fact to be noted here is that some children firmly believe that persons after dying and going to heaven will return to earth as little children. An American lady writes to me that two of her boys found their way independently of each other to this idea. Thus one of them, speaking of a playmate who had been drowned, and who was now, he was told, in heaven, remarked: " Then God will let him come back and be a baby again."

' What, it may be asked, is the explanation of this quaint childish thought ? I think it is probable that it is suggested in different ways. One must remember that as a child grows taller grown-ups may seem *by comparison* to get shorter. Again old people are wont to stoop and so to look shorter; and then children often hear in their stories of " little old " people. I suspect, however, that in some cases there is a more subtle train of thought. As the belief of the two brothers in people's coming back from heaven suggests, the idea of shrinkage is connected with those of birth and death. May it not be that the more thoughtful sort of child reasons in this way ? Babies which are sent from heaven must have been something there; and people when they die must continue to be something in heaven. Why, then, the " dead " people that go to this place are the very same as the babies that come from it. To make this theory " square with " other knowledge, the idea of shrinkage, either before or after death, has to be called in. That it takes place before death is supported by what was said above, and probably also by the information often given children that people when they die are carried by angels to heaven, just as the babies are said to be brought down to earth by the angels.'

Tisdall,[1] more recently, refers to the phantasy in connection with the belief in re-incarnation: ' Here perhaps we should mention an idea which is not uncommon among European children of tender age. The present writer, for instance, can well remember that, when a little more than three years old, he had a firm conviction that his parents would by-and-by grow little again and become *his* children in their turn. From observations made to him since by very young English boys and girls he has reason to conclude that the same strange fancy exists in not a few childish minds of to-day. He has

---

[1] St. Clair Tisdall, *Church Quarterly Review*, July, 1911, vol. lxxii., p. 337.

heard a little boy say to his mother: " Mamma, when you are little, I will take care of you." Does this throw any light on the origin of the re-incarnation doctrine ? Is it natural to the childhood of the race as well as (perhaps) to that of the individual ? And does its reappearance in adults among ourselves betoken the " second childhood " of the race ?'

The logical consequence of the phantasy, which the imagination at times does not fail to draw, is that the relative positions are so completely reversed that the child becomes the actual parent of his parents. An example of it in the sphere of religion is that of Indra, who was reputed to have begotten his father and mother from his own body.[1] Another is to be found in an ancient Egyptian delineation,[2] in which Queb, the earth-god, and Nut, the sky-goddess, are represented as being the parents of their father Schu, the air-god, who is elsewhere supposed to have begotten them.

Another way of stating this conclusion is that the child becomes identified with his grandfather, and there are many indications of this unconscious identification in mythology, folk-lore, and custom. Grandchild—i.e., great child, as grandfather is great father—is in German *Enkel*, which originally meant ' little grandfather.'[3] In the fairy-tale of ' Little Red Riding Hood,' which is a disguised birth-phantasy, the grandmother, as Rank[4] has pointed out, is treated as the equivalent of a new-born babe, as is indicated by her breathlessness on emerging (i.e., being born) from the wolf's belly. The custom of naming children after their grandparents is extremely widespread in both civilised and uncivilised races; among many it is not merely a common habit, but an invariable rule.[5] Andree[6] gives examples from North American Indians and other tribes in which the child who receives the dead grandfather's name is for some time treated with the same respect as the latter, the people definitely believing that the grandfather has returned in the person of the child; there are even complicated rites for determining which particular grandfather has returned on the occasion of a birth. The Labrador

[1] Rigveda, I. 159²; x. 54³. For comments on this see Macdonell, ' Vedic Mythology,' in Bühler's *Grundriss der Indo-Arischen Philologie und Altertumskunde*, Band iii., Heft 1.

[2] Brugsch, ' Religion und Mythologie der alten Ägypter, 1888, S. 210.

[3] Kluge, ' Etymologisches Wörterbuch.'

[4] Rank, ' Völkerpsychologische Parallelen zu den infantilen Sexualtheorien.' *Zentralbl. f. Psychoanalyse*, Jahrg. ii., S. 426.

[5] See Dieterich, ' Mutter Erde,' 2ᵉ Aufl., 1913, S. 127.

[6] Andree, ' Ethnographische Parallelen und Vergleiche,' 1878, S. 171.

Eskimos name their children after the last person who has died in the village, and Hawkes,[1] in describing this custom, plausibly connects it with the belief in the transmigration of souls.

It seems probable that the last-mentioned belief is, in large part, to be traced to the phantasy here described, but I am inclined to believe that it would be more accurate to attribute both to a more fundamental belief—namely, that in personal immortality. Neither the child's mind nor the adult unconscious can apprehend the idea of personal annihilation (as distinct from the idea of lasting disappearance of *other* people),[2] and with only a small minority of people is the belief in this possible even to full consciousness. This narcissistic conviction of personal immortality extends to persons loved or respected[3] by the ego, so that when such a person disappears it is assumed that it can only be for a time, and that he will surely be seen again, either in this world or the next. To the primitive mind the former place of reappearance is the more natural; hence our children, just like adult savages, imagine that when an old person dies he will shortly reappear as a new-born child.

While, however, this originally narcissistic conviction of immortality affords an indispensable basis for the phantasy in question, there are other important motives that contribute to its genesis. The two chief of these, in my opinion, concern the impulses of love and hate respectively. The former is a parental impulse,[4] usually of the maternal type, which manifests itself in the desire to nurse, fondle, and care for the loved parents, the illusion being cherished by the child that they are its children. That this impulse is in play is not only shown by direct observation of the child who exhibits the ' reversal ' phantasy, but is supported by the fact that in most individuals the parental instinct is awakened before the instinct to combine with a member of the opposite sex (the sexual impulse in the popular sense). This is true of both the young child and the adolescent, though more strikingly so with some individuals than

---

[1] Hawkes, ' The Labrador Eskimo,' Memoir 91 (No. 14, Anthropological Series), Canadian Geographical Survey.

[2] See Chapter XXXII. of the Third Edition, p. 593.

[3] Even in adult life this refusal to believe in death is often shown when great national leaders or heroes are concerned, striking examples being Barbarossa, Rákoczi, Napoleon, and Lord Kitchener.

[4] This term is here used in a purely descriptive sense, with all reservation as to what future analysis may dissect the impulse into ; two components at least are clearly visible—the reaction to the parents' affection and anal erotism.

with others. On the extent to which it is true depend a good many character traits in later life, the two extremes being, on the one hand, the type that, like the narcissistic child, wants to receive everything and give nothing in return, and, on the other, the type that is always burning to help or comfort everyone around. The second contributory impulse, that of hate, relates to hostility in regard to the parent or parents. The ' reversal ' phantasy then gratifies this by placing the child in the imagination in a position of power over the parent, as was illustrated in the anecdote quoted above.

The most important consequences of the ' reversal ' phantasy is the way in which it determines the later attitude of the individual towards children, especially his or her own. It is no exaggeration to say that, to a greater or lesser extent, there always takes place some transference from a person's parent to the child of the corresponding sex. A simple instance of what I mean is given by Merimsohn,[1] who makes one of his characters, an old man, say: ' My mother loved me more than the other children because I bore her father's name. He was a Rabbi in our town, and my mother used to hope that I too would become a Rabbi.' It is quite common to find a mother trying to mould a boy along her father's lines, or a father trying to mould a girl along his mother's—*i.e.*, making the child incorporate in itself its grandparent's character. The child's own personality is thus moulded, or distorted, not only by the effort to imitate its parents, but by the effort to imitate its parent's ideals, which are mostly taken from the grandparent of the corresponding sex. I have often followed this process in detail, and noticed how the parent's attitude towards quite minute specific traits, the admired ones and the disliked ones, in his or her own parent is reproduced when dealing with his or her child. The social significance of this should be apparent in regard to the transmission of tradition; it throws a light on, for instance, the considerations adduced in Benjamin Kidd's last work.[2] One has, of course, to take into account the reaction of the child, which may be either positive or negative; that is, the child may either accept the transference or rebel against it, in the latter case developing character traits of exactly the opposite kind to those it is sought to implant.

A curious and often distressing form of the transference just described is the negative one. I have studied several instances in

---

[1] Merimsohn, quoted by Kaplan, ' Grundzüge der Psychoanalyse,' 1914, S. 290.
[2] Benjamin Kidd, ' The Science of Power,' 1918.

which a person who from childhood had developed a hostile attitude towards one or other parent then took up the same attitude towards his or her own child: a woman who hated her mother and then hated her daughter, or a man who hated his father and then hated his son. The original hatred for the parent must be very strong, and usually quite manifest, for it—when transferred later—to overcome the natural parental affection for the child. I have more than once even known a man dread to have a male child—and actually avoid having any children on this account—because of his hatred for, and fear of, his father. The meaning was that he feared his son—*i.e.*, the re-incorporated grandfather—would take revenge on him for the hostile impulses he had displayed, either openly or unconsciously, usually in childhood. I will express this complicated thought more plainly in another form: *A* experiences in childhood, and possibly also later, hostile impulses directed against his father *B*, and fears that his father will punish (*e.g.*, castrate) him for them in the appropriate talion manner. When *A* grows up, he fears to have a son, *C*, lest *C*, the unconscious equivalent of *B*, will carry out this punishment on him. There is a double reason, it is true, for his fear: he fears his son *C*, not only as a re-incorporation of *B*, but also as a separate individual, his son; feeling from his own experience that sons always tend to hate their fathers. We doubtless have here the deepest reason for the constant identification of grandson with grandfather; both are equally feared by the father, who has reason to dread their retaliation for his guilty wishes against them. There are many examples of this situation in mythology. Thus, Zeus did actually carry out on his father Cronos the very injury of castration that the latter had effected on his own father, Uranos; so Uranos is avenged by his re-incarnation, Zeus.

CHAPTER XXIV

ANAL-EROTIC CHARACTER TRAITS [1]

PERHAPS the most astonishing of all Freud's findings—and certainly the one that has evoked the liveliest incredulity, repugnance, and opposition—was his discovery that certain traits of character may become profoundly modified as the result of sexual excitations experienced by the infant in the region of the anal canal. I imagine that everyone on first hearing this statement finds it almost inconceivably grotesque, a fact which well illustrates the remoteness of the unconscious from the conscious mind, since of the truth of the statement itself no one who has undertaken any serious psychoanalytical study can have any doubt.

There are, however, two biological considerations, relating respectively to the ontogenetic and phylogenetic antiquity of the physiological process concerned, that should render the statement made above a little less unthinkable, if not actually plausible. One is that the act of defæcation constitutes one of the two greatest personal interests of the infant during the first year of life, a fact which should carry due weight to any student of genetic psychology, for the basis of that science is the principle that all later tendencies and interests are considerably affected by earlier ones. With this may be correlated the circumstance that the alimentary function in general is the most constant preoccupation of all animals other than man. The other consideration is that many of the sexual processes and organs have been derived from the excretory ones, in both the individual and the race, and are very largely modelled on them; in the lower animals, for instance—and, indeed, partly so even in man —common ducts are used for both. That the primordial function of excretion, and the fundamental association between it and sexuality, should result in far-reaching effects on mental development should not, therefore, be altogether surprising.

The subject should logically be prefaced by a description of the facts of anal erotism itself, and even the question of infantile sexuality in general, but so many discussions and illustrations of this are now to be found in the literature that I can deal with the matter

[1] Published in the *Journal of Abnormal Psychology*, 1918, vol. xiii.

here very briefly. The salient features as elucidated by psycho-analysis are: The mucous membrane lining the anus and anal canal possesses the capacity of giving rise, on excitation, to sexual sensations, just as does that lining the entrance to the alimentary tract. The sensations vary in intensity with the strength of the stimulus, a fact frequently exploited by infants, who will at times obstinately postpone the act of defæcation so as to heighten the pleasurable sensation when it occurs, thus forming a habit which may lead to chronic constipation in later life. The pleasure experienced in this way is one which, as a rule, becomes repressed in very early life, so completely that perhaps most adults are no longer capable of obtaining any conscious sexual pleasure from stimulation in this region, though there are a great many with whom this capacity is still retained. The psychical energy accompanying the wishes and sensations relating to the region is almost altogether deflected into other directions, leading to the sublimations and reaction-formations which are the subject-matter of this paper. I do not propose here to touch further on the varieties of anal-erotic activities themselves or on their importance in regard to education, to psycho-neurotic symptomatology, and to the study of perversions, each of which topics would occupy a considerable chapter in itself.

In the paper in which Freud[1] originally communicated his conclusions, he confined himself to pointing out the three character traits that are most typically related to highly developed anal erotism —namely, orderliness, parsimony, and self-willedness or obstinacy. These constitute the cardinal triad of anal-erotic character traits, though a number of other attributes have also been described by Sadger and the present writer. As no systematic account of them has hitherto been given, an attempt will here be made to classify them and to point out their inter-relationship. As might have been anticipated, some of them are of a positive nature—that is, they are sublimations which represent simply a deflection from the original aim; while others are of a negative nature—that is, they constitute reaction-formations erected as barriers against the repressed tendencies.

Blüher[2] would distinguish between ' defæcation erotism,' or

---

[1] Freud, ' Charakter und Analerotik,' *Psychiatrisch-Neurologische Wochenschrift*, 1908; reprinted in his ' Sammlung kleiner Schriften zur Neurosenlehre,' Zweite Folge, 1909, chap. iv.

[2] Hans Blüher, ' Studien über den perversen Charakter,' *Zentralblatt für Psychoanalyse*, Jahrg. iv., S. 13.

erotism in connection with the act of defæcation, and ' anal erotism,' or erotism in connection with any other activities—*e.g.*, masturbation, pæderastia—relating to the anal region; he holds that the former is invariably auto-erotic, a statement not in accord with the facts of perversion. I would suggest, on the other hand, that, as all allo-erotic manifestations in connection with this region must ultimately be derived from erotism relating to the act of defæcation, there is no reason for introducing a separate term, though a useful distinction may be drawn between the different aspects of the originally auto-erotic anal erotism. One can separate thus the interest (and the character traits resulting therefrom) taken in the act itself of defæcation from that taken in the product of this act. This separation of character traits cannot be made quite sharply, it is true, for with some of them both of the interests in question play a part. Of Freud's triad, for example, the self-willedness is doubtless related to the first of the two interests mentioned, and the orderliness to the second, but the parsimony seems to be almost equally determined by both. And when one studies more closely still the relationships of the traits, the same complexity is to be found; the orderliness, for instance, passes over into pedantic persistence in the performance of duties, which is related rather to the first class of interest. Nevertheless, a certain gain in clearness is perhaps achieved by keeping distinct, so far as is possible, these two aspects of anal erotism.

Taking first the attitude of the infant towards the act itself, and the later influences of this on character-formation, we find that there are two typical features constantly noted, though, of course, to a very varying extent in different cases. The one is the endeavour of the infant to get as much pleasure as possible out of the performance, the other is his effort to retain his individual control of it in opposition to the educative aims forced on him by the environment.

The first of these endeavours he carries through by postponing the act as long as he can—children have been known even to go to the length of squatting down and supporting the anal orifice with the heel so as to keep back the stool to the last possible moment—and then performing it with intense concentration, during which he resents any disturbing influence from without. Sadger[1] has pointed out how this attitude may be mirrored in later character tendencies. Such people are very given to procrastination; they delay and postpone what they may have to do until the eleventh or even the

---

[1] Sadger, ' Analerotik und Analcharakter,' *Die Heilkunde*, 1910, S. 43.

twelfth hour. Then they plunge into the work with a desperate and often almost a ferocious energy which nothing is allowed to thwart, any interference being keenly resented. Undue sensitiveness to interference is very characteristic of this type, especially when combined with marked concentration out of proportion to the importance of the occupation. A kindred trait is intense persistence in an undertaking once engaged on, from which they allow nothing to divert them—even though considerations arising later may put the desirability or the value of the undertaking in a totally different perspective. Such people are often notorious bores. They are equally hard to move to a given course of action as to bring them from it once they have started on it. They are typically slow-minded and heavy in thought; once they have got on to a topic there is no breaking it off until they have gone up hill and down dale in saying all they want to about it, and in the meantime no one else is allowed to interrupt or get a word in on the matter—if they try to do so they are simply ignored or else their interruption greatly resented. On the other hand, these attributes are often very valuable, for the thoroughness and dogged persistence with which tasks are carried through has its rewards in the quality of the results. Such people often show an extraordinary capacity for forcing their way through difficulties, and, by their persistence, get things done in despite of apparently insuperable obstacles. The trait of persistence is often related to pedantry and obstinacy, being halfway between the two. A typical kind of behaviour when such a person is faced with the question of a possible undertaking—for instance, the preparations for a dinner-party, the writing of an article, etc.—is as follows: First there is a period of silent brooding, during which the plan is being slowly, and often only half-consciously, elaborated. At this time not only are they not to be hurried, which would only result in a flustered annoyance, but they keep postponing the preliminary steps as long as it is at all possible, until the other participants despair of the performance being ever accomplished—at least in time. Then follows a spell of feverish and concentrated activity, when all interference is resented and nothing is allowed to prevent the programme laid down being carried through to the bitter end in all its details. The self-willed independence that is implicit throughout this description comes to expression in another interesting character trait—namely, the conviction that no one else can do the thing in question as well as the subject himself, and that no one else can be relied upon to do it properly. As a result such a person cannot depute work, for he has no faith in its being done adequately unless he attends personally to every detail. Such people are therefore very hard to get on with as colleagues, for, although on occasion they will get through absolutely enormous masses of work (Napoleon !), they are subject to inhibitions during which nothing goes forward, since they refuse to allocate any of the work, however urgent it may be, to a deputy or assistant. There are many historical examples— Napoleon is again one—of persons of this type organising an elaborate system which functions marvellously well while its author, with tireless energy, attends in person to every detail, but which runs the risk of collapse as soon as the master hand is inactive; for, having assumed it all himself, he has given no one else the chance of being trained in responsibility. One notes the relation of the trait last discussed to narcissism and exalted belief in personal perfection, an association we shall have to comment on again in considering other aspects of the anal-erotic character.

It is astounding how many tasks and performances can symbolise in the unconscious the act of defæcation, and thus have the mental attitude towards them influenced by the anal-erotic character traits when these are present. Three classes of actions are particularly prone to become affected in this way. First, the task where there is a special sense of duty or of ' oughtness ' attached; therefore especially moral tasks. Much of the pathologically intolerant insistence on the absolute necessity of doing certain things in exactly the ' right ' way is derived from this source. The person has an overwhelming sense of ' mustness ' which brooks of no argument and renders him quite incapable of taking any sort of detached or objective view of the matter; there is only one side to the question, and it is not open to any discussion at all. Secondly, tasks that are intrinsically disagreeable or tedious, towards which, therefore, there is already some counter-will. This class often coalesces with the former one, when the moral duty is of an unpleasant or distasteful nature. A typical sub-group is the kind of task that Americans aptly term ' chores,' boring routine duties like tidying drawers, cleaning out a cupboard, filling in a diary, or writing up a daily report. This passes over into the third class, in which the task concerns objects that are unconscious symbols for excretory products. Some of these will be enumerated later, but a few may be mentioned here: any form of dust or dirt, anything to do with paper, any kind of waste product, money. With all these groups we may note the alternation of inhibitory procrastination and feverish concentration described above. For example, a housewife afflicted with a marked anal complex will keep postponing the doing of a necessary duty such as the cleaning out and tidying a lumber room until finally she is seized with a passionate energy for the task, to which everything else is subordinated with no discrimination as to relative importance or expediency; similarly with the getting up to date with accounts or notes, with the arranging of disorderly material, and so on. The most perfect example of all, and one quite pathognomonic of a marked anal complex, concerns the act of writing letters. There are few people who do not at times find it a nuisance to bring their correspondence up to date, but the type under discussion may show the completest possible inhibition at the thought of so doing, and most of all when thay have the strongest desire to write a given letter. When they finally succeed in bringing themselves to the task, they perform it with a wonderful thoroughness, giving up to it their whole energy and interest, so that they astonish the long-neglected relatives by producing an excellently written and detailed budget; they despatch epistles rather than write letters in the ordinary sense.

With all these activities the desire for perfection is visible. Nothing can be done ' by halves.' When an anxious relative begs for news, if only a line on a postcard, the person finds it quite as impossible to grant the request as to write an ordinary letter; he can write only after he has accumulated enough energy to produce a really satisfactory work of art; nothing less will suffice. The same tendency to perfection may further be displayed in the calligraphy of the letter, which is also related to the trait of neatness that will be considered later; such people often evince remarkable care in the fineness and beauty of their handwriting. The lady afflicted with what the Germans call a *Hausfraupsychose* will often find it difficult to attend regularly to the routine tasks of housework, and may neglect and postpone them until the unconsciously accumulated energy bursts forth in an orgy of cleaning activity.[1] These outbursts of activity are commonly followed by a marked sense of relief and self-satisfaction, to which succeeds another fallow period of apparent inactivity.

[1] Sadger, *loc. cit.*, points out that women are especially apt to display these outbursts periodically at times of suppressed sexual excitement—*e.g.*, in relation to menstruation.

It is further to be noted that with different members of the type there is a considerable variation in the relative prominence of the two phases of the process. Thus, with some, the expressing phase of thoroughness, insistence, persistence, and general energy is the dominant one, whereas with others it is the inhibitory phase of inactivity, brooding, delay, and postponement, which may even extend into temporary or permanent paralysis of various activities —such as complete inability ever to write any letters.

We have discussed so far the consequences of one feature of the infant's attitude towards the act of defæcation—namely, his endeavour to get as much pleasure as possible out of the performance of it; we have now to consider the second, correlated feature—the endeavour to retain his individual control of the process. Like the previously mentioned feature, this also has two aspects—the opposition displayed against an attempt from without to indicate conduct, and the resentment shown against any attempt to thwart conduct that has been decided on. These reactions constitute the character trait of Freud's triad which he calls *Eigensinn* (self-willedness, obstinacy), and which may attain a chronic attitude of defiance. The person objects equally to being made to do what he doesn't want to, and to being prevented from doing what he does want to. In other words, there is an inordinate, and often extreme, sensitiveness about interference. Such people take advice badly, resent any pressure being put on them, stand on their rights and on their dignity, rebel against any authority, and insist on going their own way; they are never to be driven and can only be led. As children they are extremely disobedient, there being, indeed, a constant association between defiant disobedience and unmastered anal erotism. Later a reaction-formation against this may develop, leading to unusual docility, but it can generally be observed that the docility is only partial and conditional—that is to say, they are docile only in certain circumstances, when they like and not otherwise, control of the situation thus being ultimately retained by the individual.

A curious sub-group of these character traits depends partly on the attitude described above and partly on the appreciation of value —about which more will be said presently—that the infant sets on his excretory product, in sharp contrast with that of the adult. Many infants feel it as an injustice that what they have so interestedly produced should at once be taken away from them, and this goes to strengthen the resentment against the general interference on the subject, resulting in an intense feeling against any form of injustice. Such people in later life are very sensitive on the matter of exact justice being done, even to a pedantic extent, and on all kinds of fair dealing.[1] They get particularly agitated at the idea of something being taken from them against their will, and especially if this is something that symbolises fæces in the unconscious, as, for instance, money does; thay cannot tolerate being cheated of the smallest amount. This complex often also serves to start a fear of castration —i.e., of some valued part of the body being taken away, though, of course, this has other sources as well.[2] The concept of time is, because of the sense of value attaching to it, an unconscious equivalent of excretory product, and the reaction just mentioned is also shown in regard to it; that is to say, people of this type are particularly sensitive about their time being taken up against their will, and they insist in every way on being master of their own time.

When, now, these hated intrusions and interferences nevertheless take place, the subject's reaction to them is one of resentment, increasing on occasion to anger or even outbursts of extreme rage. Brill[3] and Federn[4] have commented on the relation between anal-erotic sensations and the earliest impulses of sadism, and I have elsewhere[5] pointed out the importance played in the genesis of hatred by the earlier educative interference with anal-erotic activities. My communication referred especially to the pathology of the obsessional neurosis; in a subsequent paper Freud[6] confirmed the conclusions there reached, and also pointed out that the combination of sadism and anal erotism, a high development of which is characteristic of the obsessional neurosis, constitutes a stage in the development of the normal child, one of the stages to which he gives the name 'pregenital.' Andreas-Salomé[7] also has dealt at length with

[1] See Ernest Jones, 'Einige Fälle von Zwangsneurose,' Jahrbuch der Psychoanalyse, Bd. iv., S. 586.

[2] See Chapter XXXIII. of the Third Edition, p. 599.

[3] Brill, 'Psychoanalysis,' Second Edition, 1914, chap. xiii., 'Anal Eroticism and Character.'

[4] Federn, 'Beiträge zur Analyse des Sadismus und Masochismus,' Internat. Zeitschr. f. ärtzl. Psychoanalyse, Jahrg. i., S. 42.

[5] See Chapter XXX. of the Third Edition.

[6] Freud, 'Die Disposition zur Zwangsneurose,' Internat. Zeitschr. f. ärztl. Psychoanalyse, Jahrg. i., S. 525.

[7] Lou Andreas-Salomé, ' "Anal" und " Sexual," ' Imago, Jahrg. iv., S. 249.

the importance for later sadism of the conflict between the infant and his environment over the matter of defæcatory functioning. Where this has been very pronounced it may lead to a permanent character trait of irritability, which will manifest itself either as a tendency to angry outbursts or to sullen fractiousness, according to the degree of repression and other factors (cowardice, etc.). It is interesting that Berkeley-Hill[1] should in this connection refer to a Tamil saying which runs, ' A man who has a short temper suffers from piles.' Another ethnological example is afforded by the Cymric word ' brwnt,' which in North Welsh means ' cruel ' and in South Welsh ' dirty.' In English we often describe a man who behaves brutally, particularly to women, as a ' dirty swine.' Infantile anal erotism that has been inadequately dealt with may be suspected in anyone who is the victim of chronic irritability and bad temper, and perhaps the reason why this trait is so often seen in elderly persons of either sex is that in later life, when sexual vigour is waning, there is a tendency to regress towards a more infantile and less developed plane of sexuality; it is known that old people often show other anal character traits to a greater extent than in earlier life—e.g., personal carelessness, parsimony, and so on.[2] The reaction of annoyance and bad temper is especially apt to be brought out by intrusions on the part of the environment of just the sort described above—namely, either when the person is prevented from doing what he has set out to, or when he is made to do what he does not want to. Typical situations are: hindering the person from concentrating on a task which he has gradually forced himself to undertake, and from which he is now not to be deterred; compelling him to part with money or time against his will; pressing and urging him to undertake something at once when he wishes to brood over it; and so on. Finally, in connection with the tendency to anger and bad temper should be mentioned the vindictive desire for revenge when injured or thwarted, which in many people of this type is developed to an extraordinary extent.

It is not hard to see that many of the temperamental traits mentioned above are closely related to narcissistic self-love and over-estimation of self-importance, a fact which indicates the

[1] Owen Berkeley-Hill, ' The Psychology of the Anus,' *Indian Medical Gazette*, August, 1913, p. 301.
[2] On the other hand, Von Hattingberg points out that some of the character-traits— *e.g.*, obstinacy—may show themselves in childhood only, and disappear later; ' Analerotik, Angstlust und Eigensinn,' *Internat. Zeitschr. f. ärztl. Psychoanalyse*, Jahrg. ii., S. 244.

importance of the contribution made by anal erotism to infantile narcissism. I am referring here especially to self-willedness and all that goes with this, the insistence on pursuing one's own path regardless of the influence brought to bear by other people, the resentment at external interference, the conviction that no one else can carry out a given undertaking as well as oneself, etc. Persons of the type under consideration are apt to have a strongly marked individuality, and study of them throws many difficulties in the way of accepting Trotter's views concerning the significance of a social or herd instinct.

A character trait that I have not yet been able fully to analyse, but which is certainly related to the foregoing ones, has considerable importance for general happiness and efficiency. It consists of an inability to enjoy any pleasurable situation unless all the attendant circumstances are quite perfect. People who display this trait are extremely sensitive to any disturbing or disharmonious element in a situation; a satisfactory mood is readily impaired by slight influences; they are—to put it colloquially—easily ' put out.' The attitude is often shown in sexual situations, though by no means only here; the striking of a slightly discordant note, the thought of an unimportant duty not attended to, the slightest physical discomfort, these and similar circumstances are sufficient to abolish potency for the time being. They cannot enjoy an operatic performance, a motor ride, a social function, unless they are exactly ' in the mood,' and the right mood is only too fickle and erratic. The trait commonly goes with chronic irritability, and its anal-erotic origin is further to be suspected from its relation to the allied characteristic of being unable to settle down to any task until everything is arranged beforehand to the last detail; such a person cannot write a letter, for instance, until every article on the desk is arranged in exactly the right place, until the pen or pencil is precisely in order, and so on— an attitude which is certainly of anal-erotic origin. As may be imagined, such people are, as a rule, not only difficult to live with, but are rarely happy; they worry, they fidget, they take everything too seriously, and their life is a never-ending struggle to get things right, to arrange matters so that they may at last get some enjoyment in spite of all the difficulties in the way. In this connection it is noteworthy that pædiatrists[1] have called attention to the fact that children who suffer much from intestinal disturbances in infancy

---

[1] *E.g.*, Czerny, ' Der Arzt als Erzieher des Kindes,' 1908.

usually grow up to be unhappy, irritable, and unduly serious—*i.e.*, into the type just indicated.

Yet another character trait that is often strengthened by anal-erotic complexes is the desire for self-control, especially when this becomes a veritable passion. There are people who are never satisfied with their capacity for self-control, and who ceaselessly experiment with themselves with the aim of increasing it. This may take either a physical or moral direction. To the former category belong the people who are always doing things like going without sugar in their tea, giving up smoking temporarily, putting their legs out of bed on a cold night, and indulging in all sorts of ascetic performances in order to reassure themselves of their power of self-control and to ' show themselves that they can do it.' In the moral sphere the effects are, of course, more disturbing still, and need not be enumerated here. Although there are naturally many other sources of these ascetic and self-martyring impulses, one not unimportant one, as I have analytically illustrated elsewhere,[1] is the lasting influence of the infant's ambition to achieve *control* of his sphincters, his first great lesson of the kind.

Interest in the act of defæcation often leads to interest in the site of defæcation—*i.e.*, in the anal canal itself. Without going into the possible effects of this on the sexual development, which are, of course, of considerable importance, I may just mention a few characterological consequences that I have noted in the course of psycho-analysis.[2] The most interesting one is the tendency to be occupied with the reverse side of various things and situations. This may manifest itself in many different ways: in marked curiosity about the opposite or back side of objects and places—*e.g.*, in the desire to live on the other side of a hill because it has its back turned to a given place; in the proneness to make numerous mistakes about right and left, east and west; to reverse words and letters in writing; and so on. Another curious trait of the same origin is a great fascination for all underground passages, canals, tunnels, etc., and I have also known the same complex lead to an extreme interest in the idea of centrality; one of my patients was always restlessly searching to discover what was really the exact centre of any town he might be in, and developed many philosophical ideas as to what constituted the very ' centre of life,' the ' centre of the universe,' etc.

[1] *Op. cit.*, *Jahrbuch*, S. 587.   [2] *Op. cit.*, *Jahrbuch*, S. 581-583.

We pass now to the second of the two categories put forward above—namely, the character traits derived from interest in the excretory product itself. Some of these traits relate purely to this aspect of the subject, but most of those to be next considered relate partly to it and partly to the former theme of interest in the excretory act. They all represent either positive or negative reactions —*i.e.*, either sublimations or reaction-formations respectively. To understand them it is essential to realise the primary attitude of the infant towards fæcal material. There is every reason to think that to begin with this attitude is throughout positive, in contradistinction to the adult one. The infant regards his product as part of himself, and attaches to it a strong sense of value and of possession. He soon learns to invest the idea with a negative feeling-attitude of disgust, as for something unclean. This comes about more slowly and less completely with some children than with others, depending largely on the degree of repression. It seems likely that some of this repression may be entirely endogenous, an inherited tendency. It is much more marked in the case of other people's excreta than with their own, with liquid than with solid excreta, and with the sense of smell than with that of touch or sight. Before this reaction-formation develops, the infant's natural tendency—not always indulged in—is to keep and play with the material in question, the two typical forms of which are moulding and smearing.[1] In this stage the infant will produce and smear with excreta as a token of affection and pleasure, a demonstration usually misinterpreted by the recipient and not appreciated at its proper value.

Before we go on to discuss the character traits derived from these attitudes, a little must be said about the unconscious copro-symbols, on to which the corresponding feelings get transferred. The most natural one is food, this being the same substance in an earlier stage; many idiosyncrasies, both positive and negative, in regard to various articles of diet—*e.g.*, sausages, spinach, rissoles, etc.—are due to this unconscious association. Another obvious symbol is any dirty material, street-filth (including, of course, dung), soiled linen and other things, dust, coal, house or garden refuse, waste-paper, and, indeed, waste material of all descriptions, for in the unconscious the ideas denoted by the words ' waste ' and ' dirty '

---

[1] On the pleasure in smearing see Federn, *op. cit.*, S. 41, and many passages in Stekel's writings.

seem to be synonymous—the *tertium comparationis* doubtless being that of ' refuse.' Either disgusting or waste matter relating to the body is especially apt to become thus associated. The former of these may be illustrated by the material of loathsome diseases—*e.g.*, purulent and other secretions—and this is also the reason why a corpse is often a symbol of fæces. Examples of the latter one are hair and nails, parts of the body that are apt to get dirty and which are periodically cast off. Books and other printed matter are a curious symbol of fæces, presumably through the association with paper and the idea of pressing (smearing, imprinting).

The two most remarkable, and perhaps most important, fæcal symbols are money and children, and, as they occasion profound surprise to everyone who first hears of them, a little may be added by a way of explanation. Concerning the money symbol Freud writes:[1] ' Überall, wo die archaische Denkweise herrschend war oder geblieben ist, in den alten Kulturen, im Mythus, Märchen, Aberglauben, im unbewussten Denken, im Traume und in der Neurose ist das Geld in innigste Beziehungen zum Drecke gebracht. Es ist bekannt, dass das Gold, welches der Teufel seinen Buhlen schenkt, sich nach seinem Weggehen in Dreck verwandelt, und der Teufel ist doch gewiss nichts anderes als die Personifikation des verdrängten unbewussten Trieblebens. Bekannt ist ferner der Aberglaube, der die Auffindung von Schätzen mit der Defäkation zusammenbringt, und jedermann vertraut ist die Figur des " Dukatenscheissers." Ja, schon in der altbabylonischen Lehre ist Gold der Kot der Hölle.' [' Wherever the archaic mode of thought has prevailed or still prevails, in the older civilisations, in myths, fairy-tales, superstition, in unconscious thinking, in dreams, and in neuroses, money has been brought into the closest connection with filth. It is well known how the gold with which the devil presented his admirers changed into filth on his departure, and surely the devil is nothing other than the personification of the repressed unconscious impulses. The superstition is also well known that brings the discovery of treasure into association with defæcation, and everyone is familiar with the figure of the " gold-bug " (literally " excreter of ducats ").[2] Indeed, even in the ancient Babylonian doctrine gold was regarded as the

---

[1] Freud, ' Schriften,' *op. cit.*, S. 136.

[2] A fairy-tale equivalent is the goose with the golden eggs. For other mythological examples of the association see Dattner, ' Gold und Kot,' *Internat. Zeitschr. f. ärztl. Psychoanalyse*, Jahrg. i., S. 495.

dung of hell.'] Many linguistic expressions point to the same association. A popular German name for piles is ' goldene Ader,' golden veins. We speak of a ' dirty or filthy miser,' of a man ' rolling ' or ' wallowing ' in money, or of a man ' stinking of money.'[1] On the Stock Exchange a man who is hard up is said to be ' constipated,' and similar expressions such as ' currency,' ' liquid money,' etc., doubtless come from the same source. In insanity, and, as Wulff[2] has pointed out, also in drunkenness, the association often comes openly to expression, the patient referring to his excreta as wealth, money, or gold. In Browning's poem ' Gold Hair: A story of Pornic,' the ideas of hair, decomposition, gold colour, money, and miserliness are brought into the closest association.[3] In Freud's original article on the subject he proffered the opinion that the association is in part a contrast one—between the most valuable substance man possesses and the least valuable; but it is now known that the connection is a more direct one— namely, that the sense of value attaching to money is a direct continuation of the sense of value that the infant attaches to its excretory product, one which in the adult consciousness is replaced by its opposite, though it still persists unaltered in the unconscious. In a very suggestive paper, Ferenczi[4] has worked out in detail the stages by which the child passes from the original idea of excrement

---

[1] From an endless number of literary examples of the association I will quote the following two : ' I hate equality on a money basis. It is the equality of dirt ' (D. H. Lawrence, ' The Rainbow,' 1915, p. 431).

> ' More solemn than the tedious pomp that waits
> On princes, when their rich retinue long
> Of horses led and grooms *besmear'd with gold.'*
>   MILTON: ' Paradise Lost,' Book V.

The association is common enough in erotic art, especially in caricature (because of the connection between contempt and anal erotism). Two examples may be cited from Broadley's ' Napoleon in Caricature,' 1911: One, by Fores, depicts Napoleon and George III. as ' The Rival Gardeners'; at the side is a wheelbarrow filled with coins and labelled ' Manure from Italy and Switzerland.' The other, entitled ' The Blessings of Paper Money,' is by George Cruikshank; there is a figure of Napoleon withdrawing a large pan filled with gold coins from underneath John Bull, who is being dosed with paper money.

[2] Wulff, ' Zur Neurosensymbolik: Kot—Geld,' *Zentralbl. f. Psychoanalyse*, Jahrg. i., S. 337.

[3] In the Norse tale of Bushy Bride the heroine's hair drops gold as she brushes it. For associations in mythology between hair and gold see also Laistner, ' Das Rätsel der Sphinx,' 1889, Bd. ii., S. 147, etc.

[4] Ferenczi, ' Contributions to Psycho-Analysis,' English Translation, 1916, chap. xiii., ' The Ontogenesis of the Interest in Money.'

to the apparently remote one of money. Shortly put, they are as follows: transference of interest from the original substance to a similar one, which, however, is odourless—*i.e.*, mud-pies; from this to one that is dehydrated—*i.e.*, sand; from this to one of a harder consistence—*i.e.*, pebbles (some savages still barter in pebbles and there is in German an expression ' steinreich '—*i.e.*, stone-rich—to denote wealth); then come the artificial objects like marbles, buttons,[1] jewels, etc., and finally the attractive coins themselves (helped, of course, by the value attached to them by adults). In conclusion, I may mention a curious copro-symbol in this connection—namely, one's last will and testament; the association is doubtless the sense of value and the prominence of the idea of something being left behind.[2]

The association between children and fæces comes about in the following way: In the young child's spontaneous phantasy the abdomen is merely a bag of undifferentiated contents into which food goes and out of which fæces come. The knowledge that the fœtus grows in the mother's abdomen—a fact easily observed by children without its being realised by grown-ups, and later forgotten—leads to the natural inference that it grows out of food, which is perfectly correct except for the initial pair of cells; and then, since the child has no knowledge of the vagina, he can only conclude that the baby leaves the body through the only opening through which he has ever known solid material leave it—namely, the anus.[3] This ' cloacal ' theory of birth again has its germ of truth, for the vagina and the anus were originally one passage, in pre-mammalian animals. The baby is thus something that in some special way has been created and formed out of fæces;[4] fæces and children are, after

---

[1] Some neurotics have an intense feeling that all buttons are filthy objects, one doubtless furthered by the association between them and soiled clothes.

[2] The importance that in the anal complex gets attached to the idea of ' parting with something left behind ' may largely contribute to the sentimental attitude many people display on the occasion of parting with various personal objects which they have possessed for a long time, especially if the parting is a final one; the other source of this attitude is the death complex, where, of course, the idea of finally parting is equally prominent.

[3] This view is usually forgotten, and then replaced by the more acceptable one that the baby emerges through the navel.

[4] Clinical examples of this are given by Freud, *Jahrbuch der Psychoanalyse*, Bd. i., S. 55, and Jung, *Jahrbuch der Psychoanalyse*, Bd. ii., S. 49. Many examples of the same belief in mythology and folk-lore are quoted by Rank, ' Völkerpsychologische Parallelen zu den infantilen Sexualtheorien,' *Zentralbl. f. Psychoanalyse*, Jahrg. ii., S. 379, 380, 381. The idea has often been depicted in art, of which an example is to be found in Fuchs , ' Das erotische Element in der Karikatur,' 1904, S. 85.

all, the only two things that the body can create and produce, and the impulse to do so is remarkably similar in the two cases, especially to a young child whose feelings about its excreta are not yet what ours are. The child finds in Nature plenty of confirmatory evidence for its view that charming things grow out of matter with a bad odour—e.g., flowers[1] out of manured soil, etc., this being one of the sources of passionate delight in flowers (characteristically enough, mostly on the part of girls), which are unconscious symbols for babies. I have elsewhere[2] collected a number of words the etymology of which illustrates the association between babies, fæces, and odour. An otherwise unintelligible symbolism I have noted[3] becomes explicable in the light of the preceding considerations—namely, that the idea of stealing money from a woman can symbolise the idea of begetting a child by her. The association between the ideas of corpse and fæces—both being something that was alive and is dead—may also contribute to the belief that babies come from someone who has died.[4]

The possible reactions to these various symbols are so numerous and complex that they are not easy to classify. The anal-erotic complex is genetically related to two of the most fundamental and far-reaching instincts, the instincts to possess and to create or produce respectively. On the whole they are opposed to each other, the one being an impulse to keep, the other an impulse to give out,[5] and they may roughly be correlated with the two phases described earlier in this paper—the tendencies to keep back and postpone production and to produce feverishly.[6] The character of the person will greatly depend on whether the stress is laid on the one or the other of these two impulses. The question is complicated by the fact that the 'retaining' attitude of the first phase may extend over on to the product itself after it has been brought forth, so that a

---

[1] On the association between flowers, hair, and odour, see Scheuer, ' Das menschliche Haar und seine Beziehungen zur Sexualsphäre,' *Sexual-Probleme*, Jahrg. viii., especially S. 173; and also in this connection a note of my own, ' Haarschneiden und Geiz,' *Internat. Zeitschr. f. ärztl. Psychoanalyse*, Jahrg. ii., S. 383; and Chapter XVII. of the present volume.

[2] *Jahrbuch der Psychoanalyse*, Bd. vi., S, 192.

[3] *Ibid.*, Bd. iv., S. 585.

[4] See Chapter XXIII., p. 528, of the Fourth Edition.

[5] It is interesting that Bertrand Russell, in his ' Principles of Social Reconstruction,' 1916, should make this opposition the basis of an extensive sociological philosophy.

[6] The two might also be termed the ' retaining ' and the ' ejecting ' tendencies respectively.

hoarding tendency ensues. Further, enormous complexities result from the fact that the different attitudes possible vary with different symbols, so that the same person may in one respect show a positive attitude, in another a negative one; in one respect a sublimation, in another a reaction-formation; in one respect a giving out, in another a holding back; and so on. It is therefore only possible to delineate certain general types in a rather schematic way, and to call attention to the more characteristic reactions. At the risk of making some errors of over-simplification, I shall try to group the possible re- actions into four on the basis of two principles: that of the two impulses just mentioned, and that of sublimation *versus* reaction- formation, this one depending on whether the original sense of value is retained or not. Thus we have two groups derived from tho ' keeping back ' or possessing instinct, according as the sense of value is or is not retained, and similarly two with the creative or productive instinct. These four groups will next be illustrated in this order.

A. 1.—The most typical sublimation product of the ' retaining ' tendency is the character trait of parsimony, one of Freud's triad; in the most pronounced cases it goes on to actual miserliness. There are two aspects to the trait, the refusal to give and the desire to gather, and with a given person one of these may be much more prominent than the other; he may be either niggardly or avaricious, or both. Such people are mean, and grudge giving or lending.[1] The attitude naturally applies most to the various copro-symbols— *e.g.*, money (most of all), books, time, food (food-hoarders !), and so on. The irrational—*i.e.*, unconscious—origin of the attitude is often shown by the way in which the person will grudge giving a copper or a penny stamp (which are more directly associated symbols) much more than a considerable sum given by cheque. Sometimes the trait is marked only in a limited sphere; a common one is where a quite well-to-do person grudges the cost of the laundry, and resorts to various petty devices to diminish it; the tendency not to change underclothing more than is absolutely necessary is often doubly motivated, consciously by the dislike of parting with money—*i.e.*, sublimated dirt—and unconsciously by the dislike of parting with bodily dirt. When such people are compelled to part with more than they are willing to, they display the reaction of annoyance and resentment discussed earlier in this paper: thus, when money is

[1] We appropriately speak of such people as being ' close,' ' tight,' etc.

stolen from them, and particularly when it is stolen by their being given ' bad '—*i.e.*, ' rotten '—money[1]—that is, when they are made to excrete against their will.

The second aspect mentioned is the impulse to gather, collect, and hoard. All collectors are anal-erotics, and the objects collected are nearly always topical copro-symbols: thus, money, coins (apart from current ones), stamps, eggs, butterflies—these two being associated with the idea of babies—books, and even worthless things like pins, old newspapers, etc. In the same connection may be mentioned the joy in finding or picking up objects of the same sort, pins, coins, etc., and the interest in the discovery of treasure-trove. The treasure-trove is usually buried underground, which connects with the interest mentioned above in concealed passages, caves, and the like; the interest is also evidently strengthened by other sexual components, *Schaulust* (visual sexual curiosity), incestuous exploration in the body of Mother Earth,[2] etc.

A more edifying manifestation of the same complex is the great affection that may be displayed for various symbolic objects. Not to speak of the fond care that may be lavished on a given collection —a trait of obvious value in the custodians of museums and libraries, etc.—one of the most impressive traits in the whole gamut of the anal character is the extraordinary and quite exquisite tenderness that some members of the type are capable of, especially with children;[3] this is no doubt strengthened both by the association with innocence and purity presently to be discussed, and by the reaction-formation against the repressed sadism that so commonly goes with marked anal erotism. A curious accompaniment of this tenderness is a very pronounced tendency to domineer the loved (and possessed) object; such people are often very dictatorial or even tyrannical, and are extremely intolerant of any display of independence on the part of the loved object.

[1] *Jahrbuch, loc. cit.*

[2] In ' Paradise Lost ' (Book VIII.) we read how men, taught by Mammon,

> '. . . with impious hands
> Rifl'd the bowels of their mother Earth
> For Treasures better hid. Soon had his crew
> Op'n'd into the Hill a spacious wound
> And dig'd out ribs of Gold.'

[3] It is quite characteristic even of misers to be passionately fond of their children— *e.g.*, Shylock, Balzac's Eugénie Grandet, etc.; with the former of these, Shakespeare clearly illustrates the equivalency and unconscious identity of the daughter and the ducats.

A. 2.—The chief reaction-formation shown in conjunction with the ' retaining ' tendency is the character trait of orderliness, the third of Freud's triad. It is evidently an extension of cleanliness, on the obverse principle to the saying that ' dirt is matter in the wrong place '; presumably it is no longer dirt if it is put in the right place. When marked, this trait may amount to a definite neurotic symptom, there being a restless and uncontrollable passion for constantly arranging the various details of a room until everything is tidy, symmetrical, and in exactly ' its right place.' One illustration of this familiar trait will suffice: I have seen books, never used, kept on a table, and although they were all of the same size and looked perfectly neat, the owner could not rest without putting them in the precise order he had ordained as fit and proper; a picture ever so slightly askew would have made it out of the question for him to continue a conversation. Such people are extremely intolerant of any disorder; they are bound to clear away any waste paper or other objects ' left lying about.' Everything must be put in its proper place, and if possible put away out of sight. A more useful development that occurs in some members of the type is a high capacity for organising and systematising.

In the field of thought this tendency commonly leads to undue pedantry, with a fondness for definitions and exactitude, often merely verbal. An interesting and valuable variety occasionally met with is a great dislike for muddled thinking, and a passion for lucidity of thought; such a person delights in getting a matter quite clear, has a fondness for classifying, and so on.

The intolerance for disorder is closely related to another trait, the intolerance for waste. This has more than one source. It represents a dislike of anything being thrown away (really from the person)—a manifestation of the retaining tendency under consideration—and also a dislike of the waste product because it represents refuse—*i.e.*, dirt—so that every effort is made to make use of it. Such people are always pleased at discovering or hearing of new processes for converting waste products into useful material, in sewage farms, coal-tar manufactories, and the like.

A correlated trait, to which Freud called attention, is reliability, the capacity for being depended on. It is related to the passion for thoroughness and efficiency, with the dislike of deputing, that was discussed earlier in the paper. People having it can be trusted not to neglect any duty or to leave things undone or half done.

B. 1.—In this category comes the opposite of parsimony—namely, extreme generosity and extravagance. Some psycho-analysts would call this type ' anal-erotic ' as distinct from the ' anal character ' of the former, but it seems to me that they are equally character types derived from anal-erotic complexes, differing only in that one is positive and the other negative. One can distinguish two varieties of even the positive aspect of the ' giving-out ' type according to what is done with the product; with the one variety the person's aim is to eject the product on to some other object, living or not, while with the other the aim is to manipulate the product further and to create something else out of it. The two will next be considered in this order.

(*a*) The simplest type of the former aim may be called a sublimation of the primitive smearing impulse. An unrefined and usually repressed form of this is the impulse to stain or contaminate, found, for instance, in the perversion known as pygmalionism, the impulse to stain statues with ink, etc., and in the perverse impulse to defile women or their clothing by throwing ink, acid, or chemicals over them;[1] it sometimes lurks behind the erotic passion for young children (desire to contaminate their innocence). Two sublimations of this impulse are of great social significance—namely, interest in painting and in printing[2]—*i.e.*, in implanting one's mark on some substance. Lowlier forms of the same tendency are the common fondness of the uneducated for carving or writing their names—*i.e.*, leaving a memento of themselves which may injure and spoil something beautiful (and therefore spoilable); on the same plane there are innumerable manifestations of this spoiling, defiling impulse, usually associated with destructiveness (Freud's pregenital sadistic-anal-erotic stage of development[3])—witness the war.

When, with retention of the sense of value, the original product is replaced by money, jewels, etc., and when, further, the original sexual impulse has developed on to the allo-erotic plane, there is brought about a form of love-life characterised by the overwhelming predominance of the act of giving. It is true that, from both the psychological and physiological basis of love, the greater part of all love-life is modelled on the prototype of giving and receiving, but

---

[1] Thoinet, ' Attentats aux Mœurs,' 1898, pp. 484 *et seq.*; Moll, ' Gutachten über einen Sexual-Perversen (Besudelungstrieb), *Zeitschr. f. Medizinalbeamte*, 1900, Heft xiii.

[2] There are obviously other sources, even in the unconscious, for these interests, but the importance of the one here given is not to be under-estimated.

[3] See Chapter XXX. of the Third Edition, p. 560.

in the type in question all other aspects of love are entirely subordinated to this one act. Such people are always making presents; they woo their mate by only one method of making themselves agreeable and attractive, by giving her jewels, chocolates, etc. The immature and pregenital level of this form of love-life is shown by the fact that it is commonest with persons who are relatively impotent or anæsthetic; the usual pair who love in this way is an old man and a young girl, the former having reverted to this infantile level and the latter never having left it.

It is probable that the very desire to impregnate is contributed to by the complex in the question (see above for child symbolism), but we are here on a more adult genital plane of development, so that it is only possible to detect traces of the complex in some people.

(b) The desire to manipulate the product further and to create out of it leads to various sublimations, beginning with the usual fondness of children for moulding and manipulating plastic material, putty, plasticine, etc. The commonest sublimation is in the direction of cooking,[1] which may later be replaced by an aversion from cooking or continued as a passion for it. It finds extensive application in two other spheres of life, the industrial[2] and the artistic: good examples of the former are metal-moulding, building, carpentry, engraving, etc.; examples of the latter are sculpture, architecture, wood-carving, photography, etc.[3]

B. 2.—We have next to consider results of the reaction-formations built up against material that has been emitted, or symbols of this. The most obvious one is a strong dislike of dirt and a passion for cleanliness. Sadger[4] points out that intense dislike of dirt on the body itself is usually indicative of a masturbation complex, the anal-erotic one manifesting itself rather in an aversion from dirt in regard to external objects, particularly clothing and furniture—where with neurotics it may become exceedingly exaggerated; he gives as a special mark of an anal-erotic complex the dislike of street dirt and the tendency to lift the skirts specially high from the ground

---

[1] See *Jahrbuch*, *op. cit.*, S. 568.

[2] It does not seem altogether fanciful to correlate the enormous extension of interest in industrialism that took place a century or so ago with the wave of increased repression of anal erotism that can be shown historically to have accompanied it, especially in England.

[3] Lest it may be thought that any of these conclusions are speculative, I may say that every one is based on the data of actual analyses, as are all the conclusions presented in this paper.

[4] Sadger, *op. cit.*, S. 44.

(excepting, of course, the cases of girls where this is due rather to an exhibitionistic impulse). My experience agrees with his in this conclusion, with, however, one modification. I find that the anal-erotic reaction often extends to the *inside* of the body, there being a conviction that everything inside is inherently filthy;[1] I have known such people be unwilling even to insert a finger into their own mouths, and to have the custom of drinking large quantities of water daily with the idea of cleansing the dirty inside of the body.

In striking contrast with the character trait of loving care in regard to objects, which was mentioned above (under *A.* 1), is the attitude of the present type. Such people, so far from being proud of their possessions and productions, take very little interest in them. They are often quite indifferent to their immediate surroundings, to their furniture, clothes, and so on. As to their own productions, whether material or mental, their chief concern after the process is finished is to get rid of them as completely as possible, and they discard them with no wish to know what becomes of them. This attitude may, through the association explained above, even extend to the children produced, though such cases are rare; when this happens, the woman may delight in the process of pregnancy itself, but take no interest in the results of it.

An extension of this reaction is the exaggerated disgust and aversion sometimes displayed in regard to any idea of contaminating or spoiling. Such people are abjectly miserable at the thought of anything, especially beautiful objects, being injured, spoiled, ruined, and their life in an industrial age is one long protest against the intrusion of man, with all his squalor and ugliness, into the previously untouched spots of Nature. The staining of table-linen, the defacement of a book, the injuring of a picture, the growth of a town over what were fields and woods, the post-prandial performances of trippers in the country, the building of a new factory or the extension of a railway—all evoke the same reaction of agonised distress and resentment.

A variety of the reaction that is very important sociologically is what may be called the morbid purity complex. I refer to the purity fanatics who can only conceive of sexuality as a kind of anal erotism, and to whom, therefore, all its manifestations are necessarily filthy.[2]

---

[1] Accompanying this is often to be found a marked hypochondria, especially in regard to alimentary functioning of all kinds

[2] See *Jahrbuch, op. cit.,* S. 580.

They have so perverted the very meaning of the word ' pure ' that it is hardly possible to use it nowadays without exposing oneself to the so often well-founded comment, ' To the pure all things are impure.' My experience also tallies with Sadger's[1] in tracing to the same origin what he calls ' the theory of the pure man ' that so many neurotic girls hold—namely, the belief that a man is defiled unless he enters marriage with no previous experience of allo-erotic functioning. To such people sexuality is so inherently filthy in itself that it can only be removed from this reproach—if at all—by surrounding it with the most elaborate precautions and special conditions.

A little should be said, in conclusion, of a theme that has so far not been touched on here—namely, the psychological derivatives of the flatus complex, of the infant's interest in the production of intestinal gas. I have devoted a monograph[2] to some aspects of the part played in art and religion by this complex, the manifestations of which are a good deal more extensive than might be supposed. I have shown[3] that in the unconscious the idea of flatus forms important associations with a series of other ideas having similar attributes, notably those of sound, light, odour, fire, breath, speech, thunder, thought, mind, soul, music, poetry,[4] and that a number of mental attitudes towards these ideas is influenced by the association in question. I do not propose to repeat these here, but will simply illustrate them by a few examples. A passion for propagandism of ideas and a belief in telepathy[5] may be largely determined by this complex. So may an intense aversion for already-breathed air, with a fanaticism for fresh air, a passionate interest in the subject of breath control, and the conviction that breathing exercises afford a panacea for mental and bodily ills. With speech, quite apart from gross inhibitions like stuttering, the influence of the associated flatus complex may extend into the finest details of syntax and grammar; a man, for instance, who was habitually reticent in speech cherished the ambition, which he very largely carried out, of being able so to

[1] Sadger, *op. cit.*, S. 45.

[2] ' Essays in Applied Psycho-Analysis,' 1923, Chapter VIII.

[3] *Jahrbuch der Psychoanalyse*, Bd. iv. and v.

[4] It is noteworthy that the anal-erotic complex plays a part in relation to each of the five arts, architecture, sculpture, painting, music, and poetry, as might have been expected from the important contribution to æsthetics in general that is provided by the reaction-formation against anal erotism.

[5] See *Jahrbuch*, Bd. iv., S. 590, u. ff.; and also Hitschmann, *Internat. Zeitschr. f. ärztl. Psychoanalyse*, Jahrg. i. S. 253.

construct his clauses, on a very German model, as to expel all he might have to say in one massive but superbly finished sentence that could be flung out complete and the whole matter done with.

GENERAL SURVEY

The number of character traits and interests ranged over in the preceding remarks has been so great, and the account given of them so bald, that it may conduce to perspicuity if I once more review shortly the subject as a whole. One should keep well in mind the two fundamental phases of the process—the first one of ' keeping back ' and the second one of ' giving out ' respectively, each of which gives rise to its own series of character traits. With both of them the person strongly objects to being thwarted, to being prevented from either ' keeping back ' or ' giving out,' as the case may be; this attitude may lead to marked individualism, self-willedness, obstinacy, irritability, and bad temper. Heavy-mindedness, dogged persistence, and concentration, with a passion for thoroughness and completeness, are characterisics equally related to both phases.

Much of the person's later character will depend on the detailed interplay of the attitudes distinctive of each phase, and on the extent to which he may react to each by developing either a positive sublimation or a negative reaction-formation. The sublimations result in two contrasting character types: on the one hand a parsimonious and perhaps avaricious one, with a fondness for possessing and caring for objects, and a great capacity for tenderness so long as the loved person is docile; on the other hand, a more creative and productive type, with active tendencies to imprint the personality on something or somebody, with a fondness for moulding and manipulating, and a great capacity for giving, especially in love. The reaction-formations lead to the character traits of orderliness, cleanliness, pedantry, with a dislike of waste; they also afford important contributions to æsthetic tendencies.

It will be seen that the total result is an extremely varied one, owing to the complexity of the interrelations of the different anal-erotic components with one another and with other constituents of the whole character. Some of the most valuable qualities are derived from this complex, as well as some of the most disadvantageous. To the former may be reckoned especially the individualism, the determination and persistence, the love of order and power of organisation, the competency, reliability and thoroughness, the generosity, the bent towards art and good taste, the capacity for unusual tenderness, and the general ability to deal with concrete objects of the material world. To the latter belong the incapacity for happiness, the irritability and bad temper, the hypochondria, the miserliness, meanness and pettiness, the slow-mindedness and proneness to bore, the bent for dictating and tyrannising, and the obstinacy which, with other qualities, may make the person exceedingly unfitted for social relations.

CHAPTER XXV

THE EARLY DEVELOPMENT OF FEMALE SEXUALITY[1]

FREUD has more than once commented on the fact that our knowledge of the early stages in female development is much more obscure and imperfect than that of male development, and Karen Horney has forcibly, though justly, pointed out that this must be connected with the greater tendency to bias that exists on the former subject. It is probable that this tendency to bias is common to the two sexes, and it would be well if every writer on the subject kept this consideration in the foreground of his mind throughout. Better still, it is to be hoped that analytic investigation will gradually throw light on the nature of the prejudice in question and ultimately dispel it. There is a healthy suspicion growing that men analysts have been led to adopt an unduly phallo-centric view of the problems in question, the importance of the female organs being correspondingly underestimated. Women have on their side contributed to the general mystification by their secretive attitude towards their own genitals and by displaying a hardly disguised preference for interest in the male organ.

The immediate stimulus to the investigation on which the present paper is mainly based was provided by the unusual experience, a couple of years ago, of having to analyse at the same time five cases of manifest homosexuality in women. The analyses were all deep ones and lasted from three to five years; they have been completed in three of the cases and carried to a far stage in the other two. Among the numerous problems thus aroused two particular ones may serve as a starting-point for the considerations I wish to bring forward here. They were: what precisely in women corresponds with the fear of castration in men? and what differentiates the development of homosexual from that of heterosexual women? It will be noticed that these two questions are closely related, the word ' penis ' indicating the point of connection between them.

A few clinical facts about these cases may be of interest, though I do not propose to relate any casuistic material. Three of the

---

[1] Read at the Tenth International Congress of Psycho-Analysis, Innsbruck, September 1, 1927. Published in the *International Journal of Psycho-Analysis*, vol. viii.

patients were in the twenties and two in the thirties. Only two of the five had an entirely negative attitude towards men. It was not possible to establish any consistent rule in respect of their conscious attitude towards the parents: all varieties occurred, negative towards the father with either negative or positive towards the mother, and *vice versa*. In all five cases, however, it proved that the unconscious attitude towards both parents was strongly ambivalent. In all cases there was evidence of an unusually strong infantile fixation in regard to the mother, this being definitely connected with the oral stage. This was always succeeded by a strong father fixation, whether it was temporary or permanent in consciousness.

The first of the two questions mentioned above might also be formulated as follows: when the girl feels that she has already suffered castration, what imagined future event can evoke dread proportionate to the dread of castration? In attempting to answer this question—*i.e.*, to account for the fact that women suffer from dread at least as much as men—I came to the conclusion that the concept ' castration ' has in some respects hindered our appreciation of the fundamental conflicts. We have here in fact an example of what Karen Horney has indicated as an unconscious bias from approaching such studies too much from the male point of view. In his illuminating discussion of the penis complex in women, Abraham[1] had remarked that there was no reason for not applying the word ' castration ' there as well as with men, for wishes and fears about the penis of a parallel order occur in both. To agree with this statement, however, does not involve overlooking the differences in the two cases, nor should it blind us to the danger of importing into the one considerations with which we are already familiar in the other. Freud has justly remarked in connection with the pre-genital precursors of castration (weaning and defæcation, pointed out by Stärcke and myself respectively) that the psycho-analytical concept of castration, as distinguished from the corresponding biological one, refers definitely to the penis alone—the testicles at most being included in addition.

Now the fallacy to which I wish to draw attention here is this. The all-important part normally played in male sexuality by the genital organs naturally tends to make us equate castration with the abolition of sexuality altogether. This fallacy often creeps into our arguments even though we know that many men wish to be

---

[1] Abraham, ' Selected Papers,' 1927, p. 339.

castrated for, among others, erotic reasons, so that their sexuality certainly does not disappear with the surrender of the penis. With women, where the whole penis idea is always partial and mostly secondary in nature, this should be still more evident. In other words, the prominence of castration fears among men tends sometimes to make us forget that in both sexes castration is only a *partial* threat, however important a one, against sexual capacity and enjoyment as a whole. For the main blow of total extinction we might do well to use a separate term, such as the Greek word ' aphanisis.'

If we pursue to its roots the fundamental fear which lies at the basis of all neuroses we are driven, in my opinion, to the conclusion that what it really signifies is this aphanisis, the total, and of course permanent, extinction of the capacity (including opportunity) for sexual enjoyment. After all, this is the consciously avowed intention of most adults towards children. Their attitude is quite uncompromising: children are not to be permitted *any* sexual gratification. And we know that to the child the idea of indefinite postponement is much the same as that of permanent refusal. We cannot, of course, expect that the unconscious, with its highly concrete nature, will express itself for us in these abstract terms, which admittedly represent a generalisation. The nearest approach to the idea of aphanisis that we meet with clinically is that of castration and of death thoughts (conscious dread of death and unconscious death wishes). I may cite here an obsessional case in a young man which illustrates the same point. He had substituted as his *summum bonum* the idea of æsthetic enjoyment for that of sexual gratification, and his castration fears took the form of apprehension lest he should lose his capacity for this enjoyment, behind them being of course the concrete idea of the loss of the penis.

From this point of view we see that the question under discussion was wrongly put. The male dread of being castrated may or may not have a precise female counterpart, but what is more important is to realise that this dread is only a special case and that both sexes ultimately dread exactly the same thing, aphanisis. The mechanism whereby this is supposed to be brought about shows important differences in the two sexes. If we neglect for the moment the sphere of auto-erotism—on the justifiable ground that conflicts here owe their main importance to the subsequent allo-erotic cathexis of it—and thus confine our attention to allo-erotism itself, we may say that the reconstructed train of thought in the male is somewhat as follows: ' I wish to obtain gratification by committing a particular act, but I dare not do so because I fear that it would be followed by the punishment of aphanisis, by castration that would mean for me the permanent extinction of sexual pleasure.' The corresponding thought in the female, with her more passive nature, is characteristically somewhat different: ' I wish to obtain gratification through a particular experience, but I dare not take any steps towards bringing it about, such as asking for it and thus confessing my guilty wish, because I fear that to do this would be followed by aphanisis.' It is, of course, plain that this difference is not only not invariable, but is in any event only one of degree. In both cases there is activity, though it is more overt and vigorous with the male. This is not, however, the main difference in accent; a more important one depends on the fact that, for obvious physiological reasons, the female is much more dependent on her partner for her gratification than is the male on his. Venus had much more trouble with Adonis, for example, than Pluto with Persephone.

The last consideration mentioned provides the biological reason for the most important psychological differences in the behaviour and attitude of the sexes. It leads directly to a greater dependence (as distinct from desire) of the female on the willingness and moral approbation of the partner than we usually find in the male, where characteristically the corresponding sensitiveness occurs in respect of another, authoritative, male. Hence, among other things, the more familiar reproaches and need for reassurance on the woman's part. Among the important social consequences the following may be mentioned. It is well known that the morality of the world is essentially a male creation, and—what is much more curious—that the moral ideals of women are mainly copied from those of men. This must certainly be connected with the fact, pointed out by Helene Deutsch,[1] that the super-ego of women is, like that of men, predominantly derived from reactions to the father. Another consequence, which brings us back to our main discussion, is that the mechanism of aphanisis tends to differ in the two sexes. Whereas with the male this is typically conceived of in the active form of castration, with the female the primary fear would appear to be that of separation. This can be imagined as coming about through the rival mother intervening between the girl and the father, or even through her sending the girl away for ever, or else through the

[1] Helene Deutsch, ' Zur Psychologie der weiblichen Sexualfunktionen,' 1925, S. 9.

father simply withholding the desired gratification. The deep fear of being deserted that most women have is a derivative of the latter.

At this point it is possible to obtain from the analysis of women a deeper insight than from that of men into the important question of the relation between privation and guilt, in other words into the genesis of the super-ego. In his paper on the passing of the Œdipus complex Freud suggested that this happened in the female as the direct result of continued disappointment (privation), and we know that the super-ego is as much the heir of this complex in the female as in the male, where it is the product of the guilt derived from the dread of castration. It follows, and my analytical experience fully confirms the conclusion,[1] that sheer privation comes, of course in both sexes, to have just the same meaning as deliberate deprivation on the part of the human environment. We thus reach the formula: *Privation is equivalent to frustration.* It is even possible that, as may be inferred from Freud's remarks on the passing of the female Œdipus complex, privation alone may be an adequate cause for the genesis of guilt. To discuss this further would take us too far into the structure of the super-ego and away from the present theme, but I should like just to mention a view I have reached which is sufficiently germane to the latter. It is that guilt, and with it the super-ego, is as it were artificially built up for the purpose of protecting the child from the stress of privation—*i.e.*, of ungratified libido—and so warding off the dread of aphanisis that always goes with this; it does so, of course, by damping down the wishes that are not destined to be gratified. I even think that the external disapproval, to which the whole of this process used to be ascribed, is largely an affair of exploitation on the child's part; that is to say, non-gratification primarily means danger, and the child projects this into the outer world, as it does with all internal dangers, and than makes use of any disapproval that comes to meet it there (*moralisches Entgegenkommen*) to signalise the danger and to help it in constructing a barrier against this.

To return once more to the young girl, we are faced with the task of tracing the various stages in development from the initial oral one. The view commonly accepted is that the nipple, or artificial teat, is replaced, after a little dallying with the thumb, by

---

[1] This was reached partly in conjunction with Mrs. Riviere, whose views are expounded in another context, *International Journal of Psycho-Analysis*, vol. viii., pp. 374-5.

the clitoris as the chief source of pleasure, just as it is with boys by the penis. Freud[1] holds that it is the comparative unsatisfactoriness of this solution which automatically guides the child to seek for a better external penis, and thus ushers in the Œdipus situation where the wish for a baby[2] gradually replaces that for a penis. My own analyses, as do Melanie Klein's 'early analyses,' indicate that in addition to this there are more direct transitions between the oral and the Œdipus stages. It would seem to me that the tendencies derived from the former stage bifurcate early into clitoris and fellatio directions—*i.e.*, into digital plucking at the clitoris and into fellatio phantasies respectively; the proportion between the two would naturally be different in different cases, and this may be expected to have fateful consequences for the later development.

We have now to follow these lines of development in closer detail, and I will first sketch what I conceive to be the more normal mode of development, that leading to heterosexuality. Here the sadistic phase sets in late, and so neither the oral nor the clitoris stage receives any strong sadistic cathexis. In consequence, the clitoris does not become associated with a particularly active masculine attitude (thrusting forward, etc.), nor on the other hand is the oral-sadistic phantasy of biting off the male penis at all highly developed. The oral attitude is mainly a sucking one and passes by the well-known developmental transition into the anal stage. The two alimentary orifices thus constitute the receptive female organ. The anus is evidently identified with the vagina to begin with, and the differentiation of the two is an extremely obscure process, more so perhaps than any other in female development; I surmise, however, that it takes place in part at an earlier age than is generally supposed. A variable amount of sadism is always developed in connection with the anal stage and is revealed in the familiar phantasies of anal rape which may or may not pass over into beating phantasies. The Œdipus relationship is here in full activity; and the anal phantasies, as we shall show later, are already a compromise between libidinal and self-punishment tendencies. This mouth-anus-vagina stage, therefore, represents an identification with the mother.

What in the meantime has been the attitude towards the penis?

[1] Freud, *International Journal of Psycho-Analysis*, vol. viii., p. 140.

[2] Little is said throughout this paper about the wish for a baby because I am mainly dealing with early stages. I regard the wish as being in large part a later derivative of the anal and phallic trends.

It is likely enough that the initial one is purely positive,[1] manifested by the desire to suck it. But penis-envy soon sets in and apparently always. The primary, so to speak auto-erotic, reasons for this have been well set out by Karen Horney[2] in her discussion of the part played by the organ in urinary, exhibitionistic, scopophilic and masturbatory activities. The wish to possess a penis as the male does passes normally, however, into the wish to share his penis in some coitus-like action by means of the mouth, anus or vagina. Various sublimations and reactions show that no woman escapes the early penis-envy stage, but I fully agree with Karen Horney,[3] Helene Deutsch,[4] Melanie Klein,[5] and other workers in their view that what we meet with clinically as penis-envy in the neuroses is only in small part derived from this source. We have to distinguish between what might perhaps be termed pre-Œdipus and post-Œdipus penis-envy (more accurately, auto-erotic and allo-erotic penis-envy), and I am convinced that clinically the latter is much the more significant of the two. Just as masturbatory and other auto-erotic activities owe their main importance to re-investment from allo-erotic sources, so we have to recognise that many clinical phenomena depend on the defensive function of regression, recently insisted on by Freud.[6] It is the privation resulting from the continued disappointment at never being allowed to share the penis in coitus with the father, or thereby to obtain a baby, that reactivates the girl's early wish to possess a penis of her own. According to the theory put forward above, it is this privation that is primarily the unendurable situation, the reason being that it is tantamount to the fundamental dread of aphanisis. Guilt, and the building up of the super-ego, is, as was explained above, the first and invariable defence against the unendurable privation. But this is too negative a solution in itself; the libido must come to expression somehow as well.

There are only two possible ways in which the libido can flow in this situation, though both may, of course, be attempted. The girl must choose, broadly speaking, between sacrificing her erotic

---

[1] Helene Deutsch (*op. cit.*, S. 19) records an interesting observation in a girl-child of eighteen months who viewed a penis with apparent indifference at that time, and who only later developed affective reactions.

[2] Karen Horney, *International Journal of Psycho-Analysis*, vol. v., pp. 52-54.

[3] *Ibid.*, p. 64.

[4] Helene Deutsch, *op. cit.*, S. 16-18.

[5] Melanie Klein, communications to the British Psycho-Analytical Society.

[6] Freud, ' Hemmung, Symptom und Angst,' 1926, S. 48, etc.

attachment to her father and sacrificing her femininity—*i.e.*, her anal identification with the mother. Either the object must be exchanged for another one or the wish must be; it is impossible to retain both. Either the father or the vagina (including pregenital vaginas) must be renounced. In the first case feminine wishes are developed on the adult plane—*i.e.*, diffuse erotic charm (narcissism), positive vaginal attitude towards coitus, culminating in pregnancy and child-birth—and are transferred to more accessible objects. In the second case the bond with the father is retained, but the object-relationship in it is converted into identification—*i.e.*, a penis complex is developed.

More will be said in the next section about the precise way in which this identification defence operates, but what I should like to lay stress on at the moment is the interesting parallelism thus established, already hinted at by Horney,[1] between the solutions of the Œdipus conflict in the two sexes. The boy also is threatened with aphanisis, the familiar castration fear, by the inevitable privation of his incest wishes. He also has to make the choice between changing the wish and changing the object, between renouncing his mother and renouncing his masculinity—*i.e.*, his penis. We have thus obtained a generalisation which applies in a unitary manner to boy and girl alike: *faced with aphanisis as the result of inevitable privation, they must renounce either their sex or their incest;* what cannot be retained, except at the price of neurosis, is hetero-erotic and allo-erotic incest—*i.e.*, an incestuous object-relationship. In both cases the situation of prime difficulty is the simple, but fundamental, one of union between penis and vagina. Normally this union is made possible by the overcoming of the Œdipus complex. When, on the other hand, the solution of inversion is attempted every effort is made to avoid the union, because it is bound up with the dread of aphanisis. The individual, whether male or female, then identifies his sexual integrity with possessing the organ of the opposite sex and becomes pathologically dependent on it. With boys this can be done either by using their mouth or anus as the necessary female organ (towards either a man or a masculine woman) or else by vicariously adopting the genitalia of a woman with whom they identify themselves; in the latter case they are dependent on the woman who carries the precious object and develop anxiety if she is absent or if anything in her attitude makes the organ difficult of access. With girls the

---

[1] Karen Horney, *op. cit.*, p. 64.

same alternative presents itself, and they become pathologically dependent on either possessing a penis themselves in their imagination or on having unobstructed access to that of the man with whom they have identified themselves. If the ' condition of dependence ' (cp. Freud's phrase ' Liebesbedingung ') is not fulfilled, the individuals, men or women, approach an aphanistic state, or, in looser terminology, ' feel castrated.' They alternate, therefore, between potency on the basis of inverted gratification and aphanisis. To put it more simply, they either have an organ of the opposite sex or none at all; to have one of their own sex is out of the question.

We have next to turn to the second of our two questions, the difference in the development of heterosexual and homosexual women. This difference was indicated in our discussion of the two alternative solutions of the Œdipus conflict, but it has now to be pursued in further detail. The divergence there mentioned—which, it need hardly be said, is always a matter of degree—between those who surrender the position of their object-libido (father) and those who surrender the position of their subject-libido (sex) can be followed into the field of homosexuality itself. One can distinguish two broad groups here. (1) Those who retain their interest in men, but who set their hearts on being accepted by men as one of themselves. To this group belongs the familiar type of women who ceaselessly complain of the unfairness of women's lot and their unjust ill-treatment by men. (2) Those who have little or no interest in men, but whose libido centres on women. Analysis shows that this interest in women is a vicarious way of enjoying femininity; they merely employ other women to exhibit it for them.[1]

It is not hard to see that the former group corresponds with the class in our previous division where the sex of the subject is surrendered, while the latter group corresponds with those who surrender the object (the father), replacing him by themselves through identification. I will amplify this condensed statement for the sake of greater clarity. The members of the first group exchange their own sex, but retain their first love-object; the object relationship, however, becomes replaced by identification, and the aim of the

---

[1] For the sake of simplicity an interesting third form is omitted in the text, but should be mentioned. Some women obtain gratification of feminine desires provided two conditions are present : (1) that the penis is replaced by a surrogate such as the tongue or finger, and (2) that the partner using this organ is a woman instead of a man. Though clinically they may appear in the guise of complete inversion, such cases are evidently nearer to the normal than either of the two mentioned in the text.

libido is to procure recognition of this identification by the former object. The members of the second group also identify themselves with the love-object, but then lose further interest in him; their external object-relationship to the other woman is very imperfect, for she merely represents their own femininity through identification, and their aim is vicariously to enjoy the gratification of this at the hand of an unseen man (the father incorporated in themselves).

Identification with the father is thus common to all forms of homosexuality, though it proceeds to a more complete degree in the first group than in the second, where, in a vicarious way, some femininity is after all retained. There is little doubt that this identification serves the function of keeping feminine wishes in repression. It constitutes the most complete denial imaginable of the accusation of harbouring guilty feminine wishes, for it asserts, ' I cannot possibly desire a man's penis for my gratification, since I already possess one of my own, or at all events I want nothing else than one of my own.' Expressed in terms of the theory developed earlier in this paper, it assures the most complete defence against the aphanistic danger of privation from non-gratification of the incest wishes. The defence is in fact so well designed that it is little wonder that indications of it can be detected in all girls passing through the Œdipus stage of development, though the extent to which it is retained later is extremely variable. I would even venture the opinion that when Freud postulated a ' phallic ' stage in female development corresponding with that in the male—*i.e.*, a stage in which all the interest appears to relate to the male organ only with obliteration of the vaginal or prevaginal organs—he was giving a clinical description of what may be observed rather than a final analysis of the actual libidinal position at that stage; for it seems to me likely that the phallic stage in normal girls is but a mild form of the father-penis identification of the female homosexuals, and, like it, of an essentially secondary and defensive nature.

Karen Horney[1] has pointed out that for a girl to maintain a feminine position and to accept the absence of a penis in herself often signifies not only the daring to have incestuous object-wishes, but also the phantasy that her physical state is the result of a castrating rape once actually performed by the father. The penis identification, therefore, implies a denial of both forms of guilt, the wish that the

[1] *Idem, loc. cit.*

incestuous deed may happen in the future and the wish-fulfilment phantasy that it has already happened in the past. She further points out the greater advantage that this identification with the opposite sex presents to girls than to boys, because the defensive advantage common to both is strengthened with the former by the reinforcement of narcissism derived from the old pre-Œdipus sources of envy (urinary, exhibitionistic and masturbatory) and weakened with the latter by the blow to narcissism involved in the acceptance of castration.

As this identification is to be regarded as a universal phenomenon among young girls, we have to seek further for the motives that heighten it so extraordinarily and in such a characteristic way among those who later become homosexual. Here I must present my conclusions on this point even more briefly than those in the former ones. The fundamental—and, so far as one can see, inborn—factors that are decisive in this connection appear to be two—namely, an unusual intensity of oral erotism and of sadism respectively. These converge in an *intensification of the oral-sadistic stage*, which I would regard, in a word, as *the central characteristic of homosexual development in women*.

The sadism shows itself not only in the familiar muscular manifestations, with the corresponding derivatives of these in character, but also in imparting a specially active (thrusting) quality to the clitoris impulses, which naturally heightens the value of any penis that may be acquired in phantasy. Its most characteristic manifestation, however, is to be found in the oral-sadistic impulse forcibly to wrench the penis from the man by the act of biting. When, as is often found, the sadistic temperament is accompanied by a ready reversal of love to hate, with the familiar ideas of injustice, resentment and revenge, then the biting phantasies gratify both the desire to obtain a penis by force and also the impulse to revenge themselves on the man by castrating him.

The high development of the oral erotism is manffested in the numerous ways well known through the researches of Abraham[1] and Edward Glover;[2] they may be positive or negative in consciousness. A special feature, however, to which attention should be called is the importance of the tongue in such cases. The identifica-

[1] Abraham, *op. cit.*, ch. xii.
[2] Edward Glover, ' Notes on Oral Character Formation,' *Internationa Journal of Psycho-Analysis*, vol. vi., p. 131.

tion of tongue with penis, with which Flügel[1] and I[2] have dealt at length, reaches with some female homosexuals a quite extraordinary degree of completeness. I have seen cases where the tongue was an almost entirely satisfactory substitute for the penis in homosexual activities. It is evident that the nipple fixation here implied favours the development of homosexuality in two ways. It makes it harder for the girl to pass from the fellatio position to that of vaginal coitus, and it also makes it easier to have recourse once more to a woman as the object of libido.

A further interesting correlation may be affected at this point. The two factors mentioned above of oral erotism and sadism appear to correspond very well with the two classes of homosexuals. Where the oral erotism is the more prominent of the two the individual will probably belong to the second group (interest in women) and where the sadism is the more prominent to the first group (interest in men).

A word should be said about the important factors that influence the *later* development of female homosexuality. We have said that, to protect herself against aphanisis, the girl erects various barriers, notably penis identification, against her femininity. Prominent among these is a strong sense of guilt and condemnation concerning feminine wishes; most often this is for the greater part unconscious. As an aid to this barrier of guilt the idea is developed of ' men ' (*i.e.*, the father) being strongly opposed to feminine wishes. To help her own condemnation of it she is forced to believe that all men in their hearts disapprove of femininity. To meet this comes the unfortunate circumstance that many men do really evince disparagement of women's sexuality together with dread of the female organ. There are several reasons for this, into which we need not enter here; they all centre around the male castration complex. The homosexual woman, however, seizes with avidity on any manifestations of this attitude and can by means of them sometimes convert her deep belief into a complete delusional system. Even in milder forms it is quite common to find both men and women ascribing the whole of the supposed inferiority of women[3] to the social influences which the deeper tendencies have exploited in the way just indicated.

I will conclude with a few remarks on the subjects of dread and

---

[1] J. C. Flügel, ' A Note on the Phallic Significance of the Tongue,' *International Journal of Psycho-Analysis*, 1925, vol. vi., p. 209.

[2] Ernest Jones, *Essays in Applied Psycho-Analysis*, 1923, ch. viii.

[3] Really, their inferiority *as* women.

punishment among women in general. The ideas relating to these may be connected mainly with the mother or mainly with the father. In my experience the former is more characteristic of the hetero-sexual and the latter more of the homosexual. The former appears to be a simple retaliation for the aggressive and death wishes against the mother, who will punish the girl by coming between her and the father, by sending the girl away for ever, or by in any other way seeing to it that her incestuous wishes remain ungratified. The girl's answer is partly to retain her femininity at the cost of renouncing the father and partly to obtain vicarious gratification of her incest wishes in her imagination through identification with the mother.

When the dread mainly relates to the father the punishment takes the obvious form of his withholding gratification of her wishes, and this rapidly passes over into the idea of his disapproval of them. Rebuff and desertion are the common conscious expressions of this punishment. If this privation takes place on the oral plane the answer is resentment and castrating (biting) phantasies. If it takes place on the later anal plane the outcome is rather more favourable. Here the girl manages to combine in a single act her erotic wishes with the idea of being punished—namely, anal-vaginal rape; the familiar phantasies of being beaten are, of course, a derivative of this. As was remarked above, this is one of the ways in which incest gets equated with castration, so that the penis phantasy is a protection against both.

We may now *recapitulate the main conclusions* reached here. For different reasons both boys and girls tend to view sexuality in terms of the penis alone, and it is necessary for analysts to be sceptical in this direction. The concept ' castration ' should be reserved, as Freud pointed out, for the penis alone, and should not be con-founded with that of ' extinction of sexuality,' for which the term ' aphanisis ' is proposed. Privation in respect of sexual wishes evokes with the child the fear of aphanisis—*i.e.*, is equivalent to the dread of frustration. Guilt arises rather from within as a defence against this situation than as an imposition from without, though the child exploits any *moralisches Entgegenkommen* in the outer world.

The oral-erotic stage in the young girl passes directly into the fellatio and clitoris stages, and the former of these then into the anal-erotic stage; the mouth, anus and vagina thus form an equivalent series for the female organ. The repression of the incest wishes results in regression to the pre-Œdipus, or auto-erotic, penis-envy as a defence against them. The penis-envy met with clinically is principally derived from this reaction on the allo-erotic plane, the identification with the father essentially representing denial of femininity. *Freud's 'phallic phase' in girls is probably a secondary, defensive construction rather than a true developmental stage.*

To avoid neurosis both the boy and the girl have to overcome the Œdipus conflict in the same way: they can surrender either the love-object or their own sex. In the latter, homosexual solution they become dependent on imagined possession of the organ of the opposite sex, either directly or through identification with another person of that sex. This yields the two main forms of homosexuality.

The essential factors that decide whether a girl will develop the father-identification in such a high degree as to constitute a clinical inversion are specially intense oral erotism and sadism, which typically combine in an intense oral sadistic stage. If the former of these two factors is the more prominent one the inversion takes the form of dependence on another woman, with lack of interest in men; the subject is male, but enjoys femininity also through identification with a feminine woman whom she gratifies by a penis substitute, most typically the tongue. Prominence of the second factor leads to occupation with men, the wish being to obtain from them recognition of the subject's male attributes; it is this type that shows so often resentment against men, with castrating (biting) phantasies in respect of them.

The heterosexual woman dreads the mother more than the homosexual woman does, whose dread centres around the father. The punishment feared in the latter case is withdrawal (desertion) on the oral level, beating on the anal one (rectal assault).

CHAPTER XXVI

THE PHALLIC PHASE [1]

IF one studies closely the many important contributions made in the past ten years, particularly by women analysts, to the admittedly obscure problems relating to the early development of female sexuality one perceives an unmistakable disharmony among the various writers, and this is beginning to show also in the field of male sexuality. Most of these writers have been laudably concerned to lay stress on the points of agreement with their colleagues, so that the tendency to divergence of opinion has not always come to full expression. It is my purpose here to investigate it unreservedly in the hope of crystallising it. If there is confusion it is desirable to clear it up; if there is a divergence of opinion we should, by defining it, be able to set ourselves interesting questions for further research.

For this purpose I will select the theme of the phallic phase. It is fairly circumscribed, but we shall see that it ramifies into most of the deeper and unsolved problems. In a paper read before the Innsbruck Congress in 1927,[2] I put forward the suggestion that the phallic phase in the development of female sexuality represented a secondary solution of psychical conflict, of a defensive nature, rather than a simple and direct developmental process; last year Professor Freud[3] declared this suggestion to be quite untenable. Already at that time I had in mind similar doubts about the phallic phase in the male also, but did not discuss them since my paper was concerned purely with female sexuality; recently Dr. Horney[4] has voiced scepticism about the validity of the concept of the male phallic phase, and I will take this opportunity to comment on the arguments she has advanced.

---

[1] Read in brief before the Twelfth International Psycho-Analytical Congress, Wiesbaden, September 4, 1932, and in full before the British Psycho-Analytical Society, October 19 and November 2, 1932. Published in the *International Journal of Psycho-Analysis*, vol. xiv., 1933.

[2] Chapter xxv.

[3] Freud, 'Female Sexuality,' *International Journal of Psycho-Analysis*, 1932, vol. xiii., p. 297.

[4] Karen Horney, 'The Dread of Women,' *International Journal of Psycho-Analysis*, 1932, vol. xiii., p. 353.

I will first remind you that in Freud's[1] description of the phallic phase the essential feature common to both sexes was the belief that only one kind of genital organ exists in the world—a male one. According to Freud, the reason for this belief is simply that the female organ has at this age not yet been discovered by either sex: human beings are thus divided, not into those possessing a male organ and those possessing a female organ, but into those who possess a penis and those who do not: there is the penis-possessing class and the castrated class. A boy begins by believing that everyone belongs to the former class, and only as his fears get aroused does he begin to suspect the existence of the latter class. A girl takes the same view, save that here one should use the corresponding phrase, ' clitoris-possessing class '; and only after comparing her own with the male genital does she form a conception of a mutilated class, to which she belongs. Both sexes strive against accepting the belief in the second class, and both for the same reason—namely, from a wish to disbelieve in the supposed reality of castration. This picture as sketched by Freud is familiar to you all, and the readily available facts of observation from which it is drawn have been confirmed over and over again. The interpretation of the facts, however, is of course another matter and is not so easy.

I would now call your attention to a consideration which is implied in Freud's account, but which needs further emphasis for the sake of clarity. It is that there would appear to be two distinct stages in the phallic phase. Freud would, I know, apply the same term, ' phallic phase,' to both, and so has not explicitly subdivided them. The first of the two—let us call it the *proto-phallic* phase—would be marked by innocence or ignorance—at least in consciousness—where there is no conflict over the matter in question, it being confidently assumed by the child that the rest of the world is built like itself and has a satisfactory male organ—penis or clitoris, as the case may be. In the second or *deutero-phallic* phase there is a dawning suspicion that the world is divided into two classes: not male and female in the proper sense, but penis-possessing and castrated (though actually the two classifications overlap pretty closely). The deutero-phallic phase would appear to be more neurotic than the proto-phallic—at least in this particular context. For it is associated with anxiety, conflict, striving against accepting what is felt to be

[1] Freud, ' The Infantile Genital Organisation of the Libido,' ' Collected Papers ' (International Psycho-Analytical Library, 1924), vol. ii., p. 245.

reality—*i.e.*, castration—and over-compensatory emphasis on the narcissistic value of the penis on the boy's side with a mingled hope and despair on the girl's.

It is plain that the difference between the two phases is marked by the idea of castration, which according to Freud is bound up in both sexes with actual observation of the anatomical sex differences. As is well known, he is of opinion[1] that the fear or thought of being castrated has a weakening effect on the masculine impulses with both sexes. He considers that with the boy it drives him away from the mother and strengthens the phallic and homosexual attitude—*i.e.*, that the boy surrenders some of his incestuous heterosexuality to save his penis; whereas with the girl it has the more fortunate opposite effect of impelling her into a feminine, heterosexual attitude. According to this view, therefore, the castration complex weakens the boy's Œdipus relationship and strengthens the girl's; it drives the boy *into* the deutero-phallic phase, while—after a temporary protest on that level—it drives the girl *out of* the deutero-phallic phase.

As the development of the boy is supposed to be better understood, and is perhaps the simpler of the two, I will begin with it. We are all familiar with the narcissistic quality of the phallic phase here, which Freud says reaches its maximum about the age of four, though it is certainly manifest long before this;[2] I am speaking particularly of the deutero-phallic phase. There are two outstanding differences between it and the earlier stages: (1) It is less sadistic, the main relic of this being a tendency to omnipotence phantasies; and (2) it is more self-centred, the chief allo-erotic attribute still remaining being its exhibitionistic aspect. It is thus less aggressive and less related to other people, notably to women. How has this change been brought about ? It would seem to be change in the direction of phantasy and away from the real world of contact with other human beings. If so, this would in itself justify a suspicion that there is a flight element present, and that we have not to do simply with a natural evolution towards greater reality and a more developed adjustment.

[1] Freud, ' Some Psychological Consequences of the Anatomical Distinction between the Sexes,' *International Journal of Psycho-Analysis*, 1927, vol. viii., pp. 133, 141.

[2] When this paper was read before the British Psycho-Analytical Society three child analysts (Melanie Klein, Melitta Schmideberg and Nina Searl) gave it as their experience that traces of the *deutero*-phallic phase can be detected before the end of the first year.

This suspicion is very evidently borne out in one set of circumstances—namely, when the phallic phase persists into adult life. In applying the psycho-analytic microscope to investigate a difficult problem we may make use of the familiar magnification afforded by neurosis and perversion. Elucidation of the operative factors there gives us pointers to direct our attention in examining the so-called normal; as will be remembered, this was the path Freud followed to reach in general the infantile sexuality of the normal. Now with these adult cases it is quite easy to ascertain the presence of secondary factors in the sexual life, factors particularly of fear and guilt. The type I have specially in mind is that of the man, frequently hypochondriacal, who is concerned with the size and quality of his penis (or its symbolic substitutes) and who shows only feeble impulses towards women, with in particular a notably weak, or even non-existent, impulse towards penetration; narcissism, exhibitionism (or undue modesty), masturbation and a varying degree of homosexuality are common accompanying features. In analysis it is easily seen that all these inhibitions are repressions or defences motivated by deep anxiety; the nature of the anxiety I shall discuss presently.

Having our eyes sharpened by such experiences to the secondary nature of narcissistic phallicism, we may now turn to similar attitudes in boyhood—I am again referring to the deutero-phallic phase and in pronounced examples—and I maintain that we find there ample evidence to come to a similar conclusion. To begin with, the picture is essentially the same. There is the narcissistic concentration on the penis, with doubts or uncertainties about its size and quality. Under the heading of ' Secondary Reinforcement of Penis-Pride,' Melanie Klein[1] has in her recent book discussed at length the value of the penis to the boy in mastering deep anxieties from various sources, and she maintains that the narcissistic exaggeration of phallicism—i.e., the phallic phase, although she does not use that term in this connection—is due to the need of coping with specially large amounts of anxiety.

It is noteworthy how much of the boy's sexual curiosity of this period, to which Freud[2] called special attention in his original paper on the subject, is taken up, not with interest in females, but with comparisons between himself and other males. This is in accord with

---

[1] Melanie Klein, ' The Psycho-Analysis of Children ' (International Psycho-Analytical Library, 1932), p. 341.

[2] Freud, ' The Infantile,' etc., op. cit., p. 246.

the striking absence of the impulse towards penetration, an impulse which would logically lead to curiosity and search for its complement. Karen Horney[1] has rightly called special attention to this feature of inhibited penetration, and as the impulse to penetrate is without doubt the main characteristic of penis functioning it is surely remarkable that just where the idea of the penis dominates the picture its own most salient characteristic should be absent. I do not for a moment believe that this is because the characteristic in question has not yet been developed, a retardation due perhaps to simple ignorance of a vaginal counterpart. On the contrary, in earlier stages—as child analysts in particular have shown—there is ample evidence of sadistic penetrating tendencies in the phantasies, games and other activities of the male infant. And I quite agree with Karen Horney[2] in her conclusion that 'the undiscovered vagina is a denied vagina.' I cannot resist comparing this supposed ignorance of the vagina with the current ethnological myth that savages are ignorant of the connection between coitus and fertilisation. In both cases they know, but do not know that they know. In other words, there is knowledge, but it is *unconscious knowledge*—revealed in countless symbolic ways. The conscious ignorance is like the 'innocence' of young women—which still persists even in these enlightened days; it is merely unsanctioned or dreaded knowledge, and it therefore remains unconscious.

Actual analysis in adult life of the memories of the phallic stage yields results that coincide with the state of affairs where the phallic stage has persisted into adult life, as mentioned above, and also with the results obtained from child analysis[3] during the phallic stage itself. They are, as Freud first pointed out, that the narcissistic concentration on the penis goes hand in hand with dread of the female genital. It is also generally agreed that the former is secondary to the latter, or at all events to the fear of castration. It is not hard to see, further, that these two fears—of the female genital and of castration—stand in a specially close relationship to each other, and that no solution of the present group of problems can be satisfactory which does not throw light on both.

Freud himself does not use the word 'anxiety' in regard to the female genital, but speaks of 'horror' (*Abscheu*) of it. The word

---

[1] Karen Horney, 'The Dread,' etc., *op. cit.*, pp. 353, 354.
[2] *Ibid.*, p. 358.
[3] See in particular Melanie Klein, 'The Psycho-Analysis of Children.'

' horror ' is descriptive, but it implies an earlier dread of castration, and therefore demands an explanation of this in its turn. Some passages of Freud's read as if the horror of the female were a simple phobia protecting the boy from the thought of castrated beings, as it would from the sight of a one-legged man, but I feel sure he would admit a more specific relationship than this between the idea of castration and the particular castrated organ of the female; the two ideas must be innately connected. I think he implies that this horror is an associative reminder of what awful things—*i.e.*, castration— happen to people (like women) who have feminine wishes or get treated as women. It is certainly plain, as we have long known, that the boy here equates copulation with castration of one partner; and he evidently fears lest he might be that unfortunate partner. In this connection we may remember that to the neurotic phallic boy the idea of the female being castrated involves not merely a cutting off, but an opening being made into a hole, the well-known ' wound theory ' of the vulva. Now in our everyday practice we should find it hard to understand such a fear except in terms of a repressed wish to play the feminine part in copulation, evidently with the father. Otherwise castration and copulation would not be equated. A fear of this wish being put into effect would certainly explain the fear of being castrated, for by definition it is identical with this, and also the ' horror ' of the female genital—*i.e.*, a place where such wishes had been gratified. But that the boy equates copulation with castration seems to imply a previous knowledge of penetration. And it is not easy on this hypothesis to give adequate weight to the well-known connection between the castration fear and rivalry with the father over possession of the mother—*i.e.*, to the Œdipus complex. But we can at least see that the feminine wish must be a nodal point in the whole problem.

There would seem to be two views on the significance of the phallic phase, and I shall now attempt to ascertain in what respect they are opposed to each other and how far they may be brought into harmony. We may call them the simple and the complex view respectively. On the one hand, the boy, in a state of sex ignorance, may be supposed to have always assumed that the mother has a natural penis of her own until actual experience of the female genital, together with ideas of his own concerning castration (particularly his equating of copulation with castration), makes him reluctantly suspect that she has been castrated. This would accord with his known wish to believe that the mother has a penis. This simple view rather skims over the evidently prior questions of where the boy gets his ideas of copulation and castration from, but it does not follow that these could not be answered on this basis; that is a matter to be held in suspension for the moment. On the other hand, the boy may be supposed to have had from very early times an unconscious knowledge that the mother has an opening—and not only the mouth and anus—into which he could penetrate. The thought of doing so, however, for reasons we shall discuss in a moment, brings the fear of castration, and it is as a defence against this that he obliterates his impulse to penetrate, together with all idea of a vagina, replacing these respectively by phallic narcissism and insistence on his mother's similar possession of a penis. The second of these views implies a less simple—and avowedly a more remote— explanation of the boy's insistence on the mother's having a penis. It is, in effect, that he dreads her having a female organ more than he does her having a male one, the reason being that the former brings the thought and danger of penetrating into it. If there were only male organs in the world there would be no jealous conflict and no fear of castration; the idea of the vulva must precede that of castration. If there were no dangerous cavity to penetrate into there would be no fear of castration. This is, of course, on the assumption that the conflict and danger arise from his having the same wishes as his father, to penetrate into the same cavity; and this I believe— in conjunction with Melanie Klein and other child analysts—to be true of the earliest period, and not simply of that after the conscious discovery of the cavity in question.

We come now to the vexed question of the source of castration fears. Various authors hold different views on this question. Some of them are perhaps differences in accent only; others point to opposing conceptions. Karen Horney,[1] who has recently discussed the matter in relation to the boy's dread of the female genital, has very definite views on the matter. Speaking of the dread of the vulva she says: 'Freud's account fails to explain this anxiety. A boy's castration-anxiety in relation to his father is not an adequate reason for his dread of a being whom this punishment has already overtaken. Besides the dread of the father there must be a further dread, the object of which is the woman or female genital.' She even maintains the exceptional opinion that this dread of the vulva is not only

---

[1] Karen Horney, 'The Dread of Women,' *op. cit.*, p. 351.

earlier than that of the father's penis—whether external or concealed in the vagina—but deeper and more important than it; in fact much of the dread of the father's penis is artificially put forward to hide the intense dread of the vulva.[1] This is certainly a very debatable conclusion, although we must admit the technical difficulty of quantitatively estimating the amount of anxiety derived from various sources. We listen with curiosity to her explanation of this intense anxiety in regard to the mother. She mentions Melanie Klein's view of the boy's talion dread born in relation to his sadistic impulses toward's the mother's body, but the most important source of his dread of the vulva she would derive from the boy's fear of his self-esteem being wounded by knowing that his penis is not large enough to satisfy the mother, the mother's denial of his wishes being interpreted in this sense; the talion dread of castration by the mother is later and less important that the fear of ridicule.[2] One often gets, it is true, a vivid clinical picture of how strong this motive can be, but I doubt whether Dr. Horney has carried the analysis of it far enough. In my experience the deep shame in question, which can certainly express itself as impotence, is not simply due to the fear of ridicule as an ultimate fact; both the shame and the fear of ridicule proceed from a deeper complex—the adoption of a feminine attitude towards the father's penis that is incorporated in the mother's body. Karen Horney also calls attention to this feminine attitude, and even ascribes to it the main source of castration fear, but for her it is a secondary consequence of the dread of ridicule. We are here again brought back to the question of femininity and perceive that to answer it satisfactorily is probably to resolve the whole problem.

I will now try to reconstruct and comment on Karen Horney's argument about the connection between the dread of the vulva and the fear of castration. At the start the boy's masculinity and femininity are relatively free. Karen Horney quotes Freud's well-known views on primal bisexuality in support of her belief that the feminine wishes are primary. There perhaps are such primary feminine wishes, but I am convinced that conflict arises only when they are developed or exploited as a means of dealing with a dreaded father's penis. However, Karen Horney thinks that before this happens the boy has reacted to his mother's denial of his wishes and, as described above, feels shame and a deep sense of inadequacy in

[1] Ibid., pp. 352, 356. Ibid., p. 357.

consequence. As a result of this he can, according to her, no longer express his feminine wishes freely. There is a gap in the argument here. In the first place we are to assume that the boy at once equates his phallic inadequacy with femaleness, but it is not explained how the equation is brought about. At all events, he is now ashamed of his earlier feminine wishes, and dreads these being gratified because it would signify castration at the hands of the father—in fact, this is the essential cause of these castration fears. Surely there is another big gap in the argument here. How does the father suddenly appear on the scene? The essential point in the argument, and one on which I would join issue with Dr. Horney, would appear to be that the boy's sense of failure due to his mother's refusal leads him to fall back from his masculine wishes to feminine ones, which he then applies to the father but dreads to have gratified because of the admission they imply of his masculine inferiority (as well as the equivalence of castration). This is rather reminiscent of Adler's early views on the masculine protest. My experience leads me, on the contrary, to see the crucial turning-point in the Œdipus complex itself, in the dreaded rivalry with the father. It is to cope with this situation that the boy falls back on a feminine attitude with its risk of castration. Whereas Dr. Horney regards the feminine attitude as a primary one which the boy comes to repress because of the fear of ridicule of his masculine inferiority, this fear being the active dynamic agent, I should consider that the sense of inferiority itself, and the accompanying shame, are both secondary to the feminine attitude *and to the motive for this*. This whole group of ideas is strongest in men with a ' small penis ' complex, often accompanied by impotence, and it is with them that one gets the clearest insight into the genesis. What such a man is really ashamed of is not that his penis is ' small,' but the reason *why* it is ' small.'

On the other hand I fully agree with Karen Horney and other workers, notably Melanie Klein,[1] in the view that the boy's reaction to the crucial situation of the Œdipus complex is greatly influenced by his earlier relationship with his mother. But this is a much more complicated matter than wounded vanity; far grimmer factors are at work. Melanie Klein lays stress on the fear of the mother's retaliation for the boy's sadistic impulses against her body; and this independently of any thought of the father or his penis, though she

---

[1] Melanie Klein, ' Early Stages of the Œdipus Conflict,' *International Journal of Psycho-Analysis*, vol. ix., 1928, p. 167.

would agree that the latter heightens the boy's sadism and thus complicates the picture. As she has pointed out in detail,[1] however, these sadistic impulses have themselves an elaborate history. We have to begin with the alimentary level to appreciate the nature of the forces at work. Privations on this level—especially perhaps oral privations—are undoubtedly of the greatest importance in rendering harder the task of coping with the parents on the genital level, but we want to know exactly why this should be so. I could relate cases of a number of male patients whose failure to achieve manhood—in relation to either men or women—was strictly to be correlated with their attitude of needing first to acquire something from women, something which of course they never actually could acquire. Why should imperfect access to the nipple give a boy the sense of imperfect possession of his own penis? I am quite convinced that the two things are intimately related, although the logical connection between them is certainly not obvious.

I do not know to what extent a boy in the first year of life feels sure his mother has a genital organ like his own, on grounds of natural identification, but my impression is that any such idea has no serious interest for him until it gets involved in other associations. The first of these would appear to be the symbolic equivalency of nipple and penis. Here the mother's penis is mainly a more satisfying and nourishing nipple, its size alone being an evident advantage in this respect. Now how precisely does a bilateral organ, the breast, get changed into a medial one, the penis? When this happens does it mean that the boy, perhaps from his experiences or phantasies of the primal scene, has already come across the idea of the father's penis, or is it possible that even before this his early masturbatory experiences—so often associated with oral ones—together with the commonly expressed oral attitude towards his own penis, alone suffice for the identification? I am inclined to the latter opinion, but it is hard to get unequivocal data on the matter. Whichever of these alternatives is true, however, the attitude towards the mythical maternal penis must from the very first be ambivalent. On the one side there is the conception of a visible, and therefore accessible, friendly and nourishing organ which can be received and sucked. But on the other side the sadism stimulated by oral frustration—the very factor that first created the conception—must by projection create the idea of a sinister, hostile and dangerous organ

[1] Numerous publications in the *International Journal of Psycho-Analysis*.

which has to be destroyed by swallowing before the boy can feel safe. This ambivalence, beginning in regard to the mother's nipple (and nipple-penis), is greatly intensified when the father's penis becomes involved in the association. And it does so, I feel convinced, very early in life—certainly by the second year. This may be quite irrespective of actual experiences, even of the father's very existence, and is generated mainly by the boy's own libidinal sensations in his penis with their inevitable accompaniment of penetrative impulses. The ambivalent attitude is intensified on both sides. On the one hand the tendency to imitate the father gets related to the idea of acquiring strength from him, first of all orally, and on the other hand we get the well-known Œdipus rivalry and hostility, which also is first dealt with in terms of oral annihilation.

These considerations relating to the oral level begin to throw light on the riddle I propounded earlier—namely, why so many men feel unable to put something into a woman unless they have first got something out of her; why they cannot penetrate; or—put more broadly—why they need to pass through a satisfactory ' feminine ' stage before they can feel at home in a masculine one. I pointed out earlier on that in the feminine wishes of the boy must lie the secret of the whole problem. The first clue is that this feminine stage is an alimentary one, primarily oral. Satisfaction of wishes in this stage has to precede masculine development; failure in this respect results in fixation on the woman at an oral or anal level, a fixation which, although originating in anxiety, may become intensely eroticised in perverse forms.

I shall now try to proceed further in the answering of our riddle, and for the sake of simplicity shall consider separately the boy's difficulties with the mother and father respectively. But I must preface this by laying stress on its artificiality. When we consider the parents as two distinct beings, to be viewed separately one from the other, we are doing something that the infant is not yet capable of and something that does not greatly concern the infant in his (or her) most secret phantasies. We are artificially dissecting the elements of a concept (the ' combined parent concept,' as Melanie Klein well terms it) which to the infant are still closely interwoven. The findings of child analysis lead us to ascribe ever-increasing importance to the phantasies and emotions attaching to this concept, and I am very inclined to think that the expression ' pre-Œdipal phase ' used recently by Freud and other writers must correspond extensively with the phase of life dominated by the 'combined parent' concept.

At all events, let us consider first the relation to the mother alone. Leaving the father's penis quite out of account, we are concerned with the riddle of how the boy's acquiring something from the mother is related to his secure possession of the use of his own penis. I believe this connection between the oral and the phallic lies in the sadism common to both. The oral frustration evokes sadism, and the penetrating penis is used in phantasy as a sadistic weapon to reach the oral aims desired, to open a way to the milk, fæces, nipple, babies and so on, all of which the infant wants to swallow. The patients I alluded to earlier as having a perverse oral fixation on women were all highly sadistic. The equation tooth=penis is familiar enough, and it must begin in this sadistic pregenital stage of development. The sadistic penis has also important anal connections—e.g., the common phantasy of fetching a baby out of the bowel by the penis. The penis itself thus comes to be associated with the acquiring attitude, and thwarting of the latter to be identified with thwarting of the former—i.e., not being able to get milk, etc., is equivalent to not being able to use the penis. The thwarting leads further to retaliation fears of the mother damaging the weapons themselves. This I have even found on occasion equated with the earliest frustration. The mother's withholding of the nipple gave her the character of a nipple or penis hoarder, who would surely keep permanently any penis brought near her, and the boy's sadism can in such cases manifest itself—as a sort of double bluff—by a sadistic policy of withholding from the woman whatever she may desire—e.g., by being impotent.

Though this conflict with the mother no doubt lays the basis for later difficulties, my experience seems to teach me that greater importance is to be attached in the genesis of castration fear to the conflict with the father. But I have at once to add a very important proviso. In the boy's imagination the mother's genital is for so long inseparable from the idea of the father's penis dwelling there that one would get a very false perspective if one confined one's attention to his relationship to his actual 'external' father; this is perhaps the real difference between Freud's pre-Œdipal stage and the Œdipus complex proper. It is the hidden indwelling penis that accounts for a very great part of the trouble, the penis that has entered the mother's body or been swallowed by her—the dragon or dragons that haunt cloacal regions. Some boys attempt to deal with it on directly phallic lines, to use their penis in their phantasy for penetrating the vagina and crushing the father's penis there, or even—as I have many times found—by pursuing this phantasy to the length of penetrating into the father's body itself—*i.e.*, sodomy. One sees again, by the way, how this illustrates the close interchangeability of the father and mother *imagines*; the boy can suck either or penetrate into either. What we are more concerned with here, however, is the important tendency to deal with the father's penis on feminine lines. It would be better to say ' on apparently feminine lines,' for true feminine lines would be far more positive. Essentially I mean ' on oral- and anal-sadistic lines,' and I believe it is the annihilation attitude derived from this level that affords the clue to the various apparently feminine attitudes: the annihilation is performed by the mouth and anus, by teeth, fæces and—on the phallic level—urine. Over and again I have found this hostile and destructive tendency to lie behind not merely the obviously ambivalent attitude on all femininity in men, but behind the affectionate desire to please. After all, apparently complacent yielding is the best imaginable mask for hostile intentions. The ultimate aim of most of this femininity is to get possession of, and destroy, the dreaded object. Until this is done the boy is not safe; he cannot really attend to women, let alone penetrate into them. He also projects his oral and anal destructive attitude, which relates to his father's penis, on to the cavity that is supposed to contain it. This projection is facilitated by association with the earlier sadistic impulses, oral and phallic, against the mother's body, with their talion consequences. Destruction of the father's penis further means robbing the penis-loving mother of her possession. To penetrate into this cavity would therefore be as destructive to his own penis as he knows penetration of his father's penis into his mouth would be to it. We thus obtain a simple formula for the Œdipus complex: my (so-called feminine—*i.e.*, oral destructive) wishes against my father's penis are so strong that if I penetrate into the mother's vagina with them still in my heart the same fate will happen to me—*i.e.*, if I have intercourse with my mother my father will castrate me. Penetration is equated with destruction, or—to recur to the more familiar phrase used earlier—copulation is equated with castration. But—and this is the vital point—what is at stake is not castration of the mother, but of the boy or else his father.

After having considered the various sources of castration anxiety, and the problem of femininity in the male, I now return to the original question of why the boy in the phallic phase needs to imagine that his mother really has a penis, and I will couple with it the further question—not often raised—of whose penis it really is. The answer is given in the preceding considerations, and to avoid repetition I will simply express it as a statement. *The presence of a visible penis in the mother would signify at once a reassurance in respect of the early oral needs, with a denial of any need for dangerous sadism to deal with privation, and above all a reassurance that no castration has taken place, that neither his father nor himself is in danger of it.* This conclusion also answers the question of whose penis it is the mother must have.[1] It is her own only in very small part, the part derived from the boy's earliest oral needs. To a much greater extent it is the father's penis; though it may also in a sense be said to be the boy's own, inasmuch as his fate is bound up with it through the mutual castration danger to both his father and himself.

The reason why actual sight of the female genital organ signalises the passage from the proto- to the deutero-phallic phase has also to be given. Like the experiences of puberty, it makes manifest what had previously belonged solely to the life of phantasy. It gives an actuality to the fear of castration. It does this, however, not by conveying the idea that the father has castrated the mother—this is only a mask of rationalisation in consciousness—but by arousing the possibility that a dangerous repressed wish may be gratified in reality—namely, the wish to have intercourse with the mother and to destroy the father's penis. In spite of various suggestions to the contrary, the Œdipus complex provides the key to the problem of the phallic phase, as it has done to so many others.

We have travelled far from the conception that the boy, previously ignorant of the sex difference, is horrified to find that a man has violently created one by castrating his mate and turning her into a woman, a castrated creature. Even apart from actual analysis of the early childhood years, the proposition that the boy has no intuition of the sex difference is on logical grounds alone hard to hold. We have seen that the (deutero-) phallic phase depends on the fear of castration, and that this in its turn implies the danger of

[1] Melanie Klein, ' The Psycho-Analysis of Children ' (*op. cit.*, p. 333), answers this question categorically: ' " The woman with a penis " always means, I should say, the woman with the father's penis.'

penetration; it would appear to follow from this alone that intuition of a penetrable cavity is an early underlying assumption in the whole complex reaction. When Freud says that the boy renounces his incest wishes towards his mother in order to save his penis, this implies that the penis was the offending carrier of those wishes (in the proto-phallic phase). Now what could these penis wishes that endanger its existence have been if not to perform the natural function of the penis—penetration? And this inference is amply substantiated by actual research.

I may now summarise the conclusions reached. The main one is that *the typical phallic stage in the boy is a neurotic compromise rather than a natural evolution in sexual development*. It varies, of course, in intensity, probably with the intensity of the castration fears, but it can be called inevitable only in so far as castration fears—*i.e.*, infantile neuroses—are inevitable; and how far these are inevitable we shall know only when we have further experience of child analysis. At all events the mere need to renounce incest wishes does not make it inevitable; it is not the external situation that engenders the phallic phase, but —perhaps avoidable—complications in the boy's inner development.

To avoid the imagined and self-created dangers of the Œdipus situation the boy in the phallic phase abandons the masculine attitude of penetration, with all interest in the inside of the mother's body, and comes to insist on the assured existence of his own and his ' mother's ' external penis. This is tantamount to Freud's ' passing of the Œdipus complex,' the renunciation of the mother to save the penis, but it is not a direct stage in evolution; on the contrary, the boy has later to retrace his steps in order to evolve, he has to claim again what he had renounced—his masculine impulses to reach the vagina; he has to revert from the temporary neurotic deutero-phallic phase to the original and normal proto-phallic phase. Thus the typical phallic phase—*i.e.*, the deutero-phallic phase—in my opinion, represents a neurotic obstacle to development rather than a natural stage in the course of it.[1]

---

[1] It may be of interest to note the respects in which the conclusions here put forward agree with or differ from those of the two authors, Freud and Karen Horney, with whose views there has been most occasion to debate. In agreement with Freud is the fundamental view that the passage from the proto- to the deutero-phallic phase is due to fear of castration at the hands of the father, and that this essentially arises in the Œdipus situation. Freud would, I think, also hold that the feminine wishes behind so much of the castration fear are generated as a means of dealing with the loved and dreaded father: he would possibly lay more stress on the idea of libidinally placating him, whereas I have directed more attention to the hostile and destructive impulses

Turning now to the corresponding problem in girls, we may begin by noting that the distinction mentioned earlier between the proto- and the deutero-phallic phase is if anything more prominent with girls than with boys. So much so that when I made the suggestion that the phallic phase in girls represents a secondary solution of conflict I was under the impression that by the phallic phase was meant what I now see to be only the second half of it, a misapprehension Professor Freud corrected in recent correspondence; incidentally, his condemnation of my suggestion[1] was partly based on the same misunderstanding, since on his part he naturally thought I was referring to the whole phase. In extenuation I may remark that in his original paper Freud gave no account of the phallic phase in girls, on the score of its extreme obscurity, and that his definition—a phase in which it is believed that the sex difference is between penis-possessing and castrated beings—strictly applies only to the deutero-phallic phase, the penis being supposed to be unknown in the first one.

The difference between the two halves of the phase in Freud's conception is similar to that pointed out earlier with boys. According to him, a clitoris supremacy sets in at a certain age when the girl is ignorant of the difference between the clitoris and the penis and so is in a state of contented bliss in the matter; this I am calling for the moment the proto-phallic phase of girls, which corresponds with that of boys when they are similarly supposed to be ignorant of the sex difference. In the deutero-phallic phase, the one I had suggested was a secondary defensive reaction, the girl is aware of the difference and, like the boy, either admits it reluctantly—and in this case resent-

---

behind the feminine attitude. On the other hand I cannot subscribe to the view of sex ignorance on which Freud repeatedly insists—though in one passage on primal scenes and primal phantasies (*Ges. Sch.*, Bd. xi., S. 11) he appears to keep the question open—and I regard the idea of the castrated mother as essentially a mother whose man has been castrated. Nor do I consider the deutero-phallic phase as a natural stage in development.

With Karen Horney there is agreement in her scepticism about sex ignorance, in her doubts about the normality of the (deutero-) phallic phase, and in her opinion that the boy's reaction to the Œdipus situation is greatly influenced by his previous relation to his mother. But I think she is mistaken in her account of the connection between these two last matters, and consider that the boy's fear of his feminine wishes—which we all appear to hold lie behind the castration fear—arise not in shame at his litera l masculine inferiority in his relation to his mother, but in the dangers of his alimentary sadism when this operates in the Œdipus situation.

[1] Freud, ' Female Sexuality,' *op. cit.*, p. 297.

fully—or tries to deny it. In the denial, however, unlike the state of affairs alleged to exist with boys, there is implied some real knowledge of the difference, for the girl does not maintain the previous belief—that both sexes have a satisfactory clitoris—but wishes that she now had a different organ from before—viz., a real penis. With homosexual women, who reveal implicitly in their behaviour and explicitly in their dreams the belief that they really have a penis, this wish goes on to imaginary fulfilment, but even with the more normal girl during her deutero-phallic phase the same belief that she has a penis alternates with the wish to have one.

As with boys, the two halves of the phase are divided by the castration idea, by the idea that women are nothing but castrated beings—there being no such thing as a true female organ. The boy's wish in the deutero-phallic stage is to restore the security of the proto-phallic one which has been disturbed by the supposed discovery of castration: to revert to the original identity of the sexes. The girl's wish in the deutero-phallic stage is similarly to restore the undisturbed proto-phallic one, and even to intensify its phallic character; thus to revert to the original identity of the sexes. This I take to be a more explicit statement of Freud's conception.

Two distinct views appear to be held in respect of female sexual development, and to bring out the contrast between them I will exaggerate them in the following over-simple statement. According to one, the girl's sexuality is essentially male to start with (at least as soon as she is weaned), and she is driven into femaleness by failure of the male attitude (disappointment in the clitoris). According to the other, it is essentially female to start with, and she is—more or less temporarily—driven into a phallic maleness by failure of the female attitude.

This is avowedly an imperfect statement, which does not do justice to either view, but it may serve to point a discussion. I will call the two A and B respectively and add a few obvious modifications which will make them more exact and also diminish the grossness of the difference between them. The supporters of A would, of course, admit an early bisexuality, though they maintain that the male (clitoris) attitude predominates; they would also agree to the so-called regressive (anxiety) factors in the deutero-phallic phase, though they hold these to be less important than the libidinal impulse to maintain the original maleness. On the other side the supporters of B would also admit an early bisexuality, an early clitoris maleness in addition to the more pronounced femaleness: or—to put it more cautiously without begging any question—the co-existence of active and passive aims which tend to get associated with particular genital areas. They would also admit that there is often little apparent love for the father, who is regarded mainly as a rival, in the early stage of mother fixation; and in the deutero-phallic phase they would agree that direct auto-erotic, and therefore libidinal, penis envy plays an important part together with the anxiety factors in driving the girl from femaleness into the phallic maleness. Again, there is general agreement that the experience of seeing a penis powerfully influences the transition from the proto- to the deutero-phallic phase, though not about the reasons why it does so. Further, both views agree that in the deutero-phallic phase the girl desires a penis,[1] and blames the mother for her lack of it, though whose penis she desires and why she desires it are questions not so readily answered.

Nevertheless, in spite of these modifications, there remain differences of opinion in regard to both halves of the phase, and by no means in respect of accent only. In investigating the corresponding obscurity of male sexual development it proved useful to lay stress on the correlation between the problems of castration fear and dread of the vulva. Here I would similarly bring into prominence a correlation between the problem of the girl's desire to own a penis and her hate of her mother, since I feel sure that to explain either of these is to explain the other. And I will anticipate my conclusions to the extent of remarking that it may prove possible to combine in a single formula the male equation of problems with the female one.

In attempting to elucidate the contrasting views described above I will avail myself of two clues, both provided by Freud. The first of them is contained in his remark[2] that the girl's earliest attachment to her mother ' has in analysis seemed to me so elusive, lost in a past so dim and shadowy, so hard to resuscitate that it seemed as if it had undergone some specially inexorable repression.' We must all agree

---

[1] Incidentally, I may comment here on the unfortunate ambiguity of such phrases as ' to desire a penis,' ' the wish for a penis.' In fact three meanings of such phrases are to be discerned in connection with infantile female sexuality: (1) The wish to acquire a penis, usually by swallowing, and to retain it within the body, often converting it there into a baby; (2) the wish to possess a penis in the clitoritic region: for this purpose it may be acquired in more than one way; (3) the adult wish to enjoy a penis in coitus. I shall try to make it clear in each case which meaning is intended.

[2] Freud, ' Female Sexuality,' *op. cit.*, p. 282.

when he points out that the ultimate solution of all these problems lies in a finer analysis of the girl's very earliest period of attachment to the mother, and it is highly probable that the differences of opinion in respect of the later stage of development are mainly, and perhaps altogether, due to different assumptions concerning the earlier stage.

To give an example of this: Freud,[1] in criticising Karen Horney, describes her view as being that the girl, from fear of advancing to femininity, *regresses* in the deutero-phallic stage. So sure is he that the earlier (clitoris) stage can only be a phallic one. But this is just one of the questions at issue; to anyone taking the opposite view the process just mentioned would not be a regression, but a neurotic new-formation. And it is a question to be discussed. We should not take it too much for granted that the use of the clitoris is altogether the same thing psychologically as the use of the penis simply because they are physio-genetically homologous. Sheer accessibility may also play its part. The clitoris is after all a part of the female genitals. Clinically the correspondence between clitoris masturbation and a male attitude is very far indeed from being invariable. I have known, on the one hand, a case where the clitoris could not function because of a congenital malformation, but where the vulval masturbation was distinctly male in type (prone posture, etc.). On the other hand, cases where clitoris masturbation in the adult accompanies the most pronouncedly feminine heterosexual phantasies are an everyday experience, and Melanie Klein[2] states that this combination is characteristic of the earliest infancy. In my Innsbruck paper I expressed the opinion that vaginal excitation played a more important part in the earliest childhood than was recognised—in contra-distinction from Freud's[3] opinion that it begins only at puberty—a view that had been previously expressed by several women analysts, Melanie Klein[4] (1924), Josine Müller[5] (1925), and Karen Horney[6] (1926). This opinion I had reached first from the

---

[1] Freud, 'Female Sexuality,' *op. cit.*, p. 296.

[2] Melanie Klein, ' The Psycho-Analysis of Children,' *op. cit.*, p. 288.

[3] Freud, ' Female Sexuality,' *op. cit.*, p. 283.

[4] Melanie Klein, ' From the Analysis of an Obsessional Neurosis in a Six-year-old Child,' First German Psycho-Analytical Assembly, Würzburg, October 11, 1924.

[5] Josine Müller, ' A Contribution to the Problem of Libidinal Development of the Genital Phase in Girls,' *International Journal of Psycho-Analysis*, 1932, vol. xiii., p. 361.

[6] Karen Horney, ' The Flight from Womanhood,' *International Journal of Psycho-Analysis*, 1926, vol. vii., p. 334. She has comprehensively sustained this opinion in a paper published in the *International Journal of Psycho-Analysis*, vol. xiv., p. 57.

same class of material as Josine Müller quotes—namely, women who show strong masculine propensities in conjunction with vaginal anæsthesia. What is important about this early vaginal functioning, so deeply repressed, is the extraordinary amount of anxiety that goes with it (far more than with clitoritic functioning), a matter to which we shall have to recur. Actual vaginal masturbation is often considered by physicians to be commoner than clitoris masturbation in the first four or five years of life, whereas it certainly is not so during the latency period—a fact in itself suggesting a change from feminine to more masculine attitudes. Apart, however, from actual vaginal functioning there is extensive evidence of feminine phantasies and wishes in early childhood to be obtained from both adult and early analyses: phantasies relating to the mouth, vulva, womb, anus and the receptive attitude of the body in general. For all these reasons I feel that the question of the alleged clitoritic and therefore masculine primacy of the female infant may well be kept in suspense until we know more about the sexuality of this very early stage.

A cognate example of misunderstanding due to differing primary assumptions arises in connection with the problem of the intensity and of the direction (aim) characteristic of the deutero-phallic phase. Freud, who holds that both intensity and direction are to be explained in terms of the proto-phallic masculine phase, and that the trauma of seeing the penis only reinforces this, criticises Karen Horney for believing that the direction alone is given by the proto-phallic phase, the intensity being derived from later (anxiety) factors.[1] In so far, however, as Karen Horney is a supporter of view B—and I cannot of course say just how far this is so—she would maintain the exact converse of the view Freud ascribes to her; she would agree with him that the intensity of the deutero-phallic phase is derived from the earlier one (though with displacement) and differ from him only in holding that its direction is not so derived, being in the main determined by secondary factors. All this again depends on whether the earlier phase is regarded as predominantly masculine and auto-erotic or pedominantly feminine and allo-erotic.

Freud[2] would appear to hold that the question is settled by the very fact that many young girls have a long and exclusive mother attachment. He calls this a pre-Œdipal stage of development, one where the father plays very little part and that a negative one

---

[1] Freud, 'Female Sexuality,' op. cit., p. 296.   [2] Ibid.

(rivalry). These facts of observation are not to be doubted—I can myself quote an extreme case where the exclusive mother attachment was prolonged till near puberty, at which age an equally exclusive transference to the father took place. But they do not in themselves exclude a positive Œdipus complex in the girl's unconscious imagination: they prove only that, if this does exist, it has not yet learned to express itself in relation to the actual father. In my experience of typical cases of this kind, however, and in that of child analysts, particularly of Melanie Klein, Melitta Schmideberg and Nina Searl, analysis shows that the girls had from very early times definite impulses towards an imaginary penis, one incorporated into the mother but derived from the father, together with elaborate phantasies on the subject of parental coitus. I would again remind you at this point of the stress laid in the earlier part of the paper on the 'combined parent concept,' the picture of parents fused in coitus.

We are here led to consider the second of the clues to which I referred just now. It concerns the young girl's theories of coitus, which play a highly important part in her sexual development. They should be helpful in the present connection, since—as Freud has long ago shown—the sexual theories of a child are a mirror of its particular sexual constitution. A few years ago Professor Freud wrote to me that of the two points of which he felt most sure in the obscurity of female sexual development one was that the young girl's first idea of coitus was an oral one—i.e., of fellatio.[1] Here, as usual, he put his finger on a central point. But it is probable that the matter is more complex: at all events, this central consideration has several corollaries that are worth pursuing. In the first place, it is hardly likely that a purely oral conception would develop if the first thought of coitus occurred years after the infant's own oral experiences; and detailed analysis of this early period, especially by child analysts, confirms what one might expect—namely, that the experiences and the conception are closely related not only genetically, but also chronologically. Melanie Klein[2] attributes great importance to the stimulus given to the child's desires by the inevitable imperfections and dissatisfactions of the suckling period, and would connect the

---

[1] I may also quote the other point, since any pronouncement from such a source must command interest. It was that the girl gives up masturbation because of her dissatisfaction with the clitoris (in comparison with the penis).

[2] Melanie Klein, ' The Psycho-Analysis of Children,' op. cit., p. 326.

weaning time both with the deepest sources of hostility to the mother and with a dawning idea of a penis-like object as a more satisfying kind of nipple. That nipple wishes are transferred to the idea of the penis, and that the two objects are extensively identified in the imagination, is fairly familiar ground, but it is hard to say when this transference begins to be applied to the father in person. It is, I think, certain that for a relatively long time they apply more to the mother than to the father—*i.e.*, that the girl seeks for a penis in her mother. By the second year of life this vague aspiration is getting more definite and is getting connected with the idea of the mother's penis having been derived from the father in the supposed act of fellatio between the parents.

In the next place, the fellatic idea can hardly be confined to the notion of purposeless sucking. The child well knows that one sucks for a purpose—to get something. Milk (or semen) and (nipple-) penis are thus things to swallow, and by the familar symbolic equations, as well partly from the child's own alimentary experiences, we reach also the ideas of excrement and baby—equally obtained from this primordial sucking act. According to Freud,[1] the child's love and sexuality are essentially devoid of aim (*ziellos*), and for this very reason are doomed to disappointment. The contrary view is that in the unconscious there are very definite aims, and the disappointment is due to their not being reached.

I wish to make clear at this point that the wishes here referred to are in my opinion essentially allo-erotic. The girl infant has not yet had the occasion to develop auto-erotic envy at the sight of a boy's penis; the desire to possess one herself, for the reasons so clearly stated by Karen Horney,[2] comes later. At the early stage the wish to take the penis into the body, through the mouth, and make a (faecal) baby out of it is, though still on an alimentary level, nevertheless akin to the allo-erotism of the adult woman. Freud[3] holds that when the girl's wish to own a penis is disappointed it is replaced by a substitute—the wish to have a child. I would, however, agree rather with Melanie Klein's[4] view that the penis-child equation is more innate, and that the girl's wish to have a child—like the normal woman's wish—is a direct continuance of

---

[1] Freud, ' Female Sexuality,' *op. cit.*, p. 286.

[2] Karen Horney, ' On the Genesis of the Castration Complex in Women,' *International Journal of Psycho-Analysis*, 1924, vol. v., pp. 52-54.

[3] Freud, ' Some Psychological Consequences,' etc., *op. cit.*, p. 140.

[4] Melanie Klein, ' The Psycho-Analysis of Children,' *op. cit.*, p. 309.

her allo-erotic desire for a penis; she wants to enjoy taking the penis into the body and to make a child from it, rather than to have a child because she cannot have a penis of her own.

The purely libidinal nature of the wishes manifests itself in many ways, of which I will mention only one. The insertion of the nipple into the mouth is followed by the anal-erotic pleasure at the passage of fæces, and the cleansing process associated with this is often felt by the girl to be a sexual experience with the mother (or nurse). The point of this observation is that the mother's hand or finger is equated to a penis and is often the seduction that leads to masturbation.

      *   *   *   *   *

Now if the mother gets all this—just what the girl longs for—from the father, then a situation of normal Œdipus rivalry must surely exist, and in exact proportion to the girl's own dissatisfaction. The accompanying hostility is in direct line with that felt previously towards the mother in the suckling period, being of the same order; and it reinforces it. The mother has got something the girl wants and will not give it to her. In this something the idea of the father's penis soon comes to crystallise more and more definitely, and the mother has obtained it from the father in successful competition with the girl, as well as the baby she can make from it. This is in disagreement with Freud's[1] formidable statement that the concept of the Œdipus complex is strictly applicable only to male children and ' it is only in male children that there occurs the fateful conjunction of love for the one parent and hatred of the other as rival.' We seem compelled here to be *plus royaliste que le roi*.

Freud's fellatio account of coitus, however, from which we started, yields no explanation for the important observation on which he insists,[2] that the girl infant feels rivalry for her father. The fellatio conception of coitus, in fact, would seem to be only one half of the story. One finds also the complementary idea that the father not only gives to the mother, but receives from her; that in short she suckles him. And it is here that the direct rivalry with the father is so strong, for the mother is giving him just what the girl wants (nipple and milk); other sources of rivalry, hate and resentment in respect of the father, I shall mention presently. When this ' mammalingus ' conception, as it may be called, gets sadistically

---

[1] Freud, ' Female Sexuality,' *op. cit.*, p. 284.   *Ibid*, p. 282.

cathected, then we have the familiar feminist idea of the man who ' uses ' the woman, exhausts her, drains her, exploits her, and so on.

The girl infant doubtless identifies herself with both sides in these conceptions, but in the nature of the case her wanting, receiving desires must be more prominent than the giving ones; there is at that age so much that she wants and so little that she has to give.

What then of the phallic activity against the mother recorded by Helene Deutsch, Jeanne Lampl-de Groot, Melanie Klein, and other women analysts? We must not forget how early the child apprehends the penis not simply as an instrument of love, but also as a weapon of destruction. In the girl's sadistic furor against the mother's body, due largely to her inability to suffer thwarting, she clutches at all weapons, mouth, hands, feet; and in this connection the sadistic value of the penis, and the power it gives of directing destructive urine, is perhaps not the least of its uses which she envies the boy. We know that thwarting stimulates sadism, and, to judge from their phantasies as well as actual conduct, it would seem very difficult to overestimate the quantity of sadism present in infants. On talion grounds this leads to corresponding fear, and again it seems difficult to overestimate the depth and intensity of fear in infants. We must regard the sexual development of both boys and girls as influenced at all points by the need to cope with fear, and I must agree with Melanie Klein's[1] scepticism about the success of Freud's[2] avowed endeavour to depict sexual development without reference to the super-ego—i.e., to the factors of guilt and fear.

At this point I am constrained to express the doubt whether Freud does not attach too much significance to the girl's concern about her external organs (clitoris-penis) at the expense of her terrible fears about the inside of her body. I feel sure that to her the inside is a much stronger source of anxiety and that she often parades concern about the outside as a defensive attitude, a conclusion the truth of which Melanie Klein[3] has demonstrated in great detail in her penetrating investigations of the earliest years of female development. Josine Müller[4] has happily remarked that the anatomical fact of the girl's having two genital organs—the internal vagina (and womb) and the external clitoris—enables her to displace eroto-

---

[1] Melanie Klein, ' The Psycho-Analysis of Children,' op. cit., p. 323.
[2] Freud, ' Female Sexuality,' op. cit., p. 294.
[3] Melanie Klein, ' The Psycho-Analysis of Children,' op. cit., pp. 269 et seq.
[4] Josine Müller, op. cit., p. 363.

genicity from the internal to the external one when the former is threatened. After all, the central dread of the guilty girl—even in consciousness—is that she will never be able to bear children—*i.e.*, that her internal organs have been damaged. We are reminded of Helene Deutsch's[1] triad of equivalent female fears: castration, defloration and parturition—though the first of these needs careful definition—and of the characteristic adult fears of ' internal diseases,' particularly of cancer of the womb.

The early dread of the mother, just as the hate of her, is transferred to the father, and both dread and hate are often curiously concentrated on the idea of the penis itself. Just as the boy projects his sadism on to the female organs, and then exploits these dangerous organs as a means of destroying his father homosexually, so does the girl project her sadism on to the male organ, and very largely with a similar outcome. It is one of the oddest experiences to find a woman who has devoted herself to a penis-acquiring career (homosexually) having at the same time fear, disgust and hatred of any real penis. In such cases one gets a vista of the dread and horror that gets developed in regard to the penis, the most destructive of all lethal weapons, and how terrifying can be the idea of its penetrating into the inside of the body.[2] This particular projection is so important that one must ask how much of the girl's fear is the result of her sadistic wishes to bite away (and swallow) the penis, tearing it from the mother, or later the father, with the consequent dread lest the dangerous—because sadistically conceived—penis penetrates her; it is hard to say, but this may possibly be the very centre of the matter.

As the girl grows she often transfers her resentment from the mother to the father when she more clearly understands that he it is who really owns (and withholds) the penis. Freud[3] quotes this curious transference of hostility, resentment and dissatisfaction from the mother to the father as a proof that it cannot arise from rivalry with the mother, but we have just seen that another explanation is at least possible. It is fully intelligible that there should be resentment at the thwarting of the allo-erotic penis desire, which the father's presence stimulates, and that this applies first to the mother and then to the father. An additional tributary flows into the

---

[1] Helene Deutsch, ' The Significance of Masochism in the Mental Life of Women,' *International Journal of Psycho-Analysis,* 1930, vol. xi., p. 48.

[2] Hence, amongst other things, the frequency of beating phantasies where penetration s obviated.

[3] Freud, ' Female Sexuality,' *op. cit.,* pp. 281, 286.

resentment against the father for his thwarting the libidinal desire —namely, that this thwarting has also the effect of exposing the girl to her dread of the mother. For where there is a dread of punishment for a wish, then gratification of this wish may be the strongest safeguard against the anxiety, or at least is commonly believed by the unconscious to be so; and anyone, therefore, who denies this gratification commits a double crime—he refuses at the same time both libidinal pleasure and security.

We have to bear in mind all this background, which is doubtless only an extract of the true complexity, when we attempt to reconstruct the development of the deutero-phallic phase. At this point the girl becomes *consciously* aware of a real penis attached to male beings, and she characteristically reacts to it by wishing to possess one herself. Why exactly does she have this wish? What does she want the penis for? That is a crucial question, and the answer to it must also provide the answer to the equally crucial question of the source of the girl's hostility to her mother. Here we get a fairly clear-cut issue between views A and B, one which should prove stimulating to further research.

The answer to both questions given by view A undoubtedly has the merit of being simpler than that given by view B. According to it the girl wishes to possess the penis she sees because that is the sort of thing she has always prized, because she sees it in her wildest dreams of an efficient clitoris being realised in the nth degree. There is no serious internal conflict in the matter, only resentment, particularly against her mother, whom she holds responsible for the disappointment that inevitably ensues. Envy of the penis is the principal reason for turning from the mother. The actual value of the clitoris-penis would appear to be essentially auto-erotic, the best exposition of which was given years ago by Karen Horney.[1] The wish is almost entirely libidinal, and is in the same direction as the girl's earlier tendencies. When this wish is disappointed, the girl falls back on a feminine incestuous allo-erotic attitude, but as a second best. Any so-called defence there may be against femininity, or rather objection to it, is dictated not so much by any deep fear of it in itself, but by the desire to retain the masculine clitoris-penis position, which it imperils; in other words, by the same objection boys would have were they offered the alternative—namely, because it is tantamount to castration. This view, which in a word explains

[1] Karen Horney, ' On the Genesis,' etc., *loc. cit.*

both the hate of the mother and the strength of the deutero-phallic phase by one main factor—the auto-erotic desire to possess a clitoris-penis—is both simple and consistent. The question is, however, whether it is also comprehensive—*i.e.*, whether its underlying assumptions in the proto-phallic phase take into due account all the ascertainable factors.

The answer given by view B is that the girl originally desired the penis allo-erotically, but is driven into an auto-erotic position (in the deutero-phallic phase) in the same way that boys are—from fear of the supposed dangers attaching to the allo-erotic desires. I may here cite a few authors who illustrate sharply the contrasting views. On the one hand Helene Deutsch,[1] in accord with Freud, writes: ' My view is that the Œdipus complex in girls is inaugurated by the castration-complex.' On the other hand Karen Horney[2] speaks of ' these typical motives for flight into the male rôle—motives whose origin is the Œdipus complex,' and Melanie Klein[3] asserts ' in my view the girl's defence against her feminine attitude springs less from her masculine tendencies than from her fear of her mother.'

The masculine form of auto-erotism is thus here the second best; it is adopted because femininity—the real thing desired—brings danger and intolerable anxiety. The deepest source of resentment against the mother is the imperfect oral satisfaction, which leads the girl to seek a more potent nipple—a penis—in an allo-erotic and later in a hetero-erotic direction; the libidinal attitude towards the nipple here expresses itself as feminine phantasies associated with vulval—either vaginal or clitoric—masturbation, alone or with the nurse in cleansing operations. She is homosexually attached to the mother at this stage, but it is only from her that she can hope to obtain the desired penis satisfaction, by guile or force. This is all the easier because after all the mother is still at this early age the main source of (allo-erotic) libidinal gratification. And she is dependent on her mother not only for affection and gratification, but also for the satisfying of all her vital needs. Life would be impossible without the mother and the mother's love. There are therefore the strongest possible motives for the girl's intense attachment to her mother.

Nevertheless in the unconscious there is another side to the

[1] Helene Deutsch, ' The Significance,' etc., *op. cit.*, p. 53.
[2] Karen Horney, ' The Flight,' etc., *op. cit.*, p. 337.
[3] Melanie Klein, ' The Psycho-Analysis of Children,' *op. cit.*, p. 324.

picture, and a much grimmer one. The sadistic impulse to assault and rob the mother leads to intense dread of retaliation, which often develops—as was explained earlier—into dread of the penetrating penis; and this is revived when she comes across a real penis attached, not to the mother, but to the father or brother. Here she is actually no worse off than before—she still has a clitoris, and the mother has taken nothing away from her. She blames her, however, for not having given her more—a penis—but behind this reproach that the mother has insufficiently attended to her auto-erotic desires lies the deeper and stronger one that she has thwarted the true, feminine needs of her receptive and acquisitive nature and has threatened to destroy her body if she persists in them. View B would therefore appear to give more adequate reasons for hostility to the mother than does view A. Both agree about the pregenital thwarting at the mother's hands, but they differ in their estimate of the thwarting on the genital level. There, according to the one view, A, the mother deprives the girl of nothing, but there is resentment at not being given more; according to the other view, B, the mother both thwarts the feminine aims (towards the penis) and also threatens to mutilate the body—i.e., to destroy the real feminine penis-receiving and child-bearing organs—unless the girl renounces those aims. Small wonder that she does renounce them, always to some extent, and often altogether.

The deutero-phallic phase is her reaction to this situation, her defence against the dangers of the Œdipus complex.[1] Her desire in it to possess a penis of her own saves her threatened libido by deflecting it into the safer auto-erotic direction, just as it is saved when deflected into perversion. This shifting on to the auto-erotic (and therefore more ego-syntonic) plane, with its consequent neurotic intensification, meets in its turn with disappointment. There are very few girls who do not deceive themselves—to some extent throughout life—about the source of their inferiority feelings. The real source, as always with inferiority feelings, is internal forbiddenness because of guilt and fear, and this applies to the allo-erotic wishes far more than to the auto-erotic ones.

But there are additional advantages in this phallic position, hence

---

[1] This view, maintained in my Innsbruck Congress paper, was, I think, first put forward by Karen Horney ('On the Genesis,' etc., op. cit., p. 50), and has been elaborately developed by Melanie Klein, 'The Psycho-Analysis of Children,' op. cit., pp. 271, etc.

its great strength. It is a complete refutation of the feared mother's attack on her femininity, because it denies its very existence and therefore all reason for any such attack. And there are also still more irrational unconscious phantasies. The ambivalence towards the mother can be dealt with. On the one hand the girl is now armed with the most powerful weapon of attack, and therefore of protection; Joan Riviere[1] has called special attention to this motive. On the other hand, by the important mechanism of restitution, one to which Melanie Klein has devoted important studies in this connection, she can compensate for her dangerous wishes to rob the mother of a penis: she now has a penis to restore to the deprived mother, a process which plays an extensive part in female homosexuality. Further, she no longer runs any risk of being sadistically assaulted by the man's dangerous penis. Freud[2] asks whence, if there were any flight from femininity, could it derive its source except from masculine strivings. We have seen that there may be much deeper sources of emotional energy in the girl than masculine strivings, though these can often prove a well-disguised outlet for them.

There will, I think, be general agreement on one point at least— namely, that the girl's desire for a penis is bound up with her hate of the mother. The two problems are inherently related, but it is over the nature of this relationship that there is the sharpest division of opinion. Whereas Freud holds that the hate is a resentment at the girl's not being granted a penis of her own, the view presented here, one which has been well sustained by Melanie Klein,[3] is that the hate is essentially a rivalry over the father's penis. In the one view the deutero-phallic phase is a natural reaction to an unfortunate anatomical fact, and when it leads to disappointment the girl falls back on hetero-erotic incest. In the other view the girl develops at a very early age hetero-erotic incest, with Œdipus hate of the mother, and the deutero-phallic phase is an escape from the intolerable dangers of that situation; it thus has exactly the same significance as the corresponding phenomenon with the boy.

*   *   *   *   *

I should like now in summing up to institute a general comparison between these problems in boys and girls respectively. With

[1] Joan Riviere, 'Womanliness as a Masquerade,' *International Journal of Psycho-Analysis*, 1929, vol. x., p. 303.

[2] Freud, 'Female Sexuality,' *op. cit.*, p. 297.

[3] Melanie Klein, 'The Psycho-Analysis of Children,' *op. cit.*, p. 270.

both the idea of functioning in the hetero-erotic direction appropriate to their nature (penetrating with boys, being penetrated with girls) is absent—? renounced—in the deutero-phallic phase. And with both there is an equally strong denial—? repudiation—of the vagina: every effort is made towards the fiction that both sexes have a penis. There must surely be a common explanation for this central feature of the deutero-phallic phase in both sexes, and both the views here discussed provide one. According to the first, it is the discovery of the sex difference—with its unwelcome implication; according to the second it is a deep dread of the vagina, derived from anxiety about the ideas of parental coitus associated with it, a dread which is often re-activated by seeing the genital organ of the opposite sex.

Probably the central difference between the two views, the one from which other differences emanate and where therefore our research must be specially directed, is over the varying importance attached by different analysts to the early unconscious phantasy of the father's penis incorporated in the mother. That the phantasy in question occurs has been well known to analysts for more than twenty years, but—as a result especially of Melanie Klein's notable researches—we may have to recognise it as a never-failing feature of infantile life and to learn that the sadism and anxiety surrounding it play a dominating part in the sexual development of both boys and girls. This generalisation could profitably be extended to all the phantasies described by Melanie Klein and other child analysts in connection with what she has called the 'combined parent' concept, one which I suggested earlier is closely associated with Freud's pre-Œdipal stage of development.

Not only is the main characteristic of the deutero-phallic phase—the suppression of hetero-erotic functioning—essentially the same with boys and girls, but so also is the motive for it. The renunciation is effected in both cases for the sake of bodily integrity, to save the sexual organs (external with the boy, internal with the girl). The girl will not risk having her vagina or womb damaged any more than the boy will his penis. Both sexes have the strongest motives for denying all ideas of coitus—*i.e.*, of penetration—and they therefore keep their minds set on the outside of the body.[1]

[1] I am not suggesting that this is the only motive force at work. As Joan Riviere pointed out in the discussion when this paper was read before the British Society, it falls into line with the general tendency towards exteriorisation in the growing child's search to establish contact with the outer world.

In the two sections of this paper I used as a starting-point a pair of related problems: with boys the fear of castration and the dread of the vulva, with girls the desire to own a penis and the hate of the mother. It is now possible to show that the essential nature of these two apparently unlike pairs is common to both sexes. The common features are the avoidance of penetration and fear of injury from the parent of the same sex. The boy fears castration at the hands of his father if he penetrates into the vagina; the girl fears mutilation at the hands of the mother if she allows herself to have a penetrable vagina. That the danger is often associated, by projection, with the parent of the opposite sex, in the manner I have described above, is a secondary manifestation; its real source is hostility towards the rival parent of the same sex. We have in fact the typical Œdipus formula: incestuous coitus brings with it fear of mutilation by the rival parent. And this is as true of the girl as of the boy, in spite of the more extensive homosexual disguise she is compelled to adopt.

To return to the concept of the phallic phase. If the view here advanced is valid, then the term proto-phallic I suggested earlier applies to the boy only. It is unnecessary, since it really means simply genital; it can even be misleading, since it predisposes one to think of the boy's early genital functions in a purely phallic—*i.e.*, auto-erotic—sense to the exclusion of the allo-erotism that exists from the earliest times—in the first year of life itself. For the girls the term will be still more misleading in the eyes of those who hold that the earliest stage of their development is essentially feminine. As to the sex ignorance said to characterise the proto-phallic phase, this is no doubt true of consciousness, but there is extensive evidence to show that it is not true of the unconscious; and the unconscious is an important part of the personality.

I now come to what I call the deutero-phallic phase, the one generally meant when one uses simply the term 'phallic phase.' View A we have discussed above tends to regard the deutero-phallic phase as a natural development, in both sexes, out of a proto-phallic phase, its direction being much the same in the two. View B lays more stress on the extent to which the deutero-phallic phase is a deflection from the earlier one, comprising in important respects even a reversal of the direction of the latter. This may perhaps be most sharply expressed by saying that *the previous heterosexual allo-erotism of the early phase is in the deutero-phallic one—in both sexes—largely transmuted into a substitutive homosexual auto-erotism. This latter*

*phase would thus—in both sexes—be not so much a pure libidinal develop-
ment as a neurotic compromise between libido and anxiety,* between the
natural libidinal impulses and the wish to avoid mutilation. Strictly
speaking, it is not a neurosis proper, inasmuch as the libidinal
gratification still open is a conscious one, not unconscious as it is
in neurosis. It is rather a sexual aberration and might well be given
the name of the *phallic perversion.* It is closely akin to sexual inversion,
manifestly so with girls. This connection is so close that—although
it is not strictly germane to the purpose of my paper—I will venture
to apply to the problem of inversion some considerations that arise
from the present theme. It would seem as if inversion is in essence
hostility to the rival parent that has been libidinised by the special
technique of appropriating the dangerous organs of the opposite sex,
organs that have been made dangerous by sadistic projection. We
saw earlier to what an extent the genital sadism was derived from
the earlier oral sadism, so it may well be that the oral sadism I
suggested on an earlier occasion[1] was the specific root of female
homosexuality is that of male homosexuality also.[2]

To avoid any possible misunderstanding I would remind you that
the phallic phase, or phallic perversion, is not to be regarded as a
definitely fixed entity. We should think of it, as of all similar
processes, in dynamic and economic terms. It shows, in other words,
every possible variation. It varies in different individuals from slight
indications to the most pronounced perversion. And in the same
individual it varies in intensity from one period to another according
to the current changes in stimulation of the underlying agencies.

Nor do I commit myself to the view that the phallic phase is
necessarily pathological, though it obviously may become so
through exaggeration or fixation. It is a deviation from the direct
path of development, and it is a response to anxiety, but nevertheless,
for all we know, research may show that the earliest infantile
anxiety is inevitable and that the phallic defence is the only one
possible at that age. Nothing but further experience in analysis at
early ages can answer such questions. Further, the conclusions here
come to do not deny the biological, psychological and social value
of the homosexual constituent in human nature; there we come back
to our one and only gauge—the degree of free and harmonious
functioning in the mental economy.

[1] *Op. cit.*
[2] Melanie Klein (*op. cit.,* p. 326) traces this to an ' oral-sucking fixation.'

I will allow myself now to single out the *conclusions* which seem to me to be the most significant.

The first is that the typical (deutero-) phallic phase is a perversion subserving, as do all perversions, the function of salvaging some possibility of libidinal gratification until the time comes—if it ever comes—when fear of mutilation can be dealt with and the temporarily renounced hetero-erotic development be once more resumed. The inversion that acts as a defence against the fear depends on the sadism that gave rise to the fear.

Then we would seem to have warrant for recognising more than ever the value of what perhaps has been Freud's greatest discovery —the Œdipus complex. I can find no reason to doubt that for girls, no less than for boys, the Œdipus situation, in its reality and phantasy, is the most fateful psychical event in life.

Lastly I think we should do well to remind ourselves of a piece of wisdom whose source is more ancient than Plato: ' In the beginning . . . male and female created He them.'

CHAPTER XXVII

EARLY FEMALE SEXUALITY [1]

THIS lecture is intended to be the first of a series of exchange lectures between Vienna and London which your Vice-President, Dr. Federn, has proposed for a special purpose. For some years now it has been apparent that many analysts in London do not see eye to eye with their colleagues in Vienna on a number of important topics: among these I might instance the early development of sexuality, especially in the female, the genesis of the super-ego and its relation to the Œdipus complex, the technique of child analysis and the conception of a death instinct. I use the phrase 'many analysts' without attempting to enumerate these, but it is evident that there is some danger of local views becoming unified to such an extent as to enable people to speak of a Vienna school or London school as if they represented different tendencies of a possibly divergent order. This, I am convinced, is in no wise true. The differences are of just that kind that go with imperfect contact, which in the present case are strongly contributed to by geographical and linguistic factors. The political and economic disturbances of the past few years have not brought London and Vienna nearer to each other. Many English analysts do not read the *Zeitschrift*, and still fewer Vienna analysts read the *Journal*. And I have not as yet succeeded in making the interchange of translations between the two as free as I could wish. It is true that German work has much freer access to the *Journal* than English work has to the *Zeitschrift*, but this one-way avenue, far from perfect as it is, is not at all a satisfactory solution. The fact is that new work and ideas in London have not yet, in our opinion, been adequately considered in Vienna.

Dr. Federn has had the happy thought of remedying the present difficulty by arranging a direct personal contact and discussion. In my opinion also this is the most promising way to proceed. In the first place, I have the impression that nowadays far more psycho-analysis is learnt through the spoken than through the written word. The habit of reading has certainly declined among analysts in the

[1] Read before the Vienna Psycho-Analytical Society, April 24, 1935. Published in the *Internationale Zeitschrift fur Psychoanalyse*, Bd. xxi., and in the *International Journal of Psycho-Analysis*, vol. xvi.

past twenty years and correspondingly the habit of writing has taken on a more narcissistic bent. In the second place, this method enables speakers to be chosen who have prominently identified themselves with one or another point of view or method of investigation.

That I should have selected the present theme to discuss with you is natural. Already at the Innsbruck Congress eight years ago[1] I supported a view of female sexual development that did not altogether coincide with the one generally accepted, and at the Wiesbaden Congress three years ago[2] I amplified my conclusions and also extended them to the problems of male development. Put colloquially, my essential point was that there was more femininity in the young girl than analysts generally admit, and that the masculine phase through which she may pass is more complex in its motivation than is commonly thought; this phase seemed to me a reaction to her dread of femininity as well as something primary. Many women analysts have supported this view. It was Karen Horney who first, in her vigorous fashion, protested that the development of the young girl had been observed too exclusively through male eyes and, although her later views seem to me to be more than questionable, I would pay a tribute to the fresh stimulus she gave to the investigation of these problems. Since then child analysts, particularly Melanie Klein, have been able to get to closer quarters with them and to report direct observations of inestimable value.

Let me now review the themes of chief interest and note separately the points of agreement and of difference. To begin at the beginning. The assumption of inborn bisexuality seems to me a very probable one, in favour of which many biological facts can be quoted. But it is an assumption that is very hard to prove, so I do not think we should take it absolutely for granted and fall back on it whenever we encounter clinical difficulties.

Coming to the beginnings of individual life, we shall agree that at least in the first year, and probably later, the mother plays a much greater part in the girl's life than does the father. Of this phase Freud says, ' Everything connected with this first mother-attachment has in analysis seemed to me so elusive, lost in a past so dim and shadowy, so hard to resuscitate that it seemed as if it had undergone some specially inexorable repression.' What we evidently need, therefore, is a finer analysis of the girl's earliest period of attachment to the mother, and that, in my opinion, is what the ' early analyses '

---

[1] See Chapter XXV.   [2] See Chapter XXVI.

of young children are giving us. It is highly probable that the differences of opinion in respect of the later stage of development are mainly, and perhaps altogether, due to different assumptions concerning the earlier stage.

We begin, therefore, with the most difficult point, the crux of all the problems. Is this first stage a concentration on a single object, the mother ? And is it a masculine attitude, as clitoritic masturbation would seem to indicate ? Roughly speaking, this would appear to be Freud's view. In that case the girl has in her development to change both her sexual attitude and the sex of her love-object, and the well-known difficulties she experiences in her development would be explained by the complexity of these tasks.

In London, on the contrary, as the result partly of the experience of Melanie Klein's early analyses, but also of our findings in adults, we hold quite a different view of this early stage. We consider that the girl's attitude is already more feminine than masculine, being typically receptive and acquisitive. She is concerned more with the inside of her body than the outside. Her mother she regards not as a man regards a woman, as a creature whose wishes to receive something it is a pleasure to fulfil. She regards her rather as a person who has been successful in filling herself with just the things the child wants so badly, pleasant material of both a solid and liquid kind. Her endeavour is to get this out of the mother, and the various obstacles interposed by the delays and numerous other imperfections of feeding stimulate the aggressive components of her desires. The dissatisfaction with the nipple and the wish for a more adequate penis-like object to suck arises early and is repeated at a later period in the familiar clitoris dissatisfaction and penis-envy. The first wish for a kind of penis is thus induced by oral frustration. At this suckling stage we are still concerned with interest in a part-object, much less with father-love. The part-object is still felt to belong to the mother's body. But the father comes into account as the source whence she obtained it by the oral form of coitus which Freud has shown to be the child's initial conception of this act; indeed, in so far as the girl holds as well the converse of this theory, a mamma-lingus as well as a fellatio theory of coitus, the father is regarded as a rival for the mother's milk. In the second half of the first year, and regularly by the end of it, the personality of the father plays an increasingly important part. True feminine love for him, together with the desire for access to his sexual organ, begins to conflict with his evident relationship to the mother. In the second year we can definitely speak of an Œdipus complex. It differs from the later more familiar form in being more deeply repressed and unconscious; also the ' combined parent imago ' plays a greater part in it.

The girl's sadistic attitude towards the contents of the mother's body is recorded in innumerable phantasies of cutting, robbing and burning that body. The oral sadism soon extends to urethral and anal sadism, and it would seem that the destructive conception of excrement is even more pronounced with girls than with boys. There are two definite reasons why the girl's task of coping with this sadism, and the anxiety it gives rise to, is a good deal harder than the boy's. In the first place her anxiety essentially relates to the inside of the body and has no external organ on which to concentrate as the boy's has. There is only the clitoris, which is inferior as a source of re-assurance in the respects first emphasised by Karen Horney when she contrasted the boy's freedom in seeing, touching and urinating with his external organ. In later years the girl displaces much of her anxiety to the whole exterior of the body, including her clothes, and obtains reassurance from its integrity and general satisfactoriness, but this plays a much smaller part with the young child. In the second place, the boy has another personal lightning-conductor for his sadism and hate—namely, his sexual rival, the father. The girl, on the contrary, has as her sexual rival and the object of her sadism the same person, the mother, on whom the infant is completely dependent for both libidinal and all other needs of life. To destroy this object would be fatal, so the sadism, with its accompanying anxiety, is pent up and turned inwards far more than with the boy. In a word, the girl has for two reasons less opportunity to exteriorise her sadism. This explains the remarkable attachment to the mother, and dependence on her, to which Freud has called special attention in a recent paper. We think that these considerations also yield an explanation of what he termed the obscurity and ' inexorable repression ' so characteristic of this stage of development.

What I have just been relating of the earliest stage, say the first year of life, seems to be very differently conceived of in Vienna and London, and I am convinced that practically all the differences of opinion in respect of the later stages of development go back to these fundamental ones. Let me next try to show how this is so.

Fortunately we all agree about the importance of the oral stage, and that the oral stage is the prototype of the later femininity is also a widely accepted tenet, though perhaps less so. Helene Deutsch in this connection has pointed to the sucking nature of the vaginal function. The question of early vaginal sensibility is admittedly obscure, but several women analysts, the latest being Dr. Payne and Dr. Brierley, have produced, if not absolutely conclusive, at least highly significant evidence of its occurrence together with breast feeding. It is, however, hard to discriminate between it and vulval sensations on the one hand, and on the other hand the general retentive sensations and phantasies relating to the anus, womb and the inside of the body generally. One can at all events hardly sustain any longer the view that the vaginal attitude does not develop before puberty. The impressive facts of adult vaginal anæsthesia or even dyspareunia, with the suggestion of what they are the negative of, seem to me definitely to refute the idea of the vagina being an indifferent or merely undeveloped organ. They prove rather the erotic cathexis of the vagina and the deep fear of this. The obscurity of the organ in childhood I should attribute to three causes: (1) Phantasies relating to it, those concerning the wish for a penis and baby, are the ones most directly in conflict with the rival mother, and for obvious reasons the girl cannot display her hostility against her mother as much as the boy can against his father. (2) The vagina is the seat of the deepest anxieties, so an extensive displacement outwards takes place, both of its erotogenicity and the accompanying anxieties. It is felt, like the mouth, to be an evil and dangerous organ which must therefore be kept hidden. (3) It has no physical function before menstruation and is relatively inaccessible, facts which prevent it being used as a reality and libidinal reassurance in the way that a penis or even a clitoris can be.

We now come to the penis-clitoris question, and here the sharpest differences of opinion obtain. This is shown most clearly by considering the connection between the question and the relation to the parents. If for brevity you will allow me purposely to exaggerate the differences of opinion, one might say that according to one view the girl hates her mother because she has disappointed her wish that her clitoris were a penis, whereas according to the other view the reason that the girl wishes that her clitoris were a penis is that she feels hatred for her mother which she cannot express. Similarly according to one view the girl comes to love her father because she is disappointed in her clitoris, whereas according to the other view she wishes to change her clitoris for a penis because of the obstacles in the way of loving her father. You will agree that we have here very decided differences of opinion, even allowing for my over-sharp way of presenting them.

I have elsewhere pointed to the confusion arising from the three senses in which the phrase ' penis-wish ' is used in this connection, and will try to avoid it by defining the sense I mean. At the moment we are talking of the wish that the clitoris were a penis, and I trust that this is unambiguous. We are all familiar with the dissatisfaction and resentment connected with this wish and the part it plays in the girl's psychology. But the fact that so many girls envy boys need not blind us to the feminine attributes, her coquetry, etc., and the important fact of the existence of dolls.

Now the problem here is the motivation of this wish.. We agree that a part of it arises from the simple auto-erotic envy most fully described by Karen Horney: the freedom the boy enjoys in seeing and touching and his use of the organ in micturition. According to one view, however, this is the main motive for the wish, whereas for other authors it accounts for only the smaller part. Far more important, in my opinion, are what may be called the secondary motives for the penis-wish. These, in a word, are concerned with the girl child's various endeavours to cope with her sadism directed against the parents, especially the mother. At the risk of repetition I would again mention and lay stress on what we regard as the fundamental expression of this sadism, the wish to tear a way into the mother's body and devour the father's penis she believes to be incorporated there. What Melanie Klein happily terms the ' com-bined parent concept ' here corresponds approximately to what in Vienna is often called the pre-Œdipal stage, but we would extend the term Œdipus complex to include this stage also. The sadism so characteristic of this stage gives rise to the girl's corresponding anxiety lest the inside of her own body be similarly robbed and destroyed.

Let me now enumerate the ways in which the phantasy of possess-ing a penis attempts to allay this terrible sadism and its accompanying anxiety. I should start by saying that the value the idea of the penis has for the girl is essentially bound up with its capacity to excrete and direct the flow of urine. Helene Deutsch and Karen Horney have called special attention to this association between penis-envy and urethral sadism, while Melanie Klein and, lately, Marjorie

Brierley have dealt extensively with the intimate connection between oral sadism and urethral sadism. According to the 'isopathic principle' which I expounded before the Oxford Congress, the most successful way of dealing with this repressed urethral sadism would be by finding a way in which it can be expressed in reality and thus provide the reassurance of its not being deadly. This is what the boy can do with his urinary games, thanks to the reassurance afforded by the visibly intact penis.

The girl's idea of the penis is, of course, an ambivalent one. On the one hand, it is good, friendly, nourishing, and the fluid emanating from it is equated to milk. On the other hand, it is evil and destructive, its fluid having a corroding power. The use to which the girl puts her imaginary penis in her phantasies is therefore a double one. In so far as it is evil, sadistic and destructive it is a weapon that can be used to attack the mother in the way she fancies her father does, and thus obtain what she wants from the mother's body. In so far as it is good and beneficent it can be used to restore to the mother the penis the girl thinks she has robbed her of; this is especially so when the girl thinks her father whom she has castrated is impotent to satisfy the mother, an attitude very common in homosexuality. It can also be used to neutralise and thus make good again the bad internalised penis, the one the girl has swallowed and by her sadism turned into a harmful and self-destructive organ inside her own body; a visible and intact penis would be the best reassurance against the inaccessible internal anxieties. Thirdly, it can be used to effect restitution to the castrated father by first identifying herself with him and then developing an intact penis by way of compensation.

Behind the girl's wish that her clitoris were a penis, therefore, is the most complex network of phantasies. The aim of them is partly libidinal, but for the most part defensive—consisting of various disparate attempts to get her sadism under control and to allay the desperate anxiety it has engendered. Freud asks in connection with this phallic phase why there should be any flight from femininity unless it were due to primary natural masculine strivings. In answer I should agree with Melanie Klein's conclusion that the girl's repression of femininity springs more from her hatred and fear of her mother than from her own masculine attitude. It goes hand in hand with an excessive fixation on the mother, one which often seriously hampers the girl's development. There is, in our opinion, such a thing as a primary natural wish for a penis on the girl's part, but this we regard not as a masculine striving in clitoris terms, but the normal feminine desire to incorporate a man's penis inside her body—first of all by an oral route, later by a vaginal one.

This wish seems to us to lead on directly to the wish for a baby, the normal wish to take in a penis and convert it into a child. This again is in contradiction to Freud's view that the girl's wish for the child is mainly compensatory for her disappointment in not having a penis of her own. I could agree with Freud's description if it referred not to what we may call the clitoris-penis of the phallic phase, but to the original orally incorporated penis. I think there is no doubt that the disappointment at not being able to receive this penis (not the clitoris one) is largely compensated for by concentration on babies, usually in the form of dolls. We are familiar with the same phenomenon in the excessive maternalism of some women who, for either internal or external reasons, are deprived of sexual enjoyment. But this is not what Freud means.

I should like to say a word about the girl's attitude towards the father. She transfers to him the guilt and fear she developed towards the mother when sadistically robbing her of the penis. After all it is the father's penis as well as the mother's that she devoured, so he also is injured. There is much more envy and jealousy of the mother than of the father, and much of the latter that we observe clinically is really displaced from the former. But once there is great anxiety about the evil internalised penis, harmful because of the sadistic way by which it was obtained, the homœopathic principle again comes into play. Then the girl, as we so commonly find with homosexuals, is impelled to bite the man's penis off so as to obtain reassurance for the anxiety of the original phantasies. If, on the other hand, the relation to the mother is predominantly a good and affectionate one, that to the father will develop on less sadistic lines and will become satisfactory.

We come now to the passing of the phallic phase and the development of a manifest femininity. Here also we must expect divided opinions, since it is easy to see that the view taken of this stage in development must be profoundly influenced by that of the earlier ones. In the first place, just as I am more sceptical about the existence of the phallic phase as a stage in development, so am I more sceptical than the Viennese seem to be about the idea of its passing. It would seem to be more accurate to use the expression ' phallic position '[1] to describe the phenomena in question. We are concerned with an emotional attitude[2] rather than a stage in libidinal development. This attitude is maintained by certain forces or needs, diminishes whenever these are weaker, but persists just so long as they persist —often throughout life. The ' phallic position ' is not seldom quite as pronounced at the age of six, ten or thirty as at the age of two or three. What Viennese analysts describe as the passing of the phallic phase is rather the period in which they recognise the femininity of the girl which many London analysts think they can recognise earlier in its more repressed state. There remains, it is true, the question why the femininity is often less repressed, and therefore more visible, as the girl grows, and this question I propose to deal with next.

You may remember the distinction I drew in my Wiesbaden paper between the proto-phallic and the deutero-phallic phases, the separation between them being marked by the conscious discovery of the sex difference. This discovery often results in envy and imitation, which are the main characteristics of the deutero-phallic phase. One very important observation about which there is general agreement is that the passing of this phase—or rather the plainer evidence of femininity—is apt to be accompanied by unmistakable hostility and resentment against the mother. Freud in his explanation has coupled these two events together not only chronologically but intrinsically. The reasons he gives for the girl's emerging from the phallic phase can be summarised in one word—disappointment. The girl comes to realise that her wish to have a penis of her own is doomed to disappointment, and so she wisely resigns herself to seeking other sources of pleasure that will console her. In doing so she exchanges both her own sex, from male to female, and that of her love-object, from mother to father. The passing of the deutero-phallic phase, therefore, ushers in the Œdipus complex with its rivalry with the mother. This accords with the undoubted observation that the normal Œdipus situation is more visible after the phallic phase has weakened. As Jeanne Lampl-de Groot concisely puts it, the girl has to traverse an inverted Œdipus situation before arriving at the normal one.

[1] Cp. ' libido position,' and the psychotic ' positions ' in Melanie Klein's Lucerne paper.
[2] Not so much one of definite ideas.

In London, on the other hand, we regard the deutero-phallic phase as essentially a defence against the *already existing* Œdipus complex. To us, therefore, the problem of why the defensive phallic phase comes to an end puts itself quite differently, being not altogether unlike the problem of why an infantile phobia ever disappears.

The answer I should give resembles Freud's in so far as both could be given in terms of ' adaptation to reality.' But the way in which the impressions of reality work does not seem to me at all the same as they do to Freud. Fundamentally they strengthen ego development at the expense of phantasy. The phantasy of the penis as a defence is given up because (1) it is recognised as a phantasy and therefore not an adequate protection, (2) there is less anxiety and therefore less need for defence, and (3) other defences are available.

Let me now consider these reasons in order. We know that there are definite limits to the power of hallucinatory wish-fulfilments, at least in the normal person, a fact which Freud has often illustrated by the case of hunger. This is true whether the wish is for the satisfaction of a body need—*e.g.*, a libidinal one—or for a protection against anxiety. In this case the phantasied protection is found not to work well just because it does not give the reassurance of external reality, which is what the girl needs and is what she is beginning to find elsewhere.

In the second place, her anxiety has diminished as her ego has got stronger. She is better able to see her mother as a real and usually affectionate person rather than as the imaginary ogre of her phantasy. She is also no longer so dependent on her mother as she was in the first two or three years of life. She can therefore afford to display more sadism against her and other persons of the environment instead of locking it up and developing internal anxiety. This is the well-recognised stage when the environment finds the growing girl ' difficult ' and hard to manage.

Thirdly, the girl is now learning to exteriorize both her libido and her anxiety. She has passed the stage of part-object love and is more interested in her father or brother as a whole. This replaces the early part-object incorporated in the mother. Her anxiety is much less internal and is taking the form of the characteristic dread of desertion, one that often lasts through life.

The young girl is now much bolder in her claims, and dares for the first time to be the open rival of her mother. The resentment she displays against her has not only the meaning Freud attaches to it, of reproach that her clitoris is not a penis, but is also the bursting through of the older animosity long pent up. It is not merely the reproach that her mother gave her only a clitoris, it is the reproach that her mother had always kept the breast and the father's penis in her possession and not allowed the girl to incorporate them into her body to her heart's desire. The sight of a boy's penis is not the sole traumatic event that changes her life; it is only the last link in a long chain. Nor do I think that if a girl never experienced this trauma she would be masculine, which would seem to follow from the view that this is what drives her into femininity.

I may now sum up my contentions in a few sentences. The main facts to be explained are the young girl's desire for a penis and her resentment against her mother. The central difference between the two points of view, which for present purposes I have exaggeratedly called the London and Vienna ones, seems to me to turn on the question of the early Œdipus complex, ushered in by oral dissatisfaction. Being unable to cope with the anxiety this engenders, she more or less temporarily takes flight in the ' phallic phase ' and then later resumes her normal development. This view seems to me more in accord with the ascertainable facts, and also intrinsically more probable, than one which would regard her femininity to be the result of an external experience (viewing a penis). To my mind, on the contrary, her femininity develops progressively from the promptings of an instinctual constitution. In short, I do not see a woman—in the way feminists do—as *un homme manqué*, as a permanently disappointed creature struggling to console herself with secondary substitutes alien to her true nature. The ultimate question is whether a woman is born or made.

Put more generally, I think the Viennese would reproach us with estimating the early phantasy life too highly at the expense of external reality. And we should answer that there is no serious danger of any analysts neglecting external reality, whereas it is always possible for them to underestimate Freud's doctrine of the importance of psychical reality.

GLOSSARY

I HAVE been asked by several readers to append a glossary, and it seems only fair to do so, as the book is addressed to a double audience—a medical and a psychological one, each of whom uses terms with which the other may not be fully conversant. A definition of the terms not here included will usually be found in the text, under the references given in the index. A complete list of the translations of German psycho-analytical terms will be found in the 'glossary' published as a Supplement to the *International Journal of Psycho-Analysis*. Those who wish for a really full Glossary on allied subjects may be recommended to Dr. R. H. Hutchings' excellent 'A Psychiatric Word Book' (State Hospitals Press, Utica, N.Y.).

Aboulia.—Inability to exercise the will, in either resolutions or decisions.

Abreaction.—The process of working off a pent-up emotion by living through it again in feeling or action.

Affect.—Feeling. The essential constituent of emotion.

Agensia.—Loss of the sense of taste.

Agoraphobia.—Dread of open spaces.

Akathesia.—Inability to sit still; panicky reaction when compelled to sit down.

Algolagnia.—Sexual excitement at the presence of pain; may be active or passive.

Algophobia.—Morbid dread of physical pain.

Allo-erotism.—Erotism in connection with the idea of another human being.

Amaurosis.—Blindness.

Ambivalency.—The coexistence of opposed feelings—*e.g.*, love and hate.

Amblyopia.—Dimness of vision.

Amnesia.—A localised defect of memory.

Anaclitic type.—Choice of first love-object determined by the fact that this object had previously satisfied non-sexual needs. Sometimes applied also to persons whose later love-choice is modelled on this earlier one.

Anæsthesia.—Absence of feeling, often only so far as consciousness is concerned.

Anal erotism.—Erotic excitation aroused by stimulation of the anus.

Analgesia.—Loss of sensation to pain.

Aphonia.—Loss of speech, often hysterical.

Astasia-abasia.—Irregularity in standing or walking; an hysterical symptom.

Autistic thinking (Bleuler).—Thinking in phantasy.

Auto-erotism.—Self-generated erotism, gratified in relation to the person alone; a contrast to allo-erotism.

Autopsychic.—Pertaining to mental operations relating to the subject's personality.

Bisexuality.—Sexual feeling for members of both sexes.

Castration complex.—The idea of injury to the penis, testicles, or clitoris.

Catatonia.—A form of dementia præcox, catalepsy (also found in hysteria) being a prominent symptom.

Catharsis.—The purging of the effects of a pent-up emotion by bringing it to the surface of consciousness.

Cathexis.—Charge of energy. Investment (of an idea) with feeling and significance.

Censorship, endopsychic.—The sum of repressing forces.

Claustrophobia.—Dread of closed spaces.

Cloaca theory.—The infantile belief that the child is born through the rectum.

Coitus interruptus.—Withdrawal of the penis before the orgasm so that the emission takes place outside.

Coitus reservatus.—Coitus with no orgasm, or at all events only a delayed one.

Complex.—A group of emotionally invested ideas partially or entirely repressed.

Component instinct.—One of the elements going to make up a total instinct—*e.g.*, sadism and exhibitionism are component parts of the sexual instinct.

Condensation.—Unconscious fusion of ideas.

Constellation.—A group of emotionally invested ideas not repressed.

Conversion, hysterical.—Symbolical expression of a complex by means of physical manifestations—*e.g.*, disgust by vomiting.

Coprophilia.—Interest in excreta.

Cover-memory.—See Screen-memory.

Cunnilingus.—Apposition of the mouth to the vulva.

Cyclothymia.—Mild form of manic-depressive insanity, often not recognised as insanity.

Dementia præcox.—The commonest form of insanity.

Dipsomania.—Periodic uncontrollable desire for alcohol.

Displacement.—Transference of an affect from one idea to another.

Dissociation.—The splitting off from the main body of the personality of various, usually large, groups of ideas.

Dyspareunia.—Pain during coitus; an hysterical symptom.

Ego-dystonic.—Not consonant, compatible or consistent with the standards of the self.

Ego-ideal.—The standard of individual perfection that evokes aspiration.

Ego-instincts.—All the non-sexual instincts.

Ego-syntonic.—Consonant, compatible, or consistent with the standards of the self.

Ejaculatio præcox.—Seminal emission at the beginning of coitus.

Empathy.—Feeling with another.

End Pleasure.—The culminating point of a pleasurable process.

Epistemophilie impulse.—The instinct of curiosity.

Ereutophobia.—Dread of blushing.

Erotogenic zone.—An area of the body appropriate stimulation of which gives rise to erotic sensations.

Erythrophobia.—Dread aroused by the colour red.

Euphoria.—Sense of well-being.

Exhibitionism.—Sexual excitement at the act of displaying an erotogenic part of the body.

Fellatio.—Apposition of the mouth to the penis.

Fetishism.—Sexual gratification in connection with a part only of the loved object—*e.g.*, foot, glove, etc.

Fixation.—Remaining attached at an earlier phase of development.
Fore pleasure.—The preliminary phases, increasing in intensity, of a pleasurable process.
Fugue.—Flight.

Ganser's syndrome.—Collection of certain symptoms, most prominent of which is the giving of an approximate answer to every question.
General paralysis.—Fatal form of insanity, always due to syphilis.

Hetero-erotism.—Allo-erotism.
Hetero-sexuality.—Love for a member of the opposite sex.
Homosexuality.—Love for a member of the same sex.
Hypnagogic imagery.—Visual imagery, usually without accompanying affect, occurring just before falling asleep.
Hypnopompic imagery.—Visual imagery, usually without accompanying affect, occurring just after waking.
Hypochondriasis.—A condition where the subject believes or fears that his organs are affected with disease.
Hypomania.—A mild form of mania; often chronic.

Id.—The impersonal and instinctual part of the unconscious mind.
Idiogamy.—Possibility of potency confined to only one woman.
Imago.—An image preserved indefinitely in the unconscious and often identified with persons other than the original one.
Incest.—Sexual act with a near relative, or the desire for this; often unconscious.
Inhibition.—Involuntary restraint of a function or impulse.
Introjection.—Absorption of other personalities into the self, so that external events are reacted to as though they were internal, personal ones.
Introversion.—Withdrawal of interest from outer life on to the life of phantasy, conscious or unconscious.
Inversion, sexual.—Homosexuality. May be either objective, only the sex of the love-object being changed, or subjective, where the attitude (masculine or feminine) is inverted as well.

Korsakow's psychosis.—A form of toxic insanity, with neuritis and peculiar memory changes, most often due to alcoholism.

Latency period.—The years between about four and eleven that separate the development of infantile genital primacy from the further changes brought about by puberty.
Libido.—Sexual hunger; the love energy of the instincts.   Hence libidinal.

Manic-depressive insanity.—'Circular' insanity, with irregularly alternating phases of mania and melancholia.
Masochism.—Sexual enjoyment of mental or physical pain, usually inflicted from without, the counterpart of sadism.
Masturbation.—Auto-erotic gratification procured by manual manipulation, usually, but not always, of the genitals.
Megalomania.—A delusional exaggeration of the subject's importance, power, etc.
Metapsychology.—Used by Freud to denote the three aspects of psychology: the dynamic, the economic and the topographical.
Mixoscopia.—Excitement at witnessing a sexual act.

Narcissism.—Self-love; a stage of development in which the auto-erotic impulses are co-ordinated, but the object is still the self and not yet another person.

Nosogenic type.—Type of case classified according to circumstance and character of the onset of the illness.

Nosology.—The classification of diseases.

Nosophobia.—Dread of disease.

Nuclear complex.—The central complex of the psycho-neuroses—*i.e.*, the Œdipus complex.

Obsessional neurosis.—A neurosis characterised by the alternation of obsessive (compulsive) ideas and doubts.

Œdipus complex.—The (usually unconscious) desire to kill the father and possess the mother.

Omnipotence of thoughts.—The unconscious belief in the magical power of the act of thinking.

Onanism.—Auto-erotism. Wrongly named, for the sin of Onan was coitus interruptus.

Ontogenesis.—Development of the individual.

Oral erotism.—Erotic excitation aroused by stimulation of the mouth or lips; characteristic of one of the two forms of the pregenital stage of development.

Osphresiolagniac.—A fetishistic dependence on odour for sexual satisfaction.

Osphresiophilia.—Sexual pleasure derived from the functioning of smell.

Paræsthesia.—Perverted sensation.

Paranoia.—A form of insanity characterised by systematic delusions.

Paranoid dementia.—A form of dementia præcox resembling paranoia, but differing in that the delusions are less completely systematised and there are other symptoms present of dementia præcox.

Paraphrenia.—A special form of dementia paranoides (Kraepelin). A synonym for paranoia and dementia præcox (Freud).

Parapraxis.—Erroneous mental functioning, usually in slight matters such as slips of the tongue, forgettings, misplacings, etc.

Phylogenesis.—Development of the race.

Preconscious.—Mental process of which one is not aware at a given moment, but which it is possible, more or less readily, to recall to consciousness.

Pregenital.—Pertaining to the various sexual organisations of infancy that precede the establishment of genital dominance or primacy.

Projection.—The ascribing to the outer world mental processes that are not recognised to be of personal origin.

Psychosis.—Insanity.

Rationalisation.—The inventing of a reason for an attitude or action the motive of which is not recognised.

Reaction-Formation.—Development of a character trait that keeps in check and conceals another one, usually of the exactly opposite kind.

Regression.—Two meanings: (1) Resolution of an idea into its sensorial components instead of the usual passage onwards in the direction of action; (2) Reversion of mental life, in some respect, to that characteristic of an earlier stage of development, often an infantile one.

Repression.—The keeping from consciousness of mental processes that would be painful to it.

Resistance.—The instinctive opposition displayed towards any attempt to lay bare the unconscious; a manifestation of the repressing forces.

Sadism.—Sexual enjoyment at the infliction of bodily or mental pain; the counterpart of masochism.

Sadistic conception of coitus.—The common infantile notion that coitus consists in the male hurting the female.

Schizophrenia.—A synonym for dementia præcox.

Scopolagniac.—A ' voyeur ' (*q.v.*).

Scopophilia.—Sexual pleasure derived from the use of the eye. The counterpart to exhibitionism.

Somatic.—Bodily.

Sublimation.—The deflection of the energy of a sexual impulse to a non-sexual and socially useful goal.

Super-ego.—The unconscious conscience that criticises id impulses and gives pain to the ego whenever the latter wishes to accept dystonic id impulses.

Transference.—Two meanings: (1) Displacement of affect from one idea to another; (2) specifically displacement of an affect, either positive or negative, from one person on to the psycho-analyst.

Trauma.—Injury, mental or bodily.

Unconscious.—Two meanings: (1) All mental processes not in consciousness at a given moment; (2) specifically those that cannot be brought into consciousness by any effort of the will or act of memory. The former includes the latter, which is the typical psycho-analytical sense, together with the preconscious.

Ureteral erotism.—Erotic excitation produced by the act of urination.

' Voyeur.'—A pervert who obtains sexual gratification from the mere act of looking; the counterpart of exhibitionism. Visual sexual curiosity.

INDEX